Words
of
The
Apostles

Words
of
the
Apostles

Rudolf Stier, D. D.

Sovereign Grace Publishers, Inc.
P.O. Box 4998
Lafayette, IN 47903

*Printed In the United States of America
By Lightning Source, Inc.*

FOREWORD

The commission of Christ to His little band of followers to

Go and make disciples of all nations, baptizing them in the name
of the Father and the Son and the Holy Spirit, teaching them
to observe all that I have commanded you. . . (Mt. 28:19,20a),

was carried out by His chosen ones through the preaching of the Word. The movement of the Holy Spirit which attended their ministry is chronicled for us in the Book of Acts.

The speeches of the Book of Acts contain the answer to the lack of spiritual vigor being experienced in many areas of the Christian church today and need to be studied to determine the conditions under which Christ's commission was carried out, the content of the message which His disciples preached, and the conviction which compelled them to spread the "good news."

The result of the ministry of the disciples is well known. A critic of the times complained that they had "turned the world upside down" (Acts 17:6), or "right-side up," depending upon how you look at it.

In the book now before the reader, Rudolf Ewald Stier (1800-1862) the brilliant German exegete and Bible commentator of a generation past, delves into the history of the Book of Acts and, beginning with Peter's sermon on the day of Pentecost, expounds each message or address with consumate skill. His material is very full. He treats carefully each reference to the Old Testament, and so ably explains the thrust of each passage in keeping with the unity of Scripture, that he has earned the respect and praise of God's people.

The message of the Book of Acts (with specific focus on the teaching ministry of the Apostles) is desperately needed in the church today if the errors of extremism and the coldness of a lifeless orthodoxy are to be avoided. It is with singular thankfulness, therefore, that we welcome the reprinting of this fine work comprising the expository sermons which Dr. Stier preached to his congregation at Eisleben.

Cyril J. Barber, D.Lit.
Author, *The Minister's Library*

PREFACE TO THE SECOND EDITION (1861).

———◆———

THE first edition of this book was published as much as two-and-thirty years ago : it will not therefore be out of place if I subjoin some of the most essential matter of my former preface, so that the era of the appearance of the book, and the relation of its author to this era, may be brought more distinctly to mind.

In December 1848 I wrote as follows : " *The foundation of the New Testament on the Old, and the intimate connection between the Scriptures of the old and new covenants,* by means of which they form but one divine whole,—the due recognition of these facts constitutes the root of all believing comprehension of the Bible which understands τὴν γραφὴν ' in the mind of Christ' (1 Cor. ii. 16), and also of a true biblical theology resulting therefrom. But a failure in discerning these facts, or even an acknowledgment of and insight into them, which is deficient in simplicity or consistency and is always to some extent against the will—amounting, therefore, to a misunderstanding of the *exact* system,—this forms the radical defect, or rather the chief want, of a humanly taught system of theology and hermeneutics, which to the pure secret feeling and consciousness of faith presents a sceptical and improper treatment of those very passages in which the Old and New Testaments agree with one another and thus lay open the real Scripture-system."

" If we would fain be members and teachers in Christ's church, let us well look to the foundation on which it was built by the

Lord Himself and His first builders. This foundation is the rejected corner-stone which is spoken of in the Scriptures—Christ, who died and rose again *according to the Scriptures*—the Messiah of the Jews. The very name of our Saviour, which name indeed, as His people, we ever would and must bear, places us in the centre of the old covenant, which in the new dispensation is fulfilled and not dissolved ; and far from being cancelled, is now first instituted in its revealed spirit and nature."

" With no half-belief in the Scriptures, but with perfect faith, with no incomplete explanations, but with consistent interpretation, let us, my brethren, who hold to God's word, oppose any perversions or uprootings of the ' foundation of the apostles and prophets' (Eph. ii. 20)."

" It is no doubt true that *biblical truth* depends altogether upon *history* both in the Old, and also in the New Testament ; and for this very reason, Luke's second book, addressed to Theophilus, is called the ' Acts,' and not the ' Words' of the apostles. What they did, and how they did it, and the way in which their discourses followed their actions, and became indeed, in their power and effect, equivalent to actions,—all this at first sight contributes the chief weight to the scale of testimony.

" But, on the other hand, it is no less true that this biblical history is conveyed to us in inspired language ; and only so far as it is interpreted and revealed by the words of prophecy and teaching does it become true biblical history, that is, does it itself become a prophetico-didactic fact. Thus the *words* of the apostles throw a full light upon their *acts*. What they said, and how they said it— how the intention and sense of their entire testimony, as the *New Word* of *fulfilment*, was linked on to the Old Word of *expectation*,— this is the turning-point in the balance of confession, when we are desirous to perfect our believing comprehension of Scripture truly and systematically according to the Scripture-system itself, and not by means of some humanly devised plan in which we constrain and falsify the truth of Scripture itself."

" For the reasons I have just intimated, the oral element of the apostolic testimony, and its real practical purport, have been hitherto most surprisingly neglected in exegetical studies, and have been made to give way before an industrious and too one-sidedly zealous development of the historical and philological matter. The mere outward husk is sufficiently investigated, but the enjoyment and taste of the kernel is but little attained to."

" In addition to this, from a want of that strict and childlike belief in inspiration—in which, alas, so many modern and to some extent believing divines are deficient—the words of *Luke* are no longer looked upon as the words of the *apostles*. For this reason, too, no pains are taken to penetrate in full simplicity into the depths of these rich and terse testimonies of the Spirit, which, if closely scrutinized with a right view, afford so much matter for our consideration."

" The author of the following exposition of the ' Words of the Apostles ' is therefore led to believe that he is furnishing something which is needed by, and will be profitable for, those who desire to emerge from the narrowness, sterility, and incompleteness of a certain wisdom of the schools, and long for some freer and more lively perception of faith in the words of the Bible. According to his chief principle in all interpretation of Scripture, he does not expound the words of the apostles as if they were mere *words* of the *apostles*, but he looks upon them as the words of *the Holy Ghost through* the apostles. His chief desire is to present to the devoutly believing view the perfect oneness and harmony of the Spirit, who aforetime spake through the prophets, and afterwards, through the apostles, so wonderfully and variously refers back to the prophets. For it was in the *prophets* that *the Spirit of Christ which was in them* ' testified beforehand the suffer-

ings of Christ, and the glory that should follow'—that self-same
'*Holy Ghost sent down from heaven,*' who taught the *apostles* to
preach the gospel to us (1 Pet. i. 11, 12)."

"If, however, it is found that in this exposition the historical
matter falls somewhat into the background before the everlasting
import of the apostolic discourses; if the merely profane linguistic
philology, which does nothing in elucidating the practical substance,
but, on the contrary, weakens and levels down its divine power and
spiritual depth, is almost entirely shunned; if, generally, no learned
apparatus, with all its groundless controversy as to isolated and
secondary points, is here newly framed and compiled,—these
omissions and deficiencies must be ascribed to the deliberate intention of the author. Presupposing, as regards his learned readers,
the presence of all requisite appliances, his desire has been to
convey in a lively form to the less learned those thoughts as to
the divinely-living words of the Spirit which have been suggested
to his own mind. God grant that any portion of these thoughts
which is really His gift may find its way into the hearts and
minds of all the ministers of His word, for whom chiefly the work
has been written!"

Thus much I wrote as a portion of the preface to the first
edition; and even now I cannot more clearly describe the permanent and fundamental character of the work. But, God be
thanked, the complaints as to the prevailing spirit of theology and
exegesis which I then expressed cannot now be so forcibly repeated.
Since then, much has been done in attaining to a greater progress
in the devout and believing comprehension of Holy Scripture.

I found, nevertheless, when I was unexpectedly called upon for
a new, and of course remodelled, edition of my work, that there was
less to alter in it than I had at first imagined. It was, in the first
place, necessary to retain the youthful and vigorously grown root-
stock, in order that anything which was God's suggestion, and was

unaffected by the lapse of time, might be again communicated. In some cases certain prolixities, which extended to trifling and even edifying matters, were expunged; as also were the now useless arguments directed against authors who were then current. All that science had added to our knowledge of the subject had to be compared, and to be made use of according to its value; and all that the author had better learnt in the last thirty years had to be worked in.

I leave the book thus remodelled, in full assurance that it will continue to fill a useful position, and will perhaps receive greater acceptance than at its first appearance. I must acknowledge that a wish, which I have long entertained, of once more taking a part in discussing these subjects, is now fulfilled. So far as it is the abiding truth of God's word, I commend my work to God's blessing.

RUDOLF STIER.

EISLEBEN, *August* 27, 1860.

CONTENTS.

THE WORDS OF THE APOSTLES.

————◆————

I.

PETER'S ADDRESS TO THE DISCIPLES.

(ACTS I. 16–22.)

SUMMONS TO THE CHOICE OF AN APOSTLE IN THE PLACE OF JUDAS.

ER. 13. The men of Galilee, whom Jesus before His sufferings chose through the Holy Ghost to be apostles, whom also, on the day on which He was taken up, He charged with a message of salvation to every creature (ver. 2), saw the King of the long-anticipated kingdom of Israel disappear behind the cloud-curtain of heaven. They listened to the directions of the heavenly messengers, no longer to stand gazing up into heaven, but to turn their minds towards the future promised for the earth, the consummation of which would be the return of their King.

Then returned they unto Jerusalem from the mount called Olivet, in order to fulfil the last words of their Master, now their Lord and their God, by waiting in Jerusalem until He should again come to them in the Holy Spirit, and by power from on high should make them His witnesses even to the uttermost parts of the earth. There had they gathered themselves together in the highest part of a house, or upper chamber—some quiet Alija[1]—with **many** others who joined with them in a like hope. This room may probably have been that which witnessed the last supper, the mourning of the disciples, and Jesus' bequest of peace; but in whose house it was we cannot gather from Matt. xxvi. 18, Mark xiv. 14,

[1] As the name occurs in the Old Testament, equivalent in Hebrew to ὑπερῷον.

A

and Luke xxii. 11. Others, however, think that it was a place in the temple which, according to Josephus, was thus called, and refer to Luke xxiv. 53, "and were continually *in the temple.*" In favour of the latter opinion,[1] one might easily imagine that, after the destruction of Jesus, the rulers at Jerusalem would not think it worth while to persecute His adherents, and that the sheep might peaceably flock together even among the wolves; but this place would certainly not have been fit for a private friendly meeting, and the same remark applies to the meeting on the feast of Pentecost. Luke mentions the eleven apostles *by name,* because in the first place he wished to begin his History of the Apostles (being a separate book) with a list of this sort (as in Ex. i. the children of Israel are again enumerated), and also to call to their remembrance the *missing twelfth one,* and thus to prepare for what follows.

Ver. 14. *These all* were *of one accord* together. Thus are they here specified with this great characteristic of the Christian community, so often recurring in the apostolic history. As they might no longer outwardly look up to heaven, so much the more they continued watching and waiting inwardly, *i.e.* in *prayer and supplication,* for quiet faith during the appointed waiting-time; afterwards, on the contrary, *praise* of the God revealed to the community as Father, Son, and Spirit, became their unanimous song (Acts ii. 47; Rom. xv. 6). There were also with them *women,* or *the* women—hardly their females generally, as (from ver. 15) *disciples* only joined in this unanimity: they must therefore have been the believing women, especially the witnesses of the resurrection (Luke xxiv. 10). Among these Mary is specified by name, as was only fitting, but still without any peculiar preference being awarded her. She is mentioned now for the last time at the very beginning of the sacred history of the church, and is distinguished from the other Marys as *the Mother of Jesus*—as she who had brought forth the Son of God, now ascended to His Father. With Jesus' mother after the flesh, who now by Jesus' command was dependent upon John, stood also *His brethren*—His *actual* brethren; so distinguished by the definite article from the apostles (one of whom was at least a cousin of Jesus),—the brethren who now at last believed in their ascended Brother (John vii. 5).

Ver. 15. It was a long, grievous waiting-time, during which the above-named and many others were gathered together with

---

[1] Which, however, does not seem to be suitable to the ὅτε εἰσῆλθον, ἀνέβησαν, and to the ἦσαν καταμένοντες.

the eleven in this place; and their continuance in prayer and supplication might sometimes be a little wearisome, although Luke, on account of their unanimity, styles it *continual*. "Not many days hence" had been the Lord's words (ver. 5); but as to the exact time when this baptism of the Spirit should come upon them, they knew neither the day nor the hour, which the Father had kept in His own power. It may be well imagined that they longingly expected the speedy coming of the Holy Ghost, and the beginning of their office as witnesses, after so many and such great preparations. "Lord, how long?" might many a one both think and say. Perhaps there may have been much talk in that quiet circle about the great things which had been done, and those which were yet to come to pass. Many a look would be cast upon the book of prophecy, which the Lord had made intelligible to them. But all this would be based upon, and joined with, prayer, supplication, and—waiting. There was a wonderful union of retrospect and anticipation in this trying, quiet interval, which the wisdom of the Lord had ordained to prepare their minds for the Holy Ghost. When they contemplated their future charge as witnesses and messengers to all nations, they could not but recall to mind the lost child—him who was a devil among the twelve chosen ones. This must have been a dark point, again and again occurring to the eleven whenever they were together, and thought who it would be that, according to Jesus' words (Matt. xix. 28; Luke xxii. 30), should fill the now vacant judgeship over one of the tribes of Israel, and sit on the twelfth throne. During these days of waiting, now so long protracted, Peter, the first among the eleven, on whom the chiefdom seems naturally to have fallen, stood up, and as the enunciator of their thoughts, hitherto perhaps only half-expressed, spake to all the other disciples. These must have been those disciples of Jesus who had been accustomed to assemble in this upper room at Jerusalem : a moderately large multitude (ὄχλος)— namely, *about* (in round numbers) 120 persons; consequently ten times as many as the apostles. Still, they were but few to form the commencement of God's kingdom on earth. Luke writes *names* instead of persons, because he had mentioned the eleven and Mary by name, and also because in ver. 23 two others were to be specified by name.

Ver. 16. Peter's address—*Men*—excludes the women (mentioned in ver. 14) from the consultation and choice, and generally from any public voice in this community. The additional appella-

tion, *Brethren*, is the first recorded expression of the spiritual brotherhood in Christ after His ascension, and embraces the whole number
present, throwing aside both the apostolic office and any natural
brotherhood.   Thus the Israelitish expression (Acts xxviii. 17) is in
this smaller sphere renewed in a fuller power and meaning.—*The
Scripture must needs have been fulfilled.*   Thus did Peter, expressing neither wrath, doubt, lamentation, nor sentence, calmly consider
the deed of the betrayer, and in all the confidence which was given
him by his knowledge of that divine counsel which embraces even
the wicked, looks upon it only as an event that "must needs" have
taken place.   This way of considering the matter he had learned
from Him who had died and risen again (Matt. xxvi. 24, 54, 56 ;
John xiii. 18, xvii. 12 ; Luke xxiv. 26, 46) ; and his interpretation
of Scripture is right, for it is derived from the instruction of the
Lord (Luke xxiv. 45, 46).   By *the Scripture*, or really, as more
correctly read, *this* Scripture, he must mean the passage in Ps. xli.
10, quoted by Jesus ; but it is subsequently clear from ver. 20
that he is referring generally to everything which had been prophesied of Judas and his accomplices : so that it should be rather
translated, *that* scripture, *i.e.* the passages of Scripture which prophesy of Judas.   *Spake before* stands out strongly and vividly
after the word *fulfilled* just before.   But these things were spoken
by the Holy Ghost through the mouth of David (although David
himself might not have understood the prophetical sense of his psalm).
This view of the Scripture had been taught to His disciples by the
Risen One; and how naturally does this seem to be spoken to them,
just at the time when they were waiting for the Holy Ghost !—
Which was a guide or leader—not, as he was bound to be, to the
faith of Christ, but—*to them that took Jesus.*   This sentence connects the statement of prophecy with the reference to what had
taken place, and embraces in one glance the whole treachery of
the unhappy one (as Jesus calls him, Luke xxii. 21), from his
first negotiation with the enemy down to his great overt act in the
garden, which is thus especially called to the apostles' minds, with
Jesus' kindness towards His false friend.   This expression also
shows the point of view from which the Scripture speaks of Judas,
and an important exegetical hint is given as to the three psalms,
xli., lxix., and cix.   The false friends of the Lord are still leaders
and guides to His open enemies ; sometimes, alas, in a milder
sense, by giving rise to the appearance of evil, and by causing
scandal.

Ver. 17. *For he was numbered with us.* In this the apostle separates the eleven from the "men and brethren," and gives an intimation of what he would remind them of as to the deficiency in the sacred number of *twelve. He was numbered* both in the first choice, and also subsequently more expressly, John vi. 70. Certainly in Matt. xix. 28 the thrones only are numbered; and in the designation of the persons to fill them, the restriction is used, *Ye which have followed me.* In Luke xxii. 30 the number of the thrones is not mentioned. After the expression *numbered* had preceded, the less precise *chosen* could not well follow; but it is included in the comprehensive sentence which covers the mystery of this choice of the lost one : *and had obtained* (attained, ἔλαχε) *part* (or lot) *in this ministry.* The expression *this* is knit together with the former definition—*with us.* The word *ministry* makes amends, however, by its modest general idea, for the prominence given to the *us. Part* here means the same as the share or lot pointed out (by God) in Acts viii. 21, Col. i. 12 ; and it was assigned to Judas either generally, or, more exactly, he received the one-twelfth of the common apostleship. It is very much to be doubted if Peter intended here to hint at the nature of the approaching choice, for the drawing lots arose only from the uncertainty between the two named to be chosen from : the expression, therefore, cannot be understood in this way until ver. 26.

Ver. 18. The sin, already sufficiently made known in ver. 16, is not again described, but is only intimated in the word *iniquity*, and is placed in the background by its dreadful reward, as the theft is indicated by the gallows. *The reward of iniquity* alludes both to the wretched avarice of the Saviour-seller (cf. 2 Pet. ii. 13, 15), as well as to the words of the high priest: "It is the price of blood !" *Purchased a field*, actually *the* field,—the only too well-known potter's field, the shameful name for which subsequently follows ; which, too, was prophesied of by Zechariah, who also foretold the reward or price of thirty pieces of silver. But how was it purchased ? Probably, in the first place, the purchase was the cause of there being a "field of blood" publicly known in unbelieving Jerusalem, whose unjust rulers hired the betrayer of the Just One, and then would not place in the temple-treasury the reward and price of such manifold iniquity. This idea alone will agree with Matt. xxvii. and Zech. xi. 13. Thus possibly the sense might be, that Judas first bought, or intended to buy, for himself the barren potter's field (a wretched portion to exchange for the twelfth apostolic throne!), and then went and hanged himself in it; indeed, from ver. 19, the name of the field seems clearly to have been derived from Judas' miserable death therein. For what could then be publicly known causing this name to be given to the field? Evidently it could not be merely the private bargain for the pieces of silver, and the high priest's aversion to the returned bribe; but also especially (according to the context) Judas' end told in vers. 18 and 19—this real reward of crime, in which he bought the wished-for field only to be his place of judgment, and therein to meet his fearful death. On this point Bengel profoundly and correctly comments: "Judas initio emptionis facto occasionem dedit, ut sacerdotes eam consummarent." We will add: "Atque morte sua infesta, ut sepulturis agrum destinarent."[1] Even in Matt. xxvii. 6 the "price of blood" refers also to the suicide of Judas related in ver. 5. The name, arising from the expression used by the rulers, and afterwards given by the people to the field, bears witness not only to the innocently-shed blood of Christ, but also to the avenging death of the betrayer, threatened in his example to all betrayers of the just. The ominous meaning of this expression, and the words of the apostle pointing thereto, can only thus be completely explained.—*And falling headlong*— literally, head-over-heels—either through the breaking of the rope or some other cause, after his hanging himself, which is presupposed as well known, of which also the Scripture history had prophesied under the type of Ahithophel (2 Sam. xvii. 23)—*he burst asunder in the midst, and all his bowels gushed out.* It is a significant feature in the description of his judgment, that it struck him "in his own place;" and so shall it be with all obstinate unbelievers in Jesus. His fall could hardly have been as deep as from the rocks under which the Edomites were "broken in pieces" (2 Chron. xxv. 12); but "because he had no bowels of compassion, but from greediness of gain dealt cruelly, therefore must he suffer the just recompense in his own bowels" (Oetinger).

Ver. 19. And this miserable end of one of the twelve table-companions and friends of Jesus became *known unto all the dwellers at Jerusalem.* For if any of the foreigners at Jerusalem came to know the wonderful and dreadful things "which had come to pass there in these days" (Luke xxiv. 18), the history of the traitor would also be told them. And this is not enough. The notoriety

---

[1] A fragment by Papias says remarkably as to Iscariot's end: ἐν ἰδίῳ χωρίῳ.

extended so far, that (ὥστε) the words of aversion expressed by the chief priests in a moment of sincerity, " It is the price of blood," were conferred by an immediate public voice and naming on the field that was bought with the money, and it became the *Field of Blood.* Thus is the knowledge of the fact confirmed to posterity and strangers; and all Jerusalem testifies that the traitor had received the reward of his treachery, and acknowledges its guilty share in shedding the innocent blood ; acknowledges, too, that this blood must be upon them and upon their children, and upon all their fields and boundaries, until the devastated fold of the great city had become one vast " field of blood," on which the followers of their predecessor Judas should perish as he did ; and that the whole Jewish body, because they despised exaltation through the cross of Christ, should like him fall down from the height to which in their despair they had at last resorted, and bursting asunder should shed round about the wicked bowels and inhabitants of the holy place and land. We may thus perceive the reason why the apostle dwells so circumstantially on these things, and may remark with what scriptural wisdom he speaks, even before he had received the power from on high.—*In their proper tongue, that is to say, The field of blood.* These latter words were of course added by Luke (himself a foreigner) for the sake of Theophilus; for Peter called the field *Aceldama* only, and Luke retained this word for all who should at any time come to Jerusalem. But our arrangement and interpretation is clearly against the idea that the whole of vers. 18 and 19, or even the whole of ver. 19 only, were inserted by Luke in St. Peter's speech. It is also hardly conceivable that Luke, just at the beginning of his book, would have deemed it right to make without mention such an interpolation in a reported speech—such an addition, indeed, as nowhere else occurs.

Ver. 20. After ver. 16, it now only needed to be stated shortly, *For it is written.* Psalm lxix., as is well known, speaks of the enemies of Christ generally (as Paul, Rom. xi. 9, interprets it) ; and Psalm cix. mentions *one enemy* more particularly. This quotation is all the more suitable here, from the wonderful way in which Ps. cix. 6–19 speaks of *one* enemy (as Ps. lxix. of many), and in ver. 8 so remarkably brings forward the re-establishment of the office, together with the early despairing death of its former occupant.

Ver. 21. *Wherefore must* is the summons to the fulfilment of the above most decisive scripture, and is also the concluding pro-

position following the words, " *This Scripture must needs*," etc.,[1]
at the beginning of the speech. The *us*, referring to the apostles,
stands four times very naturally in contrast to "these men." It
did not at all follow from the Scripture passage quoted above, that
the new apostle must necessarily be (like the others) one who had
been with Jesus from the beginning; but this was a qualification in
Peter's idea for the apostolic office, in which also he followed John
xv. 27. The reference to these words of Jesus is at least probable,
because in them was the Spirit promised which "shall testify of
me," which afterwards was to recall to the apostles' minds all that
their Master had both done and taught, and also thought.—*All the
time that the Lord Jesus went in and out among us*, or dwelt and
wandered with us. A remarkable concentration of the whole earthly
life of Jesus both before and after His resurrection : both His earlier
public life, when He was *out* among the populace in the temple and
synagogue, and also when He was *in* the private circle of His disciples; also during the forty latter days, when He appeared only
to His own, and came *in* even through locked doors, and, going *out*
into the unknown spirit-world, again disappeared. This space of
time was the school of experience for him who was to testify that this
man of God, Jesus of Nazareth, well known both to us and you,
is risen from the dead, and lives for ever as Lord and Christ on the
throne of His Father. *Among us* is, I think, the correct rendering,
for otherwise the expression would fail in its chief requisite, viz.
that he had been with Jesus; and it is very correctly expressed
here, in order to connect the eleven with the twelfth, who was *with
us*, among whom Jesus was. A contrast exists between the *among
us* in ver. 21, and the *from us* in ver. 22, which is not to be passed
over. The witness was acquainted with what was then taking place,
and could also testify of that which was past.

   Ver. 22. In order to avoid any error, the apostle adds the exact
limitations. *The baptism of John*, i.e. of Jesus *by* John, is the
starting-point of Jesus' public life, and the first of the disciples
were called just after it. As to this, see Mark i. 1, Acts i. 1. But
the doings and teaching of Jesus from then down to the cross,
indeed even down to His ascension, were themselves but the beginning of His heavenly kingdom of grace, and of His omnipresent
ministry among His community on earth, which kingdom was to
be founded on the witness of the apostles. The most proper begin-

[1] Not merely for the completion of the holy, inviolable number of *twelve*
(as Löhe thinks), but especially because it was so directed in the Scripture.

ning and foundation of this consummation is the resurrection, the closing point of the time of preparation. With this event, therefore, Luke both concludes his Gospel and begins his apostolic history. But why is it that, after a mention of His being "taken up," he is to be a witness of His resurrection merely? Because this is the turning-point between the lowly Jesus and Jesus exalted to life, and in fact embraces the ascension as well; therefore, as evidence of His glorified life to those who knew only of His lowliness, this turning-point was the main thing, which everything else would follow. As this may be afterwards more completely inferred from Acts ii. 32 and iii. 15, we need not dwell further upon the subject here. The resurrection of Jesus is not to be vouched for by the chosen witness as a merely isolated matter of fact, but as the turning-point of the whole matter—as the vindication of the claim of the crucified Son of man to be the Son of God—as the warranty of Him who was numbered with transgressors and murderers to be the Saviour and the Prince of Life. Therefore the message about Him embraces not only the whole of His previous public and individual life, but also the manifold manifestations of Himself in which He subsequently showed Himself as living: first to the women and apostles, and to more than five hundred brethren at once, until that same fortieth day in which He was taken up. It is a great result, which nothing but His manifestations during the forty days could have effected in them, that the disciples, in the position in which they then stood after the second withdrawal of the presence of their Lord, should nevertheless have looked forward so assuredly to their future charge as witnesses. Yet, in the conclusion of Peter's speech, there appears a certain deficiency, which might perhaps surprise the reflective reader. The omission in it is, that it makes no mention of the promised baptism of the Spirit, so necessary for their office as witnesses; by which baptism the preparation-time after the ascension was to be ended, through which alone they could be made fit to be His witnesses, and for which even now they were still instructed to remain waiting. Peter, however, only speaks that which appears to him to follow from the words of Scripture quoted, and from his idea of the apostleship. After he has clearly brought the matter under notice in his speech, he abstains from stating what he actually wishes, and from any express summons to the choice. He contents himself with laying before the disciples the injunction that *one must be ordained;* also as to the mode and way of choice he says nothing.

RESULT OF THE DISCOURSE.

Ver. 23. *And they appointed two.* *They,* *i.e.* the disciples among whom Peter had stood up and spoken that which we have just read. The power of choice and nomination was vested neither in the chief apostle nor in the eleven only, but in the whole assembled company of disciples and brethren, to whom alone the apostle makes over the right of acting and deciding in the matter.—*One of these men.* Thus had Peter spoken ; but they could not agree as to the choice of this one, but were undecided between the two whose names are recorded. The two appear to have been alike worthy, —both he who was specially surnamed *Justus* (perhaps not until after this time), and also Matthias : the desired requirements were found in both, but whether they belonged to the seventy must be a subject of conjecture. It might be possible that the disciples were indeed willing to set forward these two men, but shrank from deciding positively on one. What was to be done? They appeal to the Lord Himself, the living God, for whose Spirit they were waiting, to directly appoint His apostle. They turned shortly and simply to Him—to Him who was living, and nigh to them.

Ver. 24. *And they prayed*—as from ver. 14 we know they had continually done, and now indeed to Jesus, who was exalted to the right hand of God (Luke xxiv. 52). They called Him *Lord,* and said, *Thou, Lord, which knowest the hearts of all men !* This is an attribute of God (Acts xv. 8 ; Jer. xvii. 9, 10), but Peter had in anticipation confessed (John xxi. 17) that it was now the attribute of Jesus also. A knowledge of the heart was what was required in the task of choosing, and they wished that He who was to choose should see into the heart, but not as men glance at that which is before their eyes. *Show us,* is their bold, confident prayer to the heart-searcher and fate-ruler, *whether of these two Thou hast chosen !* It is naturally expressed in a *past* sense, for in it they so assuredly presuppose that their preference of *these two* would be according to His will, that they thus pray to the Lord, and doubt not that one of these men would at all events be chosen.

Ver. 25. *That he may take part in this ministry and* (to wit) *apostleship.* Thus the disciples spoke, following the words of the apostle in ver. 17, or else the apostle thus repeated it in behalf of the rest. For generally, in ver. 25, the purport of his speech is briefly compressed. From this follow the words succeeding : *from which Judas by transgression fell,* *i.e.* went out, lost his office. With

this is joined the idea (in the English version *expressly*) of its being
lost in a criminal way.[1] He had done so according to God's determination and decree, *that he might go to his own place,*—a remarkable euphemism to express his punishment. The most general
allusion would of course be somewhat as Pfenninger preached from
this text : " This, in a certain sense, may be said of every one of
us. Every one of us will and must some time or other depart, to
go away to his own appointed place."[2] But it marks also the
special apostasy of Judas, in which he forsook his apostleship, and
went away—to acquire for himself a field !—to buy with the price
of blood *a place of his own !* and became the possessor of the fatal
field which was to be only his scaffold ! Thus, with a most significant grasp of thought, the spirit of the words of Scripture, speaking
through the disciples, embraces this characteristic also of Judas'
sin ; but the fundamental sense of the expression lies much deeper.
As Pfenninger further says of the horrible death of the false servant, " There are those of whose fate even the gentle Jesus must
speak harshly ; and it cannot be expressed otherwise or more clearly
than by the awful words : He also is departed, to go away to his
own place." What the place was to which Judas went, we can
only anticipate from the deeds done in his body. Every soul arriv-
ing in " Scheol" has its own appointed place ; but Judas' dreadful
place, to which he has for ever gone, and from which he will never
return, is *his own place,* which he acquired for himself, and made
himself worthy of. Jesus' betrayal is, as an event, the eternal
decree of God ; but Judas' treachery, as an act and a sin, and also
its everlasting punishment, is not of God, but of the devil, and the
result of Judas' own will (Matt. xxvi. 24).

Ver. 26. *Show us !* This was the great entreaty in their prayer.
But He whom they addressed had been taken up away from them,
and how was He to show whom He had chosen? Was He to
come again in person, or through the inward evidence of the Spirit,
in which indeed He was Himself to return? The disciples, in this

---

[1] παρέβη, *decessit,* עָבַר, cf. ἀπαράβατος (Heb. vii. 24). But we are reminded also of παραβαίνειν and παράβασις in another sense, as פָּשַׁע, to forsake
the specified way, the right position and station. Cf. Ex. xxxii. 8, Deut. ix.
12 (Septuag.).

[2] Cf. the reading δίκαιον instead of ἴδιον, and the expression in the Epistle
of Barnabas, The righteous go ἐπὶ τὸν ὡρισμένον τόπον ; also Ignat. *Epist. ad
Magnes.,* ἕκαστος εἰς τὸν ἴδιον τόπον μέλλει χωρεῖν ; and Clemens Roman. *ad
Cor.* i. ; Polycarp *ad Philipp.,* εἰς τὸν ὀφειλόμενον τόπον.

interval, were not expecting or desiring either of these two events; even now they were half-resting on the old covenant, and following the precedent there laid down, they made for themselves a visible Urim and Thummim. They thought that the man chosen might be pointed out by lot, as was Saul the chosen king of Israel, and that the share in the apostleship might be conferred by lot, as formerly their inheritances were assigned to the tribes of Israel. They would mark out the apostle chosen in the place of this new Achan, as formerly Achan the transgressor was marked out.[1] They knew for certain that a twelfth must be appointed; they had also found by deliberation that the two selected men were the worthiest for the office: the decision between them they now seek by drawing lots.

We read: *And they gave forth their lots.* They thus seek a visible exponent in the lot-drawing for the vacant apostleship, and in its visible event they are willing believingly to recognise the divine assignment of the office. In this they were justified generally; for Solomon says (Prov. xvi. 33), "The lot is cast into the lap, but the whole disposing thereof is of the Lord." They were also specially justified, inasmuch as this kind of decision is permitted to be sought by childlike faith, when the highest degree of conscientious knowledge can go no further, as in this case the *two* could indeed be chosen, but not the *one* out of the two. Finally, they were also justified because the lot-drawing of the Old Testament was still lawful where childlike faith existed, and the fulness of the Holy Ghost—the internal Urim and Thummim of the new covenant—had not yet entered. We therefore find the use of the lot is mentioned as taking place during this interval only, and subsequently the community chose without casting lots (Acts vi. 5; and Acts xiii. 2, "The *Holy Ghost said,* Separate me Barnabas and Saul for the work whereunto I have called them").

And the lot fell upon Matthias—not upon the man called *Justus*—*and he was numbered* (συγκατεψηφίσθη, by general vote; cf. κατηριθμημένος, ver. 17) *with the eleven apostles.*

Thus is it related by Luke, and we would willingly abide by his simple narrative; but still we shall venture now, even more confidently than in our first edition, to bring forward the following bold questions as to an ever important matter: 1*st,* Why does Luke say merely, *The lot fell,* and not, *The Lord pointed out or chose?* 2*d,*

---

[1] It is perhaps best rendered quite accurately: "Show the one whom Thou hast chosen."

Why does Luke conclude the section with "*eleven apostles?*" and why does he not call Matthias the *twelfth apostle?* Indeed, why does he, throughout the entire apostolic history (very probably purposely), abstain from using the expression *twelve apostles?*[1] 3*d*, Is it not really a deficiency in Peter's discourse, that at its conclusion he makes no mention of the Holy Ghost, now hourly to be expected, through whom the Lord was to return and make ready His witnesses, although he speaks of Him at the commencement of his speech? Would it not have been a natural idea, if the Spirit was to come in the place of Jesus, that the missing apostle should be nominated by Him? 4*th*, Was this "standing up" of Peter, and the lot-throwing by the disciples, consistent with the prescribed "waiting" or not? And did the Scripture prophecy, as to another taking Judas' place, summon them to *wait* or to *choose?* 5*th*, From the whole, are we not permitted to conclude that the disciples in this case, with all their intellectual knowledge of the Scripture and their childlike faith, have nevertheless erred?[2] 6*th*, Is it not the case that in Ps. cix. 8 "another" is simply and merely the expression used to denote him who was to "take" the office, and was Peter justified in adding the qualifications mentioned in vers. 21 and 22? How, if the Lord had decreed to do something special in this case, and to prepare for Himself entirely through the Spirit a father of many children in the place of the unprofitable lost child, and to bring in veritably and actually *another* in the place of the apostate? 7*th*, If the latter idea is not the correct one, what shall we say of the apostleship of Paul, which is so distinctly and remarkably asserted? Consider well Gal. i. 1, 15–17, ii. 6–9, and also the gradual progress of the apostolic history. See in Acts ix. 15, " He

---

[1] *Vid.* ch. ii. 14, "with the *eleven*" (not apostles) ; ver. 37, "to the rest of the (not eleven) apostles." And henceforward he writes " the apostles" (not the *twelve* apostles) in every place, as any concordance will show ; and the only exception is in ch. vi. 2, where it stands " the twelve" (but not apostles). I think that, as regarded his human individuality, Luke perhaps did not yet know what to think of the number of the apostles, and of Paul's apostleship, but that the Holy Ghost thus guided his words with scrupulous caution. Take notice how Paul in 1 Cor. xv. 5, 7, still leaves the matter in suspense, which certainly must have been almost clear. He only says in ver. 5, " the *twelve*," and in ver. 7, " all the *apostles*."

[2] Their infallibility at this time can in no way be inferred from John xx. 22 (quoted by Bengel) ; for the breathing on them was at most but the symbol of the arrival of the promised Spirit, just as the Lord's Supper was instituted before His body was broken or His blood shed.

is a chosen vessel unto me;" and Acts xiii. 31, from Paul's own
mouth, "He was seen many days of them which came up with Him
from Galilee to Jerusalem, *who are His witnesses* unto the people."
To this, too, add the words of Ananias, "The God of our fathers
has chosen *thee*, that thou shouldst *see* that Just One, and shouldst
hear the voice of His mouth; for *thou* shalt be *His* witness unto all
men of what thou hast seen and heard." Finally, in ch. xxvi.
16, the reference to Paul's vocation by Jesus Himself : "For I have
appeared unto thee for this purpose, to *make thee* a *minister and a
witness*, both of these things which thou hast seen, and of those
things in the which I will appear unto thee." [1] Whose name, therefore, shall be inscribed on the foundation walls of the New Jerusalem (Rev. xxi. 14)—that of Paul, the great apostle who, "through
the grace of God, laboured more than they all," or that of Matthias,
who is mentioned here, and here only ? [2] Indeed, in Rev. xxi. 14
"the twelve apostles of the Lamb" are the ones named, not the
twelve apostles of the circumcision. Likewise the limitation of the
first twelve to Israel, making Paul a separate apostle to the Gentiles, is contrary to the words of Jesus, Matt. xxviii. 19. Besides,
have not Peter and John shown themselves to be apostles also to
the Gentiles ?

These questions we modestly asked in the first edition. It has
now become so much more certain to us that Paul was the rightful
twelfth apostle, in the stead of Matthias, or in fact of Judas, that
we assert it boldly. Baumgarten's opposing theory of a thirteenth
apostle is strikingly set aside by the words, "the *twelve* apostles of
the Lamb." There is little to be said in favour of what has been
brought forward by Löhe (*Aphorisms*, pp. 26, 27, 100) ; for Paul's
title as apostle is of a different kind from that of Barnabas. Neither
was Matthias *ordained* at the feast of Pentecost with the eleven, but
received the Spirit together with the rest of the male and female
disciples.

This opinion is not one started fresh by us, but is to be met
with in old times. By Münter [3] only twelve apostles are mentioned,
including Paul, and Matthias is not thought of. Certainly also
the uncertainty appears almost surprising in reading, as *e.g.* in

---

[1] These revelations make up for the want of any intercourse with Jesus in
the flesh ; thus Gal. i. 12, and especially 1 Cor. xi. 23.

[2] The apostolic history begins with Matthias and ends with Paul.

[3] *Sinnbilder und Kunstvorstellungen der Alten Christen*, 2d Part, Altona
1825.

Lactantius:[1] "The disciples adopted Matthias *and* Paul in the place of Judas." And yet the decision is very clearly proved, as to which one of these two was chosen *by the Lord* (and not by men). It is not within my knowledge if Guericke, who in the first edition of his *Ecclesiastical History* cursorily set aside Matthias, subsequently altered his opinion. But Trautmann[2] goes so far indeed as to rightly designate this choice " an echo of the natural officiousness and impetuosity of Peter." Certainly, indeed, whoever may be too rashly inclined to refer to lot-drawing, may here find a wholesome warning against placing confidence in the result. In like manner also is he warned, who, by his deeper comprehension of Scripture, feels himself personally urged on to try and work out the fulfilment of God's words, which must sooner or later come to pass.

The discourses of the apostles begin with one delivered before their reception of the Holy Ghost, anticipating the comprehension of the Scripture, yet erring, because it was without *complete* comprehension, in order the more clearly to show us the limit of inspiration for all the following discourses—if only we are willing and able to understand it![3]

II.

PETER TO THE MULTITUDE ASSEMBLED AT THE FEAST OF PENTECOST.

(CHAP. II. 14-36.)

THE FIRST TESTIMONY TO THE GLORY OF JESUS EXALTED TO BE CHRIST.

VER. 1. And when the appointed waiting-time had ended, *and the day of Pentecost* (the fiftieth after Easter) *had fully come* (the feast of first-fruits), *they* (the disciples) *were all with one accord in*

---

[1] *De Mortibus Persecutorum,* cap. ii.

[2] *Die Apostolische Kirche,* Leipsic 1848.

[3] This will also answer Alford's objection, who, excusing my youthful work, sets it aside on this point, and is of opinion that this event would not have been made so prominent in the apostolic history, if Luke had not considered it to be the completion of the apostolic twelve, and intended to represent it as such.

one place.[1] Thus, after the true Paschal Lamb had been offered, must be introduced the true "first-fruits;" and the law of the Spirit which giveth life must be written with the finger of God, not on tables of stone, but on the fleshly tables of the heart.

Ver. 2. *And suddenly there came*—suddenly for the moment, although perhaps on this feast-day the disciples had some foreboding—*a sound from heaven* ("a voice from the temple," Isa. lxvi. 6) *as of a mighty rushing wind, and it filled all the house where they were sitting*—the room in which they were still waiting on that festival morning: filled it, as once the glory of the Lord filled the tabernacle and the temple, and would indeed henceforth fill every one of their assembly places (Acts iv. 31).[2] This wind from God was the bearer and the image of the Spirit, compared by Jesus (John iii. 8) to the wind; which Spirit the Son of man had received from His Father in the highest sanctuary, and had now sent down to the disciples, who were made susceptible to it by faith.

Ver. 3. In addition to the first sign addressed both to the hearing and to the unbelieving multitude, came a second intended for the sight, which appeared only *unto them, i.e.* the believing recipients of the power from on high, the glory of this Gospel-Sinai; just as only Jesus and John saw the dove over Jordan. But this gentle dove, now in the shape of fire, sent its cleansing gifts over and into the sanctified sinners, whose flesh was not only in the form of sinful flesh, but whose tongues and lips also required purifying. Cloven, tongue-shaped (in this predicting their immediate effect) flames of fire were borne down by the mighty wind; and in the

---

[1] The ancient opinion, that by this *all* only the *twelve apostles* were meant (Acts i. 26), has scarcely anything in its favour, and appears to be very forced, if ch. i. 14, 15 is compared with ch. ii. 1, 2, and ver. 46 is also considered. According to ver. 18, the Spirit was to come " on my servants and on my handmaidens;" and also see ch. iv. 31, ch. x. 44.

[2] The opinion that the outpouring of the Spirit, although it was in some peculiar οἶκος τοῦ ἱεροῦ, took place in the building of the temple, is in opposition to the deep sense of the words of Jesus, Matt. xxiii. 38, 39, after which "*He went out*" (ch. xxiv. 1). Our opinion must be, that the intimidated little band would have now (as Acts i. 14) sought quite a different kind of place for their unanimous assembly. Their visiting and frequenting the temple after the arrival of the Pentecostal wonder, which restored the glory of the Crucified One, is an entirely different thing (ch. ii. 46, v. 42). That the time should be shown from ch. ii. 15 to be that of the morning sacrifice is only natural, but proves nothing as to the public assembling of those who were now withdrawn from that sacrifice. Whether the house where they sat might have been in a wider sense a part of the district of the temple, is another matter.

tempest and the flames came—not the Judge, but the Saviour, *the Lord*, who now is the Spirit to us. The shower of divine power descended on the heads of these *first-fruits*, in whose earthly vessels the sacred treasure was henceforth to remain and dwell.

Ver. 4. This fire came visibly on each, both male and female; and from the moment of this penetrating baptism by wind and fire, all were inwardly filled with the Holy Ghost, which is indeed still a tempest and a fire, coming down in both, and although not actually to be perceived with the eyes, is nevertheless to be received in spirit, soul, and body. *All*—for on this occasion, as it appears, *all* were filled, without distinction of rank—began involuntarily, as it were, to pour out in a flow of words the sweet, swelling joy of the power of divine life; but, hearken! it is with tongues different in every respect from those with which they have hitherto spoken. They were *new* tongues, not " set on fire of hell" (Jas. iii. 6), but wafted down from above in the fire of the divine breathing, for the praise and evidence of this great renovation-wonder. They were other tongues, too, as regards their language; for they spoke the languages of foreign and distant nations, as a sign that the testimony now commencing was to be addressed to " every crea- ture" (Mark xvi. 17); as a sign, too, that the Spirit of God is a restorer of the unity of speech, an arranger of the Babel-like con- fusion of tongues into the one sacred Sion-language spoken by all nations. And they spake out in these foreign languages, even before others were present to understand them; but the purport of their joyful cry was ever the praise of God for His wonderful, quick-penetrating, and vast plan of salvation, a prelude to the eternal Hallelujah;—but all *as the Spirit gave them utterance.*

Ver. 5. Besides the Jews settled at Jerusalem, there were, by the peculiar providence of God, no small number of foreigners dwelling there at that time, out of every nation under heaven. They had come up for the feast of Pentecost, or for the Passover a little time before, since which many perhaps had remained. They were, however, almost entirely men who had sought Jehovah's sanctuary as proselytes, or from motives of piety. For the sound *must* go forth into all lands under heaven, that heaven was opened to all men, and that a new Sun of grace had risen on the earth.

Ver. 6. The sharp awakening sound of the mighty wind having come upon the little band of the followers of the Nazarene, the whole multitude came and assembled before the house which was marked out by this *Bath-Col.* When they pushed in, they were

B

still more astonished; for, in the wonderful confused buzz of oracles uttered by the inspired crowd, each one heard his own peculiar language and dialect.

Vers. 7–11. Then were they naturally all amazed, and marvelled at such unheard-of things ; scarcely believing their ears, they said to one another: " Behold, are not all these Galileans, who speak in this inconceivable manner ? " This, of course, was not exactly correct, but they meant the largest number of them ; having heard the name of Jesus mentioned, and having recognised them as His followers.—*And how hear we every man in our own tongue in which we were born?* It was the Saviour of them all who had taught His Galileans the languages of the world, in order to proclaim His salvation! And now it was circulated among the multitude that they were dreaming, and they wished to wake one another ; but all remains the same, and the continuance of the wonder is shown only the more clearly. " Where wast thou born ? " " I am a Parthian." " And dost thou really hear the Parthian language spoken?" " And I hear the Median!" "And we hear Persian and Syriac." Others, too, bore witness that it was the same with all. From Judea to Libya and Rome, Jews and proselytes, all must confess that *we do hear them speak in our tongues the wonderful works of God!* These unlearned Galileans speak of the high things of God, and His wonders and works upon earth, which they now all at once completely understand, and about which they can express themselves! Thus had the great God given them, through Jesus, tongues of fire, which, moreover, were the tongues of nations. The great things of God now proclaimed were (according to Joel ii. 21 ff.) much greater than those done under the old covenant ; but not, perhaps, until eternity began for them, did these inspired spokesmen fully understand what these great things were, with which the many-voiced consecration-psalm of the Christian community resounded. In our inquiries as to the giving of tongues, we must not forget the use made of them ; and that it is our part, with the new tongues which the Spirit gives us, to *praise God* as the Spirit gives us utterance.

Vers. 12, 13. *What meaneth this?* In this question was comprised the impression which the whole matter made on the better part among them, who endeavoured to understand it by natural consideration. They spoke just as the natural man would speak under such circumstances, and used just the words which the outward signs would awaken in them, so as to receive an answer in due course. They did not merely say, What is it? But, as if anticipating some higher aim in it than the mere appearance of a wonder, they asked, What is this supposed to be, to mean, to signify? Others, however, some of those perhaps who mocked under the cross at Golgotha, finding no response in their own hearts to the things said, considered it really only as a matter of jesting; others, too, who were with them, in the complete perversity of their hearts, did not even think it worth while to listen attentively, and falsely answering, broke out into the indescribably foolish words: "Nothing particular is signified! It is a mere drunken effusion! *These men are full of new wine.*" The reception which awaited the testimony of the Spirit among this unbelieving and perverted race was itself a prophecy; thus the world began to mock against the gospel, and condemned itself. This perversity of unbelieving[1] is not to be vanquished by the fiery tongues of continued prophecy, for these only tend to stir up an obstinate decision against them in the incredulous mind (1 Cor. xiv. 23); but it must be convinced by the mild influence of the Spirit in plainer and more intelligible exhortation.

Ver. 14. Enough, therefore, had now been uttered in strange tongues; the aim had been attained; the multitude had been roused; those who were susceptible of a better influence had been impelled to an apposite question, and the thoughts of all had been made manifest. Then, for the second time, Peter stood up, but not in the same way as he did some days before. He stood up *with the eleven*, although distinguished from them, very probably, in the place before the house, *and lifted up his voice*, so far at least as was necessary for commanding the attention of the multitude. His was now a different voice from that mentioned in ver. 6: it was the veritable witness-voice of the still, soft breeze; but the Lord was in this more than in the way-clearing tempest and fire. Now, too, the apostle spake with his own mouth and tongue: perhaps it was a renovated one; but at any rate he no longer spake the languages of various nations, but either the dialect of Judea, which was probably understood by the greater number, or (which is rendered the more probable by the quotation from Joel) in the then well-known Greek. And judiciously veiling the fire of the Spirit, and with spiritual wisdom rightly meting it out, he now no longer utters ascriptions of praise and songs of jubilee to the great

[1] Instead of this, Olshausen too good-naturedly finds in their conduct only "a good-natured jest."

God, but addresses a modest and effective testimony of mercy and truth *to them* (the multitude).

Ver. 14. *Ye men of Judea, and all ye that dwell at Jerusalem.* He begins by simply naming the people he is addressing; just as any other speaker, Jew or Gentile, might have done in every-day life. This bipartite address points, however, to the men of Judea, and the foreigners and proselytes especially, and therefore conveys a covert anticipation of ver. 39.—*Be this known unto you*—with a general intimation as to the glory and honour of Jesus (not as in ch. i. 19). Thus modestly is the appeal made in behalf of the divine truth; but the power from on high acts with it internally and secretly as a joint-witness, although externally everything goes on naturally, and as in the usual course of human affairs.

Ver. 15. What condescension is shown by Peter, in not only denying the accusation, which was as ill-natured as it was absurd, but also in going so far as to refute it with material reasons! The ill-nature of it he quite passes over, and exposes its absurdity by one stroke, first only in behalf of some of those who sympathizingly heard him, whose feelings might still be hurt by the echo of the rude jest, and also, as it were, to make way for his words of truth and reason. He also thus fulfils his first duty, that of defending his brethren, and standing with them as if to introduce them.—*For these are not drunken.* He appears here as their interpreter, and speaks of all the rest in the third person. Having, by his judicious designation of the multitude (ver. 14), already proved that he himself was sober, he could now speak in behalf of the others. He spoke not for the eleven only—for their sobriety was apparent enough by their coming forward with him—but principally on behalf of the whole assemblage of disciples. *As ye suppose* does not in any way sound offensive in the text; but *as ye think*, or *assume* (as the explanation of the unaccountable phenomenon), would be perhaps better. See, too, how mildly the Spirit bears testimony against the mistaken mockery! The error of the accusation under which the rest of the disciples lay is made sufficiently manifest by the words: *seeing it is but the third hour of the day.* What a drunkard must he be, who was intoxicated at nine o'clock in the morning; and besides, what a crowd there were here, all alike! (Isa. v. 11; Eccles. x. 16; 1 Thess. v. 7.) In Israel, where the more respectable tasted but little before the hour of prayer and morning sacrifice, what an unheard-of phenomenon would this be, especially at the Pentecost!—so that, in fact, the pious keepers of the feast, who were under this mistake, were the drunken ones, because they did not know what was the right hour of the day. Understand, therefore, here : *These men* are not drunken with wine ; it is rather *ye* that are drunken with your unbelieving supposition : bethink yourselves, therefore, that it is but the third hour of the day ! By the insertion in the text of the word *as* in the denial— " *as* ye suppose "—the inference arises : At all events, if we are drunken, it is with the rich bounties of God's house, with the sweet joy-cup of the commencing marriage of the Lamb, but not, after a worldly fashion, with the juice of this world's grapes ! But that this divine intoxication is at the same time the purest sobriety, is proved by the transition from the language of strange tongues to this well-arranged, temperate, and judicious address.

Vers. 16–18. From this mention of the hour of the day, the Spirit of testimony proceeds at once to the quotation of an important passage of Scripture, which should teach them what period had then arrived in the kingdom of God, and its full rehearsal would afford another proof against the accusation of drunkenness. It is very remarkable how the living, and, as it were, newly born words of the Spirit, forthwith link themselves on to the ancient writ. The *true* spirit of oral preaching in no way disdains fitting itself into some existing utterance of the Spirit, any more than the new covenant is severed from the old. The old and new Word form one great whole ; and the letter of the Old Testament, both written in the Spirit and prophesied by the Spirit, only awaited its being livingly brought forward and fulfilled in the New Testament. That which was written aforetime was written for the very purpose of being spiritually understood and made use of at the time of its fulfilment. This unity of the old and new was to be forthwith, at the beginning of the new Word, decisively proved in Israel : the further the development proceeded of that which still remained unfulfilled, the more complete would be the retrospect of the existing prophecies and promises. When Christ is enthroned with His own perfected ones in Him in the divine glory, then only is completely fulfilled the word which is written : " Behold, the man is become as one of us." This adaptation of the testimony to the existing letter of the Scripture is also peculiarly important, because it tends much to the reasonable conviction of the unbeliever ; for which very reason God has allowed future events to be previously recorded (Isa. xxxiv. 16). Thus " Apollos mightily convinced the Jews, and that publicly, showing *by the Scriptures* that Jesus was the Christ " (Acts xviii.

28); and a preacher of the gospel at the present time will obtain
a more favourable hearing through being a biblical interpreter, not
in Christendom merely, but sometimes even in the heathen world,
when the suggestion of a prophetical text may very much assist in
promoting a right understanding. *This*—which ye see and hear
(ver. 33), which some of you refer to drunkenness, and some of
you inquire about, saying, " What does it mean ?" The apostle,
speaking before the outpouring of the Spirit, had mentioned with
reverence " that which the Holy Ghost spake" (ch. i. 16); but
now is himself speaking, filled with that more complete inspiration
of which the prophet only prophesied, and easily and familiarly
refers to—*that which is spoken by the prophet Joel.* The first quotation used after the outpouring of the Spirit is not made literally,
but with free alteration, though keeping to the sense ; for the spirit
is the important matter, and not the mere letter. By this quotation also the relation between the spirit and the letter is at once
correctly set forth. The expression used by Joel in the context,
afterward, i.e. after the restoration of Israel,[1] is altered by the
apostle, who intended to refer to the secondary pre-fulfilment, into
the more general prophetical formula, *in the last days,* in the
Messianic future, in the second or last period of the world's duration (1 John ii. 18). *God saith* is here added on account of the
context.—*Of* my Spirit, according to the Septuagint, although in
the Hebrew it is *my Spirit.* This translation is correct here, as
a measure and partition are spoken of ; but the limitation of the
fulness of the Spirit thus expressed is sharply contrasted with the
more slender measure of the Old Testament by the word *pour out,*
i.e. richly, not merely to give in drops, but to baptize with it (ch.
i. 5), to fill full with it (ch. ii. 4), so that it might really at first
cause, as it were, intoxication. If we look upon the wind and the
spirit as identical, the sense arises : That of which we have drunken,
ye have heard, it is the heavenly Spirit, whose rushing noise called
you together ! But mark how the enjoyment by the disciples of
the first-fruits of the Spirit is by the apostle made subordinate to

---

[1] For as far as ch. ii. 11 Joel prophesies of the day of judgment, portrayed
first by the exile and next by the destruction of Jerusalem ; and then to the
end of ch. ii. joins an offer of mercy and exhortation to repentance, and promises the outpouring of the Spirit to come before the general judgment; and
thus the *last* reference of his prophecy stands out clearly. The apostle, however, takes the *middle* one of the three references intended by the prophet,
because the time for this had now just arrived.

the universality of the promise. What ye see in us is but the beginning of a gift promised to *all flesh;* it is but the firstling-loaf of
the great harvest which is floating down from before the presence
of God. *All flesh:* a comprehensive phrase, setting aside all the
unessential distinctions of mankind for the one great common attribute, that all, as flesh, needed the Spirit. This wide-extending
embrace is, however, rather more strictly divided. A distinction is
noted (but only outwardly, and existing according to the flesh) between sex, age, and condition; a discrimination is made (melting
away in the one source) between the various gifts of the Spirit.
These are represented by the three chief effects of the prophetical
agency of the Spirit—prophesying, seeing visions, and dreaming
dreams.[1] But it is scarcely intended that prophesying should be
exclusively promised to the children, visions to the young men, and
dreams to the elders,—a distinction which would place the Spirit
and the flesh in a wrong relation; but the various attributes are
merely combined, and each of them is promised to all, as is clearly
shown in ver. 18.   Joel, indeed, puts the old men before the young
men, but Peter places the old men last. The third distinction is not
marked by an antithesis of two members as before, but by one member
connected by the word *and;* but this is so done that the important
distinction of sex is again notified in it. This also is spoken of in
Joel, as well as the repeated mention of the chief gift of prophesying, which might well come to pass through visions and dreams,
and had indeed just been extraordinarily manifested in many kinds
of tongues. On this point Peter conveys appropriate and modest
information as to this wonderful prophesying on the part of male
and female disciples, most of whom were Galileans and persons of
low estate, without giving any special prominence to the recent
wonder of divers tongues. Finally, it is probable that Peter, following the Septuagint, added the *my* to *servants,*[2] whereby arises
a very striking addition to the sense: 1*st,* The servants are dignified with the Old Testament title as servants of God ; 2*d,* The
children, young men, and old men, by retroversion, are also col-
lectively styled the servants of God ; 3*d,* The *my* forms a vivid
contrast to the *your,* as the Spirit to the flesh ; 4*th,* Even the

---

[1] The Lord appeared to Abraham in a vision (Gen. xv. 1); Isaac prophesied
of future events as to Jacob and Esau (Heb. xi. 20) ; Jacob dreamt dreams,
and Joseph was also an interpreter of dreams.

[2] Luke has the μου twice, after δούλους and δούλας, but the ordinary text of
the LXX. has it only on the first occasion.

condition of believing submission, in which alone the Spirit can be received, is intimated by this last clause. These remarks seem to present themselves so surprisingly, that it must be acknowledged that the new and more complete Spirit purposely lends a helping hand, as it were, to the old Spirit which prophesied of Him; or more correctly, that the Holy Ghost itself completes and interprets inspiration to a higher degree.

Vers. 19, 20. These words of Joel relate, in his prophecy, chiefly to the actual *last days*, in which judgment and salvation shall simultaneously come to pass, and of which like things are predicted in Matt. xxiv. 29 and Luke xxi. 25. They are, however, to be understood, first figuratively, and then literally. But this is not all: the prophetic words embrace in their view that entire space of time during which manifold fulfilments follow one another down to the one great complete consummation. Thus, the whole period of the *last days*, as mentioned at first by Peter, which began with the birth of Jesus, is embraced in the prophecy. When the Son left His Father's throne to condescend to enter Mary's womb, then was brought to pass the first great wonder in the heaven above, and sign in the earth beneath, such as never before had taken place. When the Man from God manifested Himself with deeds, wonders, and signs on the earth beneath, and refused the oft-requested signs in heaven above, then at last was the heaven opened over Jordan, and the disciples saw Moses and Elias, and heard the voice which to the others seemed like a thunder-clap. When the blood of Christ was shed upon the cross, although the judgment-fire and vapour of smoke did not yet appear, yet did the sun veil his face in gloom,—a fearful warning-sign! And when all that had to be accomplished in the flesh, in order to obtain the Spirit, had been duly fulfilled, then appeared signs also *in* the earth beneath, when the Living One appeared among the dead, and offered the atonement once more to those who had before disbelieved it. Besides all this, there is the wonder of His rising from the dead, and of the Risen One standing on the earth; and finally, when the glorified Jesus was exalted to the right hand of God, and took again His sacred blood, that He might shed it forth upon the earth (ver. 33) in fire and vapour of smoke, then, high up in the heaven above, was the last completing wonder accomplished.[1] This eye hath not seen, nor ear heard, and yet by this

---

[1] Luke has again expressly added ἄνω and κάτω, in order to intensify Joel's word for the more developed sense.

hath God prepared an everlasting salvation and triumph for them that love Him

Ver. 21. These references were not indeed understood by those who then heard Peter, nor do we need to understand them in order to be delivered from the dread of the still future judgment, by a simple calling on the name of the Lord; but if, by God's mercy, we are among the number of the saved, we shall one day surely understand them all. To urge and force the ungodly to a penitent and faithful calling on His name, of whom the prophesying servants and handmaids, and all the accompanying signs and wonders, alike testified,—this is the aim and end of all that is taking place ere the terrible and notable judgment-day of the Lord come. The blood-bought fire of the Spirit brings deliverance from the judgment-fire and vapour of smoke ; and whosoever hears the prophecy and sees the signs on earth which testify of the wonders in heaven, let him call on the Lord, who is more ready to save than to condemn, and let him ask to be baptized with *this* fire. Thus will he escape the great retribution-fire which must consume the ungodly, and will become a blessed inheritor of the unrestricted promise to all flesh ; just as he in Israel, who then believed, escaped the judgment which came upon Israel with fire and sword (and also, according to Josephus and Tacitus, accompanied with signs and wonders). The promise is confirmed by the reiterated phrase, *It shall come to pass :* this is on a par with the same expression in ver. 17, by which also it is ratified.

Ver. 22. *Ye men of Israel*—of the people of the covenant, for whom first of all the Servant of God was raised up according to promise from the seed of David, and was sent from God as the seed of the blessing (ch. iii. 25, 26, xiii. 23). The words, *Be this known unto you,* are not again repeated here, as the speech which followed was to be concerning the publicly-known holy life of Jesus; but a hearing is again requested, though in somewhat different terms (merely *hear*). *These words*—these further words —the second part of my discourse, the connection of which with the first part will be shown by the third. But Peter no longer says *my* words, for he is about to make use of the more general term *we,* in speaking of the co-witnesses of Jesus' resurrection (ver. 32).—*Jesus of Nazareth.* This name seems to the attentive reader to follow very remarkably the mention of the *Lord,* whose *name* brings salvation, and reminds one of the signification of the sacred name which the despised Nazarene bore in common with so

many others, and yet bore, as the angel announced, in a special
sense. Jesus is specially styled *of Nazareth*, because He was thus
called in contempt, but also because He was likewise thus called
and well known in an honourable sense (Matt. xxi. 11), and, finally,
was thus designated by the angels when naming the Crucified One
(Mark xvi. 6). *A man approved of God among you*—but approved
as what? As one who had come and was sent from God, which
indeed He Himself calls Himself, with an appeal through His works
to the testimony of the Father, although He was of Nazareth,
from which no other good thing could come. Mighty works, or
miracles, are the more general expression, of which *wonders* and
signs form (according to ver. 19) the chief kinds or elements:
wonderful, extraordinary works (נִפְלָאוֹת), and both symbolically and
typically significant (אֹתוֹת and מוֹפְתִים also differing). *Which God
did by Him*: an express repetition of the leading idea contained
in the preceding words, and an important subordination of Jesus'
manhood to the Godhead dwelling in Him, as of the Son to the
Father, as if to say, By such mighty works as God only could do by
giving such power to a man. It also points to the phrase, *whom
God hath raised up. In the midst of you*: an appeal to the publicity of the Son of man among the children of men,—of the Man
of Nazareth, who had shown Himself, according to Moses' prophet-
law (Deut. xviii. 22), to be a prophet "before all the people" (Luke
xxiv. 19).—*As ye yourselves also know.* This does not of course
apply to foreigners, and hence the special address in the beginning.

Ver. 23. *Him*—the holy and just, the Prophet who had shown
Himself to be approved of God! *Him being delivered*—given up
or surrendered as a malefactor, by the provident, determinate, and
strictly ordained *counsel and foreknowledge of God*, when the fit time
had come. This parenthesis is intended, 1st, to soften down and
place in the background the heavy guilt of Israel, which could not
be passed over; 2d, to show that otherwise it would not have
been possible for them (John x. 18) to have killed the Prince of
Life, and that it was impossible that He should be holden by death;
3d, to form an admonitory transition to ver. 24. Every circumstance attending Jesus' death on the cross—as, *e.g.*, the just mentioned surrender to wicked men, and the fixing on the cross, etc.—
forms a part of the strictly ordained counsel of God, and helps to
fill the measured cup of His dying sufferings. But Providence had
also foreseen the carrying out of this determinate counsel, and had
allowed it to be foretold in prophecy (ver. 31). *And by wicked*

hands (the hands of the wicked)—by lawless heathen generally, who in this instance especially, against every legal form, gave over to death a man in whom no guilt was found—have *ye*, none the less unrighteous and spiritually uncircumcised, done it; as, on the other hand, God did His wonders through Jesus. Him, being surrendered to you by Judas (for the ἔκδοτον touches this circumstance also), ye have further delivered over to and forced upon the heathen judge, who vainly washed his assenting hands, and gave Him up to the barbarous hands of his soldiery. And thus have ye crucified and slain Him—*ye Israelites* first, by the joint-deed and joint-guilt of the whole nation (cf. Matt. xvii. 12).

Ver. 24. *Whom God hath raised up!* Let one imagine the impression these words would make on the hearers, and note the wisdom which did not express them at the first beginning, but only after that preparation of their minds which the preceding part of the discourse would effect.—*Having loosed the pains of death.* This expression can only be understood by deep consideration, and especially by reference to the declaration which follows in ver. 27. Not only ordinary expositors, but even Bengel skims over it. In the first place, in the original text it probably does not say *the pains of death*, but the *labour-pangs of the kingdom of the dead;* and this reading is not adequately refuted by the critics of the present time.[1] The human soul of Christ went down to Hades, just as every defunct human soul; and to every ordinary undeveloped soul, Hades is in general a place for regeneration in bitter labour-pangs. But the death of Christ, the Holy One of God, in whose body and soul was no stain of sin,—the death of Christ, given up into the hands of sinners, that His death might remove their sins, was completed at the instant of His last breath. For His soul there remained no pains or labour-pangs in *Sheol*, just as for His body laid in the grave there was no corruption. The perfected Son of God entered the vanquished kingdom as a conqueror: the soul living in the spirit burst asunder for itself, and hence, for all, the fetters of the great prison-house; and the kingdom of those who were under the earth received the glad tidings of the gospel earlier and more directly even than the upper world! This is the great *loosing* which took place; this is Christ's descent

---

[1] Polycarp and Irenæus so read it. The Old Testament text to which it alludes has indeed, in Ps. xviii. 5, 6, both חֶבְלֵי שְׁאוֹל and חֶבְלֵי מָוֶת (as Ps. cxvi. 3), by one another. Peter, however, affords a parallel in ver. 27, in εἰς ᾅδου, and emphatically uses this very same expression again in ver. 31.

to hell, the secret turning-point of His victory, the root and actual starting-point of His resurrection. For this very reason did the apostle express this hint to some of his hearers, who perhaps knew more about Hades and its pains than Christian biblical critics in the present day. To these deep-meaning words are added the assertion, as vast as it is clear, but only now for the first time appropriate : *Because it was not possible that He should be holden of it.* The expression *holden* is understood in too limited a sense, as referring merely to *bonds* or *fetters.* There is certainly in κρατεῖσθαι an antithesis to λύσας, but the former word expresses much more than mere *binding ;* it means *to be overcome, overpowered,* as if by one stronger both by right and might (Suidas, κρατεῖν, νικᾶν). He who was able to die only by the extraordinary gift of the Father (John iii. 16), and for whom in the world below no pangs remained, vanquished, because He was the stronger, the kingdom of death, and entered the palace of the armed man ! That it was not possible that He should be conquered by it, αὐτὸν ὑπ᾽ αὐτοῦ, life by death, thus vigorously concludes the verse, giving rise to the question, Who, then, is He ? and leading on to what follows : *For David speaketh concerning Him——* Him, the invincible by the power of hell.

Ver. 25. David, in the 16th Psalm, speaks of the Holy One of God, whom God approved, preserved, and indeed placed before His face. He depicts a man who maintained His faith and righteousness as a faithful priest of God among sinners, and yet sought not His delight in God, but in the poor sons of men, in order to bring good to them, and not to God, that they might be holy and excellent.[1] This man, however, was chastened by His reins, just as the infirm are, but yet without sin. He perished in death as sinners do, yet without corruption (1 Cor. xv. 56). He therefore did not remain in death, but made death a path to life, resumed His faithful soul and His sanctified flesh ; and with spirit, soul, and body, entered into the fulness of joy——into the incorruptible glory. He also by these means, and by communication of the same to the poor sons of men, obtained for Himself in His community a goodly lot and heritage. The apostle only points to the context of this deep-meaning Messianic psalm, and begins his

---

[1] According to the simplest translation, vers. 2, 3, טוֹבָתִי בַּל עָלֶיךָ, "my good is not for Thee" ("my delight not in Thee") ; לִקְדוֹשִׁים, but for the saints (in the saints), etc.

quotation with the praise to God for His assistance: *I foresaw the Lord always before my face;* properly in the Hebrew, "I *place* the Lord always before me," with a positive effort of faith combating the weakness which causes his reins to chasten him in the night season, and bringing again the brightness of day to his believing eye. *The Lord*—that is (according to vers. 20, 21), the Father, to whom in this psalm the Son pays all honour, and speaks humbly to Him, "Thou art my Lord" (Ps. xvi. 2). *Before me*— where a helper should stand; *for He is on my right hand,* as my defender and deliverer.[1] If we look devoutly to God, He will assist us; and He stands *by* us, that we may look to Him. He is our almighty buckler and reward, and says to us, Walk thou before me. *That I should not be moved*—by temptation, or in the utmost distress through my ungodly enemies—from perfect faith, or from the joyful confidence founded thereon.

Ver. 26. The word that is here (according to the LXX.) called *tongue* is in the original text *glory* (כָּבוֹד, not לְשׁוֹן), in the sense in which this word sometimes denotes a part of the human essence. The tripartition of the human nature is indeed not so clearly manifested in the Old Testament as in the New; but yet it is made evident to us in not a few passages. In the term *heart* (לֵב) are embraced, but still vaguely, the soul and spirit; and it can therefore, by severalizing it, stand for both. Here, however, as is generally the case, the *soul* is denoted. The term *glory*, however, stands for the spirit, the essential part that is really to be glorified, as is shown by several clear parallels.[2] The third part is next subjoined,—the flesh,[3] which *shall rest in hope*, or properly, *sleeps*, in the full confidence (בֶּטַח) of its indweller that good shall come also to it.

Vers. 27, 28. The three elements of the sacred manhood of the Holy One of God are again distinguished. As in ver. 26, heart, glory, and flesh; so now it is *soul,* the corruption of the *flesh,* and *me,* the essential *self*: Thou hast made known to *me* (the *spirit*). The soul of Him that had been slain by the enemy goes down into hell, just as His body was laid in the grave; but it is not left, made over, given to hell, not even for a moment after its descent.

---

[1] Cf. Isa. xli. 10, xlii. 1; and the contrast to Judas, Ps. cix. 6, 31.

[2] Ps. cviii. 2, lvii. 8, 9 (Luke i. 46, 47); Ex. xxxv. 21; Ps. xxxiv. 19; Gen. xlix. 6.

[3] There is good reason, as pointed out above in vers. 19 and 20, that no mention here or in Luke xxiv. 39 should be made of *the blood*.

Yet the soul does see Hades, as the body is actually laid in the grave. But just as the soul was not permitted to be troubled by the labour-pangs of hell, so the body was not affected by the corruption of the grave. It is very significant that it is just the *body*, to which corruption belongs, which is here styled "*Holy One;*" for the body of this exceptional One only was as a body without actual sin, and therefore holy, guiltless, immaculate, and cut off from corporeal stain.[1] Whilst in us the sanctification beginning in the spirit will at last lay hold of the flesh, but not without "seeing corruption," so that the "body of this death" must decay in the grave until the resurrection, the body of the One alone, though in lowliness, was still a body of life (Mark v. 30); and as, when on the cross, not one of His bones was to be broken, so in the grave no fibre of His body was to perish. Therefore had the weary flesh a perfect "rest" from the ills of man as none other had, and slept a sweet sleep (Jer. xxxi. 26).——*Thou hast made known to me the ways of life.* To *me*, that is, the *spirit*, which, bearing up the weakness of the soul and flesh with words of power, had just before exclaimed, "I trust in Thee! I place Thee always before me!" The eternal, living spirit of Jesus, committed to the Father's hand, received forthwith from Him the key of the path to the tree of life. The Cherub of Paradise gave way before the Angel of the Eternal Presence, and the soul——an element of His slain mortal nature[2]——was quickened in Hades. The soul, free and quickened in the spirit, now went and proclaimed the good tidings of the victory over death, and of the newly-regained path of life, in all the depths of the prison, where the spirits without independent life were languishing in the trammel of their souls (1 Pet. iii. 19). First down to the deepest abyss, hard by the abode of the devil, where the Titans (רְפָאִים) of the world before the deluge, having had their "foundation overflown by the flood" (Job xxii. 16), were yearning for deliverance "under the waters, with the inhabitants thereof" (שֹׁכְנֵיהֶם, Job xxvi. 5). Then through all the various stages of Hades, loosing the bonds of those who had died in faith of a future deliverance; so that they, like the penitent thief, should now be with Him in Paradise, and not in Abraham's bosom only. Then is the body also resumed, and the Risen One quickens, illuminates, and blesses His own for forty days ere He ascended to His Father and their Father. This is the new "way of life,"

---

[1] Only ὁμοίωμα, not actually σὰρξ ἁμαρτίας.

[2] Which in 1 Pet. iii. 18 is called *flesh*.

which He opened to us by the rending of His flesh—the way up into the sanctuary—to make amends for the way of death, leading down to hell, which the first man in his false wisdom had found out (Prov. xv. 24).—*Thou shalt make me full of joy with Thy countenance.* In the Hebrew it is : In Thy presence there is fulness (or repletion) of joy (more than the joy expressed in the hope, ver. 26). This is the consummation. For the non-continuance of the soul and body in death and the grave (that only which died being able to rise again) is the negative side, the starting-point of the resurrection ; the way of life for the spirit (ver. 28) denotes the transition ; and the fulness of joy before God, of spirit, soul, and body,[1] is the positive side of the event, the sitting down on the throne of absolute victory and everlasting life. *With Thy countenance* corresponds, as equivalent to what was expressed in ver. 25, to " before my face ;" and one would therefore expect the second parallel, *at Thy right hand,* and in the psalm this actually follows.[2] But the apostle breaks off his prospective glance at the ascension, in order to confirm the latter by another Scripture quotation (ver. 34), and thus, through the harmony of the Word, the better to convince his hearers.

Ver. 29. The address : *Men and brethren* appears to follow from the former address, " Ye men of Israel " (ver. 22), and to be similar to it ; but perhaps a deeper signification is betrayed by the fact that the apostle does not subsequently speak of *our* patriarch David, but *the* patriarch. In this case the Holy Ghost, in the words of Peter, alludes to the Father, high above all patriarchs ; and in calling them *brethren,* the name is given them because they are the sanctified brethren of the holy God, who were now forthwith to be called from far and near. Whilst, of course, Peter in himself only wished to address his hearers as cordially and forcibly as he could, the expression, in a prophetical light, extends to the *new,* not merely restored brotherhood, with the crucifiers of Jesus, whose hearts began to be turned and their minds changed under his discourse. Peter fitly honours David with the title of *patriarch,* which designation for this ancestor of the royal house occurs here only ; but asks for freedom to tell them that he (David) was not

[1] For the second *me* added in the translation embraces the whole human being.

[2] So that the matter of the psalm cannot be a mere reference to David returning thanks before God in the temple for his deliverance out of the hands of Saul.

the ancestor of this new humanity (the real Israel), and that he was not the Holy One of God of whom he prophesied.—*He is both dead and buried, and his sepulchre is with us to this day.*[1] This seems to form a natural climax, and thus the apostle meant it. It may, however, surprise the reader of the present day, that the apostle speaks as above, and does not say instead, David is not risen again (as in ver. 34); he is not ascended into the heavens. He does not state either that David's soul was still in Hades, or that his flesh was still in corruption: all that he says, indeed, might literally be alleged of Jesus Himself. It is highly probable that David the patriarch, prophet, and antitype of Christ, was among the sleeping saints which rose (Matt. xxvii. 52). Peter therefore expresses himself cautiously, and takes no cognizance of anything that at present formed no part of the testimony; indeed, in the meantime he builds up his proof on this very non-advertence, until by inversion David's resuscitation shall be shown from Christ's resurrection.[2]

Vers. 30, 31. The Spirit here assures us that David knew about whom he spake, although we learn through this same Peter (1 Pet. i. 10) that the prophets did not fully understand their prophecies. In this there are two different kinds of knowing: the knowledge that they prophesied of Christ generally, or, the precise precognition of the times and stages of His sufferings and glory. *God had sworn with an oath to him,* refers back both to 2 Sam. vii., and also especially Ps. cx. (Heb. vii. 21); or we might still more probably say that the 110th Psalm was composed after 2 Sam. vii. (cf. v. 19 and 1 Chron. xvii. 18), therefore before the 16th Psalm. *That of the fruit of his loins*—commonly a descendant (Ps. cxxxii. 11), who, however, was certainly more than that which proceeded from David "according to the flesh," and was also God the Lord in the highest. *To sit on his throne:* just a hint in passing, which in ch. iii. is again touched upon, that the kingdom which Jesus succeeded to was the *kingdom of David,* the throne of God—that the throne which is about to be spoken of is *David's throne.* In Christ, the Son of God and man, the throne of David (the kingly glory of the beloved man) is completely united with the throne of God (the glory of the loving Father). *He, seeing this before, spake of the resurrection of Christ:* a two-sided expression for "he prophesied." This repetition of ver. 27 is used

---

[1] ἐν ἡμῖν, with us, among us, in the midst of the city.

[2] It was perfectly lawful (ἐξόν) to speak so to the Jews.

partly for the sake of convincing emphasis, and partly to mark out three points in accordance with the pervading trichotomy of the whole discourse.[1] The words of the quotation actually referring to the resurrection are here a second time repeated, because, at all events, David's flesh had seen corruption, as shall the flesh of all of us, although *his soul*,[2] as the souls of all of us, if we believe in Him, is delivered through Christ from the power of hell (Ps. xlix. 16).

Ver. 32. *This Jesus:* not David, who had been long dead and buried. These words cannot refer merely to vers. 22-24, but link the things there attested on to what is stated of *Christ* in ver. 32 : therefore it implies this *Christ*, which title belongs to the above-named Jesus of Nazareth; as also the preterite in the repeated quotation in ver. 31 affects the testimony given in ver. 32. *Whereof we all are witnesses* — not merely of this resurrection, but of far more, of the said Jesus, of God; cf. 1 Cor. xv. 15, " witnesses of God." *We all:* first I with the eleven—those who have stood forth; but without excluding all the other disciples : for the apostleship was only a pre-eminence in the community; and the Spirit, which actually bore witness, had come upon all.

Ver. 33. The third part of the discourse is so closely connected with the second, that in its very first sentence a short continuation is given of what precedes. Here, therefore, the *address* to the hearers is expressed at the end, and not at the beginning.—*Therefore being by the right hand of God exalted.* Now is the man Jesus of Nazareth exalted by the power of God, exalted above the depth of human probationary shiftings of faith (ver. 25), and above the territories of the nether world (ver. 27). But because God cannot be a creature, it is manifest that from the beginning the eternal Son of God was in the Son of man; wherefore He alone was without sin, and stood in the " Spirit of holiness " (Rom. i. 4). See, therefore, how completely in this very first testimony the Spirit bears witness to its Holy One, and how entirely the biblical system is everywhere *one* system; so that consequently we cannot interpret and examine

---

[1] For this Pentecost discourse has the most complete arrangement, which Luke was taught and led to give it, although Peter, speaking in the fulness of the Spirit coming upon him from the newly manifested source, may not have thought of or known it.

[2] This significant expression is not permitted to be left out in the **exact** repetition.

that which is written either biblically or exactly enough.—*Being exalted to God.* And now indeed follows the virtual consummation : *having received of the Father the promise of the Holy Ghost.* In these words is drawn aside the sublime veil of the upper sanctuary, and the name of *the Father* beams forth in all its majesty and glory. The exalted Son first receives the Spirit, viz. the authority and the power, to pour out upon all flesh the blessing promised out of His flesh.—*The promise.* This is simply, in the sense of fulfilment, the Holy Ghost (Eph. i. 13; Luke xxiv. 49; Acts i. 4; 1 John ii. 25); the same also in ver. 39. The Holy Ghost is, however, the promise of *the Father*, inasmuch as everything proceeds from the counsel of the Father; the promise made indeed to all flesh, as well as to the Son Himself, to whom the power of pouring it out upon all flesh was promised, as the " fulness of joy," in the words of the prophecy. Not less also is the Spirit the promise of the *Spirit*, which had announced itself through its pre-inspiration of the prophets. *Hath shed forth,* as God; as to which it says above, " I will pour out." *This* (τοῦτο, ver. 16), *which ye now see and hear,* on this sacred day of Pentecost, as you all crowd together, *see* in our joyfulness, and *hear* from our words; which also ye shall further see and hear as the witness of power for the truth of our discourse about the Risen One.[1]

Vers. 34, 35. To ver. 33 perhaps the quotation of Ps. lxviii. 18 would have been suitable. But the apostle selects a passage of Scripture which is still more appropriate as a seal to the whole discourse. For, 1*st*, In it the Father stands forth as the Exalter of the Son in the expression of His almighty purpose; 2*d*, David in it speaks still more clearly, but yet in a way which quite agrees with the former psalm, of *another*, and not of himself; 3*d*, He calls both *Lords*, and makes Him seat Himself, according to the Father's word, on the highest kingly throne; 4*th*, Finally, the enemies of this Lord shall be subdued under Him. All this is quite applicable to the manifestation of the Father (ver. 33), and for confirming the former quotation, and for the completion of the first unfinished inference,—the attribution of the name of *the Lord* (ver. 21) to *Jesus* (ver. 36), and to the *Father* (ver. 25); also, finally, for stringently exhorting the hearers, through faith in Jesus, to deliver themselves from the punishment of His enemies, or to obtain for themselves salvation. There is now no longer any

[1] It is to be doubted if the νῦν is to be omitted. As an " explanatory addition," it adds the very strongest emphasis.

need of showing that David spoke of Jesus; but it stands forth prominently : *David is not ascended into the heavens* (as Elias), but (ver. 29) is dead and buried (it might be said, too, he was not *his own* Lord), and speaks in this psalm most evidently of the Son of God and man.[1]

Ver. 36. *Until I make Thy foes Thy footstool!* The foot of the conqueror on their proud necks ! These must be terrifying words to the crucifiers of the Exalted One.—*Until.* This leaves them some little hope of an interval of mercy ; and indeed this is now offered and opened to them, as in vers. 20, 21, redemption goes before the judgment-day. *Therefore let all the house of Israel know assuredly*—-without any doubt, the final confirmation outweighing the scandal of the cross; let them know, but not merely *know*, but understand, perceive, and then do what is requisite to be done. Consider in your minds : If these things are so, what shall we do ? The deeds, wonders, and signs done by the humiliated One, all agreeing with your prophecies; the resurrection and ascension of Him who was crucified through the counsel of God, which is to-day proved by the Holy Ghost, and testified to by us ;—everything combines to make you recognise the Messias. The concluding and crowning sentence is as short as it is weighty (*tot verba, tot pondera*). —*That God hath made.* This is the consummation of the whole counsel. *That same Jesus whom ye have crucified :* a sharp and heart-penetrating declaration to them, that they were the enemies of God and His Anointed ; and yet that through their hostile hands the everlasting mercy of the divine counsel had been allowed to be realized.—*Ye all,* not the Israelites only (ver. 22); for the sins of *all* of you were the cause of His death !—the Crucified, and now both Lord and Christ ! Thus the cross and Christ are for the first time brought close together, and Lord and Christ (*Κύριον αὐτὸν καὶ Χριστόν*). The choice lies between them : Will you have Him merely as your *Lord* and Judge, being vanquished under His feet; or will you have Him for your Saviour, through the pouring out of the Spirit, the divine ointment of salvation, on *you*, as on us— for your *Christ*—for your Messiah, invisible though believed in, working in you through the Spirit, and yet ruling in heaven ? It is this very same Jesus whom some of you perhaps knew in your own

---

[1] In this simple sentence, " David is not ascended into heaven," some have rightly discovered a hint given by Peter as to the still incomplete position of the righteous dead : for at least those who have died in the Lord, although not yet in the flesh, are to a certain extent already in heaven.

Nazareth as a charitable helper to all, as a benefactor and healer of the sick: *Him* hath God made to be both your Saviour and your King.

RESULT AND CONTINUATION OF THE DISCOURSE.

Ver. 37. *Now when they heard this,* or rather, when they *listened* to it, viz. attentively, obediently, and believingly: it would therefore be more properly, those who listened and attended to it; for not every one, but only the greater number, were minded to do that which the premonition in ver. 14 had requested. Also in ch. x. 44 ἀκούειν has this restricted meaning. "Faith comes by hearing" (Rom. x. 17), and is attentive obedience to the word of God. This listening, however, was not the involuntary hearing as of the strange tongues (ver. 11), but the willing hearing with attention (ver. 33). *They were pricked in their hearts*—through the ears into the heart; or properly, they were pierced through, sharply wounded in the heart by the two-edged sword of the words: That is your Messias whom ye have crucified!—as if the spear which pierced the side of Jesus, and the nails which transfixed His hands and His feet, had been turned back against them. The first great punishment of the sins of the world, brought about as it was by the coming of the Comforter, in that He disclosed their sin in the unbelieving rejection of Jesus, was now felt; and it was a foretoken that the consolation to be derived from Him who had now gone to His Father, whom they no longer saw, was the intention of the punishment. Those, therefore, who were seized with penitent, mercy-seeking eagerness, demanded, *Men and brethren, what shall we* (since what is done cannot be undone, at least now) *do?* They reciprocated the encouraging, friendly way of address (ver. 29), and now ask the right question instead of the former one: "What does this mean?" They dare not as yet go so far as to add, like the gaoler of Philippi, "to be saved;" but yet there is something in the question which seems to mean: "How can we make amends for this?" (cf. ch. ix. 6.) Peter, however, gives them, as Nathan in bygone days did to David (2 Sam. xii. 13), a speedy and gospel-breathing answer.

Ver. 38. All is just as it should be: Keep on and persevere in the change of mind which your question betokens; the first announcement of the coming kingdom of God does not require more. What you have to do consists only in *acknowledging* and *taking*.

This very event which brought you all together here is as good for you as it is for us : it depends only on a voluntary faith in the saving name of Jesus Christ, which pours down " good ointment" (Sol. Song i. 3), in Him who has been preached to you, that you might call upon Him (as was expressed in ver. 21). *And be baptized every one of you:* a prompt holdfast to their newly awakened penitence, and a speedy progress to the verifying confession and sealing sacrament, a prefiguring use of which was already known. The more the spiritual power of a sermon approaches in its nature the matter here enunciated, the better shall we be able to imitate without any anxiety this speedy advance, and to throw out a powerful grasp upon the whole multitude ; as in this case, by the emphatic words " every one of you," a charm like a lightning-flash is specially conveyed to every soul. *In the name, i.e.* the faithful confession, in order to seal the saving call of the name of Jesus Christ, in whom the Holy Trinity is now revealed. For the Father is only known in the Son, and the Holy Ghost only as the gift of the Father through the Son. So that the testimony and confession, Jesus is Christ the Son of God, necessarily included the prescribed form of baptism, which certainly would not be omitted on this the first time of general administration. *And ye shall receive the gift of the Holy Ghost*—the great gift from which all other gifts flow (vers. 17, 18 ; Heb. ii. 4), the ointment of God denoted in the name of the Anointed One, poured not on one king only, or one people, but over every generation of renovated humanity. The Spirit first enters as *wind* and *fire*, afterwards cleanses as *water*, and then becomes as *oil* in the bones. These are His four symbols. The order of succession is—baptism, remission, Holy Spirit. But should it not be reversed ? As regards its germ and origin, yes ; for the Holy Ghost first effects the opening and penetration of the heart ; then ensues the desire, the hope, and comfort of a remission of sins ; and not until then can the sacrament of renewal attest and perfect what has been done. But the order here indicated is nevertheless correct, inasmuch as the *perfecting* and *sealing* are alone in question here ; and the actual assignment of the remission is distinguished from its manifestation in the heart, and the pre-operating converting Spirit from the outbreaking gift of the Holy Ghost. Then began the sacramental admission into the kingdom of grace. On this admission is based the gladness of the atonement, and in this (as then, so afterwards, by speaking with the tongue) can the power of the Spirit be effica-

cious. An unusual inversion of the order of succession occurs
subsequently (ch. x. 47).

Ver. 39. *For the promise is unto you, and to your children*—the
promise of the Holy Ghost in Joel. This is again addressed to the
Israelites first, who constituted by far the greater number present,
and to whom the promises first belonged (Rom. ix. 4), though of
course under the condition of penitent and believing submission :
unto you, ye who asked the question (ver. 37). There is a beautiful contrast here to the fearful words in Matt. xxvii. 25. The
descendants are of course included in the term *children;* but a
reference to ver. 17 will not allow us to exclude the then living
children, so it cannot be denied that a slight furtherance is afforded
by these words to infant baptism. But does not Joel's promise
purport to be " for all flesh?" The following must therefore be
added : *and to all that are afar off* (cf. ver. 14),—an inclusion of
the heathen, with reference to Joel ii. 32 and Isa. lvii. 19, which
Peter himself subsequently did not understand. In the last fulfilment especially of the words spoken by Joel, it will avail to those
who are called from afar ; therefore the prophet, in the passage
quoted, concludes with the mention of them. Peter, however, in
ver. 21, had omitted the conclusion in order to add it here. But the
sense is not yet exhausted, or rather the complete sense is not hit
upon, if we think that by those afar off the heathen only are meant.
Israel also, the figuratively *near*, is essentially as far off as any of
the heathen ; and in Christ only will the two, those also who are
aliens through sin, be brought near (Eph. ii. 11-18).—*Even as
many as the Lord our God shall call.* This sentence is a definition
of the community of Christ generally, and of the spiritual Jerusalem of salvation,—an anticipation of the concluding idea (ver. 47)
ἐκκλησία, and reminds those just then called of the future deliverance of many now afar off through the same grace. It is not as if
Peter had necessarily intended a mere *local* calling to those in the
city and land of Israel, as perhaps we wrongly take it to mean in
the prophet. The new Spirit intended now to make clearly known
this sense, which from the very first lay hid under the letter.
Certainly from the succeeding history we learn that Peter did not
express this glance of the Spirit towards the heathen from his own
understanding.

Vers. 40, 41. Not, however, in all who had at first asked the
question, " What shall we do?" did the favourable impression
extend so far as to lead to baptism in the name of Jesus Christ.

Perhaps the mockers renewed their interruptions, and opposed other scandals to the allurements of the faith, which are not deemed worthy of record in the narrative. Therefore *many other words* were needed in addition to those first spoken. Their chief purport was a further testimony, and further exhortation. But the principal idea conveyed in all these " many other words" was : *Save yourselves from this untoward generation. Then they that,* willingly and spontaneously (for there was no other compulsion but the effect of the words), indeed *gladly, received his word* —chiefly, as it appears, Peter's supplementary words—*were baptized* with the baptism of salvation (1 Pet. iii. 21, 22). (And received the Holy Ghost, at least essentially in their hearts, as the first 120.)—*And there were added unto them* (on this feast of First-Fruits) *about three thousand souls.* Luke now says *souls,* whilst in ch. i. 15 he speaks of *names ;* for three thousand souls were a precious prize for the rejoicing of Jesus, for the satisfaction of the Saviour, who now saw His desire fulfilled, and had for His reward great multitudes of those for whom He had prayed on the cross (Isa. liii. 11, 12). Now were first fulfilled the words of the prophet (Isa. lxvi. 6) : " A voice of noise from the city, a voice from the (upper) temple, a voice of the Lord, that rendereth recompense to His enemies" (viz. with superabundant mercy ; Isa. lix. 18-21). Who hath ever heard the like ? Who hath even seen the like ? Can a land become fruitful in one day ? or can a whole people be born at one time ? Now indeed has Zion become fruitful, and in the same way its children are born ! Yea, they were born to Him like the dew out of the morning-dawn, and His rule began in the midst of His enemies, whom His sharp darts had pierced (Ps. cx. 3, 2, xlv. 6). And the three thousand were added through the word, therefore *called* (ver. 39) to join the 120 who were already *near.*

Vers. 42, 43. *And they,* the converted, *continued stedfastly,* now no longer in their expectant " supplication and prayer " (as in ch. i. 14), but in the four principal attributes of a spiritual community : in the further *doctrine of the apostles ;* in the *fellowship* effected and strengthened by this doctrine ; in the sacrament of *breaking of bread,*[1] confirming the fellowship (as baptism confirmed the entry to this fellowship to individuals) ; and in public and private *prayers.* Thus had those that were brought near access

---

[1] The *continuance* in this shows that on the very first day the first Lord's Supper was celebrated.

in one Spirit to the Father in *love*.   Over *every other* soul came
(at least) fear of various kinds and degrees, especially since *many
wonders and signs were done by the apostles* (the first here recorded
of them), as previously they were done by Jesus (ver. 22).

Vers. 44–47. *And all that believed :* a contrast to ver. 43, and
a return to the description in ver. 42.   The fellowship was a real
one, and forthwith brought about (a fact *not* mentioned in ver.
42) a community in all things, so that the rich brought everything
that the poorer ones had need of, and a division was made, not
with revolutionary equality, *lex agraria*, but *as every man had need*,
with consideration of circumstances and outward position.   In all
this they did not sever themselves entirely from those who were
still " afar off," so that through them yet more might be " called."
They showed their light publicly in the temple, where their Lord
and God, the Light of the World, had shone for a short time ; for
they had now become the children of this light, and had, under
the first impression of the wonder of Pentecost, to declare their
freedom.   And they also celebrated the holy sacrament of the
new covenant in smaller circles, circumspectly and retiredly, *from
house to house* (κατ’ οἶκον, *scil.* ἔκαστον).   By *this* use of the bread
and wine, they sanctified the rest of their ordinary meals.[1]   This
they did with gladness and singleness of heart, and had, though
looking only to God, *favour with all the people*, just as their Lord
had while still a child (Luke ii. 52).   A lovely picture of the
infant community !   And still more refreshing are the concluding
words : *And the Lord*, now called upon by the believing as their
Saviour, *added daily such as should be saved* (out of this " untoward
generation ") *to the* (redeemed and joyful) *church*.   This important
final word, which is based on vers. 39 and 41, and embraces all
believers (ver. 44), is opposed to the term disciples—an inadequate
expression, though derived from the gospel—and can hardly be a
gloss, as ch. v. 11 would be no very fitting place for the *first*
introduction of so large a word.

[1] From the very beginning the sacrament of the Lord's Supper is distinguished by " breaking of bread," but surely every meal among Christians may
be called a love-feast.

III.

PETER'S ADDRESS TO THE PEOPLE IN SOLOMON'S PORCH.

(CHAP. III. 12-26.)

OFFER OF SALVATION IN THE NAME OF JESUS, ATTESTED BY THE
HEALING OF A LAME MAN.

VER. 1. The community who had been called out of the " untoward generation" into the temple of the Spirit, nevertheless fre-
quented continually the actual and typical temple, the judgment
on which had not yet come. Peter and John, the chief apostles
(each in a peculiar way distinguished by Jesus), repaired thither
at the usual hour of prayer in Israel, in order, among the hypocritical crowd, to add their intercessions for the still unknowing
ones to the separate prayers of the community; also to join in the
divine and human ordinances, of which the abrogation-time was
not yet come.

Vers. 2-8. And a certain lame man, who had his begging-place
at the *gate of the temple which is called Beautiful*,[1] addressed, in his
usual way, the two apostles as they were entering the temple.
And Peter, with John (whose close association is, in the beginning
of the chapter, denoted by the ἐπὶ τὸ αὐτό, which can hardly be a
definition of time, on account of ch. ii. 44, but means *together*, as
2 Sam. ii. 13, LXX.), looked upon him closely or sharply, and
said to him, *Look on us!* Perhaps we have no right to say that
the apostles "wished to read from his glance whether he was
worthy of the benefit;" but more accurately, they desired to stir
up and find out his impressibility. The cripple, wondering at the
unusual character of this address, of course looked on them intently
and expectantly, although only under the idea that, as he desired,
something in the way of alms should be given him by them. But
Peter, who also with John, as well as before the multitude, continued
to be the speaker, because his specially powerful testimony was to
be the foundation-stone of the community, spoke the unexpected
words: *Silver and gold* (of which there was plenty on the pillars
and porch of the temple) *have I none, but such as I have give I*

---

[1] There is a contrast here, showing that the poor of Israel were not treated
with due kindness: At the "beautiful" gate of the temple, full of costly splendour, lies a beggar!

thee.[1] *In the name of Jesus Christ of Nazareth, rise up and walk.* In the distribution mentioned (ch. ii. 45), silver and gold were not considered necessary for the apostles' honour.—*In the name of Jesus Christ.* Thus spake the servant and apostle of Him who, in a similar case, had said, "I will, be thou opened." But the servant can do nothing of his own power, and it is the Lord who confirms the word by the signs which accompany it. In *His* name—thus had He promised them—" should they cast out devils, speak with new tongues, and do greater works " than even Jesus Himself had ever done (Mark xvi. 20, 17 ; cf. Luke x. 17, John xiv. 12). In *His* name : this expression can be rendered by no equivalent logical paraphrase ; but it is a name shedding power, the veritable essence of the matter, as is subsequently testified in ver. 16.—*Of Jesus Christ.* Since the first enunciation of the great proposition (ch. ii. 36, 38), " Jesus is Christ," this is now become the comprehensive holy name of their Lord and God, whom they confess, and in whose name they do all that they do, and freely give to every one all that they have. For every one who, through faith in Jesus, has received anything, can and must render it again, not in a diminished, but rather an increased measure.—*Of Nazareth.* This is added after the name of Christ, as above, the cross and Christ were brought together, in order to glorify the entire lowliness of His birth in the name of the Exalted One, and to bind closely together the name of Christ with the name of Jesus, and also to make it intelligible to the cripple, who had not perhaps heard of the things related in ch. ii., but who must certainly have known Jesus of Nazareth, as often going in and out of the temple.—*Stand up and walk.* These words, spoken to the lame man with miraculous power, are followed by an action as kind as it was impressive, leaving no interval for doubt to enter his heart, no time to turn away his earnestly fixed gaze. *He took him,* with a firm, friendly grasp, Peter-like, *by the right hand,* and almost constrained him to obey the words, " Stand up ! " This direction given to the cripple seemed little else than as if one had said to any person walking on the ground, " Fly ! " Scarcely, however, had the poor man (now made rich by the *poor* Peter) stood up, ere he felt that his feet which had never trod, and his ankle-bones which had never borne him up, had received an

---

[1] It is related that Thomas Aquinas came to the Pope at a time when a great deal of money was being counted. " The church can no longer say, Silver and gold have I none," exclaimed the Pope. " Neither can they now say, Rise up and walk," added Thomas.

unusual accession of power. This was the moment when the spark
of faith was kindled.—*He, leaping up, stood, and walked!* Whither?
Naturally with the two apostles into the temple. Feeling more and
more exultant in his *walking*—his fresh, never learned acquirement—
he could in no way either stand still or sit down, but began to jump
and leap "like a hart" (Isa. xxxv. 6), loudly and heartily praising
God for giving him this soundness in the name of one Jesus of
Nazareth.

Vers. 9–12. We find it nowhere written that this healing was
"the first public miracle of the apostles" (as Baumgarten says);
but, on the contrary, the idea is negatived in ch. ii. 43, 44, as there
"every soul" stands opposed to "all that believed." But still it
was, of course, a specially surprising sign among the many which
were wrought by the apostles; for, at least in human estimation,
the restoring of a man lame from his birth was just as great a
work as giving sight to one that was born blind. *And all the
people* that were assembled in the temple *saw him walking, and
praising God* (just as the Christian community did, ch. ii. 47).
They saw him walking, and were therefore full of wonder and
amazement as to whence this healing had come to him. They
had not much need for asking; for the restored man held fast to,
or kept close in the vicinity of, his physicians, and readily gave
them to understand that it was the apostles who had healed him.[1]
The participation of John in the whole matter, who had taken a
part both in Peter's words and in the laying hold by the lame
man, is again acknowledged here; and Peter and John must now
have actually been engaged in something or other together. We
may all learn by this to allow, as John did, the *Peters* among us
to speak and act; but also that the *Johns* should be included when
we speak of the things done by *us* or *me*, as Peter did (ver. 4
and ver. 12). And there was collected round the two a circle of
wondering people, in that same Solomon's porch where Jesus,
after the healing of the man born blind, testified that He was the
"good Shepherd," who gave eternal life by He Himself laying
down His life; saying to those who freely asked Him " if he were
the Christ," "I and my Father are one;" and in answer to those
who took up stones to throw at Him, appealed to the good works
that He had done (John x. 23). In this same place Peter bore
the following testimony, in which, as Kleuker says, it may be

---

[1] Whether he exactly held them by the hand (as χρατεῖν can only mean) is
to be doubted, as it would hardly agree with his walking and leaping.

especially noted "how clever Peter was in stating everything plainly, forcibly, and confidently;" from which also any one of his hearers who had beforetime heard Jesus, might very clearly have perceived that it was still *the same Jesus* who now was speaking through His witnesses.

Ver. 11. The Israelites are again addressed, because, after the first glance on the day of Pentecost at the calling of the heathen, the testimony was again to be limited to Israel first, and to begin first at Jerusalem, in order that the mercy of Jesus might be first offered to His enemies. In commencing thus, the Spirit has reference to the end of the discourse: "*Unto you first* God sent His Son Jesus." There is also in this address a suggestion that an Israelite, as such, had not so much cause for wonder in a miracle, because the Holy One of Israel, their covenant God, who doeth wonders, had from the beginning sent among them prophets and workers of miracles. *Why marvel ye at this* healing of the lame man? or, *why look ye so earnestly on us,* miracle-working Galileans?—coupling together the persons who were visible in the action, in order to turn the minds of the hearers to the person of the Exalted One, in whose name it had been done. It is, however, important here that Peter, who (in ver. 6), in order not to divide the glimpse of faith in the lame man at the moment of healing, felt obliged to say *I*, now again denotes John as a co-operator in the work. A state of wonder at what had happened to the lame man—this was the first step of the impression made by the thing done; the earnest looking at the apostles, through whom it came to pass, is the second step, leading from astonishment to consideration, and to a desire, at the same time, to know something of the authors. As if *we* were the effecters or the producers of this man's walking! —a more forcible and yet more humble disclaimer than was contained in the directly denying proposition (as in ch. ii. 15); for the impossibility of the idea is thus shown, and the Israelites are charged with the foolishness which could look to these men as the authors of a deed which God only could do (through men, ch. ii. 22), and for which deed even the restored sufferer himself, before all the people, praised *God* only; a foolishness, too, which also would attribute mere personal powers to these witnesses of Jesus, who were in truth filled with power from on high. That this is not done through our own power or skill is clear; and among Jesus' disciples it is not said, as of Simon the sorcerer, "*This man is the* great power of God" (Acts viii. 10). Neither is it done through our own *holiness*. Many a disciple of Jesus does not understand this; he will willingly ascribe all *power* to Jesus, but yet in his own *holiness*, *i.e.* believing and piety, he wishes to reserve a share for himself. Of course, this faith of Peter as speaking, and of John his co-operating companion, in the Spirit, conduced to the power of Jesus passing into the suffering man. Any one who had not seized hold of him as Peter did, would not perhaps have made him stand up. But whence came this faith in the apostle, except from the power of Jesus? It was not, therefore, *his own* faith, any more than it was *his own* power; but all proceeded from the power of the glorified and still more to be glorified name of Jesus: both the faith of the lame man, through which he was made whole, and also the faith of the apostle who called forth the faith of the sufferer. Well Peter knew that he, too, had denied (like the Jews, ver. 13) not only the Holy and Just One, but the accredited and acknowledged Christ, the living Son of God: he had had experience of his own weakness and godlessness, and now no longer could speak of any power and holiness as *his own*, but ascribed it solely to the gift of the Risen and Exalted One—to His Spirit working in Him. And all that he thus speaks out of his own heart he may also boldly testify to as being the feeling of the ever-loving, never unfaithful John, for before Him who alone is holy both were as nothing.

Vers. 13, 14. With the solemn title of the Covenant God, in which also Peter, by the words " *our* fathers," makes his hearers as his brethren, does the apostle in the first place excite their eager attention, and also point to the aim of his discourse (ver. 25). When God sent Moses for the typical deliverance of His people, then first He gave Himself this name (Ex. iii. 15); and the same God, sending Jesus in the Spirit for their spiritual deliverance, again by the Spirit called Himself by it,—thus uniting the beginning and the end so as clearly to reveal the oneness of His great covenant with Israel.—*Hath glorified His (child) Son Jesus.* Should it be (child) *son* or *servant?* The word παῖς may mean both; and this term, as applied to Jesus, occurs only in ver. 26, and in ch. iv. 27, 30. Although attempts have been made to settle it (as Luther does) as *child*, which meaning is perhaps well adapted to this passage, as the peculiar expression of the love of the Father, I nevertheless would adhere to the sense of *servant;* because, *1st,* Peter was here hardly speaking Greek, and in the

Aramaic there is no expression suitable for Jesus which would express the term παῖς so surprisingly placed instead of υἱός; 2d, In ch. iv. 25, παῖς occurs for *servant* immediatly before the use of the same word as applied to Jesus in ver. 27 ; 3d, By a deeper consideration of this term for Jesus, it appears very suitable and significant as a contrast to the word "glorified." If we thus translate it, the name of Jesus is joined with the term of *servant*, and yet *this* name is *glorified* by God. The name of Christ is in itself glorious, and a name of honour. But this name of Christ was not reviled by Israel; on the contrary, they would have separated its synonym, "The King of the Jews," from the name of Jesus when the latter name was made shameful on the cross, when Pilate prophetically united the two. But the holy name of Jesus Israel always reviled, and denied Him the honourable title of Christ. Israel's covenant God hath glorified His *servant* Jesus, *i.e.* has not merely dignified Him through His resurrection and ascension; the expression embraces much more than this: it comprises the entire glorification of Jesus in and after the re-surrection, as opposed to the rejection of and denial of honour to Him; it therefore includes the whole testimony to the honour of His name, beginning after the resurrection, and consisting of miracles and signs of power. Here it refers, in the first place, to the miracle which had just been done in Jesus' name : for the context is: It is not *we* that have done this; it is your God that has done it, and done it for the honour of Jesus, who has been rejected by you,[1] "whom ye have denied," and yet again, *ye now deny.* Thus boldly does Peter, who denied his Lord, dare to speak openly to the people, now that his sin had been blotted out, and all pride in his own holiness had been taken away. In this general confession he is in no way bound to publicly own this sin of his, where there is no need for it. Israel denied Jesus, *i.e.* acted as if they had not known things which they could, should, and must have known about Him ; and they did it twice : first, when they delivered Him, the servant (or prophet) and messenger of God, to Pilate, when even the chief priests denied their entire hope in a Messias (John xix. 15) in order to better accuse Jesus ; next, when Pilate, the unjust, as a judge decided rightly that there was " no fault in this man " (Luke xxiii. 4), the judges of Israel, the guardians of their law, were more

[1] Cf. John ii. 11, xi. 4, where the glory of God in Jesus, and therefore the glory of Jesus, is made manifest by miracles.

wicked even than the lawless heathen, and denied the incontro-
vertibly attested Holy and Just One (holy before God, just in
His conduct towards men). *In the presence of Pilate: i.e.* they
feigned themselves to be so hostile in spite of and in opposition
to him, that they were not ashamed to ask for the crucifixion of
an innocent man.—*And desired a murderer to be granted you.*
Thus does Peter, in a few but sharp remarks, put together the
chief points of the denial of Jesus; he freely mentions the name
of Pilate, and appeals boldly to his first judgment of acquittal, and
wisely and rightly passes over the second decision, which granted
the innocent one to His accusers (Luke xxiii. 24), but remains firm
in his statement of Israel's manifest guilt.[1]   Their request for a
murderer to be granted them is brought prominently forward, in
order to denote the shameful self-confession of those that asked
it; and also, in the continuation of his discourse, to place this
murderer in contrast to the "Prince of Life."

Ver. 15. Jesus is called the *Prince* (Lord or Harbinger) *of Life,*
and not only as the Risen One, but as the servant of God whom
they have killed.   This is an important retrospect of the benevolent,
life-waking miracles of Jesus, in which He showed Himself in every
sense to be the possessor and the dispenser of the power of life.
Here, the present miracle just performed, and His previous ones,
and the resurrection of Jesus, with its aim of giving others life
in Himself, are comprehended in one complete conception.   The
giving of life, health, and recovery, was the action of the servant,
and indeed the aim of His servantship: it is now the intention and
desire of the Lord, who wishes to serve his enemies; but Israel,
with wicked denial, has preferred a murderer to a life-giver (who
not long before had raised Lazarus), and—terrible action!—have
killed the Prince of Life.[2]   *The Prince of Life:* whom God—for His
glorification not only as Lord, but also as the minister of man's
salvation, as Jesus and Prince of Life, even to His deniers and
murderers—could not do otherwise than raise from the dead.   *Ye
have killed Him* whom *God* has raised up.   *Whereof we are witnesses,* as ch. ii. 32; but just as there the testimony of the Spirit
was included with "ours," so now is added the testimony through
miracles, and particularly through the one just performed.

Ver. 16. One must deplore Luther's inaccuracy in the first part

---

[1] He only touches upon the "delivering up" of Jesus to the cross by
mentioning the granting of freedom to a murderer.

[2] For the freeing of Barabbas was just equivalent to the destroying of Jesus.

of this beautiful verse. There are two propositions in it, the first of which is in purport: *This man, whom ye now see restored, and know* as having been born lame, has been *made strong by His name,* of which we are witnesses. But this *making strong* (although ἐστε-ρέωσε, as in ver. 7, ἐστερεώθησαν) cannot be identical with *making sound,* or else the second proposition would be the same as the first. Also ἐπὶ τῇ πίστει τοῦ ὀνόματος αὐτοῦ cannot mean *through faith, i.e. by means* of faith, for in that case the first and second clauses of the verse would be alike; and Peter does not repeat anything superfluously. We find the right clue to it in our conception of the preceding *testimony,* that it included the miracle done in the name of Jesus; also in the aim of the whole discourse, which represents the sign which had taken place as an invitation *to* faith in Jesus (cf. John i. 7; 1 Cor. iii. 5; Rom. i. 5). From this it results, as appears to us, that (narrowly following ver. 13) it should be translated: And to (promote) faith in His name, or to further the acknowledgment of His dignity and power, hath His name made this man strong; in which two things are comprehended, —both the strengthening of the lame man himself, that *he* might believe, and also the awakening the faith of others in the name of Jesus, which indeed was the aim of this *making strong.*[1] Again, it is not as if an irresistible impetus gave the faith, and left no choice to the man believing; but yet the *drawing power* of Jesus is the first motive, and then, and only then, our faith is awakened. For where would have been the faith of the lame man if Peter's word had not awakened it? And where would have been the faith of Peter himself, if the Risen One had not compelled him and strengthened him to believe? It therefore rightly follows: *And the faith which is by Him hath given him this perfect soundness in the presence of you all.* By the "faith which is by Him," Peter means the faith which is produced by the name of Jesus, in virtue of its vital power (1 Pet. i. 21): first, of course, the faith of the healed man, but also including tacitly his own faith, and that of his partner in the work, giving all the honour of it to the Lord. Thus is completed what was said in ver. 12.[2] It is as if he said:

[1] Heinrichs is correct for once: ἐπὶ τῇ πίστει, cum in finem, ut πίστις et fiducia in Jesum in animis vestrum excitaretur; ἐπί cum dat. finem et scopum innuit, ut 1 Thess. iv. 7, 2 Tim. ii. 14.

[2] I cannot make out why Alford will here understand *Peter's* faith only, and generally that of the witnesses (ver. 15), quite setting aside any faith that existed in the lame man.

Believe in our testimony, and following on that, believe in the name of the Risen One. The miracle performed summons you to this. For how was this man made strong? From faith in this name. And whence comes (to him and us) this co-operating and restoring faith? Again, only from the power of this name. Hear it, accept it, let it draw you also to faith. This is my appeal to you. See how full the apostle here shows himself to be of the all-powerful name of Jesus; and subsequently he is still more so (ch. iv. 10–12), so that the chief priests and elders were compelled to sharply threaten the Christians that they should no more " speak in this name."

Vers. 17, 18. After the sins of Israel had been earnestly represented, and their guilt in the denial of Jesus made glaringly evident, and in ver. 16 the way to salvation by faith had been intimated, then follows an offer of atonement for the crucifixion, through the cross itself. A preparation for this was, however, necessary, by somewhat softening down the things said in vers. 13–15, so as to awaken confidence, and also in order to define and limit more closely the sins which were capable of atonement, to prevent all misunderstanding. For, certainly, any one who had been once enlightened, and had " crucified to himself the Son of God, and had put Him to open shame" (Heb. vi. 4–6); who had " sinned wilfully, after that he had received the knowledge of the truth,—to *him* there remaineth no more sacrifice for sin " (Heb. x. 26): he has, like Satan, revolted against God with complete knowledge and free-will. The sin of Satan, for which everlasting fire is prepared, consisted in his fully *knowing what he did;* he was not deceived or seduced by any other serpent. The sins of men, which are capable of forgiveness, consist of a mixture of wickedness and error: it is the deceitfulness of sin which acts upon the wandering sheep, and therefore all their sins can be cast upon their Shepherd. We now first understand the deep meaning of the Lord's intercession expressed on the cross; and from this, Peter, in his confident and friendly apostrophe, " *And now, brethren, I wot,*" derives his comforting assertion, and by it reminds his attentive hearers of the forgiveness.—*That through ignorance ye did it.* This ignorance was not, however, an ignorance as to His innocence, or as to the honour due to Him as a Prophet (ch. ii. 22); for have they not *denied* the servant of God, the Son of man? but a certainly guilty yet existing ignorance as to His exact personality and dignity as Messiah, by means of which they misunderstood the Son of God. And

whence came this ignorance? It was connected with their blindness from the beginning: they did not recognise the counsel of
God, which was testified to by their prophets, as to the *sufferings of
the Messiah;* which counsel, wonderfully enough, and yet naturally,
was to be fulfilled through their misunderstanding (ver. 18, hath
He *so* fulfilled, οὕτω). Compare Paul's expressions, Acts xiii.
27 and 1 Cor. ii. 8; although in both passages he speaks of the
rulers and princes *as a body,* and does not assert that *not one* of
the rulers of Israel had known that Jesus was the Christ the Son
of God. For, of course, there were some who said, " This is the
heir; come, let us kill him, that the inheritance may be ours," who
in the actual service of hell, and with complete consciousness, crucified the Messiah of God. Jesus had warned them with faithful
menace against the sins against the Holy Ghost, " which can be
forgiven neither in this world nor in the world to come;" and yet
these sins were now committed in His Person. We, however, must
not venture to pass this judgment on any individual, Judas standing
forth as an example of it.[1] Jesus also spoke generally, " They know
not what they do;" and therefore Peter, following Him, says, *as did
also your rulers.* He mentions the rulers freely, as before he named
Pilate, and passes over their sin as gently as he did the latter's
giving up the innocent One, and so speaks that any one reporting
his words to Pilate or the rulers might be able to say : " He does
not avoid mentioning you, but he does not speak bitterly of you."
By his making a distinction between the rulers and the people, a
certain extenuation for the people is brought about; as if he said :
Ye have in ignorance imitated your rulers, and shouted out what
they put in your mouths; but thus some severity is expressed
towards those rulers, who well knew what they did, and that the
ignorance only fell to the share of the people who imitated them.
So that each, both people and rulers, might apply these few words
as their conscience dictated. The fact that no accusation follows
ἐπράξατε, is intended to more closely unite ἐπράξατε ὥσπερ καί,
and thus to increase the cautiousness of the expression.

Ver. 18. God's *covenant* of mercy is not yet spoken of, as in
ver. 25; but His *counsel* of mercy is now in question, and is denoted
as having been previously announced. The great proposition now
brought forward as a public testimony to the people, *that Christ
should suffer,* is an open announcement of what was said in Luke

[1] Yet the same thing is almost clearly expressed of Caiaphas in the solemn
words, " Thou hast said " (Matt. xxvi. 64).

xxiv. 46, and is the other element of the name of Christ, the priestly signification, in which lay the real mystery of the prophecy which Israel did not understand.   Here, however, the Holy Ghost assures us that *all* His prophets spoke both of the sufferings of Christ, and also of "the refreshing" that should come through Him (ver. 24); and this evidence we must seek for with simplicity and humility, taking into consideration that the *biblical* exegesis of the Spirit makes no distinction between the real and the unreal, the literal and the mystical sense, but comprises the whole in the one great testimony.   *He hath so fulfilled*, through your ignorant denial, in order that the iniquity should be laid upon the Mediator (Isa. liii. 6), and that the sinners should themselves slay the sacrificial lamb, that they might then understand and *repent!*   Thus, what ye thought to do wickedly, He has turned to good, and "brought it to pass, to save much people alive" (Gen. l. 20).

Ver. 19. This is the centre of the whole discourse, the summons to accept the Holy Spirit offered in Jesus.   *Repent ye therefore*— alter your state of mind—the first step on man's part to make room for the entry, through grace, of divine truth.   For Israel there must be an acknowledgment of the sin committed in the crucifixion of Jesus, and consequently a confession of the denied and rejected One.   This change of mind, at which Judas the betrayer stopped short, unable to go further, leads those sinners who are capable of amendment to *conversion*, *i.e.* a believing, seeking, praying, turning to God.   Repentance is the negative element—the penitent aversion to the bygone wickedness, through an acknowledgment of what is right; conversion is the positive element—a believing turning to the future good through confidence in mercy. Sorrow for sin without faith is a sentence of despair; but the two together form the way of life: they are therefore sometimes both comprehended in a wider sense under the term *repentance*, as *e.g.* Acts xi. 18.   When, on man's part, this penitent conversion has taken place, God shows Himself to be the rewarder of those who seek Him, and justifies, sanctifies, and redeems them.   Thirdly on man's part, but firstly on God's—*that your sins may be blotted out* —Peter again derives this mercy from the name of Christ, and indeed from His sufferings (ver. 18), in the same way as he had spoken on the day of Pentecost : Be baptized in the name (signification, *power*, anointing) of Christ, as the real baptism-water of the sacrament.— *Your sins.*   All were comprehended in the one great sin of the rejection of Jesus.   Even your killing the Prince of Life is blotted out and forgiven! We do not read here of its being merely said to the unclean, Thou art clean! But the words of justification to sinners are, at the same time, a washing of regeneration and renovation, a baptism and an anointing with power. Yet at first the positive anointing exercises only a negative action; it takes away the previous sins and guilt of sin, but it does not yet give the Spirit of sanctification. Let us imagine—and certainly it must be only imagination—a man stopping short at this stage, and not proceeding on to that which follows: his old sins are indeed actually taken away, but he continues to sin from the depravity remaining in him; and if the Christ that *died* for him does not also *rise again* for him and in him, he will remain still in his sins (1 Cor. xv. 17).

Yet this is not the case. From baptism proceeds a new man— for the death and the rising again are both one—and at the same time follows also the renovation-power of the sinner. From the washing away of sins immediately results the already begun communication of the Spirit, leading to a new and healthy life and conduct, which is sanctification. Thus, ch. ii. 38, "Ye shall receive the gift of the Holy Ghost." Thus, in Ps. li., the creation of a clean heart in a new, right spirit, follows the washing and purifying. The indication of this stage is facilitated by the context in ver. 20; and even more: it actually is the spiritual healing and making whole, which is offered through Jesus in the type of the restoration of the lame man. We now read: *when (the) times of refreshing shall come from the presence of the Lord.* It does not say *time*, but *times;* still less *the* time (as in Luther), as the article is wanting. This is usually taken to mean *the last times*, that which is now future; and in consequence the whole of the passage is generally misunderstood. *When (the) times shall come* follows immediately the promised "blotting out of sins," exactly as the latter follows the conversion; ἀνάψυξις is also, as we see, the most suitable expression for the still wanting positive element of spiritual health, the principal idea of the whole discourse. But why does it not simply say, *the refreshing,* instead of the *times of refreshing?* It is so expressed quite naturally; for the recovery from, or healing of, the wounds of sin by the oil and wine of the Spirit does not take place once for all, as the *washing* which precedes it: a longer course is needed of gradual restoration, which has its steps and stages, its days and nights of care. For sin still exists at bottom, and sprouts up again from time to time; thence come repeated penitence, conversion, forgiveness, and consequently *refreshing*, until the man is sanctified from his sins. The blotting out of sins must be sought for in the death of Jesus, and times of refreshing will begin through the direct action of the Spirit, in every one who so seeks and believes. *From the presence of the Lord* cannot mean the Son, who through the whole discourse is not called *Lord;* but it means the *Father*, of whom it is subsequently said, "and He sends Jesus." The presence of God is the source of all life and health (ch. ii. 28; Num. vi. 25; Ps. xliv. 4): it is the heaven which Jesus had taken possession of, in order to pour down the spirit of revival upon our corruption.

Ver. 20. *And He sends* ("shall send," Eng. transl.) *Jesus Christ, which before was preached to you,* or properly, *prepared, proffered* to you. The usual German translation (and also the English) quite misleads us here, by giving it: And He *shall send* Him, who now (or *before*) is (or *was*) preached to you. It is neither a *future* sending, nor is *now* used as a contrast; but that which πρoκεχειρισμένον, *paratum est,* is intended to come to you *forthwith,* and not at some future time. *And He sends* follows immediately on the coming of the times of refreshing; indeed, it stands parallel to it, and it is thus declared how and through whose advent these "times" shall come. When does refreshing come to us from God? When God sends Jesus into our hearts, in the power of the Spirit, which is Himself, as the seed of regeneration. This appears to me as the only true interpretation; and I show it, 1*st*, from the already shown close connection of the whole discourse; 2*d*, from ver. 26, where, with evident reference to ver. 20, an already accomplished *sending* of Jesus to *bless* is mentioned, and the signification of the blessing is there still clearer; 3*d*, because throughout the whole Scriptures the expression *to send* is never used in reference to Jesus' second coming; and this is not without good reason. Allowing one's self to be *sent* is the duty of a servant or minister; but when Christ comes again, He will return as *Lord*, as He Himself also represents (ch. i. 11). In the meantime, however, as Jesus, He *ministers* to our salvation, and is ever being *sent down* for a second mysterious humiliation *in* us, following His first personal humiliation *for* us; *i.e.* God sends the "Spirit of His Son into our hearts," to make us His children (Gal. iv. 6, where this sending is placed parallel to the *first* sending, ver. 4). Is it not the key-note of the discourse, that the Lord is again as a servant to minister to our salvation? Would not any of the hearers have understood this from the apostle's words? The idea was so simple: these men perform miracles, and say, "Jesus does them, and not we." Consequently Jesus is with and in them, in spirit and in power. And now they make us the offer that, if we believe, Jesus will in like manner come to us and into us. That which was sent down from heaven on the day of Pentecost is the Spirit, but it is also *Jesus Christ in the Spirit;* and it is also sent to *you*, as the gift of the Spirit is also yours.

Ver. 21. Thus much is certain, " that the whole passage marks out the first advent of Christ, which took place in the flesh, as something preliminary in relation to its consequences, not made evident until later" (Meyer); but, on the other hand, it is *not* said that the sending of Jesus at the " times of refreshing," or that the times when everything spoken by God shall be declared, denote the future return of Christ, and the perfected glory of the *last* times. On the contrary, from a more exact interpretation, it clearly results that the *immediate consequences* of His first advent are intended: therefore it is the intermediate coming of Christ *into* (*upon*) *us, into* (*upon*) the flesh indeed (ch. ii. 17), but in the Spirit, and no longer *in* the flesh ; and this is set forth throughout the whole discourse as the fulfilment of the promise of God. Through this view of it, this seldom understood passage, often quoted as apparently a proof of the " restitution of all things," will assume quite a different shape. *Who must occupy heaven* (Eng. transl., " whom the heavens must receive ")—as a throne ; must sit down, according to His Father's word, " *expecting* till His enemies be made His footstool " (Heb. x. 13).[1]—Ἄχρι χρόνων ἀποκαταστάσεως πάντων ὧν, κ.τ.λ. What does this mean ? First, what does ἀποκατάστασις mean ?[2] This substantive, which only occurs here in the New Testament, comes from ἀποκαθίστημι, and this evidently means *to restore into a previous condition.* Here, therefore, it has been translated, apparently very suitably to what precedes : " restitutio in pristinum statum." But it is followed by πάντων. Are " all

---

[1] The mistaken construction, *whom* the heavens must *receive*, is justly contradicted by Bengel as " violenta interpretatio et inimica celsitudini Christi supra omnes coelos " (Eph. iv. 10). I must, with Bengel, still maintain that it means: Christ takes up, or enters His heavenly abode, His position in heaven.

[2] As it can neither be certainly decided which of the discourses of the apostles were originally spoken in Greek and which in the Jewish language, nor even, where (as here) the latter is the more probable, can we now retranslate it with certainty into the then current Syro-Chaldee, we must treat the Greek of Luke entirely as the *original text.* For if Luke recorded the words exactly *by inspiration*, we must assume that any important and noteworthy Greek word exactly expressed the original word used.

things " the whole earth as well as the heavens ? How are the following words, ὧν ἐλάλησεν ὁ Θεός, to be understood ? Evidently
ὧν stands for ἅ; and then it would simply mean, *everything which
the Lord has spoken*. This translation is, 1*st*, The closest ; 2*d*,
quite parallel to the ἃ προκατήγγειλε, ver. 18 ; 3*d*, It expresses
the main subject of the portion of the discourse which follows,
and forms the transition to it, as a general text for the succeeding
analysis. Compare ver. 24 especially. It is the less permissible to
differ from this translation, because the construction, *the things of
which God has spoken*, remains grammatically and practically firm,
—both the accusative to ἐλάλησεν, and also the reference to *things*
instead of to *restitution* (ἣν, or *per attract.* ἧς ἐλάλησεν, προκατή-
γειλεν, περὶ ἧς ἐλαλήσεν). Therefore let ἀποκατάστασις be *restitutio ;* but πάντων are the *promises of God*. We must then ask
with Rosenmüller, " Quid esset restitutio vaticiniorum ? " and with
Morus, " Fuerantne amissa, ut restitui deberent ? Fuerantne
perturbata, ut in ordinem redigi deberent ? " Καθίστημι means,
I regulate, arrange, restore, set aright any system, organism, or
composition ; ἀπό *per se* in no way indicates repetition (as ἀνά
before ψύξις), but signifies completely, entirely. We find in
Matt. xvii. 11 it is said of Elias, ἀποκαταστήσει πάντα, where,
on account of the πρῶτον going before, it is impossible it should
mean a *restitutio in integrum*. We also find it said, Heb. xiii. 19, of
the author of the epistle, ἵνα ἀποκατασταθῶ ὑμῖν—" that I may
be restored to you." And also Acts i. 6 : " Wilt Thou at this
time restore again *the* kingdom *to* Israel ?" This cannot merely
mean, as it was at first ; for the kingdom of Israel will be otherwise than it ever was, and it is τῷ Ἰσραήλ, not τοῦ : it therefore
means (as Heb. xiii. 19) to completely restore, as *ready set up*, as
it is promised to be in the future. Ἀποκαθ-ιστανειν means very
suitably, *to cause to come anything that is promised ;* with the two
sub-ideas, 1*st*, completion or accomplishment ; and 2*d*, an arranged
harmony and connection of the whole. What are these χρόνοι of
complete co-fulfilment of all that has been spoken, of the perfectly
ordered setting forth or bringing to pass of all that is promised
(into reality) ? One cannot help regarding them as being identical
with the καιροῖς ἀναψύξεως (ver. 20), and that the two sides of the
same matter are here denoted, the refreshing that was taking place
in Israel, and the fulfilling of the words proceeding from God's
covenant of mercy ; both appear comprehended together in " these
days," ver. 24. An important reference now arises to ch. i. 6, 7,

where, in answer to the disciples' question as to restoring the kingdom to Israel, the Lord, reproving them, says, " It is not for you to know the χρόνους ἢ καιρούς," etc. The Spirit now speaks in Peter according to those words of Jesus, and testifies to the gradual spiritual setting up of the promised kingdom ; for the kingdom of God is the sum and organization of everything which was to come according to prophecy and promise. If we have got thus far, we shall now understand what is denoted by the *until* (ἄχρι). *Times* are not *one time*, nor a fixed term ; ἀποκατάστασις is also *the placing* and not *the being placed in a state of restoration ;* consequently ἄχρι is not the same as ἕως ἄν (ch. ii. 34), but is equivalent to *whilst, as long as.* Peter has here arranged the words of prophecy in two portions, as in 1 Pet. i. 11. After the fulfilment of the things prophesied as to the sufferings of Christ had been pointed out, he now promises also the completion of all that had been spoken, *i.e.* of that yet remaining which concerned the glories afterwards (certainly not without Christ suffering again in His members). He says, *holy* prophets, solemnly corroborating ver. 18 ; he adds, *since the world began*, in order to comprehend everything which had been predicted, even the things which, *e.g.*, Noah and Enoch may, unknown to us, have spoken as to the future Judge and Comforter.

Vers. 22–24. God's covenant of mercy ratified before the time of Moses with the human race—which, though under the dominion of death, was again to be restored (Rom. v. 14)—was included in the covenant with Israel, the chosen and beloved " peculiar people," first in a figure, but after Christ's resurrection, in fulfilment. Peter, therefore, who had mentioned all the prophets since the world began, now turns to the prophets of Israel, and begins with Moses, their first and great prophet (Rom. x. 19). This most important passage which is here quoted (Deut. xviii. 15 ff.), certainly can never be fully understood by those who will not allow it its manifold or full senses ; and there will always be a dispute as to the two chief references in it, so long as they are not considered *together*. On the one hand, it is irrefutable, according to the context, that Moses, after (ch. xii.–xvi.) having prescribed various holy ordinances in Israel, of which the three great feasts form the conclusion, proceeds in ch. xvii. to the institution of present and future officials ; foreseeing everything, he passes on from the judges and " people in authority at every gate " to the future kings ; over the latter (ch. xviii. 1–14) he sets the priests, and finally over both he sets the office of prophet, the highest and most glorious in Israel for all future time. That the prophet of whom Moses speaks stands in the same manifestly close relation to every future one, as the king in ch. xvii. 14 to all future kings, is proved by ch. xviii. 20–22. On the other hand, this way of understanding the passage is not to take away from us the special relation, hidden indeed at first, but subsequently made clear,—the relation to Christ, the greatest and last Prophet in Israel. In favour of this sense there are many of Moses' expressions which could be fulfilled in Him only. " A prophet *like unto me,*"—this can strictly be no other than the only One who was greater than Moses (Heb. iii. 2–6 ; Deut. xxxiv. 10). " *And will put my words in his mouth* " could only be truly completed in Christ (Isa. xlix. 2, li. 16). " Whosoever will not hearken unto *him,* shall be destroyed out of Israel," was true only in Christ ; for whosoever believeth not on the Son is already destroyed ; but unbelief in His predecessors and types was for a very long time overlooked in Israel (Acts vii. 52 ; Jer. xxvi. 2–6, xxxv. 12–16). Besides, Christ was sent by the covenant God, to redeem a people for Himself, as Moses was ; He is a leader and a prince, as Moses ; He is also, as Moses, a worker of extraordinary miracles, a powerful deliverer, a lawgiver, a covenant-maker, an intercessor, and a mediator. Moses, the first in the prophetic series, surveying in futurity the whole of the band which followed him down to the last great One, naturally comprehends them all in this last ; and the more so, that the aim and office of all the intermediate prophets was only to testify of this *One,* and to lead on to *Him.* When, therefore, after Malachi no other prophet arose in Israel for a long period, this way of understanding the passage would awaken expectation (1 Macc. xiv. 41). Thus deep and full, laid open by their fulfilment from the shell to the kernel, are the words of the prophecy. And if we ask how Peter interpreted and made use of these words, we find that he accepted them exactly as they applied, namely in this two-fold meaning.—*And all the prophets from Samuel, and those that follow after, as many as have spoken, have likewise* (as the aim of all their speaking) *foretold of these days.* Their unanimous testimony pointing to the consummation in Christ, is therefore, according to Moses' fundamental national law, to be listened to by Israel. It is clear why Peter particularly mentions Samuel after Moses ; for between Moses and Samuel there was but little prophesying (1 Sam. iii. 1), and nothing is much dwelt on in the Scriptures as to this time. The second period of prophecy opens, however, with Samuel —the typical period which was founded on David,—and therefore

the mother of him who was to anoint Israel's king was the first
to speak of the *Anointed of God* (1 Sam. ii. 10). There is indeed
no Messianic prophecy recorded of Samuel; but he is mentioned
as the precursor and chief personage, and reference is made to the
things spoken by him, as by Enoch and Noah in ver. 21. The Holy
Ghost, speaking in Peter, knew what had been spoken by all the
prophets, and not merely the things which had been written down.

Ver. 25. *Ye are the children of the prophets,* i.e. the successors,
for whom they all spake; ye live in these days, which in their prospective glance they called "the last days." But the expression
"children" superinduces another important point which must be
noticed, and on which the fulfilment of prophecy, indeed prophecy
or prediction itself, is grounded. Israel possessed prophets or prophesying, because it was chosen, called, ordained to be a kingdom
of God, which is the aim of the prophecy. Therefore the *covenant*
of God with His people is now added, in which is prefigured His
covenant of mercy with redeemed mankind.—*The children of the
covenant.* This phrase expresses more than the *children of the
prophets;* it means those most closely interested, the nearest heirs
of the childship founded on this covenant, through the one seed of
the blessing. The promise to Abraham is named, as the words
following it express, " Ye are its heirs." Its reference to Jesus is
not expressed, He having been already denoted as the aim and end
of all prophecy; but it is to be necessarily understood, because ver.
26 goes on to offer Jesus as the seed of the blessing. What, then,
is Abraham's seed, and the blessing through it? The promise of
a seed is linked on to the promise of the *woman's seed,* and is afterwards more closely defined by *thy seed,* and subsequently more
closely still by the term *Judah's* (Gen. xlix. 10) and *David's* (2
Sam. vii. 12). See how divinely simple and clear the word of God
is for any one who interprets it simply in God's light; and remark
what a beam of unity here sheds its clear light on the fulfilment,
in Jesus Christ of Nazareth, of God's whole covenant of mercy
with Israel; and how the glorified Son of God and David is predicted in the seed which was to be both Abraham's seed, and also
a seed of blessing for all the world. Yes, Jesus Christ, the new
seed promised from the beginning, born from the Godhead into
humanity, is the fruit and aim of the prophets preparing for His
appearance, and the root and foundation of the blessing disseminated
by the new covenant.

Ver. 26. Peter, having in his preceding words again testified of the call to all the heathen, now continues to address Israel, and says, *Unto you first.* The word "first" is the explanation of the term "children" in ver. 25, and allows to Israel its precedence, and to the heathen their succession, just as it was ordained in the promise to Abraham, and as Jesus had commanded, that the apostles should *begin* at Jerusalem, among the crucifiers.—*Having raised up His Son Jesus.* The manhood and Godhead of Jesus is now embraced in one glance, for the promised One was to be " of your brethren" (ver. 22), and of Abraham's seed; but yet He is in heaven as the Son of God (ver. 21), in order thence to shed down the blessing. Do we now understand the *sending* of the Saviour, who also acts as Lord *by blessing?* Do we now understand the *raising up* or *sending down* of everything promised in this One, the promised servant of God, taken out of our midst, whom God has raised up, sent down, and offered to us? The apostle has now offered the *blessing* of Jesus, but he cannot conclude without again explaining this blessing of spiritual healing and renovation in its negative sense. He therefore adds the real sting of the summons to repentance: *in turning away every one of you from his iniquities.* This is the concluding explanation of the blessing; and the iniquities, πονηρίαι (which certainly remain in spite of the "ignorance," ver. 17), are the manifold weaknesses, defects, and hurts, the marring of sin (not merely the guilt, ver. 19), from which Jesus frees and heals by the powerful blessing of the Spirit: they are the real enemies dwelling in us, from which the Messiah delivers us (Luke i. 74, 75). *Every one of you*—thus exactly following ch. ii. 38. What was there offered as the " Holy Ghost," with the clear expression of the New Testament revelation, is here brought forward, in retrospective connection with the Old Testament promise, as the " blessing of Abraham " in the advent of Jesus. In the expression *His servant* (Son) *Jesus,* which implies *being sent,* the beginning and conclusion of the discourse are united : Jesus appears as the true Isaac (the son of joy) of the true Abraham (the father of his people) ; and from the former is to proceed the true Jacob-Israel (the striving yet conquering people of the Spirit). In the middle of the discourse, the already (ch. ii.) explained name of Christ is joined to that of Jesus; but at the beginning and end, the priestly, blessing-bringing import of the name of Christ, is first made truly evident *in* the name of Jesus : so that subsequently, in ch. iv. 12, it is decided that the one only salvation is to be ascribed to the one only Saviour's name.

IV.

PETER BEFORE THE COUNCIL OF CHIEF PRIESTS AND ELDERS.

(Chap. iv. 8–12.)

SOLEMN SUMMING UP OF THE CURE OF THE LAME MAN IN THE NAME OF JESUS.

Vers. 1–3. *And as they*—either Peter *for* John, or John also with Peter, which is hardly probable—*spake unto the people,* and after they had just uttered the last necessary concluding sentence, and, according to God's counsel, *not before,*[1] there suddenly came upon them a commission of arrest which had hitherto kept in the background. This consisted of the priests who were near, the captain of the Levitical temple-guard, and a number of Sadducees. Each had reason to be vexed and inflamed with zeal by the apostle's discourse : the captain, on account of the uproar occasioned by the bold words of an unauthorized and common man ; the priests, on account of the teaching of this Galilean about Jesus ; the Sadducees also (now as in ch. v. 17), who understood everything that was mighty and great only through the contracted ear and heart belonging to their narrow system, on account of the announcement of the resurrection and therefore of the possibility of resurrection generally, shown through the great example of this Jesus, who had certainly died. And they laid hands on them, and put them in hold until the next day ; for since ch. iii. 1, during the time of the healing, the assemblage, and the discourse, evening had now come.

Ver. 4. But unfortunately they were too late in their measures! For many were won over by the word to believe in Jesus, so that on this day the Christian community at Jerusalem was increased (since ch. ii. 41) by five thousand men (exclusive of women and children).

Vers. 5–7. The matter was therefore urged along earnestly enough : hasty messages were sent round ; and as soon as the morning of the next day came, there was a full sitting of the High Council, which (almost) all the scribes in Jerusalem[2] joined. They

---

[1] We are not to assume that the discourse was actually broken in upon ; for, as far as we can see, it appears to be fully concluded.

[2] Thus, according to the reading ἐν Ἱερουσαλήμ ; which, however, might be

were *their* rulers, elders, and scribes, *i.e.* of the two prisoners, and of the believers in Jesus (ver. 4), as well as of all the Jews ; Annas *and* Caiaphas having been at that time high priests, together, or rather perhaps alternately, according to some unexplained but quite possible arrangement. Now, since the judgment of Jesus, Annas had taken precedence of Caiaphas; but the latter, as well as all the other *viri pontificii*, did not fail to be present. And they placed the prisoners before them, perhaps in the very same place in which Jesus had stood not long before, and inquired of them (ἐπυνθάνοντο, ch. xxiii. 20), *By what power, or by what name, have ye done this?* They do not ask first, whether this manifest sign had actually taken place, for it was obvious to all who dwelt at Jerusalem (ver. 16) ; and either through a remarkable dispensation of God's mercy, according to which these judges were compelled to act, or because the restored man had allowed himself to be imprisoned with his helpers, the living witness of the deed likewise stood before them (ver. 10).[1] They also say, in a reserved and close way, *Have ye done this?* thus making as little of it as possible, and thinking that they should be able to mystify, and perhaps blacken, the evident fact with their high magisterial inquiry as to the *power* and *name,* and to put down the poor Galileans with their contemptuous *ye!* O fools, who were caught in their own trap! For this solemn inquisition itself testified of the greatness of the deed, and that *these* people did it ; also of the name in which it was done! And they betrayed that they already knew the matter about which they were asking, and had received a lucid account of the healing "in the *name* of Jesus." Finally, the fact that they were most anxious to make prominent that the performers of the miracle had substituted the name of a man for that of God, in which name alone miracles were to be done in Israel—this they do not venture to speak out so boldly now, after all that had happened, as they did before (John x. 33, xix. 7).

Ver. 8. Then was Peter again filled with the Holy Ghost, as before (ch. ii. 4) and afterwards (ch. iv. 31). This marks a distinction between the transitory, special inspiration, and the more general and abiding influence of the Spirit. He who before a maid-servant had denied that he knew " the man," now—the words

an explanation of the more difficult εἰς. The latter would mean that many dwelt abroad outside the gates, and then came to Jerusalem.

[1] It is very improbable that they had cited or imprisoned the lame men with the apostles, or it would have been mentioned in ver. 3.

of Matt. x. 19, 20 being for the first time fulfilled—before the council testifies of Him whom they already knew, and announces to them the Crucified One as their sole salvation !

Vers. 8, 9. After having first acknowledged in a fitting address the authority of the rulers of Israel—omitting, however, to name the many so-called high priests[1] who were present in an irregular way—the accused next avails himself of the privilege which was allowed in every legal court, of again referring clearly to the state of the case, the matter of accusation. He expressly allows that, from the power attributable to their offices, they have the right to call him to account ; but cannot help stating that the work which was dismissed by them with the contemptuous term "*this*" carried with it its own justification. Shall we be brought to account for a good deed done to an impotent man ? Just so had Jesus spoken to the Jews in Solomon's porch : "Many good works have I shown to you: for which of these works do ye stone me ?" (John x. 32.) Thus, too, does he answer the question, "By what power or permission have ye done it ?" Surely it is permitted by the rulers to do good in Israel? (Matt. xii. 12.) He does not say, this healing of the lame man, but expresses it more generally—*the good deed done to the impotent man.* This is partly to lay down the proposition that a good deed does not need permission, and partly because he intended (in ver. 12) that the symbol should convey a more general meaning, to which the term σέσωσται conduces. *By what means,* or through *whom,* ἐν τίνι—this gives his judges to understand that he well knew that they were aware what his answer would be. Through whom *he* is made whole : thus he merely designates the witness standing by as *an impotent man ;* for the apostle intended, at the conclusion of his discourse, to comprehend himself, the rulers, and the restored man all together as impotent men, if without the help of Jesus.

Ver. 10. A solemn announcement, in which the tone of the discourse changes from that of the answer of an accused man to the message of an ambassador. Every member of the council is candidly addressed, and the testimony is delivered to the whole people of Israel through their rulers. The answer itself, beginning so forcibly and yet so merely responsively, by ascribing virtue to the *name,* scarcely needs an explanatory word : in this place, and under these circumstances, one must feel all its weight. Just as in addressing the poor man (ch. iii. 6), so now also the depreciated

[1] They might, however, have been included among the rulers ; *vid.* ch. xxiii. 5.

locality of Nazareth is added to the name of Christ: it is the same
name for princes and people. *Whom ye crucified:* the first accusation of having crucified *Christ* (in ch. ii. 36 and iii. 15 it was
Jesus only). This is a confirmation of what was said before as to
the sins of many of the rulers, and a calling to mind of Jesus'
protestation before Caiaphas, that He was the Christ. Although
in ch. iii. 17 the rulers had been mildly spoken of to the people,
in the present case nothing is said as to their ignorance and the
providence of God. *Whom God raised from the dead:* a brief
mention of the matter attested since Pentecost, which indeed the
rulers already were acquainted with (Matt. xxviii. 11). The
repetition, omitted by Luther, *even by Him,* sharpens the point of
the expression, and seems to say, Even by Him who was condemned
by you, but, contrary to your sentence, justified by God before
Israel! It adds emphasis to the words which follow: *By Him
doth this man stand here before you.* The man that was born lame,
and must otherwise have sat down or have been carried, *stands*
here *whole.*

Ver. 11. So far the two questions are answered by an appeal
to the supreme authority in Israel—Christ, the King crucified by
the rulers—and to the highest power on earth, the power of the
risen God. The proof of both consists in the man made whole
in the presence of all. By this every accusation is invalidated;
indeed, a bitter charge is laid against the High Court itself. The
matter takes a still further turn: the apostle of the crucified
Christ has more to say to the rebellious officials than merely to
answer their question: he has to declare to them God's word and
testimony as to the spiritual salvation of the world, to which this
corporeal restoration was intended to point. How could he act
more judiciously, than to bear witness before the High Council
through a passage which Jesus had reproached them with in the
temple ere they crucified Him (Matt. xxi. 42)? Thus strikingly
did Peter know how to quote the passage which Jesus had already,
though prophetically, uttered, and in this way to say more emphatically than He otherwise could: *It is fulfilled!*—thus introducing himself to the deposed officials in his actual dignity of
office as minister in the new temple and the renovated Israel. In
this example, remark again how mightily the Spirit of the new
Word handles and sets forth the letter of the old, adding the clear
interpretation to the prophetical figure.

Ver. 12. *Neither is there salvation in any other! In any other* is closely linked on to the rejected but yet vindicated "corner-stone;" as if to say, It rests upon no other foundation, and proceeds from no other source, being, power, name, or anything else. Salvation simply, both bodily and especially spiritual, the salvation of God for men, as it was promised to Israel and the whole world in the Messiah, and as we all wish to be saved. There is no other Messiah, Helper, Deliverer, or Physician of souls; this crucified Jesus is the one and only Saviour. *For there is none other name under heaven given among men:* a fortifying repetition, with an appeal to the name of Jesus, which is intimated, but purposely unexpressed. *Among men*—not merely Israel (ver. 10); among *men.* Whether they be rulers and elders, or publicans and beggars, all, like him standing in the midst of them, were impotent men through sin, which ruled and destroyed under heaven. All needed the salvation of God from heaven; and this salvation is the name of Jesus, on which whosoever calls will be saved. When everything is given and offered in one name, nothing but faith in and acceptance of this name can avail. *Whereby we must be saved:* a wonderful command, one might say, to sinners with whom mercy knew not how to reason. God not only gives the name of the Saviour, but also the command of strong paternal love, that we are to believe in Him (1 John iii. 23). The ambassador of the rejected King stands forth here full of authority over the rebels; but, at the same time, very rich in love. There is an almost impalpable delicacy in this union of dignity and humility, severity and mildness, which characterizes the close of the testimony. The concluding word in the original text is *we;* and with this incomparable *we,* which was prepared for by the general expression "men," the apostle, as his concluding point, comprises the restored man standing in the midst, all the members of the council, himself and John, the whole company of those who believed in and were saved by Christ,—including, indeed, the whole race of men in the all-embracing covenant of mercy of the Father who gave Jesus. Having responded to the haughty "*ye*" in ver. 7 with his humble "*ye*" in ver. 8, in ver. 11 he was compelled to place himself in opposition to the rulers, yet avoided mentioning himself expressly, naming Him only whose witness he was; but now he lapses into kindness to the enemy, expressing the hope that they too may believe and be saved; and concludes, making amends for the severity of his testimony with the conciliatory "*we,*" truly a shame-reflecting contrast to their haughty, threatening "*ye.*" Let every Christian, when before his rulers, learn from this all that the Spirit here teaches!

Vers. 13, 14. How was it possible that the rulers of Israel, before the assembling of the council, should not have known that the lame man had been restored through the name of Jesus, and that the disciples of the Crucified One, since the day of Pentecost, had announced salvation and resurrection in Him as Christ? In fact, they only wished to prove whether these persons were plain-spoken enough to assert their opinions before the judges of their Jesus. But the experiment went further than they expected; and the decree in Ps. cxviii. 22, 23 became realized, and they marvelled. As regards plain speaking at least, they all perceive the clear testimony of the Spirit in John no less than in Peter, for the former took a corroborative and manifest share in the words of the latter. At the same time, they understood and felt, from the tone and manner of this free speaking, that these were unlearned and so-called common people. Ἀγράμματοι, without human book-learning, of which the Spirit had no need; ἰδιῶται, without position and dignity (*privati*, not "builders," ver. 11). Added to this, they clearly perceived *that they had been with Jesus.* They knew this perhaps from the very first, as Peter, James, and John had been peculiarly accustomed to accompany Him; or perhaps from the facts related in John xviii. 15, 16. The more reasonable rulers were compelled to wonder, and some of the worst of them perhaps to dread; and yet the explanation of the joy of these "common persons" was so clear in the powerfully expressed words, *God has raised Jesus from the dead!* But to submit to this testimony, to acknowledge the Crucified One as Christ, and to seek salvation in His name,—these were things impossible for, and not to be thought of by, these chief priests, elders, and scribes, who had wandered so far in the way of unrighteousness, and had quite forgotten that they also, like every one else, were miserable men. Should they contradict his words, and consequently condemn them? But before them stood the restored man, standing with those who bore witness to the salvation in Jesus, and testifying with them; and they saw the two witnesses, and the third witness, and *could say nothing against it.* So great was the momentary efficacy of the truth, and such was the effect of the yet remaining consciousness and susceptibility of conscience of the council, that they were speechless, and were compelled to collect their thoughts ere they could venture to use threats against the truth.

Vers. 15-17. The latter course, alas, was soon taken. The witnesses were compelled to leave the presence of the council, in order that it might deliberate on folly and wickedness. *Depart!* is the language used to that which man cannot gainsay. It now goes on : *What shall we do to these men?*[1] They still cling to the external circumstances of these unlearned and private persons, and fortify their minds with the thought that the matter only concerned *these men,* and not, as in truth, every one under heaven, even themselves also, and God's salvation in Israel. That something must be done to these persons is their ready resolution ;[2] but *what?* This is ever a difficult question for those who wish to silence truth. Shall they deny it, as they had done before ? They would willingly do this, but now it is not possible even to these hypocrites ! It would be easy enough if *they only* were aware of it, but it had been publicly and openly done in Jerusalem; and although these hypocrites and unjust judges feared not God, they were afraid of the people, now as heretofore (Matt. xxi. 26, xxvi. 5). They did not indeed fear these men of God, who had spoken the truth to them, but the multitude, over whom they ruled under the title of truth.—*That indeed a notable miracle had been done by them.* This they knew from the accused before the court, and this they have now to add to their contemptuous *" these men;"* but they would not take heed to the meaning and voice of the miracle, their hearts being hardened by the repeated rejection of the miracles of Jesus (John xi. 47). But, finally, they determine, and in their folly catch at the idea, that nothing further should arise out of the thing done, and for this purpose they make provision. They think that they shall be able to manage that the matter should spread[3] no further among the rest of the people (to whom the announcement in ver. 10 applied). And how was this to be done?—*Let us straitly threaten them, that they speak henceforth to no man in this name.* Truly an impotent opposition to the name given from heaven to all men, whereby they *must* be saved ! And to this opposition the "must" stands eternally opposed. They, however, so well understood Peter's concluding words, that the *name for all men* echoed loudly even in their minds; and although from the very first they evaded mentioning

[1] Compare John xi. 47, " This man ; " and also Acts xxvi. 32.

[2] ποιεῖν τινί τι applies here as in Matt. xxi. 40, Luke xx. 15 ; cf. Matt. xvii. 12, Luke xxiii. 31.

[3] διανεμηθῇ, like a contagious disease (2 Tim. ii. 17).

Jesus, noticing only " these ignorant persons," yet at the conclusion they are compelled both to think of and utter this name.

Ver. 18. *And they called them, and commanded them*—the command of the Supreme Council of Israel against the divine " must," which indicated salvation to all—*not to speak at all nor teach in the name of Jesus.* They do not seek to show that it is not a salvation-bringing name ; they do not exercise their duty as elders towards these fanatics, but merely desire them to hold their tongues. As tyrants who had been made to look foolish by the simple testimony of a Peter, they now wish to make the whole people forget the crucified Worker of miracles, who even after His death wrought fresh wonders (Mark vi. 14), and to force the disciples to keep silence about their Master—His chosen witnesses to ignore their Risen One.

Vers. 19, 20. Now John also enters more prominently on the scene ; for their open confession has this effect, that *we two* will not keep silence about Jesus. They now reply to the uninquiring threats, but still with the same modest boldness with which Peter before spake. They repeat the fundamental idea of their first reply—the authority and command of God. They indeed appeal from the unjustly dealing judges to those who thought more rightly, speaking at first only interrogatively, *Whether it be right in the sight of God,* the Ruler of all rulers, but especially of those in Israel who ruled only in His name, *to hearken unto you* (if ye oppose God) *more than unto God, judge ye!* In this first sentence they make no mention of themselves, but are content with asking a question as to an incontrovertible proposition,[1] which, however, the more simply it is put, will the more forcibly impress these God-opposers (θεομάχοι, ch. v. 39). And not until ver. 20 do they apply the principle to their own peculiar case : *for we cannot but speak the things which we have seen and heard.* This was a conscience-smiting rejoinder to the rulers' words (ver. 16), and is connected on to them just as if the apostle had heard them. " We cannot honour men more than God:" thus speak the witnesses of truth before the tribunal of falsehood, which, alas, exists in all ages ; and God will ever help them, for counsel and action are from Him. But *we* cannot and will not pay respect to God more than to men : thus combine in saying the rebels against God and His Anointed. But what were

---

[1] Not only in Israel, but also in Athens, as Socrates (*Apol. ap. Plat.*) says : Εἰ οὖν με ἐπὶ τούτοις ἀφιοῖτε, εἴποιμ᾽ ἂν ὑμῖν, ὅτι ἐγὼ ὑμᾶς, ὦ ἄνδρες Ἀθηναῖοι, ἀσπάζομαι μὲν καὶ φιλῶ, πείσομαι δὲ θεῷ μᾶλλον ἢ ὑμῖν.

the things which they had seen and heard? They had seen the Risen and Ascended One, and had heard His words, Preach salvation in Me to every creature; and they now continually heard the command of the Spirit speaking in them, and bidding them to testify of Jesus. There was therefore a present command of God —a command through both the Son and the Spirit; yet they speak of it as briefly and modestly as possible, boasting nothing of their reception of the Holy Ghost, and of its glorious revelation, so as to mortify the convicted rulers as little as was necessary. By the modest mode of expression in ver. 20, it becomes like ordinary human phraseology, and sounds as if it were a simple appeal to the common rights of men, that any one may speak of that which he has seen and heard. Thus they turn aside not only the threatening against God's command generally, but also the special tyrannical demand that they should not utter a beloved name. They entirely pass over any distinction between private conversation and public teaching, which distinction was scarcely maintainable in the apostolic testimony; and the effect of what they say amounts to an appellative and well-grounded protestation that they will continue to speak in this name.

Vers. 21, 22. The threateners could do no more than threaten again; in fact, they enforced with threats the command given in ver. 18, and then let them go. No answer was given to the question asked in ver. 19. They dared not punish them, on account of the people;[1] for all (*i.e.* very many, many even who had not decided for Jesus), in spite of the High Council, glorified God (ἐδόξαζον; cf. αἰνεῖν, ch. iii. 8, 9, and ch. ii. 47) for that which was done. Luke, the narrator of the history of the apostles, now at the conclusion again brings prominently forward the main fact of the whole testimony, and mentions that the man who had been born lame was more than forty years old, concluding strikingly with the symbolical idea of this deed done to glorify the name of Jesus, calling it a *miracle of healing*.

---

[1] The rulers deny, the people accept. But because the rulers feared not God, whose servants they were, therefore the Lord deposed them; so that they feared to resort to punishment before the people, who should have feared them as their lords.

V.

PRAYER OF THE COMMUNITY.

(CHAP. IV. 24-30.)

ENTREATY FOR THE MIGHTY PROGRESS OF THE TESTIMONY OF THE NAME OF JESUS.

VERS. 23, 24. There were probably assembled in some particular place—perhaps the apostles' dwelling—a considerable number of believers in the name of Jesus, so that they are here called *their own company*, to whom Peter and John, returning home, related all that had happened. These persons, therefore, resorting to the weapon of prayer when they heard of the threats of the enemies of Christ, their prayer may be looked upon as the prayer of the community, inasmuch as this assemblage represented the whole multitude of " them that believed " (in ver. 32 a distinction is drawn between the two), and by means of their co-participation in the Spirit called upon the Lord with the mind, and in the name of all (cf. ch. xii. 5, 12). This is the first " common prayer " which we have—the precious fruits of the attack made upon them. Whether the voice speaking this prayer, which they with one accord sent up to God, was the leading voice of one of the apostles—perhaps Peter's, or it might be one of the others—is a matter for inquiry and conjecture. Be this as it may, it does not much matter ; and we may well consider that the community was through the Spirit fully enabled to pray with one accord by one voice, *i.e.* through one person who spoke for all, and that all could follow it with complete unanimity and simplicity. This common prayer is nowadays the more difficult the less the real spirit of prayer is poured out ; but where this is present, it can be effectually developed in every age. Of course we shall not feel ourselves bound by the title of our book, which applies *à potiori*, to exclude from consideration the prayers of the community here or subsequently, or the discourses of a Stephen, a Philip, or of the elders in Jerusalem.

Ver. 24. The apostles announced all that the lords or " gods " in Israel (Ex. xxii. 28) had said in rebellion against God's offer of salvation to all the world. We are not told whether they also reported what they replied to the rulers, but Luke's mode of expression seems rather to exclude than include this. It was quite unnecessary for them to describe how they had appealed to the will of God, and had protested against any prohibition of their testimony : the believers would readily understand all this. The praying community now elevates itself to the Lord of all lords. As it is written in Ps. lxxxii. 1, " God standeth in the congregation of the mighty, He judgeth among the gods," so now does this community call upon their God : *Lord, Thou art God which*, etc.[1] " There be that are called gods, whether in heaven or in earth ;" but to us (the community of Christ) there is but one " God the Father, of whom are all things " (1 Cor. viii. 6).—*Which hast made heaven, and earth, and the sea, and all that in them is.* A solemn title as Creator, by which the one, true, mighty, *i.e.* living God, is contrasted with and set over all false gods. This title was therefore a solemn commencement of prayer in the Old Testament.[2] Here, however, the Creator is not so much contrasted with idols as with the " gods " among men, the rulers and judges, as their supreme Lord ; as Hezekiah did against Sennacherib (Isa. xxxvii. 16, 17). The name is therefore expressed as *Lord*, and not *Jehovah* = Κύριος : for the community is about to recognise and testify to the name of Jehovah in ver. 30, in the name of Jesus ; but it is *Adonai*, δέσποτα, which is equivalent to our *Lord*. The community thus, in the obedience of holy veneration, approaches Him whom the threatening rulers would not obey.

Vers. 25, 26. The community is very certain as to the divine inspiration of the Old Testament, and accepts it in so close and strict a sense, that in a solemn prayer to the Lord of all lords it brings forward a Psalm of David with the formula, *Who hast said.* Indeed, this expression, *who hast said*, is placed parallel with the preceding, *who hast made heaven, and earth, and sea.* The only true and mighty God, who is distinguished by His creative power, is now also the only testifying and creation-loving God, in that He alone reveals Himself. So here creation and revelation are united by the words " made " and " said ;" but the revelation which was confided to Israel relates to the restoration or salvation of the creature in Christ. God having created heaven and earth, they remain before Him, waiting His nod in complete obedience, as the new heavens and the new earth shall also remain (Isa. lxvi. 22). But

[1] The disputed word ὁ Θεός is, in our opinion, not an interpolation, but almost necessarily belongs to the fulness of the address : Thou, the only true God ! Δέσποτα by itself does not exactly invoke the Creator.

[2] See *e.g.* Isa. xxxvii. 16 ; Jer. xxxii. 17 ; Neh. ix. 6.

this lower world is fallen from its obedience, and has become a raging chaos: the peoples are furious, and foam as a sea; the lords and rulers upon earth will not stand before God as λειτουργοὶ Θεοῦ, and are gathered together in vain rebellion against the Lord. This is the connection of the quotation with ver. 24, and still further back, with ver. 19. But the testimony of this rebellion of the powers of the earth against their lawful Lord was spoken by the mouth of David; *i.e.* a man after God's own heart—who, on account of his faithful obedience, was placed and *anointed* to be God's king on earth, and the ruler over God's people—spake this testimony, and added also: *against His Anointed* (Christ). This Anointed One was, as we now know, not in fact David, the *incomplete* servant of God, but He whom David prefigured, the Only-begotten and Beloved, through whom we shall be made acceptable— Jesus, the *complete* and holy servant of God, whom also God has truly anointed (ver. 27). This is God's King over the rebellious earth, the Lord of lords, sent as a servant to sinners, and, on account of His perfect obedience, set over them, that they should obey and pay homage to Him. In vers. 24 and 25 the Father only is addressed, but in a twofold way: first as the Creator-God, by reason of His power; and next as the Revealing-God, by reason of His love, who gives His Son (Ps. ii. 12) as the Anointed (Christ). This address is quite parallel to the mode of expression in John xvii. 3. Everything that is against God is also against Christ, and the powers of earth were evidently opposing God in their rebellion against God's King, as was the case in Israel (John viii. 42–47), and is also the case continually upon earth (John xvi. 3; 1 John ii. 23). But God, whose mercy is plenteous, nevertheless fulfils, through the hand and counsel of Christ's enemies, all that His hand and counsel had decreed for salvation in Jesus.

Ver. 27. The praying community recall the fact that this had already once taken place, and thus their boldness in praying for further boldness is thereby strengthened. Before closely examining these words, they may readily be taken to refer to the late gathering together of the High Council against Peter and John; and the words, *behold their threatenings*, in ver. 29, seem connected with it. "Against Jesus" might well be equivalent to "against Jesus' community" (cf. ch. ix. 5); but if παῖς here must mean *servant*, as in ver. 25, the gathering together against the Lowly One Himself is that meant. The appellation "the holy servant of God" certainly relates to the type of the imperfect servant David; and in ver. 30 also, the expression "servant" will be found most suitable. Notice also the mention of Herod and Pilate distinctly, as being appropriate to the fulfilment of the psalm (ἐπ' ἀληθείας). For Herod represents the kings and Pilate the rulers of the earth, and the people or tribes of Israel (לְאֻמִּים within the גּוֹיִים, as the רוֹזְנִים amongst the מְלָכִים) are purposely joined with the heathen. In a very forced way, a comprehensive retrospect and prevision is sometimes understood in this passage, in order to make it fully applicable to present times; but this use of Scripture, where express mention is made of names which would be thus extraneous, is a singular one. Finally, the most natural connection of thought requires a retrospect before the prayer for the present: it was impossible that the community should not think on the things which had just taken place. Thou art the Lord; Thy decree to give a Christ to the world stands fast; Thou hast revealed this when the Crucified One was glorified by Thee: now therefore give success to the testimony of Him, and further glorify His name! This is the natural train of thought. In this city—for to this the Zion mentioned in the psalm refers—in which He is set as King, He is to be really anointed; but the very "city of the Great King" will not acknowledge Him. *Whom Thou hast anointed* corresponds to *the Anointed* in ver. 26, to complete the application. But why this paraphrase: *the servant of God, whom He has anointed?* The reference to David appears a scarcely sufficient reason. There is a first and second anointing of Christ which must be kept distinct. The first took place in His baptism by John (Samuel), prefiguring His death and resurrection, as is said in Acts x. 38; and from that time forward the holy Servant of God taught and healed, being anointed with the Spirit and with power, as the man approved of God, and as such was opposed and denied. The second anointing with the awakening Spirit of sanctification took place in His resurrection (*vid.* ch. xiii. 33, 34); and His entering upon His exaltation through His crucifixion was the counsel of God carried out through His enemies; and now, therefore, the prayer is raised on account of the again rebelling powers of the world against this anointed One. As ver. 27 refers back to the former event, so the *first* anointing is intended also by the words ὃν ἔχρισας.

Ver. 28. They had gathered together to carry out their own counsel with their wicked hands—this was their idea; but God says, They have gathered themselves together to execute *my* counsel. Thus "the Lord bringeth the counsel of the heathen to nought: He maketh the devices of the people of none effect. The counsel of the Lord standeth for ever, the thoughts of His heart to all generations" (Ps. xxxiii. 10, 11). This is expressed in the words so suddenly reversing the matter: *for to do whatsoever Thy hand determined.*[1] Ὅσα, exactly so much, neither more nor less, by which the προώρισε (ch. ii. 23) is corroborated. It goes on to say, *Thy hand and Thy counsel;* for God first opposes rebels as the mighty God (ver. 24), and reverses the work of their hands by His high arm; afterwards God's counsel (vers. 25, 26) is also therein understood. It was not merely God's right hand which raised Jesus from the grave; but also, when the hands of the unrighteous nailed Him to the cross, it was even then God's right hand which raised Him up on that cross as a Saviour and propitiation for sins[2] (*vid.* ch. v. 31). God's hand ever knows what it does; but neither the hands nor even the counsel of the crucifiers knew what they did or wished to do. Also the counsel of men is only a hand for God's purpose; but God's hand is itself an almighty and omniscient counsel: the two are therefore united—*whatsoever Thy hand and Thy counsel determined before.* But in all this, the proposition "that God does what man does"—cancelling, as it does, both freedom and morality—is in no way asserted; but the distinction is accurately drawn between a deed and an event. They did (with individual sin) all that was necessary to be done according to Thy holy counsel, which turned sin to mercy.

Ver. 29. *And now, Lord,* begins the prayer against this immediate threatening, based firmly on what has been already done. For as Jesus' crucifixion prefigures all further rebellion, so is Jesus' exaltation to God's right hand the type, the basis, and the security for every future victory, and for every wider glorification of His holy name (ch. iii. 13). Ἔπιδε, behold, or more accurately, *look on to or into* (Luke i. 25),—a common expression for the easy triumph of Him who dwelleth in the heavens over the confused counsels of the sons of men (Ps. xi. 4, xxxiv. 15; Jer. xxxii. 19; Amos ix. 4, 8). For now in the first place there are *threatenings,*

---

[1] The construction of ποιῆσαι with ἔχρισας is, 1*st*, contrary to the fundamental idea of the whole (*vid.* ch. ii. 23); 2*d*, it does not suit with the insertion of the sentence, Ἡρώδης τε καί; also, 3*d*, is at variance with the previously ascertained signification of ἔχρισας.

[2] God *did not leave* His soul in hell, did not *give it up* to hell, that His Holy One should see corruption, although He gave Him up to be troubled and tormented. Thus Ps. xxii. 15: "Thou hast brought me into the dust of death."

—a result of the resurrection and glorifying of Jesus, which had been done by God's hand ; *their* threatenings—ἀπειλαί—who crucified Jesus by delivering Him up to Herod and Pilate.   *Grant*—the actual central point of this prayer, although the things prayed for are more particularly named in ver. 30—to us *Thy* hand or power, *i.e. Thy* Spirit.   *Grant unto Thy servants* this Spirit, to those who faithfully obey Thee (ch. v. 32), to the apostles of Thy Anointed now, as Thou didst to David His prophet.[1]   *That they may speak Thy word with all boldness,* now as heretofore (ver. 13), as far as is possible, seemly, and necessary ; that they may do that which was unjustly forbidden.   Grant that the word of our testimony may be *Thy* word in power and truth (ver. 31),—*that* word which is the eternal, self-testifying Word from God in the Spirit (ch. x. 36 ; Heb. iv. 12).   Grant that all our words may be only *one* word—of and in *Thy one* word—and let our joy testify to *its* divine power.[2]   They pray not against their enemies, nor for the restraining of the enemies' hands, that they may be unable to execute their threats : they are God's servants, and well prepared for everything which His counsel may decree ; they therefore only pray for help, that they may be faithful in His service.

Ver. 30. *By stretching forth Thine hand to heal* now points out more clearly the aim of the prayer,—namely, the cause that should make them bold in speaking the word.   *Thine hand ;* consequently Thy wise and mighty counsel of mercy in Christ, who is the saving arm of God (Isa. lii. 10, liii. 1).   But the hand of the arm which is stretched out for testimony, faith, and healing is the Spirit of Jesus, which raised Him up, testifies of, and brings Him.   Miracles of corporeal healing are not therefore the thing here meant ; but, on the contrary, *spiritual* healing is intended, of which the outward miracles were but the signs (ch. iv. 22).   The healing, which was originated and prepared in Jesus' wounds on the cross by Thy hand and counsel, yea, the healing of all who believe ; and power to our word, so that very many, if possible, of the fatally sick enemies of truth may believe and be healed ;—these were the two entreaties of Jesus' community to the Lord of all the world.   They pray, therefore, that power and the Spirit may be in their words (1 Thess. i. 5 ; 1 Cor. ii. 4), so that it may bring salvation (1 Cor. i. 18 ; Rom. i. 16).   They well knew that the poor servants of

---

[1] Luke distinguishes in the Greek here δοῦλοι from παῖς.

[2] Thus are Peter's words (ch. ii. 41) like God's words : ch. xiii. 48, xvi. 32, xvii. 13, xix. 20.

God have no power in themselves to speak boldly in the face of a threatening prohibition,—that all that human obstinacy and pride were capable of was at the best but a useless assertion of the word. The community therefore pray before all things for the spiritually healing power of the word, from which boldness will proceed ; for if any one knows and experiences that the gospel of Christ is a "power of God unto salvation," he is not ashamed of it, but speaks it with great certainty, so that his words do not sound vain or incomplete, but come forth with the full meaning of the Spirit. And this word of mercy may also, according to the Lord's promise (Mark xvi. 17), demand a confirmation through accompanying signs and wonders (Acts xiv. 3) ; the community therefore add, not though as the *chief* object of their prayer, but as a help and adjunct to the boldness of their testimony : *and that signs and wonders may be done.* The whole prayer, however, both the "grant" in ver. 29, and also the "healing" and "signs" in ver. 30, is all brought into one, as being *through the name of Thy holy servant Jesus.* He whom they crucified is and remains *Jesus :* He is and remains the Servant of the divine love for the salvation of men, and even for His enemies, so long as the interval of mercy continues. Thus concludes the first "common prayer" with the name of Jesus, having begun with an appeal to the Lord (Jehovah).

Ver. 31. And the Lord, who in the building of His new temple had promised that it should be done "not by might, nor by power, but by My Spirit" (Zech. iv. 6), Himself answered it ; and by shaking the place where they were assembled (which did not take place, ch. ii. 2), said to them : I the Lord have heard it, and accept it, and grant it ! Heaven and earth shall pass away, but my word that I place in thy mouth, thou community of my Son, shall be eternal ! And what they prayed for was immediately granted : *they were all filled with the Holy Ghost, and spake the word of God with boldness.* This was an apparently slighter, but in fact as great or greater effect of the Spirit, than was the "speaking with tongues," which in ver. 29 they had not specifically prayed for. Baumgarten, in his usual way of generalizing everything, sees in this a fresh step—"the extension beyond the circle of the apostles of the faculty of preaching and teaching." As to this, however, we must compare ver. 33.

Vers. 32, 33. Luke now desires to pass on from the assembly whose prayer he had just related, and to speak of the whole community, showing the effects of the fulfilment of the prayer in them also. He does this by a twofold declaration of their *unity among themselves,* and of the *external power of their testimony,* which together amounted to *great grace upon them all.—The multitude of them that believed were of one heart and of one soul.* Literally the expression is still more forcible: the heart and soul of the multitude were *one.* For the Lord, through the Holy Ghost, was in all those who had had their hearts opened and purified by faith; therefore they were all one, as the Lord had prayed (John xvii. 21): " that the world may believe that Thou hast sent me." There was " neither bond nor free, neither male nor female, but all were one in Christ Jesus " (Gal. iii. 28). The basis of unity was in their hearts, and therefore their souls also were, in their feelings and inclinations, calmed into unity and concord. The peace of God kept their hearts and minds (νοήματα) in Christ Jesus (Phil. iv. 7). From this it immediately resulted that their hearts and minds no longer attached themselves to earthly treasures, and they no more contended for them; but worldly goods were only possessed and used in love for God's purposes.—*Neither said any that ought of the things which he possessed was his own.* Luke exaggerates nothing, and idealizes as little in the history of the church as he did in that of the Lord (Luke i. 1–4); but in the grace newly poured out in answer to prayer, there might well be at first some Ananias, who had been brought into this unity, and yet not long after might give way to Satan. There are periods of grace, to which succeed periods of temptation; and this applies to communities just as to individuals. He who once has been of one heart and one soul with God's children, is on that account far from being safe from Satan and sin. Paul wrote to the Corinthians: " Know ye not that ye are the temple of God, and that the Spirit of God dwelleth in you? If any man defile the temple of God, him will God destroy " (1 Cor. iii. 16, 17). Luke in very striking language, which affords the most just rule for the possession of property by a community, tells us two things: first, that every one *possessed* that which *belonged to him;* and secondly, that no one said or thought that this property was *his own.* They consequently abolished property, as it were, without abolishing it, and possessed it as though they possessed it not. Everything, therefore, both heart, soul, and spiritual life, and also all property and worldly enjoyments, were in common, so far as was lawful and expedient. Out of this power of unity in the whole community there proceeded, according to God's ordinance for this time, a meet testimony of speaking *especially* by the apostles. The text of Scripture can never be understood too literally. *With great power gave the apostles witness*—the apostles *of the resurrection of the Lord Jesus,* the witnesses and messengers of the Risen One, whom He had ordained to preach of Him. By the general pouring out of the Spirit, the Lord shows us that we are all partakers of one calling, and of one promise; next, by the prominence of the apostles, and their selection by the finger of God, we learn that the testimony of the word must in this world have its regulations.—*And great grace was upon them all.* Luke, in conclusion, derives the great power of their great unity entirely from the grace of God ruling in their hearts, and from the consciousness that they were acceptable to God; he now again joins the apostles to the rest of the community.

VI.

PETER TO ANANIAS AND SAPPHIRA.

(Chap. v. 3–9.)

PUNISHMENT OF THEIR LIE AGAINST THE HOLY GHOST.

Ch. iv. 34, 35. The narrative is connected with ver. 32 by an intentionally repeated mention of the community of property, and by a more detailed description of the plan adopted, which opens the way for a very melancholy story. It was almost a matter of course that there were among them no indigent persons, nor *any that lacked;* for, on the whole, God's gifts are so distributed, that even in a community such as this, where there were very few really rich men, there could be no want as long as there was equality, and the overplus of one served to supply the needs of others (2 Cor. viii. 14). This was done in this case; and *so many as were possessors of lands or houses sold them,* thus employing their rights of property. Luke says ὅσοι: it therefore appears that none were excepted; but it can only speak of a wide-extending rule, of which, there being no compulsion, some well-grounded infractions may of course be understood.[1]

Thus the community rendered themselves free from, and unfettered by, any worldly abiding-places; and in addition to their prayer to God and their unity in love, availed themselves of a very

[1] A little later we find (ch. xii. 12), " the house of Mary."

judicious measure,—that of being unrestrained, provided for, and *mobile*, ready for all events, even if a persecution should follow the threats (ch. viii. 1). *They brought the prices of the things that were sold, and laid them down at the apostles' feet*, or placed them at the apostles' disposition,[1] according to which they would be distributed to any really and truly in need, not exactly by the apostles themselves, but under their inspection and management (ch. vi. 2).

Vers. 36, 37. Alas, it soon turns out worse than one would think! All of them were not, or rather did not remain, as that genuine Levite whose heart clung only to the Lord, and coveted no other possession in Israel but the Lord Himself. Even in that time of grace some were found whose hearts were no longer *one* with all other hearts, no longer upright before God, but, on the contrary, so wickedly bound up in unrighteousness, that Satan was able to *fill* them, to the exclusion of the Holy Ghost! Before giving us this melancholy example, Luke sets before us a good one in the person of a Levite of Cyprus, who simply and honestly did the same that others did. The narrator also finds an opportunity, in the new name given to this man, of bringing forward an instance of the apostles' official authority.

Ch. v. 1, 2. There was a married couple in the community who certainly possessed finer names[2] than Barnabas (the surname given to Joses); but their souls were not like their names. They disgraced their Lord's name as well as their own, for they fell back into the snares of sin after they had known the truth, and now their *names* only were numbered among the believers. They also, as the others, sold their possession, but not in faith; for they had not entire confidence in the new arrangement, and could not make up their minds to deprive themselves of all the spare money they had. If they had but made known their want of faith, and their weakness, they would perhaps have found help from the great grace which pervaded the community; but to their want of faith and avarice they now joined actual sin,—pride, and falsehood resulting therefrom. Ananias wished to appear as if he was as genuine a Levite as Barnabas; and thus testifying to his own consciousness

[1] This is the figurative meaning, but it has been further edifyingly thought that Luke also might intimate that money and goods were matters to be laid under their feet.

[2] Ananias = "God's cloud," or "God's grace" (1 Chron. iii. 21). Sapphira: *vid.* Job xxviii. 6, 16, "the beautiful." Barnabas probably means "the son of exhortation," or "of mighty power of language;" cf. Acts xi. 23, 24.

of the wrong he was doing, ventured nevertheless to lie to the apostles and the whole community.—*He kept back* (purloined, ἐνοσφίσατο, Tit. ii. 10) *part of the price, his wife also being privy to it.* This participation in it made the lie all the more wicked, since he was ashamed before the apostles to retain his land or money even with their full permission, yet was not ashamed of sinning before his wife. *He brought a certain part,* perhaps only the smaller part (μέρος τι), *and laid it at the apostles' feet,* as if it were the entire price. But Peter, as the chief, pronounced on him, and soon after on his wife, an unmasking and severe judgment.

Ver. 3. It was not their enemies without, which the Christian community had most to dread : let these execute their bitterest threats if the hand and counsel of God decreed it, and they could only kill the body. But of " Him who could destroy both soul and body in hell"[1] came a great fear upon all the church (ver. 11); so that, in their first miraculous power of the Spirit, they did not forget that they were yet in the flesh, in God's earthly territory, which yet contended with the ἐπουρανίοις of Christ (cf. Eph. i. 2, 6, ii. 6, " heavenly places," with Eph. vi. 12 in the original). Just when the community felt that there was one heart and one soul within them,—just whilst the testimony was being published in power, and the believer's state of grace was manifest to all the world,—during the time of this general and voluntary sale of property, Satan had, through money, corrupted a second Judas. An important and significant warning to churches and to individuals ! Ananias is a warning to every one who stands in the peril of spiritual assurance, who is not so much himself personally decided as merely included " in the multitude ;" and still more to every one who has forsaken his sincerity towards God and His children. It must always seem incredible to us how closely the Holy Ghost and Satan succeed one another in the human heart. *Ananias, why.* With these castigatory words begins this unmasking of his secret through the Spirit, which can neither be deceived nor mocked; and as it goes on—*has Satan filled thine heart?*—a clear beam of light is shed on the cause of the mystery. A striking contrast to ch. iv. 31, and expressing the highest degree of human sin. We are most probably permitted in this case to take the expression in all its dogmatical strictness, and it is thus similar to that used Luke xxii. 3. Since, to our natural surprise, the apostle here adds no exhortation to repentance or promise of mercy (as he did in the case of Simon,

[1] Matt. x. 28. We can only interpret this as meaning Satan.

ch. viii. 22), we may justly conclude that he, through the Spirit, knew Ananias' obstinacy in the most wicked sin, just as, without human information, he had known the deceit which had been practised. *To lie to* (or defraud) *the Holy Ghost*, which, though it cannot possibly be carried into effect, may be a possible purpose on the part of man. He knew God's truth, and yet lied against it; he is therefore Satan. According to Mark iii. 29, the "everlasting sin" of Ananias may be corroborated as follows : The Holy Ghost, in the apostle, was the Bishop and Overlooker of the community, and by Him they held their office. But the Holy Ghost dwells also in God's church generally ; and whoever publicly deceives the same by falsehood, because in his heart he despises it, deceives (or attempts to deceive) not men, but God. The sin does not hinge upon what the outward appearance and peculiar circumstances of the lie may be, whether it has to do with ten thousand pounds or a hundred pence, a trifle stolen or a costly treasure : the sin depends on the intention of the heart. As far as Ananias was concerned, the cause was now made known ; but it must be explained to the whole community, at the same time telling Ananias that his money embezzlement was a satanic lie. The amount of the price and the sum kept back are purposely not named, for it was entirely a non-essential matter : the less the little portion of purloined mammon, the worse the sin, the wickedness of which did not consist in this, but in the heart being full of evil.

Ver. 4. A child of God, when the wickedness of any sin into which he has fallen is suddenly displayed to him, is at first terrified ; but then immediately a temptation arises to think that he did this sin under fascination and infatuation, through which Satan ensnared him. He says, I knew not what I did ; and further, I myself have not done it ! Thus would man exculpate himself, although this exculpation can avail nothing, as, of course, man's will is also guilty so long as Satan does not *entirely* fill the hearts of men. In order that there might be no misunderstanding among them, Peter, who had now begun to speak for the sake of the community, places a reference to human freedom by the side of the unveiling of the satanic cause of the sin. This is naturally brought to bear by an allusion to the particular form of it. As before the reproachful "why," presupposing the consciousness of guilt, must be the first word, in order to combine Ananias' unmasking in one word of judgment : *Ananias* (the beautiful but hypocritical name), *why?* (the revealing of the wicked interior ;) so now the "why" follows as the result of the above allusion. *Whiles it remained, was it not thine own?*—meaning the piece of land, which is mentioned, as its price had not been named. Oh how merciful is the Saviour to our weakness! If only we are sincere, we are permitted to retain for ourselves any part of our property to which the heart clings, until faith is strong enough to give it up. Retentiveness of this kind becomes indeed an evil, and even an idol; but the candour which says, "Lord, Thou seest I cannot yet part from it," averts the condemnation, and atones for the infirmity. Christ will have none other than purely free-will offerings. It is infinitely better to delay in making an offering, than to do it with pretence and deceit. —*And after it was sold, was it not in thine own power?* God allows poor, weak man to alter his mind, and to draw back the hand which was about to make an offering, lest he should fall into the terrible consequences of lying, and into irreparable wickedness. Yes, although it is bad to draw back the hand from the plough, and to keep back either money or goods once destined for the service of Christ, yet if the heart is not quite given to God, it is the best thing which can then be done. It is a wholesome fear of the majesty of Him to whom man cannot lie, and at least says, "I cannot lie to God, although I can disobey the divine claim." But he who stands up among his brethren as a perfectly conscious hypocrite, and, before a community in which he knows God really dwells, asserts that a small portion of the offering incumbent on him is the whole, has fallen as Ananias fell; and to him, too, must the solemn judgment be pronounced: *Why hast thou conceived this thing in thine heart?* *Thou* hast conceived it, settled it, resolved on it, just as truly as it was before said that Satan had filled thy heart; for Satan is only fully present where there is wilful sin, and the perfect option of man fixes him in complete servitude to the wicked one. Τὸ πρᾶγμα τοῦτο, an entirely indefinite expression, quite discarding the individuality of the sin, and returning to the more general indication of it: *Thou hast not lied unto men, but unto God.* Not to men; neither to the community, nor even to the apostles, inasmuch as they are but men, and as such likewise liars (Rom. iii. 4). For the sake of the community, the necessary voluntariness of the selling of their goods is alluded to; for the sake of the community also, is it certified that their majesty, attacked by Ananias, and represented by the apostles, does not depend upon them as men, but only on God who is in them. If a man lies to other men, it can be forgiven him both by men and God; indeed,

F

he who lies against the Son of man, inasmuch as he does not completely acknowledge Him as the Son of God, may be forgiven;
but he who lies to the Holy Ghost—who has had the Holy Ghost
dwelling and working in his heart—how can this man be recovered
out of the ban of sin with which he has eternally banned himself?[1]
The apostle averts any misunderstanding, by which it might be
supposed he intended to chide and punish the contempt of the apostolic dignity in respect to any human element, and contrasts and
subordinates the whole community to the only true and only holy
God, against whom alone Ananias had sinned; he therefore designates the sin only the more forcibly: *Thou hast lied unto God.* The
doctrinal use of this passage, in which the Holy Ghost is spoken
of as equivalent to God (as 1 Cor. iii. 16, 17), is well known; and
certainly this mode of expression may influence any one who has
already a right view, but *per se* the letter of the language does not
prove much. The words in ver. 3, which presuppose *a lying to
a personality*, imply more than the mere meaning of God instead
of His Spirit. Yet Bengel's words are very striking to any who
have any feeling for the simple and distinct language of truth :
" Aude, si potes, Sociniane, ita dicere : Mentitus est non Spiritui
S. et Petro, sed Deo." Very important, too, is the parallel with
the passages which treat of the sin against the Holy Ghost, and
also the fact that in ch. iii. 20, 26 the Holy Ghost is made equivalent to Jesus, and here to God.

Ver. 5. *And Ananias, hearing these words.* " These words "
relates particularly to the last condemnatory words. The extraordinary punishment of Ananias may be compared with the judgment on Achan (Josh. vii.), which Luke appears to intimate by
his choice of the word νοσφίζεσθαι (vers. 2, 3), the same as in
Josh. vii. 1. In both cases, in the early time of a just established
community, among the first manifestations of God's glory among
them, a forcible warning example is given in the person of the
first hypocrite.[2] Achan, however, confessed his sin, which was of
a more negative character, when he was asked about it; Ananias
came to the apostles with a positive lie, and his wife afterwards
lied in answer to a question. The judgment on Ananias and

---

[1] Remark that now, *in præterito*, it can no longer be expressed ἐψεύσω τὸν
Θεόν (as ver. 3, accusative), but merely τῷ Θεῷ.

[2] The judgment on Nadab and Abihu at the beginning of the priesthood is
also parallel to this, as well as that on Uzza at the commencement of David's
divine service.

Sapphira, as the first miraculous punishment in Israel since the birth of Jesus, stands in much stronger contrast to God's mercy towards the community of Christ, than did the stoning of Achan to the stern favour of Jehovah towards His typical people. It was certainly only a demonstration of the invisible judgment which, without any such open manifestation, rests upon every previous or subsequent Ananias;[1] but this extraordinary manifestation stands here most significantly at the very commencement of Christ's church. As the Lord when in the flesh, ere He surrendered Himself into the hands of His enemies, cast them down to the ground by His words, " I am He ! " so now, but differently,[2] speaks the Lord in the Spirit. The Holy Ghost in the church, ere He comes down to be again despised by sinful humanity, again says, " I am He ; " which words even to-day ring in the heart of every false brother. *And great fear came upon all them that heard these things :* noteworthy words, which clearly show that the possibility that any one of them might become an Ananias was present to the minds of all the disciples, full of grace as they were. Without detriment to the great love testified to in ch. iv. 32, the apostolic community still needed fear, and we see thus that their love was not yet perfect (1 John iv. 18). The expression is completely parallel to ch. ii. 43 and xix. 17, and means *first* the fear of God, of His power, of His judgment; but here there is also added something which is intended to be comprehended in the full expression — the fear of the sin yet existing among them, of the seducer and destroyer who still enjoyed such power in the midst of them. " Lord, is it I ? " had been the words of the apostles in regard to Judas' treachery : a similar but still deeper feeling now pervaded the hearts of the faithful in the presence of this sign ; a feeling that Satan was still busy, and that the Saviour was also the Judge, and would be so to every one who forsook Him ; that He had allowed the judgment to begin in His community, even " the house of God " (1 Pet. iv. 17). *All them that heard*—not merely those that saw — embraces the whole absent community, among whom there were perhaps many who, like Sapphira, did not hear of

---

[1] Bengel's words, *quod gravitati pœnæ in corpore accessit, in anima potuit decedere*, will not apply, if Ananias had actually committed the sin against the Holy Ghost.

[2] For in the former case there was only *dread*, but now *judgment;* there the sin against the Son of man was committed, here the lie against the Holy Ghost was condemned.

it till afterwards.[1] But it spreads further still, and significantly embodies in one designation many others as well as the faithful; subsequently, in ver. 11, they are expressly distinguished from one another. In the midst of fear like this, neither a covetous nor indigent man would be bold enough to ridicule the disciples of Jesus on account of their community of goods.

Vers. 6, 7. No delay of the burial was necessary here, much less any preparation for it; and the carrying out of the dead body by the young men was the first thing to be done in order to remove the corpse of the wicked out of God's community. A melancholy task, and a life-long reminiscence to those who performed it! A silence, imposing reverent fear, prevailed among all, rendering impossible any idle talk about the late event: during the first few hours it was perhaps only here and there described with feelings of holy awe. Therefore, after three hours had elapsed, the wife, the participator in the sin, knew nothing whatever of its punishment. After this interval, which was granted to the weaker instrument of the crime as a period for repentance, she came, driven by a stubborn but not quite silenced conscience, in order to see how the matter had ended. Alas, in these three hours, although Ananias had not returned, her mind had not been altered; but she was, on the contrary, confirmed in the wicked denial!

Vers. 8, 9. And Peter again put to her the question, as to which Ananias had from the very first transgressed; a question in which it was in her power either to answer correctly or to lie; a question, too, which was well fitted in every respect, especially by its commencement—"Tell me"—to excite her circumspection. Also she is not first asked, For how much sold ye the land? but remarkably the question runs: *Tell me whether ye sold the land for so much?* Luke either purposely omitted the sum which Peter perhaps named, or else the information as to it was allowed to be lost as unessential. Or perhaps Peter might have pointed, without naming any amount, to the money still lying before him. The unhappy Sapphira having now by her impudent lie decidedly proved her agreement with her husband to tempt the Spirit of the Lord (*i.e.* of Christ the Saviour), her sin must likewise be sharply

[1] For there is not sufficient reason for striking out ταῦτα, so that it should mean only the audience who were present (the judgment was one to be seen). And even if the ταῦτα is wanting, the meaning must still be the same as in ver. 11.

expressed by the apostle's condemnatory "Why." More sharply, too, than in Ananias' case, in a double respect: for, first, to tempt is worse than to deceive, because it includes the consciousness of the impossibility of deceiving the Spirit;[1] and next the mutual sin is so far enhanced by the agreement to commit it, as a *mutual* consciousness is certainly the clearest, and the warning that must lie in their mutual communications is despised. The judgment is now, in conclusion, expressly named for both; and for the wife, who ought to have restrained her husband's sin instead of sharing in it, the punishment is increased on account of her participation with him whom she obeyed in opposition to God. For even if Peter, in his judgment on Ananias, had not expected or wished for his sudden death (which we do not, however, know for certain), now, since it had taken place, he could only expect a like fate for Sapphira.[2] The young men must just then have been returning from the burial of the husband, as to which Peter, speaking in the Holy Spirit, knew exactly. In the apostle's word "ye," with which in vers. 8 and 9 he addressed the widow before he distinguishes between her and her already buried husband (thus again associating her and him), there is a latent piece of instruction for those in the holy marriage-tie, which was to exist in Christ, and had here so deplorably been profaned: first the duty of community in God is pointed out as the limit of this tie, and also all husbands are warned to influence their wives to be one with them only in good things, and not in evil. Obey God rather than man! Perhaps in Ananias' case *avarice*, and in Sapphira's *the idolatrous love of her husband*, were used by Satan as snares to enslave them.

[1] " To tempt the Holy Ghost "—this only occurs here, and forms a part of the language presupposing His personality.

[2] That Peter inflicted this punishment as a first act of ecclesiastical discipline, is not so entirely indubitable to us as V. Gerlach maintains.

VII.

PETER AGAIN BEFORE THE CHIEF COUNCIL.

(CHAP. V. 29-32.)

DECLARATION IN THE NAME OF ALL THE APOSTLES OF THE PROGRESS OF THE FORBIDDEN TESTIMONY.

VERS. 12, 13. *And by the hands of the apostles were many signs and wonders wrought.* The narrative now passes from the miraculous punishment with which God's hand had smitten the community, to the signs and wonders of *healing* which were then done among the people, according to the prayer, ch. iv. 30. Nor is the fulfilment of it first related, as ch. iv. 33 immediately results from ver. 29. It was first necessary that the deceiver should be put out of the community. *By the apostles' hands*—although in the name and power of the whole community—just as before in ver. 33 with regard to the testimony ; at the same time, the laying on of the apostles' hands is intimated. Now, as before, the community gathered round the apostles in Solomon's porch, where the latter appear to have opened a kind of hospital : they assembled openly, careless of the threats of their enemies ; and now again of one accord, after the sharp purification they had undergone. *And of the rest durst no man join himself unto them*—only dared, as it were, to hang about them. By these the unbelievers and hypocrites, both within and without, are meant. These took themselves off, and only all those who were truly of one accord remained united. And in all this the people (among whom these miracles were done) in general thought highly of this beneficent community, keeping so closely to themselves, and yet so perfectly open and charitable out of doors : therefore from among *the people* believers were continually added.

VERS. 14-16. The people, though certainly in a merely popular way, thought highly of them, and magnified them—ἐμεγάλυνεν αὐτοὺς—so that even from Peter's shadow they hoped for healing. But the better ones among them were μᾶλλον δὲ προσετίθεντο πιστεύοντες τῷ Κυρίῳ—not "believers in the Lord" (as it is in Luther), but "were added to the Lord." This same expression is again used, ch. xi. 24. Before, in ch. ii. 47, it says "to the church," but now "to the Lord," not merely to the church, as Ananias.

Multitudes, πλήθη; cf. πλῆθος, ch. iv. 32 : they could not be numbered, and Jerusalem was filled (ver. 28). Men *and women*, to
make amends for Ananias and Sapphira. It must of course be
understood, that when married couples were among these believers,
their children were included in the bond of union, and were looked
upon as hallowed. It is not expressly written that the shadow of
Peter, whom the people held to be chief apostle, actually healed
any one, in order that any who might find it difficult to believe this
should not be offended. If, however, this really took place with
respect to some of them (τινὶ αὐτῶν), it was done *through faith*,
as is declared Matt. ix. 22 and Acts iii. 16. The coming in of
the people from the cities round about is also important, as the
first hint of the increase to the little community from without
Jerusalem.

Vers. 17-20. The matter developes itself. The rulers of ancient
Israel make a further attack, but the heavenly ministers of the new
Israel, on the other hand, visibly begin their office. Annas the
Sadducee, and the whole body of his adherents, who were powerful
among the great of this world, rose up full of wicked, impotent
zeal (as the apostles were full of the power of the Holy Ghost), to
fulfil their threats ; but the prison-doors fall back before the angel,
who as the minister of God says to them : Go forth, and stand
firm in your boldness, and speak in the temple of the priests and
rulers, to the people who obey the testimony of God rather than
their rulers ! Speak all the words with which you have been commissioned, without reserve ; those words of this life in Christ Jesus,
denied by the Sadducees, slain by the rulers, but now risen again !

Vers. 21-24. The apostles, at the dawn of day, obediently did
what they were afresh commanded, *and taught*. Though the
arrest (ver. 17) had been effected by Annas' adherents alone, he
now calls together not only the council, but also the " senate of the
children of Israel," in order to judge the prisoners in full session.
And now, behold, instead of the prisoners came the wonderful
message that everything was in its proper order, the prison was
safely closed and uninjured (through the ministry of the angel,
who respected order and acted as God's chief gaoler, thus making
the miracle clearer), the keepers were at the doors (who had therefore seen and heard nothing), but no man was inside. That told
them that God's power would not be restrained. This was a divine
counter order, all doubt about it being removed. Then again those
who would not confess God's power, were compelled to pause and

ask, "What does this mean?" They well knew what it was; that it was the freeness of "this life," as the angel said, baffling their prohibition and their prison.

Vers. 25–27. An officious messenger soon brought them a still clearer answer. *The men whom ye put in prison are standing in the temple, and teaching the people.* At their post, just as the keepers before the doors, without any idea of flight or concealment; with a good conscience now, as before, holding forth the forbidden testimony. Then went the captain (who had before arrested Peter and John) to bring them before the council. But he was obliged to deal gently with them; for the people, without any respect for the officers, would hardly allow them to be taken, and made as if they would stone the captain if he did anything to these people who were able so effectually to heal. Remark the susceptibility of the "people," at least to a rough impression, and the stubbornness of the "chief men" against the thousand-tongued testimony. But the apostles had no idea of appealing to violence, and again obeyed the captain's officers, as they before obeyed God's angel.

Ver. 28. No mention is made of the prison and their liberation therefrom! They had enough of miracles, so that they did not even inquire as to this fresh one. There is no inquiry as to whence they obtained the key of the prison. There is not even any reference to the former threatening; they were naturally ashamed that it had been made evident how little of it they had been able to carry out. But only, as forcibly as they could put it, *Did not we straitly command you*[1] (*i.e.* you *two* in the name of the twelve) *that ye should not teach in this name?* They could not prevail upon themselves to mention the name of Jesus, but only say "this name." And now it is only " to teach;" the prohibition of private conversation about it is now omitted. And now breaks forth the bitter reproach, quite inappropriate in a straightforward speech, in which reproach the judges do but expose their pride and evil conscience: *Ye have filled Jerusalem*—a testimony to their own impotence out of their own mouth—*with your doctrine.* " *Your* doctrine" is intended invidiously to protest and to stamp the word of God as only the word of man, and God's testimony in Israel as merely the opinion of a sect. And yet if it was only *their* doctrine, how could all Jerusalem have been filled with it? They do not again mention the frequent and open miracles, and conclude with an accusation as

---

[1] Or, according to another reading (without the οὐ), *We have commanded you!*

invidious as it is guilt-betraying : *and intend*—as if this only were the purpose of the doctrine, or rather of the teachers—*to bring this man's blood upon us.* A second evasion of the name of Jesus, and a contemptuous protestation against His dignity as Christ. But there is also here a reference to Matt. xxvii. 25 ; but they only betrayed their fear of any vengeance for the slaying of Jesus being executed, by means of an insurrection of the people against them : about the divine vengeance they did not trouble themselves.

Ver. 29. The apostles begin without any addressing title (no longer as in ch. iv. 8), as if this were only a continuation from the breaking off of the former explanation, but also as if, on account of the stubbornness of the rulers of Israel, they now spoke authoritatively to them in the full power of God's witnesses. *We ought to obey*—πειθαρχεῖν, much more forcible than the ἀκούειν in ch. iv. 19; *to obey*, properly to acknowledge as ruler, and therefore to submit (cf. Tit. iii. 1).[1] It is not properly *we must*, for one might will it or not, πειθαρχεῖν including also free-will. The apostle's speech contains no threatening, but conveys an earnest, authoritative testimony, putting before them a last invitation.—*God rather than men.* We do not speak our own doctrine, but God's testimony to Israel ; we are not mere adherents of a man whom ye, as gods in Israel, judged ; but ye are rebels against God, and we cannot obey you, because God wills that His Son should be proclaimed. They had had an express command from the angel (ver. 20), but this they do not allude to ; the command of the Holy Ghost (ver. 32) is a much more important one. Compare Gal. i. 8 with 1 Pet. i. 12. They do not say, as fanatics would: Man must only obey God, and not men ; though even this proposition has its truth for the faithful, who are only submitted to man for God's sake. But it is only where the command of man is opposed to that of God, that the actual antagonism of the testimony comes in question. They had no intimation from the Holy Ghost *not* to go before the council, and therefore they obeyed its officers. But because the Holy Ghost *had* bid them to testify, therefore they dared not submit to the prohibition of the word.

Ver. 30. Scarcely had the " ought " been put forward in opposition, than a disposition to conciliation was again shown.—*The God of our fathers.* The command comes from Him who is the Lord of Israel, of all its rulers, and of all men. This expression cor-

[1] Ammonius : πειθαρχεῖν, τῷ κελεύοντι πεισθῆναι. Xenoph. *Mem.*: πειθαρχεῖν τοῖς ἐφεστῶσι.

responds to the mention of *Israel* (ver. 31), and more distinctly
specifies "their doctrine" as not a *new* doctrine, but as the fulfilment of the *old*, and as proceeding from the Fulfiller of the promises, and intended for all Israel.—*Hath raised up* (or resuscitated)
Jesus. Very much in favour of the first rendering are, first, the
juxtaposition with God the Father; and secondly, the succession
of events referred to—the birth, the crucifixion, and the exaltation;
but the idea of a retrospect to the former testimony is quite as
much in favour of the meaning "resuscitated." There must be,
therefore, an intentional combination of the two ideas (as in ch. iii.
26). The peculiar sense here conveys the notion that the raising up
of the promised Jesus or Saviour,[1] as an offer of the same to Israel,
properly took place after they had rejected Him, and He was raised
up a second time as a reiterated offer of the gift to them. It is
now merely *Jesus;* "Christ of Nazareth" is no longer added. In
this charge of insurrection the Messianic name is quite thrown into
the shade by a new name which is to be formed from the vainly
forbidden name of Jesus, which was to be exalted to everlasting
glory. *Whom ye have slain,* or laid hands upon, διεχειρίσασθε (ch.
xxvi. 21), not justly, but forcibly—scarcely indeed with any show
of justice; in rebellion against His raising up and sending by God
the Father, thus taking away from Israel the gift of their God.—
And hanged upon a tree (or beam). Why should this new expression for the cross be used? It is not intended for an euphemism,
inasmuch as in ch. iv. 10 the word cross is used. "To hang upon
a tree" was the punishment of the Canaanite kings (Josh. viii. 29,
x. 26), and thus did the rulers of Israel to the King and Saviour,
Israel's *Joshua.* It was the punishment ordered by Moses (Deut.
xxi. 22) for crimes generally which deserved death; and thus did
the rulers of Israel to Him who had brought back, proclaimed, and
offered life,—even to the Prince of Life. These two references
would be for the then present hearers. But the reader of our days
will ask, with regard to the law of Moses, to which also another
scripture (Gal. iii. 13) refers: Why should the sinner who had
committed a sin worthy of death be hanged upon a tree? The
answer may be found in Moses' history of the first "sin unto death."
Adam and Eve ate from a tree which was to them the tree of
death, and the tree of life must be shut out from them.

Ver. 31. *Him hath God exalted, i.e.* both hung on the tree

[1] For the words "to raise up a Saviour (deliverer)" are a distinct Scripture
expression: Acts xiii. 23, Judg. iii. 9, 15 (ch. ii. 18?).

and raised up to heaven. The deed of men's hands working death, was by the right hand of God turned to life. He who, like Joseph, was sold by His brethren, is the dispenser of the bread of life, and says to sinners, "Ye thought evil against me, but God meant it for good; to bring to pass, as it is this day, to save much people alive" (Gen. l. 20). Thus the tree of death as the cross of Christ is turned into the tree of life; and through the cross, the penitent thief, the sinner redeemed from the sinner's death, enters into life, which is thereby prepared for him. See now how appropriately "the tree" is named here, when the Saviour exalted on the cross is announced; turn back to John iii. 14, 15, and compare with it Peter's remarkable words (1 Pet. ii. 24), where the tree, which is a tree both of cursing and blessing, is mentioned together with the body which was dead, and was thus made a means of life for us. *A Prince and a Saviour :* the two elements of the name of Christ, which name is here represented by these words; but the first is not merely Lord (although it contains the idea that man should obey), but also prince, leader, whose royal command tells us: Ye shall follow me, and thus ye shall be saved; thus passing to the second name, "Saviour" (Joshua, Jesus). The etymology begun in ch. iv. 12 is here completed; and from the name, which was forbidden by the foolish enemies of their own salvation, a new, clear name of mercy results. The Saviour and the cross, or the healing of our infirmity, and the conversion of our death into life, belong necessarily together. That it was spiritual salvation that was here spoken of, the High Council knew well; but because the name "Saviour" is used typically of earthly deliverers, it is here expressly followed by, *for to give repentance to Israel, and forgiveness of sins.* This refers to the *two* names: he who acknowledges Jesus as Prince, and follows or obeys Him, repents; he who experiences Him as Saviour, receives the forgiveness of sins. But is repentance to be here *given,* which in ch. ii. 38 and ch. iii. 19 was demanded as a condition? Both ideas are certainly true: in the decision it depends upon man, but the *command* to repentance by faith in the man who has risen again (ch. xvii. 30, 31) is itself a gift, without which all men everywhere would not repent; and the power of executing this purpose is again a gift, so that it is fully true that God *grants* repentance unto life to the Gentiles as well as to Israel (ch. xi. 18). And the stronger and riper the sin of the stubborn, so much the greater (as man thinks) is the necessity for the divine gift for repentance (2 Tim. ii. 25).

Ver. 32. So far the discourse is a repetition, although with
new names; but now there is an entirely new testimony of the
Spirit of testimony. To the people the apostles had certainly
already called themselves "witnesses" in ch. ii. 32 and iii. 15;
before the council they had simply come (ch. iv. 20) as men who
spoke that which they had both heard and seen; but now that
which in ch. iv. 11 had been merely hinted at comes out clearly:
We are witnesses of the Saviour! In this full authority we command even you to obey God: God, who will indeed *give* in Jesus
only! We are also the offerers of this great gift of God, which
may be received even by the rebellious, through Him who has led
captivity captive, and has ascended on high (Ps. lxviii. 19). "*His*
witnesses" does not apply to God, but to Jesus, τοῦτον, ver. 31.[1]
We are His examples of complete submission, of believing obedience to the Prince and Saviour. But the apostles do not bear
witness merely as men who have seen the Risen One, and have
heard the command "to testify" out of His mouth,—men "who
have been with Him from the beginning" (ch. iv. 13); but the
Holy Ghost (whose Godhead had been revealed to the community,
ver. 4) testifies in them (John xv. 26, 27). The apostles now take
before the council the place and right of the Israelitish prophets,
and express even more than they did: they now speak right out in the
clearest way, as to the requirement which they obey, and as to the
new time for Israel, which had since Malachi been deprived of the
gift of the Holy Spirit,—this new time beginning with the preaching of Jesus. Is, then, the apostles' testimony to be distinguished
from that of the Holy Ghost through them? In itself certainly
not, but for men, yes. The one is the declaration of trustworthy
men of things which, as men, they had humanly seen and heard:
it has a psychological and historical certainty, and a power of
persuasion as a preliminary opening the way for the other testimony.[2] But any one who accepts this human testimony of the
apostles must be led by this to the acceptance of the divine testimony *in them*, the announcement of that which they have preter-
naturally seen and heard, which is endued with a spiritual and
divine certainty, and power of conviction, as a means of real
enlightenment and confirmation. He who rejects the first testimony without any perception of the second, sins not unto death;

[1] We neither expunge αὐτοῦ, nor can we therefore assume the ἐν αὐτῷ. The
various readings arise only through the double genitive.
[2] Which indeed lies hid in it, as here, ch. v. 30-32, in ch. iv. 20.

but he who knowingly resists the Spirit speaking by them, commits the same sin of which Jesus warned the Pharisees (Matt. xii. 31, 32). The apostles recall this warning to their minds, and in this revelation of the Spirit testifying through them, disclose the sin against the Holy Ghost which the members of the council are committing. They do not, however, conclude roundly with, "which God has given *us*;" but they extend it to, *them that obey Him*. All who obey God in faith belong to this new Israel, the source of which, arising out of the old Israel, is intimated in ver. 31. Now is the summons fully completed which pervades the whole discourse: Obey, even ye rulers, God rather than men, rather than yourselves and your obdurate fellow-councillors; and the blood of Jesus will come upon you in grace and mercy, bringing repentance, forgiveness, and life! Looking back perhaps to all this, it is mentioned by Luke (Acts vi. 7) that "a great company of the *priests* were obedient to the faith;" but they were only "priests," and since Nicodemus and Joseph we read of none of the lords of the council being converted to Jesus.

Vers. 33, 34. *When they heard this, they were cut to the heart.* This was a different kind of *hearing* to that recorded ch. ii. 37, and another effect of the Holy Spirit on the heart. Before, it was a *penetration* of the heart, working repentance; now it is a *cutting*[1] of the heart, resulting in the impotent wrath of rebels sensible of the Spirit of God. Yet, in the presence of the apostles, they consult about their execution. "Away with them!" as with Jesus. They venture to attempt this. But a witness stands up in the midst of them, as Joseph and Nicodemus once had done,—one, too, whom they are not able or permitted to dismiss with contempt, as had formerly been the case. It was indeed a Pharisee opposing himself to the now predominant Sadducees; but he was a man held in reputation by all the people, and they were compelled to pay respect to him. He immediately, without further question, directs the officers to remove the apostles for a time (certainly a proper thing to be done), and speaks a few sensible words to the anger-blinded assemblage.

Vers. 35–39. He, as a man of like rank and high consequence, addresses them only in a plain and brotherly way: *Ye men of Israel, take heed to yourselves*, and well weigh what might result if ye attack these men with such wrath, and destroy them! A mild

---

[1] διεπρίοντο, cut them through the heart; which expression is repeated, ch. vii. 54.

beginning compared with ver. 28, and intended first as a warning as to earthly consequences only, as if the matter were a merely human one. *Τί μέλλετε πράσσειν*, not *θέλετε*, but in temporary wrath, contrary to your wish and consideration. After this appeasing beginning, he comes more to the point, and very judiciously brings forward two new examples, in order to restore their circumspection, and to enlarge their contracted views; and also, after the custom of politicians, to afford a proof of his words. He appears first to compare these examples to the apostles, and then almost to contrast them; but it is not so much he himself that does this, as the facts which speak for themselves. *For before these days*, when Jesus of Nazareth and His disciples are giving so much trouble to the council, we have had experience of more than one party leader. *Theudas rose up, boasting himself to be somebody* (*τινά*, perhaps a, or the, Messiah, Saviour); *to him a number of men, about four hundred, joined themselves: who was* (by the Romans) *slain*—laid hands upon (the same word as in ver. 33)—*and all, as many as obeyed him* (almost the same as vers. 29 and 32), *were scattered and brought to nought*, without your help, indeed contrary to your wish. In the same way, *after this man arose Judas, and drew away much people after him*, in like manner to revolt against established order and quiet; *he also perished, and as many as obeyed him were dispersed.* Now what does Gamaliel mean by all this? It might be well imagined that it was something like this: These men now before you are quite different from those I have just spoken of: they do not say that they themselves are something, but praise only Jesus and his name; their (or rather Jesus') followers are not to be reckoned by hundreds, but by thousands; yet, in fact, they make no insurrection, but love one another and the people, and heal the sick: finally, ye have slain their leader, and yet his adherents are *not* dispersed; on the contrary, they are become more clamorous and decided, much more so than in his lifetime: he that is dead is their Prince and Chief. But if Gamaliel had intended his words to be thus understood, would he have concluded his speech in the way he did? The above comparisons are consistent with the facts, and they may certainly have been floating in his mind, but not decisively as a principal idea; for if they had been, he would not have spoken of the *possible*, indeed to be hoped for, destruction of the party adhering to Jesus of Nazareth. He expresses it indeed conditionally: *If* this counsel, plan, or conspiracy, or rather this pretty well advanced existing *work*, be of men only, it will in any case somehow come to nought; *but if* it be of God, ye cannot overthrow it (καταλυθήσεται—καταλῦσαι). It first says ἐὰν ᾖ, and afterwards εἰ δέ ἐστιν; also Gamaliel, by his words "*ye* cannot," decidedly separates himself from their plans. Indeed, his conclusion echoes very forcibly the principal idea of the apostles' discourse: *lest haply ye be found even to fight* (impotently, and precipitating God's judgment on them) *against God!* But we must be well on our guard, lest we attribute more than its due amount of honour to this advice of Gamaliel's, welcome though it may be under the circumstances, and at all events rational and well-aimed. I say *Gamaliel's advice*, for we know not how Gamaliel himself intended it, and whether perhaps, like Nicodemus (John vii. 51), he said much less than he thought; all we have to do with here are his *words* (standing out as an example which is generally significant, and often specially recurring). And they have their bad as well as their good side—their element which can be and often is misused. Is this presumably judicious neutrality, this continual reference to *whens* and *ifs*, this waiting and wanting to see (to see what? the mere worldly and temporary immediate results),—are these things, I say, the true obedience of faith which the testimony of the Holy Ghost demands? Is the mere being on one's guard ere we stand up in the defence of a *perhaps* divine command, the *right* taking care of one's self which is required by this testimony of eternal salvation to all men? The language of the people in ch. ii. 12, and of the council in ch. v. 24, was of somewhat similar import to that of Gamaliel. If the followers of the Nazarene had actually succeeded in setting up the (carnally expected) kingdom of freedom and salvation, it would be a good thing for us that we have at least done nothing against them! This is the thought of many a one even now! It is to be feared that there is a kind of prudence like Gamaliel's, which is but little better than that of Caiaphas (John xi. 49, 50), and it is at least possible that this Gamaliel only predicted much as Caiaphas before did; still, it is also possible that he was a conscience-stricken, but more cautious Nicodemus. If Gamaliel had given his advice a year earlier, according to his idea, it would have been proved at Golgotha that Jesus of Nazareth, like Theudas, had come to nought. And what would he have said after the matters had come to pass which are told in Acts viii. 1? He whose heart is moved by the Holy Spirit, and not merely by his judgment, does not wait first to see what results may follow, any more than genuine mission supporters look first for brilliant missionary successes. No, he is added to them that believe, and becomes a professor of the gospel, should it even appear to involve his destruction ; just as in persecutions the blood of the martyrs always attracted fresh multitudes. "Man *cannot* fight against God " is the language of the meagre, feeble prudence of the cold and cautious ; " Man must believe and obey God's word," ay, even before God's work is triumphant, is the expression of the true wisdom of the penitent.[1]

Vers. 40–42. It appears, in fact, that Gamaliel had spoken with prudence only, and without any warmth of heart ; and the assembly could discover no such signs of the presence of the Holy Ghost in him, as they saw in the apostles, else they would have said to him, as to Nicodemus before, " Art thou also a Galilean ? " The fact that these rulers, who positively would not obey God, agreed with and obeyed this Pharisee ($\epsilon\pi\epsilon i\sigma\theta\eta\sigma\alpha\nu$ $\delta\epsilon$ $\alpha\dot{\nu}\tau\hat{\omega}$), would be psychologically inexplicable, and even a miracle of divine guidance, such as perhaps at that time, shortly before the out-break of persecution, it would be inadmissible to assume, if the spirit in which Gamaliel spoke had not been one that was friendly to their natural prudence.[2] However, Gamaliel's voice has great weight in the counsels of the wicked, and represents, as it were, the natural conscience of the Sanhedrim, the voice that ever testi-fies in every God-opposer, by which reason recommends them to be on their guard. Let us, with Luther, not be unwilling to make use of this Gamaliel-like feeling on the part of enemies and in-different ones, for some good may result from it ; but as far as we ourselves are concerned, let us not desire first to see the effects of believing, but let us *believe*. And now what followed ? Their

---

[1] I cannot refrain from quoting the striking words of Gen. Sup. Dr. Möller (1847) : " It never entered into the thoughts of the great apostle, once Gamaliel's scholar, to take Gamaliel for his example, and to hide himself behind the bulwarks, and to let his Lord fight without His servants. *We*, therefore, must not agree in the measured rule of the Pharisee, who was yet uncertain whether Christ's work was of human or divine origin, but we must imitate the man who, through faith in the gospel, from a Saul became a Paul." Saul, the active, zealous God-opposer, may at the proper season be quickly turned to Him ; as to his inactive, theoretical teacher, who remained, as we now say, "unprejudiced with regard to parties," we certainly read much about him in Jewish narrative, but *not* of his conversion to Christ.

[2] He had agreed in the condemnation of Christ ; subsequently also he was no friend to the Christians, if the Jewish accounts (collected by Lightfoot) are to be trusted. Perhaps his words were only the effect of Pharisaical sectarian zeal against the now predominating Sadducees, as ch. xxiii. 9.

resolution is, that they must and will let them go ; but in carrying out their resolution, *beating* and *prohibition* are added, to give a simulated appearance of authority. They considered that it *might be* God's work, and yet they beat the workmen and witnesses of it! —just as Pilate allowed the Man to be scourged in whom he found no guilt. Scourging the innocent did not much affect either Pilate or the Sanhedrim. The latter are here compelled to show somehow that they are judges, and to give some little satisfaction to their wrath. They do not examine into the testimony " that God has raised up Jesus," but resort to scourging and another prohibition. In this case the words truly apply : " He who is in heaven laughs them to scorn, and the Lord has them in derision." The apostles, however, act in accordance with the words of Matt. v. 12, and look upon sufferings on behalf of Christ as a gift of grace, in addition to the gift of the Spirit (Phil. i. 29) ; *rejoicing that they were counted worthy to suffer shame for His name.* Here the contrast between the world and the church stands out in the still closer and sharper contrast between the mock Israel and the real Israel, and there is instruction in it for all succeeding ages. " For His name:" thus writes Luke, expressing the apostle's feeling—for this unparalleled name, which no human prohibition might set aside, for the sake of which shame becomes honour, and in which the cross is glory. It scarcely need have been mentioned that they ceased not to praise the salvation in this name ; but Luke, for the sake of completeness, concludes by stating that the testimony was proclaimed both in the temple and in every house (as in the church, so in private), and makes use for the first time of the expression εὐαγγελίζεσθαι, perhaps in reference to the irrevocable command of the Saviour contained in Mark xvi. 15.

VIII.

ADDRESS OF THE TWELVE TO THE MULTITUDE OF DISCIPLES.

(Chap. vi. 2-4.)

A REQUISITION FOR APPOINTING MINISTERS OF ADMINISTRATION.

Vers. 1, 2. *And in those days* (ch. v. 42), when the apostles were without ceasing teaching and preaching Jesus Christ, *and* (in consequence) *the number of the disciples was multiplied*, there arose (another consequence) *a murmuring*. This was the first and but slight departure from the concord spoken of in ch. iv. 32 as having existed among the multitude of believers. The greater the number of disciples, the more difficult would it be to retain perfect love among them. *There arose a murmuring of the Grecians against the Hebrews*, of the Hellenists or Greek-speaking Jews (John vii. 35) against the native ones. For a considerable time there had been much jealousy and strife between these two sections. This strife now invaded the community of Christ, for disciples cannot immediately become *nothing* but *disciples :* they remain to some extent what they were before—Greeks, Hebrews, or what not ; and, by the increase of the community, the rules which had hitherto held good, met with an opposition which was brought in from without. The complaint was, that *their widows were neglected in the daily ministration*. Luke leaves it uncertain whether this grievance was founded in fact or not ; the word "because" may be the expression of the murmurers or of the narrator.[1] Παραθεωρεῖν, to neglect, sounds in the Greek both harder and milder ; it is not merely equivalent to παρορᾶν, παριδεῖν, *through overlooking* not to consider or regard, which in this case would be less in the intention than in the result, and would also be hardly credible : it means, therefore, to slight a certain one, as compared with some other in close juxtaposition, *postponere* (Hesych. κατεφρονοῦντο) ; but this more forcible expression intimates also that this could scarcely have been the case generally. Luke, in mentioning the "daily ministration," glances back to ch. iv. 35 : to every one that had need (without exception), what

---

[1] As to which the *Imperfect* does not *per se* unconditionally decide.

was necessary (and not too little) was given. We learn here that this ministration took place *daily*, with peculiar exactitude; Luke also calls it διακονία, ministry or office, as a sort of preparation for the principal idea conveyed in vers. 2–4, in harmony also with the subsequent more restricted use of the word. It appears natural that the Hebrew Christians (among whom were the most needy ones) should have the priority, if all could not be cared for at the same time; but that any had been actually and *finally neglected*, is not alleged even by the murmurers. The *overlooking* of *their widows* is the thing complained of by the Hellenists, and it is attributed to the pride of the Hebrews.—*Then the twelve called the multitude of the disciples together*—the *twelve*, not Peter alone or at their head (as ch. i. 15)—*and said*. Although *one* spoke, Peter is not again mentioned by name, as in ch. v. 29. This general appeal had the effect of setting things to rights, and perhaps silenced the murmuring before it had taken a deep hold on the community.

Ver. 2. The apostles did not order any investigation into what had taken place, as would be the case now-a-days, thereby making an important matter of almost nothing at all; neither did they dwell upon any individual cases of wrong, on which the murmuring was founded; but, acting on the principle which should ever prevail in the community, they go back to the more general and more important disadvantage by which the wrong was caused. They blame neither the murmuring, made so ungratefully in return for all their trouble, nor yet the alleged neglect; but without further question, and although they were so much occupied that it was impossible they could grapple with everything, they take upon themselves the supposed carelessness of their servants (who were only casually and not officially so). They even excuse themselves to the murmuring community, saying that the word of God must stand first; and, lest the management of their material affairs should suffer, they would rather give the latter up. This new arrangement, and the institution of the *first* public office except the apostolic (which was created by Christ Himself), took its rise in the same way as many of the regulations and laws in the Old Testament,—some occasion called it forth, and it was developed by the necessity of the case; and this is usually the best way. The apostles did not at once organize the infant society with functionaries and laws, but managed as well as they could so long as things went on well; and now, when there was a murmuring in the community, they see the necessity of taking to their assistance the seven *deacons*, just as Moses, at Jethro's advice, appointed deputy-judges (Ex. xviii.). *It is not reasonable*—or proper, just, and fit (for the future, with this increase of disciples). It may also mean, *it is no longer pleasing* (to the Holy Ghost, and therefore to us), for ἀρεστόν also is *decretum, placitum*; cf. ἔδοξε, ch. xv. 22-28. It has hitherto been fitting and pleasing to the Holy Ghost, to unite in the apostles the two offices of preaching and management; and Peter, the witness of the Holy Spirit, had not been ashamed to receive the amounts derived from the sales of property, and to share them among the indigent, doing both in the same spirit of wisdom. Therefore let no idle or perhaps eminent preacher say, "This is not fitting for me," and thus put away from himself any outward business; let him rather follow in the apostle's example the humbling instruction to give due fidelity even *ad externa*. But as soon as the *word of God* suffers any detriment through these cares of management, and it can at all be said that "the word" must be neglected or put in the background in order to prepare this register or to take care of that record, then is it readily to be pronounced, οὐκ ἀρεστόν. The apostles express themselves forcibly, so as to disclose the necessity distinctly, and anticipate the murmuring, as if to the following effect: This overlooking of the Grecian widows is not so great an evil as the neglect of the preaching of the word! Those who shared in the division had perhaps, in their first eagerness, subordinated the ministry of the word to the service of their widows; and they would thus be turned from a secondary matter to the main question for the community—the testimony of Jesus. The Holy Ghost, speaking through the apostles, rebukes any of their future followers who may be tempted to neglect the word for money and goods, and on this account the forcible expression κατα-λείψαντες is used. *To serve tables*—money-banks (Luke xix. 23; Matt. xxv. 27, in the *Greek*); not, however, excluding the idea of eating-tables, which had to be provided daily by means of the money-tables.[1] This expression is used as an intentional contrast to the *Word of God*, the real treasure of the heart and the bread of

---

[1] Löhe, with many, only understand that the widows and other poor persons *ate together*; which, however, is not so certainly consistent with what is said. At all events, the principal part of the business in which the apostles were personally busied was the purchase of the food, and the apportionment of the money destined for the purpose; therefore, with Wahl, we also prefer, as the *first* meaning of the expression, *rem nummariam curare*—τράπεζα for *abacus*.

the inward man, which is proffered and justly apportioned on God's
free table of the world. Nevertheless a community is permitted to
possess both money and property, and is bound to support itself:
consequently *tables* must be attended to as well as the word; each
is alike a ministry or charge, which is a necessity to the community. An opposite course of proceeding, to neglect worldly
management and only care for the word, is therefore not well;
for God is a God of order, and His praying and testifying community are to "eat their own bread" (2 Thess. iii. 12). For this
very reason the proceeding which follows is judicious.

Ver. 3. The apostles summon the community and require them
to make a fresh arrangement; but the right of choice is left to the
community, according to the original privilege of Christians.—
Wherefore, brethren! They are all brethren, both to the apostles
and to one another, and they are reminded of it by this address.—
Look ye out among you. Seek out,—an expression which contains
both the reason why the community are to choose, and also the
duty incumbent on them to choose faithfully with a single eye,
without any roguery or unfair distinction between brethren. The
jurisdiction given to the apostles permitted them, according to circumstances, to prescribe certain details, such as the *number of
seven;* and with the wisdom of the Holy Spirit, they begin with a
statement of the requisites. The community might think: How
many deacons will suffice for such a multitude? The proposition obviates any prolixity which might arise, and prescribes only
seven; perhaps (according to Bengel) because there were at that
time seven thousand disciples, but more probably that a sacred
seven should be annexed to them, as subordinated to the twelve.
It is not at all according to rule where twelve deacons stand round
one apostle of the word. The requisites for the office of management are partly the same as they were, according to the apostolic
rule, in every church office, viz. the Holy Ghost[1] and wisdom; and
partly special, as good report, blamelessness, and confidence with the
brethren. In every selection for an office the *special* qualification
must be the decisive one; it has therefore the first place here,
where also there is at least some slight reference to the preceding
matters. Also because good report and confidence are subsequently brought forward as general requisites for any continuous
public office (1 Tim. iii.), it is necessary that the community should

---

[1] Whether we omit the first ἅγιον or not, signifies but little; it is certainly
equivalent to the full expression in ver. 5.

assent to the choice. The twelve could not have any special knowledge of the community on this point, and it did not please the
Holy Ghost to give them this knowledge, and thus to demand from
the community faith in and obedience to the apostles' choice ; but
a humanly divine relation was to be joined to the human circumstances of the community, so that those that selected should
exercise themselves in seeking out, and that men should become or
remain aware of the power which they had in God. The good
report of the community is also only a reference to the actual
fitness which merited it ; but this fitness is twofold : first, " full of
the Holy Ghost " (πλήρεις, not merely sometimes πλησθέντας), for
in the Holy Ghost alone can the house of God be built up, watched,
and cared for : every office in it must be a function of the Spirit ;
and the management of the church's property is no such slight
matter, that a profane, mere mechanical servant can exercise it in
a way worthy of the church. Aholiab and Bezaleel received the
Spirit of God in wisdom and understanding, to fit them for their
various work (Ex. xxxi.). But where the Spirit of God is, there
also is understanding and wisdom, well able to keep the house
supplied with earthly as well as heavenly food (Gen. xli. 38, 39).
Why, then, is wisdom also mentioned ? Because there is not only
a mock spirit which is without wisdom, just as there is a mock
wisdom without the Spirit ; and both are mutually proved by one
another, as the tree by its fruit, and theory by practice ; but
there is also a certain actual gift of the Holy Spirit which is distinguished by wisdom and knowledge (1 Cor. xii. 8). Although
certainly, where God's Spirit has really given knowledge, there is
never any entire deficiency in wisdom ; yet, as a rule, an office
should be conferred only on those who have received wisdom also.
This general wisdom of the Spirit, requisite for every public office,
" is better than strength," and " more than knowledge ;" and
" the heart of the wise man, if he have it at his right hand, dis-
cerneth both time and judgment ;"[1] yea, " wisdom is profitable" to
direct everything right. So that a Stephen who is wise to speak,
is also wise to serve tables : for he who is prudent in great things
is prudent also in small, even in respect to the mammon of unrighteousness ; and whosoever wants prudence in great things is
imprudent also in small. The proposing choice of the community
stands contrasted again with the *apostolic confirmation* of the same:
Whom we will appoint, institute—" will," *not* " may," for we more

---

[1] Eccles. viii. 5, ix. 16, x. 2, 10.

correctly read it κατασστήσομεν (in the indicative), as subsequently προσκαρτερήσομεν; and this agrees best with ἀρέστον at the beginning, as if: That *we* should serve and thus neglect the word, is not pleasing to us; but it is pleasing to us to confirm the choice of ministers made by you.   In this groundwork of the apostolic system, neither the community's right of choice nor the apostles' right of appointment must be overlooked: every church office, so long as external regulations permit it, must receive its confirmation *per successionem* from the high officials appointed by the Lord.   On account, or for the sake of this necessity, the διακονία τῶν τραπεζῶν, as contrasted with the ministry of the word, is instituted; and this "deaconship" is a real necessity as well as the other ministry, even in a special sense, because it is the need of the needy (χρείαν, ch. iv. 35).

Ver. 4. If the apostolic "we" (ver. 3), spoken in the full, confirming authority of the Holy Ghost, included the community also as brethren (see ch. xv. 22), it is not so now: now the personal and official "we," the same with which ver. 2 began, stands out in complete contradistinction to the *seven men*.   This short discourse begins with the apostles, turns to the community, and then reverts again to the apostles, proceeding from the ministry of the word, through the necessity of the table-service, back again to the ministry of the word; for the latter is the great spiritual chief need of man, to which the bodily necessities of the preaching community are a subordinate condition, as the food of the labourer, which is his hire, to the actual work in the great harvest.   The loving, humble apostles promise the community that, although previously perhaps there may have been some neglect, they will now the more faithfully devote themselves to their ministry; and that after this remedy has been applied, the fruits of better arrangements will soon show themselves.   They had not ceased to testify daily, but now they will persevere in it more continuously and more zealously.   First by *prayer*.   It does not say *public* prayer, as a part of the preaching, for it is not so much the "divine service" of the community, as the more outspread testimony which is here spoken of ; also, pronouncing prayers is not a business which needs special mention in the apostolic community.   It intentionally does *not* say, to the *business* of prayer, for prayer is the general business of Christians; and the special function of every official is based only on this general all-consecrating prayer, just as the subsequent (ver. 6) laying on of hands was done *with prayer*.   The apostles conclude, thus giving their hearers to understand how onerous these pecuniary matters had been to them, and why it was not proper to lay upon a minister of the word, or on any public servant generally, a larger share of business than that for which human weakness, even with prayer, is capable.

Vers. 5–7. The ἀρεστόν of the apostles pleased (ἤρεσεν) also the whole multitude;[1] and they chose seven men, who, it is worthy of notice, have all of them Greek names. It is, however, possible that they may have been Hebrews with Hellenized names (as was often the case then), or Luke may have translated their names; but it is more conceivable that the Hebrews, with a view of restoring mutual love, had chosen Hellenists only, which would indeed have been a kind way of putting the murmurers to shame (the apostles had purposely said indefinitely, "from among you"). Stephen, as a man eminently full of faith and of the Holy Ghost, heads the list; and Nicolas, *the proselyte* of Antioch, that the proselytes might have their special representative, concludes it.[2] And these first ministers of the work of love, now to be added to the ministers of the word of faith, were set before (ἔστησαν, not κατέστησαν) the apostles by the community, as the men proposed (ἐνώπιον in ver. 6, as in ver. 5); and the apostles, following the example of the Old Testament and the synagogue, consecrated them, in the same way as every church functionary was afterwards consecrated, with *prayer* and *laying on of hands*. It is important to remark that these men were already full of the Holy Ghost; therefore in the first ordination in the church, a special communication of the Spirit is *not* expressly mentioned as a sacrament essential to it.[3]—*And a great company of the priests were obedient to the faith.* Luke, in adding this to his account of the increase of disciples owing to the renewed power of the word of God, bears the highest testimony to the force of this word, and shows the strongest cause for the immediate outbreak of persecution.—*Obedient to the faith.* In vers. 5 and 8 Stephen is said to be " full of faith "[4] and of the

---

[1] For it was not an order given with authority, but a proposal made in wisdom. But not a single one opposed it, or seemed to think they knew better.

[2] Although Stephen, like the others, was a Hellenist, yet he was a Jew descended from the fathers, as his discourse subsequently proves.

[3] It is remarkable that these public officers neither here nor elsewhere in the Acts of the Apostles (cf. ver. 8, and ch. viii. 5) are expressly called διάκονοι. The office was for some time without any title.

[4] The reading πίστεως in ver. 8 is favoured by the context, at least more than χάριτος; cf. also ch. xi. 24.

Holy Ghost; for God gives the Holy Spirit to those who obey Him in faith, so that the hearers also in faith obey their faith-derived preaching.

IX.

STEPHEN BEFORE THE CHIEF COUNCIL.

(CHAP. VII. 2-53.)

HIS REPLY, THAT HE HAD NOT BLASPHEMED THE HOLY PLACE AND THE LAW.

CH. vi. 8-10. That (as Da Costa says) Stephen stood at the head of the seven, as Peter at the head of the twelve, is not actually to be gathered from ver. 5. But he is, at all events, the first non-apostle of whom it is related that he did signs and miracles. Perhaps in this highly endowed man this gift was the result of the apostolic laying on of hands; and in its effects of blessing and increasing existing gifts, the liberty is shown which manifests itself in different persons, in different gifts, ordinary or extraordinary, but all agreeing in being for the public good. The apostles had given up the service of tables because their ministry claimed all their time; but the deacons appear now to serve the word more publicly and freely, during the whole time that their business allows them (and thus by previous exercise to rise to a superior office). For see how soon this is related of Philip. *Then there arose*, excited by this free testimony out of the Scriptures, in which Stephen subsequently showed himself so well read and enlightened, and also by the accompanying signs, certain students of the synagogue, school, or academy instituted for foreigners of different countries.[1] These men had special confidence in *their own* wisdom and intellect, and thought that they could successfully engage in disputation with Stephen. But, much as they wished it, they could not with any appearance of success resist in argument this man of faith, who set before them faith in Jesus as Israel's real

---

[1] Perhaps under Gamaliel. For Saul was most probably among these Cilicians (ver. 57, ch. xxii. 3). Others less probably assume that four or five synagogues were united against Stephen, but the ἀνέστησαν δέ τινες is scarcely suitable to this idea.

wisdom; they could not help remarking his wisdom, and through
this the spirit in which he spoke, although, as they gave not God
the glory, they would neither perceive nor confess that it was the
Holy Spirit. This was a fulfilment of Luke xxi. 15, and would be
perhaps an after-working testimony to some of these foreign scholars
of the Jewish letter-wisdom.

Vers. 11–14. But these scholars of men's learning and *the letter*
of the law would not even now be obedient to the pupil of God,
the Spirit, and Faith, but opposed by action that which they were
not able to gainsay by words (ch. vii. 51). They were ashamed to
be the personal accusers of him who had convicted them of error,
and had stopped their mouths; but they easily found men who had
accidentally heard Stephen, and were willing to bear false witness
against the words of the holy man. As with the Master, so with the
disciple : he too must be made out a blasphemer, and a ready lie converts into a crime the truths he had maintained.—*They said, We have
heard him speak blasphemous words against Moses and against God.*
Moses *and* God : a characteristic and genuinely Jewish combination, which inverts the order observed in Ex. xiv. 31, making no
distinction between the servant and his master. Then everything
is thrown into confusion ; and even a part of the *people,* who now
for the first time appear on the hostile side, are specially mentioned
as having been affected. Now also they seem (differently from ch.
v. 26) to have used unnecessary force in their increased animosity ;
and the false witnesses began before the council with the old story,
" We heard him say," supporting it now with more positive allega-
tions, which certainly sound decided enough. Again, as the Lord
whom he confessed, so the disciple is branded with the contemptuous " this fellow," and is accused of *not ceasing to speak blasphemous words against this holy place and the law.* This is again an
inverted order, setting the holy place before the law, and is also
nothing but an amplification of the similar evidence brought
against Jesus (Matt. xxvi. 61) ; with it Jer. xxvi. 11 ff. should be
compared. The charge was well calculated to affect the Jewish
ear, so easily affronted at such things. By the " holy place " is
understood, first the temple (ch. xxi. 28, xxv. 8) ; but the whole
of the holy city is included, as Stephen's answer afterwards shows,
which indeed included even the land, replying to the accusation in
its widest sense.—*And shall change the customs which Moses delivered
unto us.* Customs (ἔθη) : this is also a strictly Jewish expression,
comprehending all the most external practices, ascribing also to

Moses all the later usages, and characterizing the whole as an un-
alterable system. Stephen might perhaps have spoken of the
destruction of Jerusalem and the temple, quoting the prophets and
Christ's words; and as to the alteration of the usages handed
down by Moses, he perhaps showed a wider discernment than even
Peter, the first of the apostles, then entertained. His subsequent
discourse makes this almost probable. As a fact, Stephen *had*
acknowledged the temple and the law as far as their right extended ;
had *not* blasphemed either God or Moses; had spoken of destruction and alteration in quite a different sense from that conveyed
by the accusation; and finally, had not made these thing unceasingly his theme.

Ver. 15–ch. vii. 1. It can be readily understood that all who
sat in the council *looked stedfastly* at Stephen. This was done
partly through curiosity and amazement, that a man like this,
who appeared to have been no unlearned man, and layman as they
called it, should stand before them for the sake of "this name ;"
and partly through a trembling exasperation, which could scarcely
be restrained, that this affair about Jesus had not come to an end,
and that the testimony of it progressed more and more powerfully
in all kinds of ways. We are now told further : They *saw his
face, as it had been the face of an angel.* This may certainly have
been very far from what they actually *saw*, and only indicating
that they were disposed to flatter him, as Achish, and the woman of
Tekoah intended to flatter David in nearly the same words (1 Sam.
xxix. 9; 2 Sam. xiv. 17). Or is it a fact in the narrative of Luke?
He must then mean that something was actually seen by the High
Council in the countenance of Stephen ; but how we are to take
this, whether as a real, wonderful, miraculous light, or only as the
effect of imposing dignity, remains for each to determine for
himself. At all events, *something* of the brightness of the Lord
beamed through the Moses'-veil which was spread over their eyes
and hearts, shedding its lustre over the prisoner, so that the dignity
of his innocence and his truth[1] became perceptible to every one;
and perhaps many a one might think : This man appears almost
like a messenger of God, as Moses did when he had spoken with
God. It was also really in reference to Moses, whom he had been
accused of blaspheming, that the heavenly splendour coming from
the Spirit-Lord, and beaming down on the man full of the Holy
Ghost, shone so visibly, even to the unbelieving, on his unveiled

[1] Grotius well says : Gravitas cum summa suavitate conjuncta.

countenance ; it was the erewhile hidden brightness of Moses, which now at the end of the closing dispensation shone forth in Christ,—the now unveiled splendour of the ministry of the Spirit, which writes the new law on the tables of the heart, testifying from the temple which is above us all, where the " God of glory " is manifested in Christ and His members (ver. 2). But the still blinded, undiscerning servant of the now abolished *letter-ministry,* which was only striving against *its own* spirit, asks a question full of bitter emotion, and couched in an artificially quiet brevity, yet modified and restricted as much as was possible. The question is not, Hast thou blasphemed? or, Hast thou said these things? but with artful vagueness he says, *Are these things so?* To this the accused man with great boldness gives a circumstantial answer, which up to the turning-point (ver. 51) is characterized by truly calm circumspection, if by any means the Old Testament might even yet be opened to their obdurate minds, and the preaching of its real aim in the spiritual temple and law of Christ might produce living righteousness.

There are two circumstances of much significance in this most important discourse : one is the thorough adhesion to the accepted Greek text of the Septuagint, without any failure in essential agreement either in general or in details ; the other is the close affinity which the system here developed bears to the type of doctrine preached by Paul, now known as Saul the persecutor.

Ver. 2. *Men, brethren, and fathers.* " Men and brethren " is the natural mode of address of the brother Israelite, scribe, and candid witness ; "fathers" is that of a young man placed before the elders. By the word " hearken," his answer, which does not immediately reply to the question, is modestly introduced.—*The God of glory.* This is the expression which comes home most closely, both to the judges and also to the accused ! In ch. vi. 14 the accusers placed Moses before God, and it is the glory of this God which now shines in the countenance of the prisoner, who, in truth, had never blasphemed Him. Where glory manifests itself, it is from God ; and where God appears, there He promises, brings, and matures *glory.* The great key of God's whole mystery of the old and new covenant is proffered at the very beginning in these words. The reflected splendour of God's image in man is brought about through the *Son,* who, as the angel of the covenant and of God's countenance, appeared in the bush.—*Unto our father Abraham.* *Our father:* Stephen says this as being probably a real Jew,

although he spoke Greek: cf. vers. 11, 12, 15, 19, 38, 39, 44, 45 :
Luke i. 73.[1] *When he was in Mesopotamia* might be meant to
denote Haran, if this were not expressly excluded by the following
words; so that we see that Mesopotamia is here spoken of in a
wider sense, also the land of the Chaldeans in ver. 4 (as in Deut.
xxvi. 5, Abraham, Isaac, and Jacob are comprehended in one
"father," who was a wandering Mesopotamian). But that in Gen.
xii. 1 וַיֹּאמֶר is to be translated in the pluperfect, we may gather
from a comparison with ch. xi. 28, according to which the command to leave his *country* could only imply a removal from *Ur of
the Chaldees;* as to this verse, see Gen. xv. 7 and Neh. ix. 7, and
confirm the corroboration of Jewish tradition here afforded by the
Holy Spirit.

Vers. 3, 4. As Abraham's father had himself left his country,
and in a remarkable way, of his own free-will, turned toward that
same Canaan which the finger of God pointed out to his son
(Gen. xi. 31, xii. 5), so Abraham must now act upon His command,
and therefore leave Haran. The third sentence, "and from thy
father's house," is omitted by Stephen, because he gives a more
exact explanation of it in ver. 4, which consequently takes the
place of the words left out. The choice of the holy land, which
God points out, is entirely an arbitrary choice, and it was in no
way essential to Abraham's faith to know what land it was (Heb.
xi. 8); on the contrary, a hopeful grasp of the unknown future,
grounded on God's word, which was proved by the glory which was
manifested, is the precise essence of faith and of special merit.
God first chose Abraham, and then the *land* for him. Abraham
was brought out of the land of the Chaldeans by his father; yet we
are told *he went,* for even without his father's guidance Abraham
would have gone in due time. His purpose being anticipated by
his father was a kind of proof of Abraham's faith, to whom God
had said, "Get thee out of thy father's house." But the fact that
Terah was as if dead to Abraham[2] when the latter left Haran,
shows the gradual kindly separation of the appointed man from
his ancient stem, and the complete disconnection between the

---

[1] Also in ver. 39; *your fathers* is only a false reading.

[2] It is the actual death which Moses relates previously in ch. xi. 32; but
according to the reckoning ch. xi. 26, 32, xii. 4, sixty years of Terah's life were
still left when Abraham departed from Haran. Stephen has followed the significant tradition as to Terah's *spiritual* death through decided idolatry; we adopt
this view rather than attempt any correction of the biblical reckonings.

voluntary progress to Canaan and the obedient journey of faith.[1] That Terah was not actually but metaphorically *dead* when Abraham left Haran, was at that time just as much a recognised way of speaking, as the correct assumption that Abraham had been already called when he was in Ur. Stephen intended to convey to his hearers : I know the Scripture, and your interpretations of it, and will give the latter due force, and make use of them in speaking when they give the correct sense.—*He removed him into this land,* i.e. God removed Abraham, who in full obedience allowed himself to be led and brought. This was the fulfilment of the promise given in ver. 3, that He would *show* him the land.—*Wherein ye now dwell.* The "ye" is a second address, which in ver. 51 is followed by a third. These words emphatically connect the past with the present, as if saying : This firmly established holy land of yours is nothing but a dwelling-place, hallowed by God's will, out of which the Lord could as easily remove ($\mu\epsilon\tau o\iota\kappa i\zeta\epsilon\iota\nu$) you elsewhere, as He before brought your ancestor out of Haran.

Ver. 5. $K\lambda\eta\rho o\nu o\mu i\alpha$ is a firmer, more real, or, according to the right of man, more sure possession ($\kappa\alpha\tau\acute{a}\sigma\chi\epsilon\sigma\iota\varsigma$); certainly in another sense, according to the right of God's promise, Canaan—ay, indeed the whole world—was already Abraham's inheritance (Rom. iv. 13). Not a "foot's breadth," as Moses says of Mount Seir (Deut. ii. 5). But it was promised to him only as a future possession. Stephen now mentions his *seed,* and, presupposing the special circumstance that his and Sarah's bodies were as if dead, gives prominence to Abraham's faith in the future.

Vers. 6-8. But Abraham was inclined to be perplexed that he had as yet no son, an innumerable offspring of his body being promised him ; and his faith in this promise was counted unto him for righteousness (Gen. xv. 1-6). Stephen also omits this, because perhaps he intended to revert to the subject at the conclusion. He now extracts from Abraham's profound and significant history those facts only which form a part of his character as a whole, and conduce to the further development of the plan of his discourse. He therefore now adds the prediction of the slavery and deliverance of Abraham's seed. This would again have exercised Abraham's

---

[1] We agree with Baumgarten : " Stephen here refers back, according to the correct tradition, to the first unrevealed commencement of Abraham's calling." But we do not agree with him in thinking " that Abraham himself had a share in originating the change of settlement to Haran;" for *his* action and obedience begin only in the twelfth chapter.

faith very forcibly, and have led him to expect for his seed God's continuous, decreed, and measured guidance. The seed of Abraham, insomuch as it is the future people of God, must surely be first purified in affliction, and exalted through captivity; in it, the sin unto death and the corruption of sin must be manifested, so that its deliverance to perform the priestly service of God may be effected with a high hand. Neither the foreign land in ver. 6, nor the strange nation in ver. 7, are specified by name. And serve *me* (no longer the strange nation) in *this* place (the Canaan which Abraham was then in, no longer in a foreign land) : these words are added by Stephen, and in them he intends to comprise Gen. xv. 16, 18–21. But the language to some extent is derived, through a striking allusion easily recognised by those versed in the Scriptures, from Ex. iii. 12. It must be remarked that in ver. 6 it is said, *And God spake in this wise;* and not, God spake *to Abraham.* After the impending purification by affliction and the bringing back of his seed had been prefigured to Abraham in the smoke of the offering and the horror of great darkness, the sure covenant was (Gen. xv. 18) solemnly confirmed (Gen. xvii. 1, 9), and typically sealed by circumcision (Gen xvii. 10–14; Rom. iv. 10–12). Abraham and his seed are *flesh :* this must be put away in an offering of Isaac, a bond-service of Jacob, a captivity of Joseph, a slavery of Israel, which through grace is reckoned as "the reproach of Christ" (Heb. xi. 26); and this putting away prefigures the actual deliverance from the bondage of death and sin in the uncircumcision of the flesh (Col. ii. 13); ay, it is the circumcision of Christ, the putting off the sinful body of the flesh, fulfilled in Jesus' death and resurrection (Col. ii. 11, 12). But how much Abraham understood of all this we know not, and have no need to know : the apostolic interpretations are our light, and guided by these we are enabled and bound thus to read these scriptural types. And *so* Abraham begat Isaac, that is, *after* he was circumcised, Ishmael having been begotten *before;* the οὕτως not being without meaning either here or in John iv. 6, or in other places. Isaac Jacob, Jacob the twelve patriarchs (πατριάρχας = φυλάρχας); in both cases we must add, *begat* (as a circumcised man) *and circumcised.* Isaac's and Jacob's lives are passed over by Stephen, or rather tacitly united to Abraham's life. *On the eighth day* is, in the first place, a quotation from Gen. xxi. 4; and next, attention is drawn to the mystery of this particular number of days. Before the institution of circumcision, the Sabbath had been distinguished

by the fathers as the day hallowed by the Creator (Ex. xvi. 23),
although it was first *legally* confirmed by Moses, just as the circumcision was fixed to take place on the eighth day (Lev. xii. 3).
The fact that Moses fixed the eighth day, which might come on
the Sabbath, notwithstanding the adoption of the seventh day of
rest even among the ten commandments, may point out to us that
God, in appointing the eighth day, prefigured the abolition, or rather
the alteration, of the Old Testament Sabbath. The first week of
the child's life is, as it were, his old covenant; but on the first day
of the *new* creation week beginning in Christ his flesh is circumcised, and the whole man (no forbidden thing before God) is made
whole in the resurrection of Christ (John vii. 23).[1]

Vers. 9–11. Jealousy and selling—the beginning and end of the
sin; a seemingly trifling deviation from the love of faith, yet still a
frightful one, growing into a sin similar to fratricide, parallel to
the persecution and slaying spoken of in ver. 52. With the pious
Joseph (who is, however, not quite without blame in his somewhat
too self-sufficient speech, Gen. xxxvii. 9), the prediction quoted
ver. 6 begins to receive its last fulfilment, in that the land of
bondage which was principally meant received him as a servant.
God's mercy directs the righteous to the blessing of purification, as
the wicked to the blessing of forgiveness: all must pass through
the judgment of tribulation, Joseph with his brethren, and the old
father Jacob with them. With regard to Joseph's affliction, we
are told that in a special sense " God was with him " (cf. ch. x. 38;
John viii. 29, as applied to Christ). With his brethren in Canaan
there were Canaanitish friends and seducers (Gen. xxxviii.), but the
Lord was with Joseph (Gen. xxxix. 2, 3, 21) although he was in
Egypt; just as with Jacob in the place of which he knew nothing,
and yet it was " the house of God and the gate of heaven." Bethel
accompanies the righteous in their wanderings; and where God
dwells with believers, *there* is the holy land. Joseph in Egypt
withstood Potiphar's wife, but Judah in Canaan treated his
daughter-in-law as a harlot. Joseph's afflictions were neither short
nor slight, but his God delivered him out of them all, as He did
his father Jacob (Gen. xlviii. 16). *And gave him favour in the
sight of Pharaoh; vid.* Gen. xxxix. 4, 21, xli. 37. Pharaoh's
favour towards Joseph proceeded from God, and not from his own
eyes, as in Potiphar's wife (ch. xxxix. 7). It was indeed favour
before Pharaoh, that the king of Egypt, the land of wisdom, should

[1] As to first-borns and offerings, cf. Ex. xxii. 30, Lev. xxii. 27.

summon the Hebrew servant, and talk with him. And God, to
whom Joseph gave all the glory (Gen. xl. 8, xli. 16), gave him
also *wisdom* before Pharaoh, so that the latter was compelled to
acknowledge it, and even to give God honour for it. Here
Stephen, as if by the way, gives God the glory for *his* own wisdom,
and prays, κατὰ κρύψιν, for the favour of its acknowledgment.
The words which follow refer partly to Gen. xl. 40, 41, but more
distinctly to Ps. cv. 21. *Now there came a dearth :* ἦλθε, not
ἐγένετο, as Gen. xl. 54, for the ἔρχεσθαι of the ἑπτὰ ἔτη had been
called by God (Ps. cv. 16).[1] Egypt and Canaan are alike,
though through the blessing of Joseph's God there was bread in
Egypt; whilst in the universal great affliction the children of
Abraham found no sustenance.

Vers. 12–14. And with his wicked children, Jacob the pious
father also suffers, through the same directing mercy which aforetime sent him to Laban : the great conflict of the surrender of
earthly affections must be painfully fought in the " sacrifice " of
Joseph and Benjamin (Gen. xlii. 36), until *Israel* (ch. xliii. 6, 8,
11) gave himself up childless to the mercy of Almighty God (ver.
14). Stephen refers to all these modes of gradual development,
also to the judgment on Joseph's brethren, whereby he was not
allowed to manifest himself until the *second time.* Surely for after
times there is a deeper typico-prophetical meaning in this history,
which meaning we may now find out, whilst perhaps Stephen could
only understand the first apparent resemblance of Joseph to Christ.
—*There is corn in Egypt !* This is the marvellous cry which Jacob
has so long listened to, and cannot yet understand. But when the
judgment on his children, the sellers of the righteous one, was
completed, then his spirit revived, and it was enough for him to
see *him* and never more to die (before I die) (Gen. xlv. 27, 28).
Jacob's children are living on the bread of Egypt, and know not
that Joseph is their Prince of Life. Although they are honest, they
are always reproached as being spies, and much money, but at the
same time a cup, is placed in their sacks. Their brother keeps himself back from them, that they may be directed to a blessing, and
that they may learn to say in their hearts, We have brought these
afflictions on ourselves, and now is *his blood* required of us (ch. xlii.
21, 22). And the Egyptians abstain from eating at the same table

[1] See how the whole discourse is interwoven with quotations bearing upon
one another, as if the ancient Scriptures were completely present to Stephen's
mind.

with the Hebrews, although both are provided with Joseph's bread.
And when, finally, *God had found out the iniquity of His servants*
(ch. xliv. 16), and the aim is attained of that merciful judgment,
the visitation that was to bring them back to their lost favour,——
when Judah, as the confessing one, entreated for his father's sake,
and the acknowledgment of the sin committed against Joseph
hovered on his tongue (vers. 28, 29),—then is it in another sense
the *second time* when Joseph acknowledged his brothers as brethren,
and made himself known to them. Then, too, is Joseph's kindred
made known unto Pharaoh, and Egypt and Canaan are lovingly
united in the one maintenance of life through him who was righteous
in faith. Pharaoh knew previously that Joseph was a Hebrew
servant (ch. xli. 12); what was it, then, which was now made known
to him? Not the fact merely that they were shepherds, which is
first mentioned (ch. xlvi. 32, xlvii. 3). There is something more
expressed in this forcible expression φανερὸν ἐγένετο,—that he who
truly knew Joseph's kindred, knew also Joseph's, Jacob's, and
Abraham's God, and is adopted into the seed of Abraham (ch.
xlvii. 10). We may be allowed to trust that this will one day take
effect, when the first cycle of the type shall have its fulfilment.
There will then be no more bondage to follow; the land of bread
will not again become the land of death, nor will "another king
arise who knows not Joseph" (ver. 18). Let the devout reader
believe that the only way to comprehend rightly the historical
Joseph, is by thus interpreting his history, and by assimilating him
to his prototype; and although Stephen could only intend, in speaking to his first hearers, to allude to this interpretation as concerned
the things *then* fulfilled, still the Holy Ghost in him desires to
present it (but in a more widely grasping meaning) to all future
readers. We have alluded to the prophetic underlying meaning of
this period of history, because by the deepest conception of it we
may be the better able to show that the characteristic point of
teaching in all these occurrences is *mercy* leading back to the
blessing of *reconciliation* through the path of *judgment*. Joseph now
sent to his father, as his father previously sent to him; for now the
(typically) completely righteous man was permitted again to join his
father, as the incipient and departing righteous man was compelled
to leave him. The number of souls is stated according to the more
exact enumeration of the Greek text, the Hebrew keeping to the
round number of souls which belonged to Jacob's house. *Seventy*
and *twelve* were Israel's holy numbers, and the *five* here added

make no essential difference, but may be meant to point to the increase in Egypt made by Joseph's sons, Manasseh and Ephraim.

Vers. 15, 16. But Jacob, and also the fathers of the twelve tribes, died *out of* Canaan, but yet in faith of God's favour,—a new proof that the *salvation* waited for by Jacob (Gen. xlix. 18), and found by him through his living before God, was not in a false sense dependent on *the land*. But yet they were buried in Canaan,—a hint, on the other hand, that the fulfilment of God's promises, on which they trusted both for their own and their descendants' resurrection, would not fail to arrive even in an outward sense. With regard to Stephen's (again) briefly condensing into one reference the two accounts as to the purchase of the ground and the burial, both being well known to the orator and his audience (just as the Jewish school of antiquity was wont to do with quotations connected with one another), and his addition of the story (heretofore not biblically recorded) of the burial of Joseph's eleven brothers also in Canaan, I would refer my readers to Bengel's *Gnomon*.[1] It would be foolish to impute to Stephen a deficiency in memory; and in this mode of expression, so usual in the schools of that time, he only desired to point out—places and names not being the matter in question—the circumstance remarkable alike in both burials, that places of interment were only obtainable by the fathers by means of purchase, as strangers then inhabited the land of Canaan.

Vers. 17–19. *But when the time of the promise drew nigh:* a glance back at the first period now completed, exactly expressed by καθώς and χρόνος. *Which God had sworn to Abraham*—promising still more forcibly the fulfilment of the oath, the history of which fulfilment now begins.[2] In Gen. xv. we do not indeed read of any oath made by God, but only of a covenant; but every promise of Him that is Truth is indeed a sure covenant with us, and a firm oath in itself: refer also to Gen. xxvi. 3 and xxiv. 7. Now begins the manifestation of God's truth—of His faithfulness, infallibility, and holiness, as contrasted with the perfidiousness, falsity, and

---

[1] Or, according to v. Meyer: "Jacob was laid in the grave which Abraham had bought at Hebron (Gen. xxiii. 16, 17, l. 13); Joseph and the rest of the fathers in the piece of land which Jacob had bought at Sychem (Gen. xxxiii. 19; Josh. xxiv. 32)."

[2] We consider the readings ὡμολόγησεν and ἐπηγγείλατο as more correct, on account of the difficulty in ὤμοσεν, which, standing alone, is not suitable to the biblical usage of the language.

wickedness of all men. *The people*—now really a nation, and no longer a mere family (ver. 14)—*grew and multiplied:* a fulfilment of the promise to Abraham, in the first place, only according to the flesh. This indeed blessed seed is yet sunk into death, and needed another blessing for their deliverance. *Another king arose, which knew not Joseph,* and to whom his kindred and their holiness was not "made known;" but by whom they were, on the contrary, "evil entreated" (Ex. i. 8).[1]—*The same dealt subtilly with our kindred.* Stephen refrains from the name of Israel up to ver. 23, and only says, And evil entreated *our fathers.* The expressions κατασοφισάμενος and ἐκάκωσε are taken from Ex. i. 10, 11, where τὸ γένος τῶν υἱῶν Ἰσραήλ precedes it in ver. 9. The word κακοῦν refers also to ver. 6 above, so that in ver. 17 the promise is fulfilled, and in ver. 19 the prediction joined to it. The two fulfilments stand in opposition; for the evil treatment began in good earnest, and all artifice being cast aside, increased into open extirpation: consequently—εἰς τὸ μὴ ζωογονεῖσθαι (*ne sobolescerent*)—the ηὔξησεν καὶ ἐπληθύνθη is threatened to be abolished. The two are at variance, like the giving and taking of Isaac, and now for the people, as then for the one, point to a life from the dead, and should in Israel exalt the Abraham-like faith in the Caller of Abraham into a faith in Him who rose from the dead (Heb. xi. 19; Rom. iv. 24).

Vers. 20–22. And although Abraham's faith was almost extinct in his children, Abraham's God sent the promised deliverer at the destined time. When that time drew nigh (ver. 17), Moses was born,—the deliverer who had himself been delivered, whom God's hand had taken out of the waters of death that he might save His people. The new-born infant was already the future Moses, singled out and prepared thereto even from his mother's womb. Moses himself speaks of the special aptitude of the chosen instrument, when relating of his mother: And when she saw כִּי טוֹב הוּא (LXX. ἰδόντες δὲ αὐτὸ ἀστεῖον). It is impossible that mere outward beauty is here intended, which is scarcely observed by strangers, but which a mother almost always sees in her new-born babe. Moses' parents rested in faith, and therefore saw with eyes of faith (Heb. xi. 23). A prophetic foreboding told them that their child was specially distinguished by God; Stephen attests this by the addition τῷ Θεῷ,

---

[1] This "new king" appears indeed to have indicated, in fact, a change of dynasty; but at present no inquirer has in any way clearly shown how this may be proved, amid the dark mysteries of Egyptian history.

which some have wished to get rid of in a profane superlative of divinity[1] unusual in holy Scripture. Disposition, preservation, bringing up—these are the three chief points in the preparation of one destined for the divine "sending." Even the Egyptians are compelled to relinquish their abhorrence of the children of Israel, and to exercise love when a deliverer for Israel is to be delivered. This shows God's power over the hearts of men, and would teach the delivered one to feel some respect and gratitude towards the not quite reprobate oppressors. The daughter of Pharaoh thinks that she is bringing up a son with a hired nurse, and little knows that his own mother is suckling and secretly strengthening him with the faith of Israel, so that, among all the wisdom of the Egyptians, he may be kept firm for his despised people.—*And Moses was learned in all the wisdom of the Egyptians.* Stephen expressly adds this, following the tradition, although it would naturally result from his being adopted by Pharaoh's daughter as her son (Ex. ii. 10). In adding this, he speaks very judiciously for his purpose. As he had above, in the case of Joseph, attributed to God all the honour of true wisdom, so he now acknowledges human intervention and transmission of it, and concedes to the Alexandrians (ch. vi. 9) the merits of their ancient Egypt (although, according to Ps. cv. 22, partly derived from Moses); but he immediately proceeds to show how little the wisdom of Egypt was a full qualification for being a servant of the God of Israel. The words which immediately follow—*and was mighty in* (his) *words and in* (his) *deeds*— declare that the Egyptian wisdom was purified and quickened by the power of Israel's faith: for certainly in human wisdom words precede deeds,[2] and if the words fail in power, the deeds are also wanting; but a man of God is mighty both in deed and word (Luke xxiv. 19). As in Stephen the Spirit of Christ purified and quickened the wisdom of the schools, and added to it the *true* wisdom, so it was with Moses. But it is signified (according to the significant reading αὐτοῦ) that something was wanting to the complete dedication of Moses, and that to his might must be added a complete submission of it to the will of God. Therefore, when he began with *his* works to wish to be a ruler among his people (vers. 23–25), and with *his* words proceeded to make himself a judge (vers. 26–28), then the just question out of an unjust mouth was

---

[1] *Versio neogræca:* εἶχε θείαν εὐμορφίαν. Joseph. *Ant.* ii. 9, 7: παῖς μορφῇ θεῖος.

[2] Thus in Xenoph. *Memor.*: ἀνὴρ δεινὸς λέγειν τε καὶ πράττειν.

rightly applicable to him, *Who made thee to be a ruler and a judge over us ?*

Vers. 23--25. Moses very probably thought that, when he was forty years old, he was of the proper age to stand publicly forth (ἐπληροῦντο αὐτῷ); but he little knew that a *second* τεσσαρακονταετὴς χρόνος must be passed waiting in the wilderness for his purification, and that a *third* must be endured in the same wilderness in order to sanctify Israel (vers. 30--36). So exactly are God's times measured! As the four hundred years, so the forty years! The cause that induced Moses to call the children of Israel brethren, who were abhorred by the Egyptians, and to prefer the reproach of Christ to the treasures of the land, was certainly faith in the Unseen, and a looking forward to its promised reward ; for even his subsequent flight took place *not without faith*, although in Heb. xi. 37 it is not this flight, which was taken through fear of the king's wrath (Ex. ii. 14, 15), but the subsequent leaving Egypt, which is meant. But God's holiness is not satisfied even with a personal faith, nor even with the righteousness of faith personally made one's own, but requires a *waiting* faith in complete submission. Moses was then not yet called, but *it came into his heart,* as Stephen expressly informs us. (*Vid.* the contrast, Num. xvi. 28.) It came into *his* heart (as before *his* words and works), and also that the deliverance was to be through *his* hand; but this was not correct. For God had said to Abraham, "The nation to whom they shall be in bondage will I judge;" and when Israel was afterwards brought out by God's high hand, no Egyptian was destroyed up to the fatal night of the first passover. The result, "and they understood not," proves two things—Israel's unworthiness and Moses' officiousness; but the latter is no excuse for the former. Whoever concludes that Stephen in this part of his speech praises Moses' actions, can hardly have considered his words with right views.

Vers. 26--28. When the people of God, in addition to losing their faith in God's help, had forfeited the mutual peace arising from that faith, it was the full measure of their misery. By this their *unworthiness* was most clearly manifested, so that the " other king" would have now found no Joseph among them. Moses came to *them :* this *them* applies generally to the *they* in ver. 25, and consequently denotes that the general condition of the whole people was one of brawling and strife. Literally, *he appeared to them,* preparatory to the " appeared" in ver. 30. A higher appearance was necessary than that of a mere human deliverer. Stand up against the oppressor! Unite together in concord! These are the two human, yet correct, injunctions to an oppressed people. But certainly the second one should come first, and peace can only result from justice and faith. Where the oppressed are little or no better than the oppressors, tyranny awakens nothing but selfishness; and even a Moses, who left a palace for his brethren's sake, has to represent in vain to the poor wretches: *Sirs, ye are brethren; why do ye wrong one to another?* But he that did this wrong to his neighbour and fellow-bondsman recognised Moses also as a wrong-doer, and impudently acknowledged himself to be the guilty one; joining a second wrong to the first, he thrusts from him the peacemaker (who indeed authoritatively urged them to peace), and only boasted, *Who made thee a ruler and a judge over us?* He therefore knew not the leader, and acted with him as with one of his brethren; also he remembered not God, the God of justice and peace, whose voice he ought to have perceived in him who *appeared* to stay the quarrel. Israel had forgotten that the God of their fathers would and could help them, and that the God of His children would and must chide. *Wilt thou kill me, as thou didst the Egyptian yesterday?* Thus they "that are contentious (ἐξ ἐριθείας), and do not obey the truth" (Rom. ii. 8), fear that the purpose is to take away their meagre "life of their hand" (Isa. lvii. 10) when words of peace are spoken to them, and when redemption from death is therein offered them. *Me as the Egyptian* are words which renounce all consciousness of the " brother" whom Moses wished to avenge and see righted; and they thus disown the deliverer whom God had raised up for them.

Ver. 29. But yet Moses must have acknowledged in his conscience that there was much truth in these words of the unworthy people who thrust him from them; he could not answer, The Lord of your fathers has sent me unto you! Now therefore his power, as yet *unaccepted*, was at an end; now, too, he began to fear the king's wrath against him—*him* so wonderfully preserved and prepared; and half in faith, half in fear, he fled for the preservation of his person both from his own people and from Pharaoh. But he carried with him in his mind the saying, " Who has made thee a ruler?" for, after another forty years of life, he was to bring back the answer (ver. 35). He must first have a foretaste that the seed of Abraham are strangers and foreigners, and must lose his temporary Egyptian home. In this distant land, his protecting arm was in the meantime enabled to defend the daughters of a foreign priest, one of whom became his wife. Here, too, he may have weighed in his mind the great enigma of Job,[1] and may have learned to add to his Egyptian wisdom the virtue of keeping silence before God's ever holy truth, and to exchange his still unpurified might in words and deeds for the impotence of a servant with whom his lord is speaking (Ex. iv. 10). Stephen mentions the "two sons," to indicate how completely Moses had found a home in Midian, and also as a retrospect with regard to Joseph's two sons in Egypt, and the equally significant names of the four.

Ver. 30. *And when forty years were expired*—again the time exactly prescribed—*there appeared to him*, to Moses who had before (ver. 26) wished to appear to his brethren, the God of glory, who alone can make rulers and judges. By this second use of the word "appeared" (following that in ver. 2), Stephen clearly denotes the *second period of revelation* in reference to the former. As it was in the former "when he was yet in Mesopotamia," so now it is "in the wilderness of Mount Sinai." As before it was "the God of glory," so now it is the "angel of the Lord" (Ex. iii. 2). In the profound discourse of this scripturally learned man, who viewed and penetrated the Old Testament in the light of the New, we perceive the cause for the appearance of the *angel* on this occasion.[2] Namely, in the period of the giving of the law by the true God, who redeemed for Himself a people among whom He dwelt, is depicted the period of the *Son*, God's Messenger or Angel, who also is Himself God; who also makes Himself nigh to His people, so that He enters in among them, and "takes a nation from the midst of another nation by temptations, by signs, and by wonders, and by a mighty hand, and by a stretched-out arm, and by great terrors" (Deut. iv. 7, 34). From henceforth the Father, who Himself reconciles and pronounces us righteous (2 Cor. v. 19), is manifested in the angel more clearly than to the fathers, although in presignification of the Son who redeems and sanctifies. But the flame of fire in the bush, the symbol preceding the words of calling,

---

[1] The well-known ancient opinion, that it was here that Moses wrote the book of Job, has much in its favour, if one goes deeply into the question.

[2] Even should ἄγγελος without Κυρίου be the correct reading here, it cannot, on account of the immediate context, be translated "*an* angel;" but even with this contraction, the form of the expression is emphatical: "*the* angel," viz. the known, special angel of the Lord, from henceforth standing out prominently in the history (cf. ver. 38).

through which the person of the Caller manifested itself, is so significant that not only Stephen, but also the Lord Jesus, alludes to it (Mark xii. 26).

Vers. 31–33. *When Moses saw it, he wondered at the sight.* The first voice of the Caller was expressed in a symbol, and set forth the first name of the angel as "I am *wonderful*" (Judg. xiii. 18; Isa. ix. 6). When the Lord sees that a child of man "turns aside to see" this His great name, then the Lord calls unto him out of the midst of the bush by name, and says, Moses, Moses! O that we all may be able likewise to answer, "Here am I!" (Ex. iii. 4.) Now to the *vision* are added the voice, and the revelation of God the Father, who comes to redeem for Himself a people. For the signification and value of those great words, I am thy God! when spoken to a child of man, *vid.* Matt. xxii. 32, Heb. xi. 16. The way in which this appropriation of God to ourselves is fulfilled in the three chief points, which are depicted in the three fathers whose names are joined with the title of the God of mercy, forms a part of the one great system of Scripture, which testifies in every place both by the profundity of the type and also by the clearness of the letter. The fact that Moses trembled and did not dare to behold, is contrasted very forcibly with his former bold readiness as related by Stephen (vers. 24–26), and shows us that Moses was a man who could only be made worthy by such humiliation as this to be a type, as Israel's deliverer, of Him who was with him. When he came out from the palace to help his brethren, he was mighty in *words;* but after the Lord had spoken with His servant, "since yesterday and the day before" (Ex. iv. 10) (perhaps even before the appearance in the bush), he had become "a man of no words." It was God, and not Moses, who was to bring Israel out of Egypt; but after Moses had recognised this, and had thus become God's instrument, Israel was bound to see in him the closely approaching type of their future Redeemer. The taking off the shoes (always henceforth to be taken off) signifies the surrender of his own steps and ways, the change in his own inclinations. Where the heart of man, the thorny wilderness, has once become *holy ground* through the revelation of Him who dwelt in the bush, then he, being washed, need henceforth but wash his feet. And neither land nor place according to the flesh makes any difference; but where God's servants stand before Him, there is the "sanctitas locorum ambulatoria" which the appearance of the Everlasting One ever brings with it.

Vers. 34, 35. The well-deserved ruin of Israel is here regarded by the loving eye of the Merciful One, and is only styled *their afflictions*, grievance, κάκωσις (ver. 6), just as if the groaning children appointed unto death were suffering *injustice* (Ps. cii. 20, 21, ciii. 6–8). He calls the rebellious children, who still remain dear on account of their fathers having been chosen, *His people which is in Egypt*, who also, according to the dictates of love, must be delivered therefrom. He had heard their groaning, although it was not to Him and for His salvation that they cried, but only as all created things call for deliverance—"Who shall deliver me from the body of this death?" (Rom. vii. 24.) Stephen purposely uses the word groaning (sighing), στεναγμός, although in Ex. iii. 7 the word κραυγή is employed; he derives the former word from Ex. ii. 23 and vi. 5. Groaning is the simple expression of distress wrung out of the inmost heart of the wretched, the famine of the prodigal son; and this avails before the God of mercy as the prayer of a drowning man, who only through his deliverance can learn to call upon the name of his deliverer. *And I am come down!*—important words, in which the incarnation of the angel is announced, although distantly. He who is God's countenance came down to Babel and Gomorrah with designs of restraint and judgment (Gen. xi. 5, xviii. 21), but now comes down to redeem His people Israel out of the power of the Egyptians. And now arises (quite following Ex. iii. 10, LXX.) a second contrast to the previous self-will of him who was then not yet *sent*, calling back to his mind his forty years' schooling in the wilderness. *I will send thee*—or more emphatically, according to another reading, *I send thee* (now)! This is what was before wanting. Now, however, this same Moses, whom they had asked for his authority, is permitted to give them the following answer to their question: "The Lord, the God of your fathers, has sent me unto you" (Ex. iii. 14, 15). Stephen, therefore, in ver. 35, again sets forth this question, and calls it a *refusal* or *denial*, because the whole of Israel, to whom he justly ascribes the words of these individual members of it,[1] was thus guilty of forgetfulness of God; and he desires also to point to the previous denial (Matt. xxi. 23, when Jesus was asked for His authority) of the Redeemer—Jesus of Nazareth—now again sent from heaven. He therefore gives to Moses three names—Ruler, Judge, and Deliverer—which show forth his typical relation to the actual Redeemer. Ruler—ἄρχων = ἀρχηγός—a beginner and summoner,

---

[1] The αὐτοῖς in ver. 26 had already, as we see, attributed this general significance to the event.

a leader in arising, he who stands at the head. Judge, δικαστής =
ἐκδίκησιν ποιῶν; but among the people of Israel themselves, a dis-
poser and lawgiver for the purpose of peace. Finally, Deliverer,
λυτρωτής, actually leading out of Egypt and into the land of Canaan
(1 Cor. i. 30). In Egypt and the Red Sea Moses was ἀρχηγός;
in the wilderness he was δικαστής; and finally, he was only half
λυτρωτής, leading the people only *out of* Egypt, and not *into* Canaan.
At this point he must lay down his typical office, and yield up its
conclusion to Joshua, just as David gave up to Solomon the building
of the temple and the rule of peace. The *prefiguration* is divided
between two persons; but as the antitype, Christ is at once the beginner and the completer: He is Moses and Joshua as the deliverer
bringing in to the inheritance—the Redeemer bringing salvation.
Stephen, at the end of ver. 35, mentions only the two names *Ruler*
and *Deliverer;* and as in the expression "deliverer" he does not
really comprehend the *completion* of the deliverance, in the following part of his discourse he comes down to the fact that Moses
only brought Israel out as a lawgiver (ver. 36), that he only pointed
to the future (ver. 37), and that with his "lively oracles" he could
not give life (vers. 38–43). *By the hand of the angel,* not merely
as ἀπέστειλεν, but rather to be ἄρχοντα καὶ λυτρωτήν; that he
(Moses) did not lead them on and out through *his own* hand (ver.
25), but through the strong and high hand of the special angel,
the messenger sent from God; through whom alone any sacred
message of a child of man can be brought to pass, who also must
appear for the consecration of every servant of God, though it may
be in the bush, under the veil of an earlier revelation.

Vers. 36, 37. Because the accusers (ch. vi. 14) had placed their
Moses so strongly in opposition to Jesus, indeed almost to God,
therefore the accused man brings the person of this Moses so
closely into light. Beginning with ver. 20, Stephen has depicted
him in his entire human development, as a man who was at first
deficient in the divine warrant, and then was afterwards sanctified
by complete humility before God. In ver. 35 he points out both
that Moses was denied by Israel with injustice on their part, and
also that Moses himself only represented the Angel that was with
him, and that the Angel was the real deliverer of Israel (Isa. lxiii.
9–12). In vers. 36–38, three times he speaks of Moses as οὗτος
after the τοῦτον in ver. 35. He led them *out,* but did not lead
them in. The word οὗτος points to some future deliverer. *He*
gave them the law, which could only be fulfilled in the future.

By quitting the subject of the wilderness (ver. 36), in mentioning the forty years which Israel were to pass in it for the punishment of their disobedience, Stephen forcibly calls attention to the limit of Moses' office as deliverer, which he connects again with *Joshua* in ver. 45. The "wonders and signs" are the proofs of the strong and high hand of the angel who is with him, and also may call to remembrance the works of Jesus. There were also in the land of Egypt and in the Red Sea penal and preserving wonders—penal for the Egyptians, and preserving for Israel; but in the wilderness, the people who lusted again after Egypt and strove against the Lord received both punishment and help in long-suffering and educating alternation, ending at last with the refractory ones dying in the wilderness, not because God was unable to bring them into the land, but because Israel was not worthy of it (Ex. xiv. 3, xxxii. 12). And when the lawgiver says, Another shall come, whom ye shall hear and obey,[1] it is by this made clear that a *second* law-giving is predicted. Stephen, too, places these words of Moses *before* the law-giving spoken of in ver. 38; and by the future lawgiver being called a *prophet*, the working of the spirit as opposed to the letter of the law is made prominent.

Ver. 38. At this point of the discourse, Moses stands at his highest degree of honour, which Stephen in no way denies to him, not only as lawgiver, but also as mediator; for without being the latter he could not have been the former. By referring to the mediatorship between the angel and the fathers, even before the functions as lawgiver, Stephen closely connects ver. 37 with the further progress of his discourse (for, according to Deut. xviii. 16–19, the promise of a prophet followed the need of a mediator, and actually preceded the remainder of the lawgiving which came after the "ten commandments"). He therefore *first* specifies that element in Moses' office in which he prefigured the future and higher Lawgiver, who was also the true Mediator;[2] and *then* he limits his mention of the law to the expression *lively oracles*, or

---

[1] Matt. xvii. 5 refers to these words of Moses, indeed gives the authentic explanation of them, as contrasted to the whole series of earlier prophets (as personified in Elias) as well as to the lawgiver. When Stephen curtails his discourse, and places all the emphasis on the ὡς ἐμέ, he intends to remind his hearers of the whole well-known passage, just as if he quoted it literally and completely. Hints of this kind exist throughout the discourse.

[2] The people of the Old Testament were still so far removed that they needed a human mediator between them and the Divine Mediator; Moses had to stand between the angel and the community—to *receive* in order to *give*.

utterances. All that we read in Lev. xviii. 5, Deut. xxx. 16, 19, xxxii. 47, xxxiii. 2, Ezek. xx. 11–13, and Luke x. 38 certainly speaks in favour of the law, and contains so far a justification of the ἔθη (Acts vi. 14), as to which, alas, the New Testament divines so often imitate the Old Testament scribes; but, at the same time, it all calls to our mind (*because Israel is coming out of the land of death*) the question : Will this living law make them live ? (Gal. iii. 21; Rom. viii. 2.) And the following part of the discourse (vers. 39–43) gives a negative answer to the question. So that Moses could not actually give these words of life to the children of Israel, *i.e.* could not implant this life in them. This could only be done by Him who as Mediator entered into the cloud on another and a higher mount, and received for us out of the upper sanctuary, not only *words* of life which remain as letters for us, but also the Spirit of life in and by His purifying words (John vi. 63, 68, xiv. 26, xv. 3 ; Acts ii. 33 ; Heb. xii. 25).

Vers. 39–41. *To whom,* ᾧ, emphatically refers to Moses, who is four times distinguished by the *demonstrative*. Moses indeed had spoken the commands to them, after they would and could no longer hearken to the voice of the Lord their God. But Moses had said to them, Thus saith the Lord ! and yet even then they regarded Moses only, and not the Lord, and *thrust from them* the judge who was *now* duly appointed by God,[1] just as before they rejected the self-instituted ruler. They said, not only when they were under Sinai (in ver. 40), but even when they were by the Red Sea (Ex. xiv. 11), that *this* Moses had brought them out of Egypt. They *would not*—in spite of the signs and wonders (ver. 36), and in spite of the great and chief manifestation on Mount Sinai. *Become obedient—*ὑπήκοοι γενέσθαι : a more forcible expression than *to obey*, and comprehending the whole of the long and fruitless education which was to teach obedience. *They turned back again into Egypt*—not perhaps wishing to go back thither (for see Ex. xxxii. 4), but *in their hearts ;* turning to the Egyptian representations of an evident God (they having been forbidden to make figures and similitudes of Him), to the Egyptian meats and drinks and games, and the musical dances round the work of *their own* hands, joined to a misuse of the holy name. Israel therefore, even on Sinai, was Egyptian *at heart*—a great retrogression indeed ! They desired, and then made of their own will, an image of their God, to *go before* them. The institution of a figurative,

[1] ἀπώσαντο, as ver. 27, ἀπώσατο.

but yet *prefigurative* sanctuary, without the image of God, resulted
in bringing to light the fundamental sin of God's too sensual
people. Aaron the brother of Moses, the first high priest, took a
part in this sin of Israel, just as Moses and Aaron shared in
Israel's want of faith at the *waters of strife*, on account of which
they entered not into the land of promise (Num. xx. 10, 12).
They made a calf, ἐμοσχοποίησαν; a new, comprehensive word
being used, so as to gain an expression for all the subsequent
idolatry which began with this calf-making, and for every arbitrary outward representation and embodiment of the manifestation
of God. *In those days*—at the very time of the first lawgiving!
And offered sacrifice—to the idol, not to Jehovah, whose name was
only misused therein. Whoever makes for himself a forbidden
similitude, commits idolatry as much as he who chooses other gods:
they are the two stages of rebellion which appear in Israel, as well
as in Christendom and humanity generally.—*And they rejoiced in
the works of their own hands!* This is the idolatry and denial of
God which exists in all image-worship. Bengel very justly says:
" Deo convenit lætari in operibus manuum suarum, et nobis, in
operibus manuum ejus. Idololatræ sunt homines, qui lætantur in
operibus manuum suarum."

Vers. 42, 43. When Christendom (the chosen people of the
New Testament) again heathenizes itself on the mount of the
spiritual law, and their priesthood (as Aaron) moulds for them the
calf of an externally magnificent churchdom, then the many *lapsi*
and the many *traditores* are not far removed. The Papacy clears
the way for the antichristian apostasy. Image-worship is soon
followed by idolatry, and the desire for the return to Egypt is
answered finally by a carrying away to Babylon. For when the
children of Israel turn away from their God, who has gone before
them in power and truth, and desire to make for themselves a
thing to lead them, following their own Egypt-learned arrogance,
—when they look *only* to Moses, and so completely forget Him
who led them out through Moses' agency, that they could say,
" As to this man, we wot not what is become of him,"—when
under the mount of revelation they compelled Aaron to make them
a calf, and, Egyptian-like, rejoiced in this wicked work;—then
must God also *turn* from His Israel (although He turned not with
His heart), and must *give them up*. Now those things took place
in Israel which are spoken of the heathen in Rom. i. 21–24 (cf.
Ps. cvi. 19, 20; Jer. ii. 10, 11). But yet even now God remains

the faithful and true God, who *gives up* that He may not everlastingly repudiate, and that He may make the apostates feel what
woe and heartfelt misery is brought on them by their forsaking
the Lord their God (Jer. ii. 19), so that He might yet force them,
as it were, into the bond of the covenant, and might be enabled
to make a delivery from Babylon succeed to their delivery from
Egypt. As God's mercy blesses even in judgment, so God's faithfulness sanctifies or educates even when it gives the sinner up.
Certainly He gave them up, so that more and more, up to the time
of the exile, though with many an alternation of repentance and
mercy, they worshipped the "host of heaven." In Deut. iv. 19,
xvii. 3, this is prominently mentioned among other objects of
idolatry, and is specified as being assigned to the heathen to worship. Star-worship was the original shape of Chaldean idolatry
(Job xxxi. 26–28), just as animal-worship was the original Egyptian form. Indeed, every idolatry is so far a worship of the "host
of heaven," as the devils caused themselves to be worshipped under
the titles of idols, and they also represented themselves to be stars
or angels of light, although they were only the dark wandering
stars of the heavenly system. Amos, who not very long before
the captivity of the ten tribes rebuked the idolatry of Israel, gives
a momentous account of Israel's idolatry even when they were in
the wilderness, which account many have desired to explain away,
because it followed so long after the event; but Stephen, a man
learned in the Scriptures, brings prominently forward in its proper
place this passage, unique in its kind in the book of prophecy (*i.e.*
probably of the twelve minor prophets), and feels warranted in
using it strikingly in his severe and incisively convicting speech.
In this quotation he takes a prospective glance at the prophetic
period, and shows that the light of the prophetic censure shone on
and disclosed Israel's first sins. In ch. v. Amos has harshly censured the Israel of his own time, who sought not the Lord of life,
but dead idols, at Beth-aven, Gilgal, and Beersheba; and he has
also forcibly condemned their pharisaical worship of God as being
devoid of justice and righteousness (vers. 21–24). At the conclusion of the chapter he represents to them that they have acted thus
since the time when they were in the wilderness, and predicts their
impending captivity. He thus comprehends both the beginning
and end of their idolatry. Stephen in this quotation takes the
same survey of the whole subject. Amos, by his mention, calls to
mind that earliest idolatry, which is for the first time biblically

recorded by him, and also that God did not then require from the fathers either burnt-offerings or meat-offerings, but obedience to His voice;[1] and that the disobedient people, not caring to endure such discipline and proving (Deut. viii. 2), had therefore chosen to offer to idols. Have ye sacrificed in the wilderness to *me?* says the Lord through the prophet, *i.e.* (without contradicting Ex. xxiv., Num. vii.–ix.) to *me* wholly and purely; ay, even when ye sacrificed to me, was it actually to *me* (Zech. vii. 5, 6), that is, from your hearts? The idolatry which was unmentioned by Moses in the whole course of his history of the eight-and-thirty years, was perhaps half private, and therefore all the more wicked; this idolatry, which is disclosed by Amos so long afterwards, sufficiently reveals what then was permanently dwelling in the heart of Israel. The names *Moloch* and *Remphan* form a part of the quotation from the Septuagint,[2] and bear a general significance as names opposed to the holy title of Jehovah. We will only remark further here, that the *tabernacle* of Moloch is now already mentioned as a false and antagonistic one, before the tabernacle ordained by God is contrasted with it in ver. 44; and the *figures* which Israel had themselves made in order to worship them as their idols, before the sanctuary constructed after the heavenly model is set forth; and that consequently Stephen most significantly *leads on his discourse through Israel's idolatry to the institution of their prefigurative divine worship.* The last expression, *star, ἄστρον,* which stands in contrast to the human figure of *Moloch* (king), conclusively discloses that Israel had in their hearts gone back to Chaldea, the fatherland of star-worship: the threatening as to the exile follows therefore very suitably. Thus the captivity in Babylon was only the manifestation of that which had been in Israel's heart since their "turning back" to Egypt. *Babylon* being named by Stephen instead of *Damascus,* is only a later explanation of the words used by Amos.

Vers. 44, 45. Tabernacle and temple belong together as *one;*

---

[1] *Vid.* Jer. vii. 22 ff., and cf. Ps. xl. 7. Even circumcision was first required by God in Canaan (Josh. v.), and the whole of the sacrificial and tabernacle service was chiefly ordained for their future residence in the land. *Vid.* Deut. xii. 5–9, and remark how correctly Stephen brings the tabernacle forward in ver. 44 only.

[2] Stephen adheres so thoroughly to the Greek text, that we are compelled not only to consider him as an Hellenist, but are also convinced that he spoke in Greek before the High Council. This also must have been the language used in the disputation with the scholars of the foreign synagogue (ch. vi. 9).

for the building of the temple only declared that which was promised from the beginning, that a place should be chosen where
the Lord's name might dwell, and by the final establishment
of God's sanctuary determined the prolongation of the previous
period of uncertainty, which had been extended up to the time of
David-Solomon (Ex. xv. 13, 17). David-Solomon, king of Israel,
forms a new and important turning-point in the typical system,
before which the oppressions and deliverances of Israel in Canaan
appear as the continuation of their proving and preparing journey
through the wilderness. The Tabernacle of witness was in the
wilderness, and accompanied them in all their journeyings. But
it was prescribed through Him who spoke to Moses on Sinai and
in the tabernacle, and was not made by Israel according to their
own ideas ; and this was its sanctifying consecration. But where
God ordains anything *external*, He can thereby only shadow forth
and prefigure some *inner meaning*. The Spirit of God takes no
pleasure in unreal and meaningless figures, which would indeed be
actual untruths. *Every ordinance of God* has its eternal and divine,
though perhaps hidden meaning ; how much more, then, the appointing of His holy tabernacle in Israel ! *Vid.* Exod. xxv. 9, 40,
xxvi. 30 ; Heb. viii. 5 ; Rev. xv. 5. The actual τύποι for all
forms of Divine manifestation are to be found in that which is
heavenly ; and if anything figurative presents these antetypes to
us here below according to God's will, it is not idolatry and image-
worship, but is a holy, premonitory, and educating symbolism. It is
here distinctly stated that Joshua led them into Canaan as Moses'
successor ; and to this a mention of David and Solomon is soon
after joined. The διαδεξάμενοι with the εἰσήγαγον refers to the
change in the generation which the mention of Joshua calls to mind ;
for it was not the *old* generation which had conducted *Moloch's*
tabernacle in the wilderness, which was to bring the ark of Jehovah
into the land of promise.[1] But yet God kept His promise made to
Abraham, even to " the increase of *sinful* men " (Num. xxxii. 14),
and caused them to take possession of and inherit the land of the
Gentiles or heathen. Not because the Israelites were any better,
for in the wilderness they had on all sides lusted after Egypt, but
for the sake of the faithfulness of their merciful God (Deut.
viii. 18–20, ix. 5–7). The κατάσχεσις τῶν ἐθνῶν was the concluding point which was wanting to this last period, the fulfilment of

---

[1] But διαδεξάμενοι does not exactly mean *successores*, but that they received
the tabernacle from the previous generation as a sacred inheritance.

I

that which still remained unfulfilled in God's promise to Abraham.
Each period in the fulfilling of the promise leads on to the one
which follows : the *choice* was only completed in the *sanctification*,
and the sanctification in the *glorification* of Israel. Not only the
whole period of the judges concluding at the turning-point of Eli-
Samuel, when the prophetic office commenced, but also the time
of transition into a kingdom under the reprehensible, self-seeking
Saul, is comprehended by Stephen in *one* period, during which the
tabernacle itself was wandering in Canaan through Israel's unholi-
ness, until it was profaned at the time of Ichabod's birth (1 Sam.
iv. 21, 22). But with the days of David, the man beloved by
God and after God's own heart, a new period begins.

Vers. 46, 47. *Who found favour before God*, as a real son of
Abraham. Indeed an altogether special favour, serving as a type
of that greatest and most real favour which God shows to man.
As by his victories the capture of the land had now been finally
completed, and as the Lord had now granted him rest from all his
enemies round about, he wished in his grateful, God-serving heart,
that the Ark of God might no longer wander about and continue
to dwell under the tent of the wilderness, but that the place of
God's rest should be built. And he was right, although the building itself was decreed to be carried out by one to come, and only
the *preparation for it* was appointed for him personally. Stephen,
in speaking of this, evidently refers to the remarkable passages in
Psalm cxxxii., and still more distinctly points to what is so clearly
said in the well-known scripture, 2 Sam. vii., that the building of
the temple was accepted only in a prefigurative view, referring to
the future building in the Son of David, of whom Solomon was
the type. There is an upper sanctuary existing from the beginning, an image of which is the tabernacle of Israel during the time
of the proving, the wandering, and the victory. Read carefully
2 Sam. vii., and weigh well vers. 5, 6, 10-16, 19. This interpretation is, however, verified the most completely in Ps. cxxxii.,
to which Stephen, the scribe of the Holy Spirit, directs our attention. This psalm sings of the institution of the temple in the
light of the announcement given to David of the everlasting kingdom of his future Son, and, in David longing for and preparing
for the temple, sets before us Christ in the first half of His work.
Stephen comprehends vers. 1–5 of the psalm in his word $\eta\tau\dot{\iota}\sigma\alpha\tau o$,
and concludes with an evident quotation from ver. 5. $\Sigma\kappa\dot{\eta}\nu\omega\mu\alpha$
expresses more than $\sigma\kappa\eta\nu\dot{\eta}$, and is a $\tau\dot{\upsilon}\pi o\varsigma$ for a more secure and

perfect σκηνή, a more actual *place of abode* or rest (Ps. cxxxii. 8, 14). Let the reader now see what follows in the psalm, and acknowledge that the true temple was first found in *Bethlehem-Ephrata.* Now are the words of Moses (Num. x. 35) altered, just as they were in ver. 8 of the psalm. Now is the true place of *rest* found; now is the prediction (vers. 9–18) fulfilled in Christ. Now also is God manifest in the fulfilment as the *God of Jacob,* for Jacob is the generation of them that seek God's face (Ps. xxiv. 6). David is the suffering loved one who entreated for the temple, and prepared for it in difficulty and distress (1 Chron. xxii. 14); but Solomon is the glorified "Prince of peace," in whom David, as it were, rose again and continued to live, and through him is the house actually built. There are three stages of the expression— first, *tabernacle* or tent; next, *habitation* or dwelling (σκήνωμα; cf. John i. 14); then *house* or completed building (οἰκοδομὴ, κατοικη- τήριον, Eph. ii. 21, 22). But even in the highest stage it can only be a type; and the everlasting God cannot dwell in any house such as was Solomon's, nor can He there have the place of His rest.

Vers. 48–50. Stephen, therefore, does not use the term *temple* for this house of Solomon, but reserves the name for the true temple built in Christ, to which the type has to resign its title. He reminds his hearers of the well-known words of Solomon at the dedication of his temple (1 Kings viii. 27–30), and styles the God whom, as Solomon said, "the heaven of heavens cannot contain," the *Most High.* Ἐν χειροποιήτοις: in this expression he desires to compare Solomon's house, as soon as it is erroneously imagined that God dwelt there, to the idolatrous *works of their own hands,* mentioned in ver. 41. In ver. 48, Stephen, in the first place, intends to say: That Solomon, *as ye well know,* so spake at the dedication, and significantly adds that the prophet's words completely coincide with him. The prophetic testimony which began with Samuel bore witness in David, Nathan, Solomon, and so in all the prophets, of the impending *spiritual accomplishment* of the now outwardly completed kingdom of Israel; and their great and indeed chief theme was, by means of a *reference* to that which was *internal* and *future* in *God's sanctuary,* to rebuke the people when they pharisaically too much depended on the type, or on the other hand, like the Canaanites, revolted from it. As Stephen only brings forward one principal passage out of this mass of prophetic testimony, he does not here name Isaiah, as in ver. 42 he did not name Amos. *Heaven is my throne, and the earth is my footstool:* cf. Ps. cx. 1, cxxxii. 7, 8, xcix. 5 ; Ezek. xliii. 7 ; 1 Chron. xxix. 2 ; Matt. v. 34, 35.   Though the earth had become a den of thieves and murderers, yet in His Solomon, God again builds up a house of prayer for all nations, and raises again the temple which was rent upon the cross.   But *we* cannot build a house for Him, but *He* for us (2 Sam. vii. 11); and this is now the real place of His rest in which He is well pleased (Ps. cxxxii. 14), the Jerusalem-Hephzibah (Isa. lxii. 4), the true rest into which we now are brought by the true Joshua, who has now become as one with Solomon.   There, an eternal Sabbath is kept in an eternal temple ; for man rests in God, and God in man (Heb. iv. 10). And of this the Lord speaks on another occasion : " My hand hath made all this " (Isa. lxv. 17).   For the *groundwork* and *beginning* of the new temple of God's glory in the children of men, we must look to Isa. lxvi. 2, to the words of comfort which follow, which, however, are broken off, in order that in their stead a censure may be added on those who sacrifice falsely.

Ver. 51. But Stephen, who had already (in ver. 48) passed from his narrative into open teaching, perhaps without any sudden impulse to this altered tone, but according to the purpose of the whole of his previous speech, now himself continues the " ye " of the prophet.   The prophet promised a beam of mercy from God's glory to those who in old time were of a poor and contrite spirit, who feared God's word ; but Stephen reproaches the *stiffnecked* who, with *uncircumcised ears,* withstand the Holy Ghost's testimony of mercy.   The Holy Ghost spake to Israel through the prophets, and through Christ and the apostles, saying that everything which God makes is good, and everything which man, without God, makes is bad.   Therefore forsake the doings and works of *your own* hands (vers. 41, 48), and rejoice ye in the work of God's hand, which redeems you !   Seek with humble faith this work of God on and in you, as far as it may be found, and wait for the promised and complete salvation !   But old Israel, in that it did not perceive this great aim of its old covenant, but was " ignorant of the right-eousness of God " (Rom. x. 3, 4), was stiffnecked, refractory, and stubborn under the yoke both of the law and also of grace.   To tell them this was Moses' office, inasmuch as he was a prophet as well as a lawgiver ; to tell them this, and to manifest it to them, was the commission of all the prophets, and the theme of their words (Isa. vi. 10).   And therefore Stephen here introduces (from ver. 42) this prophetic testimony, ever more and more pushing it home to their hearts, and expressing the fact that he himself, combining in one spirit the old and new word, continues Isaiah's discourse *in the person of all the prophets.*[1] His narrative, so long, and at the beginning so calm, had set forth the acknowledged facts of history from a deeper point of view, and now the rulers are justly compelled to submit to most merited reproach.[2] Σκληρο-τράχηλοι: vid. Ex. xxxiii. 3, 5, xxxiv. 9; Deut. ix. 6, 13; Neh. ix. 16; Jer. vii. 26; 2 Kings xvii. 14.—*Uncircumcised in heart and ears!* They were men in whom the fundamental type ordained for Abraham's seed found no *essential* fulfilment. Israel's uncircumcised *heart* had often since Moses (Deut. x. 16, xxx. 6) been rebuked by the prophets; the strongest passage is perhaps Jer. ix. 26. But the uncircumcision of the ears is only once named in the Old Testament, in Jer. vi. 10. The two expressions are in no way similar, for the *heart* is distinguished as the source of all that proceeds out of a man, which can only proceed out of his own corruption (Jer. vi. 7); but the *ear* is the door for everything that either goes into the man, or is intended by God's mercy to go into him (Jer. vi. 8). Israel cannot keep the law, because it is uncircumcised in heart; but with its uncircumcised ears it hearkens not to the prophets who through grace testify of the right fulfilment of the law, and *takes not to heart* Moses' words (Deut. xxx. 11–14). But in the obedience of Christ the doors both of the *ears* and *heart* are thrown open (Ps. xl. 7–9). The uncircumcision of the heart is perhaps less reproached than declared, but the wicked heart itself first goes before the door of the ears, and wilfully stops the ears which might perhaps listen to the testimony of mercy; therefore here, on the testimony of the Holy Ghost through the prophets,

---

[1] "It is to be wondered at how the inspired man forgets all about himself, and what his fate was to be, while uttering what he had to say as to God's dealings" (Hess). In this the "scribe" and "wise man" was also a "prophet" (Matt. xxiii. 34).

[2] Many assume that now signs of indignation began to break out against the word of God (through the prophet Isaiah), and that on this account the tone of Stephen's discourse turned to one of rebuke. This may be probable, but still we do not believe that it was exactly this which stirred up Stephen to treat them more sharply: his discourse is too clearly aimed at the concluding rebuke, and his holy presence of mind is too elevated. He is not (as Neander says) "carried away by the power of his feelings;" but the Holy Ghost speaks through him, as through the prophets, with a tone of anger when the proper time comes.

Israel's unrighteousness is fully made manifest. *Believe ye in My favour!* was the call the Father made to them at the time of the patriarchs; but they sinned against God, and against Joseph, who would *not sin against God*, and thus the *want of faith* in the *chosen* people was manifest. *Obey ye My truth!* were the guiding words of the angel-deliverer, which brought them out of the land of death and into the place of God's habitation (Ex. xv. 17); but they thrust this angel from them in the person of Moses, who represented Him, and thus the *disobedience* of the *delivered* people was manifest.— *Share My glory!* Thus the Spirit of glory through the prophets testified, solicited, allured, in an ascending scale of mercy adapted to their ascending grades of corruption, but in vain. They *persecuted* and *slew* God's ambassadors; and when finally the Lord of glory Himself appeared, they persecuted and slew Him too: thus the *resistance* of those who could and were intended to *be glorified* is now made manifest! God's favour promises, Israel believes not; truth accomplishes, Israel obeys not; the glory of mercy and truth is nevertheless about to be fulfilled, Israel *resists!* The sum of all is, that Israel *always* resists. This is the large view which Stephen's words in ver. 51 (with reference also to Isa. lxiii. 10) open out to us; this, too, is Israel's great mirror, in which also the conduct of all mankind, and especially of Christendom, is reflected. For in a higher stage, the whole of the Old Testament is the period of God's promise, and the whole of the New Testament is the period of the accomplishment of that promise in the Son; and the third, the old-new, or the oldest and latest testament, will be the (millennial) reign of the temple in the Holy Spirit. *Your* fathers—emphatically says Stephen now for the first time (cf. vers. 38–45); for now, as entirely the minister of the Spirit, he stands apart from and rebukes the sinners round him.

Vers. 52, 53. The prophets were the earlier ministers of the Spirit, and against *them* Israel's resistance went as far as *persecution* and *slaying*. The office of the prophets was through their word, and sometimes even through their prefigurative fate, to pre-announce the future coming of Him, the only "Just One," who was to come to the unjust, who was Himself the last of God's prophets and messengers, and by His own word fulfilled the words of the prophets, both having spoken in the same Holy Spirit. The Just One, the Guiltless, the Holy: thus does Stephen specify, without name, Him whom the false witnesses contemptuously styled "this Jesus of Nazareth" (Acts vi. 14). In Him is the door of righteousness opened to the unrighteous (Ps. cxviii. 20) ; but in rejecting Him will Israel's unrighteousness be made conclusively manifest, and the sin against the Holy Ghost will be accomplished.[1] There is *betrayal* and *murder* for the Just One, just as there was persecution and slaying for His harbingers, who were at least not entirely guiltless. They had delivered Him, their Messiah, to Pilate, just as in a narrower sphere Judas the betrayer had delivered up his Master to the enemy ; and when Pilate the unjust judge would, notwithstanding his injustice, " have nothing to do with this just person," they had themselves put Him to death by their cry, " Crucify Him, crucify Him ! " Here, too, it is made manifest, by reverting to unquestionable matters of fact, that this very people of the law had merely *received* that law given unto them *by the disposition of angels*, and had not *kept* or preserved it. As the Lord Himself said (John vii. 19), " Did not Moses give you the law, and yet none of you keepeth the law ? why go ye about to kill me ? " Israel received the law by the disposition of an angel, as a divine command communicated by angels' ministry ; for not only were the wonders (Ex. xix. 16) effected through angels, but the Lord manifested Himself on Sinai in the midst of the heavenly host (Deut. xxxiii. 2 ; Ps. lxviii. 17). Not only, indeed, was this so, but the words themselves were spoken through an angel,—the one *angel-mediator* who was the representative of the Son (Gal. iii. 19). But now, after all these sins, the heaven is for the first time in a true sense open over Israel, and the divinely-human glory of Jesus Christ is certainly greater than the angelic glory of the old covenant (the mere preparation for that which was to come) ; truly *here* there is something more glorious even than Sinai !

Vers. 54, 55, 56. Here, on "that day" of the Lord, it is rightly shown what a distinction there is " between the righteous and the wicked, between him that serveth God and him that serveth Him not " (Mal. iii. 18). To those who obey God in faith has He given the Holy Ghost, and made them to be angels in His kingdom, indeed even to be His children in the Son, the brethren of the Only-begotten ; but for those who in stiffnecked unbelief withstand the testimony of these messengers, there is left only a hell-anticipating " gnashing of the teeth," whilst the faithful witness is contemplating the glory of God. Although Stephen, perhaps, had

---

[1] Figuratively by all who denied Him, but actually only by the most wicked among them. At all events, in the crucifixion, the measure of the iniquity of the fathers was filled up.

only just now begun to find it out, God well knew beforehand that the second division of the discourse, which he had only commenced in ver. 56, would be broken off by the malignity which would listen no longer, and therefore caused that the few first words which His servant was permitted to speak should be forcible and penetrating. The God of glory had at the beginning caused a ray of angelic splendour to light up the face of the orator; He now so opens the eyes of this man " full of the Holy Ghost," that, pausing to take breath at the turning-point of his discourse, and looking up towards heaven,[1] he sees a sight whereof he is to testify on earth for but one short moment, ere like his Lord, by a martyr's death, he enters upon its full and eternal contemplation. Stephen sees the Triune God, of whom he had borne witness in his previous speech; but he sees Him only in the One Person who is " God's countenance," whom alone it is possible for man to see, in the person of Jesus the Son of God and man standing on the right hand of the Father. He does not see (with the Son) any human representation of the God of glory, as Daniel did (Dan. vii. 13—the *only* passage in which the Father is spoken of as being visible disjoined from the Son).   Daniel's sight was perhaps only a *figure* of *prophecy*, but Stephen now sees a *real substantiality*, and no symbolic vision : and by the side of the actual risen Son of man, a phantom-appearance of the Father (an " idea of divine majesty ") could hardly appear. Luke does not tell us that he saw an *appearance* of Jesus, but that he saw *Jesus*, and in Him and round Him the (Spirit)-glory of God (the Father). The transposition of the words " God of glory " in ver. 2, to Glory of God in ver. 55, is therefore very significant. The expression *at the right hand of God* in no way presupposes any visible representation of the Father, but denotes only the glorious brightness and majesty of God's throne (Ps. xvi. 11). Thus Jesus before His judges (Matt. xxvi. 64) only said, " on the right hand of power " (cf. Luke xxii. 69, which now begins to be fulfilled); and in Heb. i. 3 and viii. 1 it only says, " on the right hand of the majesty on high" (μεγαλωσύνης ἐν ὑψηλοῖς, τοῦ θρόνου τῆς μεγαλωσύνης ἐν τοῖς οὐρανοῖς). Stephen first gazed at the heavens with merely an ordinary look ; but now *the heaven is opened*, and through the break in the veil of glory he sees right in, to the place of God's habitation, whence the voice and the dove came down over Jordan,

---

[1] Looking earnestly, ἀτενίσας, extending the longing eye of faith towards the glory of God.

and beholds Jesus *standing* on God's throne! Should it not be *sitting*, not *standing?* Yes, indeed, Jesus *sits*, after He has once for all fought and won the victory, in the *rest* of the Father, until His enemies be made His footstool (Heb. x. 11–14). He *sits*, inasmuch as in the Father He is Lord. But yet He *stands* also, as the minister and guardian of the true tabernacle for daily service to God. He *stands* also, in that He is through the Spirit the minister of our salvation, and " sends forth His seven spirits into all the earth" (Rev. v. 6). *Now*, too, He *stands*, to reach out a helping hand of power to His brother Stephen, and comes, as it were, to meet him, the first martyr, and to welcome him into His glory.[1] But Stephen in all loving confidence calls the glorious One who stood on the right hand of majesty the *Son of man*. This is the only passage [2] in which Jesus since His ascension is named as the " Son of man " (for Rev. i. 13, 14, 15 is a prophetical vision, as Daniel's; therefore also ὅμοιος is added). Why is this? Even if Stephen had known and heard Jesus in the flesh, yet none of His disciples, in speaking of Him, then gave Him this name. At this time the *Spirit of Jesus* was speaking so fully in Stephen, that it is as if the Lord Himself (who alone gave Himself this name) was uttering the name, and calling to mind His words (Matt. xxvi. 64). Stephen would now have continued to testify that the words spoken by all the prophets from the beginning of the world were fulfilled, and that the oath sworn to Abraham had been kept, in that God *grants* to us in the Son of man that we, being *delivered from our enemies*, should *serve* Him everlastingly in holiness and righteousness before the light of His countenance (Luke i. 70–75).

Vers. 57, 58. *But* his stubborn and spiritually uncircumcised hearers refused to hear any longer, and loudly cried down the voice of the man of God when he began to testify of the glory of this Son of man. They stopped their truth-refusing ears, as if to shut out a blasphemy,[3] and like a company of devils terribly unani-

---

[1] Not, perhaps, as has been thought, standing up to pronounce judgment on Israel.

[2] Luke just previously writes only " Jesus." Not merely " very *seldom* except in the Gospels " (as Baumgarten very incorrectly says), but the expression occurs elsewhere *only* from the lips of Jesus Himself.

[3] They had understood enough perhaps for some to have been able to note with ever increasing displeasure whither all this discourse would lead at the end. L. Wolff well says as to this : " As they now perceived that he had surrounded them on all sides, they prevented him with speedy violence from drawing together his net."

mous in their hatred of God, ran upon him and cast him out—
him, the apostle—just as they had thrust out from them the Lord,
the prophets, and the first typical deliverer. They cast him, indeed,
like a criminal outside the city, the holy places of which they professed to reverence, and *stoned* him. And when the false witnesses
were about to cast the first stones, and were making themselves
ready to execute their dreadful task, a young man took care of their
clothes, with cordial acquiescence in their deed (ch. viii. 1, xxvi. 10),
who himself soon after stood forth as an active persecutor of Christ's
church (ch. viii. 3), but only that he might ere long be changed
into the greatest of the apostles of the Son of man. Thus does the
world but show its impotence when it stones the witnesses for the
truth !

Vers. 59, 60. But the confessing martyr faithfully finished
his confession even unto death. He had only just begun to testify
of the divine glory of the Son of man—of the Just One who had
been murdered by the unjust ; but the result proved that the few
words he had spoken had been well understood. But the great
name of salvation, to which sinners must appeal, he had not yet
named. Now, therefore, that his confession might be completed,
this is done. Stephen calls upon his God and Lord, blasphemed
though He may be by his murderous judges, and commending his
redeemed spirit to the hands of the Son, just as the Son had surrendered His spirit to the Father, died as saints die, calling upon
the name of his Lord. But all is not yet told ! After having,
in the joyful boldness won for him by the death of Christ, assumed,
as the *first* portion of his dying language, those words which, in
the thought of His bitter abandonment, formed the *last* expiring
accents of his Master, he now takes his Lord's *former* words as his
last. He kneels down and urgently prays, all the while patiently
receiving the fatal stones, crying out with a loud voice, so that his
enemies must hear, *Lord, lay not this sin to their charge !* And
thus, as much like Jesus as it was in the power of a sinful child of
man to be, the first martyr gently fell asleep, and entered into the
glory of his God. His (symbolical) name tells of the crown which
awaited him, which will be his at the last day.

Ch. viii. 1–4. And there were many standing there whose
hearts were turned against God, and felt a satisfaction in the
sufferings of Christ and of His members. There were, however,
some among these foolish zealots who were in no way given up by
God's mercy. Of this number was *Saul*. On this same day a

general persecution broke out against the church, for now the dam was broken away from before the fearful flood. It then appeared as if Gamaliel's words were to come true, and that this firmly united community was "to come to nought;" for every one, at least all the persecuted, acted, so far as they were able, in accordance with Matt. x. 23 and Acts i. 8, and fled away, scattering themselves abroad in Judea and Samaria. The apostles alone—doubtless instructed by the Spirit—remained with the persecuted ones who were left in Jerusalem, both to strengthen them, and, by the continuance of their testimony, to stir up a fresh increase to the church in the chief city. And no man was permitted to lay hands on the apostles, for their hour was not yet come. *Devout men*, perhaps, or probably, men that had not yet been Christians, but some who now came forward to make their first profession, buried Stephen with great lamentation, as if in contrast to the great persecution which was going on. Thus was Stephen like his Lord not only in his death, but also in his burial. This kindly feeling no doubt exasperated the persecutors more and more; and Saul violently devastated and spoiled God's church, breaking into house after house to find out every place where bread was broken in Jesus' name, and casting into prison all the members of the new community whom God had elected to such a martyrdom. But was God's word thus hindered? This persecution was, in God's hand, the very means of removing His church out of their early blessedness and love, into a triumphant position as champions and witnesses for the faith. A Stephen rose up in every Christian who visited a spot where God's word had not yet been preached.[1] The enemy have destroyed God's witnesses in the flames, and the sparks have been scattered forth in all lands; ay, and on they spread, now as ever! As Luther sang of the two martyrs at Brussels:

> " Their ashes never can be washed away;
> In every land their dust shall freely play.
> Brook, pit, ditch, grave, they all in vain employ
> To hide that dust the foe would fain destroy.
> Those martyred saints, whose testifying breath
> The foe hath silenced in the calm of death,
> Though dead, yet speak; and now in every tongue
> The foe must hear their joyous triumph sung,
> On every shore and every race among!"

[1] But in no way must it be said (with Baumgarten): "The hunted and scattered Christians took up the office and work of the apostles, whilst the apostles were silent."

X.

PETER'S ADDRESS TO SIMON THE SORCERER.

(CHAP. VIII. 20–23.)

REJECTION OF HIS PROUD AND FOOLISH DESIRE OF BUYING WITH
MONEY THE POWER OF CONFERRING THE GIFT OF THE HOLY
SPIRIT.

VERS. 5–8. After Stephen's removal, Philip (who perhaps on
this account is named next after Stephen in ch. vi. 5) appears
to have taken his place to some extent : at least we hear nothing
more of the rest of the deacons ;[1] but of *Philip* we read in
this chapter that he solemnized two notable baptisms, and we
subsequently hear of him as an evangelist in Cæsarea (ch. xxi. 8).
He was now preaching Christ in a city of the Samaritans[2] (the
name of which is not specified either here or in vers. 8 and 9),
who were an ignorant and easily moved people, more free from
Pharisaism, and therefore more susceptible to the influence of
God's word.   In Matt. x. 5, Christ had forbidden the apostles to
" enter into the cities of the Samaritans, and to walk in the ways of
the heathen ; " yet in His words and actions He often showed love
and almost honour to the Samaritans, and it was to a Samaritan
woman (who looked upon the coming Messiah as not so much an
earthly king as a teacher and prophet) that He first clearly said
that He was the Christ.   Also in Acts i. 8, Samaria had been expressly specified as an intermediate sphere, standing, as it were,
between the Jewish and the heathen world, in which the gospel
should be preached.   Thus Philip, who stood first after the apostles
(who remained at Jerusalem), considered that he was authorized
and directed to preach Christ to this neighbouring people, without
caring for what the hostile rulers might say of such a connection
with wicked heretics ; and the reconciliation of this hereditary
enmity formed a beautiful beginning of the universal bond of union
of all nations in Christ.   The preaching of Philip was accompanied
and followed by no small measure of signs and wonders, by which

[1] There was no longer much for them to do in Jerusalem.

[2] If it had been the chief city, Samaria, or Sebaste, why is it twice so indefinitely indicated, as Luke usually names places ?   If it is the name of the city
which is mentioned in ver. 14, why not also in vers. 8 and 9 ?

the Lord confirmed His word, and opened the hearts of the hearers; so that first by hearing, and then by *rightly* seeing these miracles, they were constrained to give heed to that which was spoken. Unclean spirits were triumphantly driven out of those that were possessed, and the sick were healed : such were the evangelical signs and proofs of the gospel ; and thus the joy was great at the blessings both to their bodies and souls which had been brought to them in Christ Jesus.

Vers. 9-13. The poor Samaritans, to whom the salvation of the Jews had now come, had previously not known what they worshipped, and were therefore a fertile field for any necromancers or magicians to work upon who might desire to be themselves objects of adoration ; and at this time there were many of this class of men, especially in Egypt and Syria.   One of this kind, named *Simon*, for some time resident in the city, by his lying and infernal juggleries[1] (in which he assuredly did not cast out many devils or heal many sick persons) had brought into a state of stupid astonishment not only this particular city, but the whole people of the Samaritans.   He had made himself out to be an extraordinary and important man—*some great one;* but the exact nature of his assumption is purposely not told.   Old people and children, the rabble as well as persons of higher standing, had paid regard to him ; and this man had become to them the same thing which Philip now was, but yet in a different way : for *they themselves*, with a vague conception characteristic of the fanaticism of that period, had styled him the *power of God*—the so-called great personified authority of the Deity ; but Philip preached to them Christ, and not himself, in His words and works, said and done in the power of God.[2]   This wretched man, by his long-continued course of fascination, had drawn to him this large body of adherents, only to see all his honours taken from him at once by the evangelist's word ! Philip's more frequent, more important, and more beneficial miracles had diverted the attention of the people from the silly babbler and cheat, and induced them to give heed to the messenger of mercy.   And now the word that preached of the right nature of the true kingdom of God, and of its foundation on the one only adorable name of Jesus

---

[1] Luke uses the expression μαγεύων, from μάγος, in the bad meaning, as in ch. xiii. 6.

[2] Luke uses the same word in reference to both προσεῖχον in ver. 6 and ver. 10 ; but with regard to Philip it says, τοῖς λεγομένοις ὑπὸ τοῦ Φιλίππου—with regard to Simon, ᾦ.

Christ, met with such a response of faith, that the greater number of the inhabitants, both men and women, were actually baptized. What was Simon to do now? He took the best course, and truly the most natural, and considered that opposition against the evidently superior power of the truth would be diabolically wicked and foolish. We read, *Then Simon himself also believed.* Are we, on account of what follows, permitted to consider that he believed with a merely external, hypocritical confession? By no means. A correct narrator does not so tell his story, that a preceding part of it cannot be justly comprehended until some subsequent portion is read; and Luke states broadly and literally that " Simon believed," just as the others believed who are mentioned in ver. 12 : indeed it says, " Simon *also* believed." His faith, therefore, was the same as theirs in all essential requisites, and he was with them *baptized* by Philip, who would certainly have been able to distinguish any gross hypocrisy. Indeed, his baptism seems to have followed his belief [1] so much as a matter of course, that Luke only mentions it at the beginning of a fresh sentence in a participial form ($\beta\alpha\pi$-$\tau\iota\sigma\theta\epsilon\acute{\iota}\varsigma$). But in this fresh sentence we are also told something special of Simon. After he had been baptized in common with the rest, he continued with Philip. This was natural, and might denote, on the one hand, an emphatic confession that he now gave place to the true man of God; but, on the other, it might be his old pride which induced him to seek this position at least. Luke adds, that when he so closely saw the works of power and great miracles (much greater than his own) which were done continually by Philip, he *wondered,* just as the people aforetime had wondered at him. Thus had matters changed. The unprejudiced reader who has so far simply considered the narrative, will rejoice that *truth* had thus far triumphed over deceit, but will also be inclined to doubt whether perhaps things were all right with Simon, and to conjecture as to what would be his future course of action.

Vers. 14–17. These doubts and conjectures are soon satisfied. The apostles who had remained in Jerusalem heard the good news, that (a place in) Samaria had accepted the word of God, which

---

[1] The apostolic missionary rule does not recognise any long proof of perseverance in the candidates for baptism; but this sacrament was to be given to every one actually believing, although infirmity and impurity might possibly still exist in them, in the hope of their partaking in the triumph of the common grace. There is therefore here a lesson against any painful delay going to the other extreme.

Jerusalem, or rather its rulers, had rejected, and that the Samaritans were believers in Him whom the orthodox had crucified.
Then *Peter* and *John,* selected by the body in whom alone the
chief authority over individuals rested, were sent to Samaria for
the purpose of proving, confirming, and completing the work begun
by the deacon.   Although some imperfection in the procedure
may perhaps have caused this deficiency in the full manifestation
of the Spirit as regarded the persons baptized,[1] still the apostles
found, on the whole, that everything was so far done in due order,
that they prayed for the new church at Samaria that they might
receive the Holy Ghost; that is, they prayed to the Lord on their
behalf, that He would grant them authority to lay their hands upon
the church to this effect. This was done; and thus the apostles
confirmed those who had been baptized in the name of Jesus by the
important visible seal of God's power which prevailed at that time.
But *John*[2] might perhaps have looked back to the days when he
desired to call down on the Samaritans who refused to receive the
Lord another kind of heavenly fire (Luke ix. 54, 56); *now* at
least he knew " what manner of spirit he was of."

Vers. 18, 19. When Simon's turn for confirmation came, the
approach and offer of the good Spirit awoke again the *evil* spirit
within him, so that the bad intention in him was betrayed. Simon
had already seen much to astonish him in viewing the works which
had been done by the hands of Philip; but now something greater
still is presented to him; and when he contemplated the visible
extraordinary effect of the apostolic laying on of hands, then, after
gradual preparation, his old wicked self again broke out. He
might fancy that, like his own artifices, this gift of God was a
thing to be bought and sold; at all events, he offers money—as
much as he thought probably it was worth—and desires in return

---

[1] We only allow ourselves to put it as a " perhaps ; " but, at all events, the
lesser dignity of the deacon was not in itself the originating cause, but in some
way his less power or wisdom. Neander places the whole matter in a wrong
light, as if the faith of the Samaritans had been merely a faith depending on the
worker of miracles, to which the apostles by preparatory preaching were compelled to give the right substance and meaning. But there is nothing as to
this in the text; on the contrary, vers, 6, 8, 12 imply plainly the contrary.
The deficiency, as we understand it, does not go so far. If, perhaps, which is
to be imagined, all the baptized had not visibly and audibly received the special
gifts of the Spirit, it was important that the apostles should testify to the complete equality of the Samaritans.

[2] Who is here named for the last time in the " Acts of the Apostles."

for this payment a higher gift than was conferred on the rest of
the disciples. He seemed to think he had long enough stood merely
by the side of Philip. The apostles could do something which
Philip could not do ; and the poor, perverted Simon thought that
he could fill this highest position. *Give me also*, not only the Holy
Ghost itself, but *this power, that on whomsoever* (arbitrarily, with or
without baptism) *I may lay hands* (as if the power lay in the
hands !), *he may receive the Holy Ghost.* Ah! how many a successor to this Simon has wished to purchase for money, or for
money's worth, the power of ordaining others before and instead of
seeking his own true ordination !—perhaps even has desired the
power of awakening and converting others before and instead of
ensuring his own conversion ! But the *true* Simon, who is called
Peter, answers on this occasion as, alas, his so-called successors no
longer answer. In ch. iii. 6 he said he had neither silver nor gold
to give away, and now he will take nothing in exchange for that
gift of God which he had *freely* received, and could only freely give.

Ver. 20. Peter in a remarkable way begins at once with "the
money," so as to convey the rejection of his request in his very
first words, and casts it back to him as his (Simon's) own. *Thy
money perish with thee,* said Peter. What, in the first place, is the
"perishing" of money ? Its emptiness as the unrighteous mammon,
its perishableness as a thing of this world (Col. ii. 22 ; 1 Pet. i.
7, 18), whereby it is destined εἰς ἀπώλειαν, as the beasts εἰς φθοράν
(2 Pet. ii. 12). But since Simon's arrogance in endeavouring to
obtain the power of an apostle was connected with this money of
his, and was represented in his offer of it, the apostle includes him
in the "perishing" *with* the money—namely, in the φθορὰ ἐν ἐπι-
θυμία (2 Pet. i. 4)—in which, whoever doeth not the will of God,
shall perish with the world and its lusts. We learn here that this
corruption of the creature not only in a limited sense affects the
lust of the eyes and of the flesh, but also the haughty nature which
gives away money and goods in order to obtain honour, which is
more inclined to buy than to sell a birthright for a mess of pottage.
After Peter had in the σοί condemned the arrogance of Simon as a
whole, he proceeds to detailed expressions concerning it : he points
out the foolishness of his wish: *Because thou hast thought that the gift*
(or present) *of God may be purchased with money !* A complete
contradiction to his idea, and fully conveying the rejection of his
wish, which was expressed in the denunciation of him and his
money. God only could grant the Holy Ghost and the power of

conferring it, and in no way Peter, from whom Simon had demanded it as from a man : that which God gives to men is a *free
gift*, and bears no price. Peter, therefore, in these words gives a
twofold answer, both to the δότε in ver. 19, and also to the notion
involved in the ᾧ ἐὰν ἐπιθῶ, λαμβάνῃ. Among the gifts of God he
naturally first understands the *power* which was desired, and next
the possession of the Spirit generally, which Simon had lost sight
of in his eagerness to possess the power of conferring it. The Holy
Ghost is God's gift in the fullest sense, but Peter includes in the
expression all blessings and earthly good. Διὰ χρημάτων—as if a
repetition of ἀργύριον, but actually somewhat amplifying the expression, as much as to say : Away with thee and thy money ; man
may not buy God's gift with earthly goods !

Ver. 21. The sense here appears to be injured, if the ἐστί is
understood in the *future* (as by Luther), as it contradicts the admonition and possibility of repentance intimated in the following verse.
The word ἐστί, twice used in ver. 21, corresponds to the εἴη in ver.
20, so that the denunciation there expressed in the *imperative* now
appears as a mere statement in the *indicative*. *Thou hast*, on account
of the existing state of thy heart, *neither part nor lot in this matter*
(or word)—that is, in God's gift of this word, and in everything
which the term expresses, and therefore no part in God's community—because thou desirest to buy that which is a free gift.
Μερὶς οὐδὲ κλῆρος, actually share or right to a share (cf. Deut. x. 9,
2 Sam. xx. 1, LXX., and Mic. ii. 5). Perhaps also it may mean :
neither a *part* among the disciples generally, nor special *call by lot*
to a higher stage of honour (ch. i. 17, 25). Peter therefore here
ordains the exclusion of Simon from the church, yet he merely
shows to him that he has *excluded himself*. This is quite clear in
the ἐστί referring to the inner cause of the exclusion. The boon
which God gives is the abolition of corruption through His light
and life: also, no one of the church can again fall into this corruption, except he excludes himself from the benefits the church enjoys;
and this is done by arrogant perversity of the heart before God, the
mercy of the Giver being misunderstood, and His *true gift* being
despised. "Why has Satan filled thine heart?" was said to Ananias.
Now, as then, with words penetrating to the root of the matter,
Simon is told, *Thy heart is not right in the sight of God* (cf. 2 Kings
x. 15, LXX.). Thus mildly and kindly is the censure expressed :
it tends to admonition, and evidently says enough. For the second
time Simon is directed to God instead of men, for it was Him whom

Simon (like Ananias) had offended. The apostle, in the power of the Holy Ghost, could perceive how the heart was disposed towards God. We may also gather that there had actually been a beginning of faith in Simon: it says, "Thy heart *is*" (now again become) not righteous, and not "*was*" (so from the beginning).

Ver. 22. *Repent therefore of this thy wickedness*—the obliquity of the proud heart towards God. *And pray God* (or, according to another reading, *the Lord;* cf. ver. 16): this is the *third* pointing to the sin being against God.[1] Pray penitently to Him for His gift, and do not artfully demand from us that which is not *our* gift. What thou hast first to pray for is not a high stage of dignity in the church; but it is *repentance*, the first universal gift to every sinner. Those only who are penitent for wickedness in general, are permitted to pray for forgiveness of an individual sin. *Whether* thy sin may be forgiven thee is doubtful, on account of the enormity of the wickedness, and the consequent difficulty of repentance thereof (cf. Amos v. 15; Joel ii. 13, 14). The Apostle Peter could bind and loose, *i.e.* reveal and declare the existing state of the heart, and, as was only fit, could regulate matters in the church; but the forgiveness of sins belongs to God alone (Ps. cxxx. 4). This also forms a contribution to the right comprehension of John xx. 23, and is opposed to the formula of absolution, beginning "I forgive thee."

Ver. 23. *For I perceive:* here is the cause for the doubtful way in which it was put as to his *possible* forgiveness; and a return to the tone of censure marks the final declaration of the heart-searching Spirit who spoke through the apostle. *Εἶναι εἰς* means simply and clearly *to become something; ὁρῶ σε ὄντα εἰς* is therefore a prophetically warning expression for the evil consequences which must inevitably result from Simon's wickedness except he repented of it. *Χολὴ πικρίας,* gall of bitterness—a substance impregnated with bitterness—appears to allude to Deut. xxix. 18, xxxii. 32. The *εἰς* here looks back to the *εἰς* in ver. 20: Thou mayest become not only *εἰς ἀπώλειαν* as regards thyself, but mayest previously become *εἰς χολὴν πικρίας* as regards the church. And *εἰς σύνδεσμον ἀδικίας* stands contrasted with the *σύνδεσμος τελειότητος* (Col. iii. 14) and *εἰρήνης* (Eph. iv. 3).

Ver. 24. All that we learn from the tradition of the church,

---

[1] Simon subsequently speaks, in ver. 24, of prayers to the *Lord*, which may be considered to be in favour of the reading *Κυρίου;* on the other hand, with *Θεοῦ*, the third pointing to God is made more distinct.

which is at least not entirely without a groundwork of truth, alas, only confirms the view which the apostle took in ver. 23 ;[1] but this makes it still more important for us to remark, that the apostle in ver. 22 endeavoured to turn this almost desperately wicked man to repentance and consequent mercy. Simon's answer in ver. 24 sounds, however, very doubtfully.—*Pray ye to the Lord for me.* He thus refers back to the apostles their summons to him to *individual* prayer, and does it so that one might well doubt whether he spoke in derision or in truth, if it were not that he adds, *that none of these things which ye have spoken come upon me.* Simon speaks here in a very similar way to the stubborn Pharaoh in Ex. viii. 28, ix. 28, x. 17. He is afraid of " the perishing," but has no heart for repentance, and for the second time places man between him and his view of God, which course of action would probably seem peculiarly natural to him, and would spring from the old fallacies of his previous system of deceit. He only half-defiantly enunciates something which sounds like repentance, but is *not* repentance. And here Luke puts an end to the history.

XI.

PHILIP TEACHES AND BAPTIZES THE ETHIOPIAN TREASURER.

(CHAP. VIII. 25–39.)

VERS. 25, 26. *But they*—whom Simon in ver. 24 had addressed as *ye*—the apostles Peter and John, now again working together in lovely unity, after they had performed their apostolical and confirmatory duty in the new church, and had spoken to Simon not *their* words, but *the Lord's* words, speaking according to the circumstances and requirement from their peculiar spiritual impulse ; they went back from this field of labour, now so beautifully opening round them, to all the dangers of Jerusalem, preaching the gospel on the way, not perhaps without deviating from their direct road, *in many villages of the Samaritans.* But Philip, who had perhaps been peculiarly grieved by Simon's apostasy, is addressed

---

[1] This prophetical reference to the history of the subsequent heresiarch leads us also to understand the σύνδεσμος not merely of his person, as many think, but as a bundle, an entanglement made by unrighteousness.

by an angel of the Lord, and receives directions to speak the word
of the Lord to some unknown person who would be prepared for
its reception. But the messenger of the great Head of the church,
who is sent to the minister of the church, only says in the first place,
*Go toward the south, unto the way that goeth down from Jerusalem
unto Gaza, which is desert.* Whilst the apostles are preaching to
the populous villages of Samaria, Philip is directed to a solitary
abandoned path, selected out of the many roads which led to
Egypt, that he may there find a hearer for his preaching.

Vers. 27–29. Philip at once obeyed, without either doubt or
delay. *And behold:* it was soon shown to him why he had been
sent there. A foreigner, a pious Jewish proselyte, returning from
Jerusalem to a great distance off, had to be converted; and by
this a fresh transition and extension of the word, viz. to the conversion of the heathen, was to be brought about. He is an *eunuch,*
—either an actual emasculate, in which case the abolition of the
law contained in Deut. xxiii. 1 now commences as predicted in
Isa. lvi. 3 (which law, however, had been before abrogated in regard to eminent proselytes); or only officially so called—in fact,
a *chamberlain* or *treasurer.* The former is the more probable,
because δυνάστης follows, and he was servant to a *queen,* Candace
of Meroe. At all events, he was a man of great eminence in his
own country, who managed all the queen's treasure (which is here
denoted by the Persian word, which is also *Gaza*), and yet did
not hesitate as a godly man to undertake the long journey to the
temple at Jerusalem. As he was returning along the unfrequented
road, which had been purposely selected, by the way he read in the
Scriptures, just as the apostles returning to Jerusalem by the way
preached the word, each being faithful to that which it was his
duty to do. He did not take his ease, as being well satisfied with
his praiseworthy pilgrimage, now completed; nor did he merely
look about him at the country round. His aim in the whole
journey there and back had not been to perform a mere outward
act or to gratify curiosity, but to hear the word of God and obtain instruction for salvation. Perhaps he had only for the first
time procured a copy (of the entire Old Testament, or probably
of only a portion) in order to take it back with him, and was now
the more eager to obtain a knowledge of its contents, and to lay
open its treasures, which he held to be more precious than all the
riches of the royal treasury committed to his charge. The book
of the law seemed also to be less the aim of his study than was

the book of the prophets,[1]—a good sign of his eagerness for salvation. The portion of Scripture which the Ethiopian treasurer was reading was the prophet Isaiah, the prince of prophets. There was many a thing, perhaps, in the book which the man could not understand; but yet he diligently read the word of God in longing faith, and he could comprehend enough of it to cause the sense to penetrate him more and more. Bengel very beautifully says: "As spices exhale their perfume by stirring." The Scripture goes before preaching, by God's guidance awakening and preparing the future hearers. If this was the case, as here, with the Old Testament, how much more reason have *we* to send out the Bible (both Old and New Testaments) in advance of the missionary! Many a Brahmin has understood much of it before it could be preached to him. But certainly men like Philip should follow and should apply themselves to the actual teaching and baptism of those they meet with in their way. To this first Philip the way had been shown by an angel; and now the Spirit (of the Lord, ver. 39), in an ascending scale of revelation, directs him *to go near and join himself to the chariot* in which this eminent stranger was sitting, and (as directed in Deut. vi. 7) was reading aloud the words of Isaiah (in the Greek text).

Vers. 30, 31. Philip again obeys without either doubt or delay. And, behold, the same Spirit which had given him the command showed him further how it was to be carried out, and puts a simple and impressive form of address into his mouth. It must naturally have been an encouragement to Philip that the chapter of Isaiah which he heard read by the Ethiopian was that very chief chapter, as it may be called, which one would select out of the entire Old Testament as best adapted to link on with the gospel. The Spirit bids him say at once, without any circumlocution, and with a deeply significant play upon the words, Ἆρά γε γινώσκεις ἃ ἀναγινώσκεις;[2] —an opening of the conversation which, from a worldly point of view, was certainly unpolite, and yet as a divine message was perfectly appropriate,—refraining, too, from any useless salutation by the way (Luke x. 4). In the general model here presented lies the great question that must be asked in all time, which not only guides

---

[1] The Torah was easier to obtain, and perhaps already in his possession. He now had exerted himself to obtain the " prophets ; " or, if he had brought the book of Isaiah also with him, which seems less probable to us, he was now, in an inquiring spirit, reading this especially.

[2] " Legere et non intelligere nec legere est ; " cf. 2 Cor. iii. 2.

the reader on from the old prophetic word, and points him to the gospel, but also leads him on from the *new* Scriptures to a living preaching, and thus renders the minister of the word an interpreter of the text. *Understandest thou what thou readest?* The half-understanding reader of the Scriptures who is anxious for salvation will not receive this question amiss from a preacher; and if we ask it in the love and power of the Spirit, who must interpret the word, God will open the reader's heart as He did on this occasion. The good man, whose honest seeking is rewarded with explanatory preaching, which was exceptional, inasmuch as the gospel had not yet been sent to distant parts, gives an answer which is as artless as the question : *How can I, except some man should guide me?* [1] He does not plead his partial comprehension of the word to the somewhat assuming stranger, but willingly confesses at once that he does not understand : indeed, he perceives that it is a dispensation of the good God ; and feeling confident, as a man desirous to learn, that his friendly questioner is willing to teach him, he invites him, without further hesitation, to sit up with him in the chariot.

Vers. 32–35. The acknowledgment of the Old Testament for apostolic use is now completely set forth for the first time in the Acts of the Apostles. The section in Isaiah which the eunuch was reading (ch. lii. 13–liii. 12) contains the clear aim of all the previous prognostications as to the person of Christ, and depicts by itself (in the third person, which is not used since ch. xlviii. 16) His first coming in humility, in which the Lord, the God of Israel Himself (ch. lii. 12), goes before His people in the form of a servant—as their *Joshua*—makes atonement for them by His sufferings, death, and resurrection, regenerates them, and receives them into His glory. The Ethiopian treasurer, as a man without prejudice, and anxious for salvation, asks the question which would naturally occur to any such person, and says to Philip, as the teacher to whom he must appeal, *Of whom speaketh the prophet this?* It could hardly be of himself here, and therefore must be *of some other man.* Then could the evangelist joyfully open his mouth and commence his duty. *He began at the same scripture, and preached unto him Jesus.* He might also have been able to begin from some other scripture ; for whoever looks into the inner sense and context of the Scriptures in the spirit of Jesus, will find somehow, in *every* passage, a path that leads to the gospel.

[1] He speaks in harmony with the same truth to which Philip's question bore witness.

Vers. 36–38. And as the two—one preaching and the other hearing[1]—were following the path which the Lord Himself had opened out for them, this path laid down by the Lord led immediately to baptism. They came to some water, and the treasurer, who was now as quick in his belief as he had previously been anxious in his reading, and to whom Philip had probably at once spoken of baptism, says, with childlike eagerness, *See, here is water!* Perhaps, in his desire for baptism, he for the first time confessed his belief, which had so quickly and deeply imbibed the preaching he had heard. He asks for it, too, in a simple but stringent question : *What doth hinder me to be baptized?*[2] The mere presence of water was certainly not a sufficient requisite for his baptism, and it was necessary that faith should be present in him ; but the desire itself confessed this faith. Philip could therefore only say (and even if ver. 37 is really an addition of the church, which is not yet certainly determined, the tenor of it is entirely consonant with the sense and intention of Philip, and of the whole story), *If thou believest with all thine heart, thou mayest,* or, it is permitted. The tentative addition " with all thine heart," and also the strong expression "it is permitted," are both peculiarly fitting in Philip's mouth, inasmuch as he must have recollected *Simon ;* but yet he accepts with a simple heart the consolation for Simon's apostasy, which his kind Lord had in every circumstance prepared for him in the conversion of this foreigner. And also, after Simon's history, we ought anew to see in that of the treasurer, that whoever believes with his whole heart may be baptized, without any human solicitude on account of God's grace, which is *free,* and therefore *due,* to every one that believes. Was the treasurer a circumcised or uncircumcised proselyte ? Philip probably did not now ask this question ; but the former is more likely to have been the case, as is rendered probable subsequently by ch. x.[3] The treasurer answers joyfully and rightly with a summing up of the whole preaching as he understood it, by which, too, he testified to his *right* understanding of it, and expresses the groundwork of the subsequent baptismal confes-

[1] Not, as a manuscript adds, συζητοῦντες μετ᾽ ἀλλήλων.

[2] His simplicity is remarkably contrasted with the sordidness of Simon, as Olshausen remarks.

[3] Certainly only probably ; for it may be thought that God, without actual knowledge by the community, or even by Philip, may have caused this to take place by means of a direct interposition of the Spirit, which became publicly manifest at a subsequent time only. We often think that a Cornelius is the first, and yet there is an Ethiopian unknown to us who has gone before him.

sion in the church.[1] The Father and Son are named : the Spirit is
understood in the faithful naming of the former, which could only
be brought about through His effectual working. Where the Spirit
testifies, there is no need even of His name. The confessor is so
certain of the matter, that he commands the chariot to stop ; and
Philip, without further ceremony than the words ordained by God,
and the use of the water present by the road-side, without the
solemnity of a congregation, but in the presence of the joyous
angels of God—especially of the guardian angel of this treasurer—
baptizes this man, who as yet knew but little, but yet firmly, simply,
and fundamentally *believed*. No catechism of the numerous Christian duties was put into his hands. Only a short time before he
had been reading Isaiah in the semi-darkness indicated by the
question put in ver. 34 ; but now he knew Jesus' name of salvation, though he could hardly have learned much of the history of
His human life, except the great and important points of His
humiliation and exaltation ; nevertheless, through his faith he is
fit and worthy to enter Christ's church.

Ver. 39. And now the story concludes in a way as unexpected
as it is extraordinary. One would at least have expected that the
newly converted man would have made some sojourn among the
Christian community, and that perhaps there would have been a
consultation as to whether he should now return homewards or not.
But God decides immediately after the baptism (thus bringing this
ceremony conspicuously forward as the direct aim of all this special
guidance), and so directly enforces what is to be done, that no room
remains for question. *The Spirit of the Lord*, evidently in reference
to ver. 29, but at the same time remarkably mentioned *without
the article*—Πνεῦμα Κυρίου, a Spirit of the Lord—carried away
Philip ; not merely a voice of the Spirit, but, as we are shown by
the ἥρπασε which follows, a *seizure by the Spirit*, which caught
up his body : therefore a wind of the Lord, the bearer and servant
of the Spirit. We cannot doubt that it was a miraculous bodily
abstraction, as in the case of Elijah (1 Kings xviii. 12 ; 2 Kings
ii. 16),[2] which is here intended, so that the treasurer saw Philip
no more, and the latter *was found at Azotus*. The baptism by

---

[1] Even if this answer is a later addition (it has certainly existed since
Irenæus), it must be rightly assumed that the candidate for baptism would have
said something similar.

[2] The miracles of the Old Testament, such as the appearances of angels, are
renewed at the beginning of the new covenant, in order that this portion of the

the deacon is on this occasion not followed by any laying on of hands. We are, however, to look upon this apostolic confirmation as not in any way indispensable ; therefore this, and perhaps even the second sacrament, is, at least at first, withheld from the baptized person without his thus losing anything essential.[1] Though Philip is no longer there, the Spirit is still present—the Spirit which brought him and took him away ; therefore let no νεόφυτος despair though the Lord may in a like manner deprive him of his Philip, but let him joyfully and believingly penetrate into the grace of God which is opened to him in baptism. He who has the *Scriptures* and *Christ* needs not, if God will, any further human guidance. God occasionally deals wonderfully with His church, in order that we may not presume to limit wrongfully by rules the efficacy of His free and marvellous acts. He here leaves the Ethiopian to go on his way alone, but He Himself directs the converted persecutor Saul to the city, that an Ananias may there tell him what he is to do. The fact that the treasurer, comforted as he was, perhaps, by the very miracle which removed his teacher from him, *went on his way rejoicing*, shows us, finally, the great power of the Spirit which operated in this extraordinary conversion. This, too, was doubtless made evident to Philip for the quieting of his mind by the Spirit which removed him. Isa. xxx. 20, 21 may be beautifully applied to this foreigner going on his way alone.

Ver. 40 belongs more to the narrative that follows than to the preceding one. We shall, however, omit ch. ix., as the first portion of it forms a part of the discourses of the Lord Jesus, whose appearance is therein described, and does not belong to those of the apostles ; and in the second portion of it there are only two short *sayings* of Peter recorded, which are scarcely to be called "discourses." The words addressed to Æneas are like those spoken by the Lord in John v. 8 ; and those spoken to the corpse of Tabitha (ver. 40), πρὸς τὸ σῶμα, were uttered in the deepest humility of prostrate prayer, but yet with a bold simplicity. They followed closely the words of the Lord Christ, and were pronounced in the power of His name, yet without mentioning it, and naturally without using the expression, "I say unto thee." The sayings of the chief apostle on these two occasions are, to our mind, not so

sacred history may be actually sealed, and that the time of the old covenant may not retain any visible pre-eminence.

[1] The addition, πνεῦμα ἅγιον ἐπέπεσεν ἐπὶ τὸν εὐνοῦχον, ἄγγελος δὲ Κυρίου ἥρπασε τὸν Φίλιππον, has certainly originated from a feeling of doubt.

important as the short *ministerial words* of the deacon which are
recorded both *before* and *after* the preaching, which is only alluded
to in ch. viii. 35.

XII.

PETER IN THE HOUSE OF CORNELIUS.

(Chap. x. 34–43.)

COMMENCEMENT OF THE PREACHING OF THE GOSPEL TO THE HEATHEN.

Before Luke's narrative leaves for a time the persecuting
and stubborn Jerusalem—in which, however, the company of the
apostles, praying to the last, still bore their testimony of mercy—it
had been able, in the conversion of Paul, and his alteration into
an apostle of truth, to present to us a clear warning against a too
precipitate judgment; for the God of mercy—who indeed visibly
judges His stedfast opponents even on earth, and yet keeps back
and hides behind His judgment the deeper way of restoration—has
been pleased to put before us a testimony of this kind in the sub-
duing of an arch-persecutor, and his institution to an high office in
the church. There was many a Judas in Israel, although Jesus had
only revealed His decisive judgment on *one*; there was also many
a Saul, although the conversion of *one* only is made evident. The
Saviour, who appeared to him in mercy, and was able and willing
to render him submissive in three days' penance, can and will appear
in like mercy to every one who is worthy of acceptance (δεκτός), on
account of a good though mistakenly zealous conscience (ch. xxii. 3,
xxiii. 1). This Saul of Tarsus, in preaching the name which he
formerly despised, must assuredly soon experience how much he
has to suffer for the sake of this despised though saving name. The
Jews in Damascus, whom he had confounded in argument, desire
to kill him (ch. ix. 22, 24); and the Greeks at Jerusalem, who had
been unable to cope with him in dispute, also desire to kill him
(ver. 29). But the persecution as a whole had to be given up under
the compulsion of a Caligula, and the church is enabled to build
itself up in peace throughout all Judea, Galilee, and Samaria (ver.
31). Thus, after the collection of a little band of believers out of

the Israelites and Samaritans (now again acknowledged as brethren) had been so firmly begun, the great transmission of the gospel to the *uncircumcised* was being more and more prepared for. To prepare for the account of this, and as an illustrative record of the state of the community at this time, Luke brings forward Peter's two miracles wrought on *Æneas* and *Tabitha,*—thus connecting the sojourn of the chief apostle at Joppa with the preceding narrative.

Vers. 1, 2. In Cæsarea Stratonis, about eight miles distant from Joppa, a town which had been built and named by Herod in honour of Augustus, lived *a certain man called Cornelius.* Æneas also, who likewise had a Roman name, was only thus styled in ch. ix. 33, and was thus distinguished from the *saints* (ver. 32), and also from the *female disciple* (ver. 36): we see therefore at once that Cornelius was an uncircumcised man. He was also a centurion of the *cohors Italica* which was stationed at Cæsarea. But nevertheless, as Luke further states, in spite of his heathen origin and his military position (the second being significantly added to the first to indicate his Romish birth), he was *a devout man, and one that feared God.* The whole history shows us that Philip, who was preaching *in all the cities* from Azotus *until he came to Cæsarea,* had at this time not yet arrived there. Cornelius, therefore, must have become a God-fearing man, or a Jewish proselyte—a so-called " proselyte of the gate " [1]—by his adhesion to the people of Israel, and, like many heathen at that time, had enjoyed a blessing from the revelation made to him, which was missed by its proper possessor. His piety, although naturally much of an Old Testament character, and consequently still in the spirit of bondage and fear (Rom. viii. 15), was nevertheless not without life, zeal, and confidence. Its life was shown by his inducing " all his house " to worship the God of Israel ; its zeal was made known by his giving " much alms," especially to the people of God, the superiority of whom he humbly reverenced ; its confidence led him to " pray to God alway "—to that God of Israel who had become *his* God. The " much alms " appear outwardly, like those of

[1] All the reasons against it cannot induce us to deny this character to Cornelius, for we cannot believe that there were any heathen in Judæa who prayed to the one true God (at Israel's fixed hours of prayer also), and gave alms to the Jews, without at least being connected with them as " proselytes of the gate." It may be proved that the strict Jews at that time, contrary to Moses' opinion, shunned any close companionship, in their homes or at their tables, with these uncircumcised proselytes. *Vid.* subsequently, ch. xi. 3.

Tabitha mentioned in ch. ix. 36; but Luke speaks of the latter as *good works*, only because they were done from a heart purified by faith. The alms of *Cornelius* were only half-good,—a mistaken striving after justification. There is a want of understanding in the good works even of a God-fearing man, until he possesses the secret of the faith in a pure conscience; but yet there may be a good conscience to a certain degree; and where this is present, the alms given will never satisfy and quiet the heart. The seeking after justification begins with good works, and now it is decided whether the seeker is sincere or not. If he depends entirely on his works, he is wrong; but if he is honest, he must surely feel that something is still wanting—indeed, the "one thing needful;" and whilst he continues to do good, he prays to the only God without whom no one can become or continue good. Thus therefore Cornelius prayed, not with mere words and forms, as a meritorious action: he did not say prayers (προσευχόμενος), but besought (δεόμενος) God, feeling a real need and longing. He did this, too, not only at the set hours of prayer, but *alway* (διαπαντός),—by which not only an earnest, but also a faithful, seeking of peace is most strongly denoted (Heb. xi. 6).

Vers. 3–6. What took place? "Ask, and it shall be given unto you; seek, and ye shall find; knock, and it shall be opened unto you." Acceptable to (δεκτός) and willingly accepted before God is every heathen, who in a good conscience, although it may be with misunderstanding, strives after the kingdom of God and His righteousness. When Cornelius, as was his daily custom, was fasting (ver. 30) and praying at the ninth hour of the day—the prescribed hour for prayer in Israel (ch. iii. 1)—he saw in a vision, *i.e.* in a different way from the usual mode of sight, but yet *evidently* and certainly in the clear light of the afternoon, an angel of God (the God to whom he was praying for wisdom and peace) come and stand by him; he also in the same vision heard him call to him—*Cornelius!* This was the answer to his entreaties; it was as if the holy messenger had said to him in the name of the Lord, "I know thee by name, and thou hast also found grace in my sight" (Ex. xxxiii. 12). But Cornelius, looking intently on the man in bright clothing (ver. 30), naturally enough *was afraid*, as the flesh ever is in the presence of spiritual beings, and answered the messenger very much as Saul answered the Lord, although certainly with a more seeking confidence: *What is it, Lord? i.e.* what wilt Thou that I should do? (ver. 6.) And now comes the refreshing encouragement from the lips of the heavenly messenger,—that refreshment which every one feels, who, like Cornelius, has prayed long to God, and has at length found that he is heard. God knows thee, thinks upon thee, summons thee to His salvation—important tidings to every sincere Cornelius ! *Thy prayers and thine alms,* says the angel, placing them in a different order to Luke in ver. 2. There the outward acts were placed before the inward, according to the custom of men ; but now the inward feelings are placed first, as they are valued before God. The centurion's prayer was the chief thing, and the alms availed in God's sight only as deeds accompanied with prayer, as a seeking and striving after justification. Therefore both are spoken of together, and indeed in the plural, as if every single sigh and penny had been reckoned up ; and it is said that they *are come up as a memorial before God.* The angel, who was perhaps Cornelius' (now overjoyed) guardian angel, who had been the bearer of his prayers up to God's throne (Rev. viii. 4), nevertheless veils his office, and speaks only the above words, so significant to him who had hitherto felt himself so far from God, and that his prayers had been unheard.—*And now.* These words denote that all that follows is an answer to his prayer, and consequently that his prayer was looked upon as a seeking for peace, although the seeker as yet knew not that it must come through Jesus Christ. But the mere cry of any suffering soul, " Help me, Lord ! " avails before God as if it clearly said, " Grant me the Saviour ! " *Send to Joppa !* Thus the angel directs him to the regular minister of the word, to the chief apostle, who was to be the first to preach the word to the Gentiles as well as to the Jews :[1] even the tongue of an angel could not announce the remission of sins (ver. 43) from personal experience, as a Peter could. He who was to speak to Cornelius this great message, is exactly specified both by name and surname ; his city, locality, and house being mentioned, but yet no title of honour is given to him. The fact that Peter was sent for to come to Cornelius, and not just the reverse, is likewise suitable to the greatness of the event ; it forms, as Bengel remarks, the beginning of the apostles' *going forth* to preach to all nations.

Vers. 7, 8. The overjoyed man delayed not a moment to fulfil the command which seemed to promise so much. When the angel (who had not suddenly appeared and then at once vanished,

---

[1] Angelus apostolum monstrat: apostolus Christum ; tantum honorem testibus suis habuit Christus.—Grot.

but had visited him in familiar condescension) had departed, Cornelius, with judicious decision, calls two of his household servants, whose piety is to be understood from ver. 2 ; and in addition, that the message conveyed by the angel's words may be more certainly expressed, he also summons a soldier (who, like his captain, was a devout man) from among the body who waited on him, or were on guard at his house. He might now have merely said to his servants, "Go!" (Matt. viii. 9); but he manifests to them a kind confidence as to the mutual hope for their mutual piety, and declared to them the whole matter. Perhaps also it was because he could not write, and the man of God at Joppa would expect to know the reason why he should be called so far away. Enough that he sends them the same evening to Joppa, and *waits* (ver. 24).

Vers. 9–13. The acceptance of the Gentiles by the chief apostle is prepared for in an extraordinary way on both sides ; just as was (in the previous chapter) the acceptance of the subdued persecutor by the disciple at Damascus. In the case of Saul, it was the Lord Himself who interposed on both sides ; but now it is only an angel in a vision on the one hand, and on the other an ecstasy, a vision and a voice, and then the Spirit (ver. 19) ; but in all it is really God (vers. 28, 33). Whilst the men from Cæsarea are on the morrow approaching Joppa, Peter, moved by an apostolic fervour of devotion, which to the two fixed hours of prayer added a third (Ps. lv. 18 ; Dan. vi. 10), mounts at mid-day to the flat open roof to pray in quiet under the open sky, perhaps to present before his God and theirs the church at Joppa, and the owner of the house he was in. But, together with the apostle's spiritual fervour, the exigency of the flesh is also made manifest, and he is now *hungry,* indeed *very hungry,*—this being perhaps caused by some extraordinary influence. This does not completely interrupt him in his design, as might easily have been the case ; but he desires only that some small matter may be brought him to appease his appetite, and still remains on the roof. At this moment, whilst the people of the house were preparing a meal for him, the Spirit of revelation sends a vision which comes upon Peter in a trance (ἔκστασις, an abrupt alteration in the usual state of things). He sees the heaven opened (not *the heavens,* as Stephen), and a plenteous meal, indeed, descending before him on the roof ; a vessel like a great sheet, with four corners—answering to the four quarters of the globe—hanging down from heaven, and so descending to the *earth* or roof (which makes very little difference), that he was able to perceive in it beasts of the earth of all kinds, not excluding the fowls of the air. And with the vision came a voice, naturally from heaven (ch. xi. 9), saying, *Rise, Peter; kill, and eat.* The killing and eating, and the whole subsequent idea, is joined on, after the manner of dreams, to the waiting for food which was then actually existing.

Vers. 14–16. The summoning voice spoke generally of all the living things which covered this vast table, without distinction as to clean or unclean; but probably the *unclean* beasts presented themselves first at the edge of the sheet. Peter, therefore, the conscientious Israelite from his youth up—conscientious even in his trance, and faithful to the deeply rooted custom—replies, *Not so, Lord;* that is by no means fit (μηδαμῶς): *for I have never eaten anything that is common and unclean.* Hereupon the voice becomes something more—the clear and emphatic teaching of God; it speaks a second time: *What God*—the unconstrained Ruler, from whom this vision proceeds—*hath,* by this sending down from heaven and summons to eat, pronounced to be clean, and hath *cleansed, that call not thou common!* Probably Peter was at first silent, and the voice was again repeated, making the third time of its call to him; and then *the vessel was received up again into heaven.*

Vers. 17–20. Peter comes to himself,[1] and meditates doubtfully what the sight he had seen could mean. He therefore recognised that it was intended for divine instruction; as to this he was not in doubt, but was perplexed rather as to its exact signification: he must also have remarked that more was intended by it than was at first sight presented to view. For the meaning, that the Old Testament laws with regard to food were to be abolished in the Christian community, was so very evident, that he could hardly have been in doubt about *that;* it might, on the contrary, have brought to his recollection Jesus' forcible words, Mark vii. 15–23. But those words had spoken of the purity or impurity of men; and the second and third times the voice addressed Peter, it omitted (indeed significantly) the *eating,* which was only mentioned in the first call, and said with more general signification, " *What God* hath cleansed." [2] Peter must have especially meditated over this " what," and it was so intended; for as the beginning and idea of

---

[1] Understand, ὡς δὲ ἐν ἑαυτῷ γενόμενος διηπόρει; and cf. ch. xii. 11.

[2] God had already prepared Cornelius by His prevenient grace, and had so far " cleansed " him.

the vision was linked on to his own hunger, in the same way the conclusion of it leaves the explanation of its meaning to his own meditation, which was soon to be developed by God's dealings with him. Peter, while reflecting generally, and doubting as to his former Jewish ideas, is soon to be awakened to new things.

The things which were doing soon explain the things which were seen, and the meditation on the hint that had been received is developed by God's guidance and the interposition of the certifying Spirit. Peter has to pass from doubt to certainty, therefore in himself he must first actually doubt; but whilst in this doubt he must take no actual step, lest it should be a sin in him. The Spirit therefore assures him, step by step, in the matter; so that, in spite of the uncertainty which up to ver. 34 still lingered in his mind, he can both go and speak in Christian confidence. By διενθυμουμένου (ver. 19) Luke denotes both the progress to a reflective consciousness since the διηπόρει in ver. 17, and also by the διά the still remaining uncertainty. Peter reflects more on the vision in particular, than on the voice so clear in itself. It would be no reason for his going, if three or even ten men merely came to seek the apostle; but when the Spirit says, *Arise and go*, then there is no longer room for doubt. Remark the allusion to the "arise" in ver. 13, and also the divinely personal address of the Spirit: *I have sent them* (the men sent by Cornelius, according to vers. 17 and 21). These last forcible words imply: Hesitate not as to who the person may be that sends them; *I* am the actual Sender (ver. 5).

Vers. 22, 23. Peter anticipates the summons, and presents himself to them with a friendly question, although from ver. 20 he must have known that they had come to fetch him. He conceals the revelation he has received, and acts wisely, and with due respect to external order. The messengers state their business as well as they can, and in the fulness of their hearts praise their kind master, and as far as possible do away with the surprise which their demand would cause. Cornelius, they say, is a man that feareth God, and is of good report among all the Jews in Cæsarea and the neighbourhood, and therefore you need have no hesitation in venturing under his roof. A holy angel has wonderfully commanded him that he was not to go to you, but that you were to come to him: he is therefore compelled so far to presume. He is to hear words from thee, to which the angel has referred: this was a fresh explanatory hint for Peter, the minister of the word of God.

He now invites in the men who had been hitherto standing before the door, thereby breaking through the usual custom of the Jews, by entertaining Gentiles; naturally though with the approbation of Simon the tanner. The next day he takes with him six brethren (ch. xi. 12), doubling the number of the three messengers, to be the twice three witnesses of all that was to happen. How rightly, and in what harmony with God's guidance, he acted, the sequel soon shows.

Vers. 24–26. So now seven men from Israel, and three from among the Gentiles, travel towards Cæsarea; the brethren in Christ with the servants, who were soon to be brethren too, and at their head the foremost of Christ's servants. Cornelius had *waited*, as might well be supposed. In just confidence of Peter's speedy coming, and reckoning on the time of his arrival, he had invited a considerable company to assemble, not merely of his (probably few) kindred, to whom in his kind-hearted simplicity he could not grudge a participation in his blessings, but also of his close, near friends, united with him in the bond of their common piety. This kindly, simple-hearted, and loving believer is shown to us more and more as the centre and head of a considerable circle of pious Gentiles in Cæsarea, which city was now to be favoured by being the seat of the first Gentile church. The angel (vers. 6 and 32) had spoken of Cornelius only; but the latter, who possessed a generous love as well as a preparing faith, does not appropriate the promise to himself alone as a private advantage, but calls in to hear the longed-for words of salvation those whom he considered just as worthy, or perhaps even worthier than himself. And it is well pleasing to the Lord, when, in this idea, one who is himself scarcely called begins to call others: this is indeed the way in which His church is everywhere multiplied. The host was looking out to see if he whom he had invited his guests to meet was not soon coming; and as Peter—the man to whom the angel referred, who also was to tell him in God's name what he ought to do —was only just entering the house, *he met him, and fell down at his feet, and worshipped him, i.e.* according to the Old Testament expression and the Eastern usage, to which this distinguished Roman thought right to conform. He rendered him, in fact, the highest testimony of honour. There were certainly no idolatrous ideas in his mind; for Simon Peter had been mentioned to him by the angel as a mere man. But Peter does not accept this homage, as his successor receives the kissing of his feet, but raises Cornelius

L

up, and stops it, saying, *Stand up! I myself also am a man.* In the New Testament, prostration of this kind is reserved expressly for God; and herein is the Old Testament custom abolished, and a significant hint is afforded as to the worth of forms in Christian life. Luke therefore, in holy awe, has added neither αὐτοῦ nor αὐτῷ at the end of ver. 25. Peter goes on step by step, and with the words " also a man " still further prepares himself for the clearly expressed proposition in ver. 28.

Vers. 27–29. Now followed verbal salutations from Cornelius, and friendly, modest replies from Peter, and generally, a familiar conversation between the two. But when Peter had actually come into the room, and saw the *many that were come together,* who appeared to be heathen, and indeed partly Roman soldiers, he was surprised. Even if Cornelius had given him notice of it, he felt overwhelmed at this room full of all kinds of men; so that he fell from his friendliness into a certain very excusable uncourteousness. He cannot refrain, even in his salutation to them, from almost reproaching them for being foreigners, and, in fact, from excusing himself to them for having come, which certainly leads him on to a confession of his previous error, and to an open declaration that no man was either common or unclean. In this he speaks by himself as the chief person, whom his six Jewish companions follow, and calls himself simply " a man that is a Jew," and with more courtesy styles the Gentiles *men of another nation*—ἀλλοφύλους. He speaks of this separation, which was not so much a command of God as the result of a human exaggeration of the divine laws, with the term ἀθέμιτον. Now, however, he freely acknowledges that " God hath showed him"—what hitherto he had not known— that he " should not call any man common or unclean." He says nothing more now about his vision except these few indefinite and modest words, which, however, point to something corresponding to the appearance of the angel. He also classes himself as a fellow-man with all that were present under that God who had called them together, and expresses the explanation (now clear to him) of the " voice" in ver. 15. But he does not yet appear to see clearly *how far* this explanation extended; at least he asks a second time, *For what intent have ye sent for me?* which had already been pointed out to him in ver. 22. It does not suffice to say, with many, that all he wished was to induce Cornelius to make a communication expressing his feelings, as a physician or pastor of souls would act. Before the apostle's impetuous cry, expressing his own certainty (ver. 34), it was much more material to him to obtain a full confirmation of all that had been told him by the messengers.

Vers. 30–33. Cornelius, joyful that he had so far progressed, now speaks without timidity, and clearly and modestly, simply and solemnly, relates the circumstances of the event. He commences with an exact mention of the time, not forgetting to call attention to his fasting, and styles the holy angel only as *a man in bright clothing*, as if to say, "Thou (Peter) wilt best know if it was a heavenly messenger or not." He now joyfully and rightly adds that his prayer was heard, which fact he had understood from the " coming up " in ver. 4 ; but he speaks of his last prayer only, instead of the prayers generally which were named by the angel.— *And thou hast well done that thou art come.* These words betray a slight doubt on the part of the expectant man whether Peter would come. *Now therefore are we all here present;* nothing hinders that we should attain our aim, that of hearing thy saving words which are promised to us (ch. xi. 14). We are here *before thee,*[1] and desire to hear all things which are commanded thee of the *God* who has pointed thee out to us, and (according to ver. 28) has already shown something to thee, and consequently must without doubt have ordained what thou shalt say to us.

Vers. 34, 35. Cornelius, as a man, had (which may well be forgiven him) looked principally to that which was before his eyes, —namely, the person of him who had been named to him by the angel—the now present Peter ; therefore in ver. 33 "thou" and "thee" occur four times, and "I" and "we" only twice. The conclusion of his speech, which links on to Peter's words in ver. 28, and connects the appearance of the angel with Peter's presupposed instruction, is directed towards God, and in the last words expresses very rightly and satisfactorily that Cornelius intended to listen to and consider Peter's utterances as the voice of God. But this very presupposition, that Peter would speak from a previously received divine message, compels the latter, who here least of all could allow himself to receive undeserved honour, to make a respondent confession. A noble pattern of candid modesty for all those from

---

[1] For this reading is to be preferred on both external and internal grounds, and is entirely suitable to the then disposition of Cornelius, who was eagerly expecting Peter's opening his lips. Alford would willingly admit it into the text, " if it only had more authority from manuscripts." We do not miss this, looking at the other evidence for its antiquity and its internal probability.

whom, by God's ordinance, others are waiting to hear God's words!
Peter announces himself to have been in error, just as these
ignorant, erring men, ere he commences to preach God's words of
peace to the Gentiles—those words which hitherto had been only
sent to the children of Israel—and ere he appeals to his dignity,
shared with the other apostles as Christ's witnesses.—*Now of a
truth I perceive.* This second " now," answering the " now" in ver.
33, does not indeed exist in the text, but yet may very correctly be
deduced from ἐπ' ἀληθείας, and from the sense of the whole passage.
Peter replies in the *present tense* to Cornelius' προστεταγμένα in
the preterite, and makes a rejoinder to the incomplete act of reverence in a somewhat similar way to that he had before used, and
says, Yes, indeed, it is " commanded me from God" what I must
speak to thee, but it is only at this very moment that it has become fully clear and certain to me. Hitherto Peter had not felt a
full conviction of the great proposition now more and more closely
anticipated, that the gospel belongs as a matter of course to the
Gentiles also. But in an instant, when he *opened his mouth* to
begin this new preaching (cf. Matt. v. 2), it was given him by the
Spirit what he should speak, and the still erring man was merged
in the infallibility of the apostleship. Καταλαμβάνομαι really means,
I experience, i.e. I find, feel and see by means of something that is
present, I perceive by means of experience (*vid.* this word, ch. iv. 13,
xxv. 25; Eph. iii. 18). The ἐπ' ἀληθείας that precedes it is in this
passage very significant. It is looking at it in a merely superficial
point of view, to take it as an emphatic assent to Cornelius' words.
But in Peter's intention, through the sudden apprehension of the
Spirit, it means that the present clear perception of the truth (ἀλήθεια)
is contrasted with all the previous signs, doubts, and preparations,
including therefore the vision, the meditation that arose therefrom,
and the passages of Scripture which probably occurred to the
apostle during these meditations. In the completely Old-Testament
expression which follows, we must remark, in the first place, the
forcible new word προσωπολήπτης arising as a contrast to the
censured human error, from which word are also formed in the New
Testament, ληπτέω—λήψία, ἀ—λήπτως. The negative Scripture
expression is followed by the apostolic assurance, passing on in
ver. 36 into God's word by the apostle's lips.—*But in every nation,
i.e.* not only in the hitherto separated people of God. There is, in
fact, only the great contrast : God's people and the world's people ;
and this the apostle so far apprehends. Now, however, he does

not specify every person in every nation (Col. i. 28), but makes
the following limitation : *He that feareth Him, and worketh righteousness.* This limitation would seem in the highest degree necessary,
if the following word δεκτός meant fully acceptable, well pleasing,
and righteous before God. But the limitation is surprising, because
it is not this condition which is in question, but the *receptibility*
into Christ's church. Nevertheless it is entirely correct. Peter
goes further than the mere permission of his preaching, which
certainly is fitted for every heathen, the sinner as well as the
righteous, for every fallen creature, even those who believe not in
their perdition ; he speaks of the *acceptableness* of a Gentile, *i.e.* of
his preparation and ability for an actual entrance into Israel (Rom.
xi. 25), in this most decidedly controverting his previous error. He
had considered that even a Gentile thus prepared (as Cornelius
was) was excluded on account of his uncircumcision, and had been
in error not only as to the preparing, but also as to the perfecting,
grace of God. He now asserts, in the first place, what those
Gentiles are who stand, as it were, upon the threshold, and were
permitted to be called in in spite of their Gentilism. According to
human notions, he referred in the first place to Cornelius, the ἀνὴρ
δίκαιος καὶ φοβούμενος τὸν Θεόν (ver. 22) ; but the Spirit, which
in ver. 35 begins to speak, of course intends *a very universal proposition.* The humanly arranged order which is used in ver. 22 is
here reversed, as we before remarked in reference to vers. 2 and
4, and a deeply significant designation of *all prepared heathen* is
expressed. For an outward adhesion to the Israel of God, as in
the case of Cornelius, is not the only way in which a heathen can
actually fear God ; but, because the true God nowhere leaves
Himself entirely without a witness among the heathen (ch. xiv.
17), because the mysterious and yet widespread sound of Him has
gone forth into all lands, and His high-sounding but yet voiceless
words to the very ends of the earth (Rom. x. 18, if correctly interpreted), therefore can man everywhere, in some way or other,
although in very different degrees, manifest awe and fear of this
divine testimony with an accompanying obedient belief, and can
consequently have in the heart the rudiment of the true religion
completed in Christ. "Holding the truth in unrighteousness,"
with which Paul (Rom. i. 18) charges the heathen as a body, is
repeated in every individual among them designedly and consciously, although it may be only in the very slightest degree ;
and as the people to whom the truth is revealed might hold that

truth in unrighteousness, so, on the contrary, the heathen might
be obedient unto righteousness to the indestructible revelation contained in creation and their own conscience (Rom. ii. 8, 14). But
the Lord, who "looks down from heaven upon the children of
men, to see if there were any who would understand and seek after
God" (Ps. xiv. 2), who "fashioneth all the hearts of them, and
understandeth all their works" (Ps. xxxiii. 14)—He looks to "him
who is of a poor and contrite spirit, and trembles at His word"
(Isa. lxvi. 2). But it goes on to say : *And worketh righteousness.*
Are there, then, workers of righteousness among all people, just
as there are God-fearers among them ? Of course, for one proposition follows the other ; and wherever there is anything good
in the heart, there also there are outward aspirations in deeds and
works. The other side of the question is afterwards laid open in
ver. 43. There is a twofold way of using the language of Scripture, by which, on the one hand, only those who are called to God
in Christ are styled the children of God ; but, on the other, those
also who are prepared thereto, and are "scattered abroad" among
all nations (John xi. 52). On the one hand, only those who are
called through Christ are the Saviour's sheep ; but, on the other,
so are the "sheep not of this fold" who are thereto ordained all
over the world (John x. 16). On the one hand, only those
who are renewed in the Spirit of Jesus Christ are to be counted
righteous ; but, on the other, those also who seek for eternal life
by perseverance in good deeds, and strive after God's kingdom so
far as their knowledge enables them (Matt. xxv. 37). The last
case is the one in question here ; and the promise of Jesus which
is last quoted tells us what the Corneliuses of all nations have to
expect at the day of judgment.[1] We may now understand what
δεκτός actually means,—viz. able to enter, susceptible to a call,
worthy of reception ; in one word, prepared and fit for eternal life
in Christ (τεταγμένος, ch. xiii. 48). But the apostle does not say
that *only such* shall be *called;* he only asserts a fact that was to
become evident in the then position of the church, that such prepared ones were to be accepted. As regards the blind perversion
of the whole question, which asserts that equality of religion for
all nations, and a complete righteousness for the heathen without
Christ, are therein taught, it scarcely needs mention here. Against

---

[1] In our *Words of the Lord Jesus* we have, it is to be hoped, satisfactorily
proved that our Lord, in His words, Matt. xxv. 34-36, did *not* speak of *Christians,* although it has been generally so misunderstood.

this idea it might be simply said, "Cornelius might thus have always remained a mere heathen." Bengel classically says, "Non indifferentismus religionum sed indifferentia nationum hic asseritur." Only by Satan's craft can these words be thus torn away from their context. We are, on the contrary, taught by them the equality of all distinctions in the one religion of Christ, and that the acceptance of the heathen for the purpose of completing the work begun appears to be the irremissible duty of missions.

There is one doubtful point still remaining in respect to this passage which is generally brought forward, viz. the question how far this previous error of Peter, as regards one of the chief points in the plan of God's kingdom, is consistent with apostolical inspiration. The answer is to be found in the words "*apostolical inspiration*." Any infallibility of *men*, as the apostles still were, is nowhere either promised, spoken of, or maintained. Peter, as a man and Jewish Christian, might both err in his knowledge, and also go astray and sin against his better knowledge (Gal. ii. 13, 14) ; for infallibility of conduct or impeccability is nowhere taught. Jesus certainly had given strong hints as to the calling of the Gentiles, in His well-known utterances and parables ; and at last, in Matt. xxviii. 19 and Acts i. 8, had spoken of it as clearly as possible. But even His twelve apostles and chief witnesses, with a very necessary distinction between disciples and their Master, between sinners and the God-man, remain so far but frail men, in that they could only gradually grasp the vast new scheme of God's kingdom. The consecration by the Spirit which fell upon them on the day of Pentecost, in no way suddenly and for ever cancelled the whole of their former intellectual system—magically, as it were, implanting a new one in its stead ; but then was *begun* the preservation from all error, and the guidance into all truth, for their apostolic office then beginning. If we rightly take this point of view, the circumstances of the whole matter respecting the call of the Gentiles will form a remarkable proof in favour of inspiration, rather than a stumbling-block in the way of our belief. For had not Peter *in the Spirit* already testified (ch. ii. 39, iii. 26, iv. 12) of this call, he himself not yet understanding it ? And at the exact moment when he was to preach to the Gentiles, is it not suggested to him, both that he was to do so, and also what he was to say ? We see, therefore, that the Lord leads His church step by step, and only at the appointed hour, when the occasion arises, affords the necessary revealed instruction, just as we remarked as to ch. vi. 1 in reference to the regulations of the community. But since God duly instructed His witnesses at the time when their duties were to be exercised, in pertinaciously asking why He did not do this earlier, or foolishly doubting as to what would have taken place if He had not done it at all, we are like naughty children who cry out to the careful mother who is holding them, How would it have been if I had fallen ?

Ver. 36. The accusative τὸν λόγον, which is so difficult to be construed, must be perhaps supplemented somewhat in this way : Hear now *the word!* or, If I should now preach to you *the word*, learn first the history of it! The connection with δεκτός through κατά is very harsh, and is besides opposed by the separation between the preamble of Simon the man and the preaching of Peter the apostle. The idea of τὸν λόγον being governed by ὑμεῖς οἴδατε in ver. 37, which plan is followed by Luther (and also in the English translation), is grammatically awkward, on account of the ἀσυνδέτως accompanying γενόμενον ῥῆμα ; it also implies something that is actually untrue, for we are informed throughout the chapter that Cornelius did *not yet know* the message of peace. It seems simple and suitable to supply κατά to τὸν λόγον, giving it the meaning, " as respects the word." We must therefore be satisfied with this. A deeply important proposition, which is undiscernible in Luther's translation, is brought forcibly into view by our way of understanding the passage : The *word* rests upon a *history*, the *preaching* on a *matter of fact*. This plan of announcement is well fitted for the Gentile world, and leads back from the history to Israel's prophecy (ver. 43), as in Israel the acknowledged history might be interpreted from prophecy. The fact that the word ὁ Θεός is not repeated in ver. 36,[1] but that it has to be supplied to ἀπέστειλεν from the preceding αὐτῷ, shows with what a lasting emphasis the first ὁ Θεός is spoken in ver. 34, and of course somewhat tends to join the preaching with the preamble : God is no respecter of persons, although He sent the gospel first to Israel only. "The word" means the teaching of the apostles begun after Jesus' death and resurrection, so that the διὰ Ἰησοῦ Χριστοῦ belongs perhaps to εἰρήνη, and not to εὐαγγελιζόμενος. Peace is equivalent to the "remission of sins" (ver. 43); and therefore means first "peace with God," but at the same time "peace with one another." God is no respecter of persons, and therefore

---

[1] For the sake of clearness, the word is repeated in Luther's Bible (and also in the English version).

His Christ is one Lord of *all*. But if the one Lord gives peace, it is one peace for all and between all.

Vers. 37, 38. The *word* rests on the *history*, and the purport and centre of the history is the person of Jesus. Herein consists the sure ground of apostolical teaching. It was a γενόμενον ῥῆμα, a well known, or as is said, a notorious history, not "done in a corner" (ch. xxvi. 26), and consequently could not be altogether unknown even in Cæsarea, so that the preaching to the heathen may well begin with the straightforward expression, "Ye know!"[1] Our Lord, or at least the report of Him, went over all the land of Judæa (cf. Matt. iv. 24, ix. 26, 31, 35); in the populous Galilee the public ministry of Jesus began, following the loudly proclaimed and startling baptism by John. How that John announced his baptism as only preparing the way for a mightier One who was to come after; how he decreased as Jesus increased,—all these particulars fall into the background in the apostle's words before Him of whom testimony was to be given. The miraculous life of the Saviour, Jesus of Nazareth, which is here abridged into the shortest and most sublime biography which is possible for a son of man, was publicly known throughout the whole land and its frontiers; but the commencing point of it was certainly kept secret, —the anointing of the Son of man with the Holy Ghost and with power, when the heaven was opened at His baptism. This circumstance the apostle states, and in his apostolical disclosure anticipates the publicly known history by the anointing. For this part of the apostolical communication certainly belongs essentially to the history of Jesus, which can only be spiritually and rightly comprehended by its means; and it is therefore nothing but a confirmatory expression of the conclusion to be drawn from the history, that *God was with Him*. Peter clearly enough intimates the signification (subsequently to be made manifest) of the typical Saviour-life of Jesus, by describing Him as having come to destroy the works of the devil. It is remarkable that Peter says nothing of Jesus' *words* and *doctrine*: it is not Jesus' doctrine as such, and nothing further, which is to be preached to the people, but His person,—what He did (ver. 39), how He lived, and what He thereby showed Himself to be : this is the groundwork of the apostolical message of peace in this Lord ; every word of Jesus is thus developed, continued, and completed.

---

[1] Besides, the apostle might have been able to learn, in casual conversation, what Cornelius actually knew as to the history and doings of Christ.

Vers. 39, 41. *And we are witnesses.* First the history, which, however, was spread abroad to the frontiers of the land ; then the confirmatory testimony of many of those who were the closest and most trusted companions of this great Person ! Peter does not again say " in the land of Judea," but *in the land of the Jews*—a recognition of the " children of Israel " in ver. 36, and a preparation for the " they" which follows. Jerusalem, the chief city, is now named instead of Galilee : and his hearers are thus led on to Golgotha, the centre-point in the history.— *Whom* (nevertheless, καί, yet further) *they slew, and hanged upon a tree !* A forcible contrast to all that the holy Benefactor had done, and an appeal to the likewise public death upon the cross, the consummation of the public history, as the baptism by John was its starting-point. But His death is not dwelt upon on the present occasion, and the scandal of the cross is not even alluded to ; the sin, too, of the children of Israel is denoted (without pronouncing any judgment) as shortly as possible by sorrowfully saying, " They have done it." But now the veil is rent away, and the momentous apostolical testimony in its closest acceptation [1] forthwith begins. It commences with the emphatic Τοῦτον which embraces vers. 38 and 39, and refers back to the οὗτος in ver. 36, carrying on the revelation of the lowly life of the Son of man to the exaltation of the Son of God.—*On the third day.* This circumstance forms a part of the record of the history, and is as significant in the resurrection as " the tree" was in the death. The ἔδωκεν expresses an arbitrary ordering, which, however, is gracious even in its limitation; and the "showing openly" is the disclosure which now for the first time *is* made as to the reason and aim of the lowly life of Jesus. The Lord, hidden under the form of a servant, now appears in open glory. Remark how *God* still remains the subject of the sentence ; indeed, even the choice of the apostles in ver. 41 is referred back to Him, the Father. The Son of God can only be acknowledged by faith, as by His apostles in His lowliness (John vi. 69), who for this very reason were the " witnesses chosen before of God." The eating and drinking extend to the earlier table-fellowship, or closest intimacy generally (John xv. 27), most significantly concluding in the last supper, in order to form the foundation of their certainty when they again met their Master. *After He rose from the dead* forms

---

[1] The life of the Son of man in the flesh is eminently historical, and is testified to by the apostle corroboratively only ; but the resurrection of the Son of God in power is especially testified to by the words of the apostles.

a strong and again repeated confirmation of the testimony, so as to lead on to the complete revelation of the Lord and Judge in ver. 42.

Ver. 42. *And He commanded us* refers now to Christ, whose command of power impresses with its indicating seal all the mighty deeds of His lowly life ; for what is here said amounts to this : that the Father has committed all judgment to the merciful, sinner-loving Son of man, so that mercy itself now is the judge.   To whom only is power given over all flesh, so that He gives eternal life to all those whom the Father gives Him ?   To Jesus of Naza-reth, who is our Judge !   Whoever knows the Saviour-life of this Jesus, comprehends the peace of this gospel.   In naming Jesus' office as Judge, the climax of His dignity is testified to, so that then may be held out to the penitent, faith in the atonement through Him.   The solemn formula, a " Judge of quick and dead," appears here for the first time.   This, indeed, should need no explanation, on account of the noble simplicity with which all those that have died since Adam, as well as those who shall die up to the last day, are united with the present generation of living souls, who shall either soon join their departed forefathers, or shall in life undergo judgment.   In short, " quick and dead " will, in striking and expressive generality, denote every generation of men who have lived or will live from the beginning to the end; as also in Rom. xiv. 9.   " Of this ' Lord of all' (which expression in ver. 36 is a preparation for the present part of the address) we are now commanded to preach to all men in every place, that He will exercise a merciful judgment on the living first, bringing forgive-ness of sins and peace."   Thus Peter speaks, for the first time adding that it is to be preached to *the people*—an indefinite and striking term.   He intends, on the one hand, to leave the first recipients of the message in possession of their prerogative, and, on the other, to prepare for the extension of the same expression by the words " quick and dead," and " whosoever believeth" in ver. 43.

Ver. 43. At this point he appeals to all the prophets of Israel, who not only for Israel, but also for all the Gentiles, have borne witness and shall bear witness together till the end of the world ; here they are all unanimously adduced, to complete the great pro-phetico-apostolical testimony of the forgiveness of sins necessary for all the world, in the one saving name of Him whom His mes-sengers preach, according to experience, history, and prophecy. *Through His name, i.e.* through the acknowledgment of His person

as the Lord and Judge who is borne witness to. *Remission of sins,*
which otherwise would destroy everything—even the "righteousness" mentioned in ver. 35—and from the guilt of which the
"alms" in ver. 2 could not release. Cornelius certainly prayed
for the remission of his sins, and not for a reward for his alms;
and this remission every one is to receive who believes in Him,
without respect of persons, whether he be Jew or Gentile—every
individual "in every nation" (ver. 35). Although the preparing
godliness and righteousness may have been hitherto entirely
wanting, he will receive it so soon as he only believes. And thus
will this Judge of the quick and dead (beside whom God has
ordained no other) exercise His lordship over the quick and *dead*
—over the godly and *sinners* (Rom. xiv. 9).

Ver. 44. Whilst the spirit of the prophets and the apostles is
testifying through the words of Peter, the hearers believe the word
even as soon as the word "believe" is expressed, and the Holy
Ghost Himself testifies out of the newly opened mouths of the
new believers that the Spirit is truth. History, prophecy, and the
apostle's discourse—all give way before the immediate testimony of
the power of the Saviour. The grace is freely dispensed, not only
on the uncircumcised, but also without baptism, laying on of hands,
or any other outward means except the word. The church of
Christ is thus taught, not only that circumcision was abolished, but
also (which is much the same thing) that no other outward ceremony, *as outward,* even though it were baptism, ordained by Christ
Himself, is to be turned into a new circumcision in an Old Testament or Jewish sense. Baptism is nothing, and non-baptism is
nothing, but faith in the word of God. *All them which heard the
word*[1] is not intended to exclude some few who might not have
heard it, for see ch. xi. 15 as to this. In the expression of the
condition it only follows πάντα τὸν πιστεύοντα in ver. 43, placing
hearing instead of *believing,* because it is made manifest by the
Spirit that the *hearing* of the word was equivalent to a *belief* in the
word. Peter, however, naturally enough refrains from any further
preaching, since the Lord-Spirit Himself had so quickly supplanted
him in his office. Whenever the Spirit itself bears witness through
our hearers, we may discontinue our preaching, though we may
only have arrived at the *exordium.*

Vers. 45–48. This was an astonishment to the believers present who belonged to the circumcision, whose preconceived opinions

---

[1] "From Cornelius down to the humblest inmate of his household."—HESS.

were removed with overpowering might. They now see before their eyes, in this house, that the "Gentiles also" are thought worthy of God's highest gift. The expressions respecting the "pouring out of the Spirit" refer to ch. ii. 17, 33, 38, and show that there was no distinction made between this operation of the Spirit and that which took place on the day of Pentecost (ch. xi. 15). The eventual question which would occur to the Jewish mind, whether the Gentile candidates for baptism were previously to be circumcised, was so entirely dismissed that it did not at all arise; but, on the other hand, the likewise possible question, whether the existing baptism of the Spirit rendered unnecessary the baptism by water, or whether it had quite superseded it, had been already long back decided by Matt. xxviii. 19; and this was doubtless recalled to Peter's mind by the Spirit. Remark, again, how precisely the whole of this occurrence teaches us to keep the due mean between overvaluing and undervaluing any external ceremony which is ordained for an inward end, either in baptism or preaching. It is only *water* which is to follow, but yet it is sanctified by God's command. As the Ethiopian asked, in ch. viii. 36, "What doth hinder me?" so now Peter asks the brethren, *Can any one* (be he who he may, and ever so much hitherto biassed against the Gentiles) *forbid?* It is, and indeed remains, a sacrament. The chief of Christ's church, the president of the apostles' council, asks first of the lay brethren, whether either of them had anything to object. Certainly it is not "will," but "*can*," any man forbid. The brethren will as little "forbid water,"[1] and show as little objection, as when Peter summoned them to accompany him. He now causes the Gentiles to be baptized in the name of the *Lord*, through whom they had received the Spirit from the God of Israel whom they had already worshipped. Peter did not baptize them himself, doubtless by the direction of the Spirit, in order to teach that the administration of the sacrament is subordinate to the ministry of the word (1 Cor. i. 17, "For Christ sent me not to baptize, but to preach the gospel"). There is nothing here of the Old Testament priesthood, or of the *character indelebilis* of the apostle; and in the following chapter there is nothing of the personal superiority of the chief of the apostles. But much might perhaps have been told of the further

---

[1] This expression sometimes occurs as a kind of proverb with regard to rain and drinkable water, in the most ancient sacred and later profane writers: Job xii. 15, LXX.; Ovid, *Metam.* vi. 349.

preaching and narrating, of the joy and peace in the one incorporating Spirit which was heard and felt during the " certain days " which Peter, at the prayer of the newly found brethren, must surely have passed with them.

XIII.

PETER'S ADDRESS TO THE CHURCH IN JERUSALEM.

(Chap. xi. 5–17.)

VINDICATORY NARRATIVE, HOW GOD HAD ACCEPTED THE GENTILES.

Vers. 1–4. *And the apostles and brethren* — comprehending the whole church, both its head and members, the heads being specially distinguished, and yet only denoted as chief members. *That were in Judea* refers perhaps only to the brethren, as only the Apostle Peter is recorded (ch. ix. 32) to have taken a journey. Galilee and Samaria (ch. ix. 31) appear excluded; κατὰ τὴν Ἰουδαίαν, on the other hand, indicates a dispersion of the disciples in various places in the land (ch. ix. 32, 36).—*Heard that the Gentiles had also received the word of God.* Thus ran the unprecedented report which had spread abroad even before Peter's return ; and in this report the previous preaching of the word to these same Gentiles must be presupposed. But the report erred in looking at it from a human point of view ; for it should have said : God had received and accepted the Gentiles through His prompting and reconciliatory word. *When Peter returned to Jerusalem, they that were of the circumcision contended with him ;* or, as it might be put from the original text, in a rather milder way, expressed their strong doubt and hesitation as to what had taken place.[1] *They that were of the circumcision*—a remarkable appellation for the " apostles and brethren ;" for, by comparison with ch. x. 45, and from the whole context, we may almost certainly assume that the Christians generally in Jerusalem, without any limitation, are here meant. It is almost equivalent to saying, *the Jews ;* and

---

[1] For compare the same word in ver. 12. It might, however, mean : They disputed with him, reproached him with it, or pleaded as to it. Ezek. xx. 35 ; Joel iii. 2, LXX. ; Jude 9.

Luke significantly so calls the Christians, who not only were in the Jewish land, but were also in part of Jewish opinions. The reproach which the whole church cast upon the chief apostle, calling forth his vindication of himself, is strikingly characterized by saying nothing about the *preaching*, but by laying all the weight upon *visiting* and *eating* with the uncircumcised, which indeed appears to have been the principal fault. That circumcision at least should take place first, and that the full acceptance into Israel's covenant of mercy should follow,—this was the sole idea which had hitherto been formed of all the clear predictions of the opened Scripture as to the "calling" of the heathen (Eph. iii. 5, 6). For the prophets had indeed forbearingly spoken as if the entry of the heathen into the kingdom of the Messiah might appear as an addition to Israel, although this conception is true only in another sense. Peter, who at God's call had visited the Gentiles, and had also at God's will eaten with them as brethren in Christ, gives now an excellent pattern of an unanswerable vindication to all his successors in every sense of the word. He does not in the least appeal to any special personal superiority ; he accepts the reproach patiently, and with the most modest dignity relates his experience, from which a lesson is taught to the whole church, which lesson he himself had just before been compelled to learn.[1] In ver. 4 Luke assures us that the apostle made no other reply, but began at once with the explanation of what had taken place. We should in every case so act, where a mere narration suffices for vindication.

But few remarks are necessary on this repetition of the story.

The apostle's right and obedient course of action began with *prayer ;* after this, God acted in everything, and led him on step by step, so that nothing could be left undone by him. The beginning of the matter is very briefly named: the roof, the hunger, and the preparation for the meal are all omitted, as the vision itself is now the necessary point to begin from. *I saw* includes the subsequent hearing and speaking, as it is all comprised in one trance. The *article* before beasts in ver. 6 clearly shows (as πάντα in ch. x. 12) that the whole number of eatable beasts were presented to his eyes. *Entered into my mouth*—instead of " eaten," ch. x. 14— shows that Luke, who wrote ch. x. and xi. one after the other, did not unnecessarily cling to mere words: the κοινὸν ἢ ἀκάθαρτον, which

---

[1] We thus possess *three* accounts of this important matter closely following one another.

is the same in both passages, is a portion of the leading idea. The teaching of the "voice from heaven" now through Peter's lips affects the whole church. After the account of the vision there follows immediately another " Behold ! "—reality succeeding to the vision. *Into the man's house*—expressed vaguely in a remarkable way, and echoing the terms of the accusation in ver. 3, which indeed had presupposed a knowledge of all that had taken place. Cornelius' name is omitted in ver. 13 ; for the question now was not as to one particular eminent man in Cæsarea, but as to all uncircumcised men generally.—*And he showed us.* Us appeals to the six witnesses whom he had just mentioned (whom also, as it appears, Peter had purposely brought with him to Jerusalem), as to the principal matter which was now beginning. *How he had seen*—πῶς—an intimation of the closer details, which are here omitted. In ver. 14 there is the addition ἐν οἷς σωθήσῃ, κ.τ.λ., which is wanting in ch. x. 6, 22, 32 : it is either only an addition of Peter's, who might insert retrospectively in the angel's words the intention of his command, which intention was forthwith understood ; or (which we prefer) a rectified and exact transcription of the words used, of which Cornelius may have afterwards bethought himself, which Luke had hitherto refrained from mentioning. *The entry into the house,* as the result of the sending, had been specially named in ver. 12 ; the *speaking,* according to the same command, might be understood to follow, and does so at the beginning of the new sentence. *And as I began to speak,* the Holy Ghost fell upon them—itself speaking with decision, and commanding (ch. xiii. 2)— upon *them* who by the term " house " in ver. 14 had been pointed out as the rest of the " men uncircumcised," and not only the one man. It fell indeed on them, *as on us at the beginning*—denoting a new beginning for the uncircumcision, just as for the circumcision. In that wonderful manner, as has only been the case once at the first beginning. And the matter which had been clearly and more clearly commanded by vision, voice, angel, and Spirit, now attains its most decisive clearness by " a word of the Lord," of which the Spirit reminds the apostle. This word conveyed to his mind, in the first place,—the same thing exactly has happened to them as happened to you ; and this promise was not intended for the apostles only, nor only for the first disciples on the day of Pentecost, but in a general sense for believers out of every nation (ch. ii. 39). These words next convey that the communication of the Spirit is itself a baptism—indeed the real baptism. In the third place, that baptism by water is subordinated to that by the Spirit. Peter, therefore, having related all that had taken place *in the light of the words of the Lord*, now at the end of his narration implies in the most forcible way that God Himself was the author of that which man laid to his charge ; for he says, in fact, that the Lord Himself first baptized the Gentiles. And on this he takes his stand. The addition of baptism by water was to be understood from another speech of the Lord (Matt. xxviii. 19), and is omitted, like the preaching in ver. 15, being only presupposed from the concluding question in ver. 17. This concluding question affords the result of the narrative : God, without regard to circumcision or uncircumcision, has through faith alone made these Gentiles equal to us. *Has given them the like gift* means of course, in the first place, *the Holy Ghost* (ver. 15), but also (with extension of the idea) *God's gift of mercy in Christ* generally, as in ch. viii. 20, and as in ver. 18, *repentance unto life.* " Purifying the heart by faith " (ch. xv. 9) is the true circumcision ; and " in Jesus Christ neither circumcision availeth anything, nor uncircumcision, but faith" (Gal. v. 6). $\Delta\nu\nu\alpha\tau\delta\varsigma$ is taken from ch. x. 47, as well as $\kappa\omega\lambda\hat{\upsilon}\sigma\alpha\iota$, which, however, is here joined with $\tau\delta\nu$ $\Theta\epsilon\delta\nu$. Peter's concluding words (the reader of the " Acts " will be reminded of $\theta\epsilon o\mu\dot{\alpha}\chi o\iota$, ch. v. 39) make a deep impression, and shut the mouths of the members of the community, although Peter, modest up to the very last, and yet mighty in his very modesty, merely asks a question and asserts nothing, only saying, " What am I ? " and not, " What are ye ? " There is no further question as to visiting and eating with the Gentiles, since God has baptized them with the Spirit.

Ver. 18. *When they heard these things, they held their peace.* If Peter's question is an important and humbling example to us, not less so is also the silence of the community. This might perhaps have lasted a few minutes—a momentous interval for the sudden initiation into the now revealed mystery of the co-incorporation of the Gentiles, which in Eph. iii. 4 is pre-eminently called " the mystery of Christ ! " And then arose a joyful cry from all, giving God the glory, just as in ch. x. 34 from the one apostle. $\text{"}A\rho\alpha\gamma\epsilon$, of a truth we also now perceive. What God does is right, though it may gainsay the previous idea held by the whole of His church as to the Scriptures and His kingdom. Henceforth, then, " neither circumcision availeth anything, nor uncircumcision, but a new creature " by faith (Gal. vi. 15). And Abraham's prayer, " Oh that Ishmael might live before Thee " (Gen. xvii. 18), may be henceforth

M

granted to Canaan and Assur, Rahab and Babylon, Philistia and
Tyre, and all other nations (Ps. lxxxvii.).   The church says
nothing as to any previous God-fearing or joining on to Israel, but
merely " to the Gentiles."   The Jewish Christians had better have
constantly and simply adhered to these first words which the Spirit
bade them utter.

Luke now (in ver. 19) resumes the thread of his former history,
and tells of another preaching to the Gentiles, *i.e.* to those who,
like Cornelius, were proselytes of the gate ; but it is impossible that
this can have happened before Cornelius' conversion, as it would be
a contradiction to ch. xv. 7, 14 (πρῶτον).   But as Luke does not
place it expressly in connection with the events at Cæsarea, it
may be considered as an almost contemporaneous affair, and at all
events as an *independent* beginning of the preaching to the Gentiles,
and in another place.   By this the impulse and testimony of the
Holy Ghost is remarkably shown forth, in addition to all that had
been effected in the hitherto biassed mind of the chief apostle.   It
is sufficient that in Antioch, the great and luxurious chief city of
Syria, there arose, as it were, a mother church for the Gentile
Christians.   Barnabas, who was sent from Jerusalem, " found
nothing here which needed to be perfected or confirmed" (as
Baumgarten says), but could only rejoice in the great grace of
God, and exhort them to abide in it.   He having been directed by
the words of the Lord (ch. ix. 15), or in some other way, seeks
out Saul in his retirement at Tarsus,[1] and both teach for the space
of a year in the new community of Christians.   The new name of
God's new people, extending through all countries and ages, arose
first in mocking Antioch, as a term of insult for the ridiculous
folly of the Gentiles in professing themselves to be followers of the
crucified Messiah of the Jews.   The believers, however, accept the
name as an honour, as given by God.   Prophets come from Jerusalem to Antioch, and the uncircumcised brethren, understanding
the sign of the prophesying Spirit, send to the circumcised loving
assistance.   The king Herod Agrippa the elder, whom the Emperor
Claudius had established in his grandfather's kingdom, was permitted, by a mysterious divine dispensation, to put to death an
apostle—one of the " Sons of Thunder"—and to place Peter in
prison, in order to keep him for execution after the feast.   But
God answered the prayer of the beseeching community, better

---

[1] According to ch. ix. 27, he had been the first to accept Saul and introduce
him into the community.

even than the brethren in Mary's house were willing to believe. He sent His angel to deliver the quiet sleeping prisoner, who was not yet, like James, to drink of His Master's cup, but was for the present "to gird himself, and walk whither he would." The fetters fell off, the iron gate opened; and it was no vision, but a reality. Peter in the meantime "departed, and went into another place." The tyrant slew the keepers instead of the escaped prisoner, and was smitten by the angel with the fearful disease of Antiochus, the measure of his iniquity being full. But the "word of God" can be neither restricted nor repressed, but is so increased and multiplied, that the new mother church at Antioch itself, induced by an intimation from the Holy Ghost, sends those who are thereto called in order to preach the word of God to the completely idolatrous Gentiles. And thus Paul, the apostle of the Gentiles, began his course.

XIV.

PAUL'S ADDRESS TO BAR-JESUS.

(CHAP. XIII. 10, 11.)

THE PUNISHMENT OF HIS OPPOSITION TO THE GOSPEL.

VERS. 1–3. In the new church at Antioch the gifts of the Spirit had from the very first shown themselves to be mighty for the common advantage not only of this church alone, but of many which were about to be founded, so that now missions were actually sent out from this place. *Certain prophets and teachers* were now in the community there.[1] If teachers only had been named, it would be thought that they were regularly ordained teachers taken from the mass of the communities which had been collected together in various places. If, on the other hand, prophets only had been spoken of, we must have imagined that gifts of prophecy had been

---

[1] The τινές scarcely alters the sense, as these five can hardly be intended to be represented as the only ones thus gifted; yet as a gloss it is important, inasmuch as it is all the more certain that the things which follow in vers. 2, 3 were formerly understood of these *certain ones*, and not of the whole church.

manifested and acknowledged, as in ch. xi. 27. As both are spoken
of together, and indeed the prophets are mentioned first, perhaps
neither *office* nor *gift* are to be considered separately, but the manifestation of the gift is to be looked upon as a kind of office (cf.
ch. xv. 32). The κατά with the ἐκκλησίαν might be taken in the
simplest way, as in κατ᾽ οἴκους, κατὰ πόλιν, κατὰ τὴν Ἰουδαίαν, and
therefore that among the members of the church at Antioch there
were brethren possessing the gifts of prophecy and teaching. The
significance of the narrative consists in the fact that Barnabas and
Saul stood as first and last named in a list of five, and were reckoned
as members of the mission-school at Antioch, until the Holy Ghost
ordained their separation to some special functions. The order in
which Luke places the names is certainly an expression of the
ideas which were then current in Antioch, although any order of
rank in the worldly sense of the word is not for a moment to be
thought of. The Levite who was surnamed Barnabas by the
apostles, and had been sent by those at Jerusalem for the examination and confirmation of the church at Antioch, stands first, from
the value which had been there set upon him ; and Saul, who had
been fetched by the latter from Tarsus (notwithstanding the journey
to carry assistance to Judea which he took, together with Barnabas (ch. xi. 30)), occupies the last place, on account of the modest
unobtrusiveness he had hitherto shown. Whilst these *prophets* and
teachers were exercising their office as New Testament priests,[1] and
were asking the Lord in fasting and prayer, " How and where willest
Thou that we shall serve Thee ? " the Holy Ghost answered them
either by a special revelation through the mouth of one prophet
(1 Cor. xiv. 26), or in a direct address to all. The first and the
last are taken, who were already united together in friendship[2]
(ch. ix. 27), and are now to go forth (the last soon to become the
first) according to the call and gift of the Holy Ghost, which says,
Separate me them for the work whereunto I have called them, and in
which I will guide them and make ready for them. The direct
call to which Paul appeals (Gal. i. 1) had, according to Acts xxii.
21, already been made to him, and perhaps through him to his

---

[1] Λειτουργεῖν evidently specifies the particular duties of the prophets and
teachers. Chrysostom pronounces that κηρυττόντων is incorrect, but nevertheless
shows that he does *not* refer ver. 2 to the whole church.

[2] See in ch. xv. 25 the same order of precedence between the two in the
official message from Jerusalem ; compare it with ch. xv. 2, 35. Only in ch.
xiv. 14 and xv. 12 Luke places Barnabas first for special reasons.

companion; the only duty of the like-gifted brethren consisted in *separating* them from their community, and from every other claim or work, and in letting them go away with brotherly intercession whither the *Holy Ghost sent* them. There was therefore in this case no human "sending" by the church, of which in vers. 2 and 3 no express mention is made;[1] and still less were they sent by Simeon, Lucius, and Manaen: the laying on of hands after fasting is only an expression of the dismissory intercession and recommendation to the grace of God (ch. xiv. 26), and is neither the communication of a gift nor the institution to an office. This usage is employed in the apostolical church in very various significations, clearly distinguished from an actual sacrament; in the most general sense it is an image and means of showing the community of the Spirit among the members and brethren united together for God's work, by means of which the vital essence of spiritual life might flow in peculiar efficacy from one to the other.

Vers. 4, 5. Ἐκπεμφθέντες denotes the actual sending, contrasted with the dismissal by the brethren. The Spirit first directs them to Cyprus, the home of Barnabas, where the gospel had already been preached, but "only to the Jews" (ch. xi. 19). But first they preached at Salamis to the numerous Jews there. Barnabas' cousin, Mark, who had come back with them from Jerusalem (ch. xii. 25; Col. iv. 10), accompanied them, but in the first place merely as the minister of those appointed to the word, so as to "purchase for himself the good degree" of an evangelist (1 Tim. iii. 13): for the Spirit prepares and calls in all kinds of ways—one by the gift of miracles, another by ordinary teaching; one is called immediately to be an apostle, another to be a minister first; and each should abide in his vocation, and not, as Mark (ver. 13), retreat from it. But it is indisputable that even one who forsakes his vocation may, by God's grace, subsequently attain the position of an evangelist.

Vers. 6-8. They carry the gospel from one end of the island to the other; but they are first invited by an actual heathen to Paphos, the ancient seat of the impure worship of Venus. It admits of no doubt that Luke, conformably to the scheme of his book, now intends to make prominent the *first preaching to the*

---

[1] In ver. 1 the *five* are prominently distinguished from the rest of the church, and these five are naturally both in vers. 2 and 3 the subject of that which is narrated. To ascribe the λειτουργεῖν and νηστεύειν to the whole of the large community would be quite surprising.

idolatrous Gentiles, which is now disclosed as the reason for the special divine calling in ver. 2. Sergius Paulus, the proconsul or deputy-governor of the island, although not a worshipper of God, *i.e.* not a decided proselyte to Israel's God, was nevertheless a *prudent* and inquiring man. Unfortunately a *false prophet* had taken up his residence in Paphos, as in the city of Samaria. He was indeed a Jew, and, as a sorcerer, had boldly and shrewdly addressed himself to the prudent governor himself. Christ's apostles first found this Bar-jesus at Paphos, *i.e.* met with opposition from him and his adherents, when they wished to preach the word to the Jews and the proselytes. But the Lord inclined the heart of Sergius, who was prudent enough to inquire and seek for information in every direction, to call for Barnabas and Saul to come to him, *and desired to hear the word of God.* Here also it was very like the case of Cornelius : God led His church step by step, and leads her ministers always by outward means. Now was the contest to ensue as to which prophet was the true one, and to whom the poor heathen should listen. " His prudence did not so much qualify him, as render him less unqualified for faith," as Bengel ingeniously observes. The governor demanded the true word of God ; but the minister of lies, Elymas, or " the wise man," as he was styled by an Arabic name (it is now *Ulema* among the Turks), was not inclined to surrender his distinguished disciple, and did his utmost to keep him back from the right path, and *to turn away the deputy from the faith.*

Vers. 9–11. But the Lord saw into it, and gave testimony to His truth, at the same time affording an honourable revelation and confirmation in favour of His chosen vessels. In ver. 7, Luke placed Barnabas first ; but now Saul takes the lead of his companion, and, with full apostolical authority, decrees a punishment on the adversary, which resembles his own earlier discipline. That Saul now actually turned his Hebrew name (which does not necessarily remind one of David's persecutor, but has a very beautiful meaning) into a Latin and Greek one, is shown to some degree by exclusive use by Luke of the first name in the first, second, and seventh verses of this chapter. Why should not this change have been made in reference to the name of the governor, and to the revelation of the apostleship to the Gentiles made through an apostolical miracle at his conversion ?[1]   Paul *sets his eyes upon*

[1] It is well known that this was the ancient opinion of Jerome and Origen, and also held by Augustine, and it ought not to have been dismissed

Elymas in the full power of the upbraiding Spirit, and addresses him in words which, in the first place, comprise all his previous guilt in its true character and name; next, rebuke his last acts of opposition to the truth; and finally, as the measure of his iniquity is full, announce and decree his punishment. The order of the three separate addresses to Elymas (not observed in Luther's translation) is not without significance: first (as in the cases of Ananias and Simon), the revealing of the wicked impletion of the heart, in which the deceiver is fully conscious of his lies against the truth; next, giving him his true name, "child of the devil," instead of the hypocritical Bar-jesus, as the sorcerer knew well about the devil and his intercourse with him; and finally, the sharpest denomination of all, making him equal to the "father of lies," the opponent of all righteousness. This appellation looks more to externals, just as the former ones related to the actuating causes, and prepares for the "not ceasing" as regarded his conduct towards Sergius. The enemy of all that is righteous, true, and honest, ceased not (owing to his devilish disposition, which consisted in this very thing) to pervert and make crooked the right ways of the Lord, which He willed to make plain by His word through Cyprus, as well as all other lands, and constantly endeavoured to drag away honest souls from God's path, the path of faith that leads to truth, into human aberrations and errors (ver. 8). He, as a Jew, knew indeed of the Lord and His righteousness; he also, as a Jew, and still more from his sinful curiosity as a sorcerer, knew of the devil and his craft against the children of men. He knew of the great struggle between darkness and light; and yet, in his silly necromantic cunning, allowed himself to make use of the enemy, who is impotent against the almighty Lord, for the purpose of blinding even prudent people, and ensnaring them to their destruction. But the merciful God does not desire his total destruction, but forces him to *cease* (at least outwardly) from his deceits, which otherwise he would not have done. He causes His hand and His supreme power to come on "this rebel to the light" (Job xxiv. 13), and makes him, the leader of the blind, himself

so contemptuously by Umbreit (*Stud. und Krit.* 1852, 2); it need not be assumed (which would of course be improper) that the apostle chose the name "for this reason only." Wieseler does not settle it quite so decidedly, and does not question that, as a Roman citizen, he had this Roman name from the very first, and that he first resolved to adopt it exclusively on the occasion of this first mission journey.

blind, so that he shall no longer see the sun of his long-suffering Creator.[1] He must now himself seek a guide, and can no longer hinder those who are seeking for the true guide to the Sun of Righteousness. Now, perhaps, he may recognise the difference between light and darkness, and may experience what misleading into wrong paths both means and deserves. But it was only "for a season" that this chastisement was awarded him, so that he might retain the hope, by penitence and *ceasing* from deceit (ver. 10), of again seeing the sun after his night of darkness.[2] The sacred history tells us just as little about the subsequent life of this Bar-jesus as it did about Simon; but in this degenerate Jew, it places before our eyes a remarkable type of the whole of the degenerate people, which had slain the Lord Jesus, and had persecuted His true prophets and apostles, had been displeasing to God, and, in their perverted pride, were opposed to all mankind; which, also, restrained Paul and his companions and successors in every place from preaching the words of salvation to the Gentiles, until their sins were fully accomplished, and a well-deserved blindness must *for a long season* fall upon the condemned nation (1 Thess. ii. 15, 16). Here, too, the once Pharisee, a brand snatched from the burning, Paul, now the true Israelite (ch. xxiv. 14–16, xxvi. 6, 7, 22, 23, xxviii. 20), is contrasted with the false Jew Bar-jesus; the humble yet powerful apostle to the Gentiles with the proud yet impotent misleader of the Gentiles. And if we recognise in the latter a prophetic image of the interval of blindness of the people of Israel, we may perhaps in Paul perceive what a blessed time of life from death it will be when the whole of Israel, like Paul snatched out of the fire, shall change into a nation of missionaries for bringing in the heathen! Let us joyfully notice that grace is mightier than sins, and that truth overcomes deceit, as Paul overcame Bar-jesus.

Ver. 12. *Then the deputy*, when he saw *what was done, believed* that Paul possessed the true word of God, and was astonished, after his eyes (which, with all his prudence, had hitherto been blind) were opened to the clear light of grace which from the *doctrine* of the only Lord penetrated into his heart, turning him

---

[1] Ἀχλύς, not complete darkness, is used in a medical sense of a dimness before the eyes, and therefore Luke uses this expression.

[2] In all this, Paul was reminded of his own blindness, so much blessed to him, to which Luke calls attention by the "leading by the hand" (cf. ch. ix. 8, xxii. 11).

from darkness unto light, and from the power of Satan and his tools unto God.

XV.

PAUL'S DISCOURSE IN THE SYNAGOGUE AT ANTIOCH IN PISIDIA.

(CHAP. XIII. 16–41.)

ANNOUNCEMENT OF THE SALVATION PROMISED TO THE FATHERS, IN THE PROFFER OF JESUS FOR THE CLEARING FROM SIN AND JUSTIFICATION OF EVERY ONE THAT BELIEVES.

VERS. 13, 14. Henceforth Paul is the principal person, and Barnabas falls into the background in his company. The word of God proceeds freely and joyfully; but when they are at Perga, the chief place of Pamphylia, where Diana ruled, as Venus at Paphos, (John) Mark, the minister, felt certain scruples at serving any longer in this journey of the apostles. In a spirit of forbearance, it is not stated what these scruples were; but the censure for his desertion is subsequently mentioned (ch. xv. 38), when occasion called it forth. Paul and Barnabas, now without a minister, travel from the one chief city, where perhaps God had not opened the door of the word to them (for it says διελθόντες), to another. It was to be another *Antioch*, where there was to be a second church called out from among the Gentiles, and in great part indeed from among idolaters. Yet the preachers of the arrival of Israel's Messias first *go into the synagogue on the Sabbath-day, and sit down.* Whether they sat down in some particular place appointed for those that taught, thereby soliciting permission to speak, can only be conjectured. But the rulers might have had some other reasons for recognising them as men capable of teaching, and might consequently have summoned them to speak; the expressly mentioned simple "sitting down," together with the "going into the synagogue," appears actually to denote only the usual sitting down of any one who came in, especially as subsequently the rulers *sent* to them. It was therefore in due order, and modestly, as travelling

Jews, that they joined their brethren before their common God, and awaited a hint from Him to be conveyed through these brethren, to whom they were to preach the word of salvation, in spite of the small degree of faith which they could expect.

Vers. 15, 16. After the service had been opened by the usual reading of the appointed lessons or *sections* (the *Parashioth* and *Haphtharoth*) out of the law and prophets, the rulers sent the minister from their place of honour (Luke iv. 20), and, in a way which was both friendly and deferential, summoned the two modest strangers to speak forthwith. Perhaps they recognised them as learned men and Levites from Jerusalem, and expected a strictly Jewish discourse from them, according to their custom. But the words which these brethren had to deliver were of a different nature: they were words not only of *exhortation*, but of *announcement*,—a new message not only to the people of Israel, and also not only to the so-called God-fearers, but to every Gentile and sinner who suffered himself to be made through faith susceptible of eternal life. Paul, who alone stood up to speak in the synagogue, by beckoning with his hand begged for silence, that his first words might not be misunderstood.

In this discourse there is a remarkable similarity to that of Stephen, both in the fundamental ideas and the general plan. There is also a curious relation which may be observed between this sermon in the synagogue and the two chapters which had been previously read from the law and the prophets. Bengel says as to this: "In the beginning of this discourse, in vers. 17, 18, 19, there are three Greek words, which in part only occur rarely, and in part only once in the Holy Scriptures—ὕψωσεν, ἐτροφοφόρησεν, κατεκληρονόμησεν. The first of these occurs Isa. i. 2; and the second and third, Deut. i. 31, 38. Now these two chapters, Isa. i. and Deut. i., are even at the present day read together on one Sabbath, and we may therefore conclude pretty certainly that both of these were read, and read in Greek, on this Sabbath when Paul came to Antioch, and that Paul, in his discourse, had special reference to that which had been read.[1]

Ver. 16. To the dignified name of Israel's exaltation is immediately joined the likewise significant name for those Gentiles who were joined to Israel, and worshipped the one God of this people. But the two preambles which subsequently follow, clearly lead on

---

[1] Even Heinrichs allows: "Vers. 17-23. Exordium orationis ex audita pericopæ Mosaicæ lectione petitum."

to the abolition of this distinction between Jews and proselytes. For in ver. 26 it goes back beyond Israel to Abraham, in whose seed *all* the nations were to be blessed; now it is manifest that the distinction is narrowed by the words " *children of the stock of Abraham,*" but it is quite cancelled in what follows. For it now says, *and whosoever among you feareth God,* which expressly does away with the distinction in the first preamble. We should now understand by the term " God-fearers " (as the Jews then did), those Gentiles who had been received among the children of Abraham (ἐν ὑμῖν as ἐν αὐτοῖς, Rom. xi. 17); or, as may be meant, those only among Abraham's children who were really God-fearers (not only Abraham's children according to the flesh, but also through faith), together with equally God-fearing proselytes, who are spiritual children of Abraham. According to this, just as the Gentiles must become and be true Israelites, so must the Jews become and be true God-fearers, so as to be found δεκτοί (or τεταγμένοι) for the word of salvation. In ver. 38 all are fully comprehended, without mentioning names, in the words " Ye men and brethren,"—a close preparation for the πᾶς ὁ πιστεύων in ver. 39. The first preamble is introductory, and only requests a hearing for a new history in Israel closely following on to Israel's old history. The second preamble in the middle of the discourse promises an actual *announcement,* and names it as the *word of this salvation sent* from God, specifying it also as " *this* salvation," thus intimating that it proceeded only from the person of the Saviour who had come (ver. 23). The last concluding preamble briefly and decidedly sets forth that which was to be testified to, *Be it known unto you therefore,* and easily passes into the warning tone of βλέπετε οὖν in ver. 40.

Ver. 17. The merciful, good God of this sinful, wicked people —this is the meaning of the first words commencing the announcement of a Saviour for all believing sinners. *Of this people*—of one out of all the people of the earth : the free grace of God, who called Himself the God of this particular people, is manifest here. And surely it is still more manifest through the sinfulness of " this people," which from the time of Moses was continually set forth, as in Deut. i. 35 (which had just been read in the synagogue) : " Not one of these men of this evil generation shall see that good land which I sware to give unto your fathers." It is also remark-- able that Israel is spoken of in the *third* person (not as in Deut. i. 6); and this continues until ver. 25, so that the God-fearers are actually addressed in the presence of the Israelites.[1]   Certainly by the words " our fathers," this position of the Israelites is somewhat altered, and Paul thus styles himself an Israelite.[2]   He has chosen, selected, resolved upon, inclined Himself in mercy to the fathers; and only in these fathers, particularly in Isaac, is the seed called and chosen with prefigurative signification (vid. Deut. iv. 37 and the whole context, and compare Rom. xi. 28).   The *exaltation* of the people is itself the faithful carrying out of the choice, in spite of the sinfulness of the seed of the holy fathers.   The choice of the fathers, the aim of which " for all nations" is testified to at the beginning, begins to be revealed in the exaltation of " this people" above all other nations.   The word ὕψωσε, taken from Isa. i. 2 (the chapter which had been previously read as the " lesson"), embraces in a remarkable way very much in one term.   In Isaiah it means, brought up children, *i.e.* after their fathers; therefore, brought up their children, or caused them to be born and grow, *increased* them according to promise, so that they might become a *nation*, or, as we might say, "made them great" (Ecclus. xliv. 21, 22). Read Ezek. xx. 5, 6, and compare Deut. iv. 34, and remark how wonderfully the Holy Ghost, through Paul, has adopted the ὕψωσα of Isaiah as the many-sided starting-point of the many-sided τροφο-φερεῖν in Moses, and has thus made conspicuous the entire parallel of the people (a parallel grounded on Israel's guidance) with a child of God growing in grace.   *As strangers in the land of Egypt:* ἐν τῇ παροικίᾳ, with the article, refers to Gen. xv. 13, where it is ordained that the seed shall be foreigners.   The discourse, indeed, shows God's plan with Israel as a whole from the very beginning as it is in the sacred word.[3]   *With an high arm* calls to mind all the wonderful deeds done by the arm of the Lord from old time (Isa. li. 9–16; cf. lii. 10, liii. 1).   The *bringing out*, however, is the starting-point of a new series of events, the end of which—the settlement in Canaan—can only be brought about by the faithfulness of the merciful One.

Ver. 18. *And about the space of forty years* (ὡς ——); for in the fortieth year the conquest of the land began, and the provision for them in the wilderness ceased.   This important period of " forty

---

[1] Hoc dicit Pisidis, Judæos digito monstrans.—GROTIUS.

[2] For we cannot think (according to Alford) that the Gentiles also were comprehended in the words " our fathers," embracing *all* present.

[3] The substantive παροικία occurs only once in the Old Testament, in Ps. cxx. 5.

years" is often mentioned by Moses, and is also afterwards alluded to, as in Neh. ix. 21 and Amos ii. 10. As to *the bringing up* (τρο-φοφορεῖν), we must follow Bengel's copious discussion. A little child in the wilderness would need to be carried, fed, clothed, and cared for. Consider the passages which particularly speak of this, Deut. viii. 15, 16, xxxii. 10, 11, Isa. lxiii. 9 ;—and the important statement of Moses, the man and lawgiver, that *he* could not do that which the Lord only could effect (Num. xi. 11–14). In the latter place the patient " waiting" of the people crying for food is clearly depicted. There is no contradiction existing between this chief comprehension of the period in the wilderness and the other one, likewise admissible, according to which the Lord then tried and educated His son (Deut. viii. 2, 5) ; for this child was certainly from the beginning a servant possessed of consciousness and will, only that mercy looked upon his obstinacy as mere childishness. Luther's (and also the English) translation, *suffered He their manners*, taken from τροποφορεῖν, is in no respect suitable, neither here in the arrangement of the discourse, nor generally as regards the truth of this history ; because the child was not only not borne with, but was certainly smitten more than once, and at last very severely. So little did God (in this sense) bear with Israel in the wilderness, that, on the contrary, they had to die off in their unbe-lief ; but the *provision* for the refractory people of the great wilder-ness-mercies of the God who chose them and brought them out, ceased not. The new but not better generation (still therefore the people) duly came, at the end of the period of punishment, into the promised land flowing with milk and honey.

Ver. 19. Israel is maintained and nourished, but seven nations are destroyed to make room for them (Isa. xliii. 3 ; Prov. xxi. 18). The number of nations is *seven*, those only being left of the *ten* named in Gen. xv. 19, as is attested in Deut. vii. 1.[1] We know how often Moses declared to the one chosen people that they were not better than the nations which God had driven out before them. Αὐτοῖς τὴν γῆν αὐτῶν, as promised to the fathers, but yet only κατεκληρόνομησεν, not complete taking possession, on account of the unbelief of the children, who, when they were settled down, needed a continued discipline until the time that God's king, *David-Solomon*, actually reigned over the whole land, from the

---

[1] In Ex. iii. 8 only six are named, the cause for which is difficult to state (cf. Neh. ix. 8). Paul, in the number of seven, particularly refers to Deut. vii. 1-26 in its whole purport.

sea to the boundary of the river. As regards the *space of about
450 years*, we think (with Bengel) that the reading and conception
which connects this *dativus temporis* with the partition of the land
is the only correct one.   Whoever is disposed to doubt and cavil,
will do so always.   The statement in 1 Kings vi. 1 does not agree
with this, if the latter is taken to mean 450 years of the rule of
judges.   It is, however, not permissible to alter the text where it
is not absolutely necessary.   On the other hand, nothing appears
to us more simple than Bengel's reckoning from the birth of Isaac,
so that the years of the παροικία, ordained for the purification and
circumcision of Abraham's seed, are defined somewhat more exactly
than the round number named Gen. xv. 13 (similar to that other
somewhat differently arranged reckoning, Ex. xii. 40).   We also
cannot help thinking that it would be much more suitable that
Paul should have comprehended in this statement of time the *first
period*—the childhood of the seed which was to be exalted and
brought into the good land (which seed was named in and after
Isaac)—than that he should have so exactly defined the time of
the judges, for what reason one cannot tell.   In the *second period*,
with the terminating point of which (David) he at once connects
Jesus, he very fitly omits any reckoning of time, and only by his
mention of the repeated " forty years" intimates a chronological
parallelism between the two periods, which existed in fact ; so that
from the partition of the land to the building of the temple, *about*
the same time elapsed as from the promise down to the entry into
Canaan.   The " about" often used in these biblical computations
of time is not without its significance to us, who are such ready-
reckoning people.   Much might be said in reference to Bengel's
ordo temporum, of the purpose of the Holy Spirit in thus keeping
back, and yet not entirely doing away with, chronologico-historical
accuracy.

Ver. 20. The words μετὰ ταῦτα denote the turning-point to the
new period, and not unintelligibly join on to the preceding compu-
tation of time.   The constantly pervading sins of Israel are not
expressed until they culminate in the putting away of Saul.
Hitherto we are merely reminded of them, and very clearly so by
the mode, time, arrangement, and nature of God's mercies, which
were observed on account of these very sins.[1]   We are also
reminded of them by the mention of the judges, or deliverers—

---

[1] This is a fresh reason why τροποφορεῖν in Luther's translation in ver. 18
would not be suitable.

repetitions, as it were, of Joshua—as Israel was always apostatizing to the heathen, and was compelled to learn, in the sharp and yet merciful alternations of discipline and kindness through frequent falling, crying for help, and again being restored, what a difference there was between serving the Lord their God, and serving the gods of the nations, and consequently the nations themselves. Joshua himself, however, is not a judge, although the judges were counterparts of the first, and prefigurations of the second Joshua. The omission both of the name of Joshua, and also of the names of all other personages down to Samuel, is significant. In Deut. i. 38 (the "lesson" read in the synagogue) the name 'Ιησοῦς had been already mentioned, who brought them into the land, which Moses was not allowed to do on account of the sins of the people. The rare word κατεκληρόνομησεν[1] had also called him to mind, but in ver. 23 this name is to be given to the true 'Ιησοῦς; besides, Moses is not named till ver. 39, who could not give that which was reserved for Joshua only. Joshua is the mild and gentle leader of his still weak people, and it is he who conquers for them, little by little (Deut. vii. 22), the good land. Joshua is never called in the Old Testament a judge in Israel, for his personality specially prefigures the pure mercy in the giving and gaining of Canaan. But the *last* judge is also a prophet. In his person, indeed, the more spiritual office of a prophet takes the predominance over the judgeship. Samuel, the obedient servant of the Lord before Eli, who had been born through God's answer to prayer, and had been given up by his mother to be a hearer of that which the Lord says to His servant, is the actual starting-point of the series of prophets after Moses, the founder of the schools of prophets (1 Sam. iii. 20, 21). He preaches repentance to the whole of Israel, before whom he is established as a prophet (1 Sam. vii. 2-6) : he is the precursor of David, as John was of Christ.

Ver. 21. But neither the judges nor the prophets, neither the language of deeds nor the language of words, sufficed for the independence of the growing nation. Israel will have a king ; and although they thus with offensive ingratitude rejected the Lord their God, who reigned over them through the prophet Samuel, and refused that He should be the King over them, yet the merciful One granted them their desire, and Samuel was compelled in this matter to hearken to the voice of the people. According to Hos. xiii. 11, this certainly was done "in wrath ;" but yet there was in

---

[1] In Deut. iii. 28, κατακληρονομησει occurs again with a similar context.

it the clearest mercy, which must grant the request in order to prove and shame them, but will afterwards give the true King and Deliverer in spite of the misdeeds of the proud Ephraim, for the faithful One knows no change in His promises of mercy (Hos. xiii. 12–14). God gave them Saul as a king, as He gave them the judges; but the gift was merely a gift granted to their desire (ἠτήσαντο καὶ ἔδωκεν). Saul was a son of Kish, a man of the tribe of Benjamin; but he was not "a man after God's own heart," who would gently and mercifully tend His people, and thus do all God's will. Samuel, the last and good judge, shows what God's mercy can raise up; and because Israel still resisted, Saul, the wicked and first king, reveals what Israel itself is, and what it can produce.

Ver. 22. As to the "removal" of Saul, every Israelite knew; but by this allusion Paul, as we remarked above, calls to mind Israel's sins. Μεταστήσας means, in the first place, He deposed him (Luke xvi. 4; 1 Sam. xiii. 14, xv. 28): it therefore corresponds with the words, *raised up David to be king*—to be such a king as God would have him; for in the sentence, " God gave," etc., Saul is not called king, but only " a man of the tribe of Benjamin." But the expression may also mean, to remove out of life, and is so far permissible for Saul's fearful end, which was actually followed by David's institution as king. After Saul's death the μεταστήσας αὐτόν is now first completed; now first is David actually established as king—at the commencement only over the tribe of Judah (2 Sam. ii. 4). The patient contest continues until every tribe acknowledges him. Zion is won, the building of the temple (through a future one) is permitted, and the frontiers of the heathen round about are subdued. Now are the words fulfilled, ἤγειρεν αὐτοῖς τὸν Δαυὶδ εἰς βασιλέα. *Raised up* means more than the word used before—" gave:" He lifted up out of lowliness into dignity, as the counterpart of Israel, and as the type of the great future One. It is also αὐτοῖς, these very sinners who rejected God, and had demanded Saul. Here, at the conclusion of the pre-figurative historical series,[1] is manifested the sublimest mercy—the re-assumption of the revolted people under a blessed and blessing rule. Here, too, stands clearly forth the fact which, in those who understand the system of the Bible, no doubt can overthrow, that

---

[1] For all the other kings sat on David's throne; even Solomon, who only continued and completed David's person and type, is here passed over by Paul, because he desired and was compelled forthwith to preach Jesus' kingdom of the cross, so as to produce the obedience of faith.

King David himself portrays the promised God-King of Israel. The apostle also hints at this in the quotation which he adds, which he makes up of two different passages. The Spirit of revelation and prophecy had departed from Saul, but had come in a fresh measure upon David for the opening of a new sphere of promise.[1] Through Samuel it so *gave testimony* about David, that the typical reference readily shines through, and (after 2 Sam. vii.) the Spirit has clearly borne witness in many a psalm as to the future actual David and David's Son. Oh that Israel (not like Saul and Barjesus) would choose to "seek unto their God, for the living to the dead!" Then would Immanuel be their "sanctuary" and their salvation, and no longer "a stone of stumbling, and for a rock of offence." Oh that they would "seek unto the law and to the testimony" which is "sealed" to the faithful disciples of Immanuel! Then would they no longer wander about under the curse of Cain, and "curse their King and their God" (Isa. viii. 8, 14, 19, 20, 21). The first witness to which Paul here refers—the words of Samuel (1 Sam. xiii. 14)—speaks of the son of Jesse, born in sin, and the perpetrator of adultery and murder (1 Kings xv. 5), as "a man after the Lord's own heart," because it is based on the contrast (as a king) with Saul, and on David's predominant state of penitence and grace. But this contrast as a king, and this state of grace itself, has a further meaning, which Ethan (through whom God testified) intimates in Ps. lxxxix. 20, 21, referring to Samuel's former words. It is evident from the purport of Psalm lxxxix., which the apostle verily understood better than we do, that Paul glanced at the above-named passage, and that he also intended to suggest who it was that was prefigured through David. The first part of this psalm (up to ver. 38) treats of the sure promise which David received concerning a future divine King; and, after a general song of praise of God's mercies and truth in heaven and on earth has led on to a mention of His throne and kingdom among His people on earth, in vers. 20-38 the Messiah only is spoken of as this King, as we are shown by the whole context, even in ver. 20, under the name of David. In adding the words τὸν τοῦ Ἰεσσαί, Paul perhaps thought of Isa. xi. 1, 10. The conclusion, ὅς ποιήσει πάντα τὰ θελήματά μου, is indeed connected with the kingly contrast with Saul (1 Sam. xiii. 14), but nowhere occurs in this way as regards the son of Jesse, and of *him* is so far not

---

[1] At the conclusion of the prefigurative history, the prophecy began which interpreted it.

correct, as the building of the temple was reserved for some future one. The apostle, therefore, in this comprehensive expression alludes rather to Him who, instead of sacrifice and burnt-offering, delighted to do the will of His God as righteousness for us (Ps. xl. 8, 9, 10), of whom it is written in all the prophets that He (David-Solomon) shall fulfil everything that is to be fulfilled; that, as Cyrus, He shall "do the Lord's pleasure upon Babylon" (Isa. xlviii. 14), and as Zerubbabel, shall "build again the temple of the Lord"—the true *Branch* out of the root of Jesse (Zech. vi. 12, 13). This quotation of the apostle comes before us as a great general citation of the prophetic testimony as to the promised anointed One, beginning with David, and more and more concentrating itself prefiguratively in his person and office.[1] To any one who cannot accept this method of the Spirit, of comprehending the letter in the spirit, we will willingly allow that the then hearers of the discourse might not have understood this; but we certainly believe that the apostles, like the Lord Jesus Himself, often spoke above the comprehension of their immediate hearers, and that the Spirit of testimony only, as it were, satisfied itself in many deep and pregnant words, although subsequent inquirers are permitted at least to mark the depth and fulness of these treasured-up words, and to distinguish the comprehensive light out of which the Spirit spoke.

Ver. 23. In this verse, which goes so suddenly straight to its intended aim, the order of the words is very significant in the original, but is not preserved in the German translation.[2] The energetic τούτου representing David, the man of grace distinguished by the testifying Spirit of God, stands first; and Ἰησοῦν, the name of salvation, now first brought forward, concludes the verse. After David must God be named, whose omnipotence first raised up seed to David in every sense. The expression "seed" calls to mind the ancient promise to Abraham, and indeed that most ancient promise of all to Adam, of the seed of victory and bless-

---

[1] In paraphrase something like this: Raised up David to be king, as to whom He henceforth so testified through the Spirit of prophecy, that the son of Jesse was not only at first significantly contrasted with Saul as a man after God's own heart; but also his person was more and more clearly pointed out in the psalms and prophets as the type of that King David who was given by God as the King of Israel and the whole world, and actually fulfilled all God's decrees.

[2] [In the English translation, the order of the words very closely follows the Greek.—Tr.]

ing; therefore the κατ᾽ ἐπαγγελίαν which follows (without an article) points not merely to 2 Sam. vii., and the conclusions therefrom, but generally to the whole promise mentioned in ver. 32. The word ἤγαγε instead of ἤγειρε (the latter following in ver. 30 in a higher sense) is a very suitable mode of expression for the first origin of the promised One, the "letting come" of Him who was to come. Τῷ ᾽Ισραήλ—the birth of the King of the Jews from the seed of the chosen fathers avails first the people of the promise (Rom. ix. 5; Eph. ii. 12). *A Saviour:* a new, great title, due in an unprecedented sense to this One alone, who did everything which our need for help required, which also was God's merciful will. Then finally, *Jesus,* the name of consolation and of peace, explained by the angel (Matt. i. 21), and also by the apostle (Acts v. 31), with which the gospel begins and ends.

Vers. 24, 25. When He came who was to come, the minister went before the King, the voice before the Word—John, the greatest prophet among those that were born of woman, of whom likewise it was written that he should come not only as a voice in the wilderness, but also as an angel before the Angel of the Covenant; indeed, in Samuel and Elias he had been prefigured both in the beginning and the middle of the prophetic series. This man came to proclaim loudly, that God would now " perform the mercies promised to our fathers" (Luke i. 72),—that the Lord was on the way to visit His temple both in mercy and judgment, with the Holy Ghost and with fire. " Before the face of the Lord :" John predicted the entry or appearance of Jesus, and testified that He was among them, and they knew Him not. Εἴσοδος is very suitable to ἤγαγε, but by the εἰς distinguishes between the birth and the public appearance of the Saviour and Lamb of God: it is parallel to the δρόμος as regards John. The Baptist stands in the partition-door between the old and the new covenant, and preaches repentance, which is itself the partition-door, the aim and the result of the law, the groundwork and preparation for faith in the gospel. God now holds a public and solemn reasoning and reckoning with His people, as intimated in Isa. i. 18. But the result of this is, that both Jews and Gentiles are alike under sin, and consequently repentance must be desired by the whole of Israel as a baptism of proselytes. It is therefore expressed here with emphasis — *the baptism of repentance to all the people of Israel*—a thing which was new, and until then unheard of! Prepare ye to meet the Lord your God! Humble ye yourselves, that He may exalt you!

Acknowledge yourselves to be guilty, and He will show mercy to you! This is the voice of John, which must everywhere pre-announce the appearance of the Saviour. But when this wind-tempest, and earthquake, and fire had done its work, then follows that which was to follow—the still, soft voice of Him who cries not in the street, who will not break the bruised reed nor quench the smoking flax, but is the bringer of judgment in mercy for salvation and restoration. When John was fulfilling his predicted course, *i.e.* was engaged in the execution of his ministry and office (ἐπλήρου δρόμον contrasted with εἴσοδος), he called clearly with the last and loudest voice of prophecy to the now deposed rulers of Israel and to all people, *I am not He* whom ye in your great error think that I am : neither words, nor the exhortation to repentance, nor the baptism of water, can be your Saviour; but it is the power and Spirit, which He who is to come will communicate, which will effect your salvation. *The shoes of His feet I am not worthy to loose*—so elevated is He above all who are of the earth, who, although they speak in God's Spirit in a measure, yet are but sons of earth; but He who comes from heaven, and testifies without measure, the Lord over all, the Son of the Father—He who as " bridegroom " comes to free the guilty world—will decide the fate of all; either *life* through *belief* in Him, or *wrath* arising from *unbelief* (John iii. 27–36).[1]

Vers. 26, 27. The non-recognition of Jesus in Jerusalem stands likewise in condemnatory contrast to the clear and loud testimony of John; through this non-recognition, the word of salvation is transferred to the Gentile children of Abraham. The ὑμῖν also presents a contrast to the κατοικοῦντες ἐν Ἱερουσαλήμ, which is made good by the word γάρ. The Jews, scattered at that time over all lands, looked to Jerusalem and its rulers in order to learn wholesome doctrine and genuine righteousness; and it was, perhaps, with this idea that the rulers of the synagogue at Antioch summoned Paul and Barnabas to speak. But now, after the old promises and the latest testimony for Jesus had been named, it must certainly be freely told how Jerusalem, the city of God, had rejected its King, and how the rulers of this world crucified the Lord of glory. But why was this? Because they did not under-stand the secret wisdom of God, which is hidden to the natural man, but through God's Spirit is clearly manifest to faith; because,

[1] For even if these words were spoken only to disciples, they nevertheless denote the spirit of all the Baptist's utterances to the people.

also, they had mistaken the prophecies about the promised One. Bengel is wrong in disconnecting the word φωνάς from ἀγνοήσαντες—it evidently is connected with it; and with κρίναντες ἐπλήρωσαν the conclusion follows, which should be supplied to both members of the antecedent : κρίναντες αὐτὸν ἐπλήρωσαν αὐτάς. The numerous, loud, and unanimous voices of all the prophets, which resounded every Sabbath, louder in Jerusalem than in Antioch and elsewhere, awaited the voice in the wilderness as the last testimony ; but the flesh would not understand that which was spoken by the mouth of the Lord. Repentance, the door of regeneration, had long since been repugnant to them, and therefore they could not discern the kingdom of God in the Scriptures, or the Saviour when presented before their eyes (John viii. 15-19). The unlearned persons could not read it ; and to the prophets and princes, to the interpreters and eyes of the people, the book of God was a sealed book. The guilt of the non-recognition of Jesus falls, in the first place, on the inhabitants of Jerusalem in common : the misunderstanding the voices of the prophets is especially, but not exclusively, laid to the charge of the rulers. Ἐπλήρωσαν is the principal word in the whole proposition, to which both the preceding participles are subordinated ; so that the former participle denotes the reason, and the latter the mode of the fulfilment, which, although in ignorance, served to carry out God's counsels. The mystery of the atonement is already preliminarily revealed in this verse,—that sinners themselves were to crucify, and thus prepare their Saviour,—verily a mystery of mercy, before which cherubim and seraphim must bow and veil their faces.

Vers 28, 29. But it was decreed by God, and written in the prophets, that no child of man should be able, with any appearance of justice, to accuse the Saviour of sin when He came to die for us : the innocence of the accused One was, or at least would be at last, publicly manifest. The voices of all the prophets with one consent testified of this Son of God and of David, but the evidence of the false witnesses did not agree with them. *They found no cause of death in Him*, however sedulously they sought it—in Him whom God had "formed" as a "man after His own heart," and had "anointed Him with His sacred oil" (Ps. lxxxix. 20) : they were compelled to make up their minds to desire Pilate that the hated King of truth, who had come as King of the Jews, should be slain (put away, ἀναιρεθῆναι). And thus *was fulfilled all that was written of Him* (ἐτέλεσαν), the Saviour of the world, by the delivery

of whom to the heathen, Israel solemnly renounced (knowingly
and willingly) the hope of their Messiah (John xix. 15),—all that
was written, down to the draught of gall and the drawing lots for
their clothes, but not an atom beyond (John xix. 28; Luke xxii. 37).
Therefore were they permitted indeed to pierce Him, so that
thereby He might be recognised; but of the sacred body, which was
to become the new temple, not a bone was to be broken. Therefore, too, were they compelled, although He had been hung upon a
tree and numbered among the transgressors, to break through the
usual rule, by taking Him down from the cross, and allowing Him
to be placed in a grave. For thus had the prophet spoken, that
although a grave among the wicked had been destined for Him, yet
" He was with the rich in His death; because He had done no
violence, neither was any deceit in His mouth" (Isa. liii. 9). The
enemy's seal and the grave only certified to the certainty of the resurrection. Paul's omitting here to name the two counsellors, one of
whom begged for the corpse and the other brought myrrh and
aloes, and also the women and disciples who took part in the burial,
including all in the indefinite " they"[1]—meaning the whole of the
Jews and the rulers—is a remarkable example how a history can
be briefly touched upon, and yet not incorrectly narrated. For the
general expression in ver. 27 is become quite true: amongst " those
that dwelt at Jerusalem " there must have been some disciples who
acknowledged the Lord; and even among the rulers there was a
Nicodemus, who allowed himself to be called a Galilean, and professed his faith in the crucified One.

Vers. 30, 31. The Saviour of Israel, born according to promise
from the seed of David, who was misapprehended, rejected, and
crucified in Jerusalem—this Jesus remained not in the grave, the
living among the dead! For as the crucifixion and laying in the
grave by the hands of men were written of Him, so also were His
vindication and glorification by the hand of God likewise written.
And so it comes to pass. All that man was permitted and had to
do had now come to an end; but then God began to reveal His
holy arm, and again raised up the crucified One, but this time with
a true, actual " raising up " into a divine life through divine power
—He raised Him *from the dead.*[2] And when His glory (hitherto

[1] For it is evident that the same *subject* is to be understood for καθελόντες as
for ἐτέλεσαν.

[2] As to this signification of ἤγειρεν, see above, ch. v. 30. There it is
followed in ver. 31 by ὕψωσε, *manifested His dignity as the Son of God;*

renounced and given up to contempt, although testified to by the
Baptist's words) had been manifested, the living One from among
the dead *was seen* Himself, as He Himself had risen.   *Was seen*—
endued with a new, transcendent, miraculous life, as the God of
glory was seen in the beginning by the fathers.   Throughout *many
days, i.e.* on repeated days, a number of days, and then no longer,
which is made good by the conclusive ἐπί; therefore in the first
testimony a new turn of the matter is gently intimated, according
to which only the witnesses proclaim the risen One, and faith is
required.   By whom is He seen?   By them which came up with
Him from Galilee to Jerusalem, *i.e.* by the few companions, disciples, and friends who acknowledged Him, who here stand in
contrast to the inhabitants of Jerusalem, who rejected Him.   The
locality—Galilee—is named, as being the chief scene of Jesus'
ministry, indeed almost as His usual place of abode, whence He
and His disciples went up to the feast at Jerusalem.   And these
friends and companions, who knew Him well in the flesh, and had
repeatedly seen Him when risen, who were forechosen by Him, are
now *His witnesses to the people*, preaching of Him, and again
proffering the rejected One.   In a special sense of the words, Paul
makes use of the expression " to the people," in the same indefinite
sense, although applying to Israel in the first place, as Peter had
spoken them (ch. x. 41, 42).   They are *now* witnesses; *i.e.*, the
resurrection of the crucified One is now already attested and
proclaimed in Jerusalem and Judea.   And to what does all this
tend?   Is it to judgment and vengeance?   If it were so, something different would take place than the mere offer of the testimony to the faith of the people.   This much at least is implied in
the first proposition, and the following one clearly and prominently
brings forward the εὐαγγελίζεσθαι of the testimony of the risen
One.

Vers. 32, 33. *And we declare unto you :* Paul, in a modest way,
does not separate himself from Barnabas ; he omits to state how a
knowledge of the ascension of Jesus, and the extraordinary appearance of the risen One, had fallen to his (Paul's) share, and classes
himself and his brother either *among* or *with* the expressly named
" witnesses of Jesus," as each may choose to understand it.   This
was not the place for Paul to relate his own personal experience, as
he subsequently did at Jerusalem.   On this occasion he makes of
as Israel also *typically* had been raised out of the captivity and grave of
Egypt.

secondary importance the doubtful question, whether he himself
had seen and known Jesus as the witnesses had. In a plain,
confident narrative, he tells the great story, which he connects
as a consummating aim with the whole of Israel's history, narrating it only in a wonderfully comprehensive sketch. He now
begins to vouch for this history by the words of prophecy, and
speaks to the conscience of every one, setting forth in Jesus that
which the law could not give to any one. Here, however, he stops;
and in the synagogue of the chief city of Pisidia the unbelief of
the Jews is thus all the more sharply distinguished from the faith
of the Gentiles. By the " unto you," which is clearly contrasted
to " the people" (ver. 31), as the " we" to the " witnesses," Paul
already anticipates the chief address to the proselytes, which
here begins, and now offers to the latter principally the fulfilled
promise which was made to the fathers (ver. 17). In the expression (untranslateable to us) εὐαγγελιζόμεθα lies the assurance that
a *joyful* message only as to the fulfilment which had taken place of
the great promise of salvation which Israel had from the fathers, is
now to be communicated. The ever-living Jesus remains Jesus
the Saviour; mercy is now first complete in the full power of God.
By the resurrection God has first entirely fulfilled the promise
(ἐκπεπλήρωκε, more than in ver. 27); and it is indeed fulfilled to
the advantage of the children of the fathers, namely to *us* all,
without exception, as many as are here in the synagogue, both
speakers and hearers. In this " us" a brotherly evangelizing tone
is kindly implied; it lovingly embraces the ἡμεῖς ὑμᾶς, which
begins the sentence, in one common salvation, and affords a
further hint as to the spiritual sonship of Abraham (ver. 26).
How the apostle desired to have the words ἀναστήσας Ἰησοῦν
understood, may be partly seen from the fact that the promise is
now spoken of as in ver. 23, and partly that the reference to
ver. 30 is manifest, which is now to be proved from Scripture
through the language in the passage of the Psalms which follows.
The apostle therefore, in the word ἤγειρεν, intends to repeat the
ἤγαγεν, and ἀναστήσας denotes the ἐκπληροῦν of God in the full
revelation of the Son of God in the crucified Son of man. With
this, the passage from the well-known psalm, which is here called
to his hearers' recollection, entirely agrees. In this first or second[1]

---

[1] Πρώτῳ is the genuine reading, because either Ps. i., as an introduction to
the whole Psalter, is not numbered with the others, or the two first psalms
are united in one.

Psalm, the kingdom of the King of Sion anointed and instituted by God, the kingdom not to be overthrown by rebels, is first mercifully offered to faith, ere it is decisively asserted with judgment. The pervading tone of this psalm is closely allied to the apostle's discourse. The Lord Himself answers from heaven the rebels who rejected His Anointed (the crucifiers), in His overpowering omnipotence: "I establish my King with a perfecting unction!" And forthwith the appointed King, now like unto the Father, takes up the word, and proclaims as the firm and fundamental law of His kingdom, that Jehovah had said to Him, "Thou art my Son, this day have I begotten Thee." This is the contrast to the rebellion that would not acknowledge Him; the revelation that the Anointed of God is also the Son of God, and that the man of the seed of David is also God from everlasting; just as here ἀναστήσας is contrasted with the ἀγνοήσαντες (ver. 27). But the dogmatical idea of the *everlasting to-day* of the divine begetting is not just; and the mode of expression is generally not that of the Bible, for the Scriptures never speak of eternity as "a day" or a "to-day." In the *to-day of the resurrection*, the man Jesus is actually begotten and born through a second birth into an imperishable divine life. As Oettinger says, "The resuscitation and resurrection of Jesus is actually a 'begetting,' a *generatio*."[1] We also, therefore, are "begotten again" through the resurrection of Jesus Christ (1 Pet. i. 3), and fully become sons of God, ἰσάγγελοι, as sons of the resurrection (Luke xx. 36). We may now grasp the prevailing idea of the revelation and cogent "setting forth" (Rom. iii. 25, προέθετο), and consequently the complete institution to the kingly office, which are contained in this verse, as also in Heb. v. 5. In Heb. i. 2, the appointing (of the risen man) to be heir of all things is distinguished from the creation of the world through Him (the eternal Son of God); in vers. 3–5, the reassumption of the original glory, even for humanity, agrees with our passage of the Psalms, and thus in ver. 6 is styled *the bringing of the first-begotten into the world* (Ps. lxxxix. 27, 28). Certainly, therefore, according to 1 Tim. iii. 16, the resurrection of Jesus is a justification of the manifestation of God in the flesh made through the Spirit; but this also is done ἐν δυνάμει (Rom. i. 4), through the "working of the mighty power of

---

[1] Compare our remarks on ch. ii. 24. The verse is expressed very strikingly by Hess: "Thou art my Son, to-day have I called Thee forth into life." The best biblical parallel is the πρωτότοκος (Col. i. 18; Rev. i. 5).

God" (Eph. i. 19–23), which the psalm justly styles a *begetting* or *being born.*[1]

Ver. 34. The words ἐκ νεκρῶν now added do not, as it might appear, make any distinction or contrast in the matter itself, but merely mark the clearer mode of expression used as to the resurrection in another verse; and the word ἀνέστησεν now repeated also shows this. In Ps. ii. the death and resurrection of the anointed One is implied only in the hidden sense of the language, which the Spirit does not interpret until after the fulfilment. In the two quotations which follow in Paul's discourse, this great turning-point stands out clearer and more stringently *according to the letter;* indeed, in the last passage it is made quite clear, and the middle one speaks more plainly than the first. Paul therefore, by the addition μηκέτι μέλλοντα ὑποστρέφειν εἰς διαφθοράν,[2] uses the mode of expression of the third passage to explain the sense of the middle one. Isaiah, in ch. lv., corroborates God's covenant of grace, which had been made good in ch. liii., by an invitation to take and eat that which is now ready. In ch. liii. 10, 11, the *much seed* had been clearly pointed out, which through the "knowledge of the righteous Servant" should be born to justification out of the raised-up buried One. In ch. lv. another figurative expression appears in the passage, which substitutes "eating and drinking" for "being begotten;" but both are essentially the same (cf. Ps. xxii. 27–32). The Lord's Supper, now made ready, is the thing that is spoken of, and that which is to be eaten and drunken is the incorruptible God-man Jesus Christ Himself (Rev. xxii. 16, 17). In Isa. lv. 2 those persons are convincingly rebuked who seek for salvation through the paths of the law, and yet for their supposed money get only that which is not bread, and in return for their fruitless labour attain to no satisfaction. In ver. 3 these persons are invited to the obedience of faith, in order that they may attain life, according to the everlasting covenant, through "the sure mercies of David." This is the context in Isaiah; consequently the הַנֶּאֱמָנִים דָּוִד חַסְדֵי are not merely the *beneficia Davidi sancte promissa;* but דָּוִד is Christ Himself, as is shown by the "Him" which follows in ver. 4. חֲסָדִים are actual eatable and drinkable blessings—gifts of mercy,

---

[1] The *dogmatic* idea of an eternal "begetting" in God is really transcendental, *i.e.* it goes beyond the bounds of human, and therefore of biblical language.

[2] As to the vindication of the remarkable word μηκέτι (no more, no further), see Winer, § 67, 7. The sense is the same as in Rom. vi. 9.

χαρίσματα; and נֶאֱמָנִים denotes that they are to be depended upon, abiding, and everlastingly indestructible—parallel, as it were, to the everlasting covenant.   It is therefore profoundly and strikingly expressed by the LXX., τὰ ὅσια, the *holy things;* Bengel, τὸ τοῦ Χριστοῦ, *termino abstracto;* Paul also similarly, τὸν ὅσιόν σου. We might translate it, the *inviolable sanctifyings, i.e.* the powers of grace for the sanctification of mankind, which, through the killing of the Holy One of God, are no more to be destroyed, but, on the contrary, have been raised up in incorruptibility; which (powers) the חֲסִיד of God, now as the Son of God and man, possesses and contains in His essence *for us.* Rom. i. 4: κατὰ Πνεῦμα ἁγιωσύνης.   Here, therefore, is shown the reference of the resurrection *to us,* as in ver. 33 its derivation was shown to be from God.   Paul, in quoting (with the emphatic οὕτως) the remarkable utterances of Isaiah as the words of the resuscitating God Himself, also rightly adds from the context, δώσω ὑμῖν.

Vers. 35-37. This passage has been considered before.   Paul here, as Peter before, shows that the last and true David, and not the first, is meant; and he also confirms the point as to who the David in ver. 34 really is.   The ἰδεῖν is a rather more forcible expression than the previous ὑποστρέφειν εἰς.   God wills not to give up His Holy One to corruption, but will give us His incorruptible holy things.   The son of Jesse had but one γενεά as ἰδία (2 Sam. vii. 12), like all other sons of men : he served God's will as king of Israel for forty years, without being able *completely* to fulfil that will (ver. 22), and, like all other men, fell asleep, and with body and soul was gathered to the fathers (1 Kings ii. 10, 12).   He also saw corruption in the body, like all except the One of whom all prophecy testified as the promised One, whom also God had in an unparalleled sense *raised up,* who saw no corruption.   From these words Paul's hearers might first conclude that Jesus had risen *soon* after His death.

Vers. 38, 39. As to the personal address to the audience, we have already remarked (ver. 16).   Διὰ τούτου, a forcible concentration of all that had been said about Jesus in vers. 23-27,—a more impressive τούτου even than that in ver. 23, which referred to David.   Καταγγέλεται is used instead of εὐαγγελίζεται, on account of the emphatic stress setting forth the choice which is laid on the γνωστόν.   The word ἀδελφοί again makes good the kind spirit of the discourse.   Only through this Saviour, and not without Him, is preached unto you *the forgiveness of sins,* which every man needs

as his first fundamental necessity, the foundation of which consists
in the atoning sacrifice of Jesus (now intimated in His death), all
other types and preparations being now abrogated (cf. ch. ii. 38).[1]
Is the δικαιωθῆναι which follows an equivalent expression to the
above *forgiveness of sins?* and does it only mean *justification?* It is
usually understood in this way, the καί being considered as exegetic.
It might perhaps be the case that, first the negative, and then the
positive side of the question is expressed (the being *guiltless* and
righteous); δικαιοῦν also, as used by Paul generally, has for its
first meaning to *pronounce righteous*, and here there is an ἀπό
added. But from the context of the whole passage—the simple
reference to the death and resurrection of Jesus, and the preceding
δώσω ὑμῖν τὰ ὅσια—we are induced to discover an idea of actually
becoming just, which elsewhere may often be discerned in the word
δικαιοῦσθαι as used by Paul.[2] Also the διὰ τούτου and the ἐν
τούτῳ are not similar in meaning, but denote the important distinction between the *interposition* for the commencement and the
implantation for the continuance of faith. The *believing* reconciles
and brings to Christ, but the *remaining in belief* in Christ actually
justifies and sanctifies. Luther's construction of this passage is a
forced one, especially in his connecting ἐν τούτῳ with πιστεύων
instead of with δικαιοῦται; he also makes the latter mean, *is
righteous*, instead of *becomes* (is made) *righteous*. The passage
Rom. vi. 7 shows that δικαιοῦσθαι ἀπὸ πάντων (ἁμαρτημάτων) may
express the deliverance from the power of sin. But especially the
whole Epistle to the Galatians, in which this same contrast to the
impotence of the law in effecting righteousness is developed by Paul,
throughout supposes the actual becoming righteous as being possible
through faith, and arising from the commencement of being pronounced just (see ch. ii. 16, 17, iii. 8, 11, 21, 24, 27, v. 4-6).
Paul, as the conclusion of his discourse, proffers not only the forgiveness of sins in the death of Christ, but righteousness from His

---

[1] In the commencement of the apostolical preaching it was both natural and
necessary that the sacrificial death, as a ground of the atonement, should be
subordinated to the testimony of the resurrection. It is so here, as in the previous discourses of the apostles, Philip only venturing to act otherwise. The
more precise doctrine, of course, followed with the Lord's Supper for baptized
persons.

[2] 1 Cor. vi. 11, necessarily from the whole context; Tit. iii. 7; also Rom.
vi. 7, where ἀπὸ τῆς ἁμαρτίας is added, the καινότης ζωῆς and ἀνάστασις, the
μηκέτι δουλεύειν τῇ ἁμαρτίᾳ, the νεκροὺς εἶναι τῇ ἁμαρτίᾳ, the ἐλευθεροῦσθαι, are
forcibly implied.

life, just as Peter (ch. ii. 38) makes the gift of the Holy Ghost follow. Paul's words are exactly parallel to that which is stated in Rom. iv. 25. The followers of the law desired, indeed, by hearing and (so-called) obeying the law, not only to be reconciled, which the sacrifices typically effected, but actually aspired to establish a righteousness or holiness of life (Rom. x. 3) ; but man can only become holy through the merciful gifts of the holy God, not through the law, which only brings wrath. Thus the apostle includes here the sacrificial law in the law generally ; but still the prevailing and chief emphasis is placed on the precepts of the law, which could not sanctify.

Vers. 40, 41. These words which had been uttered by the great apostle of grace were scarcely against their law, and quite according to prophecy ; but a righteousness apart from the law had been preached to every one that believed (whether he possessed and kept every part of the law of Moses or not). Thus the opposition of the Jews,[1] which in the previous course of the discourse had been already noticed by Paul, now breaks forth more clearly in their countenances, and perhaps in their gestures ; so that Paul is justified in adding a sharp warning, in which, following the words of the prophet, he styles the unbelieving hearers as *despisers*. The passage in Habakkuk (ch. i. 5), under the historical prefiguration of the carrying away to and return from Babylon, refers to the scattering and return of Israel after Christ ; the Chaldeans represent the Romans, as is confirmed by Christ's allusion to ver. 8. Compare also ch. ii. 4, the important verse from the vicinity of which Paul quotes. The prophecy promises salvation to faith only, and reverses the matter to the unbelieving with a condemning judgment. The law punishes sin, and the prophecy threatens unbelief in God's atoning righteousness with the yet remaining judgment. Whoever will not believe in the salvation, must at last feel the judgment which up to the last is not believed in.

Vers. 42, 43. The traditional text here appears, at least to us, so natural, and that settled by criticism so difficult to be understood, that I could not resolve to decidedly adopt the latter in the corrected German Bible. Luke, indeed, in most cases relates in a concise way, requiring some degree of attention ; but that Paul and Barnabas, the guests invited to speak, should have forthwith gone out when their discourse was ended, without waiting for its acceptance or rejection ; or that if, in the meantime, anything had

---

[1] For which reason he more and more turned to the Gentiles.

been said or done, Luke should omit it, and merely relate as to
their going out,—these things, we must openly confess, do not
seem very plain to us.   The irritated Jews (the greater number)
went away before the time, ere the assemblage had broken up, although others, and under such circumstances comparatively many in
number (ver. 43), remained and joined themselves to the apostles,
so that the request for further preaching came from the Gentiles :
these two things fit in very congruously with the context of the rest
of the narrative.   Yet we neither desire nor ought thus entirely
to dismiss the ideas of criticism.[1]   If they are to be valid, we must
at least understand a kind of anticipation, by which the (not immediate) departure of the two must have been simultaneous with the
breaking up of the assembly (ver. 43) ; and the (in this case) indefinite παρεκάλουν must have as its subject those who followed Paul
(ver. 43) : consequently the two verses say almost the same thing.
Perhaps the rapid course of events was purposely thus denoted.
There may have been an impression shown both *for* and *against* the
discourse, on account of which Paul and Barnabas considered it
best that they should now go out and make room for further results outside the synagogue.   But it is sufficient that a number of
Jews and pious proselytes (who diligently attended the synagogue,
σεβομένων) followed the apostles, and that the latter, without
waiting for the next Sabbath,[2] on which they had been besought
again to preach, immediately began their further friendly explanations, and spoke to them during the week, exhorting them to abide
in the grace of God which had been preached to them, which also
by their belief they had received, and urging not to relax in the
spirit of *seeking, believing*, and *accepting* which had been roused up
in them; for the apostle perhaps foresaw, as Bengel expresses it,
ingruebat tentatio.   Remark here the loving confirmation of the
public and solemn preaching which was afforded by the confidential

---

[1] Which enjoin that we should briefly read it : " When they went out, they
besought that these words might be preached to them," etc.

[2] Or if, as Luther translates it, the Gentiles besought them to preach in the
week-time—between the Sabbaths—it would form a contrast to the instruction
of the Jews on the Sabbath.   Εἰς τὸ μεταξὺ σάββατον may have both meanings
without its being altered to σαββάτων.   In the later language μεταξύ occurs for
μετέπειτα, and also σάββατον for *week* in Luke (Gosp. xviii. 12) and elsewhere.
But we doubt whether the two *dies intermedii* can be meant (Monday and
Thursday), on which the people were wont to assemble; indeed, we prefer,
without positively deciding, to look upon it as identical with ἐρχομένῳ σαββάτῳ
(ver. 44).

exhortation of the souls which had been affected by the ardent
love of Christ.

Vers. 44–47. But on the following Sabbath almost the whole
city, and consequently those who were entirely heathens, and not
only the Gentile proselytes, who had hitherto taken a share in the
synagogue service, desired to hear the new word of God—most
probably, or indeed certainly, either in the synagogue or in a
place in front of it; for if otherwise, to what does the συνήχθη
point? Then the patience of the Jews entirely gave way: the
whole of their bitter Jewish zeal was roused, and they would not
allow Paul (who had again begun speaking) to preach, but vehe-
mently and blasphemously interrupted and contradicted him. They
desired to hear nothing of the mercy shown to the prodigal son, by
which their service of God and fulfilment of the law lost its pre-
eminence. Then the apostles, through the Holy Ghost, perceive
that the moment has now arrived for a decisive declaration, and
for uttering words which, although conceived in a kind feeling
towards the blasphemers, shall be forcible words, which all must
hear and understand.[1] To you Israelites, aforetime so blessed, and
yet so refractory, *it was necessary*, according to God's will and His
entire plan of salvation, *that the word of God should first have been
spoken*, even here in Antioch! Ye are of course the people which
first received the word of God, and up to the present time are so
to receive it, but now no longer so! God desires to have sinners
as believers in His word of salvation, and from them to raise up
for Himself righteous children; and as ye blaspheme, behold, He
leaves you, and out of this heathen multitude will call forth children of Abraham! We have done that which we were compelled to
do; but the unbelief (expected by us) now manifesting itself stands
out so decidedly, that ye formally and blasphemously *put from
you* the words of mercy. How, then, dare we any longer constrain
and press you? What you are rejecting is *eternal life*—an imperishable salvation in God—which we have offered to you as the
plenteous gift of mercy in Jesus Christ, who has risen! By your
rejection of it ye condemn yourselves; and before the face of
God and these believers in Him, ye show and say that ye are not
worthy, qualified for, or susceptible of this eternal life—that no
feeling of need or longing springs up in your hearts to meet the

---

[1] We might say that it would be natural and easily intelligible if they had
left the synagogue after uttering these words, but *not* if they had done it after
the first preaching.

announcement of it. Ye "wrong your own souls," and "love death" (Prov. viii. 36). God's feast is now prepared for all who come, and to it He lovingly invites you. Ye mock at us, His servants; and ye are thus unworthy guests, who must remain outside (Matt. xxii. 8). Behold the great thing, which has long since been announced and ordained, of which we conclusively warned you the last Sabbath, is now beginning to come to pass. We know what our further duty is: *Lo, we turn to the Gentiles!* Our message to *you* has come to an end, and now our commission directs us to "turn to the Gentiles"—ay, to the actual heathen, to all who believe and desire to believe like this multitude before us. This is the tenor of the charge which the Lord has delivered to and traced out for us. The word of His salvation is sent to every creature. That which Jesus' words had often prognosticated (especially, *e.g.*, in Matt. xxi. 43), which also His last commands had clearly set forth (Matt. xxviii. 19; Acts i. 8), had been made a special charge to Paul and Barnabas, according to ch. xiii. 2. Paul therefore appears, in what he says, to combine the words of ch. i. 8 and of ch. xxvi. 17, 18, and also to make use of a passage of Scripture which speaks of *a light of the Gentiles for salvation unto the ends of the earth*. The reason for his again quoting the words of Scripture is, that he thus follows the course adopted in the whole of his previous discourse, especially at its conclusion. Israel is to hear the words of her own prophet even now, when she is about to be cast off. It is also not less true, that by this passage of Scripture, brought by the Holy Ghost to the mind of these apostles called, as they were, especially to the Gentiles—brought, too, just at the moment of decision—a repeated and final command is conveyed from the God who is thus speaking to them. To the minister of the word every passage of Scripture brought to his attention by the Spirit, and rightly understood, is a special message from his Master: for many is the time that the minister of the word, in his weakness, if he wishes to be as earnest as Paul on this occasion,[1] must require some fresh message in order rightly to carry out the office committed to him; and if we *lived* in the Scriptures as the apostles did, it would be the same with us, and this Scripture passage would impress one, and that another, conveying God's commands both for the present moment and the actual future.

[1] To whom the giving up of Israel was certainly neither an easy nor light matter, humanly speaking.

Ver. 48. *And when the Gentiles heard this*—that the salvation of the Jews was suitable for and belonged to them, since the Jews had "put it from them," and that this matter had been so clearly spoken of in the prophets—*they were glad*, and perhaps afterwards anxiously opposed the main purpose of the wrath of the Jews, fearing lest they should be deprived of the good word by Israel's opposition. They were glad, in their childlike apprehension of the salvation which had been promised, and had now been revealed to them, and greeted it in the light of the Lord which had now come upon them, hailing Jesus as their King of grace. The words in Ps. lxxxix. 16 had now been transferred to them from unbelieving Israel. In this gladness *they glorified the word of the Lord*, which the Jews had thrust from them, and gave Him the glory, that it had become a divine word of salvation to *them*, sinners and unrighteous as they were.—*And as many as were τεταγμένοι to eternal life, believed.* Now what is the real meaning of this word τεταγμένοι, about which there has been so much contention?[1] In the first place, the contrast must strike us between vers. 45 and 48 : the Jews are full of *envy*, the Gentiles full of *gladness ;* the Jews *contradict*, the Gentiles *listen ;* the Jews *thrust from them* the words of their God, the Gentiles *glorify* the word of the God who mercifully offered it to them. Consequently the Jews *condemn themselves*, as being *unworthy*, and unsusceptible of everlasting life ; the Gentiles *believe to justification*, as *worthy of* and *qualified for* eternal life. That this, or something similar, must be the sense of the word τεταγμένοι, is evident to every unprejudiced reader of the context ; that the word, as Benson says, " points to the frame of mind of the heathen, and not to the decrees of God." How should an eternal decree of God be suitable now as a ground of faith, at a time when the word of God (verily not in jest and deceit) *must* first be preached to the Jews?—at a time, too, when these Jews are not saved by it, solely because they thrust it from them, and showed themselves to be unworthy, whilst nevertheless a merciful God had looked upon them as worthy to have the word of salvation sent them (ver. 26) ; finally, at a time when this unbelief of the Jews,[2] attributed to them as guilt, formed the occasion and reason for the transfer of the word to the Gentiles.

---

[1] Which Markland evaded with a strange arbitrariness : Et fidem confessi sunt, quotquot (tempus, diem) constituerant, in vitam eternam.

[2] Which is in no way so plainly referred to the divine determination and operation in Rom. xi. 11 as Baumgarten says it is.

Here I must again frankly say, that I do not comprehend the coarse predestinarian exegesis of this passage. "Non dicuntur," says Limborch, " præordinati [1] nec a Deo præordinati, multo minus immutabiliter præordinati, sed simpliciter tantum ordinati, seu τεταγμένοι." And although there may perhaps be some question as to the *præ* and the *a Deo*, there certainly can be none as to the *immutabiliter*. For the *ingens articulus mutationis*, the great turning-point, consists in the historically recorded ἐπίστευσαν, to which Luke surely did not intend to thrust in the dogmatico-Calvinistic τεταγμένοι as the one only reason of faith. It is manifestly clear that τεταγμένοι refers to the condition of heart in the Gentiles, with which the οὐκ ἄξιοι of the Jews is contrasted. It admits of no philological doubt, and has been proved by expositors to superfluity, that the participle of many verbs (and especially of τάσσειν in a medial sense) can be taken adjectively, with causality in itself; as we say *fitted, disposed, i.e.* fitting themselves, having fitted themselves. It is likewise certain that τάσσειν ἑαυτὸν and τάσσεσθαι occur principally of an army or of ministry, both in profane authors and also in the Scriptures (Luke vii. 8 ; 1 Cor. xvi. 15). It is not without importance that, according to Budæus, in Plutarch σώφρων καὶ τεταγμένος ταῖς ἐπιθυμίαις occurs of the moral state of the heart. No one, therefore, can confute it if it were translated, So many of them as were fitted or qualified, *i.e.* fitted themselves, or had fitted themselves (ἀξίους ἔκρινον ἑαυτοὺς) for eternal life; for any scruple that may be felt as to why it is written ἦσαν τεταγμένοι, and not ἐτάξαντο, ἔτασσον ἑαυτοὺς, or the like, may be removed by the remark, that an adjective and condition of being is made to contrast with the adjective ἄξιοι (ver. 46). Compare the εὐγενέστεροι, ch. xvii. 11, and the εὔθετος in Jesus' words in Luke ix. 62. Τεταγμένοι so far would be an entirely similar form to κατηρτισμένα, Rom. ix. 22, where the context completely dismisses the idea of any divine causality. The following expressions in the Bible would be suitable contrasts to the term τεταγμένοι,—the ἄτακτοι, not disposed, disorderly, and uncomplying (1 Thess. v. 14) ; the ἄτοποι καὶ πονηροὶ ἄνθρωποι— οὐ γὰρ πάντων ἡ πίστις (2 Thess. iii. 2) ; the ἄνθρωποι κατεφθαρμένοι τὸν νοῦν, ἀδόκιμοι περὶ τὴν πίστιν, *inepti ad fidem* (2 Tim. iii. 8. Compare Tit. i. 16, πρὸς πᾶν ἔργον ἀγαθὸν ἀδόκιμοι as ἀπειθεῖς.

Thus much therefore appears to be certain, that τεταγμένοι

---

[1] Although so translated in the Vulgate.

denotes the (in some way) disposed and qualified *condition* of those
who became believers. But, on the other hand, we must not stop
here, or wrongly insist that the Gentiles had fitted *themselves* for
eternal life; for in that case we should hardly penetrate deep
enough, and might overlook a fundamental truth which should not
be overlooked in the προγινώσκειν and προορίζειν of God, and
consequently lay ourselves open to the denunciations of the pre-
destinarians, who prefer to assume an unconditional decree rather
than a self-preparation of man. The word τεταγμένοι certainly
points back to a past time, to the previous origin of the now present state of things; and on this point it is certainly very true, as
Bengel says, " Etenim homo ordinare se (si modo sic loqui fas est)
ad vitam æternam non potest, nisi credendo. At hic memoratur
ordinatio fide prior, ergo ordinatio divina." We should be inclined
to add : " Minime divina, sed fides hominum quædam prævia, fides
τῷ μαρτυρίῳ τοῦ Θεοῦ, quod cap. xiv. 17, testatur, habita, eaque
ad fidem in Evangelium Christi ordinans vel aptans." Thus there
is a *prævia gratia divina*[1] in the operations and testifying of God,
which is offered to faith, as necessarily *gratia Dei semper fide
hominum prior est.* Compare Rom. xi. 35 with Acts iii. 16. The
whole state of qualification of a sinner for faith must therefore,
in fact, be traced back from the beginning to God : so it might
be said (although it is not so expressed here), *a Deo præordinati,*
but by no means *immutabiliter.* Bengel, whose profound remarks
on the term τεταγμένοι may also truly be called classical, is
completely justified, and finds out the right path between the two
erroneous opinions, when he looks upon τεταγμένοι as expressing
the *present and previous operations of God's grace,* and sees the
corresponding allowing this grace to operate in the words ἐπίστευσαν
ὅσοι. Bengel refers to the fact that the Scriptures in general
ascribe man's corruption to *himself*, and his salvation to *God;* and
also that Luke plainly is wont to bring prominently forward the
operation of God in causing belief, which operation, although
existing, is not to be looked upon as unconditional or irresistible
(ch. ii. 40, 41, 47, v. 14, xi. 21, xxviii. 28). He next particularly
compares ch. xiv. 27 with ch. xvi. 14, and, as we believe, with
great propriety specifies the ὅσοι as a *magnifica et singularis locutio.*
We (with him) understand it, that *all* who were thereto fitted and
disposed, believed, *i.e.* that there was generally present a penetrating grace upon all, and a willing acceptance in those who

[1] Also Limborch : Qui se ipsos ope præviæ gratiæ divinæ disposuerant.

believed. As many as were found δεκτοὶ were led by the power
of the word. It was a great " gathering together " of the " children of God " (John xi. 52), without resistance. We heartily
conclude in the words of the divine mentioned above : Desinant
omnes, festivum ac floridum Lucæ epiphonema tristi et suspicioso
interpretamento obfuscare !

Vers. 49–52. *And the word of the Lord was published* (beyond
the city) *over the whole region ;* although the messengers of this
word, as at Jerusalem, were persecuted and driven out beyond
their frontiers by the Jews, who were stirred up into hostility by
the instigation of " the devout and honourable women." [1] The
messengers, following their Master's command, *shook off the dust
of their feet against them*—those Jews who had become worse than
the heathen—and came to Iconium in the further prosecution of
the charge committed to them. But the new disciples, who had
been implanted from among the Gentiles into the new Israel, *were
filled with joy and with the Holy Ghost*, through their faithful continuance in the mighty grace of God which had been poured out
upon them.

XVI.

PAUL AND BARNABAS' ADDRESS TO THE PEOPLE
AT LYSTRA.

(CHAP. XIV. 15–17.)

REPUDIATION OF IDOLATROUS WORSHIP, WITH AN APPEAL TO THE
GOSPEL OF THE LIVING GOD.

VERS. 1–4. What was it that took place at Iconium in Lycaonia,
whither the messengers of God's salvation to the ends of the earth
had been driven by the persecuting Pisidians ? As far as the
faithful messengers were concerned, exactly what they themselves
had boldly stated (ch. xiii. 46) with regard to their message : they
went on preaching, wherever they were, the words of mercy and of

---

[1] It has been well remarked that in the Gospels no women are found to be
inimical to Jesus ; but in the Acts of the Apostles this mournful progress to
hostility is shown.

salvation which had been committed to them. Again as before, first of all, *they went both together into the synagogue of the Jews,* who were settled there, and had established a church. The word of God must be preached everywhere to the very ends of the earth, until sinners thrust it from them; and Israel's God still in all times and in all places stretches out His hand to the people, who gainsay it instead of listening to it, after He has so long endeavoured to dispose and prepare these sinners for eternal life. He in His long-suffering only declares them unworthy of it, when they have filled up the measure of their sins by driving away His messengers. Paul and Barnabas preached or spake in the Jewish synagogue at Iconium in a way so convincingly powerful (οὕτως ὥστε), *that a great multitude of the Jews and also of the Greeks* (or Gentiles) *believed.* Persecution had had the effect of increasing the joyfulness not only of the new disciples who were left behind at Antioch (ch. xiii. 52), but also of the apostles who had been sent away. But, on the other hand, the wrath of the unbelieving Jews was inflamed all the more bitterly. They dared to *stir up the Gentiles, and made their minds evil affected towards the brethren,*[1] blameless as they were, and doubtless honoured on their arrival, as in Antioch. The word of salvation is to go out from Israel to all nations; but when it is preached to this obdurate people, who had become unfit for their vocation, then they rebelliously and blindly take the contrary side, and vex and corrupt the souls of the Gentiles by stirring them up to unrighteousness (cf. Matt. xxiii. 13). The faithful apostles pay more attention to the great multitude of believers than to the threatening denunciations of the enemy; and they remained, waiting in faith, until they were expelled by force, continuing for a considerable and adequate time to say boldly all that they had to say, and confiding in the Lord of all their enemies, whom they preached as Christ, who also allowed *the word of His grace*—the preaching of grace given by grace—to be followed by the promised signs and wonders as a corroborating testimony. There were perhaps no signs and wonders done in Antioch; at least neither the unbelief of the Jews nor the strong, joyful faith of the Gentiles, following so immediately after the preaching, afforded much occasion for the testimony of miracles, which thus became unnecessary; and even in vers. 49 and 52

[1] Τῶν ἀδελφῶν is meant in an Israelitish sense, in contrast to ἐθνῶν. For in a Christian point of view Luke says *disciples* in ch. xiii. 22, and *apostles* in ch. xiv. 4.

nothing of the kind is related by Luke. Ver. 4 is partly supplementary to ver. 3, inasmuch as the division between the two parties,
of pretty equal strength, rendered it possible for the apostles to
make a longer stay there, and partly a progressive transition to
ver. 5, as from such a division of the whole city, arising from
religious grounds, an outbreak of violence must naturally result.

Vers. 5–7. Up to this time the apostles had remained at Iconium;
but when actual persecution broke out, they acted according to their
Lord's directions (Matt. x. 23). There arose a fierce, tumultuous
attack,[1] in which the unbelieving Gentiles and the unbelieving
Jews, with the concurrence of their respective rulers (chiefly the
Jewish elders), plotted to stone the apostles in the tumult which
was permitted. The apostles learnt this, either because their blind
wrath would not conceal it from their victims, or through being
in some way informed and warned by God's guidance. Now they
fled, but only to some of the other cities of the province, and in
the first place to the region of Lystra and Derbe, on the Isaurian
frontier. And for what purpose did they fly? In order that they
might continue to preach the gospel! This is the plan of God's
messengers, and all the persecutors do is to send the hated word of
salvation to others who are better than they.

Vers. 8–10. *And there sat a certain man at Lystra, who never
had walked*, power being wanting in his feet, *being a cripple from
his mother's womb*. But even to this poor man, who could not
leave his native city, the gospel of His salvation found its way.
The same heard Paul speak; a great mercy, which was, alas, unpro-
fitably shared by so many! But this was not the case with the
lame man, on whose sole account it is possible that Paul may have
come to Lystra.[2] The great apostle, who in his frank discourse
stedfastly regarded his hearers, not indeed with a mere human
observation of their external appearance, but in the power of the
Holy Ghost, which enabled him to see into the heart, cast his
eyes (perhaps on the poor and needy generally) on the lame man,
probably not without calling to mind Peter's miracle at Jerusalem.
He then perceived, or rather saw with the ἀτενίζειν, penetrating
into the heart (cf. ch. iii. 4), that the cripple had faith sufficient
for him to be enabled to help him. Whether this simple-minded

---

[1] Ὁρμή means more than *consilium*, and yet not the actual resulting attack,
which is first indicated by the infinitive which follows. In Jas. iii. 4, ὁρμή
means a certain *impetus consilii*.

[2] The reading ἤκουεν is important here for the continuous, attentive hearing.

man, now hearing such great things, might have heard something of the miracles spoken of in ver. 3; or whether Paul may have promised help and healing in general, so that the lame man understood it longingly in a bodily sense ; or whether this man so quickly touched was prepared to infer bodily help from the spiritual promises,—these matters Luke does not clear up, but simply abides by the condition of faith generally, which is so importantly brought forward, and purposely adds the indefinite expression σωθῆναι. Perhaps the apostle perceived that he had faith to be *saved*, because he first had faith to be *made whole*. Then the strong faith of the apostle grasped the weak faith of the Lystrian, and elevated it, as Peter with the lame man at Jerusalem : from preaching he goes on to the confirmatory work, and calls to the man sitting down, with a louder voice than that in which he had spoken to the whole multitude, *Stand up !*—just as other people— *upright on thy feet,* which shall have sufficient power to support thee! *And he leaped up, and walked,* now doing that which he had not done from his mother's womb. It may seem surprising to us that Paul, in his address to the cripple, does not mention the name of Jesus, and the reading which adds this is certainly a very welcome one. But this is only the case at the first glance, and plainly the offence caused by the omission appears to have caused the addition. As subsequently in the solemn declaration (vers. 15-17) no reference occurs to the name or person of Jesus, it is in the highest degree probable that the name was not expressed on the occasion of the miracle. Paul, who also in Athens (ch. xvii.) likewise omits to mention the saving name, probably here in Lystra preached in the first place to the *Gentiles* the gospel of the *living God,* and in general announced help from Him. At the moment when the faith of the man requiring help grasped this, he is not hindered by a complete statement of doctrine; still less is a name hitherto unknown announced to him, which would have only disturbed his faith; but the Lord, not yet named, affords a testimony beforehand in favour of the words conveying His mercy which are to follow. This is often the case in the heathen world : the Saviour, whose name is not yet known, helps the faith which meets Him half-way; indeed, it generally is so. The *name* is not the true beginning; but the God of blessing first blesses, and then reveals through whom it is that the blessing comes (Gen. xxxii. 29).

Vers. 11–13. This opinion is completely confirmed by what follows. The multitude see the lame man walking. Nothing

further is known about the matter than Paul's words, " Stand
upright;" consequently all they can imagine is, that *Paul* has
done this miracle. Such an unexampled deed, done by a stranger
before their very eyes, recalls to their minds all that they had
known and understood of godlike dealings with men (cf. ch. xii.
22). It is the deed of a god, and not of a man. They have heard
or read of their gods visiting earth in the shape of men : the bold
thought instantly arises, forced from them by the miracle, that this
is the case now, here, and in fact. The burden of the loud cry
which they raised in the (perhaps Cappadocio-Greek) dialect of the
province was, that *the gods are come down in the likeness of men* (so
that we did not at once recognise them) from their seat of Olympus
to us poor Lystrians. This unenlightened people, bigoted as they
were to the ancient form of worship of the heathen gods, rejoiced
thus artlessly in the miracle, the explanation of which they could
not yet understand, and their words foreshadow a deeper truth than
they (or perhaps our present reader) imagined. After the first
idea that they were gods, naturally follows the question as to which
gods they were, and what they were called. In front of their gates
the Lystrians had a temple of Zeus (according to some, the special
patron of this district). According to their belief, Zeus was often
in the habit of coming down to earth (as $\kappa\alpha\tau\alpha\beta\acute{\alpha}\tau\eta\varsigma$, $\sigma\omega\tau\acute{\eta}\rho$, etc.),
and had, as the story went, accompanied by Hermes, visited Phile-
mon and Baucis in the neighbouring province of Phrygia, etc.;
therefore the elderly, distinguished, and fine-looking Barnabas,
who during Paul's words had remained in dignified silence, can be
none other than Zeus ; and Paul, who had been the principal and
so powerful a speaker, and also had been the agent in the work
which had just been done, who can he be but the god of language?[1]—the usual eloquent servant and companion of Zeus, the
interpreter of the gods. Thus promptly ready are the heathen in
their god-making; and so mistaken is their view (even when it is
directed towards an actual miracle of God), not only as regards the
true God, but also as to His instruments, that they look upon the
servants to be the lords, and take a Paul for a Mercury. The
priest of Zeus, whose statue stood before the city venerated as $Z\epsilon\grave{\upsilon}\varsigma$
$\pi\rho\acute{o}\pi\upsilon\lambda o\varsigma$, $\pi\rho o\pi\upsilon\lambda\alpha\hat{\iota}o\varsigma$, or $\pi o\lambda\iota\epsilon\acute{\upsilon}\varsigma$, $\pi o\lambda\iota o\hat{\upsilon}\chi o\varsigma$ (*custos, conservator*),
is present either in childlike belief in the appearance of his god,
or cunningly determining to turn the voice of the people to the
best advantage both for his deity and himself. In all haste he

[1] In Jamblichus : $\theta\epsilon\grave{o}\varsigma$ $\acute{o}$ $\tau\hat{\omega}\nu$ $\lambda\acute{o}\gamma\omega\nu$ $\acute{\eta}\gamma\epsilon\mu\acute{\omega}\nu$.

brings up oxen,[1] and garlands to adorn them for the sacrifice, and with the joyful acquiescence of the multitude, would have slain them, and done sacrifice to the supposed gods.

Ver. 14. When Barnabas and Paul — those men who were taken for Zeus and Hermes, but were, in fact, nothing but apostles of the true God—heard this; when they noticed, from the preparations and the preparatory words of the priest, what the meaning was of this cry in the Lycaonian dialect, which was at first unintelligible to them; then they rent their clothes, being actually filled with horror at the heathen idolatry, and at finding themselves (poor fellow-sinners) in danger of being looked upon as gods,— thus affording a palpable proof that they were mere flesh and blood, as other men; and throwing aside all godlike demeanour, and putting an end to the arrangements for the offering, they rushed out among the people, and cried out to them.

Ver. 15. This is the first public testimony by Christ's apostles against the false gods of the heathen—the first at least of which we have any record in express words; for in ch. xiii. 7–12 we are not told what and how Paul taught Sergius Paulus. Here in ch. xiv. we notice, and may clearly infer, that the apostles did not begin with the person of Christ, as in the case of the proselyte Cornelius, but with the universal gospel of the living God and Benefactor; also that they spoke of, or rather presupposed, this God as the only God. Also, that in the first discourse (not recorded), which was effectual in producing the faith and soundness of the lame man, they probably did not preach expressly *against* the *false gods*, for otherwise the opinion of the people expressed in ver. 11 would be very improbable. But if, without expressing any opposition against the heathen deities, they had merely preached of their own God, the blind multitude might have considered that it was only another god added to the old ones, or that it was one of the old ones who desired to make himself known by this discourse. Compare ch. xvii. 18. But now the injurious misunderstanding of the multitude, who perhaps had only half heard, and certainly had not at all understood, is fully evident: the necessity now arises to go a step further, and to speak a bold word against the vain idols, which must have been all the bolder at a moment when the speakers were looked upon as gods, and were endeavouring, by humble repudiation of the highest honour,

---

[1] Ἐπὶ τοὺς πυλῶνας, to the gate-porch, probably of the city, under which Paul had stood to address the multitude. In this case the reading ἐξεπήδησαν might be more decidedly assumed.

to excite any healthy feeling there might exist to confidence in
their momentous words. Sirs (men)!—they address thus honour-
ably and becomingly the multitude of the city, at the head of whom
stood the priest of their tutelar deity. By this single forcible
word of address they desire to express something of this sort : Be
ye *men*, ye people, and not *children;* reflect what ye would do.
What are ye doing? or properly, *Why do ye these things?* The
intended sacrifice, from feelings of holy shame, is not once named
—the preparations betrayed, or indeed acknowledged, the purpose
clearly enough ; but in this question following immediately on the
commencing address, the apostles desire to half doubt and half
repudiate the foolish proceedings of these " men," which were a
cause of horror to them. This single incisive question appears, as
it were, to waver between two meanings : either, Surely this is not
to be a sacrifice for *us* ? or, *What is intended* by this sacrifice for us?
The latter is the more decided rejection of the divine honours
which were offered, and therefore the necessary and cogent reasons
for the repudiation now follow. We too are mortal men, as ye are
—the same reason as Peter gave to Cornelius (ch. x. 26), and also
the same groundwork for the announcement of a common salvation
for all men as in ch. iv. 9, 12.[1] *Men of like passions with you*, and
also of like suffering. Where suffering is, there is also need of
help : to any one needing it, the announcement of this help is a
gospel. To these uncultivated Lycaonians the gospel is, in the first
place, the kind message of the living God—not yet, as in Athens
(ch. xvii. 18), the tidings of Jesus and His resurrection. We
bring you the (or a) gospel,[2] to turn you to the living God from
these false, idle vanities, or idols. What does the τούτων refer to
("from *these* vanities")? Manifestly to the two deities—Jupiter and
Mercury—mentioned in ver. 12. Neither Zeus, nor Mercury his
supposed companion, nor Poseidon, nor any other of your gods, has
any real efficaciousness to benefit us poor mortals. But we ourselves are mortals like you, and we bring you an effective help,
although only as messengers, we ourselves having previously experienced the advantage of it. Ye crowd round us as if we were

---

[1] The apostles might easily have filled the places of these deities whom they
thrust out. There is danger in the present day of many persons turning to
their pastors as to some new idol. People now offer their testimonials of
honour as the Lystrians did their oxen and garlands.

[2] Ὑμᾶς must be the *acc. personæ* to εὐαγγελιζόμενοι (as ch. viii. 25, xvi. 10),
because it corresponds to the ὑμῖν in the first sentence.

your deities; but the purpose of our coming and speaking to you is directly opposed to them. This is the purport or the meaning of our gospel to you. We translate and paraphrase the passage as follows: We bring you this gospel (before heard, but, as we now see, not rightly understood) with an aim quite opposed to your present proceedings,—namely, to turn you *from* these vanities, and to turn you *to* (the only true) God—the living One. The double article, τὸν Θεὸν, τὸν ζῶντα, is not to be overlooked. The aim of the intended "turning" is first styled merely ὁ Θεός; and the latter is then specified, as an explanation of His nature, ὁ ζῶν, as before the explanatory ὁμοιοπαθεῖς preceded ἄνθρωποι, and, as the heathen deities are called, οὗτοι οἱ μάταιοι. In order still further to explain this new great name, the creation is now named, just as in ch. xvii. 24. But on that occasion, before the philosophers, only the "world" is named; now a paraphrase is used of an Old Testament character: *Heaven and earth, and the sea, and all things that are therein.* This title of Creator is naturally contrasted with the particular deities supposed to rule different portions of the universe, chiefly through the addition " all things that are therein," which in Greek (ἐν αὐτοῖς) applies to all three divisions, including the heavenly bodies (stars, angels, deities), as well as all gods, creatures, and especially mankind.

Ver. 16. This first great utterance—which, shining like a beam of light upon the darkness of heathendom, may perhaps have illumined many a soul—is followed by a second, which the questions arising out of a due comprehension of the first would naturally call forth. He has made everything, was the purport of the first utterance. Whoever realizes this in his mind must ask, What is this Living One doing now—this God to whom ye would turn us? How is it that we, His creatures, up to the present time, know nothing about Him? Whence come these deities, venerated by our ancestors, which ye call false, and from which ye endeavour to turn us away? Questions like these are answered in anticipation by the apostolical testimony, which denotes the Creator as the Sustainer and Governor, and very judiciously speaks first of the rule, and then of the careful, kind sustaining power, the latter clearing the way for the gospel of the Redeemer. In the *rule* the negative side only is brought forward, which leads to the "own ways" and the errors of corrupted humanity, and, both briefly and exactly indicating the origin and value of idolatry, obviates generally all the objections which could be brought forward against the new testimony.—*Who in times past* (or rather in passed-away generations). This commencement of the sentence implies a general survey of the history of mankind since the creation of man, especially as in the words "all nations" a comprehension of extent is added to the definition of time. What is the purport of this short but important apostolical saying as to the history of mankind, and its Creator's relation to it up to the time of Christ? *He suffered them to walk in their own ways.*[1] The people therefore found out a way of their own, which was contrary to the way of God, and was only tolerated by Him. The term *way*, in the phraseology of antiquity (ch. ix. 2, xxii. 4, xxiv. 14), signifies not only religious opinions, but also religious mode of life,—a rule for life and conduct jointly. All that is *natural* to the heathen or to the corrupt nations is in opposition to that which is given by God, and must be false and wicked; for the ground of all error and sins is the idiosyncrasy of creation. Neither the length of the time, nor the multitude of the wanderers, nor, finally, God's *suffering it*, can excuse or justify that which is false. On the contrary, after the "past times" comes the new time when God commands all men everywhere to turn to Him (Acts xvii. 30). The silence of the apostles as to Israel, the people of God, and their special guidance, is in no way to be regarded as a keeping back of the truth; for the existence of the Jewish people, and a general knowledge of their one only God, might be justly presupposed in Lystra. When Jews spoke of "the nations," it was always understood that they meant all other nations except their own. But it must not be overlooked that Israel, since the time of Malachi, had in fact been left to "its own ways;" and thus the position laid down as to the condition of the whole world at the time of the appearance of the gospel is strictly and literally correct.

Ver. 17. To the picture given in ver. 16, an explanation going deeper into the subject is now added, beginning with the forcible word of continuation, *nevertheless* (καίτοιγε). In this explanation the living God, who is now first announced to the heathen, appears, as it were, fully justified, and the sinful heathen world seems inexcusable.—*He left not Himself without witness.* He is, as we have seen, a living God actually manifesting Himself, and ἀμαρτυρότης would be a proof of ματαιότης. The intelligible witness of

---

[1] In these words, with the addition, "that they are to seek the Lord" (ch. xvii. 27), lies the whole nature of heathenism.

the everlasting power and divinity of the Creator, which in His works is continually present to all the heathen, is the very truth which is continually held by them in unrighteousness, and is nature's Bible, which bears witness to two things—law and mercy —just as the Bible of the word.   Although Paul brought it conspicuously before the corrupted Romans, that the *wrath* of God was revealed from heaven, and made itself felt in the hearts and consciences of the heathen, *now*, on the contrary, to the comparatively harmless Lystrians he sets forth only the beneficence of the Father in heaven, even towards His fallen children.   *Then* the more secret *law*, which was in existence before, and in addition to, the law of Moses, was disclosed ; *now* the more secret gospel is announced which was equally in existence before, and in addition to, the gospel of the revealed word.   God reveals Himself as the avenger of sin through the evils which He sends down from heaven, through thunder and lightning especially (Job xxvi. 14, xxxvi. 29–31, xl. 4 ; 1 Sam. ii. 10) ; next, through the judgments arising from the storms from heaven, or through these things, He threatens and prefigures punishment.   God reveals Himself as a benefactor even to the unrighteous (and consequently as a merciful God ; Luke vi. 35, 36 ; Matt. v. 45) through the blessings He sends down from heaven—the sunshine and the mild rains, and every good season, flowing from Him ; or through these things He promises and prefigures His spiritual mercies.—*Benefactor*, ἀγαθοποιῶν.   This is the second name of God announced to the heathen world.   First, *the Living One*, in contrast to the false deities ; and then, when their sins and wanderings have been disclosed, with alluring kindness towards His erring children, He is called the *Benefactor*.   Thus " their own ways " must have been, and are, ways of ingratitude (Rom. i. 21) ; but the gospel kindly summons the sinner first to thankfulness, so as to link on this purely human feeling to some higher one.   The beasts note neither the threatening in the thunder nor the mild promise in the rain, so as to be able to recognise intelligibly therein the divinity of their Creator ; but man, by means of his conscience, the still small voice in the heart, both can and should discern that starting-point of all religions, to which a Christian poet refers :

> " Thy Maker canst thou not discern, O world ?
> Far up above the starry-curtained sky
> Surely there must a gracious Father dwell ! "

Οὐρανόθεν : the blessings of the Father of all come down from

heaven, wherewith He restores the productiveness of the earth,
withered as it is by the curse, and again makes it fruitful. Heaven
is pointed out as God's habitation with typical correctness in the
order of nature, as it is with literal correctness afterwards in the
Scripture; the same heaven from which the heathen supposed
that their gods came down (ver. 11). Giving *you* rain—a more
correct reading than *us*; for it is the heathen who are spoken of as
contrasted with the preachers of the gospel, and these Lystrians
are now particularly addressed.—*Rains* (in the plural, the rains
necessary at certain times, Deut. xi. 14), and the seed-times and
harvests resulting therefrom, the "weeks of the harvest" (Jer.
v. 24), etc. These are the kindly testimonies through which the
long-suffering Benefactor above the clouds speaks to all nations.
The blessings which were promised to Israel, the people under
close and special divine guidance, as the reward of piety,[1] are
by God's long-sufferance vouchsafed even to the heathen; and
although at one time and another dearths occurred, as in the time
of Ahab, on the whole God always preserved them—the God
whose rains no idolatrous priest or African rain-maker could call
down (Jer. xiv. 22). The rains bring the water of life and growth
to the exhausted soil,[2] the true type of all spiritual blessing from
above,—"uniting," as Bengel remarks, "heaven, earth, and sea, one
with the other." The blessings which the great Giver sends down
from above (Jas. i. 5, 17), fulfil in their mild operations all our
needs, if we only receive them in a childlike spirit, and from the
fruitful years make provision for the scanty ones. It goes on to
say, *filling*, or satisfying, sufficiently refreshing, with *food* and
gladness your hearts, not your *stomachs*: for God's will is not to
give food only, nor through the latter to cause lust and wanton-
ness; but the aim of His giving food is to arouse a grateful, harmless joyfulness in His creatures. Although the concluding word
"hearts" seems at first only applicable to the "gladness," we
soon perceive that the whole proposition after ἐμπιπλῶν is determined and explained by this word. It has also been well remarked
by several expositors, that as the "own ways" are to be understood
in a religious sense, the testimony of the "benefits" standing in
contrast to them must not concern merely βιωτικά, but must in

[1] In many well-known passages; *e.g.* see the above-named, Deut. xi. 14, 15,
and the contrast, ver. 17.
[2] This general sense was on the present occasion very appropriate, as Strabo
speaks of Lycaonia as a country suffering from want of water.

some way religiously address the heart. The gladness, cheerfulness, or joy *given* even to the heathen by the God, unknown yet ever testifying, must be good and innocent. Where there is this gladness given from heaven, where there is only something of the εὐφροσύνη which the apostle here means, there too there must be some slight measure of God's grace and Spirit existing and at work. If this works, perhaps insignificantly and under the veil of the senses, in a generous and good heart, meeting half-way the gospel of the living God and Benefactor, there may arise a foretaste and a longing after that · higher food which God will send into our hearts from heaven. Thus, through the three chief points of the preaching at Lystra—the gospel, the living God, a Benefactor even to the erring—we come to the point in which man, though gone astray from his God, appears as the aim of the goodness of his Creator and maintainer, in which, too, the gospel (properly so called) of Jesus Christ may be immediately brought to bear.

Vers. 18, 19. After the apostle had so spoken as to correct the false idea of the plurality of gods, and the false light in which they themselves, poor weak men, had been looked upon, they might have entered upon the " coming down" which had just been spoken of, and have announced the Son of God from heaven (1 Thess. i. 10). But enough had been said to the people for consideration and faith; and even this was (on the whole) so little understood, *that scarce restrained they the people, that they had not done sacrifice unto them.* Consequently, of the God who made the world, who gives to every one life and breath and all things, they had comprehended but little, although He had been set forth to them so clearly, that they might feel and discern Him even in the light of day which shone upon them, and that He was not far from any one among them. Even the commencement of the address, " We are only men, who preach to you of a God," they scarcely comprehended. In the next few days the apostles might probably have testified further as to the Son of God and His kingdom ; but certain wicked enemies, who had already caused them to fly from Antioch and Iconium, now followed them hither, endeavouring to hinder the word of God in Lystra also (1 Thess. ii. 14–16). These so-called *Jews*, Satan's counterparts as opposed to the true confessors and preachers of the word of the living God, with all kinds of lies and wicked information (probably of the steps which had been taken by the rulers at Iconium, ver. 5), *persuaded the people,* the same multitude who had just (ver. 18) desired to sacrifice to the apostles (on both occasions it is τοὺς ὄχλους). The Jews were compelled first either to over-persuade them, or to do away with the impression of divine truth ;[1] but then they soon went over to the other extreme (cf. ch. xxviii. 4–6), and, with the Jews, stoned the same Paul who had spoken to them, whom also they had wished to worship as Mercury. In Iconium Paul had escaped the stoning, but here he must suffer it.[2] This is the stoning to which Paul alludes in 2 Cor. xi. 25, after which he was dragged out of the city, being supposed to be dead.

Vers. 20–22. But the man who had been stoned had many perils yet to experience in his Saviour's service (ch. ix. 16); as it says, 2 Cor. vi. 9, "As dying, and behold we live!" The new disciples, who had therefore been assembled till now at Lystra, surrounded the corpse, either to protect or bury it, or to see if there were any traces of life about it; Timothy probably among them (see 2 Tim. iii. 10, 11). But he that was believed to be dead stood up, and went into the city out of which he had just been dragged! At all events it was a miracle of strengthening, although not (from νομίσαντες or νομίζοντες, ver. 19) of actual resuscitation : for the very next day, after the wounds and bruises of a regular stoning, he vigorously departed with Barnabas to Derbe ; and here they again indefatigably preached. Here also a considerable number are made disciples. They now begin their journey back, but not by the nearest road through Syria, but by a way which led them in faithful love to visit the places where they had preached. First, the cruel Lystra (probably secretly), then Iconium, and Antioch in Pisidia. Everywhere were the new, young, and frail churches strengthened with the nourishment of the Spirit : their souls were exhorted to a continuance in the faith ; and the great disclosure was developed, both as an admonition and a stimulus to them, being shown to all the new disciples as if mirrored in the apostolical journey and their first experience—that great disclosure, that, according to the divine counsel (δεῖ), the same path which their great Head had trod through sufferings to glory had been decreed for His church ; just as the path of the typical Israel, through the

---

[1] An ancient addition to this passage is as follows : Διαλεγομένων αὐτῶν παρρησίᾳ, ἀνέπεισαν τοὺς ὄχλους ἀποστῆναι ἀπ᾽ αὐτῶν, λέγοντες, ὅτι οὐδὲν ἀληθὲς λέγουσιν ἀλλὰ πάντα ψεύδονται.

[2] This same Paul, who assisted at the stoning of Stephen—stoned for his testimony of Jesus—is now himself stoned for his testimony of the living God.

wilderness to Canaan, and through the troublous times of Saul and the judges to Solomon's days of peace.   In shoit, that the "kingdom of God" in His Messiah cannot be brought to us suddenly and ready prepared, but that *we* (apostles the same as disciples), being first purified and proved by "much tribulation," may be able to enter therein.   But however certain the tribulations may be, just as certain is the way through them for all those who abide in faith,—the way *through* them into the kingdom of God, full of "a far more exceeding and eternal weight of glory."

Vers. 23-28. In all the new Christian congregations which were the result of this first missionary journey of Paul and Barnabas, and were for the most part gathered from among the actual heathen, a form of church government was immediately established. They, the two apostles, as Barnabas and Paul are here called (vers. 4, 14), *ordained them* (*i.e.* for their behalf, according to their desire) *elders*[1]—on this occasion without any actual choice being made by the community. Newly converted heathen receive the imposition of hands as office-bearers in the church, as teachers and guides of the converted and yet to be converted brethren : they and all their brethren are commended to the Lord with prayer and fasting by the founders of the young churches ; and being left to the superintendence of regularly appointed pastors, are committed to that chief Pastor in whom they have believed.   In their journey back the word is preached at one place—Perga—where this had not previously been done, on account of the departure of John (ch. xiii. 13, 14) ; and at last they arrive at Antioch in Syria, whence, at the command of the Holy Ghost, they had been, *not sent out* (ch. xiii. 4), but given over, recommended to the grace of God for the work whereto they had been previously called by the Holy Ghost (ch. xiii. 2) : and this work they had now performed, or fully done ; but not *they*, but the grace of God, which had wrought such great things in them (ver. 27). All these things are now related to the assembled church, to their awe and admiration—the momentous result that God Himself had undeniably and actually

---

[1] It is almost a matter of course that χειροτονήσαντες αὐτοῖς does not exclude all co-operation on the part of the community ; but it is still more certain that it is not admissible to say, " that they allowed the community to choose by way of voting." Compare the language 2 Cor. viii. 19 and Acts x. 41 with the well-known passage of the pastoral letter, where Timothy appoints elders and teachers.   And it is the same with Titus in Crete (Tit. i. 5, καταστήσῃς κατὰ πόλιν, the same as χειροτονήσαντες κατ᾽ ἐκκλησίαν).

opened the door of faith to the Gentiles : that is, in the first place, that He had sent to them the preaching of the gospel ; and secondly, that He had made their faith effectual by His co-operating grace (cf. ch. xv. 7, " should hear and believe").

Some have sought to gather from this passage that there was some connection with a mother church, to which even a Paul was subordinate ; but these ideas find a limit which will prevent any misunderstanding from what we learn in the next chapter, that the mother church at Jerusalem was compelled to be silent, and, from the report of God's new work, was obliged to learn a fresh cause for praise to God and for new measures.

XVII.

PETER'S ADDRESS IN THE ASSEMBLY OF THE APOSTLES AND ELDERS AT JERUSALEM.

(CHAP. XV. 7–11.)

PROTEST AGAINST THE PHARISAICAL OPINION AS TO THE OBLI-GATION INCUMBENT ON THE GENTILE CHRISTIANS BOTH TO BE CIRCUMCISED AND TO KEEP THE LAW.

CH. xv. 1. The apostles of the Gentiles, resting after the ful-filment of their work, had spent some little time in the mother church of the Gentile Christians, devoting themselves to its quiet ministry. No one took offence at the things which God had done through these two men in Asia Minor, or troubled them and the uncircumcised converts in general. But now the dispute broke out which had been long in preparation. This soon led to an important apostolical decision, which, however, was very far from putting a stop to the contention.—*And certain men came down from Judea.* Thus Luke begins the narrative, styling these first trouble-makers τινές — certain persons — without much ceremony, their actions sufficiently describing what they were. These men could hardly have belonged to the better sort of the Jewish Christians, who were zealous for the law ; for they came down from Judea, being quite uncalled for, and *taught.* They had perhaps been scribes, but were not appointed as teachers over the Christians of

Antioch (who had no want of such, ch. xiii. 1); but yet they taught the *brethren* in common, and said, *Except ye be circumcised after the manner of Moses, ye cannot be saved.* Luke makes a contrasting distinction between these "certain men" and the " brethren;" Paul, in Gal. ii. 4, calls the like of them *"false* brethren." As Menken says, " It seemed to these men of less moment that Jews should become Christians, than that all nations, through Christianity, should become Jews." They still remained full of the ancient Jewish idea, that all uncircumcised persons went down to hell; [1] and in their pride, from which faith in Jesus the Messiah had not yet purified their hearts, they freely assumed to themselves the right of reforming this great community according to their own feelings, supplying the matters which Paul and Barnabas— those mighty men of God—and all the other prophets and teachers in the locality, had in their opinion neglected. Perhaps they made some pretence of having an apostolical commission ; at all events, they acted as if the mere fact of their being Judeans carried with it the right and authority for this reformation. Luke sums up their teaching clearly and decidedly enough : " If ye will not be circumcised after the manner of Moses, ye cannot be saved." They give the foremost place to circumcision, the indispensable covenant sign of God's church for the father of the faithful and all his children ; but they prove its necessity through its reception in the Mosaic law (John vii. 22), and seek to bring forward the second and yet harsher demand, " Unless ye keep the whole law of Moses," as subsequently appears from ver. 5. They call the law a *custom,* or manner, ἔθος, just as (in ch. vi. 14) did the false witnesses brought against Stephen. There is thus all the greater contrast with the conclusion arrived at, viz., Except ye observe this *rite*, ye cannot attain to everlasting salvation.[2] In this commencement of controversy we see reflected the whole course of the church's history. Now begins the ever increasing strife between the error and arrogance which still remained or reawakened in the church, and the free grace of God making all things clear.

Vers. 2, 3. Paul and Barnabas, with the full authority of the

---

[1] See Ezek. xxxii. 18, 19, and on to the end of the chapter, which in a pharisaical point of view might so be understood, but certainly was quite otherwise intended by the Spirit.

[2] Of course their meaning was not that a man would be saved *through* circumcision, but perhaps that *without* it the Gentiles could *not* share in the promised salvation—the grace of Jesus Christ (ver. 11).

Holy Ghost, naturally asserted the freedom which they had in Christ Jesus both for themselves and the converts at Antioch, and gave place to the unauthorized bondage-teachers, " no, not for an hour ;" yet, as was probable, the new doctrine found some acceptance among the Jews, and also among many of the overawed Gentile Christians : at least the teachers of error rendered themselves so important, that an actual *commotion* (στάσις, disturbance of order), and no slight disputation between them and Paul and Barnabas, were the results. It soon appeared that the stubbornness of the Jews was more difficult to overcome by the power of the gospel than the unbelief of the heathen. Then the community, troubled as they were, and made to doubt their mightiest teachers, exerted their influence with prudent, rapid decision. *It was determined,* in order to put an end to the disorder, that Paul and Barnabas, accompanied by certain honoured members of the church,[1] should go up to Jerusalem and obtain a certain decision as to the controversy which had arisen. It was certainly no external, indisputable authority which this second chief church thus conceded to the first ; yet it was in the highest degree natural and consonant with all freedom to act with this modest discretion, and to look for clear information and certainty as to the revelations and ordinances of God from the chosen twelve, as the superintendents of the church in the chief city in the Holy Land, with which the twelve had constantly remained in close connection. It is not clearly stated whether the false teachers accompanied Paul and his companions as their opposers, but the contrary may be assumed, as in ver. 5 it appears as if certain fresh antagonists only presented themselves. In short, the church, thereby testifying to their feelings, gave their envoys a brotherly escort for some distance, and then the latter went through Phœnice and Samaria straight to Jerusalem. On the way, however, all the brethren whom they met are fully informed (ἐκδιηγούμενοι) of the conversion of the Gentiles far off in Asia Minor to God and His Christ; and all the brethren in these regions, more unfettered than those in Judea, gave God the glory,

---

[1] According to Gal. ii. 1-3, Titus was among them, the apostolical assistant who had purposely been left uncircumcised, but is nowhere mentioned in the Acts of the Apostles. Thus, as we further learn in ver. 2, Paul, being directed by a special revelation, made a concession in seeking to obtain a general resolution on a matter that was already settled in his own mind. The other opinion, which refers Gal. ii. to Acts xviii. 22, has much against it, and is founded only on the very doubtful reading, Τίτου Ἰούστου, Acts xviii. 7.

and greatly rejoiced at all that His grace had effected in other sinners, without having their eyes and hearts narrowed by vain feelings of superiority, and by forms of worship.

Vers. 4, 5. On their departure from Antioch they had been escorted by the brethren; and on their arrival at Jerusalem they were *received* by the whole church, and the apostles and elders who stood at its head. It may be a question whether all the apostles were present, as only Peter and James are subsequently mentioned. But still, as James probably appears as spokesman for the elders, in contrast to Peter as spokesman for the apostles (of which more hereafter), all of them might have been present,—at least in Gal. ii. 9 John is also named; but, at all events, those who were present represented the whole body. The accused men, as we must call them, the apostles of the Gentiles, now the envoys of the Gentile mother church, prudently abstained from at first entering on the formal inquiry; but, gradually opening a way for the matter, they narrated again, as they had done on the way, what great things had been done, not by *them*, but by the God who evidently worked in them. Thus, by a simple narrative, they desired candidly to open the question, and also in some measure to suggest the decision. But things do not go on here as they did in Phœnice and Samaria; and in Jerusalem a long controversy must take place ere Peter can maintain the proposition, in confirmation of their story, that God Himself had done these things, and had decided the matter, as He had done before (ch. xi. 17). Now was the time when the non-Christian Jews made proselytes with fresh zeal and with tolerable success; and, according to Josephus, a proselyte king Izates of Adiabene had been compelled to adopt circumcision by the stringent persuasions of a Pharisee.[1] Such events as these, as plausible victories of the Divine law over the Gentile world, must have mightily excited the zeal of the Pharisees everywhere, and could not fail to produce an effect even in the Christian community, in which many scruples of this sort belonging to the old Jewish opinions still remained. *But there rose up*—or rather stood up in opposition, either in the assembly listening to the first accounts related by the envoys, or soon afterwards in the church generally —*certain of the sect of the Pharisees which believed.* Luke again

[1] See Hess (*Geschichte und Schriften der Apostel*, vol. i. pp. 367, 376). Eleazar, a Pharisee, said to Izates, "How long wilt thou remain uncircumcised? Hast thou never read all that the law says upon the point? Read it, and thou wilt see in what peril for thy soul thou art standing!"

calls them " certain," as above in ver. 1 ; although on both occasions, certainly at least on this, they are not to be understood as
persons of mean importance. The expression is meant something
in the same way as the τινές in Rom. iii. 3. These opponents of
the freedom of the new grace from the ceremonies of the law are
rightly to be classed among the Pharisees, but it is also added that
they believed. Their words are not, however, so harsh and coarse
as those recorded in ver. 1, inasmuch as they omit the denial of
salvation. They only maintain that, according to their ideas of
the divine economy and disposition, all those who wished to be and
remain followers of the Messiah and brethren, must at all events
be circumcised ; and more, that they must be directed to keep the
whole law of Moses. In this latter point they were only consistent (Gal. v. 3), and against it Peter subsequently protests in
ver. 10.

Vers. 6, 7. Now the great question, which had *in fact* already
received an answer in ch. x. 15 and xi. 18, became the point of
controversy. Not only Paul (the Pharisee made free by a miracle
of mercy) and Barnabas, but certainly all the apostles present
(Gal. ii. 6), with probably not a few of the elders and members of
the church, vindicated the freedom of their heathen brethren ;
but, as we subsequently gather from ver. 5, the majority inclined
to the pharisaical opinion. It was consequently necessary that an
earnest and solemn investigation of the matter should be instituted,
after and in addition to those personal negotiations which are related in the Epistle to the Galatians.[1] On account of their office,
and from a regard to order, *the apostles and elders came together,*
i.e. not alone by themselves, but (as we see from vers. 12, 22, 25)
with the whole body of the church, in order to arrive at a decision,
and to examine and make clear what proper reason and case there
might be for the words which had excited so many (they *must* be
circumcised). The apostles, and the elders acting with them,[2]
kindly conceded the point so far to this manifest error, as to
examine into it thoroughly in all due order, in order that a con-

---

[1] Paul communicated κατ᾽ ἰδίαν to the most distinguished of the apostles
his gospel and way of preaching, which had not been publicly brought forward
(Gal. ii. 2).

[2] This agreement of all the *elders* seems to us at least probable. From ver. 7
we can by no means "assume with certainty that some of the presbyters
belonged to the narrow-minded Jewish Christians" (Olshausen). A comparison with ch. xxi. 18-20 almost decides the contrary.

viction of the truth might follow without compulsion.[1] Even
Peter, the presiding apostle, who must, since the events in ch.
xi. 17, have been certain about the matter, presumed on no rights
beyond the rest of the church, and allowed the protracted disputation to continue as long as was required. Peter then stood up as
spokesman for the apostles, and uttered the following words, in
which as apostle of the circumcision he " held out the right hand
of fellowship" to the apostle of the uncircumcision, and glorified
the free grace, of which he himself had been convinced and
made by God the witness long ago in Cæsarea.

Ver. 7. *Men and brethren*—all of you, of whom a great part
are now disputing whether circumcision and the law are to be
imposed on the Gentiles or not—ye all indeed know well that some
time past God Himself decided this question. This is, in fact, the
keynote of the whole of his discourse.[2] 'Ἐπίστασθε, not merely
οἴδατε; therefore, ye know well, it is familiar to you. That a *long
time back*, in former days, ἀφ' ἡμερῶν ἀρχαίων, מִימֵי עוֹלָם or קֶדֶם
(the latter as in Ps. xliv. 1): this immediately follows the first assertion of the *knowing*, in order to intensify it, and to give an idea of
the *thing known*. It is no new and fresh thing about which ye
are now contending : the reception of believing Gentiles into the
brotherhood of Jesus' disciples took place years back, and had a
commencement which was both remarkable and well known to you :
to this fact, and the testimony of God involved in it, I now recall
your minds.   The expression ἀφ' ἡμερῶν ἀρχαίων might indeed
point to the actual *days of yore;* but this is all the less likely, as
neither can any choice or resolution of God in actually ancient
times be the subject of general knowledge here intended, nor is
ἐν ἡμῖν being placed before ἐξελέξατο at all suitable to this idea.
The arrangement in setting forth the thing well known is manifestly and emphatically this : Long ago has God Himself among
us, etc. In those days of the commencement of the conversion of
the heathen, which was similar to the other commencement on the
day of Pentecost (ch. xi. 15, ἐν ἀρχῇ). Every fresh and important
period has its קֶדֶם, its first beginning : as regards the entry of the
Gentiles into the church of Christ, this beginning was the remarkable event in the house of Cornelius ; and in referring back to this
event, which had happened ten to fourteen years before, Peter

---

[1] Those of the church who were present were permitted to speak.   As
V. Gerlach says : " So many as took any lively share in the business."

[2] Compare the like expression used by Peter, ch. x. 28, 37.

might well use this expression.[1] Those words, which are so comprehensively true, may apply here, " *In initiis principia* " (cf.
Matt. xix. 4, 8 ; Mark x. 6) ; and Peter, at the beginning of the
clear decision on this unnecessarily complicated matter, says very
justly, Ye know well how the whole thing then began. Peter's
object is to declare God's testimony to the present assemblage
through the things which took place " a long while ago ;" but
before he names these, he must go deeper, and must express God's
choice, or the " good pleasure of His will" (Eph. i. 5), which in
God precedes the testimony ; as, among the brethren, volition and
thought go before the expression of their opinion. But before
Peter expressed the word ἐξελέξατο, " among us " must precede.
We at least cannot think that the ἐν ἡμῖν is, *per Hebraismum*, to be
connected with ἐξελέξατο. For Peter could scarcely have intended
to intimate that he himself was the one *chosen*, as such a prominent
putting forward of his own person, as one chosen by God from all
the " men and brethren," would appear very unseemly. We, on the
contrary, are disposed to consider that he purposely does not make
himself, but the *events* (the ἀκοῦσαι καὶ πιστεῦσαι), the object of
the choosing, and modestly names himself only as the instrument ;
indeed, he does not go so far as to say " through me," but only " by
my mouth." Who then are the " us," among or before whom God
caused this thing to take place ? Not the *twelve*, the mention of
whom here would have no purpose or just sense, but evidently all
the men and brethren of the assembly ; indeed, so far as they were
thus represented, all the Jewish Christians generally at the commencement of the conversion of the Gentiles. Connect in ver.
7, the ὑμεῖς—ἐν ἡμῖν, in vers. 8, 9, ἡμῖν and ἡμῶν, and ver. 10,
τί πειράζετε (ὑμεῖς)—with ἡμεῖς ἰσχύσαμεν. The whole discourse
shifts about in its reference to *we* and *you*. By this interpretation,
God's *choosing* is stated to have taken place *amongst* the Jewish
Christians, and manifestly to the knowledge of them all, and by
the ἐν ἡμῖν is again as if set in their midst. In the expression
" chosen " there is something more than the mere will or counsel of
God : it is a will arising from His free grace ; so that this chief and
concluding idea, which subsequently is fully expressed in ver. 11, is
intimated at the very beginning of the speech. Peter hereby reminds
them, that both Israel and the church of Christ in Israel were only
chosen by free grace, and by the same grace which now adopted other
nations also. In ver. 14 we shall see that James thus understood

[1] Heinrichs : " ab incunabulis rei Christianæ."

Peter's words. *By my mouth:* the speaker thus points out that he was the first and closest witness of all that was done, and that consequently he had also the right to open his mouth on the subject to the disputing assembly. *The Gentiles:* thus he styles the uncircumcised proselytes at Cæsarea, and therefore equalizes them with the brethren drawn from the actual heathen, about whom the question had arisen.[1] In the former case, the church had comprehensively acknowledged, "Then hath God also to the Gentiles granted repentance unto life;" and of this remarkable exclamation Peter now reminds them. He says, *the word of the gospel,* not merely the "gospel;" that they should *hear* the *word* of the joyful message, and believe in it, and should receive the Spirit (as in Eph. i. 13), and thus become pure in heart. This is a new plan of salvation for Jew and Gentile alike, without distinction; and thus it is here *ex facto* set forth and proved that neither circumcision nor the law had any necessary place therein. *The gospel:* thus is God's word, the word of grace, styled here, which is the case only once afterwards in the Acts (ch. xx. 24). For, as Bengel remarks, "Evangelii appellatio magis congruit initiis." The gospel is here contrasted with the law, which, on the contrary, is a yoke. It is not the yoke upon their necks, but the joyful message of grace in their hearts, which God here directs should be preached to the Gentiles. Not only the "hearing," but also the "believing," on the part of the Gentiles, proceeds from God's gracious choice, although the latter is not alone and irresistible. God's choosing grace sends the word to the sinner; and this he must hear and know even against his will, so that he has no excuse: if he believes this word, it certainly in part results from the choice of his own free-will, but in part, too, it flows from the same grace which gave him the word, and only so far as "the door of grace is opened" (ch. xiv. 27). Therefore, although God has chosen in Christ every creature who needs and is susceptible of the gospel, so that they must hear it sooner or later, and should and can believe; still it may be said, relatively to all that is gradually taking place in the history of God's kingdom on earth, that God makes choice of some to believe now, and others not yet,—thus gradually sending down His gospel over the earth. But where He causes His word

---

[1] Peter's words here and in ver. 14 do not (as Sepp idly says, "because else they would be too high-flown!") confirm the idea that Peter, besides his preaching to the Gentiles in the house of Cornelius, had also preached already in a larger sphere of the heathen world and at Rome.

to be heard, there also He gives accompanying grace that men
may believe. On this account, therefore, the apostle is right in
connecting so closely hearing and believing, as also in Rom. x. 17.

Vers. 8, 9. God is He "that knoweth the heart," and therefore
from Him is the surest and most decisive testimony to be looked
for. God regards not the outward person, neither circumcision
nor uncircumcision; but the heart and the new creation within it,
which alone qualifies for admission into His present church. Man
cannot look into the heart, and therefore ought not to thrust out
or trouble any brother whom God has received (Rom. xiv. 3); but
should humbly submit to the testimony of God, the heart-searcher,
which is shown in this reception. Certainly, at the present time,
every one whom men have received and baptized is not accepted
with God; but in the apostolic age, when the Holy Ghost fell
visibly on the new believers, the testimony of God was manifestly
present. The Searcher of hearts had formerly acknowledged the
inward commencement of faith in Peter's hearers, which commencement no one could see and notice; and had given to them,
the heathen believing in His word, the testimony of the same, or
the seal of acknowledgment (Eph i. 13), in that He gave them
the Holy Spirit.[1] He gave the pure, holy Spirit of God, which
enters into nothing which is impure, and allows nothing to remain
impure; therefore the *purification of the heart by faith* (in ver. 9)
is partly presupposed, and partly effected afterwards. What
closer communion and acknowledgment was possible, than that the
Father in heaven should give the inward breath of power from
His own essence, as the highest and costliest gift (Luke xi. 13),
to the children of men; and should send the Spirit of His Son
into their hearts, which entitles and impels them to cry, Abba,
Father? What is it that ye would yet demand from these men,
whom God has thought worthy of such high honour, in order that
they should be worthy to enter *our* communion? The δούς, in
which the gracious choice is now shown, and on which the ἐμαρ-
τύρησεν is grounded, stands fast as a decided fact. They possess
something which God only could have given to them,—namely,
the gift of God in Christ to eternal life, the Spirit of power from
on high. Indeed, this gift of the Spirit was visible and audible in

---

[1] Not, He gave them faith merely, which is not implied in the words. He
gave the word and the impulse (in no way compulsory) to faith; He also gives
the operating effect of faith to those willingly believing, inasmuch as He purifies them.

outward signs and wonders. He gave it to the Gentiles, *even as unto us*. *Even as unto us*: from this a broad general inference is drawn, viz. that God Himself, as He evidently showed by the communication of His highest gifts, has made *no difference* between *us*, circumcised people of the law, and these godly people without either circumcision or law. Is the faith of the Gentiles in Christ to be of no avail with you haughty Jews, until they are circumcised and brought under the yoke of the law? Will ye then so long strive, and in some cases doubt, and, as respecters of persons, continue to make odious distinctions? Ὁ καρδιογνώστης Θεὸς οὐδὲν διέκρινε—neither doubted nor delayed a moment (ch. x. 20), and thus recognised no distinction. *No difference*: a sharp reprimand to pharisaism. Henceforth *purity* and *impurity* before God regain their valid, essential signification, now that the shadow-work has come to an end. Now it is manifest that Jews and Gentiles are alike impure from *sin*, and are alike essentially purified by *grace*, not with mere purification according to the flesh, but in their hearts. *Their* hearts—the hearts of uncircumcised persons who remain uncircumcised; and every single heart is actually and visibly purified, as is shown not only by the Holy Ghost at first, but also by the whole of their subsequent conduct. It is not *our* hearts (*i.e.* theirs and ours together, now without difference): for the question is as to the Gentile Christians; and their hearts are indeed purer than those of the Pharisees mentioned in ver. 5, to which fact Peter, a little ironically, now points. But all continued purification of the Gentiles is rooted in their faith, the only condition (as mentioned in ver. 7) to which God has not added any other; and we therefore must not require any other.[1] Faith only: but this at once obtains the Spirit, and thus attains true purity; whilst the law, only as a letter, is laid upon us as a yoke, and can never sanctify nor save Israel.

Ver. 10. The discourse now turns to the faith and grace possessed in common with the Gentiles, and mildly, but yet earnestly and decidedly, asks the question, whether they desire to be unfaithful and hostile to this common faith. Peter and Paul fully agree here in doctrine, and Peter's subsequent relapse in Antioch (Gal. ii. 11, 13, 14) was only the hypocrisy of his human conduct, and not an error of apostolical doctrine. *Now therefore*: they are enjoined not to tempt God, nor to act in opposition to this His testi-

[1] "What sort of soap, then, have ye, with which ye think ye can wash cleaner?"—GOSSNER.

mony.—*Why tempt ye God?* A hard accusation; the same which the Spirit, striving with the people, so often expressed to Israel in the wilderness and afterwards. Whosoever sees God's manifest signs and testimonies, and yet obeys not His well-recognised voice (Num. xiv. 22); whosoever hears the voice, and yet hardens his heart, and "proves God, and yet sees His work" (Ps. xcv. 7–9); whosoever desires to restrict God within the limits of his own unbelief and narrow-mindedness, and consequently to control Him (Ps. lxxviii. 41); in short, all those who have the Lord operating and testifying among them, and yet think and act under a doubt "whether the Lord is among them or not" (Ex. xvii. 7),—all these tempt God, or, with more or less consciousness, desire to put Him to the proof of His divine earnestness. The preceding statement of the divine testimony gives the apostle the right to speak thus sharply, and the more sharply as he addresses himself to the same "ye" as in ver. 7,—therefore to the majority of the assembly, who had allowed themselves to be so far excited by the zealots. But yet this censure, which applied only to the bitterest and most stubborn spokesmen, is only held out as a terror to the rest, in order that they may give God the glory, and be willing to keep silence before His testimony. This limitation of the censure is intimated by Luke by the omission of ὑμεῖς. *To put a yoke;* or properly, in that ye desire to put a yoke on the necks of the disciples! Thus sharply does the apostle designate the demand expressed in ver. 5. The Spirit's message of salvation in Jesus is a gospel to all creatures groaning under the burden of sin; but circumcision, and the law of Moses, must be considered all the heavier a yoke to the Gentile Christians, if they were so even to the Jews, who had been used to them from the time of their fathers. What, then, is it in fact which the apostle here styles, not *the,* but *a* yoke? Is it the ritual law, or is it the moral law? There has been much controversy as to this question. In the first place, it is clear that we must explain Peter's declaration by the words of the Pharisees in ver. 5: if, therefore, they intended to refer to circumcision and the ritual law only, it was these matters to which the apostle *firstly* aimed. It was not indeed the question whether the Gentile Christians should abandon adultery, stealing, lying, etc., but whether all the ceremonies of Israel were to be imposed upon them. But if we attempt to go further, and peremptorily assert that *nothing but* the ceremonies are here intended, and the moral law is *absolutely not* a matter in question; if we

positively say that the *rites only* were a burden on the freedom of
mankind, after the manner of a yoke, and that the moral law was,
on the contrary, congenial to the moral nature of man; also that
it is not called " a yoke" anywhere in the Scriptures, etc.,—in this
conviction we shall certainly err. For the decalogue [the nucleus
and centre of the whole law], and the requirement to observe faithfully and honestly, with the *whole heart, all* the commandments
and statutes of the Lord, are precepts absolutely of a moral nature.
And for *this very reason*, is not the ritual law, which otherwise
might have been observed as convenience dictated, an intolerable
yoke on the honest Israelite who feels all the force of the moral
command?   And further, does not the apostle say in 1 Tim. i. 9,
per oppositum, that the whole law κεῖται, is laid as a yoke on the
unrighteous and disobedient, ere they are made righteous by " the
glorious gospel of the blessed God?"   Or if κεῖται is here translated, *constituta, destinata est*, does not the apostle (Gal. v. 1–4)
call the *whole law*, together with circumcision, " a yoke of bondage?"
Truly, any one who honestly understands the Epistle to the Romans,
from ch. vii. onwards, cannot fail to know that the *whole* law, and
especially the moral portion of it, are there spoken of.   What, then,
are we to say as to Peter's words here?   We must not throw more
positive clearness than is really due to it upon a point which was
then obscure; but, on the other hand, we must not deny that the
decalogue is reservedly referred to in the expression by which the
Pharisees themselves *bona fide* characterized their law.   We must
also place ourselves somewhat in the position of the Jews, who did
not so philosophically discriminate between the moral and the ritual
law; but looking upon it as a whole, when the law of Moses was
spoken of, very confusedly thought most of the ceremonial part.
Peter therefore, as regards the immediate necessity, speaks chiefly
of the ceremonies; but the Holy Ghost, in His strict words, just
as certainly combines the moral law in the reference, as all that
was said was also true of the latter; and subsequently is often
intimated of it, when the wholesome doctrine of grace was further
developed.   Therefore the application of Peter's language to the
moral law is not only permissible, but is indeed legitimately grounded
on the more profound exegesis of the comprehensive words of the
Spirit.[1]

[1] As Melanchthon says, *Loci*, p. 130, ed. Aug. :—Non de ceremoniis tantum
Petrus loquitur, sed de tota lege. Nam lex ceremoniarum, ni præstes et Deca-
logum, præstari neutiquam potest. Non enim fiunt ceremoniæ coram Deo,

Upon the necks of the disciples. Thus Peter decisively styles
the Gentile Christians, and, as an inference from ver. 9, without
any distinction. They *are* disciples; and ye desire to begin to make
them so, by imposing upon them a yoke which has been now manifested to be insufficient for sanctification and salvation. God has
shown you that by the gospel of grace disciples are brought out
from among the Gentiles, and the Lord has indeed commanded
to "preach the gospel to every creature," and thus to turn the
Gentiles into disciples. Faith and baptism will save, but not circumcision and the law of Moses; and if ye would teach the Gentiles anything further, teach them, according to the Lord's words,
to hold everything which He has commanded you: for this is the
"light yoke" and the "easy burden" of Jesus Christ; but Moses'
yoke must lie heavy on the neck so long as the heart is not purified
by grace. Inquire into the whole history of your fathers, and
your own inmost personal experience. Confess it honestly, that
neither our fathers nor we were able to bear it. When the yoke
was first laid upon the fathers in the wilderness,[1] in order that
they might recognise it as a yoke, and long for deliverance, were
they able to bear it throughout all ages from Sinai onwards? Did
not the prophet speak to Israel, that they had always broken their
yoke and burst their bands, and had said that they would not be
subject to them? (Jer. ii. 20, v. 5.) In this mirror of the earlier
experience of your fathers, recognise ye your own conduct, and
acknowledge freely, with humiliation of your pharisaical arrogance,
that ye also are not able to bear it. Peter is quite willing to include himself in this "we," just as Paul (Rom. vii.) reveals his
own experience to the whole church.

Ver. 11. The discourse now reverts from a sharp, chiding tone
to a friendly intimation as to their personal faith and their own
experience, which they ought not to gainsay. The question at
first was, whether the Gentiles were permitted to believe and be
saved by grace, the same as the Jews, but without the law. As a
conclusion, the settled and legitimate faith of the Gentiles refers

nisi fideli spontaneo corde fiant. Et Petrus non hoc agebat, non posse externa
opera ceremoniarum fieri. Quid enim facilius est, quam pauculis adeo ceremoniis defungi? Num si numeres, quanto plus rituum papisticorum hodie in
ecclesia est, quam in Mose videas? Non igitur de ceremoniis tantum videri
potest in Actis egisse Petrus, sed de tota lege.

[1] The circumcision *alone* of Abraham, Isaac, and Jacob is naturally not the
matter here alluded to. In ver. 1 above it was said, "after the manner of
Moses."

the Jews back to their own faith, to which they are in danger
of being unfaithful. *We believe,* according to the doctrine and
experience from the very first, *that through the grace of the Lord
Jesus Christ we shall be saved.* Reflect now, each one of you, on
your first joy in believing. Did ye not feel something of being
under the yoke? (Gal. iii. 5, iv. 13–15.) Do not therefore contradict yourselves. It is agreed, as I hope, that we all believe *even
as they believed* (ver. 7), and by believing became pure in heart
(ver. 9). We do not expect to be justified without Christ by doing
the law, but "we through the Spirit wait for the hope of righteousness by faith" (Gal. v. 5, 6), through the rich grace open to all.
This is the last great concluding argument against the law; and
in this passage, where the Acts of the Apostles mentions Peter for
the last time, it forms the evidence of his assimilation to Paul—of
the decided *Paulismus Petri.* Ay, this is for ever a prefiguration
of the great, comprehensive, simple formula of union, which even
up to the present day must everywhere have weight, when, instead
of faith in the heart, some restrictive stipulation of "Not without
this or that"—something which obscures this faith—is sought to
be added to the sole-sufficing grace of the only Saviour. *Even as
they*—in the same way as they: καθ' ὅν τρόπον, purposely put in a
forcible way, in order to bring prominently forward the plan of
salvation described in vers. 5–7, and clearly taught to the Gentiles
as the salvation which is meant. Κἀκεῖνοι are evidently the Gentiles, and not the fathers (ver. 10), as many (and among them
Melanchthon) are of opinion; for in vers. 7–9 the Gentiles are
spoken of, in ver. 10 the Jews are placed in contrast, and in ver.
11 both are united in the same plan of salvation. The "we"
occurring twice in ver. 11 is the same "we" as that in ver. 10, and
therefore stands for the Jews only; consequently the union with
the Gentiles at the conclusion was almost requisite. The ἐκεῖνοι
is exactly suitable, as referring to something occurring some distance back in the speech. The sentences correspond: "God gave
them the Spirit even as unto *us,*" and now "*we* believe even as *they.*"
It could in no way be asserted so plainly as a thing proved and
conceded, that the fathers had been saved through the grace of the
Lord Jesus. Now, therefore, all was clear to them. But there is
one thing left on which doubt might arise. How if one of the
Jewish Christians among the audience should ask the question,
By what, then, were our fathers saved? This was a likely question, for the words in ver. 10 appeared to deny that they fulfilled

the law, and consequently to assert that they were not saved. We
believe that the Spirit's words, through Peter, settled this point
also, and that the incorrect reference of the word κἀκεῖνοι to the
fathers arose from a sense of the necessity of some declaration as
to this in the passage. This reference was not readily relinquished,
on account of the very true and important proposition, that the
fathers were saved by faith through the grace of a future Christ.
If we would seek for any intimation on the point in this passage,
we may find it in the word κἀκεῖνοι. This certainly in its principal sense applied to the Gentiles, but a deeper after-considera-
tion may make it include the *fathers* also. In this way, perhaps
—even as *all those* who were and had been saved by faith, as
the Gentiles and our fathers, both of whom had been spoken of.
It is, however, more simple to assume (with Bengel, who also justly
looks for some further intimation) that the fathers also were included in the πιστεύομεν (ver. 11), in the same way as the ἰσχύσαμεν (ver. 10). This would be a reference which would extend
the idea to the Abrahamic faith both before and after the law.

Ver. 12. The Spirit of God, through the apostle, had now put
an end to the "much disputing" (ver. 7), and the decisive reply
derived from God's testimony had been made perceptible to all.
All, and especially the more bitter among them, are startled by the
clear, sharp words, "Now therefore why tempt ye God?" But
also all, and especially the more moderate, are silenced, and are
convincingly touched, through their inmost experience and self-
conviction, by the other words, "which we ourselves were not able
to bear." This yoke—from which both we and they have been
delivered by the grace of Christ. No one has anything to say in
opposition, and no one has anything further to say in favour of
the new ideas; but *all the multitude kept silence*, notwithstanding they had previously so "much disputed." A second solemn
moment, like that before recorded (ch. xi. 18). On the former
occasion the assembled church immediately broke out into the
praise of God for the new thing revealed to them; but this time
the narrative fails to tell this. If the new disciples in Syria and
Asia Minor have received the Spirit, and if their hearts are purified
by faith, as was the case before with the Gentiles at Cæsarea,
then the former are our brethren without circumcision and the law,
just as the latter are. This much is clear, that all this might have
been presupposed by Peter, inasmuch as the apostles of the Gentiles
had at their first arrival related God's work among the latter (ver.

4). But this had taken place on another occasion, and in another assembly : it is therefore quite right that Barnabas and Paul, the Levite and the Pharisee—being, as it were, the defendants in the case—should now get up to speak. For the general satisfaction, and as a completion of the proof, they relate the accompanying and confirmatory *miracles and wonders which God had wrought among the Gentiles by them.* With great modesty, they content themselves with a mere narration, and abstain from naming to the assembly the doctrine which was to be derived from it. And now the assembly can no longer object, but are compelled to confess that through faith the hearts of these brethren also had been purified by the Holy Ghost. Their gifts and their conduct attest this, and what more can be desired ?

Ver. 13. Then they again hold their peace ; and after this repeated silence, with all due propriety and order, James lifted up his voice and spake. We, as many others, consider that this James was not the Apostle James, the son of Alphæus, but James the brother of the Lord, who was *not* an apostle, the chief of the church at Jerusalem (mentioned also ch. xii. 17 and Gal. ii. 9). Peter had given his testimony in the name of the apostles, and James answers in the name of the elders, of whom he was the head, as Peter of the apostles. And because the apostles, in the exercise of their apostolic office, had committed the peculiar bishopric over the church to this James (thus in Gal. ii. 9 he is named before Peter), therefore he, as bishop of the mother church, had the right in his own district to be the first to express his conclusion in the way of voting (ver. 19). We also consider that this same man wrote the epistle extant under his name ; and thus James' agreement with Paul, and Peter's unity with both of them, is, even beforehand, a beautiful testimony as to the true meaning of the warning doctrine as to the law and works which is brought forward in this Epistle of St. James.

XVIII.

JAMES' ADDRESS IN THE ASSEMBLY OF THE APOSTLES AND ELDERS AT JERUSALEM.

(Chap. xv. 13–21.)

HIS LEADING VOTE IN THE CONCLUSION OF THE ASSEMBLY AS TO THE GENTILE BRETHREN.

Vers. 13, 14. *Men and brethren, hearken unto me!*—thus begins James, after the assembly had listened first to Peter, and then to Barnabas and Paul. The multitude were now all the more inclined to listen in silence, as they had previously disputed so much and so loudly. But James brings the matter to a conclusion, by combining in one clear view the *beginning* and *aim* of this work of God, and by adding the testimony of the *Scriptures* to that of the *facts*, both fully agreeing. Therefore he does not mention the narrative of Paul and Barnabas, which immediately preceded his speech, although the latter individuals to some extent stood as accused men before the assembly, but connects his words with those of Peter, in order, together with him, as the second chief authority of the assembly, to conclude the discussion of the matter. He names Simon (here $\Sigma\nu\mu\epsilon\grave{\omega}\nu$) among the Hebrews by his Hebrew name, and introduces him simply as one person giving his vote the same as himself and all the others, without any special authority as the "rock" on which the church was to be built: he puts Peter specially forward, solely because the latter had again explained the beginning of God's work, and having taken a principal share in it, had exactly and clearly made it understood ($\dot{\epsilon}\xi\eta\gamma\dot{\eta}\sigma\alpha\tau o$, $\kappa\alpha\theta\grave{\omega}\varsigma$ $\pi\rho\hat{\omega}\tau o\nu$): God, as Simon had rightly declared, had *visited* the Gentiles with the manifestation of His free grace. $\dot{E}\pi\epsilon\sigma\kappa\acute{\epsilon}\psi\alpha\tau o$: this expression corresponds to the $\dot{\epsilon}\xi\epsilon\lambda\acute{\epsilon}\xi\alpha\tau o$ in ver. 7, and embraces both the choosing grace and its outward development, the *actual giving*, combining them both in one term. God visited them, *to take out of them a people for His name*: this is the completed result of what is spoken of in vers. 8, 9. He visits them not with punishment, but with grace. God Himself has accepted them in His gracious satisfaction: why should we refuse our acknowledgment? (Rom. xiv. 3.) To take out of the *Gentiles* a people,

ἐξ ἐθνῶν λαόν, עַם מִגּוֹיִם,—a beautiful contrast, which places significantly before our eyes the free choice of mercy. All the nations
of the earth are ἔθνη, גּוֹיִם, in their alienation, and deserve not to be
called λαός or עַם (cf. Deut. xxxii. 21, לֹא עָם גּוֹי נָבָל). But through
the same free choice of grace, which first took the children of
Jacob out from among the Gentiles to be a people, and acknowledged them as Israel or God's people, another people out of the
Gentiles is now again chosen and adopted (Rom. ix. 25, 26).
The Gentiles, now converted and designated by the holy name of
God as Christians and the spiritual Israel, are *a people* of God, not
merely added to a people of God. By this expression the way is
quietly opened for the new phraseology of the New Testament, in
which " people of God," as a " *nation* of God," no longer applies,
but *God's people* are to be gathered together from among all the
Gentiles. *For His name :* the correct reading is without ἐπί, that
they may now bear this name as *His* people. *All the Gentiles upon
whom my name is called,* is subsequently said ; and the " visiting"
in ver. 14 is parallel to the " returning" in ver. 16. When God
returns and visits His creatures in grace, and not for judgment, then
that which is ruined is built up ; and the name of grace, Jehovah-
Jesus, sanctifies by its outpouring power, making clean the unclean,
so that God is no longer ashamed to call a people *His* people, and
Himself *their* God ; for He Himself builds for them the city and
tabernacle, in which He may dwell with them in time and in
eternity.

Vers. 15, 16. *And to this agree the words of the prophet,* because they are the words of God through the mouth of the prophet,
—the words of the Lord who *saith* and *doeth* (ver. 17), and has
made known beforehand all His works through His servants the
prophets (Amos iii. 7). Now arrived at the beginning of God's
work, the completion of which is revealed to us in the prophecy
written by Him, these words of Scripture are brought to our minds,
and by them we are informed of its progress now at the present
time and up to the end. The decision, though, is not to be sought
for in the Scripture alone,[1] but the *work* of the Holy Spirit has
first opened out to us its right sense. After God's work has thus
unfolded to us His word, now God's word throws a light upon His
work, and by this coincidence can the church now confidently

---

[1] In this way, perhaps, as Baumgarten rightly observes, the Jewish error
triumphed through the many things which seemed to be in its favour in Moses
and the prophets.

decide and act in perfect light; for now it will be conformable to the great plan of God's work, and its resolution will be that of the Holy Ghost Himself (ver. 28). In the course of action here observed, we may gather a fundamental direction for churches and church-assemblies in every age, and also how to obtain the most complete right for the subsequent assertion of the inspiration of their conclusions. If the later councils, like this first, had weighed God's words and works in all due submission, they might have had a full right to decree with the same full authority of the Holy Spirit.[1] All the separate discourses and words of the various prophets who have spoken on the point are unanimous as God's testimony of His work for all ages; and the things which are written were also spoken (on the whole), and we may adhere to them as the true and genuine utterances of the prophets. In order that the conclusion of the assembly may be decisively corroborated by a passage of Scripture, James now quotes a very remarkable utterance of the prophet Amos, which is pre-eminently adapted to the present occasion.[2] God had very long ago (ἀφ' ἡμερῶν ἀρχαίων in a still stronger sense) before-ordained the acceptance of the Gentiles, and had included them in the great plan of Israel, the building-plan of His temple upon earth! Believers of all nations were to be partakers in the sanctuary of Israel, which, after judgment, was again to be restored! This view is laid open by James to the church at a time when the old temple was not yet destroyed, and when the preaching of the name of God to all nations had only just begun. To the teachable and intelligent, who reflected on and looked into the matter, this quotation would place this new application of the plan of God's kingdom in close connection with two principal lights in the discourses of Jesus—the prediction of the destruction of the temple, with the direction to preach the

[1] Against the Pope's proposal to institute a council, Luther, in his first objection to the first article, taught very clearly on the following groundwork: "The apostles concluded from the words and works of God—who would not desire to follow them?" Again: "A concilium sicut ab initio, such as the first were, can only be understood as a council according to God's words and works." This same Luther, who so rightly estimated the general groundwork, can yet express an opinion, "that James had gone astray a little in his proposition of mediation, and had given way to the doctrine of justification by works!"

[2] We do not, as many, assume a thing which is very improbable, that in the midst of this assembly Greek was the language used. This would have been taken badly by the pharisaical bigots at the very beginning.

gospel to all nations given at the same time and also subsequently at the ascension (Matt. xxiv. 14; Mark xiii. 10). With regard to the figures in the quotation first, what is the " tabernacle of David" which is "fallen down?" The words, " After this I will return," refer us expressly to that which has gone before in Amos' prophecy, for an explanation of this "falling down." We see there in ch. i. that it is the temple which is to be destroyed. The temple certainly denotes also the whole commonwealth of Israel as a holy building for God's habitation : if this is fallen, we revert to the time before the temple, when David had only the tabernacle; indeed it is worse, for the tabernacle has " breaches," and is ruined and spoiled. In this prophetical figure we recognise clearly the ruined house and kingdom of David, the miserable state of God's first-chosen people in their ἥττημα (Rom. xi. 12). It mentions neither house nor throne, but merely the *tabernacle* of David. The David named here is both the first historical David, the ancestor of the kings of Israel chosen by God, and also his prototype Christ, inasmuch as He is the Messiah of the Jews, and remains so, although at the time here supposed He will have scarcely a hidden tabernacle-tent among His erring brethren according to the flesh. At what period, then, does this promised rebuilding take the place of David's tabernacle, so as to become a house of prayer for all peoples? According to Amos, it was not done by Zerubbabel, for his was no time of flourishing (Ezra iii. 12), and Samaria and " the remnant of Edom" sought not then after the Lord. Nor yet by the Maccabees, who were of the tribe of Levi, and not of the seed of David. Still less was it done under the Idumean Herods, who sought more after Rome and Augustus than after Jehovah, whose temple, too, was far from being the true one, but was the very one destined to destruction by Jesus' words. It follows, that all that the Lord here promises through Amos, is still to be looked for from Him who doeth all that He saith; and James carries forward the glance of the then present church, and directs it to the full scope of that which had begun,—a point so distant, that we ourselves have not yet reached the consummation.

Ver. 17. Yes; not only for Israel, but for all mankind, will sooner or later the tabernacle of David be rebuilt as a new temple. From among all nations to whom, as chosen, the name of the Lord shall be invitingly preached, shall " the residue of men"—the *redeemed*—be gathered together; and for this very gathering of all nations after judgment will the sanctuary of Zion be rebuilt at the

end of time, and Israel shall be the "priests of the Lord" and
the "ministers of God" to the nations (Isa. lxi. 6, 9). We find
this same idea hinted at by Peter in ver. 7, and now we read it
clearly in Amos, so that the words of the prophet quoted by James
beautifully agree with Simon's narration. But if we look closely
into Amos, we find that his words do not agree with the present
quotation. We read there, "that they may possess the remnant of
Edom and of all the heathen," etc. This appears to denote a conquest or ruling by the Jews of the Edomites and other nations,
according to the false Jewish expectation. But softly, ye expositors:
look well to it, and divide rightly the word of the Lord spoken by
the prophets, else ye will misunderstand it, as the arrogant rabbis
and Pharisees long back widely erred from the meaning of the
Spirit. In the first place, in this and other similar passages, the
thing spoken of and intended is only a spiritual victory and rule
over the heathen through the power of the word, to the glory of
the one only God. To prove this here would certainly lead us too
far, and generally the whole prophetical system of the Scriptures
(still mistaken by, and as good as lost to, many divines) cannot be
developed by one prophetic utterance. We will content ourselves
by referring to Amos' literal words. From the following sentence,
"All the heathen upon whom my name is called," or " to whom it
shall be preached," it must incontestably follow to all that are
inclined to learn, that only such a "possession" of Edom, etc.,
could be meant which would be effected by their conversion to
Jehovah; also ירש is not so much a "possession" in the sense of
ruling as the promised *heirship* of the world, and the attainment to
a community and enjoyment in the Spirit of all lands and nations
(Isa. liv. 3, Zeph. ii. 9, explained by ver. 11). We are also well
aware what Edom generally signifies in the prophets. It is a
general contrasting type to Israel, and a type of the natural man.[1]
See, *e.g.*, Isa. xxxiv. 2, 5, 6, lxiii. 1, 6; Ps. cxxxvii. 7; Obad. 15,
17, 21. Even if it is assumed that our text is the correct one, still
there is no practical contradiction to the interpretation which the
Septuagint has, τῶν ἀνθρώπων for אדום, which also is given by
James in the Holy Spirit, and was recorded by Luke conformably
to his meaning, following the text of the Septuagint. A bare
adhesion to the latter is hardly to be supposed of James speaking
in Jerusalem, nor yet in Luke, after his deviation from it in the

---

[1] אדום, the red, bloody, earthly man.

previous verse. The second alteration from the present Hebrew
text is somewhat differently circumstanced, which alteration James
and the Septuagint likewise have in common: ὅπως ἐκζητήσωσιν
οἱ—τὸν Κύριον. Now, as we can neither suppose that James merely
followed the Greek text, nor that Luke in so important a passage
as this would make an alteration for the sake of agreeing with the
translation, we must certainly assume, taking into account the inspiration of James (ver. 28), and of the holy Scripture communicating his words, that there was some early corruption of our Hebrew
text in this passage. But in whatever form James had read it, at
all events the Holy Spirit pointed out to him the right sense of the
passage, which even in its present alteration remains essentially
unchanged. *The residue of men* refers, as always in the prophets,
to the judgment going before; indeed, שְׁאֵרִית may simply stand
for believers attaining true redemption—equivalent to λεῖμμα or
ἐκλογή.—*And all the Gentiles upon whom my name is called*, or to
whom my name is and shall be both preached and attributed.[1]
This sentence is pre-eminently adapted to James' purpose, and is
calculated to rouse the doubting church to a continuous preaching
to all nations, according to their Lord's last command. We have
here combined the *grace* of the Caller and the *faith* of those that
come. The Lord reveals His name of salvation as an invitation,
which name cleanses those that are called and accepted from every
impurity. Whosoever avails himself of this grace, *seeks after the
Lord*, comes to Him more and more, and thus " goes from strength
to strength, until every one of them appeareth before God in
Zion" (Ps. lxxxiv. 8). But everything, even the " seeking after
Him," is *done* and effected by the Lord Himself, by " opening the
door" and conferring the power—the Lord who saith it, and also
fulfils it—*the Lord who doeth all these things*: for He speaks, and it
is done ; He commands, and it stands fast. It is the same thing
whether we say, Thus saith the Lord, who also doeth it ; or, The
Lord doeth this, who also saith it. It is very doubtful if the πάντα
after ταῦτα is genuine ; it might take its rise from the LXX., or
from Acts vii. 50, or from ver. 18 which follows. It does not
exist in the Hebrew, in which way James appears to us to have
quoted it.

Ver. 18. The significance of the verse appears very clear to us,
and on no account should it be expunged as an interpolation and as
a *frigida sententia*. James again expressly calls attention to the

---

[1] See the same expression in the Epistle of James, ch. ii. 7.

previously mentioned agreement of the ancient prophetical utterances with the events which had just taken place, connecting his remark with the concluding words of the quotation, and setting forth the deeply grounded cause for this agreement—the omniscience of God from the beginning as to all His works. The words of the prophet are God's words; but God knew from the beginning all that He willed to do to the end of time. All things are known to Him ere they are done as well as if they were completed; therefore the predictions of His prophets stretch so far as to portray a complete view of man's history. Thus God's church, which can learn but gradually to know and guess at God's work which He does upon earth, must humbly submit itself to the progressive disclosure of the manifold wisdom of God in what He now *doeth*, which, however, He has long back *spoken* through His prophets (Eph. iii. 9–11). This present reception into Christ's church of the Gentiles who are converted unto God, is a work of Him who is clear and certain in His counsels from the beginning: it forms one of the many works all of which are embraced in the one great work of restoration. James intends to say, that as regards us, we have not now to do our share in an already accomplished matter of fact; but, on the contrary, we must beware lest we hinder or destroy it.

Ver. 19. Peter had contented himself with declaring God's testimony. James now sets forth at the conclusion, that the testimony and work are *one*, and that to gainsay the former is to hinder the latter. *Wherefore,* he says, we being warned by prophecy not to impotently hinder God's work, *my sentence is*—my sentence alone not deciding it, but only giving the first vote (therefore in the Greek the ἐγώ specially precedes)—I for my part give my vote as to the matter on the principles which have been developed. If this James had been the apostle of the name, he would not have given his vote before the first of the apostles; but James the bishop might do this, for Peter's superiority among the apostles by no means constituted any outward authoritative superiority in the church built up on him; and this is shown by the course of proceeding here. And what does James decide? That we should not make restless or cause annoyance to those that are turned to God, μὴ παρενοχλεῖν, namely, with circumcision or the law. He does not even mention the requisition made in ver. 5, which had been sufficiently refuted; nor does he use the term "yoke," as Simon did, although in his mild, deprecatory expression he seems to allude a little to this word; for whoever is submitted to a yoke, is excited to opposition and restlessness by this annoyance. But, at the same time, he goes further than Simon, in that he deprecates generally *every* disturbing or interruption of the Gentile brethren by Jewish encroachments and imputations. Wherefore and wherein, then, are they not to be disturbed? They are turned to God—to the God who, according to vers. 17, 18, had thus His work in them. Who will dare to trouble this great work of God—the sole essential and important work, as compared with all externals—and to burden it with restrictions which God has not commanded, and thus to hinder men by obstructive burdens from following on in the blessed course to their living and now discovered God?[1] Take heed, O ye disciples of Christ in every age—ye who, like the Jews, cling to any form which, in the freedom of Christ, is no longer commanded—lest thereby ye hinder any other brethren in their conversion. The increase of the new Gentile church would surely have been hindered by the discouraging yoke of the law; and there was the greater reason that this should not take place, as the poor Gentiles were now living "without God in the world" (Eph. ii. 12), and only through the faith in Christ's gospel could be turned to the God of their life.

Ver. 20. Only one demand, and that not a hard one, is to be addressed to the Gentile brethren, so as not at once to roughly embitter the existing relations. If the Gentile Christians remained entirely as heathens in their external life, the Jews would be the only party to give way, and the Gentiles would yield nothing at all; and yet, under such circumstances, both parties should meet one another, each yielding as much as possible. Or else, though the conversion of the Gentiles might not indeed be hindered, the increase in the Jewish converts would be checked, and the communion of both parties in Christ's church would be impeded by an almost insurmountable bitterness of feeling. This, however, must not be. The existing circumstances dictated the most fitting middle course. Then, as ever, the wise God had prepared for judicious innovations in His church; and at that time, by means of the numerous "proselytes of the gate," had opened the path for the progress of the gospel to the Gentile world. If now the

---

[1] Παρενοχλεῖν means more exactly, if the παρά is expressed, during, or in, any occupation, to burden in addition, as παρενόχλησις occurs with this sense. It is therefore :—The heathen are engaged in a difficult matter: in their turning away from an idolatrous mode of life, shall we give them an additional burden?

Gentile brethren would consent to comply with the demands which the Jews were in the habit of making on their " proselytes of the gate," it would be no great burden to them, and they would do well in observing these restrictions. The Jewish Christians and the Jews could not justly refuse to hold communion with them, if they fulfilled the conditions which would entitle them to enter the synagogue.[1] James therefore, led by the Holy Ghost, proposes this provisional limitation of the freedom of the Gentile Christians as a definite conclusion; and instead of saying merely that we should ask them to abstain from these things, he decides *that we should write to them.*[2] By this decided, earnest mode of expression, he desires both to pacify the Pharisees as much as possible, and also to propose the way in which their resolution was to be made known. They were to abstain from four different kinds of *pollution* or *uncleanness*, which were not merely impurities in the external Jewish sense of the word, but, from the infirmity of the newly converted, might lead to actual contamination of sin. We consider it more correct to refer the ἀλισγημάτων to *all* the *four* parallel genitives which follow it, and to translate the passage, that they abstain from pollutions of idols, and of fornication, and of things strangled, and of blood. This construction is grammatically natural, and is also corroborated by the solemnly thrice repeated καί. The ἀλισγήματα[3] may indeed principally refer to the genitive which follows it, and, together with it, may denote the flesh of the offerings made to idols (εἰδωλόθυτον, ver. 29 and ch. xxi. 25). But this by no means excludes the repetition of the ἀλισγήματα with the other three genitives as well. We paraphrase it: That they keep from the contaminations of idols generally, both, in their first sense, from the so-called meat offered to idols, as well as from the contamination of fornication, etc. We are

---

[1] " Eadem lex Mosaica Israelitis varia officia, his proselytis præstanda, injunxerat (Lev. xix. 33, 34). Jam si Ethnico-Christiani, observandis illis præceptis, proselytorum quasi personas subibant, horumque jura accipiebant; Judæo-Christiani eos in numero civium et amicorum habere, sua ipsorum lege obstricti erant. Sic ad hanc consociationem nulla opus erat legis Mosaicæ violatione; immo vinculum, quod Gentiles cum Judæis ad religionis communionem conjungeret, hujus ipsius legis ope nexum erat." Thus K. L. Nitzsch, *de consilio decreti apostolici Act.* xv. 29, Vitebergæ 1795.

[2] We at least see no reason to depart from this meaning of ἐπιστεῖλαι, immediately realized in what follows (γράψαντες, ver. 23), and to understand a mere *charging* or *ordering.*

[3] Cf. Mal. i. 7, ἄρτους ἠλισγημένους (Aqu. et Symm. μεμολυσμένους).

especially induced (with Meyer) to connect ἀλισγημάτων with πορνείας, not so much from any philological reason, as from the important advantage that would then accrue, that it would not be the mere actual fornication which would be placed among the *adiaphora* which were to be given up, but any scandalous and dangerous participation in or contiguity with the same. It is true that, in ver. 29 and ch. xxi. 25, πορνεία stands alone, and in every case any association and familiarity with the actual impurity itself will constitute impurity ; but yet the elucidation conveyed in the arrangement and intention of James' first proposition is very acceptable. We must now enter upon a closer consideration of the four requisitions. *The pollutions of idols* may be taken to mean everything in which the now converted heathen were not completely separated from their former idolatrous worship ; any degree of participation or association with which might be offensive to the Jews, and indeed dangerous to themselves, and by which outwardly they might be typically defiled, and inwardly they might be actually contaminated. But in a closer sense, this expression is aimed at the idolatrous offerings, and all that was connected with them, and therefore forbade everything that might be called *sacrifices to idols*. An abstinence from actual sacrifices would be a matter of course with the converted. The thing here meant is therefore the eating of such meat as had been in part used as a sacrifice, the remainder of which was consumed at an entertainment, or was exposed for sale in the market by the priests. On this point, read throughout 1 Cor. viii. and x., where Paul not only declares that the eating of meat so bought was *per se* innocent (ch. x. 25, 26), but goes so far as to include in this permission the eating in company at a feast with heathen friends and relations (ver. 27), even in the idol's temple (ch. viii. 10) ; but yet advises that these things should be avoided for the sake of weak consciences (ch. viii. 7–13, x. 32, 33), mentioning the confession necessary in some cases (ch. x. 28), and the danger that the eater himself would incur (ch. viii. 1, x. 6–9, 12–15). In every point of view, these chapters contain the best commentary on the passage we are considering. The second impurity named is that of *fornication*, and is here placed in close connection with the sacrifices to idols (as in Rev. ii. 20) ; either because it was often, by the regulations of the idol temples, united with the idolatrous service, or because it took place especially at the idol feasts in a more or less gross form (1 Cor. x. 7, 8) ; and also because, according to the

idea of the heathen, eating and drinking and fornication were alike
natural and permissible, against which idea Paul zealously speaks
(1 Cor. vi. 13).[1] We have no need to have recourse to any philological refinements,[2] and to try to make πορνεία in this passage
mean the meat promiscuously bought in the market; and just as
little need we limit it to incest, forbidden relationships, and the
like, or take refuge in any allegorical interpretation of fornication
derived from the heathen worship.[3] The Epistle to the Corinthians,
and the whole position of circumstances, show us clearly how
judicious, and indeed necessary, it was that a dissuasion should be
given from all further association with the carnal sins of the
heathen. Da Costa well says: "That with tender solicitude
there is subjoined a kind of holy ' Delenda est Carthago' against
the deeply rooted sins of the heathen" (cf. 1 Thess. iv. 5). The
two following items—*things strangled* and *blood*—form essentially
but one, and refer to one of the strictest and most significant food-
laws of Moses, which also had been already intimated by God to
the new generation after the flood, at the time of Noah's reinstate-
ment in the divine blessing, and the permission being given to eat
flesh-meat (Gen. ix. 4–6). See Lev. iii. 17, vii. 26, 27, xix. 26;
Deut. xii. 16–23, xv. 23; and especially the most severe and profound passage of all, Lev. xvii. 10–14; cf. ch. xx. 3 and Ezek. xx.
7, 8. Flesh which had not been purified of the blood by a proper
mode of killing (such as "things strangled"), was not to be eaten,
nor was the blood in any shape to be either eaten or drunken.
The reason for the strict command on this point is not based only
on a remembrance, on every occasion of eating meat, of the blood
of atonement poured out before the Lord (Lev. xvii. 11), but also
on a discouragement given by the abstinence from blood to all
kinds of cruelty and murder (Gen. ix. 5, 6; Lev. xvii. 14). It
was based, too, not only on a far-dividing separation from the
blood-drinking offerings of the heathen (Lev. xvii. 7; Ps. xvi. 4),
but also on the actual physical hurtfulness of a frequent feeding
upon blood, as tending to the brutalization of the natural man.[4]

[1] See the passages in Grotius, especially that of Cicero: "Quando enim hoc
factum non est? Quando reprehensum? Quando non permissum?"
[2] Such as Michaelis brings forward, and Nitzsch has copiously opposed in his
above-mentioned dissertation.
[3] Such as have been brought forward in the theological considerations in the
Evang. Kirchenzeitung (1832).
[4] In this command it absolutely is not the *only* point of view, and scarcely

Ver. 21. In this verse we consider that the cause for these re-strictions is expressed, and also that an intimation is given as to their duration. V. Meyer's remark[1] on this appears to us hardly satisfactory. We thus look upon the matter. The proposed re-solution has regard not only to the Gentile Christians, but also to the further future conversion of the Gentiles, as was expressed in ver. 19. The proposed limitation, on the other hand, is solicitous not only for the Jewish Christians, but also for the Jews, and their further conversion. Ver. 19 contains the (merely intimated) resolution and its reason combined. Now, however, the proposal of the limitations in ver. 20 is followed by its reason in ver. 21. As Moses from old times (γενεῶν, not merely ἡμερῶν ἀρχαίων) hath in every city persons appointed, who officially and regularly read out his books every Sabbath, and make known his laws, which are so strictly zealous against the least intermixture with idolatrous wor-ship, as if proclaiming and preaching him; therefore, looking at this constant publication and confirmation of Judaism, the Mosaic feelings of the Jewish Christians and Jews, thus continually re-called to their minds and stirred up, *ought to be respected.* It does not merely mean, " The poor Jews had Moses too much at heart" (Brandt's *Apost. Past.*), but acknowledges with great earnestness, " We cannot suddenly and forcibly break through these previous ordinances of God, which still have so firm a hold on the Jews." The Jewish Christian who will not yet make up his mind to leave the synagogue might easily become irritated through the reading of the law, which his brethren from among the Gentiles so completely set at defiance; or he might be made ashamed, or placed at a dis-advantage, in the presence of his Jewish brethren. The Jews, who altogether kept to the synagogue, would hardly be induced to join a community, many members of which no longer paid any respect at all to the things heard every Sabbath. It would have the effect of laying a bitter stumbling-block in the way of those Jews who were inclined to turn to Christ, if the Gentile Christians did not even give that adherence to the existing Mosaism which was required of

the *main* one, that (according to Baumgarten) " the abstinence from blood refers to a respect for the sacrificial service of Israel, the centre-point of all the Israelitish ordinances;" for then the passage Gen. ix. 4 would not be brought into question at all.

[1] " Where both Jewish and Gentile Christians heard the reasons for these commands." This would presuppose an abiding adhesion of the *latter* to the synagogue.

the Jewish proselytes.[1] It must also be added, that Moses himself
expressly included the uncircumcised strangers who dwelt in Israel
in his command to abstain from blood and the heathen fornication
(Lev. xvii. 10, 12, 13, xviii. 26). This, therefore, appears to us to
be the simple and principal meaning of ver. 21; but certainly other
and more remote references are not to be excluded.   On the other
hand, a thought is implied which was equally true and suitable, that
the believing Jews must now be satisfied, as the heathen believers
have to do the very things which for so long time have been considered, according to Moses' laws, as sufficient for God-fearing proselytes.   The words that echo in our ears, that Moses *has* people
who are everywhere and always preaching the honour of his name,
will not allow that Moses and his law should be altogether dismissed
as something unnecessary.   Did not the bigots for Moses act (vers.
1 and 5) as if the entire overthrow of his authority was suddenly
feared, and that they therefore felt compelled strictly to uphold his
honour ?   We know from ch. vi. 11 how highly the Jews estimated
their Moses.   James, at the conclusion, answers to the bigots :
" There is no need for anxiety ; your Moses is everywhere preached."
Erasmus exactly expressed this sense (certainly incorrect as the
chief sense, although Schneckenburger, Thiersch, and Baumgarten
agree with him) : " Nec est metuendum, ne Moses antiquetur."
And finally, if the cause of an ordinance ceases, and all the circumstances which rendered it necessary are changed, does not the
ordinance itself then become abrogated ?   Is not therefore an idea
of this abrogation implied in the mention of these *temporary
reasons ?*   When the existing synagogues scattered throughout the
heathen world, almost " in every city,"[2] are destroyed, and the
reading out and keeping of the law comes to an end, then need the
Gentile Christians abstain no longer from " things strangled and
from blood," and the careful consideration as to sacrificial meat
need no longer be observed ; for then the close connection between
the Jews and the Christians would be broken, and there would be
no longer a Jewish world to be gained over by this considerate
respect, or to be offended by a contrary course of action.   When
the sacrifice to idols and its abominations ceased, the first part of

---

[1] Who, as is well known, were bound to keep the so-called " seven Noachian
commands." The details are to be found in Winer, Buxtorf, etc.

[2] Unnecessary attempts have been made to soften down the forcible expression here (κατὰ πόλιν)—in cities here and there. But it should be understood
as meaning, everywhere where there are Jews.

the resolution certainly became unnecessary, and the second was also not needed when Judaism, or rather its connection with Christianity, came to an end. The reason, therefore, for the proposed limitation of liberty intimated at the same time its duration. But wherever the convert stands, as it were in the midst, between idolaters and ceremonial worshippers of God, there, in every age and in the greatest variety of shapes, the spirit of this apostolical conclusion will still hold good, breathing as it does the wisdom and foresight of brotherly love, and anxiety lest the work of God should be disturbed either in themselves or in others. But however much the restrictions on Christian liberty may be removed, it is clearly enough testified in the Scriptures, in 1 Cor. v. 6 and in other places, that fornication is not permissible for Christians under any circumstances whatever.

XIX.

LETTER FROM THE APOSTLES, ELDERS, AND BRETHREN AT JERUSALEM TO THEIR BRETHREN AMONG THE GENTILES.

(CHAP. XV. 23-29.)

EPISTOLARY COMMUNICATION OF THEIR RESOLUTION AS TO THE POSITION OF THE GENTILE BRETHREN WITH REGARD TO THE LAW OF MOSES.

VERS. 22, 23. *Then*—τότε—after these penetrating discourses by Peter and James, and also the things narrated as to God's wonderful works by Paul and Barnabas, James' words found general acceptance. But a judicious and emphatic addition was made to his proposition, which merely recommended "that we should write." This was, that special messengers should be sent (besides Paul and Barnabas) to carry the letter. After the assembly of the apostles and elders (ver. 6) had come to an agreement, they associated with them the *whole* church; and among the latter also, the well-grounded proposition of the entire body of authorities found full acceptance. *Then pleased it the apostles and elders;* but the decided expression of their opinion, and the authoritative execution of it, only took place with the co-operation of the *whole church.*

In order that any germ of jealousy might be suppressed, which might perhaps suggest that Paul and Barnabas had surprised the assembly into this conclusion, and that a lively union of love might be cultivated, which a brief and official letter might not be calculated to bring about, men chosen out of the church were to go with Paul and Barnabas to Antioch. The choice fell upon Judas Barsabas, and on Silas (or Silvanus), the subsequently abiding companion of the Apostle Paul. They were both of them men who were not elders;[1] but yet, from their character and gifts, were distinguished among the brethren, and acknowledged as chief men. And to these men was entrusted the following letter, which, as an independent commandment of loving wisdom for the edification of the Jewish and Gentile church, formed the remarkable beginning of *inspired writing* of the New Testament system, as the Decalogue did in the Old Testament. The speeches of Peter and James are compendiously made use of, but from traces in the style it appears as if James composed it; and it was naturally written in Greek, being addressed to brethren speaking this language. We have not scrupled to supplement the preceding discourses with this letter, in which we find the first transition from oral teaching to the principal form of the New Testament Scripture.[2]

Ver. 23. The letter begins in a dignified way, with the titles of the writers; and it is the right title, leaders and people together.[3] The Gentile Christians are styled the brethren of the brethren that write, with the necessary addition, *which are of the Gentiles;* but the idea, which might be misinterpreted, is quite thrown into the shade by the name of "brethren." Those (from among the Jews) who certainly were firstly and chiefly entitled to the name of "brethren," write to the *brethren which are of the Gentiles.* There must have been many a struggle ere this title of "brethren" (already anticipated by Luke in ver. 1) became so solemnly acknowledged! In this superscription, the spirit and purport of the

---

[1] For the sending of this judgment was not properly *ruling* and *commanding.*

[2] Both Luke's writings to Theophilus, indeed even the Gospel of John (remark the phrase, that *ye* may believe, ch. xx. 31), are to a certain extent *epistles.*

[3] A comparison with ver. 22 seems to demand almost decisively the same threefold title: The apostles, *and* the elders, *and* the brethren. The reading with the omission of the latter καὶ οἱ, although occurring early, and not in the hierarchical interest, gives, again almost decisively, a very strange comprehension. If the apostles and elders write as brethren to the whole body of brethren, why is there not the general brotherly salutation from church to church?

whole letter is intimated. With much foresight, too, it is not addressed to Antioch only, but also to the whole of Syria and Cilicia,
that is to say, without any distinction being made, to all the Gentile
believers in general;[1] so that, through this letter of mutual love
and acknowledgment, there might be great peace in all the Gentile
churches. The actual form of salutation is, however, remarkable—
Χαίρειν, Hail! The secular, traditional Greek salutation Χαῖρε or
Χαίρειν is used here, and not yet, as in the subsequent epistles, the
apostolic greeting, " *Grace* and *Peace* from *God* and *Christ;*" but
the Israelitish salute of Jesus and His disciples is no longer adopted,
which ran : " Peace be with you !" We find this Χαῖρε used in
the New Testament by Judas with the kiss of betrayal (Matt. xxvi.
49) ; by the mocking soldiers (Matt. xxvii. 49 ; Mark xv. 18 ; John
xix. 3) ; in the letter from the chief captain Lysias to the governor
Felix (Acts xxiii. 26) : it is also quoted as a salutation of every-
day life in 2 John 10, 11 ; and it is made use of in the Epistle of
James (i. 1). This Greek expression Χαίρειν is certainly spiri-
tualized by Christian use, and raised to its true and highest signification, just as the Israelitish שָׁלוֹם לְךָ in the mouth of the Lord :
here, however, it is a friendly mode of address to the Greek brethren,
and a greeting highly suited to the case.

Ver. 24. The ἐπειδή, *forasmuch*, opens in correct official style
the cause of the letter, and of the resolution arrived at. *As we have
heard*, or understood : thus with brief propriety the reception of the
embassy and question from Antioch is intimated. *Certain :* the
teachers of error, whom Luke in ver. 1 did not name, and as if in
rebuke throws them into the background as compared with the four
names in vers. 25 and 27 ; rebuking them, but yet at the same
time sparing them, by not recording their names reprehensively in
a permanent document, which might have again irritated them.
Certain from us : in these words the unnamed teachers of error
are half acknowledged by the apostolic assembly, and their fault is
to some extent laid upon the whole body, among whom, according
to ver. 5, a good many more such persons might be found ; at the
same time, the fact that these troublers belonged to their community
made it the duty and right of the latter to readjust what they had
done wrong. But these men *went out from them*, by their own
will, without being sent, so that they were no longer " of them "
(1 John ii. 19, iv. 1). And yet all that they did was done by
them as *coming from us*, under the false pretence of right and of

---

[1] As ch. xxi. 25 compared with ch. xvi. 4 shows.

R

authorization thereby. They have, contrary to our wish, *troubled you with words*—ἐτάραξαν λόγοις. This ταράσσειν, which is also used in Gal. v. 10, corresponds to the παρενοχλεῖν of James in ver. 19. The troubling and stirring up of a community living in quiet, taken by itself, would certainly be no sure sign of erroneous teaching; for the teaching which is effectual for the real edification of souls is often calculated to disturb a false repose. Therefore, as a proof of the falseness and error of their words, the bad consequences of them to the souls of the members of the church are immediately added; and then follows the mention of the false doctrine taught, with a most decisive contradiction of it.[1] It is as if they said: We can well believe, dear brethren, that these people coming from us, and thus recommending themselves to you, must have caused you much trouble by their words, and we willingly excuse your message of inquiry which testified to this trouble; indeed, we can well imagine that your hearts must have been troubled when ye were told that it was necessary, if ye would not forfeit salvation, that ye should adopt circumcision and the law. This expectation as to what ye ought to do is to be imputed to them only, and never entered into our minds. The forcible expression ἀνασκευάζειν does not occur in the Septuagint, and only on this occasion in the New Testament: according to Hesych. it corresponds with the word μετατιθέναι which occurs in Gal. i. 6; but the reference there is not quite the same as here. It is not here, *removing* or *taking away* your souls from anything, but *moving, disturbing, throwing into confusion* your souls: for ἀνασκευάζειν means to remove a vessel from its place, as a contrast to putting it in order; consequently to bring it into disorder and disturbance, the contrast to order and arrangement. Thus this word follows the ταράσσειν, in order to give the latter more force, and is, as V. Meyer truly remarks, the contrast to the "edification" spoken of in ch. ix. 31 and xx. 32. Remark, further, that ἀνασκευάζοντες and λέγοντες (explaining the λόγοι) are in the *present tense*; thus hinting that the teachers of false doctrine remained in Antioch. This first assembly, of course, neither desired nor were able to

---

[1] The expunging (so beloved by the modern critics) of the whole sentence, λέγοντες—τὸν νόμον, is difficult to be understood; because, indeed, then the whole letter would scarcely anywhere clearly express, and would only presuppose too briefly, what the question was about. Then, indeed, the decisive sentence in ver. 28 would have no foundation to understand it by; for the μηδὲν πλέον can be evidently only explained by some greater burden previously named.

exercise any other power than that of convincing argument and cogent advice. The infinitive περιτέμνεσθαι is correctly expressed by the words, *Ye must be circumcised;* for the contrast follows: *to whom we gave no such commandment.* But διαστέλλεσθαι does not here exactly mean to command; for Jerusalem would not desire to command in Antioch, in a hierarchical way like Rome, which afterwards took the place of the mother church.

Vers. 25-27. Now comes the conclusion to the ἐπειδή, the important first ἔδοξεν of this first δόγμα, proceeding from a council of the church of the New Testament. This ἔδοξεν ἡμῖν or *nobis placuit* is, in the first place, contrasted with the οὐ διεστειλάμεθα, and then prepares for the second actually decisive and momentous ἔδοξε in ver. 28. In the λέγοντες (ver. 24) there prevailed a false human δοκεῖν or *thinking* of individuals: now follows a just human conclusion arrived at by the whole church, a. ! in ver. 28 is added the holy *Placet* of the Holy Ghost, and of the unanimous community combined. *Being assembled together with one accord:* this translation obscures a delicate allusion in the original text, in which it says, After we had become unanimous—γενομένοις. It may certainly be also understood, After we had assembled ourselves together; but more exactly considered, it appears as if the assembly here confesses, so far as was compatible with the dignity of their letter, as to the disputation which had gone before, in which indeed this general ἔδοξε originated. The four bearers of the letter would probably give a full and open account of it; but care is taken that the letter itself should not appear to entirely conceal the preceding contest, by merely saying briefly, " We have resolved or thought right;" but instead of this, it intimates, " We resolved, after we became unanimous." It was perhaps not decided by a majority of votes, but became a unanimous matter after the holy teaching had vanquished the gainsayers. The ὁμοθυμαδόν is the New Testament sign-manual of a true community of Christ, as we have already seen in ch. i. 14, ii. 1. *To send chosen men unto you*—not one man only, but two at least, in addition to your two teachers who are now returning. It is not yet mentioned who and what they were: their responsibility is sufficiently attested by the choice. The beloved Barnabas and Paul must first receive their due attribute of corroborative praise; then the names of the joint-messengers modestly follow. Barnabas is here placed before Paul,[1] and both are called *men who have hazarded their lives for the name of our Lord Jesus*

---

[1] Although Luke subsequently, in ver. 35, again places Paul first.

Christ. Thus their beloved and eminent human names are made subordinate to the one name of the Lord, to which all honour is due; but it is also thereby intimated of them, that they rightly preached the name of the Lord only, and had shown themselves faithful in this ministry, even unto offering up their lives for it. Erroneous teachers disturb the souls of others; but true, faithful teachers give up their own lives for the ministry of the gospel (ch. xx. 24). The mode of expression used here can scarcely be taken only to mean, as Hess paraphrases it, " who have dedicated themselves with soul and body to the service of our Lord, the Messiah ;" but it must refer to the perils of death which they underwent at Iconium, Lystra, and elsewhere, on their first missionary journey. Judas and Silas were to announce to the Gentile brethren, by word of mouth, *the same things* (τὰ αὐτά). Now this announcement can hardly refer back to the praises of the two apostles [1] which had been just expressed, nor even to the mere assembly, and the cause of their being sent; but it points forward to the statement of these αὐτά, the real purport of the letter. It means: the same things which we now desire to transmit to you in a documentary form. Judas and Silas were to confirm the fact that the latter actually was the result of the unanimous resolution of the church at Jerusalem, and that Barnabas and Paul were loved and honoured there; and they were to remove every suspicion that any one might feel that these two had reported matters partially and in their own favour. They were, as living letters, to afford closer information and communication to any one who desired it, being corroborated by the letter which they brought, and they themselves also confirming the letter. Thus they were with their words to quiet those whom " those that went out " without authority had disturbed likewise by " words."

Vers. 28, 29. Now comes the decisive ἔδοξε, by which the κρίνειν of James in ver. 19 is denoted as the general decision of the whole church; cf. ch. xvi. 4, τὰ δόγματα τὰ κεκριμένα. The

---

[1] As (ingeniously supplying that which does not exist in ver. 27) Neander will have it: " They will state to you the same things which Paul and Barnabas have stated and taught to you ! " If ἀπαγγέλλειν cannot suitably stand for the oral relation of what had been determined on (we cannot conceive why), still less can it mean the preaching and teaching of that which had already been preached with so much power and blessing. It certainly did not enter into the idea of the apostolic council, to act as if they were confirming the words and works of Paul and Barnabas by the oral communications of a Judas and a Silas.

ἔδοξεν ἡμῖν may perhaps sound somewhat less decided and more feeble than κρίνομεν ἡμεῖς might have done; but it is strengthened by the addition, τῷ ἁγίῳ Πνεύματι. The assembly assumes to itself no real ἐντελλόμεθα or ἐπιτάσσομεν in the way worldly rulers would do (Luke xxii. 25, 26), and therefore does not even say —which would be an approach to it—ἡμεῖς κρίνομεν, as a development of the expression occurring in ver. 19. They do not desire to command; but they express their opinion in the way of a judgment, as desired by the brethren at Antioch, and "they think also that they have the Spirit of God" (1 Cor. vii. 12, 40). As a similar kind of expression to this (but certainly of a more forcible character when placed in the mouth of the whole assembly than when it occurs in the epistle of the Apostle Paul), we have here the prescriptive formula—*it seemed good to the Holy Ghost and to us.* We must, if possible, transfer ourselves into the fresh spiritual life of the early church, so as neither wrongly to dogmatize on this formula, nor with equal error to treat it as vain, proceeding as it did from the holy, childlike community of the Spirit. If the power and authority of the Lord Jesus Christ was present and effectual for decisive rebuke, when Paul, present in the spirit, united himself in the same sacred name with the assembly of the Corinthians; how much more must the Holy Ghost have spoken and decided in the holy assembly at Jerusalem, after they had become of one accord! We must therefore neither look upon this expression as a mere formula, as in the later councils; nor must we refine upon it, as if they said, The Holy Ghost instructed us in this in the house of Cornelius, and we now decide therefrom; as if they had been taught by that outpouring of the Holy Spirit, that these four items were to be specially imposed on the Gentile brethren! In this decretal formula now made use of, there is of course some allusive reference to the matters of fact which had been set forth by Peter, and to the Scripture that had been quoted by James, both being alike testimony of the Holy Spirit, by which testimony the assembly had been induced to come to a conclusion. The Holy Ghost leads and teaches the unanimous assembly by a reasonable consideration of the agreement existing between God's words and works, not in some (God knows how!) magical way, which the heterodox seem always to be in fear of. But the ἔδοξε of the Holy Ghost refers as much to the four requisitions of abstinence, as to the principal resolution which declared the liberation of the Gentiles; consequently it is always maintained that these four requisitions were made by the full authority of the Holy Ghost. The *personal* apprehension of the Holy Ghost, by which to Him, as to the assembly, an ἔδοξε might be fitting, need not first be remarked. It must also be noticed how the expression ἐπιτίθεσθαι βάρος connects on with Peter's words in ver. 10, and how the comforting declaration of the freedom of the Gentile brethren from the yoke of the law, which was beforehand intimated in ver. 24, is only expressed by the words μηδὲν πλέον. For, after all that God had effected in the souls of the Gentiles, it was almost a self-evident matter : the brethren at Antioch had the Holy Spirit, which had testified to them of their freedom from the law ; and the church at Jerusalem was not the first to liberate them, no legitimate " binding " having pre-existed. The phrase " no greater " serves as a transition to what follows, which thus appears to be the special and principal import of the letter; the freedom from the law having been conceded simply by this one important expression, " no greater burden." The four requisitions of abstinence are still called a *burden,* βάρος; but, under the existing circumstances, according to the opinion of the Holy Ghost and the assembly at Jerusalem, they are a *necessary* burden. Whether (according to Bengel's remark) the ἐπί in ἐπάναγκες somewhat softens the idea of necessity, we are inclined to doubt from the usage of the language elsewhere ; at all events, in this word there is a stringent reason for the actual commands which are implied in the term ἐπιτίθεσθαι. The disturbers had said that the Gentiles must be circumcised, or else they would not be saved: this resolution, on the contrary, affirms that they *need* only keep these four commands ; and that if they do not do so, that they will certainly not act as saints, and according to love. After the four points, the reasons for which we have considered above (ver. 20), are stated in succession, there follows a fraternal and frank exhortation to a frank obedience, based on grounds in which the other side of the question is gently and delicately touched upon ; that, namely, by which a failure in these four points is represented as not only offensive to the Jews, but also as dangerous to the Gentiles themselves. *From which if ye keep yourselves*—and especially from all association with the last-named item, fornication—*ye shall do well.* It does not exactly say " ye shall do *rightly,*" as opposed to doing *sinfully,* but " ye shall do *well,*" conformably to the existing circumstances both external and internal, wisely and faithfully in love and foresight (equivalent to καλῶς ποιήσετε; cf. ch. x. 33, 3 John 6). In this unfettered renunciation, ye are to keep yourselves from some things, innocent perhaps in themselves, for the sake of the consciences of your brethren, in order that God's work may not be disturbed; and your recompense for this will be, that the Jewish brethren will "lay upon you no greater burden," *i.e.* the remainder of the yoke of the law. But ye should keep yourselves from these things with cautious shunning, for the sake also of your own infirmities, for they may easily entangle you again in heathenism! Thus, in addition to the implied supposition of the one ground for the command (the necessity of avoiding any offence to the Jews), the other (the personal danger of the Gentile Christians) is at least hinted at. This is evidently the meaning of the concluding words, as if they said, "From motives of love to us, keep yourselves from these things, the abstinence from which will not only not hurt you, but will be conducive to your personal well-being." The formula, "ye shall do well,"[1] also implies the needful modification of the expression "to lay upon you" in ver. 28, far indeed removed from the *Anathema sit* of subsequent councils; so that in this first document of Christian church government, worthy as it is of imitation, liberty and command are thoroughly united and blended with one another. The whole letter concludes with the every-day but now sanctified salutation, "Farewell!"—used not without a covert reference to that which precedes. For any one who *does* well, he will also *fare* well; whoever acts according to love will be saved both here and hereafter,—an infinite difference indeed from the inflexible decree of the Judaists, which declared that, unless they adopted circumcision and the law, they could not be saved!

Vers. 30–33. The letter was delivered to the general assembly at Antioch, in order that it might from thence proceed on its further course to the other Gentile churches, conformably to its superscription (see afterwards, ch. xvi. 4). The good wishes expressed in it were soon realized: for *when they had read it, they rejoiced for the consolation;* and being declared free from the whole yoke, willingly took upon themselves the slight burden. It was not until afterwards, and in other churches, that the resolution of the assembly at Jerusalem needed any further explanation and confirmation through the teaching and epistles of Paul. Barnabas and Paul appear to have been the actual deliverers of the letter as an answer to the inquiry sent to Jerusalem, as Judas and Silas who

---

[1] Which by no means goes so far as to imply, "therein ye do our will," nor "therein will ye do a pleasure to us."

accompanied them do not make their appearance until ver. 32. They *were also prophets themselves*, like Barnabas and Paul, that is, endowed with the gifts of teaching and exhortation. It may also mean that they were filled with the spirit of gladdening—παρά- κλησις—the same as was the letter written in the Holy Ghost : the words παράκλησις and παρεκάλεσαν—the like expression being used both of the effects of the letter and the words of the two messengers—seem to point to this. The *letter* and the *words* were indeed that which was *sent* from Jerusalem, the reception and result of which Luke is relating. He also does this by referring, in the expression διὰ λόγου πολλοῦ, to the διὰ λόγου in the letter. And when we are told that they were dismissed *in peace* to those that sent them, perhaps an Israelitish שָׁלוֹם לָכֶם is hinted at as a reply to the Greek Χαίρειν in ver. 23.

XX.

PAUL AT PHILIPPI.

(Chap. XVI. 12–40.)

HIS REMARKABLE WORDS TO A SOOTHSAYING SPIRIT, TO THE
GAOLER, AND TO THE MAGISTRATES' OFFICERS.

VERS. 1–5. Paul's *second* missionary journey, undertaken (after ch. xv. 34–41) in the first place as a visitation of the churches already founded, led him in the sequel to *Europe*.[1] Luke's narrative, which from the beginning aimed at this point, now entirely leaves the history of the confirmation and spread of

---

[1] As to the " sharp contention " (παροξυσμός) between Paul and Barnabas, related in ch. xv., which led to the separation between the two allied " apostles," we will only say here, that for our part we do not impute equal fault to both— indeed, to Paul (in the chief matter, even taking into account Jas. iii. 2) we impute no fault at all—because we look upon their respective conduct as exactly described in Luke's expressions, ἐβουλεύσατο and ἠξίου, vers. 37, 38 (the latter not, as in the Vulgate, " rogabat," but *æquum censebat*) ; in ver. 40 also we find that the voice of the church is in favour of Paul. The apostle educated his assistants with a wholesome strictness : he consequently does not forgive the previous desertion of John (Mark), ch. xiii. 5, 13, so quickly as his relative Barnabas. (Subsequently he praises Mark, 2 Tim. iv. 11.)

Christ's church in Jerusalem and Judea, in order to turn its attention to the further journeys of Paul (in which Luke soon took a share) : it does not revert to Jerusalem until ch. xxi. 17, when Paul returned thither. A quick succession of governors, after the death of Agrippa the elder, afresh vexed the church ; already the preludes of the last troubles had begun to show themselves ; Judaism was once more heaving itself up in spasmodic strivings, just before its fall ; there were not perhaps many signs and wonders, or any important increase of the church to be recorded, after all that were susceptible of it had been delivered out of the corrupt mass of the " perverse generation." The apostles appear in part to have turned to foreign countries ; only James, the brother of the Lord, patiently waited with his church for the coming of the " Judge which standeth before the door " (Jas. v. 9).

When Paul revisited Derbe and Lystra, he found that the youthful Timothy had grown up in the truth, and had obtained general praise. He had been brought up by his mother and grandmother to believe in the God of Israel (2 Tim. i. 5) ; but owing to the unwillingness of his Gentile father (now probably dead), remained still uncircumcised : he had been converted to Jesus during the first visit of the apostle. Special " prophecies " (1 Tim. i. 18, iv. 14) confirmed the keen-sighted apostle in the belief that a peculiar gift for the ministry of the gospel might be implanted in this young disciple by the laying on of hands. He therefore took him and caused him to be circumcised,[1] in order to remove any cause of offence on the part of the Jews. Thus, on the one hand, in the wisdom of love he gives way not only to the Jewish brethren, but also to the whole of his own people, if by any means he may save some ; and, on the other hand, he does not omit to deliver copies of the apostolical decision as to their freedom from circumcision and the law, to the Gentile brethren whom he visits, and to recommend them to obey the four requisitions. *And so were the churches established in the faith, and increased in number daily.*

Vers. 6–12. They carry the gospel throughout Phrygia and Galatia ; Paul, indeed, in " the infirmity of the flesh," though vouched for by the deeds of the Spirit, and received " as an angel of God," indeed " as Christ Jesus " Himself by the Galatians, to whom he had brought salvation (Gal. iii. 5, iv. 13–15). Luke

---

[1] The text might be understood to the effect that Paul himself performed the operation, as was allowed to every Israelite.

passes over all this but cursorily : his narrative, conformably to his plan, hastens on towards Europe. The zealous apostle is attracted by the important *Asia Proconsularis,* and by Ephesus, the celebrated chief city of heathendom. But the right moment had not yet come for introducing the gospel there (as was subsequently so fully done, ch. xix. 1, 10), something else being then reserved for Paul. Their mouths were closed for the Lord's work in Asia by the Holy Ghost, who guided the traveller on the whole journey, and (through Paul) directed also his two associates, who could well discriminate between the spiritual leading and their own ideas. They essayed to enter the frontiers of Mysia, as if through Bithynia to turn back to Galatia, or further on to Byzantium ; but the Spirit (of Jesus), with its clear, internal voice opposing their own purposes and attempts, *suffered them not,* and pointed out the external difficulties to them as hindrances from God, not from Satan, as 1 Thess. ii. 18. Thus guided and directed, they are compelled to go down to the north coast of Mysia, as far as Troas, passing by inhabitants in all the cities who certainly needed help and salvation. Here, at Troas, having arrived at the place of passage to Europe, they are forthwith shown whither they are to go. The next night (διὰ τῆς νυκτὸς) Paul, now with the clearest manifestation, sees a vision—a representation or an appearance of a man of Macedonia,[1] who, speaking in the name and as representative of his nation, addresses to the apostle the audible supplication, *Come over into Macedonia, and help us !* Thus God allows this Macedonian to express the need which the Macedonians themselves did not recognise so far as to desire salvation ; thus also elsewhere God makes suggestions as messengers of His salvation to many a man, people, or country, whose longing need was only silently expressed. It is doubtful whether there was *more* desire for salvation and preparation of the heart to be found in Macedonia than in Asia Minor ; at all events, we may gather that the need and desire of men, as in some way or other coming to meet the word of salvation, is referred to in this expression, *Come over !* Thus is the gospel as well as Paul summoned into Europe.——*Help us !* In these words, a Paul, under the circumstances then existing, can only understand the preaching of the gospel, although Macedonia itself might wish for a very different

---

[1] That this Macedonian represented all the Greeks and Romans—indeed, the entire West—is proved by Baumgarten in his way with too diffuse and far-fetched reasons.

kind of help. He is able to distinguish with certainty between the divine vision answering his inquiries and prayers, and any natural dream likely enough in his position. When he communicated his vision to his companions, they too, after a considerate examination of the whole course of events since ver. 6, are likewise certain that, at the Lord's call, they are bound immediately to seek a passage to Macedonia, and to preach the gospel there. At this point, Luke, the narrator, modestly comes forward all at once in his own person, in the word " we : " [1] he had probably joined them first at Troas, as in ver. 8 it says that " *they* came down to Troas." From henceforth, therefore, everything is much more copiously related. Paul is the leader in the expedition, having received the command, " Come and help us," which applied to all of them : all, therefore, are to preach the gospel, each taking his share. First, the converted Pharisee and persecutor, the great apostle to the Gentiles, the mighty instrument of the Spirit of grace, ever increasing in might ; next to him, Silas the prophet, who came from Jerusalem in the place of Barnabas ; then the circumcised Timothy, an Israelite as his grandmother before him, and yet no stranger to his paternal Gentilism—the right man to act as mediator between Jews and Gentiles ; lastly Luke, the uncircumcised physician of Antioch. We see how judiciously this little auxiliary band, sent out into a country occupied by the enemy, is composed of men of various orders, and thus well prepared for every kind of association. They now sail with a *straight course*, without any stopping, with a fair wind as a good omen,[2] over against the island of Samothracia across the sea to Neapolis, and from thence, because the Spirit further directed them, up the Strymon to Philippi. This was the aim of their journey since they left Galatia. Philippi was one of the principal cities in Macedonia beyond the Strymon (*Macedonia Augustalis*), perhaps bearing the title πρώτη,[3] at all events enjoy-

---

[1] For we can never believe that, in every place where we find this " we," an account of the journey by Timothy, or some one else, has been adopted without examination or alteration ; on the contrary, nothing is more simple or more dignified than this modesty, unfortunately so seldom found, by which the author introduces himself without name.

[2] Εὐθυδρομεῖν here, as in ch. xxi. 1, is equivalent to ὀρθοπλοεῖν—a good voyage.

[3] Which several cities of the same province had received as a distinction. Other interpretations—that it was the first city in the direction of their journey (as Neapolis was only the haven to Philippi)—appear to us to be little suitable to the mode of expression.

ing the privileges of a Roman colony. Here there were waiting
for the gospel which was prepared for them, a Lydian woman in
the Jewish place for prayer, who from her origin was called " a
seller of purple," and the gaoler in the prison of the city. Here,
too, was to be established the first church of Jesus in Europe—a
church which subsequently was so specially blessed and praised.
But the apostles *abode certain days* in this city, which the Spirit
had finally pointed out to them.

Vers. 13–15. Not denying themselves some rest after their
hurried journey, and having waited till the Sabbath in order to
address themselves first to the few Jews or proselytes, the four
strangers, who were summoned and sent as *helpers*, went out from
the city to a river, where, according to custom, prayer was wont to
be made on His day by those who knew the God of Israel. In
places where no synagogue could or might be built, the *proseucha*,
i.e. place of prayer, was arranged outside the heathen city, close to
the pure water, for the Jews and God-fearing Gentiles. With this
place the gospel of Christ might very feasibly be associated, for it
disdained no expedient or means of union which, through God's
hand, might be placed in its way.[1] At this *proseucha* at Philippi,
there were on this occasion, just as now at so many times of
prayer, only *women ;* but it has often been through women that the
gospel has found its first hearing. The apostles sat down and
spake to those who resorted thither in a frank and friendly way as
to the salvation which they had to transmit to them. And a proselyte, named Lydia (very probably so surnamed from her native
country, on account of her trade, being from the Lydian city
Thyatira, celebrated for its manufacture of purple), heard them
with particular attention ; for the Lord, whose Spirit of grace
alone produces all faith in susceptible minds, opened the inner
ears of her heart, so that she gave heed with understanding and
willingness to the things which were forcibly and clearly spoken
by Paul (especially).[2] Her faith is speedily established by the
rejoiced messengers of salvation ; and this woman of Asiatic descent
becomes the first-fruits of Europe, and is baptized with her whole
house, or family. That children formed a part of the family of
this woman (who must have been a widow, as she alone is named),

---

[1] " Some particular institution or place may often for a long time appear to
be not especially productive of benefit, but yet some time or other it may do
good service in the furtherance of the gospel."—RIEGER.

[2] Chrysostomus : Τὸ μὲν οὖν ἀνοῖξαι τοῦ Θεοῦ, τὸ δὲ προσέχειν αὐτῆς.

and that these children, following the custom of the Jews as to circumcision, were also baptized with her, is rendered all the more
probable by the fact that actual believing is spoken of only as
regards the woman herself. The new Christian is very properly
ambitious to prove her faith by her love. She stringently begs her
teachers, that if they have (by baptism) acknowledged her as one
faithful to the Lord, they must come into her house, and abide
there some time, that she may minister to them, and learn from
them! *And she constrained us* (παρεβιάσατο, cf. Luke xxiv. 29)
is briefly and artlessly added by Luke. The apostles might have
desired to show first, that mere lodging and entertainment were not
their aim, and that they were somewhat doubtful as to this new and
important step. But the same Lord which had spoken to them so
clearly in favour of Macedonia and Philippi, spake to them now
also, although indirectly, through the loving prayer of their first
disciple, and let them know that the hospitality which she longed
to show them was fit and proper after her baptism.

Vers. 16-18. When the apostles were going from the house of
this seller of purple (where, according to ver. 40, they soon met
with further successful work) down to the place of prayer, a damsel
met them who, according to Luke's certain account, had a *spirit of
divination*, or a spirit which uttered through her (in a ventriloquial
manner) oracles which were ascribed to Apollo.[1] The soothsaying
of this damsel was a source of much profit to her masters, who
carried on a kind of trade in her answers to questions. This girl,
who probably against her will and consent was possessed by this
spirit and thus made use of, followed Paul and his companions
immediately she met them, and called out loudly, as those uttering
oracles were wont to cry out, *These men are the servants of the most
high God, which show unto you* (Philippians) *the way of salvation*[2]
(or, a way of help or safety)! A truly just testimony, and har-
monizing most remarkably with the words of the man of Macedonia in the vision, also not entirely without value to the strangers
who were introducing themselves with difficulty into the supersti-
tiously heathen city! Therefore the messengers of truth at first
bore with the voice of this deceitful spirit, which flattered them
from motives of fear and roguery, but yet therein spoke the truth.

[1] Hesychius: πύθων ἐγγαστρίμυθος, ἢ ἐγγαστρίμαντις. Plutarchus: τοὺς
ἐγγαστριμύθους εὐρυκλέας πάλαι, νυνὶ πύθωνας προσαγορευομένους.

[2] We (with Lachmann) hold to the reading ὑμῖν, as ἡμῖν would sound
strangely as spoken by the spirit in the name of the maid and the other men.

By this pertinacity an impression was made which might have reached the ears even of the keeper of the prison, as he showed subsequently in ver. 30. But when the stupidly cunning spirit, by the daily repetition of this cry, betrayed that its only intention was to make itself important, and perhaps even to draw the apostles into communication with it, then Paul became weary of the thing, and perceived what he ought to do in the matter, following the example of Jesus (Mark i. 34). Speedily deciding, he turns round to the damsel running after them, and says—not to her, but to the spirit which he knew was in her—*I command thee, in the name of Jesus Christ, to come out of her!* I know thee well, thou miserable wicked spirit; and, in the power of the most high God, whom in earnest thou knowest not, I am thy lord, and am far enough from needing that thou shouldst give thy authority as a witness for me! And I command thee in the *name of Jesus Christ*, whom thou couldst not name—which I, however, preach as the name of salvation given by God—I command thee not only to be now silent about us, but to entirely leave this damsel, and to discontinue thy sooth-saying, now that at last thou hast said something true!—*And he came out the same hour.* Thus, in the first place, the testimony derived from darkness is made use of for the purposes of light; but then silence is imposed on the merely self-proclaiming spirit of deceit, which becomes dangerous to the truth. The same thing is the case now with regard to many of the phenomena of magnetism so called. Luke and Paul both testify that this was no pretended spirit, but an actual one, which first spake, and then was compelled to be silent, and to go out; also that the girl was no mere impostor through whom it was *believed* that Apollo spake. All this is stated so literally, that any other explanation of the matter by believing readers of Scripture only affords a proof how far and how deeply a sceptical theology has corrupted the sense of truth among us. If it was nothing but a delusion, why did not the messenger of truth express himself just as our modern enlighteners do, and say, " I desire that ye relinquish this superstition—the idea of believing that there is really a spirit here?" But instead of this, he said *to the spirit,* "I command *thee* to come out of *her!*" and Luke adds, " *he* came out."

Vers. 19–21. The numerous masters of the damsel who had shared in the profits of her soothsaying, of course experienced the alteration which had taken place; but in it they did not recognise the expulsion of a wicked and conquered spirit through the higher power of the most high God, to whose servants even their damsel had testified. They appear, as genuine, enlightened heathen of that time, to have had but little faith in the utterances of the spirit; at least they had no foreboding of a " way of salvation" which might be necessary for them, but only a blind covetousness after earthly gain, so that whoever injured them in this was not to be asked for any other kind of help, nor to be in any way honoured or cared for. All that they perceived in the departure of the spirit was, *that the hope of their gains was gone!* At the same time, revenge and persecution against those that had expelled the spirit were both resolved on and put in execution. It was perhaps an unprecedented thing in Philippi, this expulsion of a spirit by means of a few short words ; yet it merely excited to hostility the perversely mistaken minds of those who in general scarcely knew the distinction between truth and deceit. We have here the first account of any *Gentile* hostility against the gospel which was not in the first instance stirred up by the Jews ; and it is a prelude to the uproar of the silversmiths at Ephesus. The men who had been injured in their means of livelihood seize the two chief persons, Paul and Silas ; Timothy and Luke, as their younger companions, are not noticed, or perhaps did not place themselves in their way. Luke now falls into the background in the narrative, and the " we" and " us" do not occur again until ch. xx. 5. The strangers, who had done no hurt to any one, but had only preached salvation, had been accustomed for many days to make their way through the heathen city without molestation ; but now disappointed selfishness at once drags them into the *Forum* before the rulers. They are brought before the colonial authorities—the Decurions, Duumvirs, or Prætors—with an accusation which was conceived in direct opposition to the testimony of the spirit of divination : " These men, as officious strangers, make a disturbance in our city, which ye are bound to guard and keep !" Thus, so soon after God's salvation had presented itself in Macedonia, the same accusation is brought against His servants as against their Master, the Saviour Himself. It is called " a disturbance of quiet," when an attempt is made to help lost man : spirits of all kinds may be permitted loudly to carry on their calling in the streets and ways; but directly a higher authority manifests itself, directly the idle hope of covetousness is done away with, then it is considered an uproar—then is our city in danger ! Oh that this were not the case even now, so many centuries after, in many a city of Christendom, just as it was then

in the Roman colony! After they had mentioned their privileged
city to the rulers, with clever calculation, they add that these
strangers are Jews. It is always these unquiet, godless Jews, who
have, alas, been already enough favoured, and in every disorder
should be sharply punished; it is these Jews who would excite this
fresh disturbance. This is the alteration of the Pythian utterance
which said that they were "the servants of the most high God;"
this is the way in which their blindness can and will understand it.
The conclusion of the spirit's cry, " which show unto you the way
of salvation," is also maliciously altered as follows: *And teach
customs* (ἔθη) *which are not lawful for us to receive or observe,
being Romans!* Even the gospel of the living God is considered
to aim at new customs, because the heathen had no other idea of
religion or of a way of salvation, and in the Jews' belief they saw
nothing but " customs." " To receive or observe " the same, οὐκ
ἔξεστιν ἡμῖν: in these words the complainants suggest to the judges
the law which they are bound to follow; they remind them of the
Roman law against foreign customs and new religions, which were
not allowed to be introduced by private persons without high permission; and they make a haughty appeal to the colonial authorities
of the city, which these men are disturbing. The poor Romans!
Bengel remarks on this: " Frequens exceptio civitatis mundi
adversus regnum Dei. Hodienum Romanitas Paulo repugnat."
The expulsion of the spirit, which testified rather in favour of
than against these men, is, however, not mentioned.

Vers. 22–25. In consequence of the artful language of the
disappointed oracle-dealers, *the multitude rose up together against
them,* the so-called Jews: the magistrates, unaccustomed to make
any very exact investigation in such cases, without any further
question do as the people wish; not, however, without showing some
personal ill-feeling towards these presumed trouble-makers. For
they rent their clothes from them, and caused them in the first
place to be soundly scourged. The apostles are silent both during
the tumult of the people and the highly unjust and undignified
conduct of the judges: they patiently accept the reproach of
Christ, when they might readily have brought forward their Roman
citizenship in opposition to the so-called " Romans" (ver. 21).
The messenger of Christ may often be able to testify better for
his good cause, and make a more forcible counter-impression, by
patiently receiving the reproach which is cast upon him, than by
availing himself of any earthly means of defence, which the heathen

only interpret according to the flesh. *And when they had laid
many stripes upon them* (there was no law of Moses here to fix a
limit to the number), *they cast them into prison, charging the gaoler
to keep them safely,* until it was decided what further course should
be taken with them. The rough gaoler, who was accustomed to
trouble himself very little as to the guilt or innocence of the
prisoners handed over to him, obeyed the command as strictly as
possible : he not only thrust them into the innermost, securest, and
worst dungeon ; but, as it seems, that he might sleep in security
from any possibility of their escape, he even went beyond his
orders, *and made their feet fast in the stocks.*[1] Having them now,
as he thought, in complete security (cf. ἠσφαλίσατο with the
ἀσφαλῶς, ver. 23), he cheerfully laid himself down to sleep.
Sleep like this certainly could not be enjoyed by Paul and Silas,
after their " many stripes," and suffering as they were from the
painful restraint of the stocks; but the spirit of prayer exalted
their spirits far above all the sorrows of the flesh. Paul had been
once before delivered from death by the Lord when at Lystra, and
their present journey into Macedonia had been distinctly pointed
out to them by the certain call of the same Lord ;[2] Silas, too, is
upraised by Paul to a pitch of joy in the sufferings of his ministry,
which perhaps the weaker John Mark might hardly have attained
to. Midnight finds these two servants of the most high God
engaged in *prayer,* nay, even in loud songs of praise to their God,
whom they could not but extol even in circumstances like these.
Their fellow-prisoners in this innermost dungeon, doubtless wicked
malefactors, or perhaps also the other inmates of the neighbouring
cells, heard and wondered at these sounds, so unprecedented in
such a place.[3] Which of them could have anticipated what the
next moment was to bring forth ? " After the dark day and its
events, the still midnight brings the true light" (Rieger).

Vers. 26-28. *And suddenly there was a great earthquake, so that
the foundations of the prison were shaken.* In Jerusalem, after the
angel of the Lord at high command had led out the innocent, the
prison-doors were again closed with all due order ; in Philippi, on

[1] " The heavens are silent hitherto. Who does not know that silence of the
heavens which is wont to precede the thunder-clap ?"—LAVATER.

[2] " We are intended to help them here in this country, and so in this country
we too shall be helped." This was their comforting thought, as Menken says.

[3] " It was the music by which the gospel made its entry among those who
were condemned and cast out by society."—DA COSTA.

the contrary, where angels are not known of, there must be an earthquake to testify to the whole city in favour of these servants of God, as the inhabitants would not put faith in the statement of their own oracle about them.——*And immediately all the doors were opened, and every one's bands were loosed.* The presence of the apostles among these prisoners is the means of bringing the gospel even to them, and the God of their life calls to them in this most forcible language of miracles: "Continue to listen to these men, my servants, and the bands of your minds (*animorum vincula*) will also be loosed!"[1] But the keeper of the prison wakes up out of his sleep, and sees at the first glance that all the doors are standing open: he draws out his sword, and would have killed himself. In his first terror, the only thing he could imagine was that the prisoners had escaped, and that he would have to suffer their punishment (ch. xii. 19). Remark the fierce, savage, daring nature of this man, who had previously been so ready with the stocks, who even at night had his sword close by him, and though just roused up out of sleep, immediately thinks of self-murder. Who would have thought how near this man now was to salvation, by means of the wonderful mercy which snatched him from the very brink of hell into which he desired at once to plunge himself, and fitted him, even on earth, to be a denizen of heaven? Paul can see, perhaps, through the doors what the gaoler is about to do; but the latter sees only the open doors, and does not perceive that the prisoners are still there. The gaoler was dazzled by fright; the apostle was enlightened by the Spirit, so as to be perhaps at that moment gifted with a preter-natural sight. Then the apostle calls with a loud voice, penetrating even to the sleeping-room, and uses words which are calculated to put an immediate stop to the crime.——*Do thyself no harm* (in the Greek with μηδὲν standing first for emphasis). Thus he recalls to the gaoler's consideration what he is about to do, and shows a kindly sympathy with him; at the same time, with apostolical thoughtful-ness, explaining that this miracle of God was not intended to do harm to any one. The Philippians, and especially their gaoler, have certainly done harm enough to the apostles; but the God of salva-tion who sent them does not desire to avenge His messengers by doing harm to their enemies, but only to vindicate them by saving many a family in Philippi. *For we are all here:* this follows as the appropriate reason for the first call to stay his hand. Paul, with

---

[1] Non uni sed vinctis omnibus, ut scirent, apostolos et sibi et aliis esse utiles, et per eos solvi animorum vincula.——GROTIUS.

complete humility, at the very moment of the earthquake which
had taken place *for him*, classes himself with all the other prisoners
and malefactors who were there, and says to the gaoler: " Be not
anxious about us; we do not wish to escape from you!" It was
perhaps quite natural that all the other prisoners, who had first
listened to the songs of praise, and afterwards felt the sudden earthquake opening all the doors and loosening all the fetters, should not
at first have ventured to do anything more than look at and listen
to these wonderful men, and wait for any further events that might
take place. Paul might *imagine* that all the prisoners were there,
but he could hardly have *seen* it; at all events, the same God who
raised the earthquake, could suggest at the moment these authoritative and certain words. The prisoners also thus received a kind
of direction from their inspired companion to remain where they
were, and not to think of escaping, which, besides, might not have
been possible for the malefactors after such an earthquake as this
was.

Vers. 29-31. Then the affrighted gaoler comes to himself,
and fully awakes—soon to receive a still higher awakening. He
calls for a light from some of his also awakened household, in order
to see clearly how things actually stood; he springs up speedily out
of his chamber, and comes among the prisoners with all his proper
official boldness. But he is immediately seized with trembling, from
the agony of his own conscience, when he now on close inspection
sees that all the bands are loosed, and that Paul and Silas, the men
he had only the day before so cruelly ill-treated, are standing before him full of dignity, like gods. All he can do is to fall down
at their feet (or before them). Ay, at those feet which not long
before he had fastened in the stocks! And when they naturally
had raised him up again, he immediately leads these clients of a
higher Power than his out of the disgraceful dungeon, probably
into the court of the prison. And now comes his remarkable expression to them: *Sirs* (or lords, masters, κύριοι), *what must I do
to be saved?* The day before he would not have addressed them
with this title. But now, even before he knew any details as to
who they may be, he feels compelled to give them this usual term
of honour, as if to ask their pardon for having fancied that he was
their κύριος. What, then, shall I now do? This question seems
very natural, and fitly joins on to the apostle's exclamation, " Do
thyself no harm!" But the addition to it, " to be saved," appears
to many to go too far, and to appear almost impossible, as coming

from the lips of this heathen. It is, of course, quite possible that
the ἵνα σωθῶ might mean nothing more than this : If I am to " do
myself no harm "—and, now I am come to myself, I no longer
desire it—what am I to do, so that no further harm may arise to
me out of this earthquake, and the bursting open of my prison,
and that I may be able to come out safe from the whole matter ?
Paul might (in ver. 31) have interpreted what he said in a higher
sense, and have given a reply to the bewildered man which was
very different to anything that he asked or intended. But it
appears to us, that a demand after the means of earthly deliverance, made at a moment like this, would be more unpsychological
and wonderful, than a sudden, vehement inquiry after eternal
salvation. Let Rosenmüller ask : Hominem paganum de æterna
salute cogitasse, credendum ? but we know that the heathen in
their consciences were not ignorant of the " judgment of God,"
and knew that sinners were " worthy of death " (Rom. i. 32) ; and
consequently, in a moment of sudden terror, might ask for deliverance from God's punishment. And on this occasion there was a
sudden terror under very peculiar circumstances. This rude man,
sleeping in full security, had been roused up from his bed by an
earthquake which burst open all the doors ; he had drawn his
sword for the purpose of self-murder, and had been, as it were, on
the brink of death ; he had been alternately elevated and depressed
in his inmost nature, first in his bold attempt at springing in upon
his prisoners, and then in his prostrate trembling. Might not all
these things have startled him internally also, and roused him out of
his unconcern for his sins, and, as it were, brought to the surface the
concealed depths of his conscience, disturbing all the groundwork
of his previous confidence ? All the sins of his former life, especially
those which he had committed against the prisoners in that gaol,
down to the ill-treatment of Paul and Silas on the previous evening,
and his own attempt at suicide a few moments before, all seemed
to lay hold upon him in the anguish of his heart : something he had
never felt before, the powerful efficacious prehension of the Spirit of
grace, penetrates his being. He is standing before the men whom
the inspired damsel had for many days proclaimed as preaching the
" way of *salvation;*" this testimony, hardly understood before, now
breaks in upon him with peculiar force. If in our psychology we
accept the working of the Divine Spirit, what can be more psychologically correct than the question of the gaoler, asking how he may
escape the punishment of the mighty Godhead who is protecting

those who had been ill-used by him? and this question is, in fact, his inquiry after everlasting, spiritual salvation.[1]

The answer of the apostles (which was certainly expressed by Paul) is brief, simple, and precise, without any kind of circumlocution. Why is it that the preachers of Christ ever give any other? The apostles do not question the awakened sinner for some time as to what he intends and understands by his inquiry, but they immediately receive it in its best sense. Where the Spirit of God works speedily and forcibly like an earthquake, do not intervene with prolonged and tedious catechizing and formulas. *Believe:* that is the first thing which thou shouldst do. In the first place, put faith in all that we shall preach to thee about our and thy Saviour. We are not thy *lords,* as thou callest us: there is one Lord over all, who hath sent this earthquake for the assistance of us His servants, and hath now put this question in thy mouth. Thou art not to believe in us only, but in the Lord Jesus Christ through our words—in Him[2] who lives almighty, and is and will be near to thee. Believe in Him, that He may be thy Lord—He who hath redeemed and will save thee; and then from this faith the *doing* the commands of thy *Lord* will surely follow. First of all, indeed, baptism must follow the penitence which is contained and expressed in thy question; then, when thou art become a disciple, thou must observe all that the Master has commanded. But it is not this "doing" which *saves,* but *faith* only. Believe, and thou shalt be saved—not thou only, but also *thy house.* By suicide thou wouldst have brought destruction both on thyself and thy family; but by a believing adoption of the way of salvation, which we show and open to you in Jesus Christ, thou canst save thyself and all thine house, for thy family are in the same misery of sin which thou now feelest; and if thou truly believest, thou wilt long to communicate this salvation to them also, and they too will be saved as thou (it is a matter of course), if they only likewise believe.

Vers. 32–34. After this first courage-inspiring answer, the more exact sense of which he could at first scarcely understand, they[3]

---

[1] Rieger says: "The former words, 'Come over, and help us,' were in that same hour reproduced in the heart of the gaoler to his great profit."

[2] Χριστόν, indeed, is now to be expunged; and it might be possible that the man Jesus only, in whom salvation was concluded, should have been here named to the heathen without the Jewish expression being added.

[3] *They* spake. It is thus remarkably expressed in ver. 31 also, giving Silas a share in the matter.

naturally *spake unto him the word of the Lord*—of this Lord
whom they had just named to him ; and they also spake *to all that
were in his house*, including (it must be understood) the other
prisoners. The prison was turned into a church, and the apostles
praised and confessed their God after the earthquake, just as they
had done before it.   Thus worthily the Lord introduced His
gospel into Philippi in the very abode of unrighteousness.   All
this took place in one and the same hour—after midnight.   Soon
after, the gaoler, influenced by the knowledge of Jesus the Messiah,
preached to him by the apostles in the court of the prison, more
and more reverted to a state of peace and right thinking ; and
induced by his new faith to feel for the sufferings of others, and to
exercise works of love,[1] took care of the preachers, and washed the
blood from their stripes.   But the latter also wash him (perhaps
with a portion of the same water) from his sins, and he was baptized,[2] *with all his* (his family and domestics, but, as it appears, *not*
the prisoners at the same time, which was very judicious).   Luke
concludes the verse emphatically with the word παραχρῆμα.   Our
present missionaries, when they feel that God's Spirit is working in
them and round them, might believe with greater confidence than
they usually do in the faith of their hearers, and not procrastinate
the sacrament of grace longer than is necessary.   The newly baptized man becomes more and more confident, and therefore more
and more loving towards the " lords," as he called them, who are
now become his brethren in *the Lord ;* and thus the cruel tormentor
is now become the kind host.   Even in the middle of the night
he spreads a table of refreshment for the apostles, who had doubtless been dragged off to the *forum* before their evening meal, and
the convert is filled with an entirely new and divine joy that he is
permitted to sit down to table with the servants of Jesus Christ,
who had shown him the way of salvation ; and his whole house
rejoices with him that he had become a believer in the true and
merciful God.   He is no longer anxious about the consequences of
the liberation of these men, who had been handed over to his safe

---

[1] " It would have been very excusable for him, even if he had not thought
of their stripes and wounds, their hunger and thirst, for unutterably great
things had broken in upon his soul that night.   It is all the more acceptable in
him, that, under the pressure of his new feelings, he did not think of himself
alone."—MENKEN.

[2] It may be remarked against the present Baptists, that no tank in the
court of the prison, nor any immersion, is spoken of here.

keeping. He could not perhaps foresee the events recorded in ver. 35; but yet, in his joyful confidence, he believes that the God who has so far brought everything to pass will finally settle the matter. The sins of his past life are washed away in baptism, and he looks to the future with the confidence of one who is reconciled by faith. He can therefore, like a child, enjoy the present, and can also for the first time " eat his meat with gladness and singleness of heart" (ch. ii. 46). Remark well that here too, as in ver. 15, with regard to the house of Lydia, the faith of the head of the family only is expressly mentioned, although in this case the word is spoken to some who could not all have been minors.[1] But the same thing occurs : the *entire family* is included, and not a word or hint is given that little children were excluded. The apostles receive into the church the other members of the household of a master or mistress of a family as soon as they are willing ; the faith of the one represents and guarantees in a certain measure that of the others. Any disruption of family ties by means of the gospel of peace was as far as possible avoided ; and in these Christian households a firm groundwork and a sure refuge was afforded to the infant church from the very beginning. Observe the slender commencement of that wise economy of grace which subsequently comprehended whole districts and countries in the net of the church, and how the modern theory is contradicted which desires to look upon isolated conversions as the aim and end of the apostolic mission. " The gospel," as Baumgarten says, " strikes its root into the natural soil."

Vers. 35-37. *And when it was day, the magistrates sent their sergeants* (or lictors) to say to the gaoler that he was to *let those* (only too well known) *men go.* Whence this sudden alteration in their sentiments ? Many think that the magistrates had punished the apostles the day before with great precipitation, in order to appease the multitude, but that during the night they had reflected that the privileges of the Jews had been infringed, and that they now desired quietly to set right that which they had done wrong. But scruples like these on the part of the magistrates, and especially such inconsistent conduct towards the gaoler, to whom only the day before they had handed over these well-scourged culprits for safe keeping, cannot be easily imagined without some extraordinary

---

[1] The reading σύν (ver. 32), which is more exact than καί, appears to emphasize the following of the chief person more than the application of the word to all.

moving cause. We consequently cannot refrain from believing that
the mighty earthquake had been felt in the city generally ; and we
must, as far as *this point* is concerned, give our adhesion to a certain ancient addition to the text,[1] but not as regards the other un-
feasible traditional particulars, viz. that the στρατηγοὶ came together
again in the *forum*. These, probably, were only two duumvirs :
well accustomed indeed to injustice, but yet not altogether without
conscience, they felt themselves rebuked by the earthquake (an
evil-threatening omen in the heathen idea), and more particularly
so on account of the scourging which had been inflicted on these
worthy and noble-looking Jews without any form of trial.[2] One
goes or sends to the other as soon as it is morning ; and they are not
long before they agree to quietly release these men, in favour of
whom the gods appear to speak. They must certainly be released
quietly, that the magistrates may not be exposed before the people.
In the first place, these persons must be let go ; and next, they will
further consider how the whole business is to be publicly represented. The gaoler, whose anxiety is completely removed by this
message, sees in it only what is right, and, full of joy, brings the
news to Paul, that the magistrates had sent down to say that they
were to be let go. *Now therefore depart, and go in peace !* The
good man, whose young faith the Lord had spared by so ordering
matters, is glad that the authorities are so easily settled with, and
can only think that Paul will take it in the same way. He had
already good cause for confidence in their humility ; indeed, he is so
sure of it, that he falls again a little into his official style as gaoler,
and says to them, " Ye are permitted to depart;" but as a new
brother in Christ he adds the fresh learnt blessing, " Go in peace !"
But on this occasion the Spirit directs Paul to another course of
conduct than that which Christian humility and simplicity would
have dictated in a similar case. Even the disciple of Christ is
occasionally permitted, and indeed ought, according to circumstances, to appeal to his social rights. Paul himself spoke to the
magistrates' officers, and said, *They* (the magistrates who have sent
you to us, to whom ye are to take this answer) *have beaten us openly
uncondemned*—indeed, without either trial or conviction—contrary

---

[1] This addition runs : Συνῆλθον οἱ στρατηγοὶ ἐπὶ τὸ αὐτὸ εἰς τὴν ἀγορὰν, καὶ
ἀναμνησθέντες τὸν σεισμὸν τὸν γεγονότα ἐφοβήθησαν.

[2] The heathen enmity is here hardly so stubborn as the Jewish. It is not
only susceptible of impression by signs and wonders, but has also a feeling for
the dignified endurance of innocent suffering.

to the natural rights of all nations, and especially of the Romans.
There has been a public and open shame put upon us by this great
transgression on the part of the rulers. Added to this, we, "those
men" that ye speak of (ver. 35), are Romans (more than the inhabitants of this city, ver. 21) : not only am I a Roman citizen
(ch. xxii. 25–28), but my companion Silas is so also.[1] Thus, in
their blind, inconsiderate zeal, which would not allow us to defend
ourselves, they have acted in opposition to the *Lex Valeria, Porcia,
et Sempronia ;* they have smitten Roman citizens, and cast us into
prison, as the whole city well knows.[2] But now, when they have
in part acknowledged their injustice, frightened as they are at the
divine voice raised in our favour, are they to thrust us out of prison
privily, and, as they further intend, also to expel us from the city ?
Not so ! This way of acting would not be right in many respects.
No ; let them come themselves and fetch us out, affording us all
public fitting satisfaction. Remark how boldly and with what
confidence Paul here stands up for his rights ! From his behaviour
we may learn that Christian humility is not always to abase itself
externally, and to be all-forbearing on every occasion, as the world
itself only reckons it as hypocrisy. Any one whom God has put in
possession of civil and social rights should mention them, and make
use of them, in case of need, for the service of God's kingdom.
Certainly only for the service of God's kingdom, not for his own
private benefit. It is perfectly clear that Paul did not desire any
vindication of his honour for his own sake, and that it was not
from a motive of human pride that he endeavoured to enhance
the injustice which had been done to them by the appeal to his
Romanitas, inasmuch as he, together with Silas (vers. 20–23),
allowed himself to be dragged, to be led away, to be accused, to be
scourged, and to be cast into prison. In all these things his feelings of human pride must have been much more excited, and certainly time and opportunity might readily have been found for a
few words intimating that they were Romans.[3] But now, after the

[1] That Paul should have used the *plural* here, and yet that Silas was *not* a
Roman citizen, we should hold as an untruth, and not as a mere " synecdoche,"
as is said.

[2] Facinus est, vinciri civem Romanum; scelus, verberari.—CICERO, *in Verrem,*
v. 66.

[3] We can scarcely imagine that they had at the very first appealed to their
right of citizenship, but that in the confusion it had been fruitless, on account of
rage not allowing it to be heard (as Da Costa thinks). The ἄρχοντες at least
would have listened to such an appeal with alarm ; cf. ch. xxii. 25–29.

earthquake and the blessing on his preaching had opened the way
for him, he has two reasons for desiring a public satisfaction for
the scourging and imprisonment without trial.   He therefore oppor-
tunely names the privilege which had not been previously mentioned by him: (1) That the authorities, now that they have
been touched with repentance, should openly acknowledge their
injustice, both for their own profit, and also for the advantage of
and example to the city generally ; (2) That the faith of the new
disciples in Philippi should be strengthened, and that, generally, a
clear and easy path should be opened for the spread of the gospel
in the city.   After the orders of the magistrates the apostles could
have departed uninjured ; but inasmuch as, being servants of God
and preachers of His salvation, they had become *personæ publicæ*,
the reproach of their imprisonment, from which in this way they
were so privately released, would have rested upon them, not only
with great injustice, but also with no slight injury, the heathen
and the enemy might well have said that there was something
wrong about " those men." In Jerusalem the innocence of the
apostles was well known—there they bore everything in silence ;
but here, among foreigners, on account of their ministerial office,
even the appearance of evil was to be avoided, especially when God
Himself so wonderfully placed the power in their hands.   Paul's
object, therefore, in his just demand was the honour of Christ, and
the salvation both of the persecutors and of the disciples.   In this
chapter, ere the following one brings before us the great model
discourse to the educated heathen at Athens, Luke relates the
apostle's remarkable words to the soothsaying spirit, to the gaoler,
and to the officers,—words which he made use of both before and
after the preaching of the word.   This is done that we may have
proofs how clearly and wisely (now especially on this fresh European
field of action) this apostle, in every case and under all circumstances, both says and does the right thing.   On this occasion, on
the other hand, he has kept back any account of the preaching in
ver. 14 and ver. 22.

Vers. 38-40. The magistrates, however, are only the more
afraid when they hear that their injustice of the day before had
led them into a *crimen majestatis* against the Roman state, on
account of which critical proceedings might easily have been taken
against them.   A wholesome fright is thus administered to them as
to the want of foresight they have shown in their injustice ; and
they actually so far humble themselves (perhaps bringing about an

effectual blessing for their own hearts), that they come, and now with good words seek to appease these ill-used Roman citizens : they, in fact, personally *brought them out,* and beseech these now free persons, that, for the prevention of further disorder, they will of their own accord leave the city. This request the apostles could comply with, because they did not desire to defy the enemy, and by a longer continued presence to provoke further persecution,— another proof that they desired satisfaction for their wrongs only for the sake of the business they were engaged in, and not for personal reasons. Thus they leave the prison full of dignity, in which—*i.e.* in some portion of the building—they had until now remained ; perhaps in the morning they had even returned to their former dungeon. The first place they go to is, naturally enough, their lodgings at the house of Lydia. When they have once more seen the *brethren* (of whose conversion nothing is related[1]) who were assembled there full of expectation, and had comforted them with words of leave-taking, they go forth on their journey free and unconstrained in the presence of the whole city. Their course, be it observed, was not a *backward* one, but further on into Macedonia. How it fared with the other prisoners, and how many of them were subsequently baptized, the narrative, which only follows the chief points in the history, omits to state : it also tells us nothing as to further gathering in of Christian brethren after this remarkable beginning. It is perhaps more than probable that the prisoners remained quiet in the gaol, and that no further disturbance of the usual order of things took place ; for miracles sent in favour of the gospel were not to be misused to effect a carnal liberty, nor was the arrangement of worldly matters to be interfered with more than was right.

[1] For Timothy and Luke can scarcely be the only persons intended. The former, at all events, continued to travel with Paul (*vid.* ch. xvii. 14), although Luke probably remained at Philippi, and appears again, ch. xx. 5. Compare also the expression " brethren" as used for the newly converted (ch. xvii. 10, 14, xviii. 18, 27).

XXI.

PAUL'S ADDRESS IN THE AREOPAGUS AT ATHENS.

(CHAP. XVII. 22–31.)

PREPARATIVE ANNOUNCEMENT OF THE UNKNOWN GOD.

CH. xvii. 16. The gospel of Jesus Christ was now announced even in Thessalonica [1]—one of the four chief cities of Macedonia, the province for which help was asked—and even further on at Berea; but again it was preached to the Jews in the first place, *out of the Scriptures.* A great multitude of devout Greeks, and of distinguished women not a few, had in Thessalonica believed in the suffering and risen Messiah of Israel; but the unbelieving Jews had raised an uproar against the pretended uproar-makers, and their host had to give bail for the latter, that they, the preachers of the God of truth, should do nothing against the authority of Cæsar. The Jews at Berea were " more noble," and received the word willingly, seeking in the Scriptures " if these things were so;" but even from hence Paul was expelled by the persecutors, who had followed him from Thessalonica. Silas and Timotheus, not being endowed with such mighty gifts and powers, worked more privately, and (perhaps after Timotheus had stayed some time at Thessalonica) were left behind at Berea to continue to help Macedonia; but the new brethren, in their loving care for Paul, sent him away *as it were to the sea.* [2] Having afforded a wholesome disappointment to his persecutors, he came, in the first intention generally and indeterminately, down to the sea; thence those who had undertaken to bring away Paul in safety ($\kappa\alpha\theta\iota\sigma\tau\hat{\omega}\nu\tau\epsilon\varsigma$, ver. 15), being led by human consideration and divine guidance, conducted

---

[1] Where the Jewish synagogue was not, perhaps, for the whole province, but yet for a pretty large district (including Amphipolis and Apollonia).

[2] We consider (with Winer) that the $\dot{\omega}\varsigma$ before $\dot{\epsilon}\pi\dot{\iota}$ does not intimate any dissimulation, but, on the contrary, the definite intention of the brethren, who, in conducting the apostle, only desired in the first place to get him away in safety. Probably there was no design at first to bring him to Athens; but Paul on this occasion appears to have entirely submitted himself to the divine guidance as manifested through the loving care of the brethren for him. Others assume that there was a sea voyage, which seems to us improbable, on account of the $\ddot{\epsilon}\omega\varsigma$.

him along the shore to the world-renowned city of Athens. This was something more important even than Ephesus, where Paul, at the commencement of his present journey, would have willingly preached. His companions received a message for Silas and Timotheus, that the latter should follow him as soon as possible. They returned, leaving the apostle alone for a while in the proud city, the chief seat of heathen art and wisdom, and the very centre of the glories of idolatry. Truly, for the former scholar of Gamaliel, the bigoted Pharisee with his inextinguishable horror of idol-imagery, and for the apostle of the crucified Saviour of the world, the situation was unique in its nature. No missionary heart which has any acquaintance with the ancient Grecian world, will fail to sympathize with what the man and the apostle must have now felt. Macedonia, whither he had been summoned by the vision at Troas, had been travelled through, and many of its inhabitants had been "helped" with everlasting salvation; now, through the persecutions of the enemy and the love of the brethren, the purpose of the Lord had cut him off both from his old and new brethren, and had placed him here in Athens. He knew not yet what the future commands of the Lord might be. Perhaps he anticipated that the word was to be preached here also; but he waited the time and the hour, and the impulse of the Spirit. He doubtless intended, in the first place, to wait in silence until the arrival of his companions. In the meantime, in the great city of Athens and all its glories, there was enough to occupy the apostle's sense of observation, which during this great interval was devoted to gathering matter for a wise commencement of his ministry—thus waiting patiently until the Spirit threw its interpreting light upon the darkness of the world. From all that he had seen and known in his native city of Tarsus, Greek culture and manners could by no means have been altogether strange to him; but yet his pharisaical education at Jerusalem must have taught him to despise the language and customs of Javan. Now, with his new, unfettered Christian views, he stood for the first time in this anti-Jerusalem of the heathen world. Paul's spirit was stirred within him when he saw that the proud city, with all its magnificence of art, was yet only κατείδωλος; that the *urbs fanorum referta*,[1] in spite of all its wisdom, had dedicated its images and temples to none but false gods; and that all its inhabitants, alienated from the true God,

---

[1] As Cicero expressed it. It is more forcible in Xenophon: ὅλη βωμός, ὅλη θῦμα θεοῖς καὶ ἀνάθημα.

were wandering in the ignorance and wickedness of their rebellion against Him. Thus, in the holy apostle, his religious concern overcame every æsthetic taste, and he at least could not dwell in Athens with the same feelings with which many Christians now visit the theatre or opera-house. Truly, had the blessed Saviour visited in the flesh this city of Athens, He would have mourned over it as over Jerusalem !

Vers. 17, 18. Urged on by this stirring up of his spirit, Paul now breaks through the silence which he had hitherto observed : he begins to speak both to the Jews and proselytes in the synagogue (on the Sabbath), and also in the market-place, according to the custom of the Athenian teachers, to those who every day resorted thither. In the first place indeed διελέγετο, asking questions and arguing in a conversational way, leading on their minds to thoughts about the true Messiah and the true God ; next, however, he frankly and faithfully told of Jesus and His resurrection. These strange words, spoken by a foreigner who looked like a Jew, but yet was so free-spoken with the Gentiles, made some noise, especially in the market-place. It came to pass, that some of the Epicurean and Stoic philosophers—the two most distinguished, or at least most publicly acknowledged schools—the Pharisees and Sadducees, as it were, of Greece [1]—encountered or entered into a dispute with him (συνέβαλλον αὐτῷ). The philosophers are at first very indifferent towards the evangelist who, as a Jew, had not studied in their schools, and spoke neither with classical elegance as regarded his style, nor with sophistical distinctness in his matter; but on hearing more from him, they wonder for a while at the glimmer of divine truth which beamed forth upon them from his testimony. Then matters take a turn. One party—for the most part, perhaps, the Epicureans, who inquired after truth for their own satisfaction only, and desired to find it in sensual pleasures alone—turn away from the preacher of Jesus Christ, with a cry which is indeed coarser and meaner than Pilate's "What is truth?" but yet in the main coinciding with it. After they had listened to the earnest speaker longer than suited their own frivolity of mind, they take themselves off most foolishly, just as a Parisian man of pleasure might leave a Christian, with one of those questions which do not demand an answer: "What will this babbler

[1] The more noble Platonists, who did not so much exhibit themselves in public, are not named here, just as in the Gospels the quiet Essenes are not mentioned.

say?" The arrogant, self-satisfied mind, after it has pillowed itself to rest in a life of sensuality, is content to say, "What can any one teach us which is higher and better than these enjoyments which we have already found and luxuriate in?" So spake some of them; but there was another party which, more after the manner of the proud, rigid Stoics, gave an unasked-for answer to the question of the former. "Thus much," they said, "we understand in what he says, that he appears to be a preacher of strange gods." This sounded rather more pleasantly than the other remark, but was at the same time more dangerous to the preacher. Paul had certainly freely announced to them the gospel of Jesus, and the resurrection of this Prince of Life, crucified and glorified for the salvation of the world. They either looked upon the resurrection as the apotheosis of this Jesus of Nazareth, who was consequently preached as a new and hitherto unworshipped God; or, still more obscurely, they understood that *Jesus* and the *Anastasis*[1] were *two* new divinities similar to their numerous, newfangled, ideal deifications.[2] The verbal expression of the text seems rather to point to this latter notion. At all events, they desired to call to mind that the punishment of death was awarded to all public teaching as to divinities which the State had not accepted; cf. ch. xvi. 21, and remember the prosecution of Socrates, who also is called ἕτερα καὶ καινὰ δαιμόνια εἰσηγούμενος. One party, therefore, was willing to let the apostle go on as a "babbler;" whilst the other took a stricter view of the matter, and turned it over in their minds whether, as "a preacher of strange gods," he was not introducing forbidden novelties, and thus rendering himself liable to punishment.

Vers. 19–21. With this view they seize him, and take him, although not perhaps by force, to the Areopagus. The matter becomes a serious one, and is rapidly assuming a more important shape. This was a new and difficult position for the solitary preacher of the true God, and of real wisdom and religion in the knowledge and worship of Him. Here, on this hill, was the seat of the most ancient and most esteemed tribunal of the city, the judges in which were the most honourable men in Athens; here, all the more grievous delinquencies, especially matters relating to innovations in religion, were discussed and decided upon; here, too,

---

[1] With the duplicated article, and not ἀνάστασιν αὐτοῦ.

[2] In which the modern Athenians among us have imitated them by the personification of "Virtue, Religion, Providence, Nature," etc.

had the right-minded Socrates been found guilty. Certainly we
may gather from the two questions which follow, and their explanation in ver. 21, that Paul, in the first place, was not actually brought
up as a prisoner; but in a spirit of half-mocking curiosity, he was
conducted into the place where this tribunal sat, where also philosophical and political discussions took place among the chief men.
But bringing him into this court was a suspicious sort of mockery,
as in it, if his answers exasperated them, he might be forthwith
accused. The questions which were put to him here, certainly in
the presence of no small number of the people and their principal
men, were well calculated to draw forth a plain, distinct, exact
answer. The question commences in a somewhat bantering tone:
May we know? Wilt thou, a man fond of babbling, tell us wise
men in this place what is this new thing thou desirest to bring to
our knowledge? For thou hast brought forward sundry things
which are foreign (ξενίζοντα) to our ears, and sound to them as
new, unusual, and strange. These words, which might be interpreted as half-praise and half-accusation, stand between the
courteously bantering beginning—"May we know?"—and the
more authoritative conclusion, *We would know therefore what these
things mean!* Luke adds a remark, less for the sake of Theophilus
than for future readers generally, as to the character of the
Athenians (in which the many foreigners living among them likewise partook), that curiosity was the ruling feature in it. For
they were given to nothing else, and had time and inclination
for nothing else, *but either to tell or to hear some new thing.*
This had been the description given of them by their own
Demosthenes.[1] It is just the same nowadays with both the
upper and lower classes in our great cities. It is ever καινότερόν
τι; or, as they are wont to say, one new thing supplants another.
And in this deplorable circulation of vanity, what does even the
gospel appear but as "some new thing?" Many an Athenian is
likely enough to have babbled all the week through about this
"babbler" at the Areopagus, as many an inhabitant of Berlin
now tittle-tattles of the last new church story or pulpit anecdote.
Hamann says, "Curiosity is also a kind of superstition and
idolatry;" but he adds a remark which is true only of the more
innocent kind of curiosity, "and yet it is the mother and nurse of
all science." For any one who in the strictest sense *only* seeks to

---

[1] Τοσοῦτον χρόνον σπουδάζετε, ὅσον ἂν καθῆσθε ἀκούοντες ἤν προσαγγελθῇ τι
νεώτερον.

"tell or to hear some new thing" for a season, will never by *this* seeking be led to any true knowledge. But wherever there is found any genuine desire of knowledge, and a longing after that which is requisite for it, there, of course, the inquiries of curiosity may lead to real information and understanding, if these inquiries are rightly answered. Paul looks at it in this light, and accepts the evident curiosity of the Athenians as a desire for knowledge which is represented in the question put to him. He replies *bona fide* to their only half-serious inquiries, and tells them something more than they either knew or desired to know,—that matter which is at once the *oldest* and the *newest*, the source and aim of everything about which their schools of philosophy were striving—the great light-radiating idea of the one true God, and His plan of restitution *by the One Man* for erring humanity. This discourse is one of his most important utterances, on account of the great fundamental thought contained in it, which connects the doctrines of revelation with the already existing light of nature.

Vers. 22. In that hour it was given to the apostle[1] what he should speak. This promised inspiration is shown with especial clearness in the following discourse, which may well meet with our highest praise and commendation. But better far than any so-called praise from our poor lips, is the humble acknowledgment that here it is the Holy Ghost, the Spirit of Jesus, that is speaking, and that therefore we have here a high model of apostolical procedure. *Ye men of Athens:* the apostle begins with this formula, usual in public addresses to the people, as a testimony of his παῤῥησία at the very beginning. Standing in the midst of the Areopagus, he felt that he was standing before the whole city, and therefore from this standpoint addresses confidently all the men of Athens. By no means does he desire to give information and bring the knowledge of salvation to philosophers only, but to learned and unlearned all together. Frankly and impartially he sets his own personality as that of an observer and critic in contrast to all the Athenians, and says: "*I see* that above all things ye are complete devotees!" This elevation of himself, a stranger, as an observer and critic over all the Athenians, would not be uncourteous, if the result of the observations proved to be something

---

[1] Who now found himself in entirely new circumstances, such as had not happened to him since his conversion. What a contrast there was between Athens and Berea (which he had just left), with its willing Scripture-searching hearers!

good, and gave rise to an expression of praise. Thus the vain
Athenians would always have it. It was the usual custom for
every foreign orator to begin with some praise of Athens and its
people: we find that, in the case of some proud Sophists who did
not do this, the omission was remarked on and blamed. From this
plan the apostle might not deviate, both from motives of caution
with regard to the suspicious expressions recorded in ver. 18, and
also in order that he might begin his discourse in the spirit of
his Lord's directions: "When ye enter into a house, salute that
house; and first say, Peace be to this house." When we, like Paul
at Athens, feel our spirits stirred within us at the idolatry of the
world, still even under this emotion we should not allow ourselves
to speak unwisely and roughly; but, like the apostle, we should
soften down our inward zeal to kindly utterance, and give to the
world that which is due to it from the children of God—the recognition of that measure of good that may be in it. Everywhere,
as far as possible, we should make use of that modicum of truth
which is deeply concealed in error. By no means was it from
mere prudence and precaution for his own person, but from
motives of wisdom and gospel love,[1] that Paul began with this
captatio benevolentiæ — κατὰ πάντα ὡς δεισιδαιμονεστέρους ὑμᾶς
θεωρῶ; which expression, from the whole context, especially ver.
23, can only (as in ch. xxv. 19) be intended in a good sense: Ye
are in all things devotional, religious, God-fearing; ye are altogether taken up with the worship of your gods; it is, as curiosity
likewise is, an element in *your character*. The Scriptures therefore
recognise here a certain general religionism of the heathen as something good; and if, in our overpowering zeal, we are not willing
to acknowledge this, the full force of this discourse of Paul must
be hidden from us; and in a similar position our preaching would
scarcely be much to the purpose, or be attended with blessing.

Ver. 23. Paul gives completely unanticipated reasons for his
eulogium, which eulogium was perhaps unexpected by his hearers;
explaining, in the first place, his words by some further courteous
details. He, at the same time, gives to them an unforeseen turn
and conclusion, which suddenly catches the wise Athenians in a
personal confession of their own ignorance, and opens a path to the
apostle for the introduction of the gospel of the living God. *For
as I passed through,* etc.: these words form the justification for his

[1] Chrysostom speaks beautifully as to the συγκατάβασις in this address to the
Athenians; *vid.* Neander's *Chrysostom,* i. 205.

confident statement, "I see that ye are most devout." But note
well that he does not say, "For I found *very many* holy places in
your city;" but, "I found among your many holy places an altar
dedicated to the unknown God." Thus it is not the plurality of
the other shrines, but the *one altar*, which is intimated as the
characteristic of their devotion, and the ground for his eulogium
on them. When I, as every stranger in Athens, went through
your city, and beheld (attentively considered) the numerous
σεβάσματα, *culturas*, temples, altars, images, etc.: in the first
place, another *captatio benevolentiæ* is here implied, inasmuch as
Paul frankly confesses to them that he had studied the glories of
their city, and had thus done justice to it. But certainly a Paul
had studied them from a very different point of view from that in
which a Pausanias had looked upon them. To Paul's inquiring,
thoughtful glance, seeking for some little gleam of light in all this
darkness, the numberless sacred shrines and glories were thrown
into the shade by one small insignificant altar, probably now almost
forgotten by the Athenians: on this his close observation had discovered an inscription, which addressed itself remarkably to his
spirit, grieving as it was over the idolatries of the city. The
plusquam perf. ἐπεγέγραπτο points to a certain degree of antiquity
in this remarkable inscription. As to this altar in Athens, dedicated "to the unknown God," we possess passages in ancient
writers sufficient to confirm the historical ground of Luke's relation; and yet they are not clear and coincident enough to determine
the exact nature and circumstances of this shrine. It might have
been the case that it was merely an altar which had been formerly
dedicated to some divinity, without any inscription; and that when
the memory of this dedication had died out, it came to be designated as being " (aforetime dedicated) to some (now) unknown
god;" or it might be, that the custom of the Athenians generally
(as related by Pausanias and Philostratus) of erecting altars θεοῖς
ἀγνώστοις, had its origin (as stated by Diog. Laertius) in Epi-
menides, in the lustration of the city during pestilence, causing
sheep to be sacrificed τῷ προσήκοντι θεῷ (the god who might be
the true God, although it was not known who he was);[1] or (which
does not seem so probable to us, although Bengel, Menken, and

---

[1] From which some would very superficially desire to understand in its
narrowest sense, the ambiguous praise which Paul gave to the Athenians, viz.
that they too carefully endeavoured to assure the favour of all the existing
gods, and even of those that were "unknown."

others think so) that the inscription actually meant the one true
God, placed there at the suggestion of some Jew, or perhaps of
Socrates. Suffice it to say, that one or perhaps more altars with
this inscription were existing in Athens : the origin and signification
of it was perhaps forgotten ; but, at any rate, the meaning that a
Paul would put upon it was in no way acknowledged. And yet
this inscription on an Athenian altar formed a most fitting and
significant point to which the apostle might connect his discourse.
Therefore, just as he had not closely examined into the curiosity of
the Athenians, but had put the best interpretation on it, as a desire
for knowledge, so now he does not adhere to the origin and real
meaning of this inscription, as to which he had perhaps inquired ;
but he makes it express, involuntarily as it were, the truest and
best sense, that it was dedicated not to some deity like their other
gods, although unknown by name, but to the real and only God.
Ingeniously elegant for his more refined hearers, unexpectedly
bold for those who were exasperated, and yet unassailable by the
haughty, whom he attacked both with praise and blame as regarded
their sacred matters, was the sudden turn by which the apostle
opened out the way for speaking of the true God : *Whom therefore
ye ignorantly worship, Him declare I unto you.* Not a δαιμόνιον,
but a θεός in its truest sense ; not precisely a ξένον or καινὸν θεόν,
but only the ἄγνωστον, whom ye yourselves have acknowledged as
such. There is no refutation either of the many σεβάσματα and
δαιμόνια, or of the Epicurean and Stoic systems of philosophy, but
only a positive announcement of the truth amidst the complication
of error, from which confusion an involuntary confession of their
insufficiency may be elicited. Paul could without doubt assert,
that in the most exact sense he declared to the Athenians " the
unknown God." But was it correct and really attested by this
inscription, that the Athenians ignorantly worshipped the God
whom Paul preached ? The very point of the turn[1] which Paul

---

[1] Which certainly is somewhat blunted by the more cautious change to the
other reading which is now brought forward : " *What* ye ignorantly worship,
that declare I unto you!" (just as in John iv. 22.) But we cannot make up
our minds to insert in the text this mode of expression, which so entirely destroys
the emphasis. The inscription actually testified of a θεός, and not a mere
Neutrum. And to this, in the simple progress of his discourse, Paul connects
his remarks. We think (with De Wette and Meyer) that nothing but subtiliz-
ing doubts have caused this *Neutrum* to be substituted. The contradiction to
1 Cor. x. 20, brought forward by Alford, is no real contradiction, since both
are true when differently considered. The heathen fundamentally, though un-

gives to his discourse lies precisely in the τοῦτον, which declares that the god named in the inscription and Paul's God are the same. It is a question whether there was any degree of truth in this point, or whether the apostle availed himself of a merely empty knowledge, in order to give a suitable introduction to his preaching. The latter procedure should not, in our opinion, be laid to the charge of any apostle; for an expedient of this sort, if without truth, is unworthy of the spirit of truth. Of course the Athenians did not worship Paul's God by means of this ancient altar, from the inscription on which Paul had merely derived the idea and the name, so as not to preach a *new* god; they also did not worship God with any consciousness or design, as it was to them an "unknown God;" but the Athenians worshipped Paul's God, as Paul expressly says, "ignorantly," *i.e.* without knowing that all their acts of adoration, and all true devotion in them, really pointed to and sought the true God. This is the only right, true meaning of the sentence, ὃν ἀγνοοῦντες εὐσεβεῖτε. The heathen δεισιδαιμονία, or devotion to their gods, is here divided, as it were, into its two elements. The fact that they fear their *deities*, proves their ignorance of the true God; but their *fearing* these deities is an efflux of the inextinguishable conviction of a God, and in the eyes of the merciful One constitutes a kind of worship which really avails before *Him*.[1] Wherever there is any true *religio*, fearing, humiliation, and adoration in heathenism, there the fundamental feeling of the heathen points to and really seeks the "unknown God." A Paul, therefore, could assert at Athens where an inscription like this had fallen in his way, that the devotion of the Athenians really worshipped, without knowing it, his (Paul's) God; just as, even without any such involuntary confession on the part of the heathen as the inscription afforded, a missionary might say, *e.g.* to a Hindoo, "I preach to thee the atonement which all thy expiatory actions unconsciously point to and acknowledge." The Lord said to the Samaritans, "Ye know not what ye worship;" and inasmuch as all heathenism stands in somewhat the same relation to the worship of the true God as the Samaritan stood to the Israelitish religion, this utterance of our Lord may be extended in a certain degree to all the heathen, as is here done. The language

consciously, seek after the true God; but in the performance and reality of their idol-worship they worship devils.

[1] Thus any existing (even public) exercise of religion among the heathen always conveys some benefit and blessing as regards their lives.

of mercy, because it condescendingly looks to the innermost ground
of the heart, speaks tenderly of this worship of the ignorant, which
is mistaken both in its aim and nature, and calls it, on account of
this ignorance, the worship of the unknown God. And Paul's
following words, *Whom therefore ye ignorantly worship, Him declare
I unto you*, should be the great preamble of every missionary to
every heathen people. This altar of the " unknown God" in
Athens was, without the Athenians' knowledge or will, a symbol
and a veiled confession of this reference to the true God in their
worship generally ; and therefore Paul's commencement of his discourse by this allusion is very significant.

We have here an example (and perhaps the most remarkable
and most instructive we possess) of the appropriate and striking
language which seemed to occur to the apostle, in respect to the
existing circumstances and moment. The previous chapter, too,
gave some of these words in season. Evading the accusation,
Paul says that which is in every respect the most just and suitable
thing he could say : he intimates, both that he does not desire to
preach anything strange and new to them, and also that nevertheless his announcement to them is of the very highest importance,
and something that is unknown even to the learned Athenians.
Thus he lets them know that he is neither a " babbler " nor yet
" a setter forth of strange gods."

Ver. 24. " We really know not what we worship or ought to
worship (ἀγνοοῦντες εὐσεβοῦμεν θεῖόν τι ἢ θεόν τινα) : " this is the
great avowal which, if only we give heed, is made to us by the
entire system of heathen worship ; both by its innumerable σεβάσματα (the accumulation of which knows no limit), and also by
many an express confession—like this altar in Athens—that it
does not know the true God, or that it cannot yet find deities
enough.[1] " The nature of God is really unknown to us (ἄγνωστος
ἡμῖν ὁ Θεός) : " this great confession is made to us, if we will
only understand it, by the unanimous voice of all the philosophy
of heathen sages, both by their very various assertions and as-
sumptions on the point, and also by many an express avowal, as
declared in many an inquiring book, like the inscription on the
altar. Paul consequently, in his exordium, addresses forcibly both
portions of his audience, the popular as well as the philosophical

---

[1] To which feeling belongs also the presentiment of some highest God over
all other gods, which we find at the present day even among the most debased
heathen nations.

interests, that being thus unexpectedly worked upon in their inner-most and therefore universal self-confession, they might perhaps listen to the preaching which followed, if they would but allow the ears of their hearts to be opened. The preaching, which now desires to enlighten by right *knowledge* the existing *fear*, and to purify it and turn it to a right end, commences with the same great light-inspiring thought with which Paul penetrated the heathen darkness at Lystra, viz. the idea of the creation of the world by one God, the everlasting origin of everything that is. "It is no wonder," says Roos, " that the devil has blotted out the memory of the creation in the minds of the heathen, in order to introduce idolatry. The true doctrine of the creation is the actual refutation of idol-worship." And every system of divinity either of ancient or modern times, whether it calls itself Philosophy, Dogmatism, or Theosophy, if it does not adopt as its first principle the biblical theory of creation, must take to itself the warning words of the Apostle John addressed to the church in every age, and applying to idols of thought as well as to idols of stone : " Little children, keep yourselves from idols !" Until we acknowledge *the* God whom Paul preached at Athens—that is, the God who, as the Eternal, by His personal and free will and working, in the begin-ning of time *made the world*—so long shall we, like the Athenians, serve an " unknown God," let our philosophy be ever so eminent, and our feelings of devotion and dependence ever so deep. The New Testament theory of redemption can only be rightly built up on the firm ground of the Old Testament theory of creation. Who-ever scripturally and genuinely believes the ancient words of reve-lation as to the Creator of all things, and acknowledges them in faith ; he, and he alone, can recognise, understand, and scripturally and genuinely worship " the *Man*," in whom the latest revelations of God's word are finally concluded.

The God who made the world is the self-revealing, living God ; and although, of course, believing forms a part of the acknowledg-ment of a creation, yet in this very believing we *understand* Him (Heb. xi. 3) : *i.e.*, the elevation of the mind from the works to the Creator is, so long as men dwell on earth, the most natural function of their perceptive and reasoning intellect (Rom. i. 19, 20). The apostle therefore can boldly, freely, and briefly lay down this pro-position, which is obvious to every heart which is sincere in sense and understanding. Also, when an apostle sets forth natural re-ligion (falsely so called), he does it with the authority and emphasis of revelation: he declares and settles it, without following the methods of philosophy with doubt, inquiry, and proof, and thus building up from below some supposed plan. The matters declared by revelation may afterwards be explained, and, as it were, confirmed in the depths of our own reflection; but it would be a long and fruitless labour to endeavour by means of their own inferences to bring to the truth those who are estranged from revelation. Paul avails himself of the philosophico-heathenish idea of the world current and intelligible at the time: he is not content with merely popularizing it, but individualizes it, and with the deepest signification realizes it in its concrete elements, by using the biblical expression *heaven and earth*. The world is not from everlasting: it had its beginning when God created or made it. The idea of the universe embraces every individuality in it—*all things therein*. Both universally and individually, however, the rule of the Creator over His creatures follows as a speedy and clear inference from the fact of creation. Heaven and earth have one Lord in their sole Creator, and His almighty rule so operates that everything agrees in obedience to His will. How could a temple be built for the habitation of Him "whom the heaven and the heaven of heavens cannot contain?" for the Master is to be thought of before, beyond, and above His works (1 Kings viii. 27). Thus the omnipresence of God follows immediately from the idea of a Creator; and with this is connected, in the next verse, the omnipotence of the Maintainer. The "temples made with hands" are placed intentionally in contrast with God's making the world without hands: this expression therefore conveys a reference to the immaterial spirituality of the Creator, and a repudiation of all materialistic ideas as to the creation itself. The hands of men cannot make or build anything for Him, who by Himself as Lord created the world and all men therein, together with their hands and hearts.

Ver. 25. But if He is the Lord of all men, can they not, and ought they not, then, to serve Him? Has He not created them for this very purpose? This leads up to the question as to false and true worship; and, in the first place, to the repudiation of all worship rendered by means of gifts, or maintenance by men's hands. In order to join on more suitably with the preceding verse, the negative side of the question takes the precedence of the positive: the hands of men with which they desire to worship God, are the same hands which thought to build Him a temple. But the God who has made the world, and is continually their Lord, needs nothing from those whom He has created and rules. Remark how powerfully the great axiom follows on from the idea of the one creation—an axiom which it is necessary to set forth even to Christians : *That man can give nothing to God ; the Creator needs nothing from His creature !* Now follows the great antithesis : that the creature is continually and in the highest degree in need of his Creator, who by His sustaining power, or continued creation, " upholds all things by the word of His power " (Heb. i. 3).   We do not give anything to God, but He gives everything to us : this is the relation between us and Him.   This was an idea for the men of Athens, which was as simple as it was forcible, as philosophically profound as it was popularly convincing ; but it was an idea that would subvert all their altars, and the sacrificial institutions in and round their temples.[1]   How can He be fed and supported by the lives of beasts supplied by the hands of men— He who from His divine hand giveth their life and breath both to men and beasts ?   He has not only given once for all *life* or present existence, but He also gives to all every moment the *continuance* of life or *breath*.   The living man must breathe in order to main- tain his life : he therefore needs every moment this latter gift from the hands of Him who gave him also his life.   The outer air, the material symbol of God's universal operation, enters into our lungs without our own assistance : we have but to open them.   " Breath is the special gift of God, enjoyed by man, exactly as a beggar receives anything from one who gives it to him" (Oettinger).   Cf. Isa. xlii. 5 ; Dan. v. 23.   And now, again, how wide and clear, how forcible and yet simple, is the conclusion, and the progress onwards from the Giver of *breath* to the Giver of *all things !*   Just as the first " becoming a living soul," our first breath, came to us from the *Creator* (Gen. ii. 7), so the continuance of life—every breath we draw—comes to us from the same God, as *Sustainer* of all things. And just as our breath, our most immediate and most unceasing requirement, the very food of our life,[2] comes to us from the *Sustainer*, so every want that follows, all kinds of sustenance and

---

[1] For we by no means believe that the Athenians only looked upon these words of the apostle as an explanation of the circumstance that the " unknown God " of their altar had neither temple nor priests, or that perhaps at first they thus understood the apostle's meaning.

[2] The blood (immediately after named by the apostle in ver. 26)—according to the Scriptures (Gen. ix. 4 ; Lev. xvii. 11 ; Deut. xii. 23), the seat of the natural life—is produced by the accession of the animating and vital air to the chyle, and thus the air breathed in is the real " *pabulum vitæ*."

nourishment, come to us from the same God as *Provider*. Thus
we have need of Him from first to last. We notice that Paul is
here preparing the way for the declaration he subsequently makes,
that " in Him we live, and move, and have our being." After he
has " declared " to them the *Creator*, who (in times past) made all
things, he goes on to preach to them the *Sustainer*, who continues
(at the present time) to give everything to every one. In this the
same idea of a merciful benefactor is conveyed which he had
before brought forward at Lystra (ch. xiv. 17). And in addition
he points out to them the *Ruler* who has ordained all things (by
His decree of creation), and prescribed how they shall be (in the
future to be brought on by the redemption).

Ver. 26. *And hath made of one blood :* so that all non-Israelites,
even the Athenians and their philosophers, must base their new
Christian perceptions on these revelations of the Mosaic Genesis.
The unity of the race of man, as springing from one ancestor, is
a necessary conclusion from the unity of the Creator, and the
creation of man in His image. The " *One Man*," in whom everything is concluded (ver. 31), points back, as the *second* Adam, to a
first. The apostle says here, " of one *blood*," instead of " seed," or
" ancestor," in order to denote more expressively the intimate rela-
tionship of the races of men, and also that he may mention the
mysterious seat of life, which those living in all the successive
generations of man have invigorated and continually nourished by
the breath given them. We all spring from one blood! This
fact is certified to the Athenians, who looked upon themselves as
autochthons, by a Jew whom now they felt unable to despise ; and
it is likewise certified to our modern philosophers, who, in all the
arrogance of knowledge, " professing themselves wise, have become
fools," and have vainly dreamt of a variety of origin for man.
The light of the gospel shining into the darkness of heathenism
brings with it in the Old Testament a true and certain history, in
which is shown forth God's real plan. For heathenism is based on
a false history : the perversion of the primitive revelation was a
falsification and a destruction of the records of that which God had
done. We men are all one people! This is the new, broad view
which the gospel opposed to the national feeling of the Greek, and
of the Roman, and of all the peoples of antiquity. God has from
the beginning further prepared and ordained that all nations of
men to whom He, as the Lord of heaven, has given the earth (Ps.
cxv. 16), should dwell upon the whole face of it. He has decreed

and carried out the transplanting, the spreading abroad, and the dispersion of men and nations (Ps. lxxiv. 17). The same God who created all "of one blood," wills nevertheless that there should be varieties of countries and nations, for diversity and separation are good for the fallen race of man. We now have a still closer definition, which completes the survey here given of the history of nations, in God's one plan for the *gens humana*. The *times*,[1] periods, and epochs of the development of nations, which are pre-scribed and pre-appointed by God, take the precedence : for it is according to these that the local and temporary "bounds of their habitation" are prepared ; and in this indeed is disclosed the prin-cipal idea of God's plan,—the *time*, namely, of His preparation and fulfilment (see vers. 30, 31). An unchristian natural philosophy, and an unbiblical historical science, which imagine men to be the growth of a so-called nature, and not the free pupils of the guiding hand of God, give a priority to the "bounds of their habitation" before the "times appointed by God," and derive the rise and fall of empires, as well as the wandering of nations, from the effects of soil and climate, and from the beginnings of nationalities, which have thereby developed. But Paul, who sketches out here the main idea of all genuine geography and history, correctly reverses the matter ; for our *times* are in God's hand, inasmuch as He has foreseen certain cycle-epochs of our free development, and, modifying them through His decreed influence, has thus predetermined them. According to this inner progress of mankind, and of "their own ways" (ch. xiv. 16), the change or the continuance of their boundaries is settled (Deut. ii. 5, 9, 12), and Israel is scattered into all lands, when the term of their obstinacy is come. Athens is no everlasting city,[2] and Rome is not an immortal Rome ; the glories of both fell when their time was fulfilled: for the earth in its present shape is only a temporary "habitation" of man, with a view to a higher aim, which is imme-diately after stated in ver. 27.

Ver. 27. The times and boundaries of the various nations which have sprung from "one blood" and in "one blood" are joined together as one nation and family, have been wisely ordained by their Creator, Sustainer, and Ruler (not by some dark fate which rules both gods and men). But these nations are not to have

---

[1] Καιρούς is to be taken absolutely, and does not belong to κατοικίας.

[2] The hearers are here called to reflect with earnest consideration on the past period of splendour in their own history.

various gods, as many ancient philosophers have thought; but the
one Lord (ver. 24) desires to be sought for and found by all as
their one God, after they have lost Him in guilty ignorance or
error. Finding God is in His sight (as v. Meyers remarks) "the
purpose of their habitation, and ruin and dispersion is the result of
this not being done." Through the divisions as well as the unions
of nations, through their wanderings and their settlements, through
all the dealings of God with mankind thus wisely dispersed—by all
these means are the nations to be brought back to their God. The
heathen nations indeed, who are especially in question here, are
left in freedom to "their own ways," in which God suffered them,
as a great trial, *if haply* (εἰ ἄραγε), in their own consciousness and
the light of nature, *they might feel after Him, and find Him;* and
also as a proof that, notwithstanding all the nearness of God, without a special revelation they are unable to do this. The word ζητεῖν
is connected quite as closely with the ἐποίησέ τε as κατοικεῖν is, for
the two equally formed a part of the fundamental purpose of God
in creation. The *seeking* can and is only to take place by means of
a *feeling after*, or actual *touching* or *grasping*, which comes between
seeking and finding. These remarkable words convey two points:
first, that darkness had so overshadowed the nations, that they no
longer intelligibly discerned the true God (Rom. i. 20); and next,
that "He who is not far" may nevertheless be surely and easily
apprehended. The far-off God is also the near God, because He
fills both heaven and earth. The apostle therefore continues:
though the nations, who are led from so far to find their God,
because He allowed them to follow their own ways, have Him quite
near to them in the direct testimony of their own life. The "unknown God" is a God easily discernible, and has only been thus
misapprehended through the perversion of sin. He must truly be
sought and found, not far away from us, behind the cloud-curtain
and above the stars, or in the foundations and depths of the earth.
No; every single one among us all, without exception and distinction (εἰς ἕκαστος ἡμῶν), has Him quite near.[1] Compare the
passage (Rom. x. 6–8) in which the Saviour is similarly spoken of.

Ver. 28. *For in Him we live, and move, and have our being.*

[1] "God not only cares for mankind generally as a whole, and principally
for nations and states, by manifesting Himself in their history; but He is inwardly and wonderfully near to individuals also, testifying of Himself to them
in the history of their own lives, and in the inmost deepest recesses of their own
being."—MENKEN.

This " in," which denotes the element, the breath of our existence, is the very closest " nearness." Certainly there is a distinction between the knowledge of a Creator and Sustainer, which, from the constantly existing and general acts of mercy, may be possible even to the heathen, if they were not blinded by sin, and the knowledge of a Redeemer and a Renovator, which a Christian may possess by means of special grace working in him. But yet in their meaning and extent these words were essentially true which the Spirit of truth testified to the Athenians: *in God*, all we sinners *so* " live, and move, and have our being" by nature, that by an honest, inquiring consideration of our own existence, we may rise from it to the perception of a God—indeed, to a just idea of the true God. The threefold expression, " *living, moving,* and *being*," corresponds exactly to the gifts of God mentioned in ver. 25: in Him we *live*, since He gives us *life*; in Him we *move*, since He gives us *breath* whereby we continue and exercise our life; in Him we *have our being*, since He gives us everything which makes us what we are; and our whole existence is from Him, who gives everything to all. The repetition of this triform idea seems to point to some significance in it. An ancient author has remarked: " In the Father (from whom everything proceeds) we are; in the Son (who is the life) we live; and in the Holy Spirit (who is the breath of all flesh) we move." Now that the apostle, condescending to popular and familar language (not, however, without deep allusion), had arrived at the standpoint of a natural perception of God, he quotes a verse from the poet Aratus (of Cilicia), in whom many similar passages may be found. This quotation[1] is remarkable in many points of view, as affording a satisfaction to the Athenians, by showing that the stranger was acquainted with their poets; as a striking groundwork for his forcible proposition against idol-images which immediately follows, which proposition he now infers from the words of one of their own authors, as in ver. 23 his first denunciation against them was based on their own confession; finally, as a well-selected example out of the forebodings and involuntary confessions of their sages, which actually implied the same idea as the altar to " the unknown God" symbolically set forth. The apostle quotes indefinitely and generally from " certain poets," whom he significantly contrasts with himself, by calling

---

[1] As is manifest through the poetical use of τοῦ for τούτου,—a use that only occurs here in the New Testament. Instead of εἰμίν (as Boss reads in Aratus) we have ἐσμέν.

them "*your own* poets," and refrains from mentioning the name of Aratus, perhaps because this expression is in fact found in similar words in more than one author.[1]

Ver. 29. The apostle repeats graciously and condescendingly the words of Aratus, and adopts them as his own. He emphatically places at the head of this repetition the important assertion: Γένος οὖν ὑπάρχοντες τοῦ θεοῦ. The Athenians are neither αὐτόχθονες nor γηγενεῖς; but they, as all men, are θεογενεῖς. *Offspring* is equivalent to a *descent coupled with similarity*, and consequently contains both the idea of the creation of man by one God, and also especially, the idea of the creation of man in the image of God. The apostle thus seeks to find in heathen literature the faint echoes yet remaining of the records of God, and of man's true nature and relations, and endeavours by the Greek poets to bring them back to Moses, whose sacred books would afterwards be laid before those who became believers. We have here the sole passage of the New Testament[2] which affords a sure proof as to the traces of the divine image still existing even in fallen man. As an inference from the ὑπάρχοντες, as regards human nature, there now follows a sharp protest against the errors of idolatry: *we ought not to think*, etc.[3] But this sharp protest, which is indispensably necessary as the groundwork for the command to repentance in ver. 30, is softened down by the familiar "we," and is derived from a verse in one of their own poets. Let us now cast a glance back, and note how the apostle's discourse against idolatry gradually rises from external to internal things! First he says: The God whom I preach to you dwells not in temples, and needs no sacrificial service. By this it is only hinted at, that the idols who are tended and served in houses "made with hands" can be no true divinities. Next, in ver. 27, follows the first distinct protest against any other gods except the one Lord, the knowledge of whom is prescribed for all nations; and now at last comes the authoritative decisive declaration, that it is a forbidden delusion to represent and worship the Godhead (θεῖόν τι) under the form of images made by the hands of men.

---

[1] Cleanthes, *Hymn. in Jovem*: ἐκ σοῦ γὰρ γένος ἐσμέν. Pindar, *Nem. Od.* 6: ἓν ἀνδρῶν, ἓν θεῶν γένος, etc. etc.

[2] For the passage 1 Cor. xi. 7 wavers between a reference to men generally and to the members of Christ's church; in the same way Jas. iii. 9 *might* be understood (though wrongly) as referring to the renewed image of God on a Christian brother.

[3] Or more exactly, and also more mildly, "we are not obliged, bound, or constrained to think."

The apostle, however, now makes use of a complete *deductio ad absurdum*, presupposing the natural feeling of God borne testimony to in vers. 27, 28. He rightly allows its full value to the artistic feeling displayed in these representations, but yet is compelled to reprove sharply the religious element in them. If we take *gold*, or *silver*, or costly marble (which is yet nothing but *stone*), and these materials are wrought into a sculpture (χάραγμα) by all the external art (τέχνη) and all the inward thought and device (ἐνθύμησις) which man can give them, it is nonsense to suppose that this gold or silver, formed into an image, can represent to us the Godhead (τὸ θεῖον); for if man feels that he is the offspring of God, and in all the devices of his art something infinitely higher than the dead images which are but the result of his art, must not God stand as far above man, as man above the works of his own hands? Must not He who has produced the living rational man, be Himself an eminently living and eminently rational being, whose nature can only be represented by man *per viam eminentiæ*, by thinking upwards from himself, not by descending to personations made by his own hands? The Athenians, therefore, " had comprehended mankind just as little as the Godhead" (Baumgarten). It is impossible that He who made us can be like anything we make. Compare Isa. xl. 18–26, and remark that, both here and there, witness is borne not only against the coarse superstition of actual idol-worship, but also against the æsthetical half-religion of the refined Athenians, who intend in these images of theirs to contemplate the *ideal* of some θεῖον.[1]

Ver. 30. What an unsurpassable mingling of the wisdom of the serpent and the harmlessness of the dove, of prudent caution and of bold advance, of quiet forbearance and cutting exposure, of the most exact controversy and the most impartial statement, there is in this discourse of the great apostle in the Areopagus at Athens! No sooner has he uttered this keen reprobation against the idol-worship at Athens, than he goes on to assure them of the forbearance and pardon of his and their God with regard to their foolishness; and no sooner has he announced the mercy of the Holy One, than he again sets forth His truth and justice, and in His name " *commands* all men everywhere to repent," if they desire to escape the impending judgment. Every one must have thought, and every

---

[1] Paul is speaking in view of many, and indeed the most celebrated specimens of art. Before his eyes stood the colossal Pallas Athené, and the entire Acropolis, with all its sculptures, as described by Heliodorus in fifteen books.

heart must have felt, that these were the words of an ambassador of
the true God, and of a revealer of the "unknown God." When
the anomaly and perversity of error had reached its climax, then
God, who only for the conviction of the erring ones had thus
allowed men to follow their own ways, can no longer "wink at" it;
then are the *times of this ignorance* at an end, and the God of truth
looks into it and reveals Himself. The command to repentance
now given by God follows therefore from the spontaneous contradictions shown (in vers. 28, 29) to be involved in the ideas of consummated heathenism. The *times of ignorance* correspond to the
"times" of dwelling in ver. 26; but in the former case they are
intended more as epochs of the changes of boundaries, consequently
of the rise and fall of nations; now they are intended to indicate
the intervals of time between these epochs, the general title of
which can only be "ignorance"—ἄγνοια. Let the wisdom of the
nations, in building and ruling cities, in shaping and devising either
stone or words, and in adorning for themselves their present life, be
or have been ever so great, they have all been *ignorant*, like the
sages of Athens, when they are questioned as to the chief matter,
the aim and end of their existence as a nation—the finding out
their Creator. If in Athens, the city of the goddess of wisdom,
ignorance is indigenous, how is it with the rest of the world? Still
the apostle, extending his glance from Athens over the whole of the
heathen world, uses a lenient expression in denoting the heathen in
general. In the first place, he displays the element of error, because
this is the point of view in which God's mercy regards the sins of
the children of men. But although the word *sin* is not expressly
used, it is shown pretty clearly that this ignorance is guilty and
punishable, and is indeed in itself *sin*. This is done, as it were, in
three steps or gradations: firstly, through the indulgent expression
"winked at," in which, although error is the prevalent idea, still
a right of punishment is presupposed; next, through the earnest call
to repentance, and to a dismissal from their minds of the opinions
which "we ought not to think;" finally, in the strongest way, through
the threatening of a righteous divine judgment on the men who reject and do not discern their God.[1] The important word τανῦν here
addressed to the Athenians corresponds entirely with the νυνὶ δὲ
(Rom. iii. 21), and proclaims in the Areopagus to the multitude of
those who desired to know some new thing, the great novelty which

---

[1] Μετάνοια, therefore, certainly does not stand for a merely logical, philosophical change of mind.

had been hidden from the heathen — the advent of a *new time* now commencing for the whole earth.[1] From this point, after the momentous τανῦν, the tone of the apostle's discourse is powerfully raised. In vers. 22, 23 he had spoken both as an observant courteous visitor, and as a self-vindicating defendant; in and after ver. 24, he had testified of his knowledge of the God of heaven and earth, and in a philosophically developed statement had, as requested, explained his "new doctrine;" so that the authoritative expression, "We ought not to think," etc., seemed more a logical deduction than an apostolic command; but *now* he appears as God's confidant, who knows what God will "wink at," and also as God's ambassador, through whom God "now commandeth all men everywhere to repent."[2]   Neither judge nor sage had ever spoken in the Areopagus with such plenitude of authority. Thus speaks the great apostle of the Gentiles, now without hesitation executing the duties of his ministry. This command of the long misapprehended God, that they should now penitently and believingly turn to His revelation, is issued at the time when Paul, God working in him, laboured and strove by the preaching of Christ, "to warn every man, and teach every man, in all wisdom, that he might present every man perfect in Christ Jesus" (Col. i. 25-29). *All men everywhere:* not merely the Athenians, but also the haughty, wise, and devout Athenians, no less than all other men, are affected by God's great command of repentance. Paul thus withholds from his hearers the title of " Athenians," which he at first (in ver. 22) had conceded to them, and ranks them, without any pre-eminence, among " all the nations of men " (ver. 26), in order that he may speak to them as men the words of truth and salvation in the name of their God: " Bethink ye, alter your minds, adopt other ideas both of yourselves and of the Godhead! Do this, by a willing acceptance and taking to heart of that which is now preached to you, and by a repentant confession that ye have not sought Him who did not leave Himself without testimony among you ; that ye have proudly and inconsiderately neglected to listen to the voice of creation and your own consciences, and that ye have hindered God's truth by your own unrighteousness!"

[1] " That survey was also a glance at the times and institutions which are now existing."—MENKEN.

[2] We abide by the established reading, which of course comes to the same thing ; but it might stand more accurately : " God commands men, that they should all everywhere repent."

Ver. 31. There is much seriousness in this command of God
given through the apostle, for He who gives the command will one
day be the Judge of men. His command, therefore, is to extend
to all the uttermost parts of the earth, in order that men, by conversion to their God, may be saved in this impending judgment.
—*Because*[1] *He hath appointed a day in the which He will judge.*
The apostle, as God's confidant, knew what God had appointed
(ἔστησεν)—a fixed, irrevocable, inevitable limit, a great day which
would close all the "appointed times" of man's history with an
universal judgment. This great day is precisely fixed upon by
God, although men only know that some day is fixed generally.—
In the which He will judge—μέλλει κρίνειν. It is indubitably certain,
for anything which God has appointed will positively take place.
Then will the whole earthly dwelling-place of all nations become
one great Areopagus, where the last and highest judgment shall
be truly and impartially pronounced by the Judge of all judges
on every nation and man. We see clearly that this mention of a
future judgment (in any case most appropriate) was induced by
the fact that Paul stood as one that had to give account at the
ancient and celebrated tribunal in Athens. He thus stands up in
his sacred dignity as the ambassador of his God, who is the God
of all the world, and entirely reverses the position of things by
announcing an impending judgment to those very men who might
pass judgment on him. The emphasis of the announcement becomes still more marked by the addition of the words "in righteousness." Man's judgments may always be given unjustly; but
there is a higher One than the highest upon earth (Eccles. v. 8),
who on the day appointed from the beginning will judge in righteousness, after He has in mercy so long "winked at" their ignorance. In Ps. lxxxix. 14 it is written: "Justice and judgment
(the latter disclosing and restoring the former) are the establishment of Thy throne; mercy and truth shall go before Thy face"
(alternately preparing the way). The idea of a judge of the
world is the ultimate idea of a God, which is suggested to us both
by the revelation-echo in our own reason, and the new revelation
coming to us from without. Paul has embraced within his discourse the whole Bible plan, leading on from the Creator to the
Judge; but he must also reveal the great ἀποκάλυψις, that God
judgeth no man, but hath committed all judgment unto the Son.

[1] The reading καθότι here, as elsewhere, can scarcely be distinguished in
sense from διότι.

He must describe to them the idea of the Messiah, as previously he announced to them " the unknown God." Just as Peter in Jerusalem testified to Jesus *first* as the *Lord*, whose foes were to be made His footstool, and then as the *Christ*, who would pour out the gifts of the Holy Ghost for the forgiveness of sins; so Paul in Athens preaches first of all of the Man, whose name he does not mention, that to Him all judgment is committed; and next, that by faith in Him mercy may result instead of judgment.—*Through a Man,* or *in a Man*—ἐν ἀνδρὶ. This quite unlooked-for addition, following the ἐν δικαιοσύνῃ, at once lifts the veil from off the centre-point of God's revelation to mankind, and sets forth Him who is the Mediator of the old and new covenant under His incarnate designation. Not merely to all the men of Athens (ver. 22), but to all men on the face of the earth, is there a Man given— taken out of the midst of them, ordained by their Creator, Redeemer and Judge—and by this Man shall they be judged at the last day. One Man is to be Judge over the whole world. This clearly conveys the idea of God's kingdom among men, which will be under one head in this Vicegerent, and also gives a hint as to a new commencement of human development—a second Adam. It is *a Man* who is to judge all men. In this idea is suggestively conveyed the merciful justice, or the equity and impartiality, of God, who wills that men should be judged by one of their own kind; and therefore the words ἐν ἀνδρὶ are a corroborative elucidation of ἐν δικαιοσύνῃ. Next in this momentous and crowning sentence of the apostle's discourse come the words, *whom He hath ordained*—ᾧ, i.e. ὃν ὥρισε. This relates, of course, in the first place, to the preceding words, whom He hath ordained to be a judge. But this new and great communication, ὃν ὥρισε, which is expressed so absolutely, without any close explanation as to what the ordained One is to be ordained to do, is placed between two propositions, which should be well considered in its interpretation. It is not merely the "judgment by a Man" which needs explanation,—indeed for this, the addition, " whom He hath ordained thereto," is almost superfluous; but also and especially the words which follow —*to give faith through the resurrection of this Man*—are to be explained and verified by the divine ὁρίζειν resting on this Man: consequently the interpretation which limits the idea, and only understands *whom He hath ordained as Judge*, is incorrect, as looking only at one side of the question. Paul desires to say, Whom God has ordained generally for men, and has given as " the Man"

through whom He may reveal Himself. It is only by this interpretation that the sequel becomes coherent and intelligible. In
this momentous proposition, ὁ Θεὸς ὥρισε ἄνδρα—which, although
indefinite, was calculated to awaken many a foreboding—the
apostle does not so much express as hint at the mystery of the
divine will, that all things should be gathered together under one
head in Christ (Eph. i. 9, 10). But as, on the one hand, he does
not scruple to preach this positive dogma of faith even to the philosophers in Athens (who were ignorant of the Jewish idea of a
Messiah) ; so, on the other, as a wise husbander of God's secrets,
in this his first public discourse at Athens he veils and keeps back
very much—indeed all detail as to *the Man*, in whom he has to
declare the "unknown God" as fully manifest. Thus much only
does he give them in the first place as a great leading outline : that
a Man will one day judge the world in God's name, in whose person, which is sanctified and ordained by God, in that He raised
Him from the dead, everything is to be decided through faith or
non-faith in this risen One. But this very apostle, who at Corinth
"determined not to know anything save Jesus Christ and Him
crucified" (1 Cor. ii. 2), on this occasion forbears to mention either
the saving name of "the Man," or His dignity as Messiah, so long
prescribed in the revelations of Israel, or even the scandal of His
death upon the cross. He forbears also to say that this Man was the
Son of God ; that He was indeed God in the flesh ; that His death
constituted the propitiatory sacrifice for the sins of the world, and
His new life the power of sanctification for all wrong-doers. Why
is this so ? We may get to understand it a little, by surveying the
particulars and circumstances of the case so far as they are known
to us. We are, at all events, justified in thinking that this course
of action was judged to be judicious by the Holy Spirit, which
teaches, according to the juncture, either to conceal or to announce,
either to make reservations or to speak out freely. If we take
into consideration the inquisitive, frivolous mob (as described in
vers. 19-21) before whom Paul now stood, we might well comprehend that it would be his desire to give them such an answer to
their question, that they should all of them be directed to the
living God, and away from their idol-images, and that the teachable and those desirous of it should receive an inviting intimation of the closer manifestation of this God through the *one Man*.
But the details of his "new doctrine" of Jesus and the resurrection (ver. 18) were not, in the face of this great publicity,

adapted to the ears of the multitude, or fitted to be exposed to their idle talk : they would more suitably form a subject of some of the quiet conversations (described previously in vers. 17, 18), in which they would be more fully disclosed to those who made further inquiry (as in ver. 34). A general rule for missions may be deduced from the fact (if we only knew how to understand and make use of it), that the preaching in the judgment-seat at Athens was not, in the first place, specially of Jesus.

What, finally, is the meaning of the last expression needing elucidation—*giving (offering) faith to all men?* This might easily be superficially mistaken by narrowing the reference, and *merely* understanding that He affords to every man (in the resurrection of Jesus) the reason for the belief that this Man will one day judge the world. But our previous considerations induce us to suppose something further. If, as the concluding words ἀναστήσας αὐτὸν ἐκ νεκρῶν clearly suggest, we understand this faith to be a faith *in the Man*, we know well from all the other apostolic discourses in what sense the faith in Jesus is named and demanded. It implies, of course, first and foremost, the acknowledgment of the dignity of His person as Lord and Judge. But the fact that through this acknowledgment judgment may be averted, and a reconciliation may be effected for those who believe and trust, is all the more necessary a joint-purport of this expression, since here, as everywhere before faith, repentance is demanded, and its value before the Judge is testified to. A belief and trust in a Judge and Lord—what can be presupposed in this, but that He will be (under the condition of repentance) a mercifully absolving Judge and a gracious Lord? If we consider the apostle's language more exactly, we find in it something more than mere threatening: it conveys at the conclusion both a promise and a gospel; certainly they are only intimated, and purposely so. What is the participle παρασχών connected with in the construction? Certainly not with μέλλει κρίνειν. May it be directly united with ὥρισε? This is to a certain extent right; and one is led to the before-noticed general sense of this ordaining, by this giving of faith in the ordained One of God. Considered with greater precision, however, παρασχών is properly parallel with ὑπεριδών, and both the participles are subordinate to the τανῦν παραγγέλλει. A twofold command is here given by God: Turn in penitence to the true God, and believe in the Lord Jesus Christ (see ch. xx. 21); or more exactly: The *penitence* which must result from the turning of the frightened

sinner to God is *commanded* as a beginning; but the *faith* which
is effected as a continuance of the penitence by the comforting
condescension of a merciful God applied to repentant man—this is
given him by God, *i.e.* God proffers to him the inducement to and
power for it. It is man's part to repent, and God's to give us
faith; although in the one case God's power, and in the other our
freedom, is not to be excluded from consideration. Thus forcibly
does the apostle conclude his enunciation of his "new doctrine"
with this *proffer of God*, wherein all the power and efficacy is
ascribed to God. And yet the decision of human freedom is not
shut out, for God does not compel men to believe (which is contrary to the very idea of faith): He only presents it to us stringently
and invitingly. Paul, after the requisite groundwork had been
laid by his previous announcement of the "unknown God," now
concludes his brief answer, which, saying much, foretokens still
more, and tells what sort of man the Jesus of his "new doctrine"
is, and how the matter stood in regard to "Jesus and the resurrection" (alluded to in ver. 18). At this point he breaks off, and at
least *publicly* says nothing more at present on these two great
subjects. This appears to us far more probable than that he should
have been *interrupted* [1] at this most interesting point of his discourse,
so calculated to excite further inquisitive questions; just at the
moment, too, when he was coming to the real answer to the first
questions (vers. 19, 20). The merely inquisitive ones had heard
enough for a first beginning; and those who entertained a desire
for repentance and faith might frequent the further teaching of
the apostle in a more confidential and suitable place than here in
the Areopagus. The question and demand ran as follows: "May
we know," and "We would know!" In contraposition to this
"knowing," the apostle had placed *faith*, which God gives; and in
this faith (in contrast to the "ignorance," ver. 30) had promised a
new and real wisdom in the sanctifying knowledge of a holy God.
This was giving these Athenians full measure in his *first* discourse.
The scoffers had now enough to scoff at; the babblers had enough
that was strange and peculiar to talk about; and those who were
inwardly touched with the repentant commencement of faith would
find sufficient to call forth further inquiry. "Why," they would ask,
"is this judgment to take place through a *man?* For what purpose generally is this man ordained? What is he called? Where

---

[1] As, for example, Köstlin (certainly with many others) thinks. *Der Glaube,*
p. 58.

does he live? What is to be believed of him, and how are we to believe in him? Is he dead and risen again? Will God give us faith in this risen king of man?" Questions like these, if they proceeded from a genuine desire for knowledge, the apostle would willingly answer. But imagine some stranger staying for a while in Athens, who *then* did not believe or make any further inquiry, but afterwards allowed the things he had heard to work in his heart, and was thus brought to conviction so far as this discourse could lead him, without being able to learn more: would not this man be a Christian, without knowing the name or cross of Christ? This and many other such thoughts may be suggested by this remarkable termination to the discourse. We must, however, like Luke, conclude with the conclusion, and can only examine the results as they are related to us.

Vers. 32, 33. The words "raised from the dead," which, according to the apostle's design, formed the chief point of his conclusion, are at once laid hold of by the multitude, and a division arises about it between the two principal classes of those who heard but did not believe. Although Paul had only said that God had raised Him—the ordained Man—from the dead, his hearers had naturally deduced from the idea the general problem of an universal resurrection of the dead. Some, immediately forgetting all that had gone before, which they had perhaps scarcely attended to, mocked at such foolish notions; these were probably the Epicureans. Others, however, with whose previous system of philosophy (as with the Stoics) the great ideas which had been presented to them might in a certain measure be brought in connection, said, *We will hear thee again of this matter.* Not "further," as it is in Luther, but πάλιν (or καὶ πάλιν), equivalent to "again" or "another time." These latter by no means formed a part of those that believed or were willing to believe, who, according to ver. 34, *clave unto* Paul, and as *believers* are contrasted with those who are named in ver. 32. Their language was more like Felix' plea for delay (ch. xxiv. 25); and v. Meyers rightly remarks about them, "The frivolous and those careless of repentance procrastinate the matter." Theirs was only a half-earnestness; and many of the cries, "We will hear thee again," were in no way to be distinguished from the actual mockery, which, too, might well have thus expressed itself. Therefore, after proclaiming this momentous testimony in the principal place in Athens, and having met with general indifference instead of the previous curiosity (now appeased in spite of his enigmatical conclusion), Paul goes unmolested from among them, more grieved by their present indifference than by their former persecution. They let him go, whom a little before they had so eagerly brought into the court! For the Athenians were devotees enough to worship even an unknown God; but when He was revealed to them, they mocked! Their vitiated ears did not desire to hear anything more from this foreigner: for it seemed to them a ridiculous folly to talk to them of some living God over all nations, and of a man raised from the dead by Him; and the summons to repentance, and the representation of a just judgment, were ideas to be shrunk from.[1] Paul had fulfilled his mission to these Athenians, and now departed. "Never did Paul endeavour to adapt himself to foreign peculiarities with more love and earnestness, and scarcely ever did he meet with so little success" (Baumgarten).

Ver. 34. But yet it was not quite in vain that he uttered his energetically bold and (till the obscure conclusion) luminous testimony among these æsthetic, literary, and philosophical triflers and devotees. *Certain men clave unto him:* their hearts having been smitten, they feared not to cast aside their old opinions, and to turn to a righteous and good God. These men became believers after further teaching and exhortation. And among them was Dionysius the Areopagite (according to tradition, chosen to be the first bishop there); and besides the distinguished magistrate—the member of the σεμνότατον καὶ δικαιότατον δικαστήριον—there is also mentioned a woman named Damaris (at all events remarkable for some cause or other). She was perhaps a courtezan, who shared with the honourable councillor a common salvation. Luke also mentions *others with them,* but does not name or enumerate them, hastening on to the account of the commencement of the gospel in Corinth. But yet in the third century Origen was enabled to refer

[1] In matters of religion they wished for something at most *philosophically* new to dispute about, but only within the limits of their old accustomed ideas as regarded the positive groundwork. If the new *teaching* is intended to convey a new *faith,* entirely under the condition of a repentance to consist in the first place of turning away from their beautiful idols, then their curiosity is soon brought to an end. J. D. Michaelis says on this point both severely and forcibly: "The Greek was more irrational than the savage, when religion was philosophized about. He laughed when he heard of the resurrection of the dead, for the doctrine was not a fashionable one; but when he was told that our souls would one day pass into cows, oxen, donkeys, etc., he was less opposed to it, for this idea did not seem so new or strange to him, the Pythagoreans having taught it."

to the Christian church at Athens as a brilliant example of the fruits of Christianity.

XXII.

PAUL'S ADDRESS TO THE ELDERS OF EPHESUS.

(CHAP. XX. 18–35.)

A VALEDICTORY EXHORTATION TO FOLLOW HIS EXAMPLE IN MINISTERING TO THE CHURCH.

WE now omit a period of about five or six years in Luke's apostolic history, which, since the beginning of ch. xvi., has confined itself to an account of Paul's journeys. During this period we do not meet with any discourse suitable to be commented on.[1] In the meantime, the apostle preached the gospel in the luxurious Corinth to the Jews first, proceeding from preparatory, persuasive discussions (ch. xviii. 4), to an earnest testimony of Jesus Christ (ver. 5); next turning to the Gentiles, and strengthened by a vision of the Lord Himself, he preached to them for some considerable time. The Jews who persecuted him " with one accord" were disappointed in their appeal to the kind-hearted Gallio. Paul then came to Ephesus, first only for a short time, for he desired to be at Jerusalem for the feast. After he had saluted the church *there*, and had stayed some time in Antioch, and had also travelled through Galatia and Phrygia, he came back, according to his promise, to Ephesus, where Apollos had been in the meantime labouring, though imperfectly. The twelve Christians, according to John's baptism, whom he found at Ephesus, were asked by him the great test-question, " Have ye received the Holy Ghost since ye believed ? " And when it was shown that they had only received the ordinance incompletely, Paul completed it, and through baptism in the name of Jesus, led them on to the baptism of the Spirit. After these introductory wonders, he was able to preach the gospel freely for the space of three months; but then the accustomed

---

[1] For such isolated utterances as ch. xviii. 6, 21, xix. 2-4, 21, xx. 10, are not to be classed among our Words of the Apostles. The necessary observations on the words spoken about Eutychus follow in their place.

enmity broke out which led to the first actual separation among the disciples. The gospel was next preached for two years in the school of a certain Sophist; and through the success which attended it, and the corroboration it acquired by the "special miracles" of Paul, it extended and prevailed over all Asia. But it is in the ancient seat of the magical arts that the power of the name of Jesus (when adduced by a Paul and not by "vagabond exorcists") was to manifest itself in the lordliest way, so that an entire costly library of magical books was burnt by the hands of the believers. Shortly before Paul's intended journey into Macedonia, Demetrius the silversmith was indeed enabled to stir up the multitude against him and his companions, so that "all with one voice, about the space of two hours, cried out, Great is Diana of the Ephesians!" and Alexander the coppersmith (2 Tim. iv. 15) was not allowed to speak. But the town-clerk stilled the tumult, and referred all complaints to the proper tribunals; because, as he said, the disciples of Jesus had not behaved either as robbers of temples, or as blasphemers of the goddess. Paul after this journeyed, as he intended, into Macedonia and Greece, and then, being impelled by the Spirit, he commenced his last journey to Jerusalem. On account, however, of the "laying in wait of the Jews," he travelled again through Macedonia and Asia Minor. In Troas, where a number of travelling companions awaited him, he recalled back to life[1] Eutychus, who had fallen out of a window, doing it without any disturbance, and, as it were, concealing the miracle, so that the preaching of the word, and the Sacrament should not be interrupted or delayed. He afterwards departed, and, although he had been speaking the whole of the night, went alone on foot[2] to Assos. From thence he proceeded on board ship to Lesbos and Samos, and passing by Chios, so to Miletus.

Ch. xx. 16, 17. *For Paul had determined to sail by Ephesus* (κεκρίκει), in order that he might not, against his will and determination, be compelled, by the claims which would be brought before him there, to lose time in Asia. His fixed aim was to be in

---

[1] Schneckenburger justly defends the actual raising from the dead as a parallel to Peter in the case of Tabitha. Luke relates, ἤρθη νεκρός (not as ch. xiv. 19); and again, ἤγαγον δὲ τὸν παῖδα ζῶντα. As regards the apostle's words in ver. 10, who bids us to supply, "his life is *yet* in him," instead of "his life is *again* in him?" And who gives us leave to translate the words just before (as Stoltz and Seiler do), "He was taken up *for* dead," or "*as* dead?"

[2] Though πεζεύειν might mean only a journey *by land*.

Jerusalem, if it were possible, at the feast of Pentecost; and he was therefore so much hurried, that it seemed to him to be a loss of time even to visit and strengthen the brethren in Asia. The alms for the poor brethren in Judea, which had been collected in Macedonia and Achaia, were to be delivered to the saints in Jerusalem as an offering at the feast; and the apostle to the Gentiles must make himself acceptable to the Jewish brethren by his adhesion to their law at Pentecost; and he must also again bear public testimony before the unbelieving Jews. But the central Asiatic church of Ephesus, which he had so faithfully planted and watered, which, too, he had lately left in somewhat doubtful circumstances, was so dear to his heart, that, passing so near, he could not refrain from ministering to it. He must have known from revelation that he should see their faces again no more, and denied himself this visit to the church (which had been to him like a second Antioch), only because he was "bound in the spirit" to hasten towards Jerusalem. Under these circumstances, he sent from Miletus to Ephesus, and summoned the elders, overseers, or bishops of the church[1] to come to him, that from the fulness of his fatherly and brotherly heart, and looking back at the whole of his apostolic work at Ephesus, he might give them a parting exhortation, and might solemnly commit them, and those under their charge, to that God " who was able to build them up."

Ver. 18. *Ye know :* thus does Paul begin the representation of his own faithfulness to his ministerial work, by means of which he desires, as he is leaving, to exhort the elders now committed to God's charge. Such is the humility of a Paul, that without pride, or the appearance of pride, he is able to point to his own virtues, and through them to set forth the goodness of Him who had called him, whom through grace he now serves. We are not to think that genuine humility consists in ignoring the goodness we have received from God, and possess and exercise only in Him. If this were so, the great pattern of humility Himself could not be called humble, because He said, " Learn of me, for I am meek and lowly of heart ;" and, " Who can convict me of sin?" The apostles were charged by the Lord that they should themselves humanly represent His holy pattern, and that the disciples should be pointed to

---

[1] There must certainly have been more than " three or four " of these men (to which number Menken strangely limits them). Neither the reading ὁμοῦ ὄντων αὐτῶν (ver. 18), nor the certain text ἐξ ὑμῶν αὐτῶν ἄνδρες (ver. 30), would otherwise be suitable

the apostles as an example, and through them to the Lord. This Paul often did (1 Cor. iv. 16; Phil. iii. 17; 1 Thess. i. 6; 2 Thess. iii. 9). This charge they also transmitted to those whom they appointed not only as bishops and leaders, but also as "en-samples to the flock" (1 Pet. v. 3; 1 Tim. iv. 12; Tit. ii. 7). The apostle, therefore, here exhorts the bishops and elders of Ephesus that they should follow his holy example, in which humility before the Lord shone so conspicuously (ver. 19), that a reference to the humility exhibited during three years could not appear as any sign of pride.[1] "Happy he who can so open his discourse!" exclaims Bengel in commencing his consideration of this speech of the apostle. There is much significance in the fact that the apostle appeals first to his life before he speaks of his teaching (in ver. 20); for the seal of the teaching is the humility, purity, and un-selfishness of a life devoted to a ministry of love.—*From the first day that I came into Asia;* or more exactly—ἐπέβην, since *I set foot in Asia.*[2] Paul desires to say: Ye know and can recall to recollection the whole period of my presence among you, from its very first commencement! Paul emphatically combines the *first day* and the *whole time* (τὸν πάντα χρόνον, meaning more than merely *all the time*).—*After what manner I have been with you.* This expressive phrase, "after what manner," comprises the whole of his conduct to them. He was not merely *before* or *among* them, but μεθ᾽ ὑμῶν ἐγενόμην, entirely *with* and *for* you—altogether *yours.* There is implied in this a certain ὑμῖν δουλεύων, which is significantly contrasted with the subsequent δουλεύων τῷ Κυρίῳ; as if to say: I have devoted myself entirely to you, and have lived as your minister with and among you.

Ver. 19. By his being, both in body and mind, with and among the church which he had founded, ministered to, and nourished, he was not so much serving men as the Lord, to whom the church belongs, who had purchased it with His blood; he was also serving the Holy Spirit, who had made him the planter and nourisher of the church at Ephesus (ver. 28). His preaching was not for the pleasing of man, but according to the precepts of Christ, even

---

[1] "True humility never even knows that it is humble; for if it knew it, it would become proud in the contemplation of this lovely virtue." These words of Luther, beautiful enough in their sphere, apply only to those Christians who have not yet attained to the apostolical elevation in Christ, and their universal application is here contradicted by Paul's words.

[2] Compare the reading ἐπιβαίνειν, ch. xxi. 4.

when " to the weak he became as weak," and became " all things
to all men " (Gal. i. 10; 1 Cor. ix. 21).   Thus at the very beginning he sets forth the great fundamental basis of his whole conduct,
and then proceeds to a closer delineation of it as regarded its outward manifestations.   First and foremost among these stands the
humility or submission, which here is not to be considered as a
mere internal sensation, but as the outward expression of it, by
which is represented and demonstrated the thorough surrender of
himself to the church for God's sake, and to the requirements and
fatigues of his ministry.— *With (many) tears and temptations.*[1]
These two expressions are not meant to be disconnected, as if it
were the fatherly tears of a faithful admonisher which are spoken
of (ver. 31); for the latter would belong to the faithfulness of
the testimony (ver. 21), and not to the humility or self-surrender
which was manifest in the willingly endured temptations (oppositions); συμβάντων also refers both to δακρύων and πειρασμῶν.[2]
The apostle, in the first place, calls to remembrance the tears
which he had shed owing to the temptations and troubles of his
ministry; thus beautifully acknowledging his feelings as a man,
and repudiating all appearance of self-exaltation.   We are not to
think of the apostles as unfeeling Stoics, but as men like ourselves,
and feeling like us in their many persecutions, and in the misin-
terpretations and calumnies they were liable to, all of which they
suffered for the sake of their apostolic office.[3]   But we must note
this, that when an apostle weeps on account of " lyings in wait "
and oppositions, the tears are shed much less for his own personal
sufferings than for the sins of the enemies of Christ (Phil. iii. 18 ;
Rom. ix. 2).   In order to represent to the elders the sufferings
which might fall to their share for the sake of their ministry, Paul
reminds them of the opposition he had experienced in Ephesus,
exciting him even to tears.   In doing this, the faithfulness with
which he nevertheless remained with them, and laboriously carried
out the Lord's work among them, is still more prominently displayed.   Yet, just at the commencement of his address, he does not
desire to suggest to them how difficult his task had been made to

[1] Πολλῶν may perhaps be expunged, but certainly not πειρασμῶν.

[2] The tears here spoken of do not exactly refer to tears shed on account of
the sins of his own ministry, as Brückner, with well-justified application to all
of us, imagines.

[3] " In Paul, the 'man' was quite given up in the 'apostle;' but the
' apostle ' did not stifle and annihilate the ' man.' "—MENKEN.

him by the church itself, through their indolence, disobedience, and unfaithfulness, by which indeed his faith had been peculiarly exercised and put to the test, and tears of a different kind had been drawn from his eyes. His intention is not, in this his tender farewell, to bring any accusation against the elders to whom he is speaking, or their beloved church; he therefore pauses after the mention of the "lying in wait" of the Jews, which was actually the most grievous thing to him. Demetrius' plot against him, and the like, he does not even mention; but the rancorous enmity of the Jews—his own countrymen (to which Luke in ch. xix. 9 only slightly alludes)—was most bitter to him. His not having taken much consideration for the latter, that he might minister to the church according to God's will, and his now styling them "*the Jews*"—thus (as the apostle of the Gentiles) casting aside, as it were, his own people—constitute here, as everywhere, the seal of his apostolic faithfulness. He now proceeds to the actual statement of the things which he had done for the Ephesians.

Vers. 20, 21. These tears and temptations were not, however, able to induce him to *keep back* anything, or, from a want of courage and confidence, to conceal anything which his duty called upon him to communicate. By the word ὡς, which is connected with the πῶς in ver. 18, he appeals more forcibly than he could have done by a mere ὅτι to something which was already known in every respect.—*Nothing that was profitable*. Among all the points which were profitable and wholesome, not even one has the apostle kept back or omitted: this is, of course, to be understood of things *truly* profitable or advantageous. Many a thing might perhaps have been lawful for him; "but all things are not expedient and edify not" (1 Cor. vi. 12, x. 23). On the other hand, perhaps, many a thing came hard to him, but yet it was good for edifying: he therefore omitted the former and did the latter. The idea of profitableness refers principally to the first of the three points of apostolic duty which follow—to the *preaching* or *making known*—for with this the *keeping back* is directly contrasted. It is consequently intimated, that the faithfulness of a messenger of salvation by no means consists in freely proclaiming to new converts, either at the very first or too soon, all those mysteries of God which, through God's grace, he himself may know; but that matter must be kept back which, according to the knowledge and perception of the mind, is not profitable for edifying, and, although it is true, may even do harm. As the Lord acted with His disciples (John xvi. 12), so

also did the apostles act with their churches (Heb. v. 13, 14, ix. 5).
The "faithful and wise servant" will "give the meat in due season"
out of his Lord's provision (Matt. xxiv. 45), and will give it in
fitting measure, "rightly dividing the word of truth" (2 Tim. ii. 15).
But, on the other hand, under this pretext, especially in the presence of "temptations" and troubles, an improper system of negli-
gence and omission may creep in; and therefore the συμφέρειν,
understood by the light of the Spirit in a good conscience, is the
only rule of action to guide us as to what should be made known,
and what should be kept back.   The συμφέροντα which the apostle
here intends, are, however, the three chief points of apostolic duty,
which he forthwith names, and thereby desires to intimate that he
has not omitted one of them, and has not been content to stop short
at fulfilling the first or the second, etc.   The whole of the official
duties of a preacher as such, *i.e.* his duties concerning *the word*,
are divided here into the following three heads : 1*st*, To preach or
make known all that is profitable or necessary, so that the hearers
may know it, and it no longer remains concealed from them.
2*d*, To teach or explain, setting forth argumentatively and con-
secutively the whole counsel of God, so that the disciples may
understand it, and it no longer remains obscure to them.   3*d*, To
testify, or to certify and affirm from faith and experience, with an
implanted surrender of the entire impulsive personality ; *i.e.* to represent the path of repentance and faith with such arousing and
hortatory results, that those appealed to follow it willingly, and
are converted and edified ; or that some, in various degrees, should
even against their wills receive conviction.   The resources and
provision which a minister of the word needs for this threefold
efficacy are : *first*, a knowledge of the truths which he has to
preach ; *secondly*, an understanding of the plan of salvation which
he has to teach ; *finally*, a confidence in the way of grace to
which he has to testify as the only and certain means of salvation.
The usual stages of the course of action of God's word in the
natural man are these—the people first hear something which they
did not know; and where the word touches them, they understand
the profitable matter which it teaches them, and they receive the
doctrine; and from this they go on to the reception of the exhortation, or to practical conviction. *Repentance* and *faith* must proceed
from the free-will of the hearers through the operation of the grace
of God.   Of these two conditions of the heart, repentance towards
God would seem to refer principally to the Greeks, and faith

towards our Lord Jesus Christ to the Jews; but yet both of them apply equally to each people.[1] Repentance and faith are the beginning of all that is "profitable;" and they must not only be preached and taught, but must also be testified to : then only will nothing essential be kept back. He who only preaches without making his subject intelligible—he who only teaches from the pulpit, as if it were a lecturer's chair, without testifying that it is life and death which he is laying before his congregation ; he also who only endeavours to exhort and rebuke, without taking suffi-cient care to make his words understood—he who in his doctrine takes for granted things which should be first communicated to his disciples — he who is constantly demanding repentance without alluring on to faith, or bids the impenitent only to believe—he who always calls men to God, and keeps in the background that they can only come to Him through Christ, or preaches of Christ with-out showing forth the true God and Father in Christ, and turning souls through the Son to the Father,—all these men fail in finding the right way of fulfilling the apostolic office, the way which Paul so strikingly points out in his present discourse. Also as to *time* and *place* he adds an important prescript—*publicly* and *from house to house*, *i.e.* in the synagogue or lecture-room, and in families ; even in the market-place when it was fitting, and in the chamber when opportunity offered. The preaching of the gospel must be in public to the multitude, and in private to the disciples. The ministry of the word, apostolically considered, knows in its inner nature no limitation of any kind in respect to churches, pulpits, and Sundays. If a messenger of God's salvation—a shepherd in the name of the good Shepherd—is sent to a community, he may and must preach the word "in season or out of season" (2 Tim. iv. 2). A minister of the Lord speaks, teaches, and exhorts,

[1] It is not as if (according to Olshausen) the idea of strict justice was expressly implied in God the Father, and the idea of mercy in Christ. But " God " is at first the general and unspecified God (by no means already is He the Father), when we find Him at our first conversion ; then the same God as the Father reveals Himself more closely in Christ as the Gracious One. Every sinner both in Israel and Christendom must, in the first place, as the heathen (Acts xxvi. 18), turn to *God;* his first prayer cannot run : " Lord Jesus Christ, be merciful to me a sinner ! " *Repentance to Christ*—who even among us ever says this ? But the faith presented, offered, and commanded to us now, since Christ has appeared, is to be in this " appointed Man " (Acts xvii. 31) and given Saviour, and in Him God is to be recognised and appropriated as a mer-ciful God.

according to his Lord's command, wherever it is profitable to do so, and will not hold back because it is not in the church, although it may be desired to confine the word of God thereto ; and he will also not forbear to speak even in public places—in cases where it is only permitted to utter privately the voice of truth with clearness and stringency.   To sum up briefly : Paul's faithfulness in Ephesus consisted in having preached everything—to every one, everywhere, and in every way ; and this is the model which he holds out to his successors.   He does not say a word as to the numerous and surprising miracles (ch. xix. 11, 12) which had accompanied his testimony, for these miracles had nothing to do with his faithfulness : they were not the thing essential, and they were not to continue to be worked ; and the apostle desired so to describe his fidelity to his duty, that the elders might be able to imitate him in all points.

Ver. 22. The above applies specially to show how he had proved his faithfulness in the care of one particular church at Ephesus ; but as he was manifesting the self-same faithfulness in his present journey, he must, in order to present a pattern to the elders and pastors who were remaining behind, now proceed to declare his more general fidelity to duty taken as a whole.   The office of an apostle, and especially of a Paul, did not consist in ministering to one church, but in " the care of all the churches " (2 Cor. xi. 28).   Although his heart had been devoted for three long years to tending with fostering care one now blooming flower, the Lord had commanded him to pass it by ; and his fidelity to his duty consisted at present in tearing himself away, and in obe-diently following the path which the Spirit pointed out.   Thus his faithfulness in his present journeying to Jerusalem, is still more displayed through his former faithfulness in remaining at Ephesus. The ἐγώ prefixed is intended to call attention to this, and means (as had already been intimated by the νῦν ἰδού) the same as the αὐτὸς ἐγώ, Rom. vii. 25 : I, the same man who for so long gave himself up entirely to Ephesus.   The expression δεδεμένος τῷ πνεύματι, as to which there has been much exegetical controversy, is parallel with δουλεύων τῷ Κυρίῳ (" being bound " is the most constant service) : consequently " the spirit " is not, in the first place, Paul's own spirit, his inmost heart, in which he felt the binding ; but it is the Lord who is the Spirit, and as such directed the apostle's journeys (ch. xvi. 6, 7).   Certainly we must also include the idea, that the Spirit of Jesus worked and spake in

Paul's spirit, who willingly submitted his personal inner life (ψυχή, ver. 24) to God's guidance; consequently it is *bound in* (not merely through) *the Spirit,* inasmuch as and because the latter had become, and would continue to be, the Lord and Pervader of Paul's spirit, the power and chief element of his inner life. The " binding" is also least of all to be considered as an affliction and anxiety, as many have interpreted it : it is also not merely an expectation and presentiment of the actual bonds a'luded to in ver. 23 (with the consciousness that I shall become bound or imprisoned). But it is, in the first place, the stringent command, the inevitable obligation to take this journey, communicated through the internal clear command of the Holy Spirit. The apostle had already said (ch. xviii. 21), " I must *by all means* keep this feast that cometh at Jerusalem ;" and we are further told, at the conclusion of his blessed labours at Ephesus (ch. xix. 21), " Paul purposed in the spirit (ἔθετο ἐν τῷ πνεύματι), when he had passed through Macedonia and Achaia, to go to Jerusalem, saying, After I have been there, I *must* also see Rome." From this it follows, that in this passage the apostle had purposed not in his own mind, but in the Holy Spirit, this great termination of his effective ministry in Ephesus, and the " must" was the result of a revelation (as in Gal. ii. 2). Remark the confirmation of this from the Lord's lips in ch. xxiii. 11. Paul here makes use of the forcible expression " bound," in order to confess that there was a natural human self-will existing in him, although he willingly allowed it to be " bound," and that it must actually in a certain measure be bound and overcome by this command of the Spirit. This general state-ment is now followed by a further reference to the temptations or dangers in which the self-same faithfulness is always shown, because the Christian counts not his life dear unto him, so that through afflictions he may finish his course with joy. All the elders well knew Paul's " tears and temptations" at Ephesus ; but as to the things which were to befall him at Jerusalem accord-ing to God's ordinance and dispensation, and as to what afflictions he was now journeying to meet, these even Paul himself was ignorant of, at least with respect to all their detailed circumstances ; and most of all, he could not foresee the final result, whether it was life or death which awaited him (not like the Lord Himself, Luke xviii. 31). His earlier glance, which was turned to Rome after Jerusalem (ch. xix. 21), now falls into the background in the apostle's mind, compared with the increasing stringency of his call to Jerusalem, until his "bearing witness" at Rome is again suggested to him by the Lord Himself.

Ver. 23. *Save that the Holy Ghost witnesseth*, or distinctly certi-fieth to me, while I am on the road, from city to city (almost in *every* city),[1] *that bonds and afflictions await me.* Often must the disciple of Christ thus pursue his prescribed way, without knowing what is to happen to him, except so far that he is about to meet with many sufferings. The same Paul, who in vers. 25 and 29 prophesied to the Ephesians, must leave his own course to be prophesied about by others: the two subsequent examples of this (ch. xxi. 4, 11) were not the first, as is here shown, and he had often received such predictions before he came to Miletus. But at Tyre all the disciples in common "said to Paul through the Spirit, that he should *not* go up to Jerusalem;" and here Paul is "bound in the Spirit" to go up to the same place. Is there not then a contradiction? Or have we not wrongly interpreted the word δεδεμένος, and might not Paul have been stubbornly striving on this occasion against the dissuasions of the Holy Spirit? By no means, as is unconditionally shown by the passage already quoted (ch. xxiii. 11). Was it not then, if we may so speak, a contradic-tion on the part of the Holy Ghost Himself, who inwardly urged Paul on to Jerusalem, and outwardly restrained him from it? And was it not leading His disciple into temptation? Again by no means, as a closer consideration, very instructive in all similar cases, will clearly show. Of course, this apparent contradiction was a trial of the apostle, similar to that in which a prophet once came to an evil end (1 Kings xiii. 8–32); but there could be no false temptation by an actual contradiction on the part of the Spirit of truth. The disciples in Tyre perceived correctly enough, that bonds and afflictions awaited Paul at Jerusalem: this prescience was through the Spirit; but the advice deduced from it, that Paul should now give up the journey, was a merely human inference and an arbitrary addition made by these inexperienced prophets. They imagined that this foreknowledge was given to them for this very purpose; and in their good intentions they too hastily mixed up the prediction of the Spirit with their own merely human opinions. But God does not always show us the afflictions to come in order that we may avoid them, but often that we may be better prepared to meet them. Even should brethren through the Holy Spirit predict the "bonds" which are to come upon us, with the

[1] We assume the μοί here to be genuine.

good intention of keeping us from them, we must nevertheless hasten on to these very bonds, if we are thereto inwardly " bound in the Spirit," and thus enlightened as to the merely human character of the prophet's advice. It is clear that this was the nature of the case ; as, in Cæsarea (although none of the four prophesying daughters of the evangelist did so), the prophet Agabus predicted the " binding" in the most emphatic way (ch. xxi. 11). Not only all the disciples in Cæsarea, but also the whole of the travelling company (even Luke, as he confesses in ver. 12), understood the prediction wrongly, and thought that Paul was biassed and deluded by his own self-will : they therefore besought him, in the presence of such manifest dissuasions of the Holy Spirit, to abstain from his journey to Jerusalem. But Paul, although his heart was well-nigh broken by their weeping, remained firm to his purpose, and pointed them to the simple truth, which in their love they had overlooked, that the prophecy must be fulfilled, and that it was not his duty by turning back to make it a lie, but, on the contrary, to prepare himself for its sure fulfilment. Agabus had indeed distinctly said, " The Jews at Jerusalem shall bind the man that owneth this girdle, and shall deliver him into the hands of the Gentiles ; " but Paul's only answer was, " I am ready thereto " (ver. 13). And finally all the others understood it, and said rightly, " The will of the Lord be done." The above explanation appears to us necessary, in order to do away with the apparent contradiction between vers. 22 and 23, and to point out how surely Paul believed and knew that which the Holy Ghost testified to him, even as *he* testified the gospel both to Jews and Greeks.[1]

Ver. 24. *But none of these things move me.* He who is in the Lord's path, who once for all reckons not his life dear unto him, takes no account of either bonds or afflictions, even when they are so repeatedly predicted by the Holy Ghost that all the disciples think that they are intended for dissuasions. This mode of expression is used, in the first place, as referring to an actual martyrdom, which might result from his being bound and delivered up to the Gentiles, and so far names the highest possible example of those things, none of which, as he said, moved him. But secondly, there is also implied the inward death of self-renunciation which every Christian must die daily, being crucified with his Lord ; and as the inward binding included the external bonds, so does the inward

---

[1] The whole of ver. 23 stands in contrast to the words "I know not" in ver. 22.

dying the actual death. In this he commences the transition from the fidelity shown in this particular journey, to his fidelity to his office generally, and to its origin in his fidelity as a disciple. This transition was necessary here, in order that Paul should compare himself as a brother in office with the elders, and hold out his own example as a pattern available for them. Every quiet disciple who in the contest prescribed for him holds not his life dear, but readily lays it down, having through the Holy Ghost his own will entirely bound to the cross of Christ, is thus essentially like the apostle, who let another gird him and lead him away, glorifying God by a noble martyrdom (John xxi. 18, 19). But no unlicensed throwing away or contempt for life is here meant; for neither the disciple nor the apostle and bishop are permitted to consider their mental faculties and fruitful ministerial life as things in themselves unworthy and without value : they are before God purchased dearly for the service of His kingdom, and belong to Him (Rom. xv. 30, 31); for it merely says, "I count not my life dear ἐμαυτῷ, *unto myself*," so far as I might rob God of it, and appropriate it to my own sinful and slothful individuality.[1] A disciple, and still more a minister, may and must take care of his life for the sake of the church, but not for himself. The Holy Spirit, his guide, will teach him to distinguish between the two motives. The thought of a martyr's death as the possible end of his present journey, raises the apostle's view to the issue of his life-journey generally, and thus leads on most suitably to a glance at the zeal of his own "course." First, serving the Lord, or a surrender of self to His work; then, still more forcibly, a sufferance of being "bound in the Spirit" to do something which is painful and grievous; and finally—the hardest thing of all—his not counting his own life dear unto him, and the absence of any desire to preserve it for himself personally. In the expression "course" the apostle understands his present journey as a type of his whole life, which was but a journey to the heavenly Jerusalem above; but at the end of this journey we "know the things which shall befall us there,"

---

[1] "A foreknowledge of that which will happen to us is not so much the thing implied, as the power (derived from the gospel) of depriving the enemy of any opportunity of finding us to be lovers of our own lives."—RIEGER. This beautiful and profound sense of the apostle's words, which extends to a constant surrender of life, and consequently to a constant preparation for death, is destroyed by the exegesis of this passage, which only understands a foreboding of death.

—namely, everlasting joy and bliss. Whoever in this sense
" finishes his course" certainly resigns his life, but only to receive
it again eternally in imperishable renewal as a crown of righteousness (2 Tim. iv. 7, 8). After his tears (ver. 19) and afflictions
(ver. 23) are past and gone, the apostle will one day finish with
joy in the everlasting bliss of heaven, both his present journey and
his whole " course" and ministry as a witness for Jesus. Now
therefore he is joyful and blessed in this hope, and considers not
" the light affliction which is but for a moment, which worketh for
him a far more exceeding and eternal weight of glory" (2 Cor.
iv. 17). He has received his ministry (ἀποστολή) as a gift of
grace (χάρις) from the Lord Jesus, whom he well knows, and in
whose service alone he is saved ; and whatever the Holy Ghost
may witness to him of afflictions on the way, he must and will continue on to the end testifying whithersoever his Lord may send him
of the gospel of the grace of God, which in repentance towards
God produces a saving faith in Jesus.

Vers. 25–27. This is the solemn, forcible, earnest, and holy
farewell addressed to the elders by their former teacher and ex-
horter. At this point, perhaps, the tears of the elders began to
flow ; and the emphatic declaration of the apostle, now about to be
separated from them for ever, *I am pure from the blood of all men,*
sank deep into their hearts. That his words may be more affect-
ingly penetrating, the apostle prefixes the disclosure that they shall
see him no more.[1] Καὶ νῦν ἰδού, ἐγώ—a similar commencement to
that in ver. 22 ; for the day of his setting o   for Jerusalem is also
the day of his farewell to Ephesus. In order to show that he did
not foresee much about *himself*, but that he did distinctly foresee
this about *them*, he uses the words, " Ye shall see my face no more,"
addressing the elders thus as a preparation and groundwork for the
exhortation in ver. 28. We are not exactly to lay an artificial
emphasis on the word *all*, to make it mean, " Thus, united as
ye now are, ye shall see me no more ;" or, " Ye shall not *all* be
alive or present if I ever return :" for the subsequent obscure life-
history of the apostle contains nothing decisive as to any further
visit to Ephesus.—*Among whom I have gone*, in my apostolical
course. The apostle still uses the figure he adopted in ver. 24, and
his now terminated sojourn is called by him a journey among them

[1] " At every word which he now adds, they might well think that it was the
last which he would speak to them."—MENKEN.

preaching the kingdom of God.[1]   As the purport of his gospel, he had preached, or freely and loudly announced to them, the kingdom of God,[2] its presence among them, its nature, its aim, and the only sure way thereto.   The last testimony with which the testifying and exhorting messenger of the kingdom is to conclude his ministry, is the assurance that he has declared everything to them, and that he is pure from the blood of those who would not follow his words. In the energetic yet holy earnestness of his loving zeal, the apostle says to the believing leaders of a flourishing church to some extent the same thing which he said (ch. xviii. 6) on abandoning the reviling Jews.   He may and must thus resign his ministry, for he has neglected nothing that was profitable for them; and yet he can see in the spirit, that from among those to whom he is speaking a root of bitterness shall grow up (ver. 30).   He has declared to them the whole counsel and will of God—repentance and faith (ver. 21) as the gospel of grace (ver. 24)—that they might enter into the kingdom of God (ver. 25), the end and crown of which would be the glorious inheritance of the saints in light.   If any "against themselves reject the counsel of God" (Luke vii. 30), they shall "die in their iniquity;" but the apostle has "delivered his own soul" (Ezek. xxxiii. 9).

Ver. 28.   *Take heed therefore*—take care both of yourselves and the ministry confided to you, for which ye have been duly instructed and authorized by me and the Holy Ghost; so that by a faithful performance of your special duties ye may faithfully finish your Christian course, and may save yourselves and those who obey you.   First, take heed to *yourselves :* this is the necessary groundwork for all $\epsilon\pi\iota\sigma\kappa\sigma\pi\dot{\eta}$ over others.   And next to the *flock,* not *your* flock : for it is only teachers of error who seek to "draw away disciples after them" (ver. 30) ; but the flock is *God's* church, dearly purchased by Him.   And it must be *all* the flock, without distinc-

---

[1] Because the closely implied sense of these words has not been understood, it has been very unjustifiably assumed, that besides the elders from Ephesus (ver. 17), others were present from the whole district round about, so as to explain better his "journeying through them" here, and the "three years subsequently" (in ver. 31).

[2] Merely *to preach the kingdom* (without $\tau o\tilde{v}$ $\Theta\varepsilon o\tilde{v}$, as many now wish to read it) is a mode of expression so unusual, and here so entirely without motive, that we must from internal criticism protest against the external.   "Paul," it is said, "felt himself to be the harbinger of a King and of His kingdom ; " but this interpretation is altogether too artificial amid all the precision of the whole discourse, which everywhere speaks distinctly of God and Christ.

tion, partiality, or omission of any, as Paul (according to ver. 31) warned every one. In the beautiful expression " flock," introduced from the Old Testament by the words of Jesus, is conveyed the two ideas of *guiding* and *feeding*, both of which are here brought forward. *Among* which, not *over* which, ye are placed—in the Greek, ἐν ᾧ ὑμᾶς; among whom the Holy Ghost hath raised you by special appointment, without taking you out of the flock or raising you above it. The bishop is and remains a sheep of the flock, and must thus exercise his oversight both on himself and the whole flock. The office of the cure of souls, where rightly discharged, is not to consist in the gown and bands, or in any official robe which would separate the shepherd from the flock, but must be exercised in brotherly love, as by a friend and fellow-pilgrim. Let the only efficacious authority for episcopal exhortations and warnings be the Holy Ghost, which alone, although by means of human interposition, and even by the choice of the church, can make and appoint a true bishop. The Holy Ghost is the doorkeeper who throws open the fold to the shepherd (John x. 3) not merely at first and once for all; for it is He alone who can and will continue to open the mouth of the shepherd and the hearts of the sheep. These bishops were appointed by Paul, but not by the man or even by the apostle Paul, but through him by the Holy Ghost, who should outwardly (and indirectly) appoint, and inwardly (and directly) endow to every office in the church. In this it is not merely the first and inmost origin of the office which is stated, but also the continuous and enduring source and provision from which they, poor weak sheep themselves, can alone derive the power of *guiding* and *feeding* others. These two ideas contain the two great tasks of the ministry (1 Pet. v. 2): here, in the *feeding* (ποιμαίνειν which is due to a ποίμνιον), the *guiding* is also included; but, on the other hand, the title of office, ἐπίσκοποι, now given them (and henceforth to be honoured by the church), is derived from the other idea of *oversight* or *guiding*.[1] The office of the guide or guardian

[1] On account of the word ἔθετο, we cannot say (as Luther) that this term ἐπίσκοποι does not stand here as an official title, but merely to express the obligation of the " overlooking;" on the contrary, we think that the obligation is derived from the official title, and is explained by the very essential addition ποιμαίνειν. For what good would a shepherd and guide be to the sheep if he did not feed them? Every pastor should even now be a bishop, and not a mere preacher. " It is not right that a man should only preach a sermon every Sunday, and after that pay no regard to the people" (Gossner). But this regard is paid to them only in order to provide for them. Brückner, with deep

is properly confined to the above : he is not the *food-giver* who can make the pasture grow; but he who tends a flock must lead them with due care to that pasture which God has prepared for all through the blood of Christ. Now, after the origin and duties of the episcopal office have been generally stated (just as in ver. 24 the apostolic duties were specified), follows the entirely unfigurative and emphatic designation for the flock, "the church of God,"—a name which should make it very dear to the shepherds, in that it was "purchased with His own blood." Paul had in succession testified of himself, that he counted not his life dear to himself in the ministry of the gospel of the grace of God, in the preaching of God's kingdom, and in the declaration of God's whole counsel, and had thus designated himself as a servant and apostle in the ministry of the gospel of God, and through His will, as indeed he almost always does in his epistles.[1] In like manner he now, with deep significance, closely connects with God these mortal men whom the Holy Ghost had appointed to be bishops or watchmen to take care both of themselves and the whole flock, and says that they are to feed *God's* church; which, according to ver. 21, is formed by "repentance towards God," and according to ver. 32, is perfected by God's power to receive its inheritance.

Ver. 29. This is the *fourth* emphatic ἐγώ which Paul here makes use of in holy dignity to specify his person now departing; see above, vers. 22, 25, 26. *I* know, I your father, who obey, though with the reluctance of a father's heart, the revelations of the Spirit which summon me away from you—that Spirit which urges me whither it will, although I never shall cease to think on you, my children, before God;—I *know* not merely by experience and observation of your condition and circumstances, but also in the spirit of prophecy, just as I knew that ye would see me again no more. I know *this*—τοῦτο—a mournful and dangerous thing, which must call for the highest vigilance in you, if my former words have not yet effected this. *After my departure*[2] refers back

comprehension, perceives in the *feeding* the proffering of that which is given to the church by God ; and in the preceding *guiding*, the interposing to carry out (and expressing) that which is done by the church before God. Here, *à potiori fit denominatio*, the *feeding* is named, the *guiding* merely included, and indeed only as leading *to* God *for* food, so that God remains the sole doer and giver.

[1] Rom. i. 1, xv. 16, 17, 32; 1 Cor. i. 1; 2 Cor. i. 1, vi. 4; Eph. i. 1; Col. i. 1; 1 Tim. i. 1; Tit. i. 1.

[2] This signification is improperly denied to the word ἄφιξις; it is the only one suitable to the context.

to ver. 25, in which the former "I know" was given, and is now a most decisive, comprehensive expression. Glance back at the gradual stages in the apostle's discourse : "I have been with you" (ver. 18) ; "now I go" (ver. 22) ; "ye shall see my face no more" (ver. 25); "this day" (ver. 26) ; "my departure" (ver. 29). When even the most faithful and effective shepherd is no longer present, then, as is usual after such a departure, will the wolves come. They shall *enter in among you*—εἰσελεύσονται—shall break in upon you with wanton arbitrariness, without right or reason, not as if appointed by the Holy Ghost (an ἐπιβαίνειν of quite a different kind from that of Paul's (ver. 18), and like that described in John x. 1). The expression denotes the violent disturbers and renders of the flock (λύκοι βαρεῖς), attacking with power and hard to be repulsed, who in their cruel avidity desire to feed on the blood of God's church, and will not pay the least respect to or *spare* the flock, like foreigners and enemies coming from without. Compared even with this, the prediction which now follows is still more mournful.

Ver. 30. *Also of your own selves* means the elders or bishops who were present, for these are the only ones addressed throughout, since they were comprehended with the church in general in vers. 18–20. As in vers. 25–28 these elders only are meant, so in ver. 29 the εἰς ὑμᾶς is also addressed to them : the wolves will break in among *you* as teachers and chiefs. The flock or church and the disciples are always spoken of in the third person ; thus in ver. 31 only ἕνα ἕκαστον is said, and ὑμῶν is not added. "Men shall *arise*" —ἀναστήσονται—in the like sense of arbitrariness as in the previous εἰσελεύσονται. "*Men* shall arise"—no longer to be called bishops or shepherds—who shall speak perverse things ; not the counsel of God (ver. 27), but lies and false doctrine, arising from a perversion and misrepresentation of the truth ; not, as would be right, preaching, teaching, and exhorting, but *speaking* their own ideas. And with what aim will this be done ? In order that the disciples, who should all be disciples of only one Master, should be *drawn away* from the Lord, to whom these very elders ought to lead them. Certainly this misleading could only take place through perverted, false, and dishonest speaking. Drawing away disciples *after themselves*, that they should follow these "men," and be *their* disciples, and that they should be the masters, stealing away from God His own people, and "glorying in the flesh" of the children of God (Gal. vi. 13). Thus in his forcible warning does the apostle depict the character of an unfaithful bishop, who has become a wolf instead of a shepherd, and has turned from being a guide and fosterer of the flock, to be a misleader and destroyer. The two chief characteristics are perverted speaking instead of wholesome teaching, and an egotistical seeking after a peculiar body of adherents; the latter for the express purpose of the wicked enjoyment of devouring their flesh and shearing off their wool, or that these men themselves may idly act the master. As the apostle *knew* that "men" of this kind would arise from among those elders to whom he was speaking, how earnest and anxious must have been his appeal to them, " Take heed therefore to yourselves! "

Ver. 31. How emphatically this is followed by the reiterated exhortation, *Therefore watch!* Γρηγορεῖτε, be vigilant and awake, —a call pregnant with meaning to the shepherds when the wolves are about to break in upon the flock, and destroyers of the sheep are to arise from among these very shepherds themselves. It is a forcible substantiation of the προσέχειν and ἐπισκοπεῖν (ver. 28). In order to make yourselves watchful, keep in mind continually my three years' watchfulness for you and your church. *Three years* is a kind of round abstract (which was more suitable here than naming the exact period) of the time which Paul had abode in Ephesus; see the " three months" (ch. xix. 8) and the " two years" (ver. 10), and, besides, the indefinite time " for a season" (ver. 22).—*Day and night*, or in Greek, " night and day," *for the space of three years.* This is saying much, and the nightly watchings especially are a bright type and example of faithful vigilance; but in this the sleep which was requisite even for an apostle is not denied. Where the literal sense would be nonsense in all languages, such expressions must be taken as speaking with aphoristic exaggeration. Compare the expressions Luke ii. 37, 1 Tim. v. 5, and understand here, warning even *by nights,* whenever a good and urgent reason existed; consequently equivalent in meaning to the εὐκαίρως ἀκαίρως (2 Tim. iv. 2). Of the ἕνα ἕκαστον[1] we have previously spoken; the " warning"—νουθετεῖν—is a corroboration of the " testifying" (ver. 21), but expresses greater familiarity. *I ceased not* expresses the perfection of faithfulness in office. The

[1] We at least feel most decidedly prevented, by the whole disposition and plan of the discourse, from referring (as many do) this ἕνα ἕκαστον in a narrower sense to the *elders only.* Not only in that case must an ὑμῶν be added, but also the " constant warning with tears" seems but little suitable in the case of the bishops appointed by the Holy Ghost.

whole description is completed by the glance now first disclosed at the *tears* arising from his loving zeal in the ministry : the tears previously spoken of were called forth by suffering and temptations. The two emotions correspond ; but the last-named tears are the more precious, and also the more moving. The apostle wept them under the most unfeigned heartfelt impulse of love, which, even where they themselves did not weep, lamented over the disasters of his dear children and wards, so as in any way to overpower them, and make them wise unto salvation. These holy apostolic tears, this admirable loving zeal, this immeasurable self-devotion, considered as the actions of a weak man, are explicable only as being derived from the power of God. How great must have been the efforts of Paul at Ephesus, in teaching, exhorting, and adjuring ! how much must he have implored, wept, prayed, and striven, to be able now to venture to speak thus ! And did he not do the same in all the churches to which he ministered, and, as his epistles testify, never forgot them when they were far distant from him ?

Ver. 32. Now comes the actual moment of farewell—the severance of the apostle's human person from the church at Ephesus, and his solemn committal of them to God. This moment is more forcibly indicated by the ταυῦν (occurring only in the Acts of the Apostles) than by the νῦν in vers. 22 and 25 (cf. ch. iv. 29, xxvii. 22). Now also παρατίθεμαι is used without the ἐγώ—I commend or surrender you to God. His last verbal exhortation having been given, the apostle resolves to quit his beloved ones, and to leave them in the hands of his and their God, who has thus ordered it, and without the apostle's help can further care for and perfect them. Before the God to whom he commits them, he now for the first time names them *brethren.* Hitherto he had addressed them in all the dignity of a father, and had thus reminded the elders that he had both educated and appointed them ; but now they become his successors in the office which he is giving up.[1] Formerly even these elders formed a part of his flock, as in ver. 31 in ἕνα ἕκαστον both the church and their overseers were included ; but now he gives up the flock entirely into their hands, and both together into the hands of God. He commends them to God and to the

[1] Because a form of address appears to be wanting at the beginning of the discourse, some few manuscripts have the word ἀδελφοί there also. But here, in connection with the ταυῦν of this heartfelt and sublime farewell, we cannot make up our minds to expunge the ἀδελφοί, so that it should not once occur in the whole discourse.

word of His grace, i.e., in the first place, to the gospel of the grace
of God (ver. 24, ch. xiv. 3), by the interposition of which the
grace is testified, offered, and further shown ; to the unadulterated,
one only word which points to God, which, too, is opposed to the
" perverted speaking" in ver. 30.   But why does he commend
them just as much to this " word" as to God ?   He does not say,
" to God, who is able to build you up *through* the word of His
grace," as some would artificially construe it : the necessary continuation of this " who through the word can give you the inheritance" seems unfitting.   But he names *the word* independently and
as well as God, as he names Christ in vers. 21 and 24.   It is therefore, according to the biblical idea, the independent " Word" in the
preached word—the λόγος, so far as it is efficaciously manifested
in the apostolical preaching.   In reference to this idea, Heb. iv.
12, 13 is the principal passage.   Τῷ δυναμένῳ does not apply to
the word, or even to God and the word together, but to God alone,
to whom the accomplishment and completion of the work in the
church is to be ascribed.   It was God alone who, through Paul's
word, had previously built up the church at Ephesus ; and He can
and will do and give all else that is necessary : for even without
Paul the " word of His grace" remains with the church, and can
open all willing hearts to the grace of God, who alone can lead on
and finally perfect all (Rom. xvi. 25 ; Eph. iii. 20 ; 2 Tim. i. 12 ;
Jude 24).   Remark how Paul desires to afford neither time nor
opportunity for giving vent to the grief of the farewell, but forthwith concludes with sublime consolation.   The bishops of the
church, now left by the apostle, have no need to tremble; for He
who through Paul had laid the foundation, can even without Paul
" build up" all that is wanting.   This is the proper sense of ἐποικο-
δομῆσαι.[1]   Where " the foundation of the apostles and prophets,
Jesus Christ Himself being the chief corner-stone," is duly laid by
the powerful word of grace, as the apostles and prophets unanimously preach it, there God will further " build up" His saints
and household, until all " grow together unto an holy temple in the
Lord " (Eph. ii. 20, 21).   The aim of this building up is the completion of all the gifts of God's grace—the *giving* of the promised
inheritance (1 Pet. i. 4, 5.; Heb. ix. 15 ; Ps. xxxvii. 18 ; Isa. lviii.

---

[1] We retain here (with Tischendorf) the *compositum* ἐποικοδομεῖν, which is
suitable here if anywhere, and we might almost say indispensable to the sense.
It occurs three times in Paul's epistles (besides Jude 20), reckoning 1 Cor. iii.
10–14 as one, viz. Eph. ii. 20, Col. ii. 7.

14). The blessedness of this glorious inheritance, which from the beginning of the Old Testament was shown forth under a material type, is thus exalted and completed, so that it is received in common, and is enjoyed with or among "all them that are sanctified." In this last expression the apostle signifies much. In the first place, it means that God was able by His power to preserve them also through faith unto salvation, and to give them a right to and a share in the inheritance among all them that are sanctified. Secondly, this ultimate communion of saints points beautifully to another and real meeting after the present farewell. Finally, in the *sanctification*, which is to be the fruit of the *building up*, the indispensable path is shown, the end of which is the inheritance ; for the term ἡγιασμένοι by no means implies the same as ἅγιοι—in a more general sense for κλητοὶ or πιστοὶ : still less does it mean (according to Bengel) the Gentile Christians principally, but rather the Jewish Christians, as may be seen from ch. xxvi. 18. The mode of expression of the New Testament points to its precise meaning as being *moral purification* in the fountain of the spiritually powerful *word of truth*. Thus the Lord in John xvii. 17 prays, "Sanctify them by Thy truth : Thy word is truth ;" and in ver. 19 says, "And for their sake I sanctify myself, that they also might be sanctified (ὦσιν ἡγιασμένοι) in Thy truth." In Rom. xv. 16 Paul desires "to be the minister of Jesus Christ to the Gentiles, ministering the gospel of God, that the offering up of the Gentiles (the Gentiles themselves being offered up to God) might be acceptable, being sanctified by the Holy Ghost." Consider also 1 Thess. v. 23 and 2 Tim. ii. 21, and remark how in our present passage the "building up" is referred to God, but the sanctification to the word of His grace. Paul here makes use of an expression which the Lord Himself spoke to him in the heavenly vision (see ch. xxvi. 18), where the precise meaning of ἡγιασμένοι is shown by the context. He now adds πᾶσιν in order to contrast the universality of the sanctifying with their own special glance at Ephesus, and also that he may conclude with the animating and consolatory idea, that *all* who will be sanctified through God's word shall certainly one day receive the inheritance together.

Vers. 33, 34. If we lay stress upon the human element in this discourse, we might suppose that the apostle had desired to conclude with ver. 32 ; but that the "giving" by God which he had just mentioned had impressed him to add an exhortation to disinterestedness *in giving*, taking himself as an example. The con-

nection is at least implied in it. God's grace gives us everything
up to the attainment of the inheritance; God's minister therefore
should consider giving to God's church as more blessed than receiving anything from it,—thus following the pattern of Paul, of
Jesus, indeed of God Himself. But this concluding idea must
necessarily form a part of the apostolical discourse as a finished
whole, and therefore cannot have been added from merely human
feelings.[1] An exhortation to a disinterested self-devotion must be
contrasted with the selfishness and self-seeking mentioned in vers.
29, 30; and the example of the apostle previously set forth, merely
in reference to what he had *said*, must be completed by a declaration of what he had *done*; and finally, it was necessary that the
whole apostolic example should be cast into the shade as compared
with the pattern of Jesus and God. All this now follows in the
real conclusion, after ver. 32. In order to urge upon the elders
the fundamental thought which he has in view, Paul at once, with
a sharp and striking contrast, says that he has coveted no man's
gold, silver, or apparel[2] (nourishment or food is due as a matter of
course to the workman who, according to Matt. x. 10, "is worthy
of his meat"). Then he again (as at first in ver. 18), appealing
to them, says : *Ye yourselves know*, that not only for my own
necessities of every kind, but also for them that were with me, who
came with me, and afterwards remained and dwelt with me, *these
hands have ministered*. Whilst, therefore, Paul with his whole soul
and spirit served the Lord through His church, his hands at the
same time were serving his companions,—a most eminent example
of disinterestedness in such faithfulness as that described in ver. 31.
Luke has previously related, with regard to the sojourn in Corinth
only (ch. xviii. 3), that Paul worked as a tent-maker. We see
here that the same thing also took place at Ephesus. Paul had
come in the name of Jesus, not to be ministered unto, but to
minister, and to entirely give up his life for his brethren. Very
probably he now exhibited to them his hands, hard and horny with
toil; at least the emphatic conclusion (in the Greek) of the sen-

[1] "Something was still in the apostle's heart which he longed to say, and
longed *so* to say, that it should remain indelible; but he had been unable, if
I may so speak, to find the right opportunity for it. *Here* the right place for
it is disclosed as it were spontaneously to his heart." Thus Menken forcibly
expresses himself; but we would rather say that *here* the guiding Spirit had
prepared and kept in reserve the proper place for it.

[2] The somewhat similar farewell of *Samuel* (1 Sam. xii. 3) spoke also of
" not taking."

tence, αἱ χεῖρες αὗται, *these* hands, lead us to suppose this. As in his whole course of conduct among them he had not only *taught*, but *shown* (ver. 35), so now, all that he has to say to them, looking at the impending dangers, he desires to say *demonstratively* (δεικτικῶς). These toil-worn hands of Paul, which at the moment of his departure he showed to the elders, may have started up before the eyes of some who in after times were tempted to covet silver or gold, and may have proved a shame-causing vision to hold them back from "arising," like the "men" named in ver. 30, in perversity and self-seeking.[1]

Ver. 35. To those among whom he ministered, Paul had, in his own conduct, *shown all things*, including the unselfishness which he had just mentioned to them. He had not only taught them by words, but had also shown them by his own actions, what was right and good, what was holy and blessed. This *showing* by means of the conduct fully corroborates the *testifying* by words, and makes his entire presence among them one great living doctrine, and a real example or ὑπόδειγμα (to which the expression ὑπέδειξα points). If, therefore, we would become ministers of Jesus, and workers in His church, we must thus labour and strive; not merely with the work of the hands, but generally, in all the painfulness of a perfect service.[2] We must interest ourselves in the *weak* in mind (Rom. xiv. 1; 1 Cor. viii. 9, ix. 22), and help those who may thus be lifted up and sustained; also, where it is possible and requisite, we must in a loving spirit assist and minister to others, even through the work of our own hands. Generally, too, we must not be burdensome (1 Thess. ii. 6–9), or make ourselves great or important *over* the church, but must take the lead *in* the church with a disinterested self-denial. All this we shall do if we rightly keep in mind the Lord Jesus, our great leader in the ministry, and His words so often and so emphatically summoning us to follow Him. The recurrence to the words of the Lord Jesus now predominates over the reference to Paul's exhortations in ver. 31. Think how I thought on Jesus, and through me contemplate

[1] On this passage Menken observes, that "the deceitfulness of riches is the most plausible and strongest of any—a deceitfulness like magic." We might also refer to 2 Pet. ii. 3.

[2] According to this (not to be overlooked) *general* sense of these last words (here only concretely exemplified), the apostle in his discourse, so entirely prefigurative of the ministry in God's church, uses, at the conclusion of it, language of a large and wide-spreading tendency. "To support the weak" is a matter which concerns the church now more than ever.

Him !—this is the apostle's concluding appeal to them.   His whole
conduct was nothing but an emanation from and a copy of one
deep-meaning utterance of Jesus.   He concludes with Jesus, not
with himself, mentioning the " words of the Lord Jesus " generally
(τῶν λόγων),[1] which contain so much holy teaching; but he brings
forward only one of them which we do not find recorded elsewhere,
although the sense of it is contained in several of our Lord's sayings, as e.g. in Luke xiv. 12–14.   It is remarkable, as regards the
living tradition in the apostolic age, that Paul should be the apostle
to hand down to us an utterance of Jesus, with the simple assurance, " how He said."   And what a beautiful thought it is—*It is
more blessed to give than to receive!*   Most assuredly a maxim of
the Lord Jesus, and in complete opposition to the mistaken wisdom
of this world, which considers that it is more fortunate to receive.[2]
But as God desires not to receive offerings, but to grant His grace,
and being the richest Giver is the most blessed of all, in the same
way His Son, His personation on earth, and His unspeakable gift,
manifests the same sublime disinterestedness.   If we would follow
Him, this must be our watchword—we must look upon even the
things we are permitted to receive as a detriment to us, if by giving
we may be more like Jesus and God.   This mode of thinking and
acting has its reward not only in the world above, but contains a
blessing for us even here below.   The more blessed we would be in
our labour and painstaking in behalf of the weak, the more must
we (impelled thereto by the Spirit of grace) endeavour to penetrate
into the love which, in every sense after God's pattern, would
rather give than receive, both as regards external necessities, and
even in respect to the very love itself.[3]   This view of God's loving
heart, as revealed to us through Jesus, and of the blessedness
that a concurrence with it involves—so that, as Brückner says,
" in giving, we receive back more than we give"—this is the *last*
reflection which Paul, out of the depth of his apostolic heart, was

---

[1] According to the correct reading, which we acknowledge.   Τὸν λόγον or τοῦ
λόγου (in which Luther follows the Vulgate) is certainly wrong, and has only
crept in through lack of understanding.

[2] Artaxerxes is reported to have said : ὅτι τὸ προσθεῖναι τοῦ ἀφελεῖν βασιλι-
κώτερόν ἐστι.   Similar things are found in Aristotle and Seneca.   But these
ideas (as Lechler reminds us), with all their proud, grand style of expression,
do not come up to the profound words of the Lord Jesus, which give pre-
eminence to the blessedness of giving in itself.

[3] " Though the more abundantly I love you, the less I be loved."   Thus
Paul writes in 2 Cor. xii. 15.

able to tender to the bishops and shepherds who were ordained to give God's gifts to others. He now ceases, and prays with them all to the most blessed Giver of all good. Then, as a follower of Jesus, and a pattern to us, he goes on his apostolic way, leading through the blessing of tribulation to the everlasting blessing of the glorious inheritance reserved for those who are sanctified in affliction.

XXIII.

THE ELDERS IN JERUSALEM TO PAUL.

(Chap. xxi. 20-25.)

A REQUEST THAT PAUL WOULD, AS FAR AS WAS LAWFUL, ACCOM-
MODATE HIMSELF TO CIRCUMSTANCES, IN ORDER TO OBVIATE
A CERTAIN MISUNDERSTANDING.

Vers. 15, 16. *The will of the Lord be done!* Thus did the Christians in Cæsarea and Paul's companions at last express themselves, when he would not allow himself to be persuaded by them, and would not try to evade the "binding and delivering over to the Gentiles," which had been so certainly predicted by Agabus. The apostle must have been almost heart-broken in refusing a request which sprung from such strong affection, yet he remained "bound" by that which was made certain to him by the Spirit; and holding out firmly against all their love, was prepared both for bonds and also death in his imitation of the Lord Jesus. They immediately packed up ("took up their carriages") and proceeded towards Jerusalem. Certain disciples from Cæsarea accompanied them, in order to procure (at least for the present) a safe and convenient lodging for the travellers at the house of one Mnason of Cyprus. This man was one of Jesus' earliest disciples,[1] and was liberal-minded enough to be freely willing to entertain the apostle

---

[1] Does ἀρχαῖος μαθητής mean one who had had a personal knowledge of Jesus Himself? We must confess that it is doubtful whether his becoming a disciple dated back to the commencement at the Pentecost, or to an association with the Lord Himself. The expression μαθητής appears here to be better adapted to the latter idea.

of the Gentiles. This was a welcome kindness at the feast-time, which filled Jerusalem to overflowing, and was also a friendly introduction for Paul, in the face of the prevailing disposition of the Jewish Christians against him and his gospel work among the Gentiles.

Vers. 17-20. The purpose for which the disciples of Cæsarea had travelled with them was fully answered, and Paul and his companions met with a kind and willing reception from the *brethren in Mnason's house.* This is perhaps the most correct way of understanding ver. 17, as in ver. 20 *all* the *Jewish* Christians as a body are described as being provoked against Paul, and the elders are not in question until ver. 18. Without delay, on the day following, Paul goes with his whole company to *James,* with whom we have already been made acquainted. None of the apostles were now left in Jerusalem; following their Lord's directions, after they had borne witness to Christ long time enough in the holy city, now hastening on to its destruction, they had sought a further sphere of activity, some in Judea and Samaria, and some in more distant lands, even to the very ends of the earth.[1] All that could have been done had been done: the state of things was becoming more and more sanguinary and involved under the rule of the governors; the present one being Felix, soon to be admonished by Paul. The last and not unimportant band of all those Jews zealous for the law, who still had to be won over to Jesus the Messiah, was tended by the faithful James and the elders associated with him, with all the love and patience of Christ. James immediately, on Paul's arrival, with wise determination summoned an assembly of the chief men, in order to arrange and turn to the best account the beloved but yet critical presence of their valued guest. Paul fraternally saluted his venerable brother, and with the greatest circumstantiality related to the eager and willing leaders of the Jewish Christians all and everything that God had done among the Gentiles through his ministry. Luke, who here keeps to the chief matter, does not relate anything as to the collection which Paul brought with him, which was probably now handed over as the fruit of love from the Gentile brethren, and as a seal of their common brotherhood (Rom. xv. 28). This, however, he relates, that the whole assembly, with Christian recognition and candour, pleased at these fresh works of God, though disconnected from the

---

[1] Whither the Lord from the very beginning had directed them, not having retracted this command and given it exclusively to Paul.

church at the head of which they stood, in the first place " glorified
God " for what they had learned ; and next looking at the disposition of their community, they proceeded to give advice which was
no less friendly than wise and determined.   We must either consider that James, as the head of the assembly, spoke in the name
of all, which seems most likely, or that Luke combined in a pithy
abstract, entirely in conformity with the truth, the sum-total of all
that was spoken by the many.   At all events, this particular form
of the narrative, according to which the elders speak *directly*, is a
highly important and decisive testimony that even James, in his
acknowledged position, possessed no peculiar official title, or any
authoritative pre-eminence.

Ver. 20. The commencement of this request, addressed as it is
to Paul in full confidence, seems very gracious.   Those who speak,
acknowledge with praise to God all that had been done among the
Gentiles through Paul's ministry, and are very far from entertaining any feeling in their hearts against the valued apostle who had
so convincingly laid everything before them ; without any reluctance, they call him *brother*.   They, however, had been appointed
to a forbearing, much-enduring, and slowly-guiding ministry among
the *Jews*, and therefore cannot but pay attention to all that concerns *their* charge.   They themselves are personally no zealots for
the law : if they had been, the apostles and James would not have
instituted them as elders.   But " *thou seest, brother,* how the
matter generally stands, and especially so with our community
here :" this is the commencement of their address.   Most suitably
they, in the first place, appeal to something which Paul already
knew, and now on his arrival might assure himself of by observation, perhaps even in one day, because the existence of ceremonial
observance is so outwardly conspicuous.   *Thou seest* : this implies a
half-sad, half-candid confession of the imperfection of their flock,
as to which they agreed with their brother Paul without saying
much about it.   There is also a decided reference to something
which existed, and consequently could not be overthrown by force,
but must be treated with love.——*How many thousands* (or properly
myriads) *there are of Jews which believe !* They call the Christian
brethren still *Jews*, although they are believers, in antithesis to the
Gentiles, about whom Paul had been relating ; and also from an
acknowledgment of their slow progress, on which account they
were only to be called *Jews* who believed as regarded the chief
matter, and not full and free believers from among the Jews.

There were, too, many myriads of these men! Even if we assume that all the strangers from the provinces now assembled in Jerusalem (for the zealot for the law was to be recognised from this pertinacious attendance at the feast), or indeed all the believers in Judea, were included in this number, it certainly seems a strong expression.[1] The elders made use of it (with truth, as a matter of course), in order to intimate through the great number of the erring brethren how necessary it was to show forbearance to their error. For all these Jews were certainly believers,[2] and as such to be respected; but yet they were all (with perhaps few exceptions) *zealous for the law.* Not merely observers of it, as indeed James and the elders were, but *zealots,* with a still Jewish, unchristian bigotry. What was it, then, that they believed in? In the grace of Jesus Christ. And yet could they be zealots for the law? Is not this a direct contradiction? Completely so, no doubt, as Paul often shows in his epistles. Here, however, we may see in a highly significant and world-widely spread example, that complete contradiction may still exist in those who already form a part of God's church—contradiction, too, even in important points; that this may take place so long as the faith laid hold of by the heart is not yet established in a clear confession, and an exact consistent theory is not derived therefrom. This confession and theory, even in main points, is by no means the principal thing in believing unto salvation. As God so long suffered the Jewish Christians until, in His good time, "that which was decayed and waxed old was ready to vanish away" (Heb. viii. 13), so in all ages He bears with the weak until they become strong. We must not therefore despise those whom God has received (Rom. xiv. 3), but must consider that any zeal of ours against them would be as Jewish as their own, and would be nothing but a "zeal for the law" which would turn the free-making faith in the pure truth as it is in Jesus into a form and a commandment, instead of making it a matter of unfettered life and growth. Thus the apostles and elders thought of it: they would not and could not forestall God's work by their impatience, but understood and honoured God's wisdom therein. It was a

---

[1] Neander (against Baur, *Pflanzung*, etc., p. 358) has settled that τῶν πεπιστευκότων ought not to be expunged, because speaking merely of the many *Jews* who were there to see would have been entirely useless; and also that the great number of believers is perfectly credible even in those early days.

[2] They believed rudimentally, as it were, and had not yet sunk into apostasy, as many of them probably did afterwards.

matter precious to their love, that so many Jews, their brethren
after the flesh, should be delivered out of the general destruction
of the " untoward generation," and should be grounded in the faith
of the crucified Jesus, and that thus the source of all further
wisdom and grace should be rendered accessible to them. They
awaited the abrogation of the Judaism that yet remained, which
abrogation would result in the course of time through the grace of
Jesus, and the impending destruction of the temple and city. And
Paul also agreed with them, the apostle of the Gentiles, who must
have dreaded these believers almost as much as he did the heathen,
and yet looked upon and ministered to them as God's " saints "
(Rom. xv. 31).[1] The words of the elders, therefore, met with his
full acceptance : the latter must have known this beforehand,
addressing him, as they did, with such fraternal confidence. Remark how beautiful and lovely it is when brethren, who are
anointed with the strength of the Spirit more than others, understand one another so harmoniously as to their respective spheres of
action, and their mutual forbearance to the weak. This is the
work of mercy, and the love of God is thus manifest in us more
predominantly than when greater haste is shown, and those only
are included in the church of God who have been able without
delay to become strong, and from their faith to develope a theory
which is consistent in all points.

Ver. 21. *And they are informed about thee;* or, as the word
κατηχήθησαν almost implies, purposely apprised about thee, intentionally instructed by repeated communications. We may easily
imagine that it was partly the unbelieving Jews, and partly the
pharisaical Christians, who were the eager tell-tales in this matter.
They have been informed, not *we,* who presuppose it to be a false
report, particularly after the narrative you have afforded us. If,
however, these men are zealous for the law, and have also received
false reports—in these two things there is to be found a good-
natured excuse for their feeling against you. Prejudices and false
rumours combined have stirred up among disciples in all ages
many an unjust enmity. The elders speak prudently, and impart
to the honoured apostle their unpleasant information with equal

---

[1] Oh that at the time of the Reformation this feeling had prevailed! Then
we should not have had two evangelical churches opposed to one another, any
more than a Pauline and a Petrine church of God in the apostolic age. That
these two divisions existed from the beginning, is but a fiction of incorrect
history.

circumspection and love. The reports spoken of contained a two-fold misunderstanding arising from a distortion of the truth. 1*st*, That which Paul only *permitted*—namely, that all who were firm in the perception that the types had been superseded by their substantial fulfilment, and felt free thereto in love, might give up these types—this was stated to be *taught* or commanded by him. 2*d*, The second misconception was, that whilst Paul only preached freedom from the law to the *Gentiles* as such, and dealt tenderly with the Jews, who were painfully and rigorously accustomed to the law, it is here said, to the contrary, that he taught " the *Jews* who were among the Gentiles," and indeed *all* of them. The matter thus strikingly conveyed in such few words is further explained and corroborated by the explicit addition : that thou *sayest* (in thy teaching of all the Jews), *i.e.* that thou *prescribest*, " that they ought neither to circumcise their children" (the innocent children, thus early torn away from Moses, and deprived of the holy sign of the covenant !), nor (themselves generally) " to walk after the customs."

Vers. 22, 23. *What is it, therefore*, which must now be done, both by us as well as specially by thee ? How are we to demean ourselves in such a position of matters ? It might seem, as many interpret it, that the question as to what the principal men should do is answered in the words δεῖ πλῆθος συνελθεῖν, that they should assemble the church ; and that Paul's conduct under the circumstances is pointed out by the subsequent words τοῦτο ποίησον. But for several reasons it cannot be an intentional calling together of the church which is spoken of in ver. 22. 1*st*, Τὸ πλῆθος τῶν μαθητῶν is indeed used in ch. vi. 2 of the assembly of the whole church ; but here not only the qualifying words τῶν μαθητῶν are wanting, but also the article is not used : it is not *the* multitude, but *a* multitude, a crowd. 2*d*, The term συνελθεῖν instead of συγκαλεῖσθαι, as well as the cause for the multitude, which is forthwith stated—"*for* they will *hear* that thou art come"—evidently denote an unprompted assembling, caused by the news of Paul's arrival, and not a duly summoned meeting at the desire of the elders. The words πάντως δεῖ,[1] which are apt to mislead to a different interpretation, must therefore be explained, *it is necessary*—nothing else can be thought or expected ; as in Matt. xviii. 7, ἀνάγκη γάρ ἐστι. 3*d*, To have formally convoked a general assembly would

---

[1] These words are certainly not rightly to be expunged ; for how would any interpolation of them be explicable ?

have been rather an unsuitable and doubtful measure ; indeed, Paul's subsequent ceremonial proceedings would have lost the greatest part of their judicious character, if they had not been impartially left to his spontaneous perception, but had been brought before a special assembly with all the appearance of an expressly advised matter. *4th,* In ver. 24 neither is any such assembly spoken of (as it is merely said, καὶ γνώσονται πάντες, *and all shall know*), nor does Luke relate anything about it in vers. 26, 27, but, on the contrary, joins on the apostle's visit to the temple to this assembly of the elders, and the former is directly followed by the apostle's arrest by the people. We therefore understand that it was a kind of anxious, spontaneous, and unauthorized flocking together of the multitude caused by the arrival of the supposed transgressor ;[1] and we interpret the τί οὖν ἐστι not exactly as, *Quid tibi (nobis) faciendum?* but in a more undefined way, as, " What will (or is to) be the result of this ?" This again resolves itself into two points : first, what would necessarily take place without the elders' will or agency ; and next, what was Paul to be advised to do. The simple sense is : If the multitude is now (here and there) assembled, ought we not to endeavour to quiet this critical excitement (which may easily lead on to something bad) by something which will modify their zeal for the law as directed against thee, and give the brethren something else to speak of and think of about thee, instead of that which only prompts the ardour of their bigotry ? Thus, in ver. 23, it follows most fittingly : *Do therefore this that we say to thee!* A worthy preamble to their fraternal, peace-desiring advice, which this assembly of elders addresses almost as a request to the apostle. An actual command is in no way implied : on this point we must think on the kindly and confiding expression " brother" with which the address began.

Ver. 24. Besides the customs and ceremonies which Moses once for all ordained for all Israelites without distinction, there were, according to this law, several spontaneous offerings, vows, and dedications to be performed as opportunity and impulse dictated ; among which the vow of a Nazarite—the ancient custom having been confirmed by Moses—stood in the foremost place, and might be called simply *a* or *the vow.* Compare ch. xviii. 18, and read Num. vi. 1–21. This vow might be undertaken for as long a time as was desired ; certainly, according to the later rabbins, the shortest period was a month. But Moses did not prescribe anything

---

[1] Schott : Nequit evitari, quin multitudo confluat.

on the point,[1] and here at all events it follows from ver. 27, that
in Paul's case his association with the other Nazarites, as well as his
own vow, lasted for only a week.[2] A spontaneous vow of this sort
was a peculiarly fitting testimony that he did not despise the law
of Moses ; and his bearing the expenses of some other poor Nazarites served as a sign of commendable religious zeal. We read in
Josephus of other instances of this generosity. As just at this
time there were some poor Nazarites among the Jewish Christians,
what better thing could have been advised, than that the apostle
should join these men engaged in the vow, and hold them completely free of all charges? The matter was offered by the
circumstances themselves, and was as unsought for as it was judicious : it would serve to show that Paul not only acknowledged
the keeping of the law in other Jews, but that he did not reckon
it as any sin that he himself should take a share in all due form in
the customs of Moses. Paul, with spontaneous devotion to the
forms of the law, and with all earnestness of heart therein, had
also done the same thing before at Corinth, in order to pacify
the Jews who were stirred up against him as being an enemy
(vid. ch. xviii. 12, 13, 18).—Εἰσὶν ἡμῖν, there are among us. This
statement, which connects the advice about to be given with the
narrative of the existing state of things, is emphatically prefixed
by the elders, in order to show that it is not so much they themselves who give the advice, but that the Lord Himself appears to
speak through this apposite and favourable circumstance. The
word ἡμῖν denotes that the four men were Christians, as indeed
was necessary : the indefinite expression εὐχὴν (which is found in
Num. vi. 2, 6, 7) is explained by the subsequent mention of the
shaving of the head, as well as by the formula ἔχοντες ἐφ' ἑαυτῶν.
For the latter is the legal expression used in Num. vi. 7 ; whilst
εὐχή, or נֶזֶר, stands for the sacred hair itself. These men take to
thee, παραλαβὼν, coming among them as their chief who pays all

---

[1] For Num. vi. 9, 10 is not to be interpreted as referring to this point, but
as applying to the seven days of purification.

[2] Now in our second edition we abide by this view of the matter, although
Wieseler (Chron. des apost. Zeitalt. p. 105) has brought forward several arguments against it. We omit any refutation of them, as extraneous to our subject,
and leave it to our readers to decide ; certainly thinking that an unprejudiced
reader will certainly be inclined to deduce an actual Nazarate on the part of the
apostle from the words ἁγνίσθητι σὺν αὐτοῖς (ver. 24) and ἁγνισθείς (ver. 26).
This Nazarate is also opposed by Baumgarten. Wieseler brings forward many such
novelties, against the plausibilities of which it is necessary to be on our guard.

charges. Two things now follow which are to be done: ἀγνίσθητι is the legal expression (Num. vi. 2, 3, 5), and δαπάνησον is used by Josephus (*Ant.* xix. 6, 1) in similar cases.—*That they may shave their heads.* In this are meant the offerings of purification prescribed in this vow (ver. 26). Now, since their conduct will certainly be accurately observed, and the purification will take place publicly in the temple, *all* (the whole of the " multitude coming together," ver. 22, and the πάντες ζηλωταὶ, ver. 20) must know, perceive, and mark in a perfectly unconstrained way (γνώσονται, by which expression the matter narrated in ver. 21 is now distinctly brought before us as a misunderstanding). But what are they to *know ?* That there is *nothing* in all the information they have received concerning thee—at one blow dissipating the lies, and contradicting them by public evidence ! For how couldst thou with bitter zeal " teach all the Jews to forsake Moses," and forbid their circumcision and keeping the law, if thou thyself (καὶ αὐτὸς) enterest into a spontaneous vow as an observer of the law ? From this present acquiescence in the vow of a Nazarite they may (not altogether with reason) conclude, that thou everywhere and always keepest the law ; or they may only go as far as to recognise that thou art not hostile to the law and its ceremonies. The former delusive conclusion may tend to peace ; but the latter idea, that thou dost not consider a fraternal connection with the zealous keepers of the law to be any sin—this is, at all events, the main point, which they may be persuaded to in all truth. On this point it is (as Baumgarten rightly remarks) taken for granted by the elders, that the apostle's fulfilment of the law would make more impression on the Jewish Christians than the loving gift collected for them by the Gentile brethren ; and this would be but natural.

Ver. 25. It scarcely needs proving that it was permissible for Paul to undertake the vow of a Nazarite, although in his inner consciousness he stood above any such forms, and was enabled to contemplate the reality of these types, and the achieved end of all these preparations. Because Christian freedom stands above these forms, any coercion to which must give way before it—for this very reason is it also free to take these forms upon itself when it is required by the love which tends to spare a brother's feelings, in order that the Lord's work may not be disturbed. If Christ, the Son of God, was placed under the law, and if He, although the children of the heavenly kingdom were free from the foreigner's tax, paid as if to His Father the external temple-tribute, so that He might not embitter those in the midst of whom He was working, what is it that we are not *permitted*, indeed *bound*, to do in imitation of Him? Therefore, ye better class of separatists, purify yourselves with your weak brethren, although ye through faith may be already pure; and ye who are more bitter—who look upon any such adaptation to circumstances as a sin—understand this, that ye yourselves are but slaves to your own pride, and by no means free in the liberty of Christ Jesus, the Servant of God and man. In many an accommodation to circumstances, and especially in the matter here advised, one thing must be especially considered,— whether a wrong and pernicious misunderstanding might arise from it. When any giving way to the weakness of others might be taken as, and be, an express confirmation of their error, then it would be both forbidden and wrong. This was Christ's position in His whole course of life under the law, and yet He testified freely enough both in words and works for the freedom of the spirit over the law. Especially, however, when, as in Paul's case, a misunderstanding was to be obviated, the question must be asked, whether a more bitter misunderstanding might not be caused. If by the apostle's vow as a Nazarite any one might have been led mistakenly to conclude that Paul adhered so firmly to the law, that he would desire to persuade the Gentile brethren thereto, that he had confessed his previous error, and would now commence to be zealous for the law like them, etc.—in this case the advice of the elders would have been unwarrantable and dangerous. But the general and well-known resolution in regard to the Gentile Christians was opposed to any such ideas; and this is the relation in which the mention of the latter stands to the preceding discourse. It is not, as many say, "Thou art thyself of Israel, and not a Gentile Christian; thou art therefore permitted to take upon thee a Mosaical vow:" for the resolution in question did not forbid the law to any Gentile Christian, if he was spontaneously willing to observe it; it merely removed any compulsion thereto. The true relation of the reference to this resolution is as if they said, "As regards the believers from among the Gentiles, none of our zealots for the law can demand anything from them except according to this resolution, which is both well known, and up to the present time has never been abrogated.[1] By this resolution we shall abide, and

---

[1] Μηδὲν τοιοῦτον, εἰ μὴ, refers back to the expressions used in the resolution: Μηδὲν πλέον πλὴν. It ought not to be omitted, but forms a part of the quotation of the original resolution.

thou needst not fear that any one should wrongly interpret thy conduct, or that we shall require anything from thee which might dangerously tend to any change in the Christian freedom of thy Gentile brethren." Thus at the conclusion the elders assure the apostle, that in main points everything should remain undisturbed ; only that, on this occasion, he as a Jew might all the more readily adhere to the law in the same spirit of brotherly love in which the Gentiles were necessarily willing to yield something to the spirit of Judaism.

XXIV.

PAUL'S ADDRESS TO THE MULTITUDE ASSEMBLED IN JERUSALEM.

(CHAP. XXII. 1–21.)

A VINDICATORY NARRATIVE OF THE MIRACULOUS ORIGIN OF HIS CHRISTIANITY AND APOSTLESHIP.

CH. xxi. 26–29. *Then*—τότε—Paul at once agreed with the advice which had just been given by his brother James and the elders. In ver. 24 he was bidden to take the men to him, and purify himself with them; and now immediately he does take the men to him, and purifies himself with them.[1] *The next day* (cf. ch. xxiv. 1, 11) he went into the temple and showed himself to the priests in all due form and order; thus professing before the whole multitude, who were observant of his conduct, that he desired, in conjunction with these men whose expenses he paid, to take upon himself the vow for the (least) number of days requisite (namely seven); for the dates fitted in together so well, that at the termination of a week the longer (and perhaps various) periods of the vows of the other men also came to an end, and the votive offerings of each of them were presented on the same day.[2] But all that the great apostle wished in his loving condescension to do (with the best

---

[1] This means, and can literally only mean, as v. Gerlach understands it, that he began his Nazarate with the others for the week yet remaining.

[2] Neander is of opinion that these four men also only made a vow for a week ; but this is not only improbable, but directly contrary to ver. 24.

intentions) towards his Jewish brethren, was interrupted by the tumultuous, blind hostility of the unbelieving Jews, and was hindered from being completed. Whilst he was thus proceeding, according to the law of Moses, as one making a vow to God, and was about to make his offering in the temple (although he knew the aim and end of all these foreshadowing types, and thus showed most clearly his love to his people), then is he accused of apostasy from his people, of enmity to the law, and of desecration of the temple. Now, as one vowed and dedicated to Christ according to a *new* law, he must prepare himself for a long imprisonment, and in reproach of all kinds, to lay down those last powerful testimonies as to the hope of Israel fulfilled in Jesus which form the conclusion of the Acts of the Apostles. *And when the seven days were almost ended,*[1] he was seen in the temple by some of the Jews from *Asia propria* who had come up to the feast, and from his ministrations at Ephesus and elsewhere, knew Paul only too well. These men stirred up the people, rushed after Paul as if he had been an arrant villain, laid hands upon him in their angry zeal, and cried out, "Men of Israel, help!" The accusation by which these zealots (quite in the mode in which blind Judaism was wont to vent its rage at that time) stirred up the whole people against the quiet Nazarite, was much to the same effect as the charges brought against Stephen (ch. vi. 14).—*This is the man* (although he now seeks to conceal himself under the mask of legality) *who teacheth all men everywhere against the people* (politically), *against the law* (theologically), *and this place* (ecclesiastically, against this holy temple in which he ventures to show himself). The accusation would conclude somewhat feebly with nothing but mere "teaching" (compare the accusation against Christ Himself, Luke xxiii. 5). They therefore add an overt act, in which they pretend that they have caught the transgressor in the fact: "Added to all that we know of his teaching, he has also openly sinned in his actions; and just at this time, when all are resorting solemnly to the sanctuary, he has introduced Greeks, or Gentiles, into the fore-court of the Israelites, and has therefore maliciously and coarsely made common, desecrated, or defiled, these holy places." The fore-court of the temple, intended for the Israelites only, contained the following inscription on various columns: Μὴ δεῖν ἀλλόφυλον ἐντὸς τοῦ ἁγίου

---

[1] This "seven days" certainly does not point (without any proper connection here) to the week before the feast of Pentecost (as even Lechler protests, in opposition to Wieseler).

παριέναι; and (according to Josephus) even a Roman might be put to death if he ventured to set foot in it. Nothing could have been better adapted to raise a commotion among the hotheads who formed the greater part of the oppressed and besotted Jewish people, ready enough as they were to be roused at the slightest cause. One might almost be inclined to impute too much to these Asiatic Jews, and to consider that this last impudent accusation, which they added after the general description of the heretical teaching, was nothing but a completely conscious lie. But Luke, on purpose to dispel this idea, adds in ver. 29: *For they had seen before with him in the city Trophimus, an Ephesian* (their fellow-countryman, ch. xx. 4, 2 Tim. iv. 20), *whom they supposed that Paul had brought into the temple.* What a conclusion to arrive at! As Bengel pungently says, "Zelotæ *putantes* sæpe errant." What malice it showed, to stamp such a supposition as this as an accusation before Israel, and from this one Trophimus forthwith to make out "Greeks" in the plural! Paul had undertaken the vow in love for the Jewish Christians, and was indeed far from desiring, as they "supposed," to desecrate the temple; but it would be carrying his submission too far to give up all public intercourse with his beloved Trophimus. The enmity of the blind zealots laid hold of this fact in a remarkable way; and the apostle, who was at this very time engaged in the temple in a concession to the law, is accused of being a breaker of the law and a defiler of the temple.[1] But thus, in the imitation of Christ, it often happens to His disciples that they come to be called the very opposite of what they really are.

Vers. 30–32. The whole city fell into commotion through this tumultuous cry which was raised in the temple, and a crowd of the people collected round the poor apostle, actuated as he was by nothing but holy love. Those who are close to him seize him tightly, and drag him by force out of the temple, all those who had been in the temple following. As soon as this had taken place, the doorkeepers of the temple close the entry to it,—a thing which was only done under highly critical circumstances. On this occasion it

---

[1] We cannot (with v. Gerlach) confidently assert "that the result might justify the opinion that Paul and the elders had given way more than was right, or indeed even than was prudent." Rieger, on the contrary, says very justly: "The violence which was exercised on Paul might indeed have broken forth under various other circumstances; and the fact that it broke out in the temple in consequence of an action in conformity to the law, afforded a serviceable testimony in favour of Paul's innocence, and put to shame the fury of his enemies."

was either for the sake of preserving the sanctuary from further
tumult, and perhaps murder, or perhaps to prevent Paul from
claiming an asylum in the temple, if such a thing could be in
question at this era.   When the multitude, in their mad rage, were
actually desirous of beating Paul to death, tidings came (through
some one who was ordered, or who felt himself called upon to send
them, perhaps through the tower-watch who looked down into the
court of the temple, or some well-meaning Christian), just in time
to save the precious life of the defenceless apostle, to the tribune
of the Roman cohort, which, on account of preserving tranquillity
at the feast-time, was stationed in the Castle of Antonia.   The
tidings were to the effect that " all Jerusalem was in an uproar."
The *tribunus militum* (named Claudius Lysias, ch. xxiii. 26) lost
no time, but in a moment hurried down to the temple with soldiers
and centurions.   When the infuriated mob caught sight of the
tribune himself, accompanied with such a numerous guard, they
ceased beating Paul; a little later, and perhaps his life would have
been lost, if we may be permitted to speak humanly of God's ways.
These blows, as the reproach of Christ, were the apostle's glory,
and as the cross of Christ were the killing of his " old man."   Not
long after he was able to stand up vigorous and active, much as he
did after his stoning at Lystra, and to testify before all Jerusalem
of the Lord before whom he had been cast down to the ground, so
that in His power he might again rise up, and might walk according
to " all things which were appointed for him to do." [1]

Vers. 33–36.   Then—τότε—the chief captain ventured to approach the man against whom he saw that all were raging, took him
(ἐπελάβετο as ἐπιλαβόμενοι in ver. 30), and, without in the first
place questioning him, *commanded him to be bound with two chains*;
thus fulfilling Agabus' prophecy (ver. 11). [2]   After this he sought
for information from the people on two simple points: first, who
this villain was; and next, what was the actual wickedness that he
had done.   But very few among the people knew anything rightly
about this, and they all with great noise cried out confusedly all
kinds of things against Paul; so that the chief captain, with the intention of appeasing the people, was compelled by the duty of his

---

[1] Baumgarten's exclamation is here applicable : " What power and what
love had the Lord caused to dwell in this man !"

[2] Its essential meaning is here fulfilled : " The Jews shall bind thee," *i.e.*
shall by their enmity cause thee to be bound, and " shall deliver thee over into
the hands of the Gentiles."

office to preserve law and order, and to conduct into the barracks (παρεμβολὴν) occupied by his troops this man so strangely seized upon and accused. The Roman guard at the time of the feast was stationed in the castle on the hill. This castle was first built by John Hyrcanus, and afterwards repaired and strengthened by Herod the Great, who had named it *Antonia*, after his friend Antonius. From this the fore-court of the adjacent temple could be looked down upon, and the castle was connected with the outer-most hall of the latter by means of a high flight of stairs. The soldiers are now obliged to *carry* Paul up these stairs in order to rescue him from the people, who were violently crowding after him; behind him resounded the wild cry, "Away with him!"[1] (Luke xxiii. 18.)

Vers. 37–40. Up to that time Paul had submitted to the drag-ging, beating, thrusting, carrying, and crying out, leaving himself in the hand of his Lord and his God, and in the calm conflict of prayer awaiting the issue of this inroad of the predicted affliction. Now when he is withdrawn from the people, and is about to be brought into the soldiers' quarters for safe custody, Paul, impelled by the Spirit, finds a suitable moment to say a few words, and to implore that he may first utter another testimony to the excited people. He speaks to the chief captain in Greek, the language of society and intercourse at that time, perhaps taking for granted that he was ignorant of the vernacular language of Judea, and respectfully and quietly asks him: "May I speak unto thee?" The chief captain wondered that the supposed bandit could speak Greek; and the idea thus occurred to him which led to the question whether Paul was not the Egyptian who some time before raised a public disturbance.[2] A robber-chief, a leader of four thousand

---

[1] Baumgarten speaks of a "complete indifference of the Jewish Christians as to Paul's danger of death." But where do we find anything about this? It does not follow as a matter of course, from Luke's silence about it; besides, what, under such circumstances, could the Jewish Christians have done for the apostle?

[2] We find in Josephus further details about this Egyptian: he speaks (but only through an incorrect reading) of his having 30,000 followers, while the chief captain only mentions 4000 sicarii. The false prophet first led his ad-herents into the wilderness, where they considerably increased in number; he then brought them to the Mount of Olives, promising them that the walls of Jerusalem should fall in ruins before him. His followers were, however, scat-tered by the governor Felix, but their leader escaped. Whether this latter event took place before or after Paul's capture, is still a question.

sicarii or assassins, provided with concealed short daggers (of whom there was now a bold and dangerous multitude): this is the character, Paul, now "counted among the transgressors," is supposed to be, and is at once asked if he is not the man. Certainly he did not look as if he were this insurgent, but nevertheless the rage of all Jerusalem against him led the chief captain to this idea. Paul did not reply to him with a mere awkward "No," but said plainly, and indeed with a certain dignity (prefixing a courteous Ἐγὼ) repelling the slanderous supposition: *I am a man which am a Jew* (not ἀνήρ, but ἄνθρωπος): this is his modest commencement. But then he more boldly adds: *of Tarsus in Cilicia, a citizen of no mean city!* With a quick-witted transition, expressed in elegant Greek, from his previous modesty to a certain degree of pride, he calls the well-known, ancient, large, and especially cultivated chief city of Cilicia,[1] "no mean city." As a citizen of Tarsus, having obtained a sudden influence over the chief captain, he ventures upon the request that he may be suffered to speak unto the people. It was of course a somewhat surprising request from a prisoner in Paul's position, and in the face of such a great uproar among the people; but the captive is in the power of the guard, and the disposition of the people is entirely against him. Also the chief captain can scarcely understand the admirable words in which this supposed wicked reprobate designated himself and made the request: in short, he permitted him to speak, and *was compelled* to permit it. For although it bore the appearance of an apostle of the gospel having before speaking to ask permission of a Roman tribune, yet, when a testimony preordained in the whole course of God's word had surely to be delivered, the permission did not in fact rest with this tribune. Indeed, the whole of a tumultuous mob are compelled to be silent at the beck of a man who was odious to them, whom but just now they had almost beaten to death: they must be silent, because the Lord willed it, and conferred power on the mere intimation of Paul's wish. Thus it now happened: Paul stood before the eyes of all, under the protection of the heathen guard, on the stairs a little way from the door of the castle, opposite to the whole mass of the people; and from this lofty pulpit, which was higher even than the temple itself, and as it were commanded all Jerusalem, *he beckoned with his hand unto the people.* What a

[1] Which (as Neander says) was considered, as a seat of literature, to be the equal of such cities as Athens and Alexandria, and is indeed by Strabo placed before both.

different position from that in which he stood in the Areopagus at
Athens! The apostle, too, now speaks differently; but on both
occasions he speaks equally and only as a witness for the Lord his
God. Now conscious of a higher protection than the Roman
guard, and bold in his duty, he controls in quiet confidence the
very sea whose foaming billows had but just now carried him help-
lessly along, and threatened to swallow him up.—*There was a great
silence.* "The fury had now partly exhausted itself, and many
were now all the more eager to hear him, because they did not
rightly know what was the real cause of the tumult:" thus does
Hess, in his way, bring forward the natural element in the cause
of this silence. We, however, must not forget the miraculous part
in it, as it is perhaps only through this that the silence is perfectly
intelligible. Paul would have been able to speak to the people in
Greek, and he would have been in a great measure, or almost
generally understood; but he wisely commences his address in the
Hebrew,[1] *i.e.* in the Syro-Chaldee tongue, which was the vernacular of that time in Judea, which, even if it were not more
intelligible, at least went more to the hearts of the people.[2] It
was as a man that was a Jew, and educated in Jerusalem, that
Paul wished to speak to the "brethren and fathers," and to tell
them about the true Messiah, Jesus of Nazareth, who, when He
came down from heaven to appear to *Saul,* spoke to him in Hebrew
(ch. xxvi. 14).

Ch. xxii. 1, 2. As the holy and almighty God, who is the Judge
of all the world, honoured man created in His own image, even in
the persons of rebellious, stiffnecked sinners; as Jehovah bore with
apostate Israel, and lovingly calling on them to return to Him,
still allowed them to bear the name of Israel; and as Christ
acknowledged the unjust violence used to Him as the result of
power given down from above; so Paul, the servant of Christ,
after he had compelled the frantic and blind mob to keep silence
at his beck, addresses them in the following modest and respectful
way: "Brethren and fathers," or still more impressively in the
ancient tongue, Ἄνδρες ἀδελφοὶ καὶ πατέρες, just as Stephen
addressed the high council (ch. vii. 2).—*Hear ye my defence now
made to you!* This most unjustly accused and ill-treated man

[1] Remark the term ἑβραϊστί (John v. 2, xix. 13).
[2] The special mention of the Hebrew language here gives us to understand that many, if not most, of the discourses of the apostles were delivered
in Greek.

desires to vindicate himself, and expressly adds, *to you* : he also
further adds *now*, *vvví*, less perhaps because hitherto they had not
heard him on account of the noise, and that *now* there was silence,
than that *now* the great moment had arrived for an eminently
public explanation as to his whole life and conduct generally,
which had been so hateful to the people.   Hear me, brethren and
fathers, young and old, common people and rulers of my still beloved people !   I will accept your tumultuous assemblage against
me as a duly arranged and legitimate tribunal for inquiry into my
case ; the quiet induced by my beckoning gives me courage and
confidence, and I beg and hope that ye will afford me willing ears,
and will actually listen !   I will therefore now, before all Jerusalem, give a general account about myself and my business; and
yet it is not *my* business !   Thus, in the most gracious way, does
the apostle beg and sue : long back th. Lord had said to him,
" Get thee quickly out of Jerusalem, for   ey will not receive thy
testimony concerning me" (ver. 18).   For the same God who
foreknew that men would become corrupt and turn from Him,
and, ceasing to be His children, would become " their own spot,"
and " a perverse and crooked generation " (Deut. xxxii. 5), says
nevertheless of them, in His compassion and great mercy, " Surely
they are my people, children that will not lie " (Isa. lxiii. 8).   That
is, even to the obdurate and refractory ones, whose final destruction
He foresees, He allows the fullest privilege of the course of mercy
and of the testimony of truth, just as if faith and salvation might
be thereby produced.   Paul's final vindicatory speeches, forming
the close of the Acts of the Apostles, show very plainly this over-
flow of God's faithfulness, by which He caused the testimony
which (since ch. vii. and viii.) had been gradually withdrawn from
Jerusalem once again to revert to it with a final and most mighty
power, ere, as regarded Israel, the cycle of God's patience was
closed for this period.   Oh that they had *now* really hearkened to,
accepted, understood, and believed in this self-vindication of the
apostle which beamed down upon them as a light from heaven,
clearer than the brightness of the sun, and in their own familiar
Hebrew appealed to them in the utterance of their rejected
Saviour, " I am Jesus, whom ye persecute !"   Oh that they would
have really listened to, accepted, understood, and believed in this
irrefragable testimony, which in every word bore in itself the unmistakeable stamp of divine truth !   In the first place, we now read
that *they kept the more silence*, as this man who had been so blindly

considered by many as being of this or that different character now spoke to them in their familiar vernacular tongue. If they had been " of the truth," they would have gone on to understand and willingly listen to the language of truth, the common mother tongue of all God's children (John viii. 43).

Ver. 3. We find no defence made as to the special, detailed points of accusation named in ch. xxi. 28, at least not expressly and at first ; no mention made whether Trophimus had actually come into the temple or not ; no account of the Nazarate which he had undertaken, which would have been nothing but the plain truth (hitherto so disgracefully misunderstood), and would have tended to the pacification of the people and the vindication of the man Paul. No, a disciple and messenger of Jesus can and may now and then avail himself in his own defence of a vindication which is content to rest on the special existing circumstances ; but the apostle, in his defence before Israel, pushes forward through all the particular instances of injustice, and justifies not himself, but the gospel. Thus, at this great moment, he leaves in the background everything which affected himself only ; and his vindication, although he appears to speak only of himself, actually consists of nothing but a simple, quiet narrative of the miraculous grounds of both his hope and teaching, on account of which he was persecuted, and Jesus in him. If his enemies accept this, all other error and enmity would be removed ; if, on the other hand, they withstand this testimony, what would he attain by a mere paltry, personal vindication, but the shame of seeing himself delivered perhaps from danger, and the gospel, for the preaching of which God had sent the " great silence," despised and set at nought ? He therefore here testifies to them as to the sure, experimental ground of his faith (as subsequently, ch. xxiii.-xxvi.), and its agreement with the Scriptures and their pharisaical doctrine ; and *this* is his vindication ! All indeed who suffer the persecution of the world only because they wish to live godly in Christ Jesus, may, when called on to vindicate their principles, learn the principle of the apostolic testimony. Many a bold sophist might perhaps say : " What good was there in embittering the mob by such a public assertion of things so repugnant to them, and thus exciting their hostility ? Why should life be hazarded, when, according to certain testimony (in ver. 18), nothing more was on the whole to be hoped for ? And did not Jesus say, ' Be ye wise as serpents ;' and, ' When they persecute you, flee ? ' " Language of this serpent-like wisdom[1] may really *often* be right, but *not always:* this is the important point. Wherever, as here, the Holy Ghost impels to testify, its holy right forcibly changes all the holy and unholy wisdom of men's thoughts into the "harmlessness of the dove." Words spoken from this impulse constitute an indispensable portion in the great building of God's kingdom, although to us they may appear useless: they will surely bear their full fruit, though it may not be until hundreds and thousands of years have passed away, just as this discourse of Paul is profitable, as forming a part of the Acts of the Apostles, for the instruction of the church of Christ: they *must* be spoken, so that the Judge may one day appeal to such addresses as this narrative of Paul. It was notorious, even among the heathen everywhere, that he who was formerly Saul, now as Paul called on and preached the name of Jesus of Nazareth; but many a one present now learnt for the first time *how* Paul had been changed to what he now was, by a direct and overpowering vision of this Jesus. This highly credible narrative of Paul's odious yet otherwise inexplicable alteration and present stedfastness, was now first told simply and regularly to many there. Paul knew through the Spirit that the mightiest force of his testimony lay in the simple account of the things which had happened to him; therefore, presupposing the well-known facts, he only relates the miraculous *how* and *wherefore* which constituted the ground of his Christianity and apostleship. In the first place, however, he prefixes (somewhat widely expatiating on it) a copious mention of his early zealous Judaism, in order to appease the minds of his hearers, and to form a sure groundwork for all that follows. He does not plainly say, "I am Paul who once was Saul;" for by this many of those who had crowded together, without actually knowing against whom they were shouting, might have been suddenly excited, and those who did know him would have been newly embittered. He only allows his name to be expressed in the course of the narrative—in ver. 7 by the Lord, and in ver. 13 by Ananias. *I am a man that am a Jew:* it is ἀνήρ now, not ἄνθρωπος as in ch. xxi. 39. He thus comes forward with dignity and freedom before the multitude, at once representing

---

[1] These ideas are yet further extended by Blumhardt: " Would it not have been better if Paul had paid attention to the well-meant advice and wa~ ᵢⁿᵍₛ of his Christian brethren, and, instead of venturing himself into the embittered party conflicts at Jerusalem, had remained among his churches in Asia Minor and Greece, or had carried out his plan for a journey into Spain ? "

himself as the fellow of every one of his hearers. That it may be quite accurately stated, he adds : *born in Tarsus, in Cilicia*, no mean city, one of which he had no reason to be ashamed. *Brought up in this city*, which he was then looking down upon from those steps—the holy city of God, the chief city for the Jewish world in every country. Inasmuch, therefore, as education decides the home and usages of a man more than his mere birth, he was most essentially their countryman and fellow-citizen. Still more :[1] *At the feet* [*i.e.* as the scholar] *of Gamaliel*, the celebrated and most austere Pharisee, known and respected by all the people, Paul had been instructed and taught, and had pursued his regular studies in the best and most complete way. Remark from this that a Christian may make use even of his worldly origin and advantages in order to increase the weight of his testimony in the eyes of the world ; also, that all our experience, be it ever so erring and sinful, may retain some advantage for us even in our Christian vocation. The strictness and accuracy—ἀκρίβεια—are not to be understood as the *diligence* of instruction, for then it must have gone on (ἐν) τῷ πατρῴῳ νόμῳ (cf. ch. vii. 22) ; but ἀκρίβεια indicates the character and school of the teaching, and specifies the pharisaism represented by Gamaliel. In " the law of the fathers " are also here included the *traditions* of the fathers, which were not only made equal to, but even set before, the law of God (see Gal. i. 14). As before in ch. vi. 14, τὰ ἔθη included both law and customs in an indefinite way : I am a man who has been educated in Jerusalem, taught by Gamaliel, and am well-read and learned in the pharisaical law. In this first proposition is implied an answer to their vague cry, " This is the man who teacheth against the law and the people ;" but it also conveys a great pacification and allurement to the people, inducing them to listen to the defence made by this well-read Jewish scholar. It was an apostle of this character who was to vindicate " the unlearned and ignorant men," as they were called (ch. iv. 13), and to remove completely from the city of God this paltry pretext against God's salvation. The pharisaism imbibed in the school of Gamaliel produced in the apostle not only knowledge and science as regarded the intellect ; it also in a great measure, even pre-

---

[1] His education as a learned Jew embraces a threefold idea : in Jerusalem, under Gamaliel, and according to the perfect manner. The two participles ἀνατεθραμμένος and πεπαιδευμένος are really parallel, but forming a climax. The comma may be placed differently at will, either *before* or *after* παρὰ τοὺς πόδας Γαμαλιήλ. We prefer the former.

eminently ($\pi\epsilon\rho\iota\sigma\sigma\sigma\tau\acute{\epsilon}\rho\omega\varsigma$, Gal. i. 14), pervaded the whole of his being, influencing his way of acting and real course of life : in his practical Jewish zeal he proved his Jewish knowledge and feeling. *And was zealous toward God*, although not with understanding : this is a very striking and yet a very mild designation of pharisaical Judaism, which (as the haughty Ishmael) the faith in the word and law of God had begotten with the Egyptian Hagar before the true Isaac came. He expressly says $\pi\acute{a}\nu\tau\epsilon\varsigma$ $\acute{\nu}\mu\epsilon\hat{\iota}\varsigma$; but in ch. xxiii. we learn to distinguish the vast difference between a Paul who persecuted even Jesus with a good conscience, and such " whited walls" as Ananias the high priest. This $\pi\acute{a}\nu\tau\epsilon\varsigma$ is therefore spoken with the kind wish of screening the wicked, and in the confident, conciliatory idea which we have named above as the general and leading characteristic of this discourse ; which Peter also made use of (ch. iii. 17), following the example of Jesus' words upon the cross. Paul does not now *blame* these men who were " zealous towards God," and by their ill-treatment of him had shown themselves to be true *zealots*, in the special sense of the word at that time ; he rather *praises* them, or at least gives them the testimony which was due to them, as in Rom. x. 2. But as in his case, nothing but the (before deficient) perception of the misunderstood and persecuted Lord was requisite in order to turn his fundamentally honest heart to an acknowledgment of this Lord ; so now, wishing and hoping that *all* his hearers would likewise be thus honest, he addresses his narrative to those who were honest-hearted in the main, and not yet hardened enough to sin against the Spirit. He desires that the narrative should touch them, as the events narrated had worked upon him, and that he might be thus made the mere channel of the manifestation of Jesus, afforded indeed to him personally, but through him to many others.

Vers. 4, 5. It is rather remarkable that the apostle does not yet desire to name the teaching of Jesus and His disciples, but the first mention of the sacred name is reserved for the Lord Himself (ver. 8). He speaks therefore from the standpoint of the time then present, and calls Christianity " *this way*,"—a mode of expression which would be easily, and as a matter of course, understood by his hearers. It would imply the teaching and way of life which is now called heresy by *you*, as once it was by *me* (ch. xxiv. 14)—this presumptively dangerous and erring " way" of the Nazarene (ch. ix. 2, xix. 9), which ye are now persecuting in me. I once took the very same part which ye are now taking against me. Remark the wise and yet so incisive and deeply forcible mode in which their minds are prepared for the great conversion which was about to be related. *Unto the death* implies, in the first place, the highest degree of zeal, but at the same time has its own special historical truth. Although in ch. ix. 1 the "breathing out threatenings and murder" is, in the first place, to be understood only of "murderous threatenings," and the verse following only speaks of taking prisoners and binding them (as here in ver. 4), yet the aim and end of taking these prisoners and bringing them bound to Jerusalem was actually ἵνα τιμωρηθῶσιν—*for to be punished* (ver. 5), either by torture and imprisonment (as ch. xxvi. 11), or where possible, by the punishment of death (as Heb. x. 28, 29). Compare ch. xxvi. 10, and in ver. 20 in the discourse we are considering, the mention of the shedding of the blood of Stephen. "At least it was not my fault," Paul seems to say, "if I did not execute the sentence of death on the hated heretics. All that I could do, I did as zealously as possible. I bound them, and delivered them over faithfully and securely into prisons (φυλακὰς), in such numbers that one prison would not suffice—both men and women, not sparing even the latter in the bitterness of my animosity. In former times I bound those who confessed the name of Jesus—I, who now stand bound before you for the sake of this very name." Thus appeals the former Saul to his well-known activity in the first general persecution of the Christians, as to which the high priest and all the estate of the elders can and must even then bear witness for him. Subsequently, in ch. xxvi. 5, he says yet more forcibly: "My manner of life from my youth up know all the Jews, which knew me from the beginning, if they would testify." Now the testimony is presupposed as not being refused—ὡς καὶ μαρτυρεῖ μοι—and the chief authorities are purposely brought prominently before the people, partly in order to show forth the notoriety and importance of his earlier life, and partly also to bring them in connection with the authority-conferring letters which were given him to take to Damascus. The "high priest" was the high priest of the former time spoken of—Jonathan by name, or more probably his successor Theophilus; at all events, according to the way in which Paul speaks of him, it must be assumed that he was still living. With an unusual mode of expression, which comprehends the dignity of the several members and witnesses, the Sanhedrim is here called πρεσβυτέριον. One step further in the history of his persecuting zeal, and the apostle arrives at the theatre of the great

miracle which he desires to confess and testify to. Being provided
with letters of authority from the high priest and council (which,
according to ch. ix. 1, 2, he expressly *desired*[1]—here, however, he
only says briefly, δεξάμενος), he wished to apply to his then brethren
—in the first place, the chiefs of the synagogue, who were among
the Sanhedrim—in the great city of Damascus, which contained
many Jews and Jewish synagogues, and was under a governor set
there by the king Aretas of Arabia who was favourable to the
Jews, and to request the help and authority of these brethren to
arrest the heretics there, and bring them, like a zealous inquisitor,
to Jerusalem. "After he believed he had purified the holy city
from this wicked sect, the report coming in that members of it,
scattered here and there both within and without the land of Judea,
not only continued their meetings, but continued to annex new
disciples, he was forthwith impelled by his spirit of bigotry to
extend the persecution as far as possible."[2] The words "*also*, who
were there," which must not be overlooked, refer to this extension
and generalization of the persecution by the hands of Paul (cf. ch.
xxvi. 11), "even unto strange cities." According to ch. ix. 2, he
was still uncertain whether he should find any of "that way" there,
and he made the journey only on the chance. He calls them here,
indefinitely, τοὺς ἐκεῖσε ὄντας. Mark the undefined way in which
he designates them without any name: "those who were there."
This excellently expresses the contemptible character which the
Nazarenes then held in his estimation, without requiring him to
now give utterance to any name of reproach, or anything evil or
untrue. Paul now desires neither to name and acknowledge them,[3]
and thus anticipate his narrative, nor yet to revert to his former
expressions concerning them: he therefore adheres to this vague
designation, which was in fact none at all, although clear enough
under the existing circumstances.—*That I might bring them bound.*
This is not like ver. 4, in which he is said to have bound and delivered them over: the latter actually came to pass; but this plan
extending to Damascus, proved nothing but a vain, unaccomplished
design, for in ver. 6 we read another "it came to pass." Thus did
Saul breathe out torture and murder against the disciples of the

[1] And indeed from a high priest who was a Sadducee, although he himself
was so strict a Pharisee. The letters are in the plural, as being addressed to
the several various synagogues at Damascus, according to ch. ix. 2.
[2] Hess, *Geschichte und Schriften der Apostel*, i. 179.
[3] As in ch. xxvi. 10 he subsequently does, saying "many saints."

Lord, whom he still was opposing. Many a one, since his satisfaction at the death of Stephen had first stirred him up, had he " shut up in prison ; and when they were put to death, given his voice against them, being exceedingly mad against them" (ch. xxvi. 10, 11). Thus " exceedingly mad" against God's saints, whom he looked upon as the most obdurate heretics, he is now journeying towards Damascus, his full authority for persecution in his pocket. Yet Paul persecuted the heretics with a good conscience ; not like a hypocrite, from miserable motives of self-interest, *but with conviction.* Already even he must have put to shame the miscreants who made use of his zeal as a welcome instrument and were much more wickedly guilty. His business was fully settled for him. What are the *words* which can open the eyes of the blinded man ? He was being hurried forcibly along his path of error ; and what can stay him therein, except *seeing* and *hearing* the Just One whom he persecuted ? And, behold, this came to pass. The risen One showed himself to a Thomas, that the faithless one might touch Him with his fingers and hands. And now He that is gone up into heaven is not too high above an erring Paul but that He is able to cast him down to the ground, and then to raise him up again into the way of truth.

Ver. 6. Remark the simple emphasis of the commencement : *And it came to pass, that, as I made my journey*—in my full persecuting zeal. Now falls from heaven the great " Corner-stone" down into the middle of his path ; but he is not " ground to powder" (Matt. xxi. 44). It reverses his course, and turns the persecutor of God's church into a founder of many churches. The position and circumstances of the persecutor were, *as I journeyed ;* the place and time of the event, *nigh unto Damascus,* and *about noon.* Saul is already near the end of his journey, but he must be made another man ere he enters the gates of Damascus. That which is written of the ancient Saul, " God gave him a new heart," is to be fulfilled on him in a much larger sense (1 Sam. x. 9). In the bright noontide suddenly there shone down from heaven round about him (" and them which journeyed with him," ch. xxvi. 13) a great and actual light, easily to be distinguished from the usual light of the sun ($\phi\hat{\omega}\varsigma$ $i\kappa\alpha\nu\grave{o}\nu$; cf. ch. xxvi. 13, $\acute{u}\pi\grave{\epsilon}\rho$ $\tau\grave{\eta}\nu$ $\lambda\alpha\mu\pi\rho\acute{o}\tau\eta\tau\alpha$ $\tauο\hat{v}$ $\acute{\eta}\lambda\acute{\iota}ο\nu$). " Who coverest Thyself with light as with a garment" (Ps. civ. 2) : This applies also to the Son of man exalted into the glory of the Father. It is in the *shekinah* of the new covenant that the Messiah, who had hitherto been misapprehended by him,

appears to the erring disciple of the old dispensation. God commands "the light to shine out of darkness" suddenly into Paul's soul,
that "the light of the knowledge of the glory of God in the face
of Jesus Christ" may arise in his heart. Many understand that
Paul now only saw a brightness, and heard a voice, and that it was
not until subsequently that the figure of the Lord became visible to
him; and in all the three narratives of the event (here, ch. ix., and
ch. xxvi.), this of course appears to be the case at the first glance.
If, however, we reflect that his companions (just as Dan. x. 7 and
John xii. 28, 29) also heard the noise and saw the flash of light,
but heard no voice and *saw no one* (below, ver. 9, and ch. ix. 7), we
may come to the conclusion that by antithesis it is intimated that
Paul not only heard the voice, but also *saw some one.* It says also
in ch. ix. 17, "The Lord, even Jesus that appeared unto thee in
the way" ('Ιησοῦς ὁ ὀφθείς σοι); and still more explicitly in ver. 27,
"He declared unto them how he had seen the Lord in the way,
and that He had spoken unto him." It appears to us to be a very
forced interpretation if we allow these passages to refer merely to
the flood of light in which, from the evidence of the voice, Jesus
was present. Added to this, in ver. 14 of the chapter we are considering, the *seeing* the Just One, and the *hearing* the words out
of His mouth, may with the highest probability refer just as well
to the events which had already taken place as to something future.
We therefore cannot hesitate for a moment in assuming that Paul
actually, but *suddenly,* caught one hasty glance of the figure of
Jesus in the midst of the heavenly light; that he then did not
again look up[1] after he had been hurled overpowered on the ground;
and that it was only when the fear was removed that he recognised
in the further visions Him that had appeared to him. It appears
to us natural that Paul might not and could not afterwards utter
(at least publicly) the slightest word as to this lightning-glance, in
which the figure of Jesus rather looked on him than he on Jesus;
but that he should have delicately concealed this inmost heart-
opening commencement of his forgiveness.[2] It is also just as
natural that Luke, following Paul's sentiments, should have related

---

[1] It is very clearly intimated in ch. ix. 8 that "he saw no man." He was
completely blind when he again desired to open his (hitherto closed) eyes in
order to go, as commanded, into Damascus.

[2] Although his appeals to the fact that he had seen the Lord (1 Cor. ix. 1,
xv. 8) might be very naturally intended to be understood of this first glance
of him, but not excluding his further visions and revelations.

the event with a like delicacy, although in ch. ix. 7, 17, 27, he allows perfectly clear hints to follow. By this assumption we obtain two points : first, the *recognition* (in the subsequent visions) of Him who looked upon Paul first, which connection adds a peculiar force and significance to the later visions ; next, we find distinctly impressed in this miraculous story the following divine idea both of warning and encouragement : Thinkest thou that only a Stephen in his martyrdom is permitted to see the heaven opened, and the Son of man in the glory of God ? Even to a Saul, who with satisfaction held the clothes of the murderers, overflowing pity is able to vouchsafe for an instant an equal or similar view—not, however, for judgment, but for salvation.

Ver. 7. The light from heaven shines round the persecutor, and he falls to the ground (εἰς τὸ ἔδαφος)—to the earth (ch ix. ἐπὶ, ch. xxvi. εἰς τὴν γῆν). This forcible beginning is associated with the interpreting voice—the voice which laid entire hold of the sinner and persecutor with its thunder-like utterance. Fallen on the earth, lying in the dust before the might and the glory of heaven —this is indeed the right position for Saul, the haughty Pharisee, which a single glance at the persecuted Son of man had at once pointed out to him. As he is lying in the position fitting for him, and in all his impotence and wretchedness, unable to endure without trembling the divine glance, the mighty voice from heaven seeks him, resounding down from the miraculously terrible and yet beautiful figure of radiance, now no longer seen. Saul veiled himself, as Adam hid himself : his " good conscience," that was valid towards men, and, in relation to other men, even before God, had not yet become the really good, pure conscience, sprinkled with the blood of the Lamb. Ah ! the inmost recesses of his heart— wicked and impure as it was, yet to a certain extent honest even in its error—were pricked and penetrated by the divine voice calling unto him, " *Saul! Saul!* " This calling by name denotes and affects the whole innermost man: " Saul! Saul!" This was as a second call of the Creator to the naked one : " Adam, where art thou ? " Where is now the goodly garment of his pharisaical righteousness ? Melted away before the first flash of the radiance of his Saviour and Judge, it was no longer able to screen his nakedness. The voice calls out his name a second time, that the repetition may penetrate deeply, as if one were awaking a deep sleeper with a reiterated call. Now is the sleeper wakened. He finds himself lying on the ground without either power or privilege, and given up to the wrath of the God of Israel, on the mercy of whom his heart felt not yet any claim. Above him resounds the voice of the mighty and majestic One, for whose honour and name he had hitherto fancied himself zealous; for in the first few moments after his glance at Jesus, Paul could perhaps scarcely think anything else than that it was Jehovah Himself, or an angel in Jehovah's name, who was calling to him. Now, too, must the sin of the prostrate and awakened man come out clearly into God's light in explicit terms, and the Saviour Himself begins His thunder-like divine preaching with a statement of Saul's sin. The whole internal striving of the Pharisee against the hitherto overlooked glimmer of God's light and the unheeded voice of divine truth, is compressed into but a small compass, and is hurled down upon his head in the question, " Why persecutest thou Me ?" When the Lord Himself deals with an adversary and unbeliever, He does not make use of many words, as we do. One word from Him has the force of all ; and on every occasion he chooses the right word. Saul's perverted knowledge and the wickedness of his will were chiefly manifested in his persecution of Jesus' disciples. Engaged as he had been on a journey for the purpose of persecution, he is now prostrate on the ground ; therefore the voice, speaking of the present time, grasps the entire circumstances of the sinner. It is very remarkable how often the Lord Jesus, when on earth, penetrated the hearts of people by means of questions. A simple question of this sort, penetrating the inmost recesses of the conscience, now proceeds from the great Searcher of hearts. If some poor child of man had asked Paul, " Why dost thou persecute the Nazarenes ? " he would perhaps have justified his right to do so by a hundred reasons ; indeed, he would have proved the compatibility with duty and the meritoriousness of his zeal in the persecution. But now the Lord simply and briefly asks him, " Why persecutest thou *me !*" and he is at once silenced. The spirit of persecution comes to an end, and he only asks, " Lord, what shall I do ? " On this occasion the miraculous vision certainly gives an emphasis to the words ; but if it is well-pleasing to Him, the power of the Spirit of Jesus Christ can, without the thunder and the lightning-flash, impart the same emphasis to any mere apostolic voice ; and it has ever been the case, that the fiercest foes have been compelled to fall vanquished before the question of a man or child of God asking, " Why doest thou so ? " All that now remains for our consideration is, duly to regard the little word " me " as coming from the lips of

Jesus, and to recognise therein the fact, that in the first words which He spake on earth after His ascension (connecting them with Matt. xxv. 40, 45), Jesus acknowledged and confirmed His oneness with His brethren on earth—*Me, i.e.* Mine, My church, and Myself in it. The real depth of these words is not yet understood by Paul; he could only fully grasp them, when they are repeated to him in ver. 8: "I am Jesus of Nazareth, whom thou persecutest."

Ver. 8. "Why persecutest thou *me?*" This last "Me" is really for the first moment inexplicable and incomprehensible [1] to Paul; and in this fact his innocence is again shown by the side of his guilt. Had the divine question run, "Wherefore—whom—dost thou persecute?" or, "Who gave thee letters and authority to persecute the Nazarenes?" he must then have become speechless from guilt, inasmuch as he would suddenly have been made aware of his inward impurity, and of the impiety and selfishness of the zeal with which he persecuted these remarkably holy people. But the form of brightness, either Jehovah or Jehovah's messenger, asked him, "Why persecutest thou *me?*" He was not yet actually conscious that he had been striving against heaven, and an inhabitant of heaven, although he had earnestly thought that the Nazarenes were heretics, however slight a cause (as he now felt) there might have been for such an opinion. Saul was not among those who knew or might know in their hearts that Jesus was the Christ, and yet, sinning against the Holy Ghost, hindered the progress of the truth: he was not one of those who said, "This is the heir; come, let us kill him, that the inheritance may be ours" (Matt. xxi. 38). Had the Lord appeared to any one of such enemies of God and Christ as these were, and had asked the above question, it would have consumed him with the flash and thunder of judgment; at most, he could but have cried out with the devils, "What have we to do with Thee, Jesus, Thou Son of God? art Thou come hither to torment us before our time?" (Luke viii. 28; Matt. viii. 29.) Saul certainly was something very different: he had grievously sinned and erred, but he had not consciously persecuted the Messiah, or him who might be He. Therefore, although he is lying on the ground with his face hidden, he is able at once to summon up courage for the trembling inquiry, *Who art thou, Lord?* In any case, he addresses as "Lord" the being that had appeared and spoken to him, and thus re-echoes his deep impression of the sharp contrast between "thou" and "me." Who art thou, then, that sayest that I perse-

[1] In spite even of the addition here omitted, which we find in ch. xxvi. 14.

cute thee? For the moment he can ask this question with the real privilege of ignorance. Art thou not the God of Israel, for whose honour I zealously thought I was persecuting the people that followed "this way?" Was I God's enemy when I considered that I was zealous *in His cause?* Or who is this heavenly being who so identifies himself with the Nazarenes, that their sufferings become his? To this last question we may remark, that Saul only needed to have well thought over his inquiry whilst he was expressing it, in order to have immediately found a reply in his conscience and understanding, ere the Lord said to him, "I am Jesus of Nazareth." Who else could it be who thus identified himself with his disciples, except their Master Himself, the Risen One, the Living One, the Messiah exalted to God, whom they represented their Jesus to be?—*I am Jesus of Nazareth, whom thou persecutest!* The Lord Himself, speaking from heaven, calls Himself by the same name as that by which the Spirit since the first Pentecost had named and glorified Him. Although He utters the majestic "I" from out the glory of God, yet He calls Himself by His name of lowliness and shame, which now in His glorification is also glorified. I am Jesus of Nazareth! Thus the Lord Himself from heaven seals the testimony as to the resurrection and ascension of the son of Mary, and solemnly attests the identity of his present Person with the Person of the Lowly One, adverting even to the years of His childhood and boyhood at Nazareth, on which He now in everlasting splendour looks back from God's throne. *Whom thou persecutest*—an emphatic repetition, giving an elucidation of the first question, "Why persecutest *thou me?*" which now appears in perfect clearness. If we now reflect, as we may and ought, on the signification of the name of *Jesus,* meaning as it does, *Helper, Saviour,* the large meaning of the above question, Why persecutest thou the *Saviour?* will be evident to all hearers and readers of this narrative; and it must have struck Paul when he afterwards considered it. "Why persecutest thou" Him who has helped so many, and desires to help all, even thee also? It is as if He said, "What evil have I done to thee, that thou shouldst be so hostile to me, and shouldst hinder me in my work as a Saviour!" (John x. 32.) Thus does the majestic and severe reproach implied in the disclosure, "I am Jesus," immediately change into the tenderly mournful and pathetic accusation and complaint: "I am Jesus of Nazareth, the friend and helper of man, as on earth so in heaven," against whose lovingly

intended sceptre thou "kickest." Thou wilt not accept Me thyself,
nor wilt thou permit others to accept Me, saying, as it were, "Why
wilt thou not allow Me to help both thee and others?" Oh, how
often must we even now exclaim of our Emmanuel, "His name is
Wonderful," ere we come to a right perception of His other name!
What rays of deep revelation beam down upon us in these few
simple words of the Lord, as we more and more regard them from
all points of view! We see clearly that the words "I am," etc.,
which properly convey the distinct judgment on a sinner, were at
the same time spoken in overflowing clemency and kindliness, and
that the sin was forgiven and condoned even whilst it was being
named : this we may readily infer, from the words which Paul (in
ver. 10) immediately found the heart to utter. This clemency
was already implied in the arrangement of what was said : First,
the chiding reproach, "Why persecutest thou Me?" Now the
loving complaint of misapprehended and rejected love, "I am
He whom thou persecutest!—even now see and hear Me!" Thus
the Lord ofttimes reveals certainly the gracious name of Jesus
(by which name He loves best to call Himself and hear Himself
called) to many Sauls who have really misunderstood Him : at the
right juncture He powerfully and stringently addresses every man
who is thus to be won over, and appeals to him with the words,
"I am Jesus—even now acknowledge Me!" The great time will
certainly come some day, when all who have a veil before their
eyes shall lose it, and shall see the Son of man as He is ; when
every knee shall bow at the name of Jesus, the name which is
above every name, and every tongue shall confess that Jesus Christ
is the Lord ; and certainly also (for Jesus is Jesus, and God is
love) all who have not, as consummated sinners, blasphemed against
the Holy Ghost, shall see and confess Him to their salvation. The
Lord's ways had hitherto been miraculous ways, which are unsearch-
able to us. This much, however, we may clearly see in the whole
course of His testimony from the resurrection onward, that the
Lord desired to procure for His people the greater blessedness of
not seeing, and yet believing, and therefore appeared only to pre-
chosen witnesses that they might announce Him to all nations : to
a Thomas, that others might be ashamed and believe without
seeing; to a Saul, that all Jerusalem might hear from his lips the
testimony of this vision, and that, according to the order of God's
kingdom, right faith might come by hearing, and not through
seeing. Thus, through Paul's words the Lord appeals to the Jews,

and says, " I am Jesus of Nazareth, whom ye continually persecuted, and are now again persecuting in this very Paul, the witness
of my vision." If any one knew about this vision, and although
unable to explain the wonderfully altered life of Saul except by
faith in the miracle narrated, continued nevertheless to persecute
as before—this man now no longer persecuted the Jesus whom he
misunderstood, but the Saviour who was testified to him—he became
indeed a blasphemer against the very Spirit of testimony. But
any one in whose inmost heart some Nathanael-like feeling could
be stirred up, must have acknowledged this Jesus (who to Saul does
not call Himself the Christ, because the name of Jesus is a higher
name) to be the Living One, God's Messiah now exalted to God.
This simple narrative of all that Saul saw and heard on the way to
Damascus, in connection with the whole subsequent life of the
apostle, has in it a far greater power of proof and conviction for
the gainsayer than one would cursorily think ; and therefore it is
written three times [1] in the brief and succinct narrative of the Acts
of the Apostles. It contains, indeed, the seal which He who had
gone up to heaven impressed on all the other testimonies ; and Paul
thus became the apostle whose apostolic warrant confirmed, as it
were, those of the others. The other apostles were more or less
God's, ere they were given to Jesus (John xvii. 6) ; in their case,
even the miraculous nature of the testimony had a certain natural
connection, so that it was blindly contradicted because it proceeded
from simple-minded, pious Galileans. But Paul, the strict Pharisee
and learned pupil of Gamaliel, thought that he was zealous on *God's*
side against Jesus of Nazareth, even as all the rest; and, behold, it
is all at once made clear to him from heaven, that he is persecuting
God's Saviour in His church, and that, against his knowledge and
will, he is an enemy of God in his dreadful and guilty blindness.
A whole life full of deeds of power and words of wonder, full of
holy and fiery zeal for the cause of this Jesus, was now begun
at this place near Damascus, where Jesus appeared to him ; and
when, after the lapse of years, the witness and object of this
miracle, standing in the midst of his persecutors, desired to give an
account of himself, and state the reasons for his change, he only
once more relates this " heavenly vision " (ch. xxvi. 19). Let us

---

[1] On this Zeller forcibly remarks : " In ch. ix. it is related for *Christians;*
in ch. xxii. the story is told before a tumultuous assemblage of *Jews;* in ch.
xxvi. Paul narrates it to *Festus*, and Agrippa principally, with reference to
Gentiles."

ponder upon, and thoroughly appreciate in all its bearings, the weight of this testimony as regarded Jerusalem, and the long-suffering of Jesus, who again and in such a way gave it.

Ver. 9. All that (according to vers. 6–8) is said to have taken place is not to be believed on the mere word of the narrator: it has witnesses in its favour, just the same as Saul's previous zeal in persecuting Jesus (according to ver. 5). Those who were with Saul also saw and heard something which they could vouch for, and certainly did vouch for many times, inasmuch as a persecutor was at once changed into a disciple. They soon stood up again (whilst Paul was lying on the ground; *vid.* ch. xxvi. 14), but they were speechless and motionless from fright and fear (ch. ix. ἐννεοὶ or ἐνεοὶ, here ἔμφοβοι): they saw the flash and the light, although they did not see any visionary being; and they heard a loud voice, perhaps like a thunder-clap, although in this voice they did not understand any intelligible words. This half-perception of the extraordinary things happening to Saul (which was sufficient for external evidence) only increased their fear, and the whole affair must have made a deep impression upon them. An unprejudiced person will hardly doubt that ch. ix. 7 and ch. xxii. 9 may be harmonized in this way: if, however, any one prefers to charge Luke with writing contradictions in his own book, we, at least here, have nothing further to say to such an one.[1] That φωνὴ may also mean *thunder*, and ἀκούειν to *understand*, is not to be denied; and he who has found the testimony of the Scripture generally all agreeing as to Jesus, will certainly desire to understand correctly the different expressions of these three narratives.

Ver. 10. *And I said, What shall I do, Lord?* The fact that this persecutor, now quelled, overpowered, and checked in his course, can, immediately after the disclosure of his sin, ask a question like this, is, in the first place, a most decisive proof of that honesty in his persecution, distinguishing him from the more wicked enemies of Jesus, which we have already several times spoken of: it is also evidence of the clemency and kindliness of Jesus' words contained in ver. 8, already considered by us. After the second representation made to him of his persecution of the true Messiah and Saviour, he does not continue in his fright and

[1] We do not desire to discuss the matter with those who (as Olshausen formerly) now again, still with the best intentions, are led away by a too great obsequiousness towards scholars, and consider it their duty to maintain the existence of differences in the various accounts.

amazement, so as only to be able to wail out, " Ah, Lord, what have I done ? " and to be powerless either to think or perceive anything further.   No ; this revelation of the Jesus hitherto misunderstood by him, was all that he required to work a change in him as decided as his previous persecutions, so that he now only asks to know the will of his recognised and acknowledged Lord. The whole of the actual sin of which the words of the visionary appearance had convicted him, is at once forgiven by the mercy of Him that appeared, not to judge, but only to reveal Himself. Amidst all his trembling and timidity, Paul has deeply felt this much from the last words of Jesus of Nazareth : from the very words which disclosed his sin, a comforting breath of pardon has flowed in upon his heart.   In short, he takes heart again to look forward, and, with the offer and surrender of the whole of his future life to the service of those he has hitherto persecuted, to ask with childlike confidence, " Lord, what shall I do ? "   Thus, after repentance, a sinner who is enlightened and converted through grace asks, " How may I now serve Thee, O my Saviour ? Show and grant me fresh work, instead of my former wicked actions."   In Saul's case, however, the main points of his conversion were suddenly and closely crowded together.   Still his speedy inquiry after the will of the Lord had this special cause founded on the circumstances attending it, that he was close to Damascus with his authority for persecution in his pocket, now repudiated by him through the divine countermand : he might therefore well be eager for some particular directions as to what he should now begin to do, and must be expecting these directions from the mercy of Him that had appeared to him.—*And the Lord.*   Thus does Paul now name Jesus of Nazareth, freely acknowledging and testifying to Him before all Jerusalem, now that he had just related how he was first brought so to call Him.—*The Lord said unto me, Arise, and go into Damascus*—" But rise, and stand upon thy feet," as it is in ch. xxvi. 16.   This gracious summons, this auspicious command of the Saviour's mercy, has in this position a peculiar weight and importance : in it is implied the second main point involved in the things which, through Jesus' overwhelming appearance, had successively and so suddenly happened to Saul.   First the voice of the Lord hurls him down to the ground, now it raises him up again : the same thing occurs, although not in so extraordinary a manner, to every sinner and enemy of God whom the Lord overpowers, converts, and changes into a disciple and a servant.

Whoever is prostrate on the ground before the Lord, shall, however, surely be permitted to rise up again, and henceforth walk
according to the Lord's will.—*Arise and go*, or travel on the
journey you have begun, *to Damascus*, but as an altered man.
But, very remarkably, the Lord does not give him a direct answer
as to the things which were appointed for him to do ; but by
Jesus Himself Saul is referred to Jesus' disciples, as the angel
referred Cornelius to the apostle.—*There* (in Damascus) *it shall be
told thee*—it is expressed quite indefinitely, σοὶ λαληθήσεται : some
one whom I shall appoint thereto will tell thee.   Saul is thus sent
to some one of Jesus' disciples at Damascus, because, *in the first
place*, by this means he would be immediately brought by the
Lord into communion with the disciples, and the latter (hitherto
looked upon as heretics) would be thus sanctioned and sanctified.
The Lord not only certifies that he who persecutes Jesus' disciples
persecutes Jesus ; but also, that he who hears His disciples hears
Him.   Therefore, in His first appearance after the ascension, He
vindicates and glorifies in a twofold way " His saints that are in
the earth, and the excellent in whom is all His delight" (Ps. xvi. 3).
This reference was given, *secondly*, in order that the work of the
conversion of this blasphemer — a work so extraordinarily and
miraculously begun—should have an ordinary and regular conclusion ; also, that the miracle should be brought into a closer
connection with the regular order of things, and that the latter
should have its share in the work as well as the miracle.   We now
come to another reason why Jesus thus acted on this occasion, viz.
thirdly, that a *humiliation* might be added to the peculiar honour
with which this proud Pharisee had been dignified through the
direct vision which had been granted him, and that the prostration
of this previously haughty man might be confirmed by sending
him to the once despised Nazarenes,—thus at once trying, disciplin-
ing, and strengthening him.   We read, indeed, in 2 Cor. xii. 7, that
Paul was subsequently in danger of being over-exalted by the high
revelations which had been afforded him ; and in this first dealing
of the Lord with him, perhaps he felt an influence which would
tend to induce humility in the presence of all the brethren in
whom also the Lord dwelt.   How often, in all ages, has the Lord
dealt with man exactly in this way !   He Himself makes the
beginning in all His power, but the conclusion of the matter is
left to His disciples : *He* strikes down with a sudden efflux of His
own power, and renders the sinner helpless and prayerful ; but *we*

are permitted to complete the work[1] in His name and according to His mighty preparation—the work of raising up, enlightening, and directing to practical activity.   The Lord therefore greets His children upon earth with, as it were, a loving, faith-strengthening greeting, when He makes over to them for further care and provision some captured enemy—some strong and learned man made both powerless and ignorant.   The promise to Paul is, however, large enough to excite in him further expectation.   His inquiry, "What shall I do?" is accepted more decisively and significantly than the asker had at first any reason to hope.   The Lord's answer conveys an important idea, embracing indeed his whole life—that there were many things ordained for him both to do and to suffer, some portion of which Ananias was already acquainted with (ch. ix. 15, 16); but that in Damascus he should receive information as to the whole matter (at least as regards all the main points), compare vers. 14, 15 below.   Finally, the last expression calling for remark on these words of Jesus are: "of all things which are *appointed* for thee"—τέτακταί σοι.   We must not say that this merely stands for ἔταξα; but we find here, from the lips of the glorified One, a reference to the Father, from whom (according to Matt. xx. 23) all prescription proceeds, especially for His witnesses and their positions: we are at least subsequently told in the disclosure through Ananias which corresponded to the vision: "The God of our fathers hath chosen thee, that thou shouldest see that Just One," etc.   In *another* vision, which follows in ch. xxvi. 16, the Lord Himself ordains Saul "to be a minister and a witness;" but now, just at the conclusion of this first vision, in all its majesty, so peculiarly condescending and benign, the slight reference to a higher power involved in the indefinite τέτακται (ch. ix. 6, τί σε δεῖ ποιεῖν) occurs very suitably.   A beautiful contrast is also brought about with the equally indefinite expression λαληθήσεται—it will be *told* thee (by men) as to all things which are *ordained* for thee (by God).   Whoever asks in full earnestness, "What shall I do, Lord?" him the Lord will surely tell, or cause to be told, all that is ordained for him.

Ver. 11. Paul does not omit to state that the brightness or glory (δόξα) of the light in which the Lord appeared to him, caused

---

[1] Also to give further instruction, which in Paul's case was not a matter in question, as he "received not his gospel of man" (Gal. i. 12).   Ananias only communicated to him, once for all, that which was (in the first place) ordained for him to do.

him to be *blind* for a season. It was, in fact, an evidence for the
certainty of the vision, and could be vouched for by those who
were with him, who "led him by the hand." According to ch.
ix. 9, he was "three days without sight," and, in his deep prostration and continuous conflict of prayer, "neither did eat nor
drink." Now the vast experiences and perceptions which, with
the flash and the thunder, had been brought home to him, first
began gradually to apportion themselves out in his mind, so that he
was abidingly conscious of them. The Lord had pointed him out
to Ananias as one that prayed (ch. ix. 11); but all these further
details, as merely affecting his own personality inwardly and individually, are here omitted by the apostle in his plain, open narrative
of that which happened to him. Now, before this multitude, he
does not desire to say much of things concerning his own heart and
his own prayers, but only to relate in all its main features how the
Lord had laid hold upon him, directed him, ordained, and sent him.
He concludes the account of all that happened to him on the road
near Damascus with the simple words, *I came into Damascus*—the
place which (according to vers. 5, 6) I was journeying to in all my
bold self-will; but now I enter it "led by the hand," and following Jesus' directions, because the glory of Jesus of Nazareth had
dazzled me and rendered me obedient. As a matter of course, the
persecuting mandate of the high council must remain unopened
and unused. I was overpowered; my Jewish zeal came to an end;
I was now compelled to acknowledge that Jesus of Nazareth was
my Lord and my Saviour; and I now for the first time obeyed
Him, in that I went to Damascus. This is the impression which
this first conclusion is intended to make on the hearers.

Vers. 12, 13. The apostle evidently hurries on in his narrative
to the further directions promised by Jesus. He does not, however, press on so hurriedly but that the person and characteristics
of Ananias are somewhat copiously and closely described, for this
was important and pertinent to the matter in question. This man
"one Ananias"—through whom the Lord continued His manifestation to Saul, was *a devout man according to the law*; perhaps
not a proselyte, who had adopted the whole law—for in ver. 14 he
speaks as a Jew by birth of the "God of *our* fathers"—but a pious
Jew, zealously and blamelessly observing the law. In ch. ix. 10 he
is called "a disciple;" and that he was so is a matter of course,
and perfectly clear from his own words; but Paul on this occasion
emphatically holds out to view his *legal devotion*, which even as

Christian he still retained. A disciple who also observed the Jewish law is thought worthy by Jesus to announce in Jesus' name God's will to Paul. This is a second and very decided answer and contradiction to the vague cry (ch. xxi. 28), the first answer being given in ch. xxii. 3. The emphasis with which Paul appeals to this man as another witness and joint defendant in the matter, is fully completed by the fact that all the Jews dwelling in Damascus could and must testify in a laudatory way to Ananias' devotion to the law. Paul now omits everything which (according to ch. ix. 10–16) in the meantime happened to him and to Ananias, and merely leaves it open to be remarked, that Ananias must have received a distinct revelation and intimation from the Lord before he would have ventured to approach and speak to the persecutor, hitherto so much dreaded. We remark generally, that the further we proceed with Paul's address, the more haste we notice in treating of the accidents of the matter in question, and in hurrying on to the more striking main points which it was intended to set forth. Paul perhaps saw that the people began to become more restless, and that he could no longer reckon on any lengthened period of silence; and therefore the more important disclosures, which were better calculated to engage the attention, were introduced in quick succession. Hence the omission of the visions by which Saul and Ananias were mutually directed by the Lord to meet one another; hence the abridgment of Ananias' first words to him, and the speedy mention of the vision (ver. 17) which occurred three years later. The Lord had appeared to Ananias in a vision, and not in visible glory as to Saul, and had directed him to the straight street, to the house of Judas, to Saul of Tarsus, that he might lay his hands upon this subjugated enemy, and restore him to sight. Saul had also in a vision seen Ananias coming to him. "Behold, he prayeth!" Thus doth the Lord point out the new penitence of the persecutor, of whom it is said by the very lips of the Lord, that he is no longer an enemy, but "a chosen vessel." But Ananias, quite in terror at the mention of the notorious name of "Saul of Tarsus," seemed almost to forget everything else; and being not unaccustomed to discourse with his Lord, at least in the intercourse of prayer, and in the vision being removed from any former dread of Him, in full confidence made the objection, that there were many who spoke evil of this man, and that at this very time he had come with a mandate of persecution against all who called upon the name of Jesus—just as if the Lord had erred, and did not yet know all this! He is then told, "Go thy way, for he is a chosen vessel unto me"—not only to call upon my name, as he is now doing, but "to bear my name before the Gentiles, and kings, and the children of Israel;" indeed, as a martyr, he shall himself henceforth suffer many things for my name's sake, which he has persecuted. Presupposing these things, Paul now relates that which took place in consequence of these directions: That Ananias came to him, stood by him, and spake to him all that the Lord inspired him to speak. "Came," "stood by," "spake,"—all this shows the hasting on to the important words, whilst Ananias himself is not slow in fulfilling the Lord's command, and does not allow the blinded, supplicating Saul to wait long for the full light of healing mercy. At once stretching out his hands to place them on Saul, he thus introduces himself to the blind man, kindly addressing him as "Brother Saul." It was not from any anxiety as to his reception, but for kindly encouragement, that Ananias vindicates his position by the words which we read in ch. ix. 17 : "The Lord, even Jesus that appeared unto thee in the way as thou camest,[1] hath sent me that thou mayest receive thy sight (now through me), and be filled with the Holy Ghost" (in the complete community of grace). All this Paul now comprehends in the single expression, "Look up," which was perhaps actually uttered, or is perhaps only intended to denote the sense and result of Ananias' address.—*And the same hour I looked up upon him.* In these words, referring to ver. 11, he simply points out the restoration of his sight, by which Ananias most completely proved himself to be sent by the Lord as the interpreter of His will. In ch. ix. 18 we read : "And immediately there fell from his eyes as it were scales." This was a true and right type of the "veil of Moses" which was thus removed from Saul's eyes and heart (2 Cor. iii. 14–16).

Vers. 14, 15. *The God of our fathers:* thus begins the address of the pious Jew to his Jewish brother who, in his confession of the Messiah denied by his people, had now become still more closely his brother. This Messiah, Jesus, contradicts not the Old Testament, but rather fulfils it; and in Jesus, the God of Abraham, Isaac, and Jacob is manifested (ch. iii. 13). "This way" is no sect, heresy, or apostasy from the people, law, and temple; but in the faithful acceptance of that which is the aim, the end, and the

---

[1] In ch. ix. 10–16 the Lord said nothing about this to Ananias; He must therefore have suggested it to him just before, or even in the course of, his address to Paul.

living fulness of the whole law, is the only true and genuine
Judaism. The expression "hath chosen thee" evidently refers, as
already remarked, to the "appointing" mentioned last by Jesus
in ver. 10; so that the first words of the promised disclosure are
joined on to the last words of the promise, and the grace and the
choice of grace in the vision afforded to Saul are comfortingly
confirmed. What is it to which the former blasphemer, persecutor, and reviler, is to be fore-ordained by God the Father? In
the first place, *to know His will.* This is denoted by the first thing
which happened to him near Damascus—the revelation of the misapprehended One whom in unbelief and self-will he had ignorantly
persecuted (1 Tim. i. 13); and the *seeing* and *hearing that Just
One* (whom he had considered as a deceiver) also declare this first
sense of the expression. But perceiving and knowing God's will
refer back to Paul's question, "Lord, what wilt Thou have me
to do?" and give the promised answer to it: they therefore include
everything to which Paul was appointed, up to the end of the
"knowledge of the Son of God," to the "measure of the stature
of the fulness of Christ" (Eph. iv. 13), consequently his apostleship (ver. 15). Paul therefore, in the beginning of his epistles,
calls himself "an apostle by the will of God." The tree is determined by the germ, and the end of a long career is often indicated
by the starting-point; just so Paul comprehends the beginning
and end together of all that to which the grace of God had called
him, when he says in Gal. i. 16, "to reveal His Son in me." Not
until the aim of sanctification is attained, and we join in the
eternal worship of the saved, shall we fully and perfectly get to
know God's will; but this gracious will of God, the knowledge of
which effects our sanctification and salvation, is determined in the
knowledge of the Just One, the one Holy One who in humanity
perfectly knows and fulfils God's will, and we in Him. Remark
how Paul intimates to the Israelites who heard him, that it is the
will of the God of their fathers—whom, although zealous towards
God as they think, they nevertheless misunderstand—that Jesus
was to be known and testified to as the *Just One.* To know Him,
the Just One, and by the knowledge of Him to be made righteous,
constitute the ordinary task of all Christians, and the will of God is
the common aim of all; but Paul is now ordained to an extraordinary way and means of attaining to an ordinary end—"to *see*
that Just One, and *hear* the voice of His mouth." By this the
vision which had already taken place is evidently intended in the

first place; but an idea of the promise of further and still clearer appearances of the Lord cannot be excluded from it. The subsequent vision—in which Paul more calmly saw the Lord, and seeing, heard Him—may therefore be hinted at in the conclusion of these words, that he should hear His voice *out of His own* (on this account visible) *mouth.*[1] Finally, we cannot leave unmentioned the remarkable ancient opinion, that Paul, in addition to the various visions of the Lord, which are expressly mentioned, received also a direct extraordinary revelation of the whole of *Jesus' history,* of which the other apostles were natural eye-witnesses. Although there may be something strange and justly incredible in this idea, taken in its full extent, yet it appears to us that there may be some truth concealed in it; and we could very well imagine that not only the institution of the holy communion of the Lord's Supper, but also many other such things, were revealed to the apostle in the Spirit. Ponder well Paul's utterances, 1 Cor. xi. 23, and xv. 3, with its context; also Gal. i. 11, 12, 18–20; and the remarkable words in ch. xxvi. 16, *those things which I will cause to appear unto thee,* properly, will cause thee to see of me—ὧν τε ὀφθήσομαί σοι. Of course, whether any such entirely miraculous position as an eye-witness of the shape and words of the Just One be secretly conveyed in Ananias' words in ver. 14 or not, the miraculous, extraordinary "seeing and hearing," by which Paul was to know the will of God in Jesus, have for their cause his further ordained *office as a witness,* as added in ver. 15. As an apostle, it was necessary that Paul should have seen Jesus Christ (1 Cor. ix. 1).—*Thou shalt be His witness, of what thou hast seen and heard.* This is an exact description of the apostolic office (cf. ch. x. 39, 41), and is true in a special sense as regarded Paul. If we cannot make up our minds to see in ver. 14 any idea of a mysterious revelation supplying the want of ocular testimony (2 Pet. i. 16; Luke i. 2), we may find it hinted at in ver. 15. Thou shalt, as the other apostles, testify of *that which thou hast seen and heard.* Thou shalt be *His* witness, in His almighty hand, sure guidance, and inviolable communion, for the honour and spread of His name.—*Unto all men.* In these words especially, as well as in the verse generally, there is a pretty clear pre-announcement of his office as the apostle to the Gentiles, which is expressly spoken of in the latter portion of the

---

[1] If it should be maintained that Paul, when near Damascus, did not properly *see* the Lord, these words must be interpreted, "both to see and also to hear," *i.e.* to see Him subsequently, just as thou hast heard Him now.

discourse. That the things which he had *seen* and *heard* were to
be testified to by Paul, points out the credibility as well as the
necessity of the testimony. In relating so plainly to the assembled
Jews the divine directions he had received through Ananias, Paul
defends himself much in the same way as Peter and John before
the high council (ch. iv. 20), when they said that they could not
but speak the things which they had seen and heard.

Ver. 16. *And now, why tarriest thou?* With such a prospect
in view of the future ordained for thee, of further *seeing* and
hearing, and *testifying* before all men, why shouldst thou delay
another moment in beginning to take the first decisive step in
entering on thy path as a disciple and witness, by sealing thy confession in baptism? To whom much is appointed to do, let him not
linger in making a beginning. Τί μέλλεις is here evidently equivalent to τί βραδύνεις, ὀκνεῖς; μέλλειν often having this meaning.
Through this opportune question[1] of Ananias, Paul now asks the
Jews whether, after such events, prospects, and demands, he could
well hesitate in confessing himself to be a disciple of Jesus. "Must
I not," he would, as it were, say to them, "obediently follow as
I am led and directed by the God of my fathers?"—*Arise* (or,
arising) *and be baptized!* Thus runs the powerful, encouraging,
inviting voice of the disciple, distinctly calling Saul out of the
sorrow of repentance into the peace of reconciliation by a full surrender of himself to Jesus; the Lord Himself speaking in the
disciple's words. The words of Ananias, following the intention of
the Spirit of inspiration, are connected on to the first "Arise"
spoken by the Lord (ver. 10); and the baptism which made Saul a
publicly confessing disciple of the Lord was his spiritual "arising"
and "taking courage." In this sense Luke relates (ch. ix. 18, 19),
"He arose (from his praying repentance), and was baptized; and
when he had received food *he was strengthened—ἐνίσχυσεν—*again
became strong." First baptism, and then the bodily strengthening
after the three days' fast; for baptism was itself the spiritual
invigoration and strengthening in which Saul henceforth "increased the more in strength"—*ἐνεδυναμοῦτο* (ch. ix. 22). Further
instruction was not necessary for one so powerfully instructed by
the Lord Himself: his deep humiliation was the best preparation
for the sacrament which received him into grace, the comfort of

[1] It was not indeed irresolution which needed to be removed, but the procrastinating humility of the prostrated man, who did not grasp at the full means
of grace so quickly as might be.

which was not now for a moment to be delayed. *Be baptized*, and thus *wash away* thy sins : take them entirely away, and obtain pardon for them ; so that, forgetting all that is past, thou mayest joyfully begin a new life.—*Thy sins.* It is this expression only which satisfactorily sets forth in words the implanted and inmost wickedness of the former Saul, as to which the whole narrative (vers. 6–10) gave some hints ; but this one expression is quite sufficient for all Jerusalem to clearly understand by it that the whole of Paul's former life before his knowledge of Jesus was looked upon by him only as *sin ;* that his pharisaical zeal, and his "blamelessness touching the righteousness of the law" (Phil. iii. 5, 6), were also counted by God as *sin,* and all the profit and glory in it were considered only as shame ; but that baptism in the name of Jesus, the Just One, *washes away* sin, and by the power of a sufficient grace and pardon establishes in us true righteousness before God. *Calling upon the name of the Lord,* or, according to the more correct reading, *His name*—referring back to the Just One (ver. 14).[1] By this calling in the first place is meant the confession of the name by baptism to or in this name ; so that all three expressions, baptism, washing away, calling, denote together one and the same thing. But the calling on the Just One which begins with baptism, in which we are made righteous to the satisfaction of the Father, is a continuous "calling." The first confession promises continuous confession, and the first granting of grace promises, and is an earnest of, renewed grantings of grace. It therefore, of course, also means, Call continually, with all the other disciples of Jesus, on His name ; *i.e.*, according to a mode of designation usual in the New Testament (*e.g.* Acts ix. 14, 1 Cor. i. 2), *Become one of Jesus' disciples.* We have now come to an end of the first division of the discourse. It needed not to be told that Paul did not "tarry," but was forthwith baptized. Indeed, Paul does not so much desire to relate the bare facts of his being made a disciple, and ordained an apostle of Jesus, as to set forth the "how and the wherefore" of the change. In mentioning the last words which Ananias addressed to him, Paul puts, as it were, the unuttered question, Could I, ye brethren and fathers, well do otherwise than I did ?

Vers. 17, 18. *And it came to pass*—happened to me—*when I*

---

[1] Not perhaps (as Grotius will have it) on *God the Father*, with whom the whole address begins ; στόματος αὐτοῦ (ver. 14), μάρτυς αὐτῷ (ver. 15), and now ὄνομα αὐτοῦ, all correspond.

was again come to Jerusalem. This emphatic commencement is
exactly similar to the important beginning in ver. 6—in the Greek,
ἐγένετο δέ μοι πορευομένῳ — ἐγένετο δέ μοι ὑποστρέψαντι.
The attention of the hearers is thus called to a fresh vision of the
Lord, tending to confirm Paul's further behaviour. The return to
Jerusalem, pointing out the date of the vision which, rapidly passing over an interval of time, is made to follow, is of course the *first*
return thither after his journey thence to Damascus. This, however, did not take place until after three years had been spent in
mysterious quiet, as we learn from Gal. i. 17, 18. Paul therefore
omits all that is related in ch. ix. 19–22, as well as the account in
ch. ix. 23–29 of the detailed circumstances of his return to Jerusalem.[1]   During his solitary abode in Arabia, much may have
taken place in his soul, which will one day be manifest to the
praise and glory of grace before both angels and men. Also, of
the visions and revelations of the Lord which Paul, as it appears,
several times received, but very little is recorded for us: the
revelation related here may have been the one next following the
first, but perhaps not. Luke's relating nothing about it in ch. ix.
is fully justified by his intention of causing the apostle to give an
account of it here.   How, then, does he now tell it?—*While I
prayed in the temple.* He thus controverts the third division of
the accusation against him, by certifying to the peaceful relation
in which he and Christianity in general stood towards both the
people and the law. Paul was praying to the God of Israel in
the name of Jesus, calling upon that "Just One," his Lord standing at the right hand of the Lord (ver. 16): he was praying,
too, in the *temple,* which through the patience of this Lord was
still standing, and by His and His people's forbearance continued
to be acknowledged, and was in no way opposed or desecrated.
Ananias as a disciple of Jesus observed the law, Paul as a disciple
of Jesus prayed in the temple — both acting just like many
thousand believing Jews in and round Jerusalem, who were all
zealous for the law, as all Jerusalem knew and saw. It is indeed

---

[1] In ch. ix. the "three years" mentioned in Gal. i. 18 must be brought in
either between vers. 22 and 23, or between vers. 25 and 26. The former is by
far the more likely, and is adopted by many (*e.g.* by Neander), as the ἡμέραι
ἱκαναί in ver. 23 may point to this interval. Against Wieseler's far too confident assertion, that Paul in ch. xxii. speaks of the same trance as that mentioned in 2 Cor. xii., we have raised our voice and arguments (*Reden des Herrn
Jesu,* etc. p. 38).

God the Father who is appealed to in Jesus the Messiah (ver. 14). And yet more! Here, in the temple, Paul falls into a *trance*, or an unwonted elevation of the spirit beyond the usual limits of body and mind (ch. x. 10; 2 Cor. xii. 2), and again sees the Lord Jesus. Jesus Himself, therefore, appears to His disciple in the sanctuary of Israel, which He by no means considered unclean, contaminated as it was; and He is so little displeased with His servant for his acquiescent veneration for it, that it is in this very place that He honours him by His appearance. The *trance* is also, as is clearly shown here, a new kind and stage of manifestation, not so direct as the actual appearing near Damascus, and also more direct than the vision of Ananias. *And saw Him*—briefly and yet solemnly expressed, glancing back to the promised "seeing" and "hearing" promised in vers. 14, 15. We may remark generally, that in the whole narrative, on one occasion only—at the great crisis of the matter—does the Lord Himself express His own name as "*Jesus of Nazareth?*" previously and subsequently He is named neither Jesus nor Christ; previously, any mention by name of the then blasphemed One is avoided; but subsequently, in ver. 10, He is called the *Lord*, in ver. 14 *that Just One*. Afterwards, in ver. 16 (according to the correct reading), vers. 18 and 21, the solemn term "He" is used: He who is now testified of, and the confession or rejection of whom is now in question.—*I saw Him speaking to me*—in the Greek, ἰδεῖν αὐτὸν λέγοντά μοι. This arrangement of the words evidently implies a reference to the greater closeness, clearness, and duration of time with and during which Paul now saw Him standing and speaking, as compared with the momentary glance at Him in the flash of light, and his merely hearing a voice. This reference we also find hinted at in ver. 14, in the words, "and hear the voice of His mouth." But what is the purport of this new, direct command which Paul, here in the temple, receives from Jesus Himself? It is an injunction to abandon Jerusalem, and to preach to the far-off Gentiles! First, we have the stringent, authoritatively decisive recall from Jerusalem: *Make haste, and get thee quickly out of Jerusalem. Quickly*—ἐν τάχει: speed is thus twice emphatically commanded; and the fresh and direct intimation whither Paul was to go (as in ver. 10, "Go into Damascus") merely says, "out of Jerusalem," as a counter-order to his own well-meant return and revisitation to it (ver. 17). This command to abandon the holy city is issued in the very midst of it, and in the sanctuary of the temple itself.

The temple, in which the Lord now forbearingly appears, is no longer a worthy and hallowed type of heaven ; Jerusalem is no longer the city of the great King, for it has rejected God's King, who sits above at God's right hand.—*For they will not receive thy testimony concerning me.* This is the cause for Paul's recall as stated by the Lord, who knows all things beforehand, even the belief or unbelief of all men ; and we see here that He takes away and keeps back His testimony from no one who will believe ; but, on the contrary, in His due time, sends it yet once more even to the unbelieving, as on this occasion to Jerusalem through Paul His ambassador.

Vers. 19, 20. Paul was an Israelite as good and as faithful as any. Even after he had recognised Israel's Messiah in the lowly Jesus, rejected by the blindness both of rulers and people—even then he clung with affection to his headstrong fellow-countrymen. This was his " heart's desire and prayer to God for Israel "—Israel, which he saw to be " zealous towards God, but not according to knowledge"—that they might be saved through the knowledge of the righteousness of Christ, which is " the end of the law" (Rom. x. 1-4). He has again come to Jerusalem, the sacred, well-beloved scene of his early education, and the theatre of his former sinning against Jesus. Here he feels himself compelled to testify, and, in his newly awakened zeal, thinks that *his* testimony *must* be accepted. He therefore cannot at all reconcile himself to the Lord's command, " Go out from Jerusalem." Certainly the Lord had condescended to state the reason for the command, and had emphatically said, " They will not receive *thy* testimony (σοῦ τὴν μαρτυρίαν, not even thine), exactly because it is *of me.*" But Paul acts like all newly converted witnesses who are just entering on their work, especially after a wonderfully sudden conversion : he omits to notice the emphasis with which the Lord has certified that they would not be willing to hear anything of Him, even if Paul said it, and remains confident in himself and his testimony. He seems to think they *must* receive the fact of *his* conversion, although hitherto they have paid no regard to the words and deeds of Peter and John, and all the other apostles. My conversion, and the contrast between my present testimony and my former life, are so surprising, that they cannot help acknowledging God's power in me, and believing what I say. Under this idea, which kindly counted on others being affected by the conscience which had so overpowered him, he urges to his Lord the confident objection : *Lord, they*—even those of whom

Thou sayest that they will not accept my testimony—*know well* (ἐπίσταται) *that I imprisoned and beat in every synagogue them that believed on Thee.* Will they not believe *me*—he means to say—*now* that I, who did these things, believe on Thee, and testify of Thee? The apostle, however, is in error, partly from an amiable and partly from an evil sentiment. In him we may observe the idea existing in so many of us—that *our* testimony will at once avail for good where that of many others has failed. In his three years' solitude Paul has learnt *a little* "to know God's will:" he has thus become more confident, and somewhat goes beyond the limits of the unconditional obedience of his first question, "Lord, what shall I do?" He desires also to talk over that which is ordained for him, and has his own reflections on the point, with certain suppositions as to his own personal importance in the kingdom of God. The Lord has most decisively given him the command, "*Make haste,* and get thee *quickly* out"—thus giving him to understand that snares and dangers for him were at hand: He even added a reason, and, as the Omniscient One, announced what would take place. Nevertheless Paul brings forward his objection, and would fain remain in Jerusalem, neither obeying nor believing in the Lord. Is it permissible for us to blame him much for this? We certainly would not desire to extenuate the amount of self-interest and egotism which, as the germ of spiritual pride, is contained in his words. This much is, however, clear, that opposition of this kind on the part of a disciple is not the most unpleasing and offensive in the sight of the Lord; for it is almost inseparable from the feelings of human nature, and has withal an element in it of something good and amiable, and acceptable to the Lord. In the apostle's words we may notice the *love* of the apostle to his people and his city, whose rejection he can scarcely make up his mind to believe, because he does not see so deeply as the Lord sees; the (in itself) not improper *wish*, that in the very same place where he had so grievously sinned, he might be permitted to retract his sins, and, as far as he could, make restitution for them; his joyful *readiness* to give his testimony under every circumstance of opposition, hostility, and great danger; finally—which, too, is the main point, and the loveliest in the eyes of the Lord—the confiding candour with which he opens out before the Lord all his conflicting thoughts. Dost thou in thy heart and mind feel a spirit of opposition against the command of the Lord? Out with it freely and quickly! This is so far a duty, and is pleasing to the Lord, who willingly, and with kind condescension,

confers with His disciples. We still have to consider the second
part of Paul's objection. He appeals in general to his well-known
zeal as a persecutor in former days, in order to hint at the probability of their belief in his present testimony; although he only
states his reasons against the Lord's command and announcement,
and does not venture to express the direct counter-assertion which
may be deduced from them, viz. that they *will* receive his testimony. But whilst in the presence of the Lord he is looking back
to these former days, the image of Stephen is brought before his
mind, and he perceives as it were the counter-objection which the
Lord might make: Ah! they have outrageously rejected the clear
testimony of many a man of God, and amongst them that of
Stephen, as thou thyself well knowest. To this he now believes
that he both ought and can reply; but just as in ver. 19 he only
expresses the groundwork of his thoughts, and not the thoughts
themselves, so now he cannot find heart or words to speak out plainly,
but evidently continues only the reminiscence of his former conduct in persecuting the Christians. But the Lord, who understands
the intention of our words, perceived here that it was not Paul's
desire merely to give the details of what he had said in ver. 19,
and that his meaning was: Even if the same thing should happen
to me as befell Stephen, I am prepared for it. Allow me then to
suffer a like martyrdom in Jerusalem. This interpretation of ver.
20 is confirmed by the intimation of danger which is implied in the
summons to "make haste" (ver. 18), and by the expression, "the
blood of Thy *witness* Stephen," as I now also am [1] (vers. 18, 15).
However blinded the satisfaction may have been with which Saul
had assisted at the stoning of Stephen, the man who, with, as it
were, the face of an angel, looked up and saw heaven opened, and
the Son of man standing at the right hand of God; still a deep
impression of the divine glory, which shed its beams down upon
the martyr, had unconsciously sunk into the young man's mind, so
that, after his conversion, the picture imprinted on his recollection
stood out resplendent in very different colours. Paul now knows
how glorious a thing it is to suffer martyrdom as Stephen did, and
longs that he might now testify and be persecuted to the death
in the very place where he had himself persecuted. But such self-
surrender to martyrdom must give way before the command and
mission of our Lord; for he only is a faithful messenger and wit-

[1] *Now*, in his sufferings and bonds through the hostility of the Jews, some
of these things for which the apostle offered himself had fallen to his lot.

ness who remains where he ought to remain, and goes whither he ought to go. In Paul's rejoinder we must remark, first, the fearless, confident mention of his former sins, proving that they were *washed away* by the baptism in the name of Jesus (ver. 16); further, the conscientiousness with which his merely standing near and showing satisfaction at Stephen's death,[1] and his taking care of the murderers' clothes,[2] are designated by him as a joining in persecution; finally, the very artless way——showing as much confidence as boldness——in which Paul relates the whole of this event to the Jews, freely declaring to them the precise words of the Lord: " They will not receive thy testimony concerning me." He thus points out to them that his presence among them on this occasion, after he had been before called away from them, is an overflowing measure of mercy now again presented to them, but chides them, at the same time, in the name of his Lord for their unbelief. The position which the apostle takes up towards his hearers in this last narrative is a wonderful compound of mildness and boldness, of confiding love and incisive truth, all uttered in the name of the Lord.

Ver. 21. *And He*——that is, the Lord, who is again the person intended——*said unto me* (repeating the recall already expressed), *Depart !* This word supplies the place of any confutation of the servant's thoughts : it is sufficient that the Lord has graciously given heed to them, and does not chide the opposition to His command. Now follows even a second reason for this command : *for I*——whose word and will are to be henceforth sufficient for thee—— *will send thee far hence unto the Gentiles*——will send thee away as an apostle——ἐξαποστελῶ σε. Whether these Gentiles would receive his testimony or not, is on this occasion kept back by the Lord; but in ch. xxvi. 18 we find a promise on the point. It is, however, sufficient reason for thy going, that I shall send thee. We must remark this, that long before he was separated to the work by the prophets at Antioch, even before Peter had received the revelation concerning Cornelius, the great Gentile apostle had been called in this

---

[1] This would be expressed still more strongly if we omit the τῇ ἀναιρέσει αὐτοῦ, as being taken from ch. viii. 1.

[2] Sepp's idea (*Leben Christi*, part iv. p. 29) as to Paul's *official* functions in taking care of the clothes, and that he acted as a delegate or commissary of the Sanhedrim, is conceived in too strong and decided a tone, as the stoning was of a tumultuous character, and took place without strict form. We have, however, acknowledged that there was *something* official in the act in the *Reden Jesu*, etc., p. 42.

quiet vision by the Lord Himself to undertake His work among
the Gentiles : this is alluded to in ch. xiii. 2, "The work whereunto
I have called them." Although it does not expressly say, " Thou
shalt *testify of me* to the Gentiles," this is manifestly implied in
the " sending," especially after Paul had intimated his impulse to
become a witness for God. It is as if the Lord said : Thy zeal
for testifying is good, but obedience must be added to it ; I will
make use of it among the Gentiles, and not here. Even if Paul had
entertained any doubt as to this meaning of the Lord's words, on
further consideration, a comparison of Ananias' expressions to him
in ver. 15, " a witness to *all men*," must have guided him to a right
conclusion. Nothing is said of anything further which might have
been spoken by the Lord in this revelation ; Paul did not intend
perhaps to close his discourse at this point, but after these last
words he was interrupted by a cry.[1]   They had, in fact, been
compelled to keep silence until Paul's ac nce had attained to a
satisfactory conclusion. Until these last words were spoken, the
accusations in ch. xxi. 28 had not been fully answered, nor had it
been truly disclosed what was the moving cause and the real state
of the case as regarded Paul's " teaching all men everywhere," and
his relations to Greeks and Gentiles. He had simply told them
how, with overpowering might, he had been ordained by the Lord
Jesus Himself to be an apostle to the Gentiles, not without some
opposition on his part, caused by his love for Israel and his hope of
their appreciation of the truth ; also, in this account of his first
call, he was enabled to testify that he was praying in the *temple*,
and that Jesus appeared to him in the *temple*,—consequently that
his teaching and Jesus' purpose were certainly without any intention of showing contempt for the *temple*. The fact that he had
satisfactorily defended himself, and that the truth of his discourse
had shone out as clear as the light of heaven, was sufficiently
vouched for by the effects on the consciences of his hearers, manifested by the cry, " Away with him ! " which they now raised.

Vers. 22–24. Even up to this point the assembled multitude had
scarcely contained themselves so as to listen quietly to the testimony
about Jesus of Nazareth. But the divine bonds restrained them
until the few last important words had been brought home to them
—those words which told them that Jerusalem, on account of its
unbelief, is given up by the God of their fathers and by the Messiah,
and that God's salvation is made over to the Gentiles. This idea

[1] We must compare what follows in ch. xxvi. 16.

constitutes the limit of their endurance, here as well as in many
other testimonies of which we are told in Scripture; compare not
only ch. xxviii. 25–29, but also in Luke iv. 25–29, the conduct of
the Nazarenes towards Jesus Himself. Their blind Jewish pride—
which, amid all their unrighteousness, clung to God's special choice
of them as a kind of property, and despised all other nations as
for ever excluded—was roused up by Paul's clear language. They
cannot gainsay it in their hearts; but Paul's last words about
the Gentiles are sufficient to set them violently against the whole
speech, the Hebrew language of which had at first pacified them,
and to induce them to regard as unheard all that had preceded, and
with blind denial of the clear truth to cry out, " *Away with such a
fellow,*" who values the Gentiles more than Jerusalem, against whom
no other proof or evidence is requisite beyond his own words against
our city. *For it is not fit that he should live:* he does not deserve
to stand upon God's earth, as we are wont to say of an arrant
villain.[1] Thus do they calumniously intensify and confirm the
cry, " Away with him," which they had before raised (ch. xxi. 36),
and formally and solemnly thrust from them the word of God, just
as their brethren in Antioch (ch. xiii. 46). They directly contradict the " will of God" first announced to them by Paul, saying as
it were: " Is *he* to go far hence among the Gentiles ? Why, he
is not worthy to be upon the earth !" Even thus are they compelled to fulfil and confirm Jesus' prediction which had just been
uttered (ver. 18). The very few individuals among the multitude
who, being perhaps touched by the truth, might not have joined in
this cry, are here naturally enough omitted in the narrative, which
confines itself to the matter as a whole; nevertheless it can scarcely
be assumed that, after such repeated testimonies of Jesus' salvation,
those who were susceptible of faith should have remained till then
in a state of unbelief. Suffice it to say, they thus cried out against
Paul, and shook or threw up their clothes,—a usual custom in great
assemblages to indicate the noisy, bustling clamour of unanimity
and satisfaction; also throwing dust into the air, or raising the
dust by the stamping of their feet as a sign of malice and uproar.[2]

---

[1] Looked at more exactly, there is perhaps implied in καθῆκεν (the correct
reading, instead of καθῆκον) a bitter reproach against the Roman power, as if
to say, " It was not right to prevent us from killing him." If the tense is to
be insisted on, this comprehension seems more suitable than merely : For a long
time past it was not right that he should have lived.

[2] Not "a symbolical expression of disquietude and perplexity," as Olshausen

The Roman chief captain understanding nothing of the Hebrew language, and of all this shouting of the Jews, was then again confirmed in his opinion that the pretended citizen of Tarsus must have perpetrated some wicked crime. He has him taken into the castle, and orders that he should be examined by scourging,—a Roman torture for extorting a confession in cases of grave suspicion. The chief captain, whose conduct in this case was quite of an every-day character, and is not specially to be blamed, desired to ascertain from the very lips of this Greek-speaking man, what was the true cause of the people thus crying out against him.

Vers. 25-29. On this occasion, however, the torture of scourging was not to take place, and Paul received permission in the Spirit to evade it in a proper and legitimate way. Although, as re-garded the Jews, neither his education and erudition as a Pharisee, nor the incontestably vouched for appearance to him of the Mes-siah from heaven, availed him anything, yet among the Romans the right of citizenship—that privilege so honoured and beloved throughout their whole empire—had its due influence. Paul was not only a citizen of Tarsus, but, as we learn from ch. xiii. 37, he was also a *Roman* citizen. He had not sought to avoid the *bonds* which had been predicted for him, just as at Philippi he had patiently endured the scourging and harsh imprisonment. If he had so wished, this same privilege must always and everywhere have shielded him both from fetters and scourging ; but formerly he endured both, in order to be honoured by bearing the reproach of Christ. But on some occasions, when it would better serve the cause of the gospel, and doubtless in every case through some in-ward spiritual direction, he made use of his worldly rights, as he now does. When the persons appointed for the purpose (*lorarii*, μαστιγόφοροι, who were to torture him) were about to lay hold of him, to stretch him out or bind him to receive the leathern thongs with which his back was to be lashed, Paul said to the centurion who gave the command : *Is it lawful for you to scourge a man that is a Roman, and uncondemned?* His meaning is : In any case, it is an injustice to scourge a man that is unheard : ye ought first to calmly interrogate me, and not immediately put me to the torture before I have shown any stubbornness in my reply to accu-sations which are certainly very probable ; but besides this, as a Roman citizen, whom in general it is not lawful to scourge, I first

thinks. It was, perhaps, rather a symbol that with justice they desired to stone Paul, if only they dared, as Baumgarten, Grotius, and others are of opinion.

at least demand a hearing.   He thus to some extent expresses himself with modesty, not immediately demanding his full rights, but yet at the same time imposing a sufficient check on what was being done, by asking with some degree of severity, Is it lawful for you to do a thing which is forbidden by the laws throughout the whole Roman empire?   *When the centurion heard this, he went and told the chief captain, saying, Take heed what thou doest!*—reflect on the orders you have just given, and retract them; *for this man is a Roman,* according to his own very confident and credible assertion.   The punishment of death was indeed awarded to any illegal assumption of this right of citizenship; but Paul had no appearance of having been impelled by fear to risk this punishment.   The chief captain therefore took the trouble to come to him and address him with official emphasis, saying : *Tell me*—without any deceit or pretension, which can only have the effect of bringing more trouble upon you, and aggravating your fate—*art thou a Roman?*   To this laconic question Paul replies more briefly still, with a dignified and confident " Yes."   This answer bore but little appearance of being a silly lie dictated by a fear of the torture. The chief captain, from a direct conviction of the truth, at once accepted and believed this simple " Yes."   He addresses the Roman citizen with a confiding spirit of inquiry, and also with some degree of respect : *With a great sum obtained I this freedom*[1]—as if to imply, " Why, thou art as good as I am ; and I should be only despising my own privilege, which has cost me enough, if I did not pay due respect to it in thy person." [2]   This somewhat familiar communication may also involve a question of surprise, asking : " How didst thou obtain this freedom?"   On this presumption, Paul replies to the chief captain in a way certainly unlooked for, but quite conformable to the truth : *But I was free-born*—there was no need for me to buy it, and I consequently stand in a higher position than thou.   As we know from sure data that Tarsus was not a Roman colony or municipality, but merely a free city retaining its own regulations, we are compelled to assume that some

[1] " Lysias " was probably the Greek name, to which " Claudius " was then added.   It was not until this degraded period, at the time of Claudius, that the Roman citizenship could be bought with money.

[2] It was not said with a feeling of distrust, implying : Thou dost not seem to me to have been rich enough to be able to buy it.   For this Paul, who had at first wrung from him the permission to speak, and then had been able to preserve the listening attention of the raging people, had now made such an impression by his dignity and calmness, that his word was certainly trusted.

ancestor of Paul had either purchased for his family an hereditary citizenship, or that it had been conferred upon them on account of merit; in the latter case, we have a right to infer a distinguished parentage for the apostle. From all that Luke says, it is likewise clear that every one born in Tarsus was not on that account a Roman citizen; for else Paul's statement in ch. xxix. 39 would have sufficed to have shielded him from the fetters and scourging. The chief captain now stands confused before this mysterious man, against whom the people were so infuriated, and is unable to do anything with him. Those who were to have tortured him straightway leave him, and the chief captain himself *was afraid*, now that he indubitably understood by closer inquiry that the man whom he had caused to be bound with two chains was a Roman. The word ἐπιγνούς probably implies some closer investigation of the matter; compare the same word in ch. xxiv. 8. However great the degree of credibility which might be inferred from the personal characteristics of this man, whom Israel indeed would not believe in his testimony of Jesus' manifestation to him; however clear the confidence which was shown in his simple "Yes," still we may very well believe that more certain proofs of his assertion must have been subsequently given or alleged. Thus more and more begin to be developed the features of Paul's long imprisonment, in which, like the Saviour, he was continually being accused by the Jews before the Gentiles; and being found guiltless by the latter, was only kept in captivity to give pleasure to Jews. Finally, his appeal to Cæsar is the means of bringing him to Rome, there also *to testify*, as he had testified at Jerusalem (ch. xxiii. 11).

XXV.

PAUL BEFORE THE HIGH COUNCIL.

(Chap. xxiii. 1–6.)

THE TWICE BEGUN AND TWICE INTERRUPTED DEFENCE OF HIS ORTHODOX JUDAISM.

Ch. xxii. 30. In order to come as soon as possible to a certainty about the strange and unpleasant legal matter in which he had involved himself by his interference in the uproar of the people, the next day the chief captain exercises all his authority, and convokes a meeting of the high council to interrogate the prisoner, against whom no just cause for imprisonment was alleged (ch. xxv. 27). From a just spirit of official zeal and sense of justice, with which perhaps some more bitter feeling may have been mixed up, he desires to know something certain—the positive and correct truth (τὸ ἀσφαλὲς ; cf. ch. xxi. 34, xxv. 26)—why he was thus accused by the Jews. Could he not first have amicably and closely questioned the prisoner, who, be it remembered, spoke Greek ? One reason, perhaps, why he did not do this was based upon the pride of the tribune ; another was his somewhat irritable desire that the Jews should themselves clearly inform him why they thus raged against Paul. The first thing, therefore, which the chief captain did the next day, was to release Paul from his fetters. He wished in some way to evince the respect with which the apostle had inspired him: he therefore, renouncing all prejudice on his part, placed him before the council, temporarily at least, free from his fetters ("ut sine præjudicio causam diceret," Grotius). Looking at the constantly increasing degradation of Jewish rights at this time, we can scarcely doubt that the *tribunus militum* of the feast-watch had the power, in extraordinary cases of this sort, of actually ordering a convocation of the high council to inquire into the cause of any general tumult ; at least we find here the same simple term ἐκέλευσεν which is subsequently used in commanding the soldiers (ver. 10). The whole of the high council must therefore have been assembled in their usual place of meeting,[1]

---

[1] For even ἐλθεῖν (instead of which συνελθεῖν is the correct reading) might point, on account of the word καταγαγὼν which follows, not to a coming into

not so much for the purpose of pronouncing any real judgment
or decisive verdict (which Paul subsequently, ch. xxv. 9, 10, as a
Roman citizen declined to recognise), as merely for preliminary
information for the chief captain himself. The chief captain led
his prisoner down from the Castle of Antonia, and placed him
unfettered (he himself remaining with him), not *before*, but rather
among, in the midst of the council (εἰς αὐτούς).

Ch. xxiii. 1. Thus, therefore, the incontrovertible witness for the
hated Jesus of Nazareth, of whose preaching among the Gentiles
report had told so many important and grievous things, now stood
before the Sanhedrim, as the day before he had faced the assembled
multitude. The matter had, indeed, almost assumed the appearance of its being the council which had to give an account of the
origin of the uproar against this man, instead of the latter having
to defend himself. They now, for the first time, had so closely
before them the notorious Paul—him who was once their own
associate Saul! This, then, was the learned scholar of Gamaliel
and zealous Pharisee, once the hope of his sect, now a fellow-
witness with the poor Galilean laymen; this was the man who
not only, like the latter, testified of Jesus' resurrection and ascension, but also asserted that he had been afforded several visions of
Him who was now in heaven! They might well need some little
time for considering him, ere their evil consciences could suggest
any suitable commencement for the investigation. But Paul had
no cause for delay, or for any timidity in entering on the question:
with a good conscience he earnestly and significantly looked upon
the council for a while, and then, all unquestioned, himself began
the proceedings. He perhaps recollected many things about them,
and might well fix his eyes upon these associates in his former
bigotry, although he had never taken a part in their hypocrisy,
now so evident to him. The thought perhaps entered his mind,
that if Jesus had not redeemed him from his sins, he too might
have been sitting upon that judgment-seat, and adjudicating about
Jesus' witnesses, just as once he had received letters against the
saints from this very council! In short, he felt that he had a
special liberty, both in the sight of his God and of these men, to be
the first to speak, and to address the embarrassed council in bold
but true language.

the presence of the chief captain, but only to the usual συνελθεῖν. The council
had not for a long time held its meetings in the temple, which would have been
inaccessible to the Romans.

Standing among these men, some of whom he had known in former times—among these Sadducees and Pharisees, these voluptuaries and boasters, hiding their hypocrisy under the veil of their office—the apostle, with a comprehensive glance, surveys his former and present feelings and convictions, and permits himself to boast of his *good conscience*, as contrasted with that of the deceivers who were sitting in the seat of honour to judge him. Thus he begins his defence with a candid, open assertion of the character of his inmost individuality, and is able to propound his own honesty of purpose. Having thus (as was indeed necessary) renounced and separated himself from these Jews, he is enabled in a second commencement (ver. 6) to testify that he, as an orthodox Jew, possessed in Jesus Christ that very hope which, except in Him, could not be rightly and truly possessed, for which at least the orthodox party among the Jews were still waiting (ch. xxiv. 15); that, consequently, he ought not to be condemned by them; and besides, that he could not in any way allow himself to be judged by the *Sadducees*. We thus far enter into the discussion of the whole address, so as better to understand the necessary position and significance of the first commencement. No longer is the council addressed by the witness for Jesus, as they were in ch. iv. 8, nor even as in ch. vii. 2 by Stephen: they are now *men*, who are opposing God, to whom God's messenger gives more than their due, when, as fellow-men and brother Israelites, he calls them *brethren*. In addressing the people the day before, Paul had styled them "Men, brethren, and *fathers*" (ch. xxii. 1), in order, before the multitude of common men, to give honour both to age and official position. But now, in the midst of the council itself, in the presence and hearing of the chief captain,[1] he calls all the high priests and lords of the council merely "*brethren*," as joint-members of the same nation which has thrust him from there, although he did not desire to give them up (cf. John xviii. 35; Acts xxviii. 19), making himself equal to them all as a scribe, as an Israelite, and as a *man*. His "living before God" refers, in its deepest sense, to the last of these terms; but an intimation of his Judaism is not excluded: for πεπολίτευμαι τῷ Θεῷ means, properly, something else than mere "living (or walking) before God." This somewhat

---

[1] It may be well imagined that Paul now spoke in Greek, on account of the tribune who would desire to hear and understand him. In his address, therefore, to all the people the day before, he had used the Hebrew tongue; but now, before the sacred authorities of Israel, he speaks Greek.

remarkable expression is by no means one and the same thing with ζῆν, πράττειν, ἀναστρέφεσθαι, βιοῦν, etc., in a general sense :[1] it also contains the sub-idea of living in a *state*, according to a *law*,— as living and behaving in a certain way as a citizen of a kingdom.[2] As Luke informs us by his selection of this Greek word, Paul on this occasion intended to express to the high council of Israel that he had lived as a citizen of God's kingdom, as an orderly member of God's people, both in outward position and inward sentiments ; in short, that he had been an Israelite of good conscience, and remained so up to that very day.—*In all good conscience.* This is the somewhat bold expression which requires a more exact consideration. In the first place, the truth of this assertion, in a *relative* sense, as regarded the Sanhedrim, is tolerably clear; in this sense, the words " until this day " have application, and the whole sentence may be understood as meaning : Populares, ego summopere sanctitati vitæ studui ad hunc usque diem (Morus). Always according to the best knowledge I had, and *now* quite as much so and in a purer way than heretofore. I have never ceased to be a citizen before God in a good conscience ; I have not sinned or become an apostate by my confession of Jesus, but can confidently claim from you, up to this very day, the testimonials which ye once afforded me. Hess says, both forcibly and justly, " My conscience bears me witness, that up to this day I have remained faithful to our religion." Also Bengel : " Loquitur Paulus *præcipue* de statu suo *post* conversionem, nam de statu pristino nemo ei controversiam movebat." But though we may consider this sense appropriate as regarded the Sanhedrim, and may think that this laying claim to his former good report was eminently suitable as regarded the time he had spent in the service of Jesus, still the important question arises, how Paul himself, as a disciple of Jesus, could have thus expressed himself in the true spirit of Jesus, without any tinge of jesuitical equivocation, and could have thus combined the periods *before* and *after* his conversion as one and the same " living before God in all good conscience ? " Even if we should desire to assume the subterfuge of thinking that Paul, in his words on this occasion, accommodated himself both in expression and meaning to those who were around

---

[1] As *e.g.* Morus asserts, and yet allows that it is " contra omnem Græcæ linguæ consuetudinem."

[2] Refer to the passages from the ancient writers in Wetstein on Phil. i. 27, especially Basilius, πρὸς Θεὸν, ᾧ ζῶ καὶ πεπολίτευμαι ; and Origen.

him, and that he only intended to assert that before men and in the sight of men he was even then as honest a Jew and as blameless a Pharisee as any of them were,[1] even then the expression τῷ Θεῷ will deprive us of the benefit of this loophole. It must indeed remain clear enough, that Paul speaks of what he had been and was *before God*, and not *before men*—what he was before or to God, in relation to Him, and for Him. As a contrast to the " men and brethren" who were sitting there to judge him, and did not know how to begin, he evidently appeals to God *as* a witness of his honesty. By this means, in all the holy consciousness of his dignity, he makes a distinction between himself and the Pharisees present, the whole of whose righteousness was " before men" (Matt. vi. 1, xxiii. 5), and is thus enabled, without detriment to his own inward personality, to subsequently associate himself with them, and side with them against the Sadducees. He speaks, indeed, chiefly of his life in Christ, in which he had been acknowledged before God, although no longer before men, as an honest servant and citizen, and uses without distinction the same expression in regard to his earlier life. Finally, he says also, " In all good conscience." Now it is certainly not permissible to interpret this phrase of mere external righteousness. We see, therefore, that Paul must *in himself* have felt justified in asserting that a " good conscience" of this sort was consistent even with his former path of error, and that, *for the Sanhedrim*, he maintained it in this way with regard also to his present belief. Also in his familiar epistle to his own disciple Timothy he writes: " I thank God, whom I serve from my forefathers with a pure conscience" (2 Tim. i. 3). We must therefore allow (with Bengel), " Et tamen in pristino quoque statu, quanquam in errore versabatur, *conscientiæ fuerat obsecutus;*" and with Steffens, " Saul had persecuted Christianity in *honest* and open enmity, and became a Paul." Remark how the apostle describes his early life in Phil. iii. 4–6 : as touching the law (κατὰ νόμον) a Pharisee, *i.e.* in his outward party, and in all main points, an orthodox Israelite; touching the active disposition of his mind, or faithful obedience of his inmost heart to the acknowledged and supposed truth (κατὰ ζῆλον), a persecutor of the church; and, finally, in his actions done in all sincerity according to the best knowledge he had, and so far as was possible in regard to the supposed righteousness of the law, he was

---

[1] As Bengel expresses it: "Neque quicquam commiserat, cur in foro externo reus fieret."

blameless (ἄμεμπτος). Those who attribute to Christianity a gloomy condemnation of, and a certain injustice towards, the natural man, and that which is good in him, or even those real devotees who, going beyond the truth, think badly of and inveigh against themselves and their former life, may learn here from Paul's example, that a regenerate man may rejoice before God and man even in his former relatively good conscience when in a position of error and sin, if his present conscience in Christ bears him witness[1] that he has not belonged to the class of gross hypocrites.[2] True it is, that this same man Paul, who now in God's light, in the presence of these hypocrites, could call God to witness as to his good conscience in former days, fell to the earth without excuse before his Saviour when He visited him in judgment; subsequently, also, to his own disciple Timothy he styles himself the "chief of sinners" (1 Tim. i. 15). We must therefore make a due distinction between these two standpoints and modes of expression, which were before considered in the case of Cornelius (ch. x. 35). There is the more deeply penetrating way of speaking, according to which the most honest and upright *natural* man is before God but a deceiver and a hypocrite of impure conscience; also the other, which graciously acknowledges that which is but half-good, and, distinguishing it from the more wicked grades of sin, allows it to receive, even before God, its but half-true name.

Ver. 2. As soon as we confess Jesus in good earnest, the world, and especially the Babylon of an erring church, desires to hear nothing more either of our previous or present honesty of mind. The Sanhedrim cannot brook Paul's bold language, and the high priest becomes the medium of their common wrath. Oh how much it must have irritated these men, who had long back decided the matter in their own hearts, and cared not to hear any further of God's truth, to see the apostle standing among them unbound, and under the protection of the tribune,—able, therefore, to look them in the face joyfully and freely, and to begin the proceedings boldly, without giving them any title of honour, or using any *captatio bene-*

---

[1] As Bengel beautifully says: "Nunc, cum bona vetera non abjecit, sed meliora accepit, ex praesenti statu lux in pristinum sese refundebat."

[2] When a warrior, honourable in his vocation, is taunted after his conversion as a devotee and a hypocrite, he may boldly say: "Brethren, I have always been an honest and good comrade to you; trust me that I shall be so now."

volentiæ, by telling about his " good conscience !"   " The language
seemed all too bold as coming from the lips of a man whom the
fiery zeal of bigotry had already condemned to death ; it appeared
almost a blasphemy, as proceeding from an apostate who had proved
faithless to the council, faithless to his mandates of persecution,
and faithless also to zealously orthodox Judaism " (Hess). But if
we go to the root of the matter, it was the high priest Ananias'
own evil conscience which chiefly and actually embittered him to
that extent, that he himself commanded the officers that they should
smite him on the mouth. This was meant for an admonition that
it was not Paul's place to speak first, but that he ought to keep
silence. It was an unworthy outrage to commit on a Roman
citizen, whom the chief captain had the day before feared either
to scourge or fetter ; it was committed, too, in the very presence of
the tribune, and was not only a mean treatment of a once highly-
honoured Pharisee, but also unkind conduct towards a prisoner on
the part of one who not long before (as we shall state below) had
himself tasted the indignity of captivity.[1]

Ver. 3. Paul's rejoinder was *not* contrary to the gentleness of
Jesus, but was spoken as by a servant of the Lord, in the name
of God, just as if by any one of the prophets. He availed himself
of this undignified blow to unmask reprovingly in an explanatory
antithesis the hypocrisy of the high priest and the council, and
thus to rightly evince to them the true sense in which he appealed
before them to his good conscience.—*God shall smite thee, thou
whited wall !* Thus, in the first place, he hits upon the whole
general hypocrisy of the man, and gives judgment upon it, as if he
(Paul) were seated upon the judge's seat, and the high priest was
standing as a condemned sinner before him. And in the eye of
the Spirit, and before God, was not this actually the case ? Should
not one of God's saints be permitted to impeach miscreants, although he may be standing before their judgment-seat ?   Paul
does so here, and calls Ananias what he was, *a whited wall*—using a
proverbial expression which is found in these very terms in Seneca
and other ancient writers. We must leave it undecided whether,
in the *fitting* title which, according to God's truth, Paul conferred
on the miserable president, he meant in any way to point to his
white robe of office, or to the grey hairs of the aged sinner : it

[1] Baumgarten rather arbitrarily assumes that the passionate command was
not carried out, and that Paul was not actually smitten ; the execution of the
order is, I think, to be inferred from the narrative.

seems more probable to us that he desired to call to mind Jesus'
words about "whited sepulchres" (Matt. xxiii. 27, 28), just as
Peter in ch. iv. 11 referred to what the Lord said as to the rejected
corner-stone. If there is any fear of our taking offence at these
words of Paul, which are a degree milder than those of Jesus, we
are at least taught by the Spirit to compare them with the utterances of Him who was most humble and most gentle. In case
any should desire to put to our consideration whether Jesus Himself, if before the council,[1] would not have behaved more meekly,
we shall bring forward some points which are of a contrary tendency. In the first place, Jesus' words, " If I have spoken well,
why smitest thou me ? " are not so very different to those of Paul
as might be thought. Next, at a time when the Sanhedrim had
become more and more degraded, that treatment was not unfitted
for them, even before their public bar, which (treatment) Jesus
only caused them to experience in private. Further, that the disciples of Jesus were to be permitted to bear swords, and use them
(Luke xxii. 36–38), although their Master before them suffered in
silence, for the simple reason that *only He* had to drink of the *cup*
that was ordained for the salvation of the whole world (John xviii.
11) ; but it was soon necessary that His disciples should serve the
then existing kingdom of Christ both with patient endurance, and
also with energy of language and the power of the sword. Finally,
the servant who stands up in the name of his Lord is commissioned
to make use of greater severity and loftiness of language than was
permitted to the Lord Himself, owing to the special decree as to
the patience of the latter. Majesty itself may majestically keep
silence when its ambassadors are bound to speak. There is therefore nothing to prevent us from maintaining that Paul on this
occasion announced to Ananias, in the name and Spirit of Jesus,
the just retribution for this wicked smiting, and that his words
were words of prediction and not of abuse.—*God shall smite thee !*
In saying this, the apostle does not express a wish that evil may
befall the aged hypocrite, but *predicts* it (τύπτειν σὲ μέλλει), and
as it were *prophesies* in the place of the high priest (John xi. 51),
completely reversing their positions. He consequently speaks here
as a prophet of the new covenant, just as in former days many
of the old prophets had rebuked both kings and priests. It is

[1] As *e.g.* Heinrichs, who says : " Apparet tamen, quantum inter mansuetu-
dinem Jesu et vehementiam Pauli in ærumnis, quibus objiciebatur uterque, per-
ferendis discrimen intercesserit."

also worthy of notice, that we learn from Josephus that, not long
after this, Ananias together with his brother were miserably slain.
God therefore confirmed His apostle's words. In the second half
of the verse we read Paul's special charge as to the illegality of
Ananias' present conduct. For dost *thou* (the so-called and osten-
sible high priest) sit here on the seat of justice, in order to judge
me *according to the law,* and commandest thou me to be smitten
contrary to the law? Remark Paul's recognition not only of the
external seat of judgment, but also of all that might be delivered
legally from Moses' seat, even by an Ananias. Remark also the
incisive question as to the complete opposition shown by his judges
between their title and their persons, their office and their conduct,
in the deepest meaning of which is disclosed the key to Paul's
whole position before this assembly : he was to be judged by the
unjust in the name of the Just One, and appeals against their
judgment to God's law : hypocrites and heretics wished to condemn
him in the name of Israel ; but he, on the contrary, styles himself,
in contrast to them, a genuine Israelite. It may be a matter of
question, whether by the " smiting contrary to the law " the apostle
desired to point to any distinct ordinances as to impartiality and
accurate investigation in courts of justice (*e.g.* Lev. xix. 15, Deut.
xvii. 4, cf. John vii. 51), or merely to allude to the general injustice of such conduct ; the latter is, however, the more probable, on
account of the Greek expression παρανομῶν being used (and *not*
παρὰ τὸν νόμον). This expression touches generally on the preceding rebuke administered to the hypocrite, as a law-breaker and
unjust man, who cared nothing for right and equity.

Ver. 4. Paul therefore on this occasion, as before the Gentiles
(ch. xxii. 25), appealed to justice and to law ; but Israel is more
unjust than the Gentiles. The apparitors standing by, who in the
name of Ananias the president were desirous of defending the order
which they had executed, ill-naturedly turned upon him with a
ready reply, saying, " Revilest *thou* God's high priest ?"—*thou,* who
assertest that thou hast lived before God in all good conscience,
and desirest not to suffer anything *contrary* to the law ! They
forget that Paul (vers. 1, 3) had called *God* to the remembrance
of these *men,* who were now no longer to sit in judgment like gods
in God's name, but were to die like other men—these judges in
Israel who had long acted in complete opposition to their duties.
He had appealed from them to the highest Judge in God's church,
and had announced the punishment of this Avenger on all unjust

judges. With a very natural and almost unavoidable misconception—interpreting, as they did, the holy apostle's words as if they were every-day language used by one of themselves—the officers look upon his *prediction* as nothing but a wishful invective,[1] and consequently with a certain appearance of justice, say, " Revilest thou God's high priest?" Compare the words of one of the officers (John xviii. 22) to the Lord Jesus, and also the somewhat similar reproach of the lawyer when Jesus called down a "woe" on them as "graves which appear not" (Luke xi. 45). The question, as they intended it, conveys something of a cutting and criminating character—a forcible retort to the question Paul had put. Paul had asked, "Sittest thou here as a legal judge, and dost thou act illegally?" He is met with the rejoinder, "Dost thou assert thyself to be innocent before God, and yet dost thou despise God in the dignity which His law attributes to His high priest?"

Ver. 5. The answer which Paul gives to this question has been frequently and variously discussed by expositors; and the only result which most of them have been able to elicit from this difficult matter is, that one of the weaknesses of human nature must be laid to the apostle's charge.[2] But it is only the human weakness of the interpreters, who mistake the deep-meaning language of the Spirit, expressed here in a form to which they are not accustomed.[3] We desire to consider this answer, basing our comprehension of it on faith, and doubting rather our own wisdom than the holiness of Paul's conduct on such an important occasion, and shall endeavour, in explaining it, to see if, by believing impartiality, or as some might say, partiality, its natural drift and bearing may not lead us to the goal of a satisfactory explanation of it. Paul, while acknowledging the remonstrance of the officers, turns (as was fitting) in his reply away from the latter, and addresses

[1] The corresponding Hebrew expression (יְבָכֶּה אֱלֹהִים) was, in fact, a common form of rebuke, which the Mischna quotes as such.

[2] "One of the 'manifold moral infirmities' in the apostles which the history allows us to get a sight of." Thus says R. Rothe (*Stud. u. Krit.* 1860, ii.).

[3] We still adhere in firm conviction to the points we maintained in our first edition, now thirty years ago, viz. that Paul on this occasion committed neither sin nor error. Let the majority—the most eminent even of believers—continue to persevere in their blame of the apostle, we desire once more to oppose this opinion; and we rejoice at Baumgarten's opposition to a prevailing misinterpretation, agreeing as he does with all we said long ago (although he does not mention our name).

himself to his judges, still calling them in a quiet and composed way his "brethren," as he had done before, and says to them : *I wist not that it was the high priest*, or that he (whom I reproached) is the high priest—οὐκ ᾔδειν ὅτι ἐστὶν ἀρχιερεύς. *For it is* (certainly) *written*, as I well know and acknowledge, that *thou shalt not speak evil of the ruler of thy people*. This is his remarkable reply. We shall now, with Chrysostom and many other of the ancient writers, as well as others, among whom we may now reckon Da Costa, endeavour to make good that Paul's excuse—"I knew not," etc.—is literally true. Various reasons have been brought forward in order to give some probability to this "not-knowing" of Paul. It is said that the meeting of the council might have been irregular, and not quite correct according to all due form; that Paul, having been so long away from Jerusalem, might hardly have known who the present high priest was, as he was shifted almost every year, and the dignity (which became venal under the Roman authority) was transferred from one to the other with increasing rapidity and confusion; that the high priest did not wear any distinguishing robe of office except in the temple; and other reasons of a similar nature are alleged. But the closer the matter is looked at from all points of view, the more incredible it seems that the apostle did not actually know or see that it was the high priest. There is nothing at all said as to the meeting being an irregular one; on the contrary, from ch. xxii. 30, we are led to expect that it was convoked solemnly and in all due form, so as to make an impression both on Paul and the tribune. The person of the ruling or presiding high priest was still so conspicuous,[1] that Paul, during his eight days' sojourn among the Christians at Jerusalem, would probably have had his attention drawn to him. On this occasion the presiding high priest must have been clearly evident, if not by his robes, at least by his *seat*, and by the officers (according to ver. 2) standing round him. When Paul "earnestly beheld the council" (ver. 1), he must have sought for and descried this president, as subsequently he detected the Pharisees and Sadducees[2] (ver. 6) : therefore in his words, "Sittest *thou* to judge me," etc.,

---

[1] It is well known that it was not always necessary for the high priest to preside over the Sanhedrim, although he generally did so.

[2] Alford seeks to infer from the ἀτενίζω in this passage, and in ch. xiii. 9 and xiv. 9, that Paul, since the events at Damascus, had retained a certain infirmity of vision, and therefore did not perhaps recognise the high priest. But this is a groundless supposition.

he most probably referred to the president of the court, upon whom fell the administration of its legal order. This is rendered still more probable by the words καὶ σὺ κάθῃ in the original. Thus Bengel interprets it : " Tu quoque, non modo ceteri ; tu qui defensor legis vis videri ! " Almost all expositors, although they differ in other points, are now agreed in this, that Paul *must* have known that he was speaking to the high priest. How, then, are the words οὐκ ᾔδειν to be treated ? As far as I know, it has been reserved for the audacity of the Tübingen school to be the first to assume that Paul *lied* in order to excuse himself. The only thing that remains is to understand εἰδέναι in its more unfrequent meaning, *to recollect, to think of* ; in favour of this, Bengel adduces an abundance of passages, to which, however, more might be added.[1] On this point most are agreed, that Paul intended to say, *I did not think of it, I did not reflect upon it*, and so far, *I did not know it.* Subject even to this comprehension of the first words, the intention of the whole of Paul's utterance may be very differently understood, according to the two points of view in which it may be looked at—either by first taking the quotation of the law which follows, and from this interpreting the preceding words, or the reverse. Those who do the former, find an *earnestly* asserted quotation of the law, and consequently an excuse on the part of Paul,[2] to the effect that he had really *forgotten*, or had not *thought of*, the dignity of the high priest, and had thus offended against this law. Ancients and moderns, believers and unbelievers, have not shrunk from imputing this offence to the apostle.[3] But we ourselves,

---

[1] 1 Cor. i. 16, xii. 2, xv. 34 ; Phil. iv. 15 (Eph. vi. 8 ; Col. iii. 24) ; Luke ix. 55 ; 2 Sam. xix. 22 ; Lev. v. 4.

[2] "The passage which Paul quotes for his own correction." This, alas, is said in the beautiful and popular *Introduction to the New Testament* by Wucherer (*Das Wort der Wahrheit*, Nördlingen 1848–1850).

[3] Even Jerome most surprisingly says: " Ubi est illa patientia Salvatoris, qui quasi agnus ductus ad victimam non aperuit os suum, sed clementer loquitur verberanti ? Non apostolo detrahimus, sed gloriam Domini prædicamus, qui in carne passus carnis injuriam superat et fragilitatem." Hess says: " Paul expresses this in the first ebullition of his feelings, regardless of time and place. Immediately he is asked, ' Revilest thou God's high priest ? ' he became sensible that he must recollect whom he was before." Morus: " Indicat Paulus, se festinasse, non satis cogitasse, cui dixerit hoc. Et quidni Paulum hominem indignatio, cum vix aperto ore pulsaretur, non movere potuit, ut paullo ardentius loqueretur ? Satis est, eum admonitum non defendere hoc, sed retractare quodammodo." Kuinoel : " Fateor, me æstuantis animi impetu abreptum (quamvis injuria mihi sit facta) paulo liberius esse locutum, nec ad animum

isolated though we may be in our opinion, do very much shrink
from this imputation ; not from any mere vague repugnance to
attributing to the apostle this error of weakness, but from evident
reasons derived from the existing context. First and foremost,
the Lord's declaration, which follows in ver. 11, induces us not to
impute any error to the apostle on this occasion. In the next
place, as we have seen above, Paul, in his words in ver. 3, expressly
points out the high priest ; and he could not, without a strange perversion of the truth, have said that he did not think of him. Can
it, too, be supposed, that in this first and most important appearance
of the great witness before the high council, the grace (so mighty
in him at other times) would have deserted him, and that the Holy
Spirit, specially promised in Matt. x. 19, 20 for such a case as
this, would not have led him ? [1]   It is the more difficult to make
up our minds to assume this desertion, the greater we consider
Paul's human deficiency to have been. Even psychologically it
appears to us inexplicable that this same man, who had been so
long exercised in shame and suffering, and the day previous, when
in imminent danger of death, had been able to speak with the
greatest presence of mind and most unselfish love, should have so
suddenly altered ; that in the intervening night, instead of obtaining strength and calmness from his Lord, he should have so changed
as to be unable to endure a blow (such as Jesus received before
Annas) without losing his self-command.   No, we cannot believe
it.   If Paul had really asked to be excused for his most just words
of rebuke and sentence (by no means words of reviling[2]) on the

revocavi mihi cum pontifice rem esse." Neander: " Although Paul allowed
himself to be carried away by a momentary feeling of just indignation, he
was soon able to obtain the mastery, and to act as his vocation demanded."
Thiersch : " He allowed himself to be impelled to revile the Sadducean high
priest." Alas, even v. Gerlach says : " In his feelings of wrath, he transgressed
by unseemly words." But, latest of all, the eminent Van Oosterzee has, inconceivably and unjustifiably, expressed himself most severely (*Predigten über
Moses*, p. 151) as to Paul's conduct and words.

[1] Rougemont says very boldly : " Paul's words of contumely to Ananias
gainsay the papistical theory as to *office ;* which theory maintains that he who is
invested with certain functions, be he even a Borgia, is in some magical way
preserved from error." Added to this, a page previously he says, " Paul did
not always act, speak, and write in his capacity as an apostle." In opposition to
this, we should confidently ask when and where Paul ever acted in " his capacity
as an apostle," if not on this occasion when before the high council.

[2] Olshausen, *e.g.*, considers it " incongruous" that the apostle should use
" words of contumely." Did not the Lord Himself (Matt. xxiii.) use still more

ground of human infirmity, he must have brought shame, not only on himself, but on the cause of his Lord; for in the presence of this wretched Sanhedrim, and from the enemy's point of view, the two were identified. If, also, Paul had by his own conduct (at least in the view of the malicious enemy) given the lie to his proud boast in ver. 1, it would tend to stagger our belief in the mercy of the Lord shown by His appearance before the council of Israel, and by the patience and overflowing long-suffering exhibited in sending yet again this last witness. Finally, we are influenced by the account (mentioned above) of the subsequent murder of Ananias. God Himself did not retract the words uttered by the apostle; how, then, could Paul have done so? If, therefore, the words "*I wist not*" cannot be looked upon as false, nor yet as true, either in the sense of actual *knowledge* or in that of *non-consideration*, what is left for us to assume, except that which holds the middle course between truth and falsehood—viz. an *ironical figure of speech?* This is constituted by saying something which in literal words is untrue, but the untruth of which is at once laid open to the hearer by the well-understood but hidden sense of the expression.[1] Many expositors since Calvin, Camerarius, and Pricæus, have thus understood Paul's words, with more or less fulness and depth of insight into this holy irony. The superficial sense, though ironically expressed, of course still holds good, as if to say, "I did not think of it, and must make that my excuse;" but the idea which was intended to be conveyed, which explained the irony to the knaves (who deserved nothing better), is to the following effect: "Ye are yourselves in fault if I did not know and acknowledge your high priest, in spite of his seat and his robe. What! is this your high priest? Why! I never should have thought it. Should not the fact be seen and known from his conduct? Certainly, certainly; the high priest must be honoured: that I am

---

bitter words of contumely? And with regard to the authorities before whom Paul was speaking, had they not in fact forfeited all the privileges, respect, and dignity due to their office, through their opposition to God, notwithstanding all His patience towards them? And is not this just the very meaning of the apostle's ironical apology?

[1] "*I wist not* are words which, literally understood, would be a complete absurdity and impossibility as coming from the lips of a scholar of Gamaliel, and a former legate of the Sanhedrim,—spoken, too, in the presence of the latter. The contradiction between the purport and the meaning must lead any intelligent person to infer some sense hidden under the mere words."—BAUMGARTEN.

well aware of!" In this way Paul emphatically parodies the
hypocritical language of the officers, and intimates by his tone and
look that at all events he did not acknowledge this man as high
priest, and that (in ver. 3) he had not spoken to him as such. In
this only half-intended excuse there is implied (as Bengel nicely
discerns) something more than a mere mockery and mortification
of the wicked hypocrites; it also tends to conciliate and make
allowance for the kindly disposed (if there were any) among the
judges and the officers who had admonished him. Here again we
recognise the whole individuality of the incomparable Paul in the
ready lightning-like flash of his holy banter, which blends the
most incisive keenness and the deepest earnestness with the most
delicate discretion and the most subtle emotion of raillery, leaving
it to the Spirit which inspired it to bring it home to those it concerned. Can we, in fact, imagine that the law referred to (Ex.
xxii. 28) altogether forbade the application of any rebuke to the
rulers of the people,—thus constituting them as infallible popes?
Does it not merely indicate the ordinary regulation for the human
will of the Israelites, to which rule exceptions might constantly be
made, whenever (not man, but) God Himself, the King of Israel,
by the mouth of some one inspired by Him, rebuked and reproached
a guilty servant, no ruler in His sight? Did not all the prophets,
whose office is set above all other positions of authority (Deut.
xvi.-xviii.), reprove many a priest and king in Israel?[1] Did not
Nathan speak of David as a man doomed to death? and did not
both the "man of God," of whom we read in 1 Sam. ii. 27, and
even the little child Samuel, predict God's judgments on the high
priest Eli? Paul had only said, "God shall smite thee," speaking
as a prophet, just as Micaiah to Zedekiah (1 Kings xxii. 25). If,
therefore, the command, "Thou shalt not curse the ruler of thy
people," applied only to the feelings of human will, could Paul have
quoted it here in all earnestness, and as if confessing that he had
infringed it? We also perceive that the quotation following the
quasi-excuse is to some extent only *irony;* but it also implies a
modifying reference to the ordinary rule, which in its proper application is acknowledged and confirmed. Any ordinary Christian,
without the special impulse of the Spirit, was not to be permitted
to rebuke the high priest.[2] Even Paul himself, after he had spoken

---

[1] Is not this command, therefore, in fact abolished as regards this prophetical
privilege?

[2] Alford maintains that on this occasion Paul, at all events, did not follow

as a prophet, reverts to a show of respect, and expresses himself to the effect that he had not cursed him in God's name *as the high priest;* and if his words, which God would make good, were too hard for them, he would again, if they wished it, show respect to their high priest; also that it was not from any ignorance of the law that he had spoken in a way which seemed to violate the law. This very law, which Paul quotes as well known to him when the officers called his attention to it, contains also an earnest admonition to all the rulers in Israel, not to contradict by their conduct the dignity and sanctity of their persons, and not to stir up evil words against them, but so to conduct themselves that no one should have right or liberty to calumniate them. Remark, finally, that Paul quotes only the latter part of the law, וְנָשִׂיא בְעַמְּךָ לֹא תָאֹר, but premeditatedly omits the words which precede, אֱלֹהִים לֹא תְקַלֵּל—Thou shalt not revile the gods (judges), who stand in God's place (Ex. xxi. 6, xxii. 8 ; Ps. lxxxii. 1, 6). He again acknowledges Ananias " as the high priest," partly in irony, and partly from a just submission to the state of things which by God's patience was still permitted to exist; but neither ironically nor forbearingly will he designate him as אֱלֹהִים in God's stead, as " God's high priest," as the officers called him. Thus, therefore, by deeper investigation we perceive, if we are desirous and able to perceive it, how the different points in the question, as dealt with by various expositors, when taken separately, lead to incorrect results; but when united, form truth : thus here, the three ideas, " I did not think about it," " I do not acknowledge him," and an " ironical untruth." We see, further, how mistaken and inept our natural understanding is for comprehending the Holy Spirit, when the latter condescends so far as to the use of irony, for the sole purpose of reaching the inaccessible hearts of men. Irony and modesty are here united, and there is no element of the pride which pervades our generally ill-natured irony. On this occasion Paul replied in the most judicious way possible, by ironically taking upon himself the fault of forgetfulness, and tacitly causing it to be understood how he intended it. Would it have been better if he had appealed to his just privilege as a prophet, or if he had continued to rebuke, or if he had entered into a diffuse explanation of the whole matter? Grotius answers these inquiries : " Nec id quidquam isto loco profuisset." Many

our Lord's example, and that his conduct might serve as an excuse, but never as an example. We say, on the contrary, " First become like Paul, and then thou mayest act as Paul."

have thought (as Grotius) that there was some irregularity in Ananias' tenure of the office of high priest. At all events, we learn from Josephus that this Ananias, the son of Nebedæus, was high priest under Cumanus, the predecessor of Felix, and had been sent as a prisoner to Rome by Quadratus, the *Præses* of Syria, to answer for his conduct in respect to a contest between the Jews and Samaritans; and that he was subsequently set free by the Emperor Claudius at the intercession of Agrippa the younger. It is assumed that he returned and usurped authority, as having been high priest before, without being again appointed to the office in due and proper order. It is also assumed that, after the murder of his successor Jonathan, there was, at the instigation of Felix, a period of abeyance and anarchy, and that Ananias (whose conduct in other things is much disparaged by Josephus) usurped or bought the office. Even if we set on one side the uncertainty of this conjunction of stories and suppositions, and allow that Ananias, being merely a *vir pontificius*, had assumed the office without due appointment, we must take care how we refer the apostle's weighty utterance to such pettinesses as these. Ananias is called by Luke (ver. 2) simply ὁ ἀρχιερεὺς, with the article; and the officers also call him τὸν ἀρχιερέα, as distinguished from the numerous ἀρχιερεῖς mentioned ch. xxii. 30. It was not Paul's concern to investigate into the means by which Ananias attained his position. How, indeed, could any high priest be appointed in a theocratically legal mode at that time? No; since the rejection of Jesus and His Spirit, the dignity was no longer valid in the sight of God. After Paul in ver. 3 had passed judgment on the high priest, in ver. 5 he rebuked the inward hypocrisy of the whole council, and not any special illegality in the position of the high priest.

Ver. 6. Luke does not inform us of the impression which Paul's words made upon the council. He probably desires to intimate that Paul only left them as much time as was necessary for the full appreciation of the sting of his words, ere he began the second division of his defence. He had shown them how elevated he in his good conscience felt himself to be above their easily discovered hypocrisy: this he had done both by his open protestation (ver. 1), and also by his rebuke to the presiding high priest (ver. 3), and the expression of his opinion as to the entire court in his ironical words (ver. 5). His ready quotation of "that which is written" affords him a suitable transition to his second protestation of his own orthodoxy.—*But when Paul perceived*—γνοὺς δὲ ὁ

Παῦλος—that one part were Sadducees and the other Pharisees. In the lifetime of Christ the party of the Pharisees had the sway in the council and among the high priests (Matt. xxi. 45); but since that time matters had changed, so that the Sadducees had the pre-eminence, as we before remarked in reference to Acts iv. 1, 2, v. 27. Ananias himself belonged to this party; and being the majority, they are mentioned by Luke as first in order. Then Paul cried out in the council, standing as he did among and before this Sanhedrim, which could so easily be split up into two factions, and gave utterance to a fresh matter which, to their utter confusion, revealed their incompetency to judge him. "Ανδρες ἀδελφοὶ, ἐγώ —the same commencement as in ver. 1, only, from what follows, the name of "brethren" tends on this occasion to some closer association.—*I am a Pharisee, and the son of a Pharisee.* Many understand that "son" stands here for "scholar." This, however, would be mere tautology, and we are disposed to adhere to the usual sense of the word, which appears still clearer in the probably correct reading, υἱὸς Φαρισαίων, in the plural. This expression is similar to that used Phil. iii. 5, ʽΕβραῖος ἐξ ʽΕβραίων, and points to ancestors of an orthodox pharisaical character,—a fact to which Paul again refers, 2 Tim. i. 3. But to this glance at his pharisaism by descent and early education is annexed another view of the matter, which applies this pharisaism to the new Christian opinions. On account of the *hope and resurrection of the dead* I am now accused before you, and am called in question. These words have also given rise to another outcry on the part of expositors, that the apostle, influenced by human prudence, extricated himself from his difficulty by this assertion of his pharisaism, throwing down an apple of contention to his judges so that he himself might get free. Unfortunately, too, some of the best expositors agree in this, although they adopt a most moderate tone.[1] But the same

---

[1] Morus says : " Arte utitur aliqua expediendi se ex istis injuriis." Kuinoel : " Cum videret, se nihil proficere, sed judices cæco odio præcipites ferri, ut ex his injuriis sese expediret, et tribuno præsenti se nullius criminis esse reum probaret, prudenter dissensione inter Pharisæos et Sadducæos in rem suam utebatur, ut Pharisæos judices sibi faventes nancisceretur." Hess : " His presence of mind now suggested to him a plan which was not only innocent in itself, but the most prudent conduct under the circumstances. He saw a way open to him by which he might be able to bring over to his side (at least in the first instance) a considerable portion of the Sanhedrim." This " *vafrities*," as Bullinger calls it, is praised to the utmost by Grotius, who says : " Non deerat Paulo humana etiam prudentia, qua in bonum Evangelii utens, columbæ ser-

reasons which we expressed with regard to ver. 5, to which other
and stronger arguments may now be added, forbid us to attribute
blame to the apostle—blame which cannot be correctly excused
by the Saviour's expression, "wisdom of serpents." If we have
correctly interpreted ver. 5, Paul, speaking as he did in the full
and clear consciousness of the Holy Spirit, was far removed from
any common human anxiety, weakness, or prudence : it was not, as
some would say, "his presence of mind," but the Spirit of Jesus,
which inspired him with this appeal to his pharisaism. We
find ourselves compelled to interpret these words also ἀποστολο-
πρεπῶς or χριστοπρεπῶς. In the first place, it must strike us that
this invocation of the party spirit existing in the Sanhedrim was a
highly legitimate and (before God) well-founded, solemn protestation against these unbelieving heretics—the Sadducees—sitting in
the high council of Israel ; it was, too, an emphatic testimony as to
their (ch. iv. 2) already mentioned hostility against the preaching
of a resurrection of the dead through Jesus. This appeal also
implied a public declaration that Paul could not allow himself and
Jesus' gospel (the main point of which was an assertion as a fact
of the resurrection through Jesus) to be judged by a party which
denied this resurrection in hypothesi, but that he would prefer to
appeal to the orthodox party, and to associate himself with them.
We adhere to Bengel's words : " Hic in bonam partem valuit illud :
Divide et impera. Non usus est Paulus calliditate rationis aut
stratagemate dialectico, sed ad sui defensionem simpliciter eos
invitat, qui propius aberant a veritate.' As far as the Sanhedrim
were concerned, Paul had a full right to assert that even now,
and eminently so as to the main point of his doctrine, he was a
Pharisee. Comprehending alike his life both before and after his

pentem utiliter miscebat, et inimicorum dissidiis fruebatur." Oh that I had not
to add to this list the esteemed Rothe, who says (Ethik, iii. § 1095) "Disposi-
tions which are distinguished by their energy in the prosecution of a design are
not always sufficiently careful in the choice of means, although their aim may be
of the most noble character : they are too much inclined to seek the aid of any
policy which is supposed to be judicious." Added to this, there is the note :
" This meets with confirmation in the case of the Apostle Paul, to whom some
slight tinge of policy was not foreign (cf. Acts xxiii. 6)." But what was this
design which the Apostle Paul was prosecuting? Was it to save his life ? Or
was it only to " shield himself from further ill-treatment," as Da Costa says ?
Refer to ch. xx. 24, xxi. 13; and we may infer that, on the contrary, his aim was
to bring forward the testimony of Christ with the utmost importunity, if per-
chance any might accept it.

conversion (as ver. 1), Paul was not merely once a Pharisee (Phil. iii. 5), but was so now, by his firm adherence to the "hope of the promise to the fathers" (Acts xxvi. 5–7), and by his belief in the whole Scripture of the law and of the prophets, the fulfilment and confirmation of which in Jesus was the very thing he maintained and proved. "According to their doctrine, the pharisaical party were the better, and there was indeed something good among them," as Hess rather too slightingly says; for Jesus Himself, in His lamentation over their hypocrisy, says first, "All whatsoever they bid you to observe, that observe and do" (Matt. xxiii. 2, 3). When the witness for Jesus professed himself a Pharisee in opposition to the Sadducees, it was not only truth and justice, but also the most judicious course of action which could be suggested by the Spirit of testimony. In this profession, mildness and sharpness, mercy and judgment, were mingled in the wisest way. On the one hand, it was nothing but mildness and mercy that the well-known gospel of Jesus, with which the judges had been long acquainted, which indeed had been presupposed in the whole business as the subject of the accusation, should condescendingly appeal to the only link of union now left. God was trying the utmost with His blinded people to induce them to hear and understand Him, and to receive His salvation in Christ. With this intention, Paul, in this his last great testimony in Jerusalem, the more blindly they thrust him from them, only endeavoured the more closely to associate himself with them, where any association was now possible, and the more stringently followed them up, testifying unceasingly that his was the genuine and true Judaism. He therefore connects his own cause with the contest between the factions of the Pharisees and Sadducees which was now existing in full fervour, and needed but a word to kindle it up in the Sanhedrim; and as the witness of the fulfilment of prophecy in the risen Messiah, taking that side in the doctrine in which some little truth might be found, he appeals from the dead formula to the living fact itself. His declaration seems to say: "The question ye are striving about with vain words is, in my system, an established fact." This constitutes one aspect of the wisdom of the Holy Spirit in Paul's course of action — the gracious condescension to existing feelings. But, on the other hand, here as ever, there was certainly intimately joined with this a sharp denunciation of the apostasy even of pharisaism, and a well-deserved rebuke of their squabbles as to empty forms. As in vers. 1, 3, 5, the hypocrisy of the council as a body was reproved, now, the heresy of a great part of them is held up to censure.

Vers. 7, 8. It is now made plainly evident what sort of an assembly this so-called "*Synedrium*" really was. As soon as Paul said that he was accused *as a Pharisee*, because he asserted and hoped for the resurrection, then an uproar arose (στάσις, a disorderly dissension and rising up against one another of those who were sitting together as a court). The sacred assembly, being thus broken up into an unofficial, promiscuous multitude, *was divided.——For the Sadducees* (as Luke adds by way of elucidation) *say that there is no resurrection, neither angel nor spirit; but the Pharisees confess both.* The Sadducees deny with idle, lying pertinacity against the truth, but the Pharisees acknowledge or allow it. This intimation made by Luke is a decisive passage, fully confirming that in Matt. xxii. 23. They therefore, in the present form of their doctrine, denied generally everything which overstepped the transitory and material world; and although they accepted the Pentateuch, in which angels are spoken of, and acknowledged a faith in God, they, like many expositors of the present day, looked upon angels as mere figures of speech : their faith in God must also have been dead and unprofitable, and could hardly have been entertained in good earnest. These people now sat in the judgment-seat in Israel and condemned the gospel, because in their system they would not allow of any spiritual existence beyond the life of the body. That they denied the being of angels, is confirmed in Matt. xxii. 30, where Jesus expressly speaks of angels in opposition to their ideas. But the most profound and striking argument against the internal inconsistency of a belief in a God joined to a denial of a spiritual life beyond the transitoriness of matter, forming indeed the real overthrow of their system, is found in the words which Jesus spake to them (Matt. xxii. 32) : "God is not the God of the dead, but of the living." If there is a God, and a revelation from Him, there is also a world of immortal spirits. The word πνεῦμα is not to be understood here as meaning *afflatus*, ἐπίπνοια, or inspiration ; but, as results from ἐλάλησεν (in ver. 9) being applied both to πνεῦμα and ἄγγελος, it must signify a *disembodied human soul*, in which sense the word occurs, Luke xxiv. 37, Heb. xii. 23, 1 Pet. iii. 19.

Ver. 9. In the incoherent fury of faction, the uproar became more and more unseemly, and *there rose a great cry.* The scribes and champions of the Pharisee party (since, as Bengel remarks, in every sect the "*literati*" constitute the "*os partis suæ*") arose still more in opposition to the Sadducees, who were striving for the supremacy, and contended with all their might. At last, in the heat of the contest, they gave up and sacrificed to the interests of their party all their inclinations against the cause of Jesus, crying out, to the extreme vexation of the Sadducees, "We find no evil in this man; but if a spirit or an angel has spoken to him—" Thus they show that they were not ignorant of that which Paul had the day before uttered before all Jerusalem; but in their foolish zeal, and notwithstanding Paul's testimony that *Jesus of Nazareth* had appeared and named Himself to him, all that they are willing to allow is that an angel or spirit had spoken to him. The spirit of party urges them to this indefinite supposition, but further they will not go: it is impossible for them to mention the name of Jesus! They would indeed willingly allow that a thousand spirits—good or bad—might have spoken to Paul; but not the one who is Lord and Master of all spirits, who since His resurrection in the body is no longer *only* a spirit. At this point their obduracy fixed its limit. We must not pass over the remarkable words: *We find no evil in this man!* "Thus party spirit sometimes even forces us both to do and say things which a love of truth and justice would never have extorted from us" (Hess). Remark also how in ch. xxiii. 29, xxv. 18, 25, xxvi. 31, 32, similar words are repeatedly used as testifying of the apostle's innocence, much in the same way as Pilate and Herod spoke of Jesus. With regard to the conclusion of the Pharisees' utterance—μὴ θεομαχῶμεν—it seems to need no further controversy: its non-genuineness may be inferred both from external and internal reasons. It was very natural that the Pharisees should not know how to conclude the sentence they had so hastily begun. The deduction which followed from the hypothesis they had indeterminately enough adopted, must have reminded them that they had already conceded too much, and that they would do better to stop short.[1] Whoever it was that attributed to them this echo of Gamaliel's expression, gave them more credit than was due to them. A bald, feeble conclusion corresponds more suitably to the existing state of their hearts.[2]

Ver. 10. As the tumult and quarrelling continued to increase, and the person of Paul himself began to be in peril, it was neces-

[1] With Stolz, Fritzsche, and others, to assume that a question is asked, is still less suitable.

[2] They again creep back into a state of irresolution as to the main point.

sary for the chief captain to take care that his prisoner was not torn from him by the frantic judges. What could the astonished man have thought of such conduct on the part of the venerated college? What a disgrace it was for Israel in the sight of the heathen!—worse almost than the cry of the high priest for Barabbas which was addressed to Pilate. However little the chief captain might understand of the whole matter, he now saw clearly at least this much, " that Paul's examination did not touch upon any civil delinquency, but concerned some matter of belief—a thing about which the high council had said nothing to him" (Blumhardt); cf. ch. xxv. 18, 19. He was well aware of the fanaticism of the Jews in matters of belief; and, lest the members of the Sanhedrim might in the tumult do some injury to this man in his (the chief captain's) presence—a man, too, who seemed worthy of respect, and had shown himself to be a Roman citizen—he ordered a detachment of soldiers to come down from the castle and to drag Paul from the midst of them (ἁρπάσαι, to take him away by force), and to take him into the barracks.

Ver. 11. After the close of this eventful day, during which Paul had stood before the highest authorities of his people, which in all its blindness was still dear to him, and, doing that which the Lord bade him, had denounced " the whited wall;" and then, after having conceded to them the fact of his being the high priest, had appealed to the Pharisees for the protection of the doctrine they held in common with him,—in the night following, when all the deep feelings and thoughts crowded in upon him which agitated the human soul of the holy apostle simultaneously with and subordinate to the suggestions of inspiration, and when, too, it was probable that some anxiety as to the result of this complicated business had begun to disturb him, *then the Lord stood by him*, and strengthened and comforted him with praise and promise. Far be from us any participation in the Sadducee-like unbelief which, despising the plain words of truth in the Holy Scripture, can discern nothing in this nocturnal appearance of the Lord but a dreamy embodiment of the apostle's self-satisfied feelings and hopes.[1] When Paul was strong and courageous in the spirit, then he is said to

[1] According to Heinrichs, " the apostle felt courageous at everything having turned out so fortunately, and resolved, as soon as the least injury was likely to happen to him, to appeal to Caesar;" and, " Was it wonderful if, with such ideas, the very same things which he himself felt and intended should occur to him in a dream as the words of Christ?"

have sought out some prudent expedient from motives of fear; but when anxiety was in fact aroused in his heart, then he is said to have comforted and praised himself by mere self-satisfaction. Thus does our folly misconstrue the lives of the saints, when we fail in grasping the right mode of understanding them.

We, however, cannot consent to pass over this verse as speedily and lightly as possible, as many expositors have done: we must not only heartily rejoice in it, but must accurately examine it, in order to fully understand how the faithful, kind Saviour tenderly comforts His servants, and appears just at the right moment to furnish them with fresh light for their path. We have no reason for thinking that Paul enjoyed any hard and stoical elevation above the common feelings of humanity. Paul, the *man in Christ*, animated and urged by the power of the Spirit, spoke and acted with outward expression of joy; but Paul the *natural man* might in his inward personality oft-times feel his own weakness. We may thus very well imagine, that just at this moment—when, amid all the complications between the chief captain, the Sanhedrim, and the people, appearances seem to point to nothing but a wearisome imprisonment and hostile plots—despondency came over the apostle, and he who had stood up so boldly before the council now humbly and meekly implored his Lord for fresh strength and new light. We shall more correctly comprehend the character of the Lord's manifestation to the apostle, if we attribute to the latter a certain degree of anxiety and weakness combined with doubt and inquiry,—a desire to know what would become of him, and whether his "purpose in the Spirit" (ch. xix. 21) to go to Rome would be fulfilled or not.—*Be of good cheer*—θάρσει; and then the revelation is made: *for as thou hast testified of me in Jerusalem, so must thou bear witness of me at Rome.* As certainly as the former event (which was long previously indicated to thee by the Spirit) has now taken place, so surely shall the other come to pass in due time. Thou shalt testify as thou hast before testified, and I will continue to guide thee. This is the comfort which the Lord affords to His servant, who in all his weakness is still anxious to testify. In the two chief cities of the world at that time—in the city of God and in the city of Cæsar—was this "chosen vessel" to confess and preach the name of Jesus. In the first part of the Lord's words the apostle's testimony at Jerusalem is (as we have already remarked) acknowledged and confirmed; and then a like blessed destiny at Rome also is promised to him, who had up to that time faithfully fulfilled his commission. The words τὰ περὶ ἐμοῦ are intended to refer not only to the public narrative to the people (ch. xxii.), but also to Paul's assertion to the Sanhedrim in respect to the resurrection, for the latter were well aware to whom this resurrection was meant to point ; indeed, two years after, the life of the dead Jesus is stated by Festus to have been the main point in question (ch. xxv. 19). The emphatic conclusion of the whole of the Lord's words is contained in the δεῖ, *thou must.* In this Paul's entire future is certified and pre-ordained ; cf. Matt. xvi. 21, Acts ix. 6. This divine " must," the expression of irresistible absolutism, is as a clear light tendered to the faith of the apostle. Before this decree, all dangers, hindrances, and snares must succumb, and are indeed converted into joint-helpers in the apostle's destiny.

XXVI.

PAUL BEFORE FELIX THE GOVERNOR.

(Chap. xxiv. 10-21.)

PAUL'S DEFENCE AGAINST THE COMPLAINT OF THE JEWS MADE THROUGH TERTULLUS THE ORATOR.

Ch. xxiii. 12--35. The next day more than forty blind zealots[1] vowed, with rigorous oaths and curses, that they would neither eat nor drink until they had done God a service by slaying Paul. In the terrible blindness of their zeal, they mention their intention to some of the high priests and elders, with a proposition and request that the latter, in the name of the Sanhedrim, would demand that Paul should be again produced, in order to " inquire something more certainly concerning him." If this were done, they, the men bound by the oath, would waylay and kill this chief of the Nazarenes ere he came near to the Sanhedrim, so that no suspicion should rest upon the latter. The miserable rulers, who scruple neither to smite nor slay contrary to the law, accept this bold proposal just as willingly as they embraced Judas' offers against Jesus. Luke does not expressly mention their acceptance,

---

[1] Whose συστροφὴ (ver. 12), by the reading οἱ Ἰουδαῖοι, is ascribed to the whole people.

looking upon it as a matter of course. But God had decreed that this snare, as well as all future attempts against His chosen instrument, should be brought to nought, and had determined that, in spite of assassination, accusers, just and unjust governors—ay, through storm and shipwreck—the imprisoned evangelist should be brought safe to Rome. His good providence, who can command angels and earthquakes to His purpose, and can also bend the ordinary course of things to the advantage of the people of God, on this occasion makes use of only natural means. Paul's sister's son [1] (we only learn accidentally, as it were, of Paul's kindred in Jerusalem) heard of the plot, which must have been divulged in some thoughtless way, and hasted to give an account of it to his uncle. In this report, however, Paul immediately recognised an intimation of the means by which, in the ordinary course of events, the wonderful promises made to him the night before were to be fulfilled. He adopted the most simple, prudent, and discreet course which was possible : he caused a centurion to bring the young man before the chief captain, to tell the latter the whole of his certain and credible story. Paul makes no special request to the tribune, but, believing in the Lord's promise, confides his own and the Lord's cause to the justice and prudence of the heathen, which had already been contrasted with the wicked fury of Israel. This confidence in Lysias was not misplaced : the latter, with a kindness which could not fail to inspire trust, takes the young man by the hand, and prudently takes him aside privately in order to listen to his disclosure. The apostle's nephew spoke with perfect freedom on his uncle's behalf. He very properly first mentioned the request that was to be looked for on the part of the Jews, that Paul should be re-examined, and then told of the murderous vow that was connected with it, concluding with the assurance : *and now are they ready, looking for a promise from thee.* The chief captain, as a just man, saw immediately what his duty was towards his innocent prisoner. Commanding the young man to keep silence as to his communication, he ordered two centurions to prepare their two hundred soldiers, adding to them seventy horsemen and two hundred of the body-guard (δεξιολάβους, or

---

[1] From this Da Costa would conclude that this nephew of the apostle " was, without any doubt, one of the same faith." We, however, cannot understand this. We may, though, certainly assume this much, that he had not just lately come with Paul to Jerusalem ; for more notice would have been taken of a fellow-traveller of this kind.

sharpshooters, δεξιοβόλους). With this honourable escort, more than sufficient to guard against the forty Jews, and able even to ensure the apostle's safety against any bands of predatory zealots, at nine o'clock the same evening Paul is sent away to Felix the procurator at Cæsarea.

We learn, not only from Josephus, but also from Tacitus and Suetonius, that Antonius Claudius Felix, a freedman of the Emperor Claudius and his mother Antonia, was now procurator of Samaria, Judea, Galilee, and Perea, under the *Præses* of the whole of Syria, whose court was at Antioch. Felix had a brother, one Pallas, a freedman who was in high favour with the Emperor Claudius, and especially with the notorious Agrippina, and through his influence obtained the procuratorship of Samaria. At the same time Ventidius Cumanus was procurator of Judea. When the latter gave dissatisfaction on account of a disturbance between the Jews and Samaritans,[1] and a formal investigation into the matter was made by Ummidius Quadratus the *Præses*, Felix, who was perhaps equally guilty, was, at the instigation of his brother, appointed governor over Judea, Galilee, and Perea. Tacitus speaks badly of him, as being unjust, cruel, and voluptuous.[2] Josephus, too, tells us that he caused the high priest Jonathan to be assassinated in the temple. Thus much we supply in order to introduce the apostle's new judge, before whose judgment-seat he is now to be placed, in that same Cæsarea in which, some few weeks before, he had so faithfully withstood the prophecies and warning of the brethren (ch. xxi. 8–15).

Lysias the tribune sent a letter to Felix with Paul, which Luke has judged to be worthy of insertion in the Acts of Apostles, not so much perhaps as a document in favour of Paul's innocence (as Hess thinks), as for an honourable memorial for Lysias, in contrast to the disgrace of the Sanhedrim; chiefly, however, as an historical record how the powers of this world were compelled to give their protection to the kingdom of God.[3]

The four hundred and seventy men conduct Paul the same

---

[1] The same which we before mentioned in Ananias' history.

[2] *Annal.* xii. : Cuncta malefacta sibi impune ratus. *Histor.* v. : Per omnem sævitiam ac libidinem jus regium servili ingenio exercuit.

[3] The question, how Luke became possessed of this letter, may be answered in various ways, without assuming, with the good Seiler, "that Paul subsequently bought, for a large sum of money, all the documents connected with his trial!"

night to Antipatris; and the next day, as there was little or no further cause for fear, they left the seventy horsemen to escort him to Cæsarea. When the governor had seen the man and read the letter, which was in fact rather a testimonial of innocence than an accusation, he asked him, in the first place, as to his extraction and province, and then ordered him to be placed as a prisoner, not in the common prison, but in Herod's *Prætorium*—so called from Herod, who buil.. it—until his accusers should come, and regular judicial proceedings could be held, which, according to the Roman law, required both parties to be confronted.

Ch. xxiv. 1. Paul's accusers do not delay the matter, and spare no pains to achieve their purpose. Their deliberations as to the unexpected turn things had taken lasted only five days, and then they did not hesitate to proceed personally to Cæsarea, and to bring forward their accusation in the ʌst regular and effective way. In the first place, there is An. ʌs, who is here again merely called *the* high priest, with many ʌf the elders, although the whole Sanhedrim (*in pleno*) was probably not present: an official appearance before the throne of the governor would have been too great a humiliation. Remark that these eminent accusers had not sufficient confidence that they could plead their cause skilfully and influentially enough before this heathen judge, but hired a certain Tertullus, a ῥήτωρ learned in the Roman law and language, *i.e.* an advocate or counsel, to address the governor in their name, in accusing Paul. The holy apostle confronts them, without any advocate, in all the boldness of conscious innocence, and joyous in his confession of faith: he is not now *bound*, but probably (according to ver. 2) " called forth" as a free man.

Vers. 2–8. Luke, whose narrative of this last imprisonment of Paul is in general very circumstantial, gives us the purport of Tertullus' speech, as a dark contrast to the apostle's address which follows. Although we may readily allow that this speech is probably given only in abstract, and not complete and literally, and that Tertullus, notwithstanding his promise of brevity (ver. 4), must have pleaded the cause at some considerable length; still, on the other hand, it must be maintained that this abstract expresses the essential character of this flattering, deceitful speech, and its affected confidence. This may be fully proved by an exact analysis of it, if we may be allowed to take so much notice of Tertullus when discussing the words of the apostles. We will therefore make but a few remarks on the more prominent points. The orator commences with courtly flattery, and praises the " great quietness" which the country enjoyed under the governor, and also the " worthy deeds" or regulations (κατορθώματα, or in another reading διορθώματα = reforms, improvements) which were carried out by the " providence" (πρόνοια) of the " most noble Felix." These benefits, the orator says, they " accept always, and in all places, with all thankfulness." The first-named cause for this eulogy — the peace enjoyed — might have been founded on the fact that Felix had lately got rid of some rebels and impostors,[1] although this be-praised governor was himself a wicked robber and oppressor. But Tertullus has no desire to detain the most noble Felix with any protracted enumeration of all his virtues and merits, and forthwith begs the favour that, with his accustomed " clemency," he will listen to his complaint, which shall be as brief as possible. In the beginning of his preamble, Tertullus, by the first person singular, distinguishes himself from " this nation ;" at the conclusion of it he says, " that thou wouldest hear us," thus identifying himself with the Jews, speaking as if he were one of them. If he had been hired in Paul's behalf, he would doubtless have spoken as a Nazarene. He now, with imposing dignity, states that " we have found this man a perfect pest to the country and nation "[2] (cf. much the same thing said about Jesus, Luke xxiii. 2). As in the case of Jesus, the " perverting the people," and " forbidding to give tribute to Cæsar," were the first things alleged, and then came the more exclusively Jewish matter, that He says that " he himself is Christ a king ;" so now Tertullus first brings forward that which is the most odious to the Roman authorities, viz. that Paul was " a mover of sedition among all the Jews" throughout the whole Roman empire : after this he accuses him of being " a ringleader of the sect of the Nazarenes." Ver. 6 is intended to make good the whole accusation ; the " going about to profane the temple" (both as a rioter and a heretic), on account of which Paul had been laid hold of with a view to his just punishment, is made the most of, though with much vagueness.

This was the real point of proof for the whole case ; but the only further testimony alleged for it by the advocate is, " whom we took, and would have judged according to our law." He at once conceals this deficiency in testimony by confidently complain-

---

[1] Especially a notorious robber called Eleazar.

[2] As in Cicero : Pestis civitatis, patriæ.

ing of Lysias, just as shamelessly as just before he had flattered
Felix. With skilful vagueness he confuses together the uproar of
the people and the assembly of the council (which things were
clearly enough related in Lysias' letter), and makes complaint of
the forcible intervention of the chief captain, by means of which
Paul was sent to Felix (in opposition to the freedom of the Jews
to judge him according to their law). They had, in fact, no wish
to judge him according to law, but their desire had been to kill
him, first openly, and then in a more private way; "Vim vocant
opem vim prohibentis," as Grotius says. Remark the crowning
point of this masterpiece, the malicious and presumptuous conclusion: "by examining of whom (*Paul*)[1] thou thyself mayest take
knowledge of all these things whereof we accuse him." This
evidently is intended to mean, as Hess observes very justly, that if
Felix only used force, he would get everything out of Paul and
compel him to confess.

Vers. 9, 10. Poor Paul, what would have been his fate had not
the Lord become his advocate in the conscience of the governor,
and his protection and shield in the midst of the unrighteous! *The
Jews*, in the name of whom Tertullus had spoken, now, as it were
verbally, subscribed to all that the orator had said (συνεπέθεντο,
equivalent in fact to the gloss συνέθεντο, must mean, acted as joint
plaintiffs, confirmed and substantiated the accusation by their
evidence), and declared with much dignity and assumedly honest
importance (φάσκοντες), *that these things were so*. The governor,
however, with silent dignity only replied by a beckoning, or
intimation to Paul to enter upon his defence. Paul, who had
hitherto maintained perfect silence, and had formed his plan, was
ready with an address in which the *true dignity* of innocence and
truth was made evident, both to the accusers and judge, in striking contrast to the hired eloquence of Tertullus. The result of
Paul's discourse was the putting to shame of his accusers and the
perplexity of his judge.

Ver. 10. "Paul's very preamble stands in remarkable contrast
to Tertullus' speech:" thus Hess remarks, and adds the proper
point of view from which Paul's commencement is to be considered.
In this introduction to his address, Paul desires to show himself a
worthy opponent of the hired orator, and, as it were by the way,

---

[1] Referring to the last αὐτοῦ, and certainly not to Lysias, who indeed was
not present. Could Tertullus have merely desired that which Felix answered
in ver. 22?

to convey some covert rebuke to the conscience of the latter, ere
he turns his attention to the matter in question, and to the Jews
who were principally concerned. This rebuke is conveyed with as
much plainness as delicacy, and generally in this preamble, so full
of dignity and so superior to the babbling of the speech-maker, an
efficient groundwork is laid for the defence which is to follow.
Tertullus commenced with deceitful flattery; Paul contents himself with acknowledging the many years' existence of Felix's
official position, giving him to understand that he was acquainted
both with his person and rule. Tertullus spoke of gratitude for
various praiseworthy matters, which in fact had no existence;
Paul, on the contrary, by the mention of his long-existing title
as *judge*, recalls to his mind the duties and obligation of his
office. Tertullus, with courtly affectation, prayed for an indulgent
hearing; Paul, without any such request,[1] declares—as before
his judge he had a right to do—that he will " answer for himself;" only expressing a kindly expectation of justice, and the
more confidently as he is speaking before Felix. Tertullus said
much more than he was cognizant of; Paul utters only what he
knew, and could express without uncourteousness. Tertullus
spoke as the hired servant of others; Paul desires " cheerfully
to answer for himself" (τὰ περὶ ἐμαυτοῦ). Thus the review we
have made of Paul's short and pithy preamble, in comparing it
thoroughly with Tertullus' speech, has brought under our notice
nearly all the significant points : there still are, however, one or
two things to be considered. Felix had been a *judge, i.e.* governor
or chief authority, for *many years* over *this nation.* For although
it was only about six years since he had succeeded Cumanus, he
had, as stated above, ruled Samaria for some time previously : he
must therefore have been for a considerable period well acquainted
with the customs and laws of the Jews. It is to this knowledge on
the part of Felix of the dogmas, ideas, and parties of the Jewish
nation, that Paul desires to appeal. Any one who had for some
time ruled over " this nation," would have been aware of its restless, tumultuous, hypocritical, and fanatical feelings, often leading
to the bitterest persecution of innocent individuals : he also would
have experienced how often he was called upon to act as " judge,"
and to set matters straight (instead of the " great quietness," ver. 3),
and how little he could reckon on the gratitude of " this nation :"

---

[1] Which under other circumstances (as ch. xxvi. 3) he was indeed permitted
to make.

he, too, could and should seek to maintain his office in justice only, if he wished to retain it long. Any one who had long filled this position must have been on his guard against deposition, for it was not an easy matter for the governors to retain their office so long. We see what a variety of circumstances and relations these few words of the apostle, as it were, touch upon ; to us, it seems to form a part of complete interpretation to fully show forth these allusions. The apostle desires to " answer for himself," here as in ch. xxii. 1 using this modest expression. Of course a declaration of innocence, and even a counter complaint, which this address turns to, may in a general sense be called a reply or defence, when an accusation has been previously made.

Ver. 11. *Uproar* and *heresy*—στάσις and αἵρεσις—these were the two heads of Tertullus' accusation against Paul. The second of these two charges is brought forward in very general terms of vituperation, and has to be in fact inferred from the first, the uproar leading to a desecration of the temple. Paul denies and contradicts the charge of uproar ; and freely confessing the faith " which they call heresy," intimates that on account of this faith they are seeking to charge him with making a disturbance, but that in doing this his accusers are involving themselves in heresy, or an apostasy from genuine Judaism. Paul commences, just as any other defendant, with asserting a denial of the first charge (ver. 12), and then adds a free confession as to the second (ver. 14). Having, as it were, at his first start laid down correctly the real matters of fact, he commences to relate accurately all the events which the eye-witnesses (if they had been present) would have been compelled to tell as to the first charge ; and finally, with regard to the second, he appeals to the meeting of the council,—a fact which had been cleverly slurred over by his accusers. Thus his defence shapes itself into four stages or steps : the denial of the accusation, the confession of the truth which is attacked, the correct narrative of the events, and an appeal to the well-known disunion and perversity of his accusers, mounting ultimately to a counter accusation. The confession of the truth attacked is put forward ironically as a kind of concession ; and his appeal to the quarrel in the council as to his belief in the resurrection is made with still keener irony, as showing the one wrong thing (ἀδίκημα) they could find in him.

Because that thou mayest know : this refers to Tertullus' malicious words in ver. 8 (δυναμένου to δυνήσῃ). Paul implies that

there is hardly a need for any special ἐπιγινώσκειν or ἀνακρίνειν for
Felix to ascertain with certainty that he (Paul) had only twelve
days before set out from that very Cæsarea where he was now
standing, and had gone up to Jerusalem : a mere inquiry would
establish the fact.   The affair with which the first accusation is
connected had taken place but a very short time ago, and was easy
to investigate : Paul can easily prove that he came up as a good
Jew, and indeed *to worship*.   This first general counter-assertion
gainsays the accusation of profaning the temple, and in it is also
comprehended a claim to orderly conduct and orthodoxy as opposed
to the charges of uproar-making and heresy.   We may well believe
that Paul had actually gone into the temple, the downfall of which
was now so close at hand, with the express purpose of praying to
the God of Israel, although certainly this was not his *chief* purpose.   This chief purpose he does not now desire to mention ;
indeed, in ver. 17 he speaks of some other intention.   All he wishes
to intimate is, that he entered the temple with reverence, like any
other orthodox Jew, and was very far indeed from any intention of
profaning it.   Finally, as regards the enumeration of the " not
more than twelve days," which has needlessly been considered a
difficult matter, and indeed looked upon as incorrect.   Bengel is of
course in error in reckoning only the seven days of the purification
(ch. xxi. 27) and the " five days" mentioned ch. xxiv. 1, as there
are several other days intervening.   It is, however, the simplest
plan not to include the five days at Cæsarea (which Neander does
not question, Olshausen and v. Gerlach simply agreeing with him
as if it were a matter of course) ; so that we must look upon Paul
as speaking only of the days which he had spent in Jerusalem, the
only time in which he could have raised an uproar, either in the
temple or in the city (ver. 12).   The twelve days would then be
reckoned as follows : The *first* day after his arrival, the assembly
of the elders (ch. xxi. 18–25).   The *second* day, the purification,
or the commencement of the Nazarate (ver. 26).   Then *six* days
must be added, the uproar arising on the *seventh*,[1] making eight
days altogether.   On the *ninth* day, the meeting of the council
(ch. xxii. 30, xxiii. 11).   On the *tenth* day, the conspiracy (vers.

---

[1] If, according to Bengel, the five days mentioned in ch. xxiv. 1 are reckoned,
the uproar must have taken place on the *third* day of the Nazarate, which
appears inconsistent with the language in ch. xxi. 27.   It might then be, ὡς δὲ
ἔμελλον ταῦτα συντελεῖσθαι, which Bengel's translation gives, *cum ea fierent,*
quæ Paulus ver. 26, susceperat, but not αἱ ἑπτὰ ἡμέραι.

12–15), and Paul's escape in the night (vers. 16–31). On the *eleventh* day, the journey from Antipatris to Cæsarea (vers. 22, 23). This reckoning would make *twelve days* between Paul's arrival at Jerusalem and at Cæsarea, including the day of his arrival at one of the two places.[1]

Vers. 12, 13. *And they neither found me:* this is the first counter-protest against his accusers' words, "For we have found," etc. (ver. 5). By the addition of the καί, Paul's assertion follows as an inference from the expression προσκυνήσων, which precedes it; as if to say, he who comes to *worship* in the temple is not likely to raise a tumult there, or even outside: at least any right-minded worshipper (as Paul was, much more than his opponents) would not do such a thing. Nor did Paul permit himself to hold any protracted doctrinal or controversial discourse with any one in the temple; still less had he "raised up the people," or intruded himself as an extraneous teacher into any of the synagogues. Generally, too, he had behaved himself quietly throughout the whole city (κατὰ τὴν πόλιν). Fully confiding in the truth of his counter-protest, the apostle also maintains " that they cannot prove the things whereof they now accuse him." Παραστῆσαι, to produce or show as proved (ch. i. 3), is equivalent here to the ἀποδεῖξαι, ch. xxv. 7, but combines a glance at the necessity for the presence of eye-witnesses to prove the accusation, or even to duly arraign him. All they could do was to accuse him, and say, "For we have found this man," etc., and that "he hath gone about to profane the temple;" but this was far from being any legally valid plea of so grave a charge. In asserting that he is innocent generally "of the things whereof they now accuse him," Paul includes among the charges that of heresy as a Nazarene, which charge he now goes on specifically to deny.

Ver. 14. He denies it, too, in an ironical way, with some intimation of a counter-charge, by confessing his genuinely Israelitish belief, hope, and worship, which his accusers wrongly call αἵρεσις. Paul declares, with a plain and distinct contradiction of the charge of heresy, and not with a mere "mild deprecation" (as Lechler says), that perfect orthodoxy is very much more on his side of the question. "But I confess *this* unto *thee*, even to thee, the Roman

---

[1] Another reckoning (by Auger) counts the five days (ver. 1) rather artificially, so that the day on the evening of which Paul left Jerusalem is taken as the first. But then ver. 1 ought to run, " Five days after this departure," or the like. The text can only be understood to mean so many days after (ver. 35).

judge, just as to my countrymen, and to every one. I confess
unto thee willingly all that I have to confess, without being sharply
questioned and tortured. For, according to the Roman law, the
actual Jewish religion has been for long past acknowledged and
privileged. My 'way' (ch. xxii. 4) is indeed called by them,
through their mouthpiece Tertullus, a 'sect' (ver. 5), *i.e.* an un-
orthodox party, professing doctrines and customs in opposition to
true Judaism; but I truly worship the God of my fathers." In
saying this, he in the first place intimates that, although a Roman
citizen, he was born a Jew,—a fact which his accuser (in ver. 5, by
the plausible contrast of " this man " to " all the Jews ") had placed
in the background. A προσκυνήσων (ver. 11) might have been
a proselyte, or indeed a heathen worshipping for the first time;
this expression is now closely defined. In the second place, he does
not say, as elsewhere (cf. ch. xxii. 14), τῷ Θεῷ τῶν πατέρων μου,
but significantly, τῷ πατρῴῳ Θεῷ, *Deo patrio*, echoing the heathen
idea of *dii patrii*, whom to serve truly was honourable religious
fidelity, in contrast to new, foreign deities, whose worship was
heresy. My God the Nazarene's God—is none but Israel's God,
whom the Roman authorities generally acknowledge. Paul therefore confesses that he is a " Nazarene," accepting this name as the
honourable reproach of Christ: he only wishes to avert the invidious and false stamp of sectarianism which some desired to impress on " this way," whether he was a πρωτοστάτης to this στάσις
and αἵρεσις or not; only as a Nazarene, the same as all the others,
he confesses this his faith. In this one ὁμολογῶ he had acknowledged everything; and as Felix already well knew about " this
way " (ver. 22), he had no need to make any further confession.
All that was requisite here was to testify with accurate proof to the
relation which this " faith in Christ " (ver. 24), and the " superstition of one Jesus who was dead, but yet lived " (ch. xxv. 19),
bore to orthodox Judaism, *i.e.* to its unity with the latter. I also
so (οὕτω) worship Him, that I believe all the Scriptures, and have
hope of the complete fulfilment of all the things promised therein.
Faith and hope are the two cardinal points of religious conviction;
and the two are properly one—a trusting grasp on things invisible,
and not present, which are only morally demonstrable. Belief or
faith, in a narrower sense, is a conviction of things past or present;
but in a wider and far higher sense it embraces the future too:
hope, therefore, is nothing but faith applied to things to come.
Faith and hope are shown in the life by that which was before

called "worship," or devotion and love towards God and men
(together *pietas*), as we see subsequently in vers. 16, 17. When
Paul says, "I believe *all* things which are written," he gives his
adhesion in the closest way to the *letter of the entire Old Testament*,
and emphatically places the outward ground of his faith in that
which is written,—a fact which can never be sufficiently set forth
in our time, which is so given to set aside the letter of the Spirit in
favour of a false and fickle intellect. In his further assertion, "I
believe all things which are written in the *law*," it is evident that
he speaks here of the *promises* contained in the law, or of the law,
so far as it embraces or veils promises and prophecy; otherwise
how could we reconcile Gal. iii. 12? The observance of the commandments of the law, so far as Paul still observed them, had
already been included in the "worshipping." In *believing the law*,
there is a strange (and for the Jews, a striking and yet profound)
contrast to their false but highly extolled keeping of the law, which
is intended to develope, where possible, the inner heart of their religion, now dead in pharisaism; in John v. 46, 47, the Saviour spoke
to them in somewhat the same way. The weighty import of the
apostle's words, which contains the key and the emphatic meaning
of the whole, is, that a Jew should believe all that is in the law,
or that Moses has written. He must believe not merely outwardly
in the first table of the Decalogue, but also inwardly in the second,
and especially in its last words—not to lust after things forbidden;
and therefore must essentially acknowledge and seek to obey the
first prohibition of strange gods. He must not merely believe that
he is to keep it all, but that he is cursed unless he keep and observe
it all perfectly. He must not merely acknowledge that the Lord
is his God, but also that He is his guide out of the land of Egypt
for all time,—for his body out of the outward and material land,
and for his heart out of the inner land of idolatry and deceit, of
lust and death. He must not merely take to himself the curse of
the law, but must also believingly grasp the prophetical blessings
of Moses, and must look for their fulfilment in the Mediator and
Prophet, who by Moses' command was to be hearkened to after
himself. He must not only accept the commanding words of
thunder which Moses brought down from Sinai, but must also seek
to understand the prophesying spirit of his priestly and sacrificial
institutions, and sincerely inquire after " the word which is very
·nigh, in the mouth and in the heart," of which Moses testifies at
the end of the law (Deut. xxx. 11–14).

How clearly in this verse the true relation between Judaism and Christianity is set forth!—that Christianity is nothing but fulfilled and completed Judaism,—that a Christian remained, or rather became a true Jew, and that a genuine Jew must be a Christian (ch. xxvi. 27, 28). How justly does this verse, by its contrast, define the idea of *sect*, the invidious pretext for a rejection of the full truth! He who believingly accepts all God's revelation, in its plan, connection, and aim, and in hope of its consummation grasps and holds fast every proffered fulfilment of the promises—that man rightly worships the living God, and belongs to His Israel. But he who adds and takes away according to his own human ideas and self-will, and despises the lively apprehension of the whole revelation—this man is in αἵρεσις—" quæ est humani arbitrii," as Bengel says: he does not yet walk in the " way " prescribed by God—the way which even to the present day " is everywhere spoken against " (ch. xxviii. 22), the so-called *sect* of either Nazarenes, Moravians, Pietists, Methodists, Mystics, Fanatics, Literalists, Millenarians, or any other name which the Pharisees and Sadducees of the visible church apply to the members of God's community.

Ver. 15. Of hope, as the culminating point of faith, by which the latter is perfected so as to produce a life faithful to its belief, we have previously spoken (cf. Heb. iii. 6, vi. 11, 12). This is the hope " as an anchor of the soul, both sure and stedfast, which entereth into that within the veil " (Heb. vi. 19) ; *i.e.* it is a " hope toward God"—ἐλπὶς εἰς τὸν Θεόν—and, moreover, to the God of the fathers : the future is sealed by the past ; and God, who has hitherto adhered to His word, will complete everything to the very letter. God *can* do it, for He is God ; God *will* do it, for it is impossible for Him to lie ; and we have His word for it, from Genesis down to Revelation, inclusive, *not* exclusive. As we see the old serpent of the Pentateuch (now looked upon as mythical and non-authentic) always seducing over the whole earth those heathen who know not or will not know the blood of the Lamb ; so also will the same old serpent, which is the devil, be bound at the appointed time for his thousand years, and finally, after his last deceiving, will be cast with Gog and Magog into the lake of fire, where also the " beast " of Sadducean sensuality, and the " false prophet " of all Sadducean and pharisaical worldly and religious wisdom, will have their part. After this will earth and heaven flee away before the face of the

" seed of the woman," who thus " will bruise the serpent's head ; " and then will come the *resurrection of the dead, both of the just and unjust !* [1]

We must be excused for having here referred to the New Testament in order to show how we are now to apply to ourselves the apostle's great confession : the inward sense and essential connection was, however, with him the same as with us, although he had but the Old Testament in view. Malachi connects the prophecy of the last day with the law of Moses; and Daniel, the precursor of the Apocalypse, concludes in ch. xii. 2, 13, with a glance at the Revelation which was to be written, the aim of hoping faith. The two-sided expression, *the resurrection of the just and unjust,* appears to refer here specially to the passage in Daniel. The important contrast between Paul's *having* the hope, and the Jews' *waiting for* (or allowing) it, which is intimated here, we have previously spoken of. Paul only, as a Christian, can properly use the words " hope of the resurrection " with any real, living hope coming from the bottom of his heart, for he knows Him who is the resurrection and the life. His accusers *wait for* (or allow) this hope, *i.e.* they use some such language and entertain some such doctrine, but hitherto it had been neither living nor consolatory, and therefore not actually *hope ;* for they had denied Him in whom life and immortality were brought to light, and in whom the resurrection is preached. It is much as if Paul said : " The certain, living, and comforting hope of a resurrection which I have in Christ, which hope I share with all the Nazarenes as the consummation of our faith, agrees with your (the Jewish) doctrine, which, however, in your case must certainly be rather a terror than a hope : our faith, like yours, is grounded on the law and the prophets, although we are so widely asunder in our mode of comprehension and treatment." *Spem* in Deum, resurrectione Christi confirmatam, firmiter *teneo*, eamque *eandem*, quam etiam isti secundum sanam doctrinam *statuentes*, tale quid *expectant*, nimirum fore, etc. The sharply defining phrase αὐτοὶ οὗτοι prominently distinguishes the Pharisees from the other accusers who were present, as the former alone awaited a resurrection. But the Sadducees also are not excluded (and this is still more the case in the same words (αὐτοὶ οὗτοι) in

---

[1] Whether νεκρῶν be genuine or not is not very important. In its omission Alford desires to recognise a degree of subtlety—that the direct connection " resurrection of the *dead* " was purposely avoided by the apostle, as a paradox which was likely to lead to mockery.

ver. 20), so that their wicked consciences might be touched, and
they might be brought to the confession—which must ruin their
whole cause before Felix—that, in denying Paul's doctrine, they
were denying the doctrine of the Pharisees, and the belief of this
important and considerable party among their learned men.   If we
may venture to assume a matter which according to Josephus is
very probable, that a fresh party had arisen among the Pharisees
themselves, which asserted that *only the righteous* (cf. Luke xiv.
14) would attain to a resurrection of the body, the conclusion of the
verse would be very significant as directed against these heretics :
in this conclusion Paul confesses his hope in a future resurrection
" both of the just and *unjust*."   We see then most fully, that in
this his confession he reproves their deviations from his faith as a
whole, although asserting their partial agreement with him.   Of
course the mention of the " unjust"—which, however, naturally
results from the passage in Daniel—is so far suitable, inasmuch as
the apostle so falsely accused of heresy directs his "hope" to the
future and certain shaming and punishment of the injustice which
was being done to him, and also affords a serious hint to the conscience of Felix his judge (cf. ver. 5).

Ver. 16. Thus Paul freely used before Felix much the same
language which he spake before the council (ch. xxiii. 6).   We will
now therefore only remark that the hope of a blessed resurrection
with Christ, the Risen One, is really the truest and deepest basis
and main point of Christian faith, as the Messiah's promised kingdom of glory is first fulfilled in the resurrection.   Of this a very
complete proof is subsequently to be given in ch. xxvi. 6, 7.   Paul,
too, testifies most clearly in 1 Cor. xv. 12–19, that " if there be no
resurrection of the dead," the preaching and faith of Christians
were alike " vain," and the apostles were " false witnesses of God ;"
that if the disciples " have hope in Christ in this life only," they
are " of all men most miserable."   But *now* he entertains no vain
faith, who with lively hope pursues and grasps the future glory
opened out in Christ, and living a life which is holy and active in
love, purifies his conscience to serve the living God.   Of this
holiness of life as the result of his faith, the apostle now speaks at
the end of this first portion of his address, and refers back again to
the beginning, as the innocence asserted in vers. 11, 12 now appears
as the natural fruit of his belief.   He is far removed from the
delusion of the hypocrite who, " on account of his faith, fancies
that he can dispense with all earnestness of conscience—in whom

faith and conscience dwell in separate chambers." [1]—*And herein—* *i.e.* in belief in the whole Scripture, and in a sure expectation of a resurrection of the just to eternal life, and of the unjust to eternal shame and reproach[2]—*do I exercise myself to have always a conscience void of offence.* Not merely to live inoffensively in externals; no, my faith works in me an inner conscientiousness, by which my outward life is, as it were, spontaneously directed. Paul repeats the same language which (in ch. xxiii. 1) he first spoke before the council, but with a certain modification and explanation. He does not say, I *have, possess,* or *hold firmly*—as just before with regard to the hope—but less decidedly, *I exercise myself to have* (ἀσκῶ, scil. ἐμαυτὸν), that is, I seek to preserve myself in it with earnest labour and self-mastery. *Toward God and toward men* is added to strengthen the former proposition, and as a comprehensive expression for the whole sphere of obligation; also as an acknowledgment that the apostle was kind and courteous with men, precisely because he knew "the terror of the Lord," and was "made manifest unto God" (2 Cor. v. 11); lastly, as a transition to a fresh portion of his speech which was to follow.

Vers. 17–19. *Now after many years* of my possession of this new faith, firm hope, and conscientious principles, and after I had long time exercised myself to have "a conscience void of offence," and had been by no means "a mover of sedition throughout the world" (ver. 5), *I came* (to Jerusalem, as mentioned above in ver. 11) *to bring alms to my nation, and offerings* (to be presented in the temple). Alms therefore for men, offerings for God, in love and devotion,—an allusion to the "God and men," ver. 16. The προσφοραὶ are evidently the intended offerings of purification, during the preparation of which, on the seventh day, the Jews seized the apostle. Paul had not indeed come to Jerusalem for the express purpose of making offerings (as above, ver. 11, προσκυνήσων), but still he by no means states anything that is untrue: for in addition to the προσκυνεῖν he might also have intended to bring certain προσφορὰς; also καὶ προσφορὰς is added with only a general, vague mode of expression, so that the ποιήσων is only to be referred strictly to the ἐλεημοσύνας: "I came to bring alms," (and also) "offerings." The alms were the "certain contribution"

[1] Tholuck, *Gewissens-, Glaubens-, und Gelegenheits predigten,* p. 22.
[2] Or as John xvi. 30, ἐν τούτῳ merely for *therefore* (as Winer would have it)? But we are of opinion that this rendering would only be a weakening of the fundamental sense of the passage.

sent to the Jewish Christians (Rom. xv. 26), and their mention is
opposed to the λοιμός in ver. 5.   The question would naturally
arise : Is this man a " pestilent fellow," who came to bring gifts of
love to his brethren, and to worship in the temple ?   It may also be
asked how these collections presented to the Christians could be
called " alms to my nation."   This has been answered by the idea
that the apostle brought the alms to them as *Jewish* Christians,
and this is quite correct ; or that the apostle looked upon the believers in Israel as the real pith of the nation, and this is perhaps
equally right.   But τὸ ἔθνος μου must evidently mean here *all the
Jews generally*, including also the unbelievers in Jesus.   The question indeed has been about *them* in almost every verse (vers. 10,
12, 13, 14, 15) ; and the expression " my nation " appears to be
connected with the words " this nation " in ver. 10, and the " God
of my fathers," ver. 14.[1]   Others have thought that Paul had perhaps also brought some contribution to the general poor fund of the
temple ; but would not this be impossible, whoever might maintain
it ?   We may, however, propound as the simplest solution, that εἰς
τὸ ἔθνος μου refers to the παρεγενόμην, and not to the ἐλεημοσύνας :
I came to my nation, with brotherly love towards them as " my
nation "—which was a deep truth in Paul's heart — just as in
ver. 11, " I went up to Jerusalem " with devotional desires, and
actually to worship in the temple.   Thus Paul, as would indeed
be most fitting, would entirely omit the mention of those for whom
the gifts of love were brought, and in what way the offerings were
presented : it is sufficient for him to say that he was occupied in
works of kindness and devotion.

'Ἐν οἷς, in these innocent, nay praiseworthy, purposes and
employments, especially in the preparation for the " offerings "
mentioned last, *they found me in the temple*.   This is the second
vindication of his conduct against the accusations in vers. 5 and 6.
That, in ver. 12, he stated what they did *not* find, and now he says
what the real state of the case was.   They found *me*—me only, and
no Gentile with me, brought in by me to profane the temple ;
on the contrary, they found me as a Nazarite—ἡγνισμένον—not
making an uproar among the people, but altogether in the state
which was fitting for a Nazarite.   Paul does not relate that the
fact of their thus finding him in the temple and seizing him (thus

---

[1] To refer the whole expression, as Baumgarten almost does, specially and
only to expenses of the Nazarate (taken out of the money collected), is not at
all practicable.

profaning the rites of purification) was the real cause of the tumult
and uproar: the people to whom this charge would apply, and
whom alone he could personally accuse, are not present. It is
sufficient for him to summon these eye-witnesses when the complaint would be of some use.

He therefore goes on to say, that those who " found him" were
not those who stated, through Tertullus their spokesman, that they
had found him, but were *certain Jews from Asia;* that he was not
seized by any official persons, but by foreigners, who did it without
right, and of their own arbitrary will. These, he says, as eye-
witnesses, *ought to have been here before thee,* and *object if* (with any
right and reason) *they* had ought against me.[1] Those who now,
through Tertullus, say "*we* found him" (although the high priest
is indeed present), were not eye-witnesses of the events in the
temple, and are consequently, in default of this, incompetent
accusers. The eye-witnesses, however, make no accusation, but
have wisely kept away and withdrawn from the whole business.
Paul entirely forbears to accuse these Jews of having ill-used him,
or to complain of the nearly fatal maltreatment he had experienced
from the people: he only desires to intimate that the case could not
be justly investigated, as the real witnesses were absent, and that
they would certainly have been present, and have been produced
by the distinguished accusers, if there had been anything which
they could have deposed against him (Paul) in the presence of the
governor.[2]

Vers. 20, 21. Paul now reverts to the accusers who were present, and desires to know from them whether, the first point of the
accusation having failed, they had anything to say or prove as to
the second, which would render him liable in the procurator's court
either to death or bonds. In the discomfiture of the first point of
the accusation (so wanting in all proof) with which these accusers
had so forcibly attempted to ensnare him, it was shown that in
fact it was the way which they called αἵρεσις, his hated faith, which
was the real cause of their so readily accusing him of uproar, and

---

[1] The apostle modestly and hypothetically uses the word ἔδει: the reading
δεῖ would be too peremptory to the judge.

[2] " Nunquam majores solœcismos mundus etiam contra suas leges com-
mittit, quam in persequenda fide" (Bengel). And these weak points are discovered and laid hold of for the sake of the truth. In this case the Asiatic
Jews had absented themselves through fear of a long suit, or else the lords of
the council, in their first excitement, had not thought of seeking out and summoning these first witnesses.

that any actual turbulent conduct of the Nazarene was *not* the reason of the charge.—*Or else let these same here say*—εἰπάτωσαν, distinctly and clearly, legally, and not with mere invective in general—*if they have found any evil thing in me*—any actual infringement of the law, or guilt (ἀδίκημα)—*while I stood before the council.* Remark how incisive in its character is the apostle's simple vindication — perhaps involuntarily on his part. At the conclusion of his defence, after he had remarked on the absence of the actual witnesses, he summons them to speak, but on a point about which it was almost impossible for them to say much before Felix. They had perhaps wisely allowed their orator Tertullus to leave the untoward trial before the council quite in the background. Paul, on the contrary, proclaims loudly that he had previously stood before their legal court (ver. 6), and that they could bring nothing against him, owing to their own divisions.

His sharpest and most striking language, however, comes at the last: *Except it be for this one voice, that I cried* (freely and loudly) *standing among them* full of confidence: *one* voice, for owing to their uproar I could not utter a second. Herein there again occurs a kind of ironical concession, similar to the ὁμολογῶ δὲ τοῦτο in ver. 14 (here ταύτης φωνῆς). This results from the idea that this belief in the resurrection which he pretends that he confessed before the Sanhedrim, perhaps as an ἀδίκημα, he had previously (vers. 14, 15) maintained to be an orthodox belief, and founded on the Scriptures.[1] The accusers who were present were eye-witnesses and auditors only of this appeal to the pharisaical belief in a resurrection, and the consequent confusion in the most wise council, and of the words of the pharisaical scribes, "We find no evil in this man;" so that *this* was all they could say against him. Paul, shaming them, summons them to speak. And what could they bring forward? If Lysias had been present, he would perhaps have told everything, and Paul may any moment appeal to him. Thus are the persecutors caught in the trap of their own foolishness. Paul now uses the same language which he had before uttered before the council, only he omits the ἐγὼ Φαρισαῖός εἰμι, because he does not desire to mention the party matters which had been quite omitted by Tertullus; and for the sake of emphasis adds, *by you* this day, which he might have said on the former occasion, and at all events meant. Thus the

[1] How is it possible that Heinrichs can acknowledge this irony, and yet say, "Sentire videtur Paulus, clamore se isto contra auctoritatem Synedrii peccasse?"

variously hinted at counter-complaint, that they had unjustly
accused and persecuted him on account of his genuinely Jewish
faith, is now openly expressed, and the defence closes with a disclosure of the real reason for the accusation, which was, in fact, no
reason at all. " They have persecuted me unjustly, and can prove
nothing against me done against either their law or that of the
Romans ; I, however, can prove to them that a portion of their
council actually acquitted me, and I merely appeal to them to say
what took place in the presence of Lysias." We thus see how the
apostle's apology, denying that which was false, and disclosing their
perplexity, closely follows Tertullus' accusation in vers. 5 and 6 ;
but with regard to the matters brought against Lysias in vers. 7
and 8, Paul says nothing, but in all due order adheres to the right
he had claimed at the very first : τὰ περὶ ἐμαυτοῦ ἀπολογοῦμαι.

Vers. 22, 23. What ought Felix, as a just judge, to have now
done ? Of course he ought to have required the accusers to give
the details as to the result of the meeting of the council, which
details were demanded by Paul, especially as they are so suspiciously
silent in answer to the εἰπάτωσαν of the accused man. But being
perhaps in some perplexity about the matter, he does not act justly,
though with a certain prudence ; and wishing neither to condemn
Paul, nor to behave uncourteously to the high priest and the elders,
he adjourns the matter,—a very frequent expedient in such cases,
and the way of the world generally in things concerning the truth.
He cannot convict Paul; his defence is too conclusive. Also
Lysias' privity of the whole affair must be taken into account, and
deters the governor from any open injustice. Finally, Paul had
warned his conscious judge of the higher judgment that was impending. Besides, Felix had *a more perfect knowledge of that
way*, which, from his residence in Cæsarea and his marriage with
Drusilla, a Jewess, was exceedingly probable : his heart is, in fact,
a little touched, as we may also gather from ver. 24. Many indeed
(as Beza, Grotius, and others) are not inclined to allow the ancient
and simple rendering of the word εἰδώς, and translate the passage,
" *When* I shall have obtained more perfect knowledge of this way,
then, *i.e.* when Lysias the chief captain shall come down, I will
pronounce a decision in your matter." But this construction is
very forced : we shall therefore adhere to the clear meaning of the
words, that Felix *then* had an accurate acquaintance of the circumstances of Christianity. But he did not altogether wish to repel
the high priest and elders, who (in ver. 3) had so undeservedly and

unexpectedly praised him. Felix therefore adjourned the case, which was in fact ripe for decision, or at least would have been through a more prolonged hearing. *When Lysias the chief captain shall come down* (which would probably be the case soon after the conclusion of the restless period of the feast, during which the presence of the cohort was required in the Castle of Antonia), then (after closer investigation) I will pronounce a decision, or come to a conclusion, in your matter.[1] *Διαγινώσκειν* must be held to mean, *to pronounce his judgment after further inquiry.* Felix satisfies them as to the delay, by promising them both further investigation and a decisive sentence, intending, without prejudice, and indeed fittingly, to inquire of Lysias about the uproar; but perhaps he was not aware how unacceptable this reference to the witnesses of the popular tumult and the uproar in the council must be to the accusers. Suffice it to say, the latter must go away, together with their advocate, without having accomplished their object.

Felix, however, had acquired so much respect for Paul and his cause, that both his heart and conscience impelled him to deprive the latter's unnecessarily prolonged imprisonment of any great hardships. He orders the centurion who was in charge to keep Paul in custody (*τηρεῖσθαι αὐτόν*; cf. ch. xii. 5, xxv. 4, 21), but *to let him have liberty,* i.e. some relaxation or ease in his imprisonment; indeed, he expressly adds, that *he should forbid none of his acquaintance to minister or come unto him.* We may well imagine that here in Cæsarea, where Philip the evangelist dwelt—where, too, not three weeks before (ch. xxi. 8-14), the disciples had so tenderly cared for the apostle, and warned him as to his journey to Jerusalem—Paul would experience every kind of loving sympathy.

Vers. 24, 25. *And after certain days* of this confinement to his house or room, the imprisoned evangelist is summoned to preach to his judge. *Felix came with his wife Drusilla, which was a Jewess,* and *sent for Paul.* He came either from his palace in Herod's *Prætorium* (ch. xxiii. 35), or, as some have conjectured, from a journey in which he had fetched his wife Drusilla; with which idea, however, the *ἡμέραι τινές* does not very well harmonize. This Drusilla was a daughter of Herod Agrippa the elder (ch. xii. 1), and sister of the existing king (ch. xxv. 13). She was first married to Azizus, king of Emesa, who had therefore adopted circumcision; but Felix, being inflamed with love for her, had (through one Simon, a Jewish go-between) alienated her affections

[1] Cf. διεγνώκειν, Num. xxxiii. 56, and διεγνώκει, 2 Macc. ix. 15.

from her lawful husband, and Drusilla was now the consort of the heathen governor. Paul could not keep silence as to a case like this, somewhat similar to that which John the Baptist once rebuked in the person of Herod Antipas. Felix and his wife Drusilla—now almost become an apostate from Judaism—desired to hear Paul, not judicially—for then the woman would not have been present—but partly from curiosity and other reasons, and partly from some incipient desire to hear the truth, and to know what his doctrines and belief really were. And Felix *heard him* quietly enough so long as he spoke in general about *the faith in Christ*.[1]

But Paul was not the man to confine himself, before such auditors, to any merely general language as to "the faith." As we read in Hess: " He cannot and will not speak of the doctrine of the Messiah to any one merely to gratify curiosity, but he will lay it before them in all its practical tendencies. To entertain a Felix and his spouse with a narrative of signs and wonders[2] would be a thing but little worthy of him; just as our Lord refused to gratify the curiosity of a Herod by answering his inquisitive questions, or by working any wonderful miracle. Paul therefore turns his discourse to those subjects which would be likely to most deeply affect his distinguished auditors. Before Felix, who was now before him as his hearer and not as his judge, he *reasoned*, like John the Baptist before a former Herod, *of righteousness, temperance, and judgment to come*. And he so 'reasoned,' that Felix could not avoid applying it to himself." Oh ye court preachers, imitate the Baptist and Paul; and when ye have princes before you, not as princes, but as hearers, and ye address them, not like Paul as a prisoner, but clad in the garb of office, speak not to them of the merely general doctrines of the "faith in Christ," but bring home to their consciences those points which may be specially efficacious for repentance and amendment of their sins; and do this so that they cannot avoid applying it to themselves! Paul on this occasion spoke of " righteousness " to an unrighteous judge;[3] of chastity, or " temperance," to a sensual, luxurious pair,

---

[1] In Christ *Jesus* is perhaps a correction. Certainly the apostle spoke also of Jesus; yet the more general expression leads only to the *Christ* of the Jewish promise and doctrine.

[2] We add to this: or to foster, or even allow him to retain, any ideas he might have (common enough at that time) as to some magical means of expiation existing in Christianity.

[3] Recollect the accounts of this governor which were given above.

who, incited by fleshly lust, had been unlawfully united ; of " judgment to come," when all *impune malefacta* of this life will find
their retribution before the great Judge of the world, who now
offers Himself to men, either as a Saviour or a Judge, which they
will.   Paul cared not whether by his free language he might not
aggravate the unpleasantness of his imprisonment : for himself he
had no thought ; he yearned for the two souls to whom the Lord
had appointed him to preach repentance and forgiveness of sins.
The power of the truth so mightily wrought, that *Felix trembled*,[1]
or became afraid, and anxiously stopped him, saying, " *Go thy way
for this time ; for the present I have heard sufficient ; when I have
a convenient season, I will call for thee.*"

Vers. 26, 27.   Many, after a similar answer, never seem to find
this " convenient season" for God's word, although they have plenty
of time for all the amusements of the world ; but numerous opportunities must have been offered to Felix.   *But*—and this " but"
spoils all—he does not listen to God's word with a pure heart, his
first answer being given with a covert and wicked idea.   ᾽Αμα καὶ
ἐλπίζων is connected with the ἀπεκρίθη, and the ἅμα καί denotes a
coincidence with the ἔμφοβος γενόμενος.   It was therefore not
entirely, although chiefly, from the workings of his own conscience
that Felix gave this procrastinating reply, and adjourned the business of his own salvation as well as Paul's trial : he had also
another good reason, in the crafty hope *that money should have been
given him of Paul, that he might loose him.*   " Go thy way for this
time," said the alarmed conscience ; but the addition, " When I
have a convenient season, I will call for thee," was made by the
covetousness of the " *servile ingenium*."   Paul was one of the chief
men of the now considerable sect (ver. 5) ; he had brought alms to
Jerusalem.   In Cæsarea itself there was no small number of Nazarenes who, following the permission given (ver. 23), might manifest
much interest in Paul.   A prospect like this of inducing the apostle
to purchase justice could not but allure a Felix.   Perhaps the hope
of a ransom may have had some effect in his mitigation of Paul's
captivity, which mitigation we have attributed to more honourable
reasons ; at least we see further, in ver. 26, that Felix must have

---

[1] Nothing is said about Drusilla, and the " hearing" in ver. 24 seems to
apply to Felix only.   She appears therefore to have accompanied the latter
partly out of curiosity, partly perhaps with a view of averting by her presence
any too bold or confident prominence in the preaching of those matters which
her conscience led her to expect ; but this purpose she failed in effecting.

been a somewhat strange character, who almost impudently trifled
with the feelings which the truth extorted from him, and continuing
his plans, was willing to listen to further persuasion to righteousness and justice, in order to realize a profit for that which simple
legality demanded from him : *wherefore* (in order to give him and
his friends the requisite confidence, and perhaps a pretence for the
purchase of his freedom) Luke says, *he sent for him the oftener,
and communed with him* in a familiar way—ὡμίλει αὐτῷ. But
Paul did not understand this kind of talk, and therefore remained
two years in his easy imprisonment at Cæsarea, being neither
condemned nor acquitted—sometimes perhaps listened to by the
governor as to the " faith in Christ." He was doubtless supported
and visited by the Christians of the place, and may perhaps now
and then have been tempted to purchase his freedom, but yet remained waiting patiently in the Lord's " way." " Two years !"—
a significant interval of unaccustomed quiet and strengthening for
the apostle to stimulate him to fresh activity,—an interval which
Luke passes over in one line. All this time was the great apostle
confined in Herod's judgment-hall, and withdrawn from his beloved
church ; all this time, too, he must have failed to see how the promise " that thou must bear witness also of me in Rome" should
come to pass ; but the Lord's words, " Be of good cheer, Paul,"
must also all this time have been present to his faith. The Jews
who had sworn to kill him must now make up their minds to break
their vow, and eat food, thus rightfully bringing down their curses
on their own heads.

After these two years—which, as regards his salvation, he had
so miserably wasted—Felix was removed from his office ; and in
order, on his departure, to please the Jews, lest he might be accused
by them at Rome, *he left Paul bound,* whom he might perhaps have
set free.[1] Thus do the children of the world seek to give pleasure
to one another at the expense of the children of God ; thus does a
Felix conclude his government by courting worldly favour, after
having for two years slighted the testimony of God's mercy. But
this final act of favour, after so many years of persecution, was but
of little avail to the crafty Felix. Accusations were brought against
him to the Emperor Nero, and he was very hard pushed, so that

---

[1] He might perhaps, had he been base enough, have done the Jews a still
greater pleasure, and have delivered Paul into their power (*vid.* ch. xxv. 3) ;
but he was prevented from doing this by God's counsel through the now
notorious Roman citizenship.

nothing but his brother Pallas' influence with Agrippina saved him.[1] It is worthy of remark, that during these very two years of the apostle's captivity, tumultuous risings took place amongst the Jewish and Hellenist inhabitants of Cæsarea, which gave rise to complaints as to Felix's conduct in the affair. Thus we see how the quiet waiting of the apostle, who disdained even to buy his liberty, must have evidently contrasted with the uproar round him, and must have destroyed the accusation that the Nazarenes were the uproar-makers. Porcius Festus, who succeeded Felix, is praised more than the other governors for his justice and clemency, and this praise is to some extent justified by his treatment of Paul.

Ch. xxv. 1–5. Now when Festus was come into the province, *i.e.* when he had reached his palace at Cæsarea, *after three days he ascended from Cæsarea to Jerusalem*, in order to show himself to the authorities as their new governor. The first thing which the high priest and elders ask him is to send Paul back to Jerusalem; so little, even during the lapse of two years, had they subdued their enmity against the quiet and patient confessor of Jesus of Nazareth. They urgently solicit Festus, making manifold accusations against Paul, that as the governor's first favour to them he would have the prisoner immediately brought from Cæsarea to Jerusalem. They, however, would lay in wait to kill him on the way, as they had fully intended two years before. But now *the high priest and the chief of the Jews* spontaneously purpose a repetition of the murderous attack; *before* they had only been stirred up to it by others, and were well pleased at it.[2] Festus, however, is unwilling to grant this surprising request, that he should send to Jerusalem a prisoner who was impeached before the governor's court, and on his first appearance in Jerusalem maintains his somewhat invaded rights. He partly refuses and partly grants their demand, and answers them to the effect that Paul was kept safely and duly in custody, and that he (Festus) would depart shortly for Cæsarea.— *Let them therefore among you which are able* (that is, to bring the accusation, or to whom the journey is not too troublesome), *go down with me, and accuse this man* before my court, *if there be any wickedness in him* which can be proved. Thus were the apostle's enemies, who would willingly have murdered him, again referred to a legal

---

[1] Drusilla, together with her and Felix's son, subsequently (at the time of Titus) met with a miserable death in an eruption of Vesuvius.

[2] One Ismael had now become high priest in the place of Ananias. Another reading, however, says οἱ ἀρχιερεῖς.

prosecution, from which even less success could now be hoped for. God, through the justice of the heathen, protected His servant against the malice of His apostate people.

Vers. 6–8. Festus did not remain more than ten days in Jerusalem. Having again come down to Cæsarea, and arranging everything briefly and plainly, he seated himself the very next day on his new judgment-seat, that Paul might be brought before him. He was no procrastinator, like Felix. The Jews were compelled to make up their minds to a second prosecution before this judgment-seat ; but now they *stood round about* the tribunal in greater numbers than before, *and laid many and grievous complaints against Paul ;* but yet it is said of all of them, *which they could not prove!* (οὐκ ἴσχυον). The more incapable of proof the matters which they allege, the more surprising becomes this accumulation of charges. Paul answered both distinctly and emphatically : *Neither against the law of the Jews* (when rightly understood and applied), *neither against the temple* (as they specially charge me, but cannot prove it), *nor yet against Cæsar* (by turbulence, which before this tribunal is the chief matter), *have I offended anything at all.* From what is said in ver. 19, we may justly conclude that Paul also bore witness as to the resurrection of Jesus.

Vers. 9–12. Festus cannot discover the grievous guilt in the man which he had supposed he should find, and perhaps remarks that it is a controversy as to matters of faith and doctrine which urges on the accusers to so many and such grievous charges. He therefore desires, now that he has asserted the right of his court over the prisoner, to grant, if possible, the favour requested by the Jews—in fact, to " show them a pleasure " at his first coming, as Felix at his departure. Festus little knew, or even guessed, what turpitude the rulers of the Jews were capable of under the guise of justice. But, like a man who wished to act with all the justice and prudence possible, he asks the Roman citizen whether he would voluntarily acknowledge the decision of the Sanhedrim given in the presence of the procurator. He does not require him to condescend to the judgment of a lower tribunal, but says, *Wilt thou go up to Jerusalem, and there be judged of these things before me ?*—that is, by the Sanhedrim, in *my* presence and under *my* superintendence (ἐπ' ἐμοῦ, as in ch. xxiii. 30 and xxvi. 2). He wishes to please the Jews as much as possible, and to transfer to them this matter of belief, as he takes the whole affair to be ; but in order to guard against any injustice, and to have the whole circumstances brought closely before him, he will himself be present.[1] This was a proposal which certainly would not have been acceptable to the Sanhedrim, except as far as "killing him on the way" was concerned. Now at last was the juncture arrived for Paul, when he might avail himself of his citizenship, and, according to the Lord's will, reach Rome; when indeed he *must*, in order not again to fall into the hands of the Jews, from whom the Lord had once delivered him, appeal to Cæsar. His short speech (vers. 10, 11) contains three main points : I am subject to Cæsar, not to the tribunal of the Jews; I desire nothing but justice; for this very reason I appeal unto Cæsar. *I stand at Cæsar's judgment-seat* probably refers to the procurator's court, before which he was actually standing, and in Roman law was equivalent to that of the emperor himself. To the question, "Wilt thou be judged before me?" Paul answers, "I already am standing before *thy* court, or indeed Cæsar's, where I ought to be judged; that is generally the proper tribunal for me, owing to my Roman citizenship." *To the Jews have I done no wrong, as thou very well knowest*—judging from thy present examination, and thy questions and language. Why, therefore, should there be a new trial before those who can now bring nothing against me? I desire nothing but justice. If I have done any wrong, or committed any crime worthy of death, I ask not that my life may be spared. *But if there be none of these things whereof these accuse me, no man may deliver me unto them*, and, granting their request as a favour (ver. 9), give me up to certain death from an unjust judgment, or from still more cunning plots.[2] Rather than allow this to take place, and acknowledge the Sanhedrim, *I appeal unto Cæsar.* Every Roman citizen had a right to this *appellatio ante sententiam*, as a protest against any lower tribunal. These important words, the mere utterance of which was enough for the court, were spoken by Paul, being certainly impelled by the suggestion of the Holy Spirit (cf. ch. xxiii. 11), as well as under a necessity arising from the

[1] Which was by no means a "weak security." This Festus had no evil intentions, and only gave way so far as he might safely do, and still retain a certainty of justice. His whole character is subsequently clearly depicted in ch. xxv. 24-27.

[2] The apostle makes no complaint as to what the Jews had before done against him and what they further purposed to do (which at the conclusion he only slightly glances at). He always confines himself in his counter accusations to the matters which concern his defence. He is very far from wishing to bring before any human tribunal the murderous plots which affect his life.

judge's question (cf. ch. xxviii. 19). The minister of the gospel of Christ protests against Israel's chief authorities, now no longer valid before God, and prefers to appeal to the justice of a *Nero!* This was a great and significant moment in the apostolic history, repetitions of which often occur in the church of Christ. Festus, as a man who proceeded carefully and orderly in all points, first confers as to the matter with his council; and when the latter thought that the appeal should be accepted, he speaks his decree to Paul: *Hast thou appealed unto Cæsar?*—although only conditionally, rather than be judged by the Sanhedrim. It is well! That thy long trial may be ended as soon as possible, thy request is granted, and I unconditionally accept thy proposal: *unto Cæsar shalt thou go.*[1] Thus is Festus rid of his strange prisoner, with all justice, and indeed by the prisoner's own wish. Thus is the important decree pronounced to Paul, that *now* was to take place that which the Lord had promised him two years before; which, too, he had for a still longer period revolved in his own mind,— that his path should lie towards Rome, and to the presence of Cæsar. Whether he was to go as a prisoner or as a free man, he was not to ask; sufficient for him were the words, "Thou must bear witness also of me at *Rome.*"

XXVII.

PAUL BEFORE KING AGRIPPA.

(Chap. xxvi. 2-23.)

VINDICATORY CONFESSION AND TESTIMONY AS TO HIS FAITH AND DOCTRINE.

Ch. xxv. 13-21. Festus was now waiting for some suitable opportunity of a passage for Paul, in order to send him to Rome. In the meantime, however, God had ordained that a remarkable

---

[1] Festus' reply has usually been considered a bitterly impudent retort to Paul's language, "that no man may deliver me up to them." But this hardly harmonizes with the intervening conference with his council, and still less with the passage, vers. 25-27.

and important opportunity should be afforded to Paul to stand
and testify in and before a very distinguished auditory (ver. 23),
that Jesus of Nazareth was the Christ, and that He "should
suffer, and that He should be the first that should rise from the
dead, and should show light unto the people and to the Gentiles"
(ch. xxvi. 23).—*And after certain days, King Agrippa and Bernice
came unto Cæsarea to salute Festus.* This man, Herod Agrippa
the younger, was son of Herod the elder, and great-grandson of
the so-called Herod the Great, and also brother to Drusilla. He
was, on the whole, a much better man than his odious father. He
had received his education at Rome as a special favourite of the
Emperor Claudius; but when his father died (ch. xii. 23), who
had retained the entire kingdom of Herod the Great, he was too
young (being only seventeen years old) to succeed him. Claudius
therefore sent Cuspius Fadus into the land as procurator, who
was followed by Tiberius Alexander, Ventidius Cumanus, and
Felix. Subsequently, two years later, when King Herod of
Chalcis, uncle of the youthful Agrippa, died, the latter obtained
first Herod's small kingdom or principality; then, after four or six
years, he received instead the former tetrarchy of Philip (Luke
iii. 1), which had hitherto been administered by a procurator,
together with that of Lysanias, including therefore Batanæa,
Auranitis, Trachonitis, and Abilene.[1] Like all former tetrarchs,
he caused himself to be styled "king," and, as Herod of Chalcis
before him, possessed the right of control over the treasures of the
temple, and also the power of nominating the high priest, although
Judea, Galilee, and Samaria were ruled by a governor (now
Festus). Agrippa was the last Jewish "king," and long survived
the destruction of Jerusalem. The Bernice (or Berenice, Φερενίκη)
who here appears with him was his and Drusilla's sister, and had
been married to the above-named uncle,[2] Herod of Chalcis. Having become a widow at his death, she came to stay with her brother Agrippa, and a very general public report accused the pair
of living together in incest. To avert this suspicion, she again
sought for matrimony with Polemon king of Cilicia, whom, however, she abandoned in a short time, although for her sake he had
adopted circumcision. She then returned to her former connection

---

[1] Added to which, Nero, in the first year of his reign, conferred upon him
several townships.

[2] Whether such a marriage was prohibited in Lev. xviii. 14 is doubtful; but
the prohibition appears the more probable conclusion.

with her brother.[1] She must have been a person of the greatest
beauty, and as regards this point no slight jealousy must have
existed between the sisters Bernice and Drusilla. According to
Tacitus, Bernice subsequently much endeared herself both to Ves-
pasian (" seni quoque magnificentia munerum grata ") and also
to Titus (as " florens ætate formaque "): the latter, according to
Suetonius, would have made her his empress, if the dissatisfaction
of the people had not deterred him, and compelled him to send her
away.[2]

These, then, were the personages before whom Paul the
prisoner was to testify of the King, Saviour, and Judge of the
world — of Jesus of Nazareth, Him who died and rose again.
They had come to Cæsarea to congratulate Festus on his accession
to the vicegerency, and also to exhibit themselves to him in all
their pomp and dignity, and thus seek the Roman favour and
friendship which was so important to their interests. No doubt
many compliments were passed and festivities took place ; then,
after they had spent several days there, and had had a sufficiency of
frivolities and merry-makings, there came a serious conversation as
to this remarkable Nazarene. *Festus declared Paul's cause unto
the king—ἀνέθετο* ; that is, perhaps, only related to him the state
of the case, in order to enable the Jewish king to give him some
advice in the matter, thereby both paying the king a courtesy, and
also obtaining the benefit of his counsel. Festus did not, as some
have understood it, transfer the whole cause to Agrippa, for him to
pronounce judgment upon it. For as regards Paul's appeal, and
its acceptance by Festus, all was now settled, and the only point in
question was the account which the governor was to transmit with
the prisoner (vers. 25, 26). Festus' explanation to Agrippa (vers.
14–21) is very characteristic : throughout the whole of it we may
recognise the new official in the circumstantial details as to his
previous management and present doubt in this his first difficult
task ; and also the mere Roman, who, notwithstanding all his show
of advice seeking courtesy towards Agrippa, desires first and foremost to praise the impartiality and method of Roman justice.
Against Paul, he says, *the chief priests and elders of the Jews*

---

[1] Baumgarten remarks, that Luke hints at this equivocal connection by not
mentioning her as Agrippa's sister, or indeed in any way.

[2] This is naturally enough turned by Suetonius to special praise, as an
example of the self-restraint of the much-lauded emperor : " Berenicen statim
ab urbe dimisit invitus invitam."

informed me, desiring to have judgment against him (κατ᾽ αὐτοῦ δίκην, *i.e.* καταδίκην, this more exact reading being now brought forward). *To whom I answered, It is not the custom of the Romans to deliver any man*—εἰς ἀπώλειαν (a correct gloss)—*before he that is accused have the accusers face to face, and have licence to answer for himself.* In like manner Scipio said to Allucius, "It is not the custom of the Romans to avail themselves of any power of which they may not justly avail themselves." Felix was a Roman, and yet he "left Paul bound," in order to "show the Jews a pleasure." Festus himself similarly desired to "do the Jews a pleasure" (ch. xxv. 9); and not until Paul represented to him that "no man may deliver me unto them" (χαρίσασθαι, just as in ver. 16), did he accept his appeal, so as to avoid letting him go free, as justice demanded. What, too, did the Roman Pilate do with Jesus? Yet Festus was a Roman, like the proud, indeed nationally proud, and just men who are always to be found in the world clamouring for the truth. He further extols his own diligence in holding his court "without any delay" (ver. 17), and candidly states that no heavy transgression, as he had been led to expect, had been brought forward against Paul, at least *which could be proved* (cf. ver. 7); but that the whole point in question against him turned on some matter concerning their religion. Περὶ τῆς ἰδίας δεισιδαιμονίας, the same equivocal word being used as in ch. xvii. 22. In the presence of the Jewish king the courtly Festus might not have intended any term so harsh as "superstition" would have been; but yet as a heathen he could not speak quite piously and reverentially of Judaism. He therefore chose an intermediate word, which among the polite would convey a certain smack of indifferentism. It only concerned certain (properly *useless*) questions of their own system of religion: this was the whole affair! Thus at least Festus thought he ought to speak about the matter in the presence of the Jewish king, enlightened as he was by his Roman education. Festus shrinks from appearing to insult the king by saying "*your* religion."[1] "And of a certain man," he continues, "whom they, as I recollect, called *Jesus*, who was dead, whom Paul confidently asserted (ἔφασκεν) to be alive." Whether or not He died upon the cross was all the same to Festus; sufficient for him *He was dead*, and yet Paul said that *He was alive*. No doubt Festus looked upon it as a piece of innocent fanaticism on the part of the

[1] Although τῆς ἰδίας only expresses this indeterminately, as if to say, "I know not indeed whether it is *thy* belief also."

otherwise guiltless man, and actually no worse than all the δεισι-δαιμονία of the Jews generally. " Περί τινος 'Ιησοῦ—ita miser Festus loquitur de eo, cui omne genu flectetur"—thus exclaims the pious Bengel in regard to this passage. But the reproach against many *doctores theologiæ* in Christendom[1] still remains, who, like the heathen prætor Festus, look upon the gospel, trodden down as it is by their self-satisfied arrogance, as a questionable superstition—that a Jesus who was *dead* is, according to the apostolic φάσκειν, *alive*, and has become *life* to all men! We also learn from this verse, that Paul in his examination (vers. 7, 8) had expressly testified of the resurrection of Jesus. The remainder of Festus' speech (vers. 20, 21) needs no further remark; we only observe, that to us the περὶ τούτου (as masculine) appears to refer back to the περί τινος 'Ιησοῦ.

Vers. 22, 23. Agrippa is curious, as Herod formerly was (Luke xxiii. 8). The question about the Christians was one by no means unknown to him (ch. xxvi. 26, 28): his father had put James to death, and had laid violent hands on Peter.—*I would also hear the man myself.* With this idea many a man of the world goes to listen to a preacher of the gospel, and, as was the case with Agrippa, knows not beforehand what may be the result of his hearing. Festus makes a courteous reply—perhaps, as Heinrichs remarks, at the same time inviting him to a banquet : "To-morrow," he says, "thou shalt hear him." *And on the morrow, when Agrippa and Bernice had come with great pomp*, they went into the audience-chamber—the ἀκροατήριον, the stateliest room in the house, and best fitted for the entertainment which Festus desired to afford his noble guests by his display of the apostle. This took place, as Wetstein observes, in the same city in which the father of the king was eaten by worms as a punishment for his sins. Oh, if Agrippa had on this occasion but set aside all his pomp, and listened willingly to the man in quiet privacy, who knows whether he might not have been *not almost*, but *altogether*, persuaded " to be a Christian !" Many a lord and prince loses, through his " great pomp," the best opportunities for his everlasting salvation. There were present not only the king himself, together with his constant com-

---

[1] " The heathen Festus has in few words expressed the 'summa theologiæ Christianæ' more distinctly than innumerable doctors of divinity have done. It can only be considered as bitter irony against Christianity, whenever the persuasion of the reality of the resurrection is declared to be unessential to Christianity."—Fr. v. BAADER.

panion Bernice (who had been for a time queen of Cilicia, Paul's native province), but also the *tribuni militum* (of whom there were five in Cæsarea) and the principal men of the city, *i.e.* the highest military and civil authorities, whom Festus had commanded to be present. This was the company before whom, at Festus' command, Paul was brought. The testimony has to be delivered with the utmost completeness ere the witness departs for Rome. In *Jerusalem* the long-suffering of the Lord toward the despisers was now exhausted. In *Antioch*, the court of the *Præses* of Syria, the new chief church, composed both of Jews and Gentiles, was now flourishing. Here, in *Cæsarea*, the court of the governor, the testimony had commenced in the house of Cornelius the centurion ; but now it had made its way up to this brilliant assemblage of all the authorities of the place in the presence of the last king of the Jews. It was indeed a prisoner who testified, but it was a prisoner of whom it again had to be certified that he had " done no wrong ; " and however much and condescendingly the noble personages might look down upon " this man," " this man" would change places with none of them, and could joyfully record his wish before God, that all his hearers in that distinguished audience were *such as he was.*

Vers. 24–47. Festus thus opens the proceedings : " *King Agrippa, and all men who are here present with us, ye see this man about whom all the multitude of the Jews have dealt with me, both at Jerusalem and also here, crying that he ought not to live any longer* (cf. ch. xx. 22—the inflexible consistency of ·malice). *But when I found that he had committed nothing worthy of death* (as Paul said, ver. 11), *and that he himself had appealed unto Augustus* (Σεβαστόν, the most honourable, his majesty), *I have determined to send him* (at the earliest opportunity)." After Festus had thus, with some degree of pride, communicated his decision in this case, he makes amends for it by the following ingenuous confession, which affords another opportunity for an act of courtesy towards Agrippa : " I had indeed intended to send him," he says ; " but *I have no certain thing to write unto my lord.*" Therefore all the high officials present, but specially the king Agrippa, being well acquainted with the Jewish religion, after another investigation of this case, which had already been so fully investigated, were to give advice as to what the judge of the highest court was to say about the prisoner ; " *for,*" he says, " *it seemeth to me unreasonable* (ἄλογον) *to send a prisoner, and not withal to signify* (or clearly describe) *the crimes against him.*"

Festus openly avows the embarrassment in which he had in-

volved himself, by having (to please the Jews) accepted the validity
of Paul's appeal, which was at least only conditional, instead of at
once setting free the man that had been found to be innocent. But
before the authorities, this confession on the part of the judge, that
by his decision " to send him" (ver. 25) he had entangled himself
in ἄλογόν τι, is made to appear as nothing but a courtly exaggeration, intended to flatter king Agrippa, by making him out to be a
better judge in the matter.

Ch. xxvi. 1. Agrippa, who, in his anxiety to hear the man
speak, could perhaps hardly brook the delay of this long introduction, immediately addresses him, saying briefly, but not without
dignity, *Thou art permitted* (by Festus and me) *to speak for thyself*.[1]
Then Paul, after the custom of ancient orators, frankly stretched
forth his hand—the right hand—on which was the fetter and chain
(ver. 29), and, full of the wisdom and power of the Holy Spirit,
began his second vindication. He, however, spoke less *for himself*
than of the Lord, whose servant and witness he was, and related
again that which he had seen, and during his lifetime must have
often and willingly related. Following God's inspiration, his present discourse *confesses* more, *testifies* to more, and *reveals* more
than his former one, and is perfectly arranged even in the smallest
and most delicate details.

Vers. 2, 3. This remarkable man, whose testifying—φάσκειν—as
to the resurrection and life of the crucified One (called indeed the
Messiah) Agrippa had desired to listen to, had nevertheless been
treated by the king as an ordinary prisoner, and had been told by
him that he was permitted to speak for himself, and to bring forward anything that might tend to his vindication and acquittal.
But the apostle looks upon the distinguished company before whom
he is arraigned as nothing but an assembly of sinners, to whom he
longs to testify of *their* acquittal and redemption through Jesus
Christ. He therefore answers the king in the character of a happy
prisoner and a joyful witness : *I think myself happy, king Agrippa,*
—far more than thou thinkest or knowest, ay, even in this my imprisonment—even with these fetters on my hands, stretched forth
as they are as I speak for God's unfettered word. The apostle does
not expressly say this ; but the mode of expression, that he thinks
himself happy that he is permitted that day to defend himself
before the king, arises, if we inquire into its real groundwork in

---

[1] Of course περὶ σεαυτοῦ occurs here quite in the sense of ὑπὲρ σεαυτοῦ, as
Paul similarly says in ver. 2, ἀπολογεῖσθαι ; cf. τὰ περὶ ἐμαυτοῦ, ch. xxiv. 10.

the mind of the apostle, from his general state of happiness and
blessedness amid the persecutions for Jesus' sake (Ἥγημαι ἐμαυτὸν
μακάριον, as Matt. v. 11). Ἐπὶ σοῦ is a well-chosen expression, as
he thus denotes his mere presence without acknowledging him as
his judge. The μάλιστα (ver. 3) is, however, by no means to be
connected with γνώστην ὄντα σε,—making it, because thou art
especially conversant, a distinguished expert in all Jewish matters :
for, in the first place, it is a question if so much could be justly said
of Agrippa ; besides, μάλιστα evidently denotes here the same idea
as the comparative εὐθυμότερον in ch. xxiv. 10, only more forcibly
expressed. Paul thinks himself happy generally in being accused
for Jesus' sake, and still more when opportunity is afforded him
for his defence and testimony, for both of which he ever stood
in joyful readiness ; but most of all he rejoices that, after his repeated examinations before Romans, he now is permitted to speak
and testify before a Jewish king. Certainly Agrippa was only
an Idumæan—a half Jew—and Paul consequently does *not* say
expressly, Ἰουδαῖον ὄντα σε, but somewhat obscurely, γνώστην ὄντα
σε—an expert in all the *customs* (in practice) and *questions* (in
theory) *of the Jews.* As we see both from this passage, and also
subsequently, this must have been specially the case as regarded
Agrippa. Thus Paul's " feeling of confidence in the presence of a
man who understood him " (Blumhardt) was all the more natural
after his examination by Festus, who was not acquainted with the
circumstances of the case, especially as Agrippa, although well
acquainted with Judaism, was no blind zealot of schools and sects.
Before him Paul could entertain a good hope in all the confidence
of faith and love, and was therefore able to express himself more
fully than we have remarked him doing since ch. xxii. On this
occasion, by his request for a patient hearing, he intimates that he
will not be able to treat the matter very briefly, and also that other
points will be added to the defence he was (ver. 1) permitted to
make *for himself.*

Vers. 4, 5. Now follows once more the indispensable, far-
stretching retrospect of his whole life, from his youth up. The
discourse henceforward presents much similarity to that in ch. xxii.
We have already spoken of the comparison between the two, and
the reasons for the differences which may be noticed. The *manner
of life*—βίωσις—embraces his whole conduct and deportment ; his
course of life and behaviour in reference to his present position as
a criminal. The word ἔζησα at the end of ver. 5 has the same

meaning; cf. Gal. i. 13, ἀναστροφὴν ἐν τῷ Ἰουδαϊσμῷ. *My manner of life from my youth know all the Jews*, because from the very beginning this youth was spent at Jerusalem. In ch. xxiv. 17 he expressed somewhat later in his discourse the idea that the Jews were, both by descent, and on his part by his attachment to them, *his nation:* this he now brings forward at the beginning. The ἄνωθεν in ver. 5 is equivalent to ἀπ᾽ ἀρχῆς in ver. 4 ; and προγινώσκειν points out that the Jews were well acquainted with him, as a result of the sojourn of Saul the student at Jerusalem, before all their present accusations and persecutions.—*If they would* (only) *testify.* Harsher language is used now, after his experience of their obstinacy and enmity, than he employed in ch. xxii. 5. The world is apt to forget all former honourable conduct and ability in the disciples of Christ ; even of the man whom, as one of themselves, they delighted to praise, worldlings will refuse to testify, because they feel that by doing so they will only rtify to God's work in the change that has taken place. Paul had actually lived *after the straitest sect* or party of the Jewish cultus, that is, as a Pharisee : he had, indeed, altogether thought and behaved with all zeal as a Pharisee, and had not, as many others, been merely classed among that party. By using the rather indefinite, equivocal word θρησκεία, Paul somewhat approaches the standpoint of his heathen audience, with whom, nevertheless, he contrasts himself and Agrippa together by adding the ἡμετέρας. Also in using the term αἵρεσις he intimates that the αἵρεσις was on the part of the present Jews, but that he (Paul) had turned from this αἵρεσις to the full truth. The adjective ἀκριβεστάτη is the proper description of the pharisaical party, just as κατὰ ἀκρίβειαν τοῦ πατρῴου νόμου in ch. xxii. 3 ; for Josephus calls the Pharisees, οἱ δοκοῦντες μετὰ ἀκριβείας ἐξηγεῖσθαι τὰ νόμιμα—οἱ περὶ τὰ πάτρια νόμιμα δοκοῦσι τῶν ἄλλων ἀκριβείᾳ διαφέρειν. In saying this, Paul desires to intimate that, in his former blindness, he had omitted nothing whereby, according to his then existing knowledge, he might hit upon that which was right ; but that all this supposed, although often highly erroneous, strictness and precision in fulfilling the law and interpreting Scripture had neither brought help to his heart, nor enlightened his eyes as to Him who was the fulfiller of all law and all prophecy—Jesus of Nazareth. His present lively, clear *hope* (ver. 6), with which he now contrasts his former pharisaism, is indeed something entirely different from that dead, blind ἀκρίβεια, although there is a certain resemblance between them; inasmuch as in this hope all that was right in his former opinions is not relinquished, but, on the contrary, is completed, and by the fulfilment in Jesus is now made lively and true.

Ver. 6. *Καὶ νῦν* expresses forcibly the twofold relation of similarity and contrast, by which Paul connects his present *ἐλπίς* with his former *ἀκρίβεια*. Bengel briefly hints at it : " Etiamnum —I hold to the hope of Israel." This is one side of the question, which is implied in the *καί*; the other lies in the *νῦν*, which intimates the distinction, the change which had since taken place. *Ἐπ' ἐλπίδι*, etc., naturally stands first (in the Greek), in order to make the *ἕστηκα κρινόμενος* follow with all the more surprising emphasis as a molestation of his orthodoxy. We have seen above, in ch. xxiv. 15, that in the expression *hope*, taken in all its inmost depth, are embraced the joyful recognition and firm grasp of the fulfilment. Here, too, this must be understood; for the faith in the promises of God made to the fathers, is the faith which firmly holds the beginning of the fulfilment, and looks forward in joyful hope to their consummation. *The promise made of God unto our fathers* is here intended to mean the *things promised*, which now have begun to appear (ch. i. 4, ii. 33, 39). The kingdom of the Messiah is therefore the thing meant, the kingdom of God which was to be founded in the promised King and Saviour, the kingdom of peace and glory. For this is the essence and aim of all the promises, and can therefore be considered as *the promise.* This promise was made to *the fathers,* that is, to the forefathers gene-rally, during the whole time of the divine revelations and promises, up to the completion of their great period of development in the last prophet. Yet must we not therefore exclude the *fathers* specially so called—Abraham, Isaac, and Jacob ; for under the type of Isaac a new seed of blessing from God's quickening power was promised to Abraham, to whom again, in receiving Isaac, the resurrection of Christ from the dead was prefigured (Heb. xi. 19).

Moreover, in this general reference to the kingdom of the Messiah, the reference also implied to the resurrection is by no means excluded, but, on the contrary, specially included. We cannot fail to be convinced of this by ver. 8, in which the resurrec-tion of the dead, which Paul (according to ver. 9) believes, hopes, and testifies of in the person of *Jesus of Nazareth,* is described as the main point of Paul's assailed and impugned hope. On this Grotius rightly remarks (though one-sidedly, without glancing at the kingdom of the resurrection as a whole), " He means the hope

of the resurrection, just as in ch. xxiii. 6, xxiv. 15 ;" and in order
to show that *this promise* belonged to the *fathers*, Abraham, Isaac,
and Jacob, he justly adds, " God promised that He would be the
God of Abraham, Isaac, and Jacob.   In this life, however, these
men possessed nothing more than others, and had only the ground
for their sepulchres : we may therefore perceive that further and
greater blessings awaited them after death (Matt. xxii. 32)."   Some
innovators now most incorrectly deny that the apostle (in vers. 6
and 7) referred to the resurrection, although the fact is unques-
tionably pointed to in ver. 8.   On the one hand, their mode of interpretation is too narrow, and prevents them from combining the
two ideas, that Paul spoke both of the promised kingdom of the
Messiah and also of the resurrection ; and on the other hand, they
do not desire to allow the wonderful idea that, even to the fathers,
the resurrection was clearly spoken of in the Old Testament.   In
ch. xxiv. 14, 15 the apostle asserts that the resurrection is written
of both in the law and the prophets ; and according to the Master,
in Luke xxiv. 44-47, whoever opens his understanding to the
Scriptures, will find that the resurrection of the Messiah is written
of as the groundwork of His kingdom, as in so many passages,
from Job xix. 25 and Ps. xvi. to Zech. xii. 10, xiii. 7-9, Mal. iv. 2.
Look back to Acts xiii. 32-37, and the interpretation given of that
passage : there, in vers. 32, 33, the institution of the promised
Messiah is spoken of, but therein is implied that this was done
through His " raising up ;" and in vers. 34, 35 it is shown by two
quotations that the promised institution of the Messiah's kingdom
is comprehended in Jesus' resurrection.   We must thus understand
the present passage : The kingdoms of the Messiah and of the
resurrection are one both in the promise and also in the fulfilment ; both the groundwork and commencement of this kingdom
are recognised by Paul's faith as depending on Jesus living again ;
and the resurrection of all, thus vouched for and fully certified,
is looked upon by his hope as the aim and consummation of this
kingdom.   We have, I trust, recognised in all its deep groundwork the reason why Paul, in his last testimony at Jerusalem,
should constantly bring forward the resurrection : the Jews at that
time, in the then existing state of Christianity, could not be either
reached or helped except by this combination of the announcement
of the Messiah with the doctrine of the resurrection.[1]   If the apostle

[1] As perhaps many of our present Christians may still be helped by the
assertion and proof of the true, completed humanity in the person of Christ.

desired to declare to them that Jesus of Nazareth was the Messiah,
he was compelled to maintain not only that He was risen, but also that
His kingdom of the Messiah was a kingdom of the resurrection, and
that thereby all the promises were fulfilled which the Jews vainly
expected in *their* hope of the resurrection. By this means also there
was brought about an eminently well-grounded and judicious appeal
to their consciences; he appealed to them by the future, so uncertain
for sinners, and said to them: In vain ye hope to attain the resurrection taught by your Pharisees in the kingdom of the Messiah,
unless in the risen Jesus ye acknowledge the true Messiah of the
true kingdom of the resurrection. He who clearly perceives these
circumstances and relations, will no longer entertain any doubt as
to the connection of vers. 6–9, which is as profound as it is clear.
Ere we proceed further, we will only remark as to ver. 6, that
the $\dot{\eta}\mu\hat{\omega}\nu$ corresponds with the $\dot{\eta}\mu\epsilon\tau\acute{\epsilon}\rho\alpha\varsigma$ in ver. 5; also that the
addition—*made by God*—points to the certainty of the promise,
and consequently to the confidence of the hope ($\epsilon\dot{\iota}\varsigma$ $\tau\grave{o}\nu$ $\Theta\epsilon\grave{o}\nu$, ch.
xxiv. 15); also that the $\dot{\epsilon}\sigma\tau\eta\kappa\alpha$ contrasts with the $\kappa\rho\iota\nu\acute{o}\mu\epsilon\nu o\varsigma$, and
tends to annul it, pointing to the preservation of the guiltless
prisoner through God's assistance,—an idea which is brought for-
ward still more strongly in the $\dot{\epsilon}\sigma\tau\eta\kappa\alpha$ $\mu\alpha\rho\tau\nu\rho\acute{o}\mu\epsilon\nu o\varsigma$ in ver. 22.

Ver. 7. *Unto which*—$\epsilon\dot{\iota}\varsigma$ $\dot{\eta}\nu$—*our whole nation hope to come.* To
what does this refer—to the *promise* or the *hope*? The *promise*
appears to be the more likely and the more natural; but most
expositors justly take it to apply to $\dot{\epsilon}\lambda\pi\acute{\iota}\delta\alpha$. For, in the first place,
the explanation follows, $\pi\epsilon\rho\grave{\iota}$ $\dot{\eta}\varsigma$ $\dot{\epsilon}\lambda\pi\acute{\iota}\delta o\varsigma$ $\dot{\epsilon}\gamma\kappa\alpha\lambda o\hat{\nu}\mu\alpha\iota$; and secondly,
we must compare ch. xxiv. 15, $\dot{\epsilon}\lambda\pi\acute{\iota}\delta\alpha$ $\dot{\epsilon}\chi\omega\nu$, $\dot{\eta}\nu$ $\kappa\alpha\grave{\iota}$ $\alpha\dot{\nu}\tau o\grave{\iota}$ $o\dot{\nu}\tau o\iota$
$\pi\rho o\sigma\delta\acute{\epsilon}\chi o\nu\tau\alpha\iota$. In the present passage it is expressed more forcibly,
"To which *hope* they *hope* to attain." And is not this striking,
indeed graphic, language to use as regards that blind Judaism
which, discontented and unappeased, although zealous in the outward service of God, strove for a never-attained *future*, which,
when arrived, is not acknowledged? The Messiah's kingdom, and
the resurrection of the just in that Messiah, is the aim and end of
the religious service of all Jews—"tota religio eorum tendit in
futurum" (Bengel)—and yet they themselves knew not what it
was they waited for and sought. They based their hopes on the
letter, and not on the spirit—on the mere purport of the dogma,
without any inward confidence and certainty. They thought that
they were ardently striving after it with all zeal; but when it arrives
in a shape different from that which they had set their hearts on,

then they reject it, and would rather continue to wait.[1] They, in fact, sought after *seeking* instead of after *finding* : how then, after all, could they find it ? Paul complains : This is what " our twelve tribes "—τὸ δωδεκάφυλον ἡμῶν, that is, all the Jews, both those in Palestine and also those that are scattered abroad—are now doing, so many of them at least who claim descent from the fathers (ver. 6), and appropriate to themselves the promises.[2] This language also is perfectly correct ; for although certainly there was a Sadducean section who denied the resurrection, yet, looking at the matter *in toto*, it was true of the whole body of Jews that their worship of God sought after the future fulfilment of the promise. Some, or indeed many, might no longer understand and believe what the things promised were ; yet, rightly considered and interpreted, the blinded tendency of the whole of Judaism continued to be directed to that which could only be really developed in Jesus of Nazareth. This is what Paul desires to call attention to in everything that he says. The expression λατρεύειν, made more forcible by the ἐκτενείᾳ, corresponds with the θρησκεία in ver. 5, and the vivid description of their blind zeal, ἐν ἐκτενείᾳ νύκτα καὶ ἡμέραν, plainly intimates that the Jews had substituted a self-chosen worship for that which was ordained by God ; that their θρησκεία, by which they had sought, since the days of Abraham, to set up their own righteousness against God's testimony (ζητοῦντες στῆσαι, Rom. x. 3), was thus become ἐθελοθρησκεία (Col. ii. 23) ; and their groundless, although firmly held, faith in the reward of such a worship was turned into a superstition. Thus the true relation between Christianity and pharisaical Judaism is as follows : On one side a genuine faith in the word, on the other a superstitious belief in the human mystifications by which it is involved ; on one side a worship of God the Father according to God's own " way " (ch. xxiv. 14), on the other a self-chosen service following all kinds of sects and schools ; on one side an apprehension of the coming kingdom of the Messiah in the risen Jesus, on the other an endless waiting for a Messiah's kingdom framed according to their own notions,—which kingdom can never come, all the truth and reality

[1] Kuinöl feels something of this when he says : " Erat Paulus a Judæis in jus vocatus, quod hanc spem non fovebat, quoniam Messiam venisse docebat."

[2] Baumgarten adds here a long dissertation on the existence of the ten tribes now apparently lost. This I do not desire to go into here. From many passages (among others Jas. i. 1) this much is, however, certain, that these ten tribes still exist.

which their ideas can boast of being but the echo and shadow of that which actually will come to pass in Jesus. After the apostle had thus laid down the real position of the matter, he goes on to annex a statement of the ground of his complaint as a kind of counter-accusation.—*For which hope's sake, king Agrippa, I am accused,* and strange to say, *by the Jews !* These words are in fact only a corroborative repetition of ver. 2 : ἐγκαλοῦμαι is the term used in both cases, only now βασιλεῦ 'Αγρίππα is added before ὑπὸ 'Ιουδαίων ; and, following the explanation he has just given, Paul says, περὶ ἧς ἐλπίδος, instead of περὶ πάντων ὧν, the rather vague expression he before used. Thus the emphasis of the repetition seems to say, "This hope is the only matter in question."

Ver. 8. The apostle now intimates that by his "hope" (ver. 6) he intended a believing acceptance of the kingdom of the Messiah, begun in the risen Jesus, as the spiritual kingdom of the resurrection. This idea he fully reveals by a question which must have come home to Agrippa, and thus passes on to a more precise notice of the heavenly life of Jesus. His transition may be thus paraphrased : " Ye well know what my words mean ! That Jesus who is dead, of whose resurrection I testify, Him I believe to be the Messiah , and in *this* fulfilment of the promise to Israel, what is there so incredible and absurd, that ye so absolutely reject it ? " In the *you* Paul turns entirely to Agrippa, whom indeed he had twice addressed, including him in the " our " in vers. 5 and 7. He also purposely appeals to him personally in vers. 13 and 19. For throughout the whole of this discourse his confidence and trust apply only to Agrippa, as he himself intimates in ver. 26. Probably the Sadducean principles which prevailed in the family of the Herods (Mark iii. 6, viii. 15) had been handed down to Agrippa, ---more, however, in a practical shape than as a matter of theory. Paul now addresses himself to those undecided principles as stringently as afterwards in ver. 27, and asks with some degree of wonder, *Why should it be thought a thing incredible* (ἄπιστον) *with you, that God should raise the dead*—the dead generally, and in particular Jesus of Nazareth, who had indeed died ? This mode of interpretation seems to us more probable than the other, which would run, " What ! is it held incredible by you ? " etc. This latter sounds as if Paul was scarcely aware of the general practical denial of any such fact; but his desire really was to express a certain wonder at the groundlessness of this denial, and by the " *why?* " to appeal reprovingly to their consciences. It was like

Jesus' question to Paul himself, "Why persecutest thou me?" We may also notice that the εἰ in this verse by no means merely stands for ὅτι, as many usually take it, but retains its proper signification. If we undertand it to mean *that*, Paul would be directly contradicting what he said in ver. 7. For how could he (in ver. 7) attribute the hope of the resurrection to all the Jews, and then (in ver. 8) ask why they *disbelieved* in the resurrection? Even if we assume that in ver. 8 by the ὑμῖν the Sadducees only are meant, he would be contradicting the question he subsequently puts in ver. 27, in which he evidently does *not* treat the king as a decided Sadducee. We see, therefore, that the ὑμῖν refers generally to the words preceding, βασιλεῦ ʼΑγρίππα, ὑπὸ ʼΙουδαίων, and embraces the king as a Jew with all other Jews. The word εἰ contains properly the point of the question, as if to say, "Why do ye deny it, in opposition to the aim and end of all your worship, *when now, in fact*, the resurrection of the dead (in Jesus) has taken place, and that promise is commencing to be fulfilled for which ye *wait*?"—or, indeed, will have to wait; for without some future aim of expectation, the whole of the Mosaic and traditional cultus is without either sense or meaning. Lastly, we must not overlook the significant contrast between ὑμῖν and Θεός. "Why do you deny with your human opposition that which God, your God, who gave the promise to your fathers, the God of wonders from the beginning, now actually *does*?" If it be marvellous (impossible, יִפָּלֵא) "in the eyes of the remnant of the people in these days, should it be also marvellous (impossible) in my eyes? saith the Lord of hosts." Israel as a body, whatever they may teach as a dogma, nevertheless obstinately deny that fact testified to a thousand times, in which their God surely reveals Himself to be that which He actually is, and desires to be, for His Israel; and the spirit of testimony now asks the rebuking question, "Why is this?"

Ver. 9. This question of the reproving spirit is, however, spoken by the lips of a man who had previously dealt with it, and now again reverts to his former confession, and for the first time after this astonishing preparation, fully relates how he had been overcome, and turned from this denial and persecution of the Risen One. Certainly I know well how this denial comes to pass, and I have had experience what answer to this "why" lies hidden in our wicked hearts. I too once absolutely would not believe that Jesus of Nazareth was living in heaven as the Risen Messiah, and from thence could rule and influence His people on earth. In the perse-

cution of Jesus I acted as a Sadducee, although I was a Pharisee,
and denied Him in all His reality whom with much false ἀκρίβεια I
desired to find in the Scriptures. *I verily thought,* ay indeed, *with
myself*—that is, even in these false opinions, with an inward truth
and honesty which did not exist in all the persecutors of Jesus—
that I (and generally every one) *ought to do many things contrary to
the name of Jesus of Nazareth.* In this δεῖν the apostle describes
his blind honesty even more strongly than in the ἐμαυτῷ, in which
it is only hinted at. He does *not* say, as we have it in the uncor-
rected German Bible, *I also;* for in many of the blinded enemies
of Jesus, their conscience loudly and clearly expressed that which
Gamaliel put as a caution to the consciences of the Sanhedrim
(ch. v. 38, 39) ; but they looked upon the matter in quite a different way—that they *must* forbid teaching in this name on account
of maintaining their own consistency, and so as not to be compelled
to do the righteous works " meet for repentance" (vers. 20, 21).
It was not so with Paul ; and although these feelings existed in
the inmost depths of his heart, into which Jesus afterwards cast
a beam of heavenly light, it was not with *consciousness ;* and this
constitutes the great difference between those who did know and
those who did not know what they did. Paul thought that, in
consequence of his obligation to aid Israel's salvation, he *must*
destroy the heretics and fanatics, and do all in his power against
the falsely honoured and adored *name* of Jesus, ignorant as he was,
that in this he was persecuting the living and glorified Jesus Himself, the Messiah.

Ver. 10. Ὁ καὶ ἐποίησα—καθὼς ἔδοξα δεῖν πρᾶξαι. The very
zeal of his mistaken opinions, as shown in actual persecution, was
a proof of his (to some extent) good conscience in the matter. He
thus even in this went beyond the many other revilers and calum-
niators, who did not make the outward persecution of the saints a
matter of heart and conscience. Paul did what he thought he was
obliged to do, first in Jerusalem, where he lived among his nation
(ver. 4) ; and many of the saints he shut up in prison. Πολλούς
follows the πολλά in ver. 9 ; and the emphatic ἐγώ denotes that *he*
personally did it from zeal, so that he singly made prisoners of
many. The fact that he here (*not* as in ch. xxii. 2, 5) calls the
Nazarenes *the saints,* is quite in harmony with the generally joyful
and testifying tone of this discourse ; it is also a prospective glance
to the words of the Lord Himself in ver. 18, in which He gives to
believers in Him the title of ἡγιασμένοι. But the apostle says,

πολλοὺς τῶν ἁγίων, and thus describes the then existing and former confessors of Jesus together as those who, as God's saints, in the power of the Spirit and of love, had shown themselves to be in opposition to this conscience of Paul's, indeed as *the* true saints exclusively, as contrasted with all the rest of the Jews. He here employs for the Nazarenes this honoured title, so esteemed in the Old Testament, showing that he looks upon *them* as the only true Israelites before God, and considers anything done against them as impious and wicked. The language is fundamentally the same as that used by Paul in Gal. i. 13, " the church of God," the true church, in contrast to the " Jews' religion"—'Ιουδαϊσμός—which he had just before named.—*Having received authority* (for this unrighteous persecution of God's saints) *from the chief priests*, the great authorities in Israel. *And when they*—a great many of whom I had imprisoned for this purpose—*were put to death ;* this seems the natural connection here ; and it is incorrect to say that the plural—after the preceding forcible plural πολλούς—stands for the singular just because Luke in ch. vii.-ix. tells of the death of Stephen only. We are here told by Paul's lips of " many." Standing between the previous πολλοὺς and the πολλάκις αὐτούς, and αὐτοῖς occurring afterwards, this αὐτῶν cannot possibly refer to one single case only. The διωγμὸς μέγας in ch. viii. 1, and ἐμπνεῖν ἀπειλῆς καὶ φόνου in ch. ix. 1, point to much that is not related by Luke; as, for example, the " compelling to blaspheme," the mention of which immediately follows. Many therefore, besides Stephen, may have attained to the martyr's crown.

What share does Paul now ascribe to himself in the putting to death of the saints? Κατήνεγκα ψῆφον—*calculum adjeci, sententiam meam addidi.* This expression certainly admits of our understanding an actual delivery of his vote as a judge; but yet, looking at ch. vii. 58 and xxii. 20, it is impossible to think that the νεανίας had then a seat in the council. We must therefore take the words in a more general sense, as meaning " I agreed with them," which would be a stronger way of putting the " consenting" in ch. xxii. 20 and ch. viii. 1. For we must, of course, consider that he *principally* alludes to Stephen, the first and most notable martyr, whom also Paul specified before the Lord in ch. xxii. 20. We must, however, by no means overlook and fail to apply what is implied in Paul's language, viz. that he acted *as if* he had been a judge in the matter. Paul desires to intimate most forcibly, that his guilt before God is just as great as it would have been if he had formally assisted in the condemnation. It is as if he said, " In my fervid zeal, I gave, at least in thought and wish, my *suffragium*, just as much as if I had sat in judgment as the others."[1] And this was not all : by his bitter accusations, his fervid exciting language, etc., Saul actually *acted* overtly, so much as in him lay, not only as a witness, but even as a *judge of life and death*, and, as Hess says, " helped in carrying out the sentence of death."

Vers. 11, 12. We have before alluded to the reason why Paul on this occasion again tells the story of his heavenly vision, and why this seal of all the testimony of the living ministry of the Lord is given *three times* by Luke in his Acts of the Apostles. He who thinks that he can destroy this testimony—he who continues to entertain no sense of the indisputable power of proof of the conversion of Paul—must be classed by us (as far as human opinion can go) as almost at least among the obdurate. This was, in fact, the *last* testimony which the Saviour allowed to be brought before the obdurate Jews ; henceforward there is none more forcible than this.

The first journey of the persecutor, ever anxious as he was to extend his persecutions to " strange cities," constituted his last steps in the path of blindness. On this journey he was met by the inconceivably wonderful and adorable *light*—that light which was to transform his inmost being, and turn him into the right way. On this occasion Paul relates some particulars of his blindness, in which he, the persevering chief persecutor of God's church, went beyond all their other foes. He not only *punished them oft in every synagogue* (of Jerusalem), in which they were " scourged" (Matt. x. 17), but also *compelled them to blaspheme* ; that is, by all kinds of tortures caused them to forswear their Lord and Saviour, and thus to renounce their reverence for Him. A devilish masterpiece of malice this, which in subsequent persecutions of the followers of Jesus was often repeated. Perhaps it was but a small number who thus allowed themselves to be compelled by Saul " to blaspheme ;" for in later times a Pliny writes : " Quorum nihil cogi posse dicuntur, qui sunt re vera Christiani." But yet *some* fell, as is distinctly shown by the decisive word ἠνάγκαζον, together with τιμωρῶν.[2] What a heart-stab it must have been for the feelings

[1] To which must be added something of an official character, in Saul's taking care of the clothes, on which we remarked in considering ch. xxii. 20.

[2] We have no right to fall short in our interpretation, and say that it only means, " did all that he could in order to compel them."

of a Christian, to think that by his means saints had been forced
by torture to blaspheme! Paul, to whom " the grace of the Lord
was exceeding abundant with faith and love" (1 Tim. i. 14), fully
and deeply felt all the horror of what he then did, but yet had
sufficient *faith* in the complete certainty of his forgiveness, to
enable him to make public mention of this wickedness ; and by
his *love* he is forced to add all this blasphemy of the saints, as his
present confession calls it, to the sum of his own pardoned sins,
using the words, " I *compelled* them." Having thus arrived at the
very pinnacle of his blindness, he characterizes himself as *mad*, or
furious against them, and connects with it the last stage in the
progress of his persecution : *I persecuted them even unto strange
cities*. The journey to Damascus came under our consideration
in ch. xxii. ; we shall therefore only refer to anything which is
specially brought forward in this narrative. The καί after ἐν οἷς
in ver. 12 might be understood as pointing out that Saul had
visited other " strange cities" with a view to persecution ; but the
connection of ch. viii. 3 (which, on account of the word " houses,"
and what follows in ver. 4, can only apply to Jerusalem) and
ch. ix. 1, 2, as well as ch. xxii. 5 (in which καὶ εἰς Δαμασκόν is
equivalent to καὶ εἰς τὰς ἔξω πόλεις in the passage we are considering), clearly shows that Damascus was the first " strange city"
to which he travelled ; so that the καί here must be more generally
connected with the comprehensive ἐν οἷς.

Vers. 13, 14. It was not merely power and right, but also a
command (ἐπιτροπή, *commission*), which Saul received from the
chief priests on earth, ordering him to punish the saints. But the
merciful and mighty High Priest above came out from within the
veil, into which He had entered for us ; and the enemy, converted
into a patient witness, soon stands endowed with the divine power
of faith, and the command and commission of God the Saviour,
who was his hope (1 Tim. i. 1). One heavenly apparition converts
him to faith, another ordains him as a witness ; the two, however,
are but one " heavenly vision" of the living One whom he now
obeyed. The fresh address, Βασιλεῦ, after εἶδον, denotes the commencement of the account of the great vision ; and now the
omnipotent " from heaven" overrides the mere earthly title.
Compare how again, in ver. 19, Paul's bounden obedience to the
" heavenly vision" overrides his reverence for the earthly king.
But this light, which flashed down from heaven into Paul's darkness, was not like the mere rays of the sun : it shone down from

the upper heavens *above the brightness of the sun.* Jesus on the mount of transfiguration " did shine *as* the sun ;" and at " the end of this world" the righteous, too, shall " shine forth *as* the sun" (Matt. xvii. 2, xiii. 43) ; but the glory of the revelation of the irresistible One must now flash down brighter even than the brightness of the sun. The order of the words (in the Greek) is also very significant : *At mid-day—in the way—I saw, O king— from heaven—above the brightness of the sun—shining round about me—a light—and on them which journeyed with me.* The light shone round about both him and them ; but according to ver. 14, although all fell to the ground, Paul *only* heard or understood the voice speaking to him. The fact that in ch. ix. and xxii. Saul alone is said to have fallen to the ground (ch. ix. 7, indeed, stating that those who accompanied him *stood*), is no contradiction to the present narrative. On this occasion, the *commencement* of the vision before the voice is spoken of ; before, it was the end of the vision, after the voice, which was in question, when Paul himself had again stood up. It is also most natural that those who tra- velled with Saul likewise fell to the ground, and also that they again stood up when they saw the latter rise. It is now for the first time mentioned as a highly important circumstance, that the voice spake *in the Hebrew tongue.* In ch. ix. Luke perhaps desired to keep something back for the two subsequent repetitions ; in ch. xxii. Paul spoke in Hebrew ; but now he was speaking in Greek, and very suitably expressly specifies the language in which Jesus spake to him from heaven.[1] In this mention of the language there is, in the first place, implied a forcible representation of the clearly audible, and therefore objective and perceptively real, character of the vision, as opposed to any mere inward mental suggestion, in which no particular language would be distinguishable. Secondly, herein is attested the identity of the Person who so spake at Nazareth, and on earth generally.[2] Lastly, however, and indeed the main point, the *sacred* language of God's chosen people, and consequently the choice of Israel, and the future reserved for them, is thus acknowledged from heaven by their Messiah and King. Ay, we must rejoice that He, whose Spirit knew and taught all languages, employed on this occasion the sacred lan-

---

[1] Alford well remarks, that Luke, by retaining in all three passages the form Σαούλ (not Σαύλε), desires to point out that Hebrew was spoken.

[2] Refer to what was said in our *Words of the Lord Jesus*, p. 16, as to the abiding humanity of Jesus, both in body and soul.

guage of His people. From this, too, we have reverentially to gather, that even in His heavenly glory He is the Son of *the chosen people* : that as a man, He is and remains a Jew; and as the Saviour of the world, He is and remains the Messiah of the Jews. And who can tell whether Agrippa, the half Greek and half Roman king of the Jews, hearing this account of the Hebrew utterance of the glorified Messiah, may not have felt and been compelled to feel all that directed him reprovingly to the exact fulfilment of all the words of the prophet in this Jesus of Nazareth?

But the most important matter, which is here told us for the first time, is the utterance of Jesus which follows His first words to Saul,—the two sentences together forming " the voice" which first arrested him in his path of error. Σκληρόν σοι πρὸς κέντρα λακτίζειν—קָשֶׁה לְךָ לִבְעֹט עַל הַדָּרְבֹנוֹת—*it is hard* (or injurious) *for thee to kick against the pricks!* It is now generally acknowledged that these words in ch. ix. are not genuine, and were subsequently introduced in an improper place. Luke, in the previous account, abridges his own narrative, leaving the full details to be related by the apostle himself. But in ch. xxii., in which the apostle only combined the chief features of the matter, he omits both the three days' fasting and praying, and also the words as to " kicking against the pricks," both of which concern the apostle's own innermost personality. In the passage we are considering, in which Paul opens his lips in the most joyful way to speak from his very heart, we consequently read this latter circumstance for the first time. The expression is a proverb derived from agriculture, from the plough and draught oxen which in dull obstinacy kick against the sharp-pointed goad of their driver—the only result being that they make the goad more painful to them, and wound their own feet. The fundamental meaning of the proverb, therefore, is a stupid and vain opposition offered to a superior power, producing thereby harm to the opposer, not merely generally (according to Grotius), " de his, qui res sibi male cessureas moliuntur," but those who strive *stupidly* against a superior power. In passages from the ancients we find it emphatically used as applying to opposition against the gods.[1]

---

[1] The following are remarkable passages :—Terence: "Nam quæ inscitia est, advorsum stimulum calces ? " Plautus : " Si stimulos pugnis cædas, manibus plus dolet." Euripides : πρὸς κέντρα μὴ λάκτιζε τοῖς κρατοῦσί σου. *Ib.* : θύοιμ' ἂν αὐτῷ μᾶλλον ἢ θυμούμενος πρὸς κέντρα λακτίζοιμι θνητὸς ὢν θεῷ. Pindar : χρῆ δὲ πρὸς θεὸν οὐκ ἐοίζειν, Φέρειν δ' ἐλαφρῶς ἐπαυχένιον λαβόντα ζυγὸν ἀρήγει. Ποτὶ κέντρα δέ τοι λακτίζεμεν τελέθει ὀλισθηρὸς οἶμος.

We perceive, therefore, that the sense of these words as used here by Jesus is in the first place an explanation of the previous sentence, " Why persecutest thou me ? " The meaning that was only hinted at in the conscience-piercing question is in the words following fully brought home to the understanding, and seems to say, " I am too powerful for thee." This is very suitably followed in ver. 15 by the declaration, " For I, this heavenly and glorious One, am Jesus, against whom with thy persecution thou vainly kickest, but only to thine own hurt." The words σκληρόν σοι (ἐστί) explain at once the question, τί με διώκεις, in some such way as Benson well expresses it, " Why persecutest thou me, who, as thou seest, am invested with such mighty power, which, if thou perseverest in thy contumacy, must ultimately destroy thee ? " But in this paraphrase something is intimated which we must further notice. The question may be raised, that Saul was already kicking against the pricks in his persecution of Jesus. But in reply, we may urge that hitherto he had not recognised Him *as the Lord*—he did not yet bear His yoke ; therefore in his hostility he did not as an ἄτακτος oppose an overwhelming divine τάσσειν (τέτακται, ch. xxii. 10). He only who recognises Jesus, and stands consciously under the influence of His Spirit, can in the full sense rebel against Jesus' sceptre. It is to some extent true, and we indeed allow it, that Jesus here first reveals Himself to Saul as the irresistible One—as He who bears in His hand the rod of iron, to execute sentence on all the heathen. But, on the other hand, we must not overlook the fact that the blindly striving sinner, although indeed he does not yet clearly perceive who it is that bears the rod, nevertheless observes and feels to some extent the superior power against which he is vainly and foolishly striving ; and that thus, from the angel-like countenance of Stephen, and the evident holiness of the saints, warnings and shocks sufficient for this end had come home to Saul's conscience, only *half-apprehended* indeed, but none the less *existing*. The more Saul raged against the church, the more indestructible did he everywhere find it ; the further his rage progressed, the less it seemed likely to attain its proposed end. Only a few of the Nazarenes " blasphemed : " the greater part, even under their torments, testified to the name against which he desired " to do many things ; " indeed this persecuted name, in its living, miraculous power, showed itself to be the sceptre of a Lord against which he vainly " kicked," and only more and more corrupted and injured his mind and conscience. But Jesus now all at once reveals and gives to the persecutor *light*—in the first place as to the past. He had actually proved Himself to be, and now shows Himself as, the irresistible One, so that Paul can no longer resist acknowledging Him. The question, "Why persecutest thou Me?" now contains the addition, "and thereby, in fact, persecutest only *thyself.*" This, therefore, is one view of the expression, according to which Jesus' words apply to the before-named persecution, and seem to say, "Why dost thou toil and trouble in persecuting a power that is incomprehensible to thee? Take care, and see how thou art circumstanced, and what thou art doing; thou art only kicking against my sceptre!" But from the moment that these important points are brought home to the conscience, they assume a more forcible sense, which is then for the first time entire and complete. They seem to say, "Wouldst thou now further oppose Me? Reflect how hard, useless, and vain it would be for thee so to do." And this reference to the *future* appears to us to be the *principal* signification of the wonderful words of the revelation, wavering as they do between the *past* and the *present.* We understand the translation of this passage as follows: "In the future it shall be hard, much harder than it has been, indeed impossible for thee, to further strive against Me. Perhaps even in past times thou hast been able to notice that, in dealing with the Nazarenes, thou hast had to do with a power which is superior to thine own. *Now* I will constrain thee in another way with my rod! Behold my sceptre! Dost thou now feel it, and wilt thou continue to oppose Me? Or wilt thou patiently accept *my yoke,* and be willing to turn in thy course, and to be employed in my service? Hitherto thou hast been a dull and obstinate ox under my yoke; yet my holy mercy has determined to make thee obedient, and woe, woe to thee if now thou followest not Me!" Thus, we think, the full meaning of Jesus' words may be amplified and paraphrased, although the expression of all the thoughts contained in them did not require many words. It is evident from ver. 19 that Jesus' words do not refer to the irresistibleness of grace. Σκληρόν has a different meaning from ἀδύνατον, and makes known only the difficulty and ruin which follow a vain opposition. The whole passage may perhaps be most intelligibly analyzed by connecting the assertion *interrogatively* to the previous question, as if to say, "Is it not true that it went hard with thee in opposing my power in my saints? Dost thou now perceive why this was so? It was my rod that was against thee and over thee!" But at the same time the promise is given:

" I will make it more and more hard and painful for thee if thou followest not Me!" Remark how Saul in ch. xxii. 10 immediately answers, "Lord, what shall I do? Turn me, and I will now follow Thee!"

We still have one thing to remark at the conclusion. Jesus, speaking from heaven, not only employs the Hebrew language, which He used on earth, but in lovely condescension deigns to speak to men in their own aphorisms, and to infuse a divine sense into a homely formula. Compare with this passage the figurative language of the letters to the seven churches in the Revelation of St. John, and rejoice that it is the self-same Jesus of Nazareth who, even on His Father's throne, remains faithful to His divinely-human wisdom of love, emphatically as *ours* for *us*.

Vers. 15, 16. Paul's question has been already commented on in ch. xxii. There it merely continues, "And He"—He who in the voice uttered the "Me"—"said." In the passage we are now considering, a proposed reading would convey the more joyful testimony, " *The Lord* said." Bengel thinks that in the declaration *I am Jesus*, the addition " of Nazareth" was omitted by the apostle from a feeling of forbearance for Agrippa, so as not to refer reproachfully to the hostility of the Herods against the Nazarenes; but in this idea he must overlook the fact that this full name had been already mentioned in ver. 9, and mentioned indeed in connection with the practical enmity against it. We prefer to consider that, in the omission in ver. 15 of the full name as given in ver. 9, Paul is beginning the summing up of the result or purpose of the vision, in which summing up he blends his present revelation with those which follow in ver. 16. On the other hand, Bengel very strikingly calls attention to the significance that the words from heaven would have for Festus: "I am He, the Jesus who was dead," who therefore still lives. Although bringing prominently forward no other portion of the Lord's utterance but the words, " *Arise, and stand upon thy feet,*" Paul desires to intimate all that we assumed in ch. xxii. to be the meaning of this expression, viz. the promise made at the end of the first vision, that he should be ordained to a new course of activity in the service of Jesus. This, too, may clearly be inferred from the words that follow: *For I have appeared unto thee for this purpose,* that thou shouldst henceforth *stand* before me as my minister and witness, through my deliverance and help. From the further details, so circumstantially related in ch. ix. and xxii., it is certain that Paul's ordination as an apostle to the Gentiles, which now immediately follows, was *not* communicated to him on the occasion of this first appearance to him of Jesus. This conclusion also is necessarily to be inferred from the facts of the case. Paul was, in the first place, directed to proceed to Damascus with instructions, the full purport of which was concealed from him ; and Ananias, to whom the Lord revealed His intention concerning Paul, communicated at first only in general that he was to be Jesus' witness to all men. It was not until three years afterwards that the Lord Himself said to His witness in the temple, " I will send thee far hence unto *the Gentiles*."

How, then, are we to understand the narrative given in this passage ? In the first place, as believing expositors, to whom it is not permissible to impute anything against the truth of the inspired word, we must protest against that view which either coarsely, or with a greater degree of delicacy, would make out that the Lord did not actually Himself thus speak to him who relates it. Can it be that the apostle attributed to the utterance of the Lord either his own subsequent thoughts, or (wonderful and groundless assertion !) the things which were so distinctly said to him by Ananias ? Although we may indeed allow—learning it, as we do, in so many instances from the different accounts in Scripture— that in God's word the time and letter are not matters of primary importance, and that consequently the apostle might with perfect justice, in speaking before Agrippa, unite the *words spoken by Jesus* at different times and places, combining them into one vision and address, we must, nevertheless, unconditionally maintain that all these words were actually *words of Jesus*. That either the sacred orator or penman could have elaborated his own thoughts and passed them off as the words of the Lord, is an idea which could only be entertained by one who had formed no adequate and comprehensive idea of the inward relation subsisting between these holy witnesses and their most holy Lord and Master. The form of words they might indeed supply, for the very reason that we are not directed to the mere letter of the Lord's words, but to their *sense*—the real *living word* contained therein ; but on every occasion the Spirit of truth must have *inspired* them with this *sense*, so that they were perfectly certain that it was actually the word of the Lord they were recording whenever they ventured to attribute any utterance to the lips of Jesus. Even then he suggested it to them, and they did not of their own accord attribute it to Him. The self-same apostle, who before the elders of Ephesus, in ch. xx.

35, with deep veneration contrasted with his whole discourse one single utterance of Jesus which He had spoken in His *lowliness* on earth, now before Agrippa would hardly ascribe to the *heavenly appearance of the glorified One* anything which He had not actually uttered.[1] This much, therefore, is sure, that the Lord had Himself spoken to the apostle the words that are given here in vers. 16–18. Although the Lord might not have spoken them at His first appearance, did He perhaps utter them on the occasion of the other vision which is related in ch. xxii. 17–21? This, too, can hardly be assumed, although it might be so plausibly said that the words here are only a continuation of the account which was suddenly broken off in ch. xxii. 21; for, in the first place, the promised *sending to the Gentiles* was there uttered in quite another connection, which had its own deep and necessary signification. It does not seem suitable that Jesus should have expressed that which is written in ch. xxvi. 17, immediately after the words in ch. xxii. 21. Next, it appears to us significant in ch. xxii. (as we there remarked), that the apostle is told that in Jerusalem they will *not* receive his testimony, but he is not yet told that the Gentiles *will* receive it; also that, in requiring obedience, and to crush all his objections, he is merely told, "Depart, for I will send thee." In the present passage, however, a great promise is given (in ver. 18) as to the result of his work among the Gentiles especially. Finally, in ch. xxii. it runs only, ἐξαποστελῶ σε (*Vulg.* "mittam"); but here it is, εἰς οὓς ἐγὼ νῦν (or νῦν ἐγώ) σε ἀποστέλλω (*Vulg.* "nunc ego"). There is at least sufficient ground for maintaining the νῦν as the right reading. We have therefore in this passage a subsequent fulfilment of that which was at first pointed out as future, consequently *another* vision of Jesus *after* that described in ch. xxii. 17.

Now as regards the words themselves.—*I have appeared unto thee for this purpose.* This is a summary of all the previous appearances of Jesus to Paul, including them all in their one aim and end —his appointment as a witness. It is exactly in this reference to

---

[1] There is a vast difference between "clinging slavishly to the letter and the isolated circumstances" (as Lechler says), and "being bound in reverence before the Lord to understand His own most high word as exactly as we can." What historian, or what faithful subject, when describing a mere ministerial rescript in a royal commission, would turn it into a direct cabinet order, giving such prominence to its *directness* as is done in this passage? But one might despair as to the rudeness of some learned divines, who, in all their "scientific" freedom, seem in matters of holy Scripture to forget the common laws of human society.

the matters of which Paul was to testify—viz. those things which he had seen, and those which were to appear unto him—that the various " visions and revelations of the Lord " (2 Cor. xii. 1) which were vouchsafed to him all coincide in one single *revelation* of the Son, whom he was to preach (Gal. i. 16). The apostle can appeal to this groundwork and source of his testimony as to one single " *revelation of Jesus Christ*" (Gal. i. 12),—a " heavenly vision" to which in faith he was " not disobedient" (ver. 19). The Lord Himself thus combines them all in one in saying, *For this purpose have I appeared unto thee* (before), *to make thee a minister and a witness both of those things which thou hast seen, and of those things in the which I will appear unto thee* (yet further). ῎Ωφθην and ὀφθήσομαί σοι are the beginning and end of the sentence. Paul, therefore, in combining in his narrative all the different visions, is only following the Lord Himself, and the spirit of the Lord's words. Προχειρίσασθαι evidently means here to *ordain*, appoint, nominate, or to communicate a destined commission, exactly as in ch. xxii. 14. With regard to this solemn ordination of Paul to be an apostle, we have already spoken in reference to the question as to Matthias' apostleship in ch. i. 26. He who at the first vision was described as an ox impatient of the goad, has now for a time so well submitted to the " bit and bridle" (Ps. xxxii. 9), that he can receive the most solemn dedication and confirmation of his apostolic office from the lips of his Lord. In this ordination—which, as it were, rises in ascending stages—the Lord seems to us to acknowledge lovingly the three ordinary steps of office in the church : first *minister*, then a mere *witness*, next a *witness of things seen*, or an *apostle*. As if Paul already stood in the first two positions, the Lord now expressly consecrates him not only to be a minister (cf. ὑπηρέτης, ch. xiii. 5), but also to be a witness (cf. μάρτυς, ch. xxii. 20) ; and not as a mere witness only, but as a witness of that which he *had seen* and *was to see*, consequently as an *apostle*,—an apostle, indeed, who was distinguished by continuous visions of the Lord, whilst the others testified only of that which they *had seen* up to the time of the ascension. Paul, then, was to be a special eye-witness of the glory of Jesus ; Peter, on the contrary, though the chief of the former twelve, only calls himself " a witness of the *sufferings* of Christ, and also a *partaker* of the glory *that shall be revealed*." Remark, too, how through this one among the apostles, who was " born out of due time," who calls himself the " least among the apostles, that am not meet to be called an apostle," through " the grace of God" more was done than was vouchsafed to all the rest (1 Cor. xv. 8–10). Refer again to our remarks on ch. i., and decide each in his own mind who it was that was ordained *by Jesus* to be a fellow with the eleven—Matthias or Paul.

Vers. 17, 18. It is very clear that the word ἐξαιρεῖσθαι cannot here be equivalent to ἐκλέγειν, and mean to *choose*, to *select*, although, strangely enough, many (as *e.g.* Schleusner's *Lexicon*) so interpret it. Elsewhere it often means *to select*, and in many places in the Greek Old Testament it corresponds with the Hebrew נָתַן; but in the Acts of the Apostles it means *to deliver* (ch. vii. 10, 34, xii. 11, xxiii. 27; cf. also Gal. i. 4). Very frequently, also, the Septuagint has it for הִצִּיל, הָלַץ, פִּלֵּט, מִלֵּט; and in the whole of the New Testament it nowhere means to choose. The foolish reason given in the interpretation of Hesychius, that Paul here expressed in a different way the σκεῦος ἐκλογῆς of Ananias (ch. ix. 15), has been already dismissed; and the preceding προχειρίσασθαι shows us the very reverse, that the choice cannot follow the ordination, at least the words must then have been in the aorist. And what is there to tell us that Paul was thus selected and chosen *from the Jews and from the Gentiles?* What is there, too, to tell us that he was selected from *all men?* But why is this paraphrase used? Paul was, in fact, chosen from the Jews, and not from the Gentiles. Thus much we urge against an incorrect exegesis, which by wrongly applied philological consideration has made its way even into the lexicons. Nothing can be more suitable here than the promise of *assistance* against the plots, chiefly of the Jews, but also of the Gentiles. Paul himself refers back to *this* promise, when in ver. 22 he prides himself in "having obtained help from God" (ἐπικουρίας τῆς παρὰ τοῦ Θεοῦ), by which he continued to *stand*, according to the Lord's first words (ver. 16). If we combine the *promise* and the *sending*, which immediately follows, we have in the ordination of the twelfth apostle those two main points which we also find in that of the eleven ("Go and teach all nations; . . . and, behold, I am with you"). It may be asked whether the οὕς applies to "the people" and the Gentiles together, or only to the Gentiles. Bengel refers it to both, comparing it with vers. 20 and 23; he also, in ver. 18, connects specially with Israel the "darkness" and the "forgiveness of sins," and with the Gentiles "the power of Satan" and the reception of the "inheritance," just as in ver. 20 "repentance" and "turning to God" may also be thus assigned. In our first edition we strongly opposed this view; but we subsequently withdrew this opposition. We formerly found the principal grounds of our adverse opinion in the relation between this vision and that mentioned in ch. xxii. 17. If Paul on a former occasion received a charge to leave Jerusalem, because the Lord desired to send him far away unto the Gentiles, how could the Lord subsequently send him to "the people" and to the Gentiles? These discrepancies are, however, reconciled, inasmuch as on the former occasion Jerusalem only was expressly spoken of; and on the other hand, Paul, even as the apostle to the Gentiles, retained his mission to the people of Israel. In his epistles, we find Paul testifying of one mission as well as the other; and in Acts ix. 15 (cf. ch. xxii. 15) exactly the same thing is pointed out. The apostle, who is here relating his story to king Agrippa, but also to Festus, who belonged to the *Gentiles*,[1] speaks just as decidedly of his calling as the apostle of the Gentiles, as he had already done before the Jews in ch. xxii.; but as he is now preaching in part, indeed principally, to the Jewish king, he immediately (in ver. 20) goes on to speak of the application of his ministry to both Jews and Gentiles together, and in ver. 23 refers to the words of Jesus: "unto the people and to the Gentiles." Although the promised result (ver. 18) of his preaching was fulfilled in a proportionately much less degree as regarded Israel, nevertheless, always and everywhere, there was a selection, whenever the path to the Gentiles led through the synagogue, or the testimony of the Gentiles reacted on Israel (Rom. xi. 5-7, 13, 14). Assuredly, therefore, the "*delivery* from the *people*," preceding the *sending* therein presupposed, is also meant for them.

The important and deep purport of the divine words in ver. 18, and how they are still to be taken to heart by every one who is sent out as a messenger of Jesus, and to be adopted as his personal instructions for his ministry, might be expanded into a little volume, so clearly is it shown that the Lord Himself spoke these words. The one matter, properly speaking, with which Paul is charged, is *opening the eyes* of Jews and Gentiles through the words of his testimony. Any further result is to be contemplated by the apostle as the aim of his testimony, and to be striven for with all faithfulness on his part; but all he himself can do, is to

---

[1] In considering ch. xxii., we quoted Zeller's statement as to the threefold narrative. But that (according to Baumgarten) Agrippa is also to be looked upon as a heathen king, and indeed represented to Paul the presence of the emperor, appears to us rather a strange idea.

bring before the eyes of the blind the awakening light of true
knowledge. He indeed cannot actually " turn them," nor can he
give them " forgiveness of sins," and the " inheritance" of the
saints. To effect these ends, free-will and God's mighty power
must work together both in Jew and Gentile, in the faith which
is inspired by God's power, and is confirmed and strengthened by
Him for His own aim, the salvation of their souls. Indeed,
Bengel's remark is most essentially true, that even the ἀνοῖξαι
refers to the action of the Lord, who sends His minister; for
certainly it is He alone who gives " light to them that sit in darkness" (Luke i. 79), and alone does and confers everything which is
to be done or conferred. Bengel takes the words τοῦ ἐπιστρέψαι
transitively (as Luke i. 16, 17; Jas. v. 19, 20; also Acts xiv. 15
and iii. 9, as we interpret it), and would refer them to Paul, and
τοῦ λαβεῖν, on account of the αὐτούς with it, to the recipients of
the preaching; so that the following catenation would arise:

> *I* send thee—
> in order *through thee* to open their eyes—
> *so that thou* mayest turn them—
> *so that they* may receive, etc.

But the inner substance of the words leads us to analyze them in a
different way, and in the ἐπιστρέψαι and the λαβεῖν to recognise
the conditions implied in man's freedom, and the endowment for it
promised by God's grace; both of which, indeed, are included in
the concluding words, " by faith which is in Me;" that is, through
a confident turning to Me, the giver of forgiveness and the inheritance, in the way of sanctification, by the power of my grace. So
that we should arrange the catena thus:

> *I* send thee—
> *that thou* mayest open their eyes—
> *in order that they* may be turned—
> *and may then* receive, etc.

This conception of the word ἐπιστρέψαι is corroborated in two
ways. Firstly, through the close connection it has with the
opening of their eyes ; for the first thing which any one would do
whose eyes were opened to his wretchedness and the path of error
he was walking in, and indeed the natural result of his recognition
of the fact, would be to *turn away* from his wretchedness in search
of help, from his path of error to the way of salvation now pointed
out to him (compare the same connection in Luke i. 79). Secondly,
because it is more usually and frequently said of the Gentiles, that

they turn to God (Acts xv. 3, 19; 1 Thess. i. 9; and here, in ver.
20, μετανοεῖν καὶ ἐπιστρέφειν ἐπὶ τὸν Θεόν). Also the idea that
the apostle was to open their eyes has its peculiar significance.
Firstly, through the unmistakeable reference to that which the
Lord had done *in him*, and, by the restoration of his outward and
material blindness, had most clearly prefigured. Paul was now, as
it were, to deal with all men (ch. xxii. 15) as Ananias in the Lord's
name had dealt with him, and to say, " Brethren, the Lord hath
sent me that ye may receive your sight, and may be filled with the
Holy Ghost." Next, we have here the description of something
which the testimony can and has to do to men against their wills;
consequently of the real official charge which is carried out, even
when the intended aim of " turning" remains unfulfilled, through
the want of faith in the hearers. The apostle, through the power
of his word, bringing light and conviction, can open their eyes;
they, on the other hand, can obey the convincing testimony or not.
The Gentiles can *turn* from darkness to light; indeed, even the
doubly darkened Jews, who had been apostates from the light, can
turn again to it, because their eyes had been opened, and God's
light had shone upon them, to invite them to return to God. They
can *receive* the benefits of mercy, because they have believingly and
longingly turned to the original source of mercy. Lastly, they are
sanctified, because in the " forgiveness of sins" the groundwork
thereto had been proffered to them, and by the hope of the rich
inheritance an impulse is given to perseverance.

The first term by which the condition of all the unconverted is
here described (merely as a condition) is *darkness* (an expression
which of course chiefly applies to the heathen, but also as a cause of
shame to Israel also). All those, indeed, who have left the right
path are " walking in darkness and the shadow of death " (Prov.
ii. 13); every one also " who has lost the name of the Lord, in
whom the nations are to hope, and his God, on whom he might
rely " (Isa. l. 10). Without the light and life of men, without the
mercy of God in Christ, the state of the world is *darkness* (John
i. 5). But God, through His messengers, calls all those " who in
times past were not a people, but are now the people of God, out
of darkness into His wonderful light" (1 Pet. ii. 9, 10). God
says to Christ, and the ambassadors in Christ's stead: "I give
thee for a covenant to the people, for a light of the Gentiles; to
open the blind eyes, to bring out the prisoners from the prison, and
them that sit in darkness out of the prison-house " (Isa. xlii. 6, 7).

The commencement of " turning," based upon man's free obedience of faith, which as the first step is called conversion, is in itself not a complete change of condition, but yet in it everything is commenced : both the evil cause of the darkness is revealed, and also the glorious aim of the divine light is shown (afar off at least), to the opened eyes and the anticipating heart. The *clear perception* of this evil cause and this glorious aim is a second stage of conversion, in which it becomes complete and known. For this purpose the Lord's holy word further points out the origin of the darkness (viz. " the power of Satan ") and the source of the light, with which the glorious aim is ultimately to become one *in God.* What is it that the sinner first sees in this new light ? That his darkness arose from the " power of Satan," and that God is the light to which he now " turns" from Satan's bondage. All darkness is, as Isaiah says, a prison-house, and its fetters and chains are the prison of hell (2 Pet. ii. 4 ; Jude 6). Mark well, ye that think that the Lord spoke on earth *of a Satan* only to please the Jews ! The Lord here, speaking from heaven, directs and teaches not merely the apostle himself about Satan, under whose kingdom and authority all men must remain unless they turn to God, but He also commands him to preach among *all the Gentiles,* that with all earnestness they should guard against the *power* of *this Satan.*

It is, besides, worthy of remark, that in contrast to the " power of Satan," it merely says " unto God ;" for the name of God alone is sufficiently powerful to obtain the victory over all " power." God's might is not an enslaving fettering, like Satan's power. " The light" is not merely another prison-house, into which man passes out of the prison-house of darkness ; and we shall not become the slaves of God, as we have before been the slaves of Satan and of sin. In the light there is freedom ; with God there is the inward power of the Spirit, changing the freedom itself, and making it truly free. He who is delivered from the power of Satan, in which he lay enchained, is " translated into the kingdom of God's dear Son" (Col. i. 13) : he treads an open, free path, the course of which ultimately leads straight on to God. With the first " turning" to this God of love, with the first step on the way leading to mercy, commences our *receiving* from Him : whoever *turns* to God, begins to *receive.* The first mercy (which we receive only under the condition of repentance), the great gift and favour arising from the atonement of the second Adam for the sin of the first, the basis of every life that is sanctified in God, is the *forgive-*

ness of sins. For although we stood under the power of Satan, we nevertheless acquiesced in it until we turned away from it to God: we have rejected many a preparatory beam of true light, and have loved the darkness rather than light. Forgiveness will wash away every sin with the blood of the Son in the love of the Father, and a new life is begun in God's light. The aim of this forgiveness, the last gift completing all the former ones, is the *inheritance*, the child's portion in the glory of the Father, now to be restored to the again accepted son, which the Father has reserved and destined for us, so that every one may receive the full glory of God.

We see in Paul's testimony to the Gentiles why the Lord first names the *beginning* and *end* of His mercy, and afterwards the *sanctification*, which is only possible through a knowledge of the destined aim, although the former certainly contains the condition for the attainment of the latter. Sanctification, which proceeds only from God's perfecting, and is accomplished at His will, is much more a *gift* of God than the *turning* to Him, which must precede all giving on His part, and in its *first* volition is promoted by us, being afterwards brought to completion by God's impulse; and yet sanctification, inasmuch as we must acquiesce thereto with full and firm fidelity of faith, is also a continuous condition of all future gifts. We receive the first gift, the forgiveness of sins, so that we may not sin (1 John ii. 1). If we do not correspond to this its aim, it will be taken away from us, like the kingdom of God from Israel. The last gift, the "inheritance in light," is to be received by the "saints" only (Col. i. 12); for "without holiness no man shall see the Lord" (Heb. xii. 14). Not among all that are called, for many do not "give diligence to make their calling and election sure" (2 Pet. i. 9-11), but "among them which are sanctified," shall we, if we are saved, find our entrance into the everlasting kingdom and inheritance. The οἱ ἡγιασμένοι whom the Lord here speaks of are the οἱ ἅγιοι whom Paul had previously mentioned in his narrative (ver. 10), only they are now described in the participial form, as having fully become "saints." Lastly, the community with all them that are sanctified, and the participation with them in the inheritance, is an essential exaltation of his blessedness,—an idea which the apostle had already brought prominently forward in ch. xx. 32 by the addition of the word πᾶσι.

The conclusion of the Lord's words is all that now remains for us to consider: *by faith that is in me.* This faith evidently applies neither to the *sanctification* only, nor merely to the gifts of *forgive-*

ness and the *inheritance*, but also and equally to the *turning* to God's light, which is henceforth to be effected by believing in the name of the Son. The Lord therefore comprehends all in one, and points out the *one and sole great means* for attaining all.[1] Faith, as spoken of here, and also in many other passages of the New Testament, embraces not only the *confidence* wherewith we turn to God in Christ, not only the *trusting apprehension* by which we attain our justification, but also the firm and persevering fidelity which, after " the course is finished," receives the " crown of righteousness" (2 Tim. iv. 7). All the conditions of the believer are but steps of the faith growing and working in us, through which we become free, righteous, holy, and glorified. And this faith is faith *in Jesus*, as He Himself emphatically says; πίστει, *by faith*—τῇ εἰς ἐμέ, *which is in Me*. Faith in the *name* preached draws us from the power of darkness, so that we turn to and approach God, the Father of this Saviour; faith in *Him who died* for us gains for us forgiveness of our sins; by faith in the *Risen One* we acquire and retain the power of sanctification; finally, faith in the glorified One in heaven gives us a sure hope of the inheritance which He will one day grant us, " to sit with Him on His throne" (Rev. iii. 21). Thus by faith in the *whole Christ* shall we attain our *whole salvation*. Mark well how majestically the Lord declares that nothing but faith in *Him* can lead to God and to God's glory. Ay, verily, He to whom the Father has given all things for us, He works out everything in us, gives everything to us, and finally grants us the inheritance; and to this loftiest and most difficult aim we are surely and certainly led by the simple and easy path of faith in Him, which faith is all that He requires of us; so that *through it*, step by step, He Himself may be able to work out in us and give us all things.

Vers. 19, 20. The apostle has now concluded the narrative of his heavenly calling to faith and testimony—a calling vouchsafed by Him in whom he believes, and of whom he testifies. " He Himself," the apostle seems to say, " has told me, I am He; how then can I not believe in Him?" " He Himself has commanded me to preach faith in Him; how then can I fail to testify of

---

[1] *Faith*, in its closer sense and usual acceptation, inasmuch as (as ch. xx. 21) it follows repentance, is the hand and the ὄργανον ληπτικόν to grasp everything; but repentance and turning to God only result from a preliminary faith in the truth and reality of the word of the Lord which calls forth the repentance, and of the promise which allures thereto.

Him ? " With great emphasis, therefore, he continues : *Where-upon, O king Agrippa* — on account of this revelation of and sending by the King of all kings, and although all the kings and emperors on earth condemned it—*I was not ἀπειθής to the heavenly vision !* We have already remarked how the words οὐράνιος ὀπτασία, referring back to vers. 13 and 14, embrace all that Paul believes in and testifies to as *seen.* 'Απειθής, however, scarcely means *incredulous* (for how can a man disbelieve that which he was compelled to *see ?*) ; it is better rendered *disobedient,* and refers chiefly to the second part of the vision—the command to testify —as indeed we may gather from Paul's subsequent language in ver. 20. After such a vision of the Living One, it need hardly have been said that Paul believed in the life of Jesus Christ : he was compelled to believe, as some day all will be compelled, when He comes in the clouds of heaven, and every eye shall see Him, those even that persecuted and pierced Him. But that he was not silent about this his belief, but testified of it " to small and great," that they also might believe—this is what he means to say, grounding it upon the command of the Lord Himself. What ! could it have been possible that Paul should *not* have obeyed the Lord's charge ? By all means, just as possible as the prophet Jonah's flying from the face of the Lord, because he feared to preach in Nineveh. The Apostle Paul, who thoroughly knew the hostility of the Jews against the name of Jesus of Nazareth, might well have been not only influenced by a fear of the same kind, but also kept back from his ministry. And although Ben-gel's words, " Ne Pauli quidem conversio irresistibilis fuit," are only true in a certain sense (for it was at least in the first place psychologically impossible that Paul could further persecute Jesus, although his heart might still deny Him), this much is perfectly clear, that he might have conferred much with " flesh and blood " about the testimony. But in Gal. i. 16 he says, that with regard to his call to preach the gospel among the Gentiles, in the first place he " conferred not with flesh and blood." " The Lord God hath opened mine ear, and I was not rebellious, neither turned away back. I (willingly, like Jesus) gave my back to the smiters. . . . For the Lord God will help me, therefore shall I not be con-founded " [1] (Isa. l. 5-7). This was perhaps Paul's thought. The same vision which had given him new light had also endowed him

---

[1] Where the LXX. has ἐγὼ δὲ οὐκ ἀπειθῶ. Grotius also remarks, " Respi-citur locus, Jes. l. 5."

with new power, and he trusted in the deliverance which had been promised him (ver. 17). This reference is also implied in the expression ὅθεν; Bengel therefore appropriately remarks: " Inde facultatem accepi obediendi." In the *negative* expression, the apostle hints at the temptation to disobedience which would be caused by the persecution stirred up by the nature of his testimony, and so goes on to a statement of its purport. *I showed*—and, in the first place, to *whom?* Henceforth unremittingly to all to whom I was sent; and as the *first* appearance of Jesus was near Damascus, naturally enough first to the (Jewish) inhabitants of that city (ch. ix. 20–22); then, after a quiet sojourn in Arabia and other places (which are not recorded), I came to *Jerusalem* (ch. ix. 26–29; Gal. i. 18); next, in all the regions of the land of Judea (which is *not* contradicted by Gal. i. 22; cf. the subsequent journey, Acts xi. 25, 30, xii. 25); lastly, according to the Lord's *later* command, chiefly to the *Gentiles* (from Acts xiii. 46 onwards). What was it that Paul preached to all men without exception, at Damascus as at Jerusalem, in the land of Judea and also among Gentiles? He preached that with which the Lord had charged him, which had indeed been first effected in himself, viz. *repentance*, or a change of mind—a repentant turning *away from* all wicked works, and *to* God. Paul thus explains what was said in ver. 18; μετάνοια from wicked works is " a turning from darkness" (John iii. 19), and ἐπιστρέφειν ἐπὶ τὸν Θεὸν is that literally which was spoken by the Lord. The state which in ver. 18 was considered as a *receiving* of forgiveness, and an " inheritance among them that are sanctified," is now described as a *doing;* thus certifying to king Agrippa that the apostle, in Jesus' name, required of men not merely feelings and intentions of repentance and turning, but *works meet for repentance.* Thus, too, he testifies that, as we have already remarked (ver. 18), the sanctification resulting from faith is certainly *given;* but its *acceptance* is likewise required as a proviso, and the works required are those which correspond with a repentance from Satan's darkness and a turning to God's light, therefore *good* works, works of light, " wrought in God" (John iii. 21). The mention of the works has also another cause and aim. Paul here relates that he had preached this " turning to God" even to the Jews at Jerusalem and in the land of Judea; this being the message with which the Lord had charged him, both to *the people* and the Gentiles. He therefore desires to intimate that even God's chosen people were living in darkness as apostates from God, and thus mentions these *good works*, "the works of Abraham" (John viii. 39), which were altogether wanting in Israel, and had been in vain required from them by John the Baptist. This intimation is at once made perfectly clear, by his going on to tell how the evil-doers *for these causes* showed hostility to him, and persecuted him.

Ver. 21. Ἔνεκα τούτων contrasts sharply and emphatically with the preceding ὅθεν, and completes the clear disclosure of the whole state of the case. Jesus of Nazareth has Himself, in an undeniably heavenly vision, given me faith, and commanded me to testify; I *therefore* preach in His name that which is good and right—repentance towards God and diligence in good works. But Israel is apostate from its God, and is living in evil works, and will not entertain the idea of the "works meet for repentance:" *for these causes* the Jews accuse, nay, persecute me. This is the whole of my offence, that I require from every man good works wrought through repentance towards God in His Christ. This is the real cause of their hatred, and not the matters which they complain of and charge me with: I suffer persecution for the sake of truth and righteousness, as all the prophets in Israel once suffered it, and as my Lord and Master, the crucified One, for the sake of whose name I am now persecuted, just as I once persecuted Him in His saints. It was not because I wished to profane the temple, but because they hated my doctrine, that *the Jews caught me in the temple,* and from that time forward not only laid all kinds of things to my charge (vers. 6, 7); no, they also *went about to kill me,* they sought to lay hands upon me (διαχειρίσασθαι), to put me out of the way (cf. ch. v. 30, of Christ). They complain that I *attempted* to profane the temple (ch. xxiv. 6); but I have to complain of quite another kind of *attempt* on their part. Paul alludes primarily to the first concourse of the people (ch. xxi. 31) after his seizure in the temple; and secondly, to the oft-repeated cry that it was not fit that he should live (ch. xxii. 22, xxv. 15, 16, 24), and the plot discovered by his nephew (ch. xxiii. 12). Paul had not, perhaps, any exact information as to the repetition of this plot recorded in ch. xxv. 3; but thus much he certainly knew, that ever since the Jews seized him in the temple, up to the then present time, they had done all in their power to compass his death. For this cause he had declined (ch. xxv. 10) to acknowledge the jurisdiction at Jerusalem, and now before this solemn assembly says right out in comprehensive words that he well knew the feelings of the Jews were against him; at the same time, he lays no legal counter-accusation against them, but merely for his own vindication states what is true.

Ver. 22. But although they have *attempted* up to the present time, they have not *succeeded*. In spite of all, *I continue unto this day* in the power of my Lord, although an accused man (ver. 6), yet in the joyfulness of faith and hope *witnessing both to small and great*, and confidently fulfilling the "ministry which I have received of the Lord Jesus" (ch. xx. 24), as a preacher of righteousness even in bonds before both kings and lords. This is the cause. I enjoy the assistance promised me by God against all men—the people and the Gentiles. Ἐπικουρία is the hastening for deliverance on the part of one not present; and so far perhaps the word refers in the first place to the divinely sent interposition of Lysias the tribune, when the Jews sought to kill Paul in the temple, through which interposition he came into the power and under the guarantee of the Roman authority, which preserved him from all plots and "layings in wait" of the Jews. Of course, as the main ground of his trust, Paul means the continuous miraculous assistance of God, manifesting itself both outwardly and inwardly, which had hitherto turned all circumstances to his benefit, and had endowed him with the spirit of perseverance. Thus, being strengthened and encouraged by God's help, Paul now testifies to every one, both small and great; that is, probably, not to the *young* and *old*, but to the humble and distinguished in rank, even before Agrippa and Festus, and the most eminent men of the court. The whole of his testimony, in behalf of which he can appeal to the direct revelation of Jesus, can, however, likewise be vindicated as regards its truth for Israel through the *Scripture*, which was the testimony of the promise possessed by that people. Everything that Paul teaches and testifies of Jesus and the faith in Him, agrees most completely with "all things which are written in the law and the prophets" (ch. xxiv. 14); Paul's hope embraces nothing but the fulfilment of that which is Israel's real and true hope according to the law and the prophets (ch. xxviii. 20). The apostle protests that he asserts nothing but this—nothing new, arbitrary, or heretical; *none other things*, in fact, *than those which the prophets and Moses did say should come*. The *prophets* are here placed first (differently from ch. xxiv. 14 and xxviii. 23), so that the mention of Moses should follow with still greater emphasis as the prophet who had spoken of the sufferings and resurrection

of Christ. Paul in his long captivity might certainly have diligently searched the Scriptures, and through the enlightenment of
the Spirit might have discerned in the prophets a light for the
Gentiles, more and more clearly the more nearly he approached to
his journey to Rome. We may learn from the Spirit which inspired Paul where Moses said this which the apostle ascribes to
him. If our merely humanly taught theology had not fallen away
from the apostolical standpoint, and thus lost the simple appreciation of Jesus and the apostle's holy words, it would not so often
have denied the interpretations of the Old Testament which have
been disclosed to us by Jesus and the apostles as the purport of the
same.

Ver. 23. What, then, is this purport? Although always and
everywhere beaming down and reflecting itself in the most various
shades of light, yet it is only one and the same great *light*—the
sufferings and resurrection of Christ, and the salvation resulting
therefrom for all the world. Christ is the consummation of the
Old Testament, and the centre-point of the New. Here also, as
in ver. 8, the εἰ is not merely equivalent to *that*, although in this
case it more nearly approaches this signification : it by no means,
however, signifies as much as ὅτι, but hints at an *if* implied in the
that; so that there is here intimated a kind of *whether* referring to
the doubts of the Jews. We thus understand it : " I say nothing
but what the prophets have said ; but the latter have clearly enough
said whether (*i.e.*, in fact, in opposition to the doubts of others) the
Messiah should suffer, rise from the dead, and be a light to the
Gentiles, or not."[1] The prefixing of the disputed proposition παθη-
τὸς ὁ Χριστός, by the acknowledging of which in the Scriptures
the acknowledgment of Jesus was almost attained, leads us very
clearly to this view of the εἰ ; cf. Luke xxiv. 26. The blinded
Jews could not find in the Scriptures even the possibility of suffering and death for the Messiah ; Paul here certifies that he leaves it
to the correct interpretation, or rather unfolding of the prophetical
words, to decide whether Christ was promised as a suffering Messiah.
He is often, sometimes clearly and sometimes more obscurely, so

---

[1] So that the sentence beginning with εἰ (ver. 23) is not properly connected
with the λέγων of the apostle, but to the ἐλάλησαν of the prophets ; as the
παθητός, and still more the repeated μέλλει, show. Remark, besides, how
boldly and easily the apostle combines the three main points of the Messianic
prophecy which were then subjected to be called in question : the suffering (of
death) ; the resurrection ; and the being a light for the Gentiles.

promised and described—as a sufferer indeed even to *death*, and further as the first in the *resurrection* from the dead.   Paul, again, shows forth the great central point of the whole—the resurrection of the Messiah as the basis, source, and surety of the general resurrection ; and at the conclusion points out completely what he intended both here and in ch. xxiii. 6 and ch. xxiv. 15. Πρῶτος ἐξ ἀναστάσεως is equivalent to πρῶτος ἀναστὰς ἐκ νεκρῶν, the First-risen, " the First-born from the dead " (Col. i. 18).   But all who through the Spirit of holiness attain to His resurrection, are as the brethren of this First-born (Rom. viii. 29).   And in reference to this the Scriptures often prophesy of the new " seed," " people," and " generation," which in the power of God shall be born to this one (Ps. xxii. 31, 32).   According to prophecy, as understood by the apostolical spirit, from the resurrection of Christ results the light promised for all the world, the light of God, to which all the Gentiles were to turn, leaving behind them the darkness of Satan. In this expression Paul combines the first " opening of the eyes " with the last " inheritance of the saints in light :" here, too, "the life is the light of men ; " and in Him, the Son, is this life for all (John i. 4).   From the new life of the risen Son of man proceeds the new quickening light of God as the awakening " dew of herbs," as Isaiah expresses it ; and this is the true light of life, both for " the *people* and the *Gentiles*." Of the " light to lighten the Gentiles " Simeon had already spoken (Luke ii. 32) ; cf. Acts xiii. 47.   Christ Himself shows the light, by causing it to be shown by His messengers through His Spirit ; and the beginning of this manifestation was (according to the Scripture, Luke xxiv. 47) to take place at Jerusalem and among the chosen nation, although certainly afterwards it was to pass over to the Gentiles.   In con-cluding with the words, " unto the people and to the Gentiles," the apostle most clearly describes the kingdom of the Messiah recognised by him according to the Scripture, as a world-wide kingdom of sanctification and resurrection through the faith in Jesus ; and he embraces in what he says both Agrippa the *Jew* and Festus the *Gentile*.

Ver. 24. But the heathen Festus, when he hears the prisoner testify with such boldness of *a light for all nations* springing from the resurrection of this Jesus who was dead, and that in his testimony Paul appeals to the Jewish Scriptures in which the whole matter is clearly set forth, cannot refrain from interrupting him angrily, and crying out with a loud voice, " *Paul, thou art beside thyself !* "

The resurrection appears to him as strange a thing as it did to the Athenians (ch. xvii. 32), and he is promptly ready with his refusal of the great words of salvation. He discerns something unusual and extraordinary in Paul; but as he neither knows nor perceives the Spirit of grace from whom it proceeds, and is also actuated to some extent by peculiar hostility in his nature against the divine inspiration, he declares it to be *madness*. This word μαίνεσθαι cannot, as many think, be intended for a *fury of inspiration*, or (fanatically asserted) enthusiasm; but it must mean an actual, although not complete, *derangement of the intellect*, as we learn both from Paul's reply and Festus' additional remark. Festus feels, as he hastily utters his angry words, that by themselves they go too far, and are quite unfounded. Since the events recorded in ch. xxv. 6, he had sufficiently observed the wisdom and prudence of his prisoner, and must even now rem. much good sense in his so-called crazy language. In order to ress in a prudent and proper way the fitting name to that which was incomprehensible in this language, he characterizes the madness of the orator as *foolishness* arising from *too much wisdom*, or a distraction caused by too great an amount of erudition.[1] Τὰ πολλὰ γράμματα, the incessant study of thy " prophets " (vers. 5, 6, 22, 23), σὲ εἰς μανίαν περιτρέπει, has at last made thee mad, as at least thy present language shows. In Festus' second sentence we recognise a softening down of his language, especially in περιτρέπει, which, being in the present tense, is intended to denote a temporary tendency of Paul's learning to fanaticism—a momentary giving way of the intellect in the zeal of his discourse. It is as if he said, "Paul, thou art out of thy senses! Much learning causes thee now to talk nonsense!" We must not omit to remark that, as a novice in the land, Festus possessed no adequate idea of the Jewish Scriptures, and that he was perhaps annoyed at Paul addressing Agrippa only: he thus ascribes the πνεῦμα speaking in the apostle to πολλοῖς γράμμασι, and the living testimony of life to dead books. Oh that even now in Christendom there were not many such people, who know as little

---

[1] This remark is intended by Festus in all earnestness, and certainly not, as the ever good-natured Olshausen would have it, only as an " unseemly jest," intended to turn aside or destroy the impression made. It is certainly true that, in the strictest sense of the words, he did not consider the apostle " mad," or " out of his senses; " but notwithstanding this, our interpretation retains its value. That he for the moment acted passionately, and not in joke (as his " loud voice " also shows), is rightly stated by Chrysostom : θυμοῦ ἦν καὶ ὀργῆς ἡ φωνή.

as Festus of the contents and meaning of the Bible, and the Spirit of God therein! Oh that even now there were not many witnesses compelled to hear both from ignorant and learned a *Maívŋ* of this kind.

Vers. 25–27. Paul had previously said in ver. 11, that once in his life he had been "mad;" but now the clear light of his preaching is reviled by one whose eyes were not yet opened. What does he do? He brings forward the simple counter-proof in calm and well-ordered language, in which he ceases to address Festus for the present, and turns to Agrippa, with whom the whole speech had its due weight. At the commencement of the apostle's first testimony it was said that they were drunken; and Peter answered in the name of all, "These are not drunken." Just so the apostle now replies, *I am not mad.* The Master had Himself supplied the model for such a reply, when he said to the Jews, "I have not a devil" (John viii. 49). As a proof of what he says, now follows the humble and proper address, *Most noble Festus!*—κράτιστε Φῆστε (cf. ch. xxiv. 3),—a fitting parallel to the previous address, Βασιλεῦ Ἀγρίππα. Thou seest that I know well before whom I am standing, and that I am quite in my senses! *I speak forth the words of truth and soberness* even now at this moment, while I am calmly maintaining the fact. My words are words of *truth* as regards their purport, and of *soberness* (σωφροσύνης, Mark v. 15, Luke viii. 35, a contrast to nonsense) in their form and style: this is a twofold counter-assertion, answering to Festus' implied twofold accusation. By these two words Paul makes a profound distinction between the *subject* of his testimony and *his own personality*, and declares that he testifies quite reasonably of something existing, and is not speaking of some fanatical idea which was only to be found in his own feelings. The first question is the most important—whether his words are *true;* for there is plenty of rational and sober language used—indeed only too naturally rational, and clear as water itself—which language springs from an understanding sound enough in its way, but knowing nothing whatever of the real and highest truth. But the second question is also important; for the Spirit of truth desires us to utter His eternal truths with all due order and reason, and not in any mere fanciful, spurious, and crazy enthusiasm. With regard to this point, many a witness of Christ lays himself open to a similar reproach, without being able to reply as Paul replied. Ἀποφθέγγομαι—*I speak forth,* certainly not without the dignity due to my subject, and the warmth befitting a frank,

hearty speech. Παῤῥησιαζόμενος λαλῶ—I speak with joy and
confidence, without any detriment to my soberness ; and *that* is
what thou callest madness ! This joy of mine applies, however, to
the king, and not to thee—to the king, before whom thou thyself
hast produced me, and to whom alone, with thy permission, I now
speak.[1] To *thee* I should certainly have spoken ŏtherwise, and
should not perhaps have excited thee to so much anger.[2] It is only
because thou art not acquainted with all those things which in my
language to Agrippa I was allowed to presuppose, that they appear
to thee so nonsensical ! Remark how delicately the apostle intimates the right answer to Festus. " Thou dost not," he seems to
say, " understand the matter, and therefore perfectly clear language
is described by thee as nonsense." Three times does Paul describe
the subject of his testimony as being well known to Agrippa. The
first τούτων applies principally to the γράμματα mentioned by
Festus, consequently to the scriptural prophecies as to the Messiah's
kingdom. The second τούτων embraces both the prophecies of
Christ, and their fulfilment in Jesus. Lastly, the third τοῦτο lays
a stress only on the things which had taken place.

We thus get at the best arrangement of the clauses in this
appeal to Agrippa's knowledge. First, the king well understands
when I speak of God's promise to our fathers, of the aim and end
of all our worship, and of what the prophets and Moses have said
about the Messiah. We see here, and still more from ver. 27,
that Agrippa must actually have had a special knowledge of the
Jewish doctrines, and perhaps also of the Scriptures ; and on this
was grounded the joy and freedom with which Paul endeavours
to work upon his feelings. The apostle then goes on : *For I am
persuaded that none of these things are hidden from him*—can have
escaped him, or have remained obscure and ambiguous to him
(λανθάνειν αὐτὸν, as with Festus). That is to say, Agrippa will
understand me (and therefore will not pronounce it nonsense) when
I testify of my hope fulfilled in Jesus, and declare the Risen One
who has appeared unto me to be the Messiah of the Scriptures :

---

[1] Five times from ver. 2 to ver. 27 does the apostle address thus solemnly
this last king of the Jews—the first *king* before whom he had to bear witness.

[2] Thus much is true, and is implied in the apostle's words. We have nevertheless already remarked and acknowledged, that his discourse on this occasion
to a certain extent " preferentially paid a regard to the heathen intelligence"
(Baumgarten) ; because if, on the other hand, he had spoken before the king
alone, he would also have spoken differently.

he at least is well acquainted both with Judaism, and also with the new, much spoken of sect arising from it, the Christians, who venerate Jesus as the Messiah who has now come. Then follows with the greatest joy and freedom : *For this thing was not done in a corner,* but openly, before all the people. *" This thing,* in the knowledge of which (the key of the whole of my language to Agrippa) thou, O Festus, art deficient !—for thou knowest nothing of the teaching, sufferings, and death of Jesus, and of the testimony and confession of His resurrection and Messianic dignity by a great number of those who believe in Him." The apostle is now indirectly addressing the king, whose emotion during the discourse he had joyfully noticed. In the full consciousness of the notoriety of his cause, he describes Agrippa to the governor as a man who was well acquainted both with Judaism and Christianity, and could readily understand the assertion that Christianity was in fact true Judaism, and that Jesus was the true Messiah of the prophets. He now turns suddenly, yet confidently, to the king himself, and appealing to his heart and conscience in the presence of all that brilliant assembly, says, *" King Agrippa, believest thou the prophets?* I do not ask if thou believest me or in the 'heavenly vision ;' all I ask is, 'Believest thou the *prophets?'* I will then prove to thee what they say about Christ, and thou canst not help perceiving that this is fulfilled in Jesus : then thou wilt believe me, and also in Jesus." The holy witness, who, moved by a feeling of hope and love, is momentarily drawn to this king of the Jews, now grasps with a yet firmer hold the heart which he had already touched, if by any means he may induce him to acknowledge the true King of Israel.—*I know that thou believest!* Two different ideas are probably combined here. In the first place, I know that thou dost not decidedly deny the prophets ; but that, on the contrary, thou hast read them, and believed them (we have no information how the apostle knew this, but he distinctly says so here). Secondly, it may be taken half interrogatively, as if to say : Is it not a fact that thou believest now, when I point out Jesus to thee in the prophets ? I can perceive it in thee, that thou art almost inclined to believe that I have said nothing to thee beyond that which the prophets have said.

Vers. 28, 29. And behold, Agrippa, impulsively touched by these sudden words, proceeds without reluctance to tell before the whole assembly how his heart, or rather perhaps his mind, was affected. Paul's speech had scarcely penetrated his *heart:* his feeling was more a conviction of the understanding, an assenting faith, in which the apostle wished in the first place to confirm him.[1] Much is not required for me to believe what thou sayest, or *almost thou persuadest me to be a Christian!* A remarkable utterance this to be expressed by the last king of the Jews on the occasion of the last great apostolical testimony, which was indeed given before a Gentile authority. From ver. 29 we must assume that the ἐν ὀλίγῳ is used in the sense of *almost;* and it is quite certain that the language of the king is intended seriously, and not scoffingly, as many have viewed it ; as if it implied, " Dost thou fancy that with thy short discourse thou hast suddenly made me a Christian ?—that would be a rare success for thee."[2] This interpretation of the words is opposed not only by the fact that the apostle in ver. 29 takes them quite in earnest, but also still more in vers. 26 and 27 by Paul's παῤῥησιάζεσθαι and his confident οἶδα. Are we justified in giving the apostle credit for so little apostolical acuteness, that he should mistake a mocker for one inclined to believe, with whom perhaps some good might be done ? Would we ascribe to Paul so much common, weak good-nature, that after this manifest ridicule he should reply to Agrippa in a friendly way, just as if he were in earnest ? This is decidedly contrary to our view of the matter ; and we should prefer to give the king credit for being touched, at least as far as his understanding was concerned, by Paul's clear and powerful language. Thus, too, his utterance would contrast finely and significantly with that of Festus. Both speak freely from the momentary impression made upon them. One cries out, " Thou art beside thyself ; " the other, on the contrary, as if to make amends, confesses, " Almost thou persuadest me." Agrippa

---

[1] Mistaking the whole situation, and thus marring the whole history as regards its most significant point, Olshausen looks upon the words of the king as " something of a jocular character," but still as being assumed, because " he wished to conceal his internal emotion." We consider that this emotion was expressed without any concealment.

[2] Neander's interpretation is worse than Olshausen's : " Agrippa being annoyed at this confidence on Paul's part, replied to him, ' Truly, in a short time thou wilt make me a Christian.' " Baumgarten, alas, looks at it similarly, and considers the king's words " not devoid of a dash of irony : " " In so short a time, or with so few words, wilt thou persuade me to be a Christian ? " But whether ἐν ὀλίγῳ be taken either as *temporal* or *instrumental* (which is most doubtful), or however it may be rendered, μὲ πείθεις can never mean, " Thou *wilt* persuade me," or " *wilt* thou," etc. ; but it must simply signify what it expresses, that Agrippa feels and confesses at this moment the over-persuading power of the apostolic testimony.

seems to say, " If thou continuest to speak but a little longer so clearly and persuasively, I shall be forced to be a Christian. *Thou*, the captive chief of the Nazarenes, almost persuadest *me*, the king Agrippa, who indeed was only induced to hear thy defence from a feeling of curiosity." This is a graceful and candid confession to be made without hesitation before the whole of the distinguished company, without any fear of offending the governor, who looked upon Paul's words as merely the effect of madness. Added to this, the king, who had a thorough acquaintance with all these matters, uses the unprejudicial term of *Christian*, which, of course, was considered a milder and less abusive term than Nazarene. It was a name given to the new party, and was equivalent to calling them *Messianists*—those, namely, who believed that the Messiah had already come. This signification seems very suitable to Agrippa's meaning—that, like Paul, he almost believes that the Messiah had come (in Jesus). But even with the most friendly acceptation of Agrippa's candid words, they nevertheless have their weak and bad points, which do not lie so much in the language as in the thought and intention of the king. In the first place, he only says ἐν ὀλίγῳ, only *almost*, not yet *actually*, and thus at once recalls what he appears to allow. He remains standing without the doors of salvation, and will not enter in. Ah! he knew not how *much* this supposed *little* matter was, which was still wanting for his full conviction. In the next place, he only says, " Thou persuadest me, thou subduest me with thy forcible language ; " but a *persuasion* is something much less than *faith* or *conviction*, and may, as in this case, come to an end with the words which called it forth. Paul had asked, " Believest thou ? " But to this Agrippa was unable simply to reply, " I believe." But he leaves his belief in the prophets an undecided matter, and only confesses, not without some slight reproach to Paul's great energy, " *Almost* thou persuadest me." Lastly, the way in which he expresses the result of this persuasion is merely external—" to be a Christian," thus suddenly to join thy party—instead of saying, " As the result of my judgment, I believe the prophets, and therefore I believingly accept thy testimony about Jesus."

The apostle now replies with incomparable appropriateness to these *three shortcomings* on the part of Agrippa. With heartfelt and melancholy earnestness, he prays to God that the words might be true which the king had just uttered. But he does not forget to at once represent that becoming a Christian is not a thing of so sudden a character as might perhaps be thought. He does this both delicately and kindly, by holding out *himself* as an example of a Christian, and joyfully wishing that the whole assembly were in his position, with a graciously courteous exception of his state as a prisoner. " Ah, truly," he begins, with a heartfelt sigh, " I would, nay more, I pray to God, that thou wert a Christian." In this, Paul in the first place expresses his gratitude to the king for the candour he had shown, and manifests both the love which would supplicate for his salvation, and also the hopes he entertained from the present hearing. But, at the same time, he testifies to the fact that *becoming a Christian* was no such sudden matter, but that there was still much that was necessary to be prayed for. He also contrasts the merely human *persuasion* with the indispensable inward, vital *conviction*, which was to be wrought out by God only, and turns their attention from his own testimony to the Spirit who suggested it, who alone can make it effectual. Whoever becomes a Christian must be *made* one by God, and not by the mere persuasion of man. He now goes on to say, still more candidly, although with much delicacy of allusion,[1] καὶ ἐν ὀλίγῳ καὶ ἐν πολλῷ. These words might be understood, *almost or quite*, and ἐν πολλῷ would stand for *completely, entirely*,—thus continuing Agrippa's mode of expression by a contrast. This would appear to do very well, but it will not harmonize with Paul's intention. Paul desires to say, that in " becoming a Christian," it must *not* be merely a matter of *almost*, but of *quite* being so ; but here he would, on the contrary, say, " I would to God that ye were Christians, *either* almost *or* quite,"—thus making the *almost* a thing to be prayed for to God. We should then be compelled to say that the words were used ironically, as if to say that they might be almost or quite Christians, but that it was a matter upon which he did not then lay any special stress. But such irony, immediately following his earnest, heartfelt commencement, would be very unsuitable. We should therefore understand it : οὐ μόνον ἐν ὀλίγῳ, not only if *little* were wanting, ἀλλὰ καὶ ἐν πολλῷ, but even if there was *much* still wanting, even although they might be *far indeed* from being Christians, still I would wish and pray that they might become so. This rendering links on still better to Agrippa's words, at the same time adding force to them, and implying, " Although thou hadst said

---

[1] This allusion appears to us to prove that Agrippa did not intend his ἐν ὀλίγῳ to mean either " in a short time," or " in a few words," but as the apostle took it, *almost*, or *little being wanting*.

ἐν πολλῷ, instead of ἐν ὀλίγῳ, and hadst found *much* instead of *little*
preventing thy belief." Taken in this way, Paul's words are a
correction to Agrippa's, and almost go so far as to tell him that
much more than he thought was still deficient in him. And was
not this so? Whoever merely says to one of Christ's witnesses,
" Almost thou persuadest me," ought to say, instead of this, " I am
yet very far from believing." Every " almost" of this kind implies
a state where much is still deficient. But these words were uttered
not only to Agrippa, although in him much might still be wanting.
This ἐν πολλῷ applies with incisive truth chiefly to the " all that
hear me," especially to the governor. This last reference is decidedly in favour of our interpretation, and is quite lost in any
other. Bengel justly remarks: " *In multo* pertinet ad Festum,
cujus nomini Paulus parcit, et ad alios auditores, Festi similes, quos
ad fidem invitat : *in pauco*, vel *utrumvis*, ad Agrippam." In this the
" utrumvis" is not to be overlooked. In him who pronounced
Paul's testimony to be madness there was in fact much still wanting, and it is therefore as if the apostle said, " *Little* may be
wanting, as *thou* thinkest ; but there is *much* wanting (in *thee* perhaps, but certainly) in Festus, judging from his former words."
The rest of Paul's hearers all stood at various stages of *nearness*
to or *distance* from the truth, between the two extremes expressed
in Festus' " Thou art beside thyself," and Agrippa's " Almost thou
persuadest me." This striking contrast of different opinions, which
the apostle must often have experienced, is here immediately given
up ; and he assures *all* those that heard him, those nearest to and
those furthest from the truth, of his interceding love, which longed
for the personal salvation of each one of them. *All that hear me
this day ;* reminding them solemnly of God's great mercy in affording them such a testimony, and of the responsibility which God
would attach to every hearer of that day's discourse. It was also
a hint to them, that having heard him speak that day, was through
God's Spirit sufficient to enable them to attain to faith.[1] There is
also an intimation implied, that he would willingly speak still more,
if only he could thereby ἐν πολλῷ win over every one.

Now he comes to the point of " being a Christian "—to the
Χριστιανὸν γενέσθαι. He keeps to the γενέσθαι ; for all must
surely *become* something *new* and *different*—something they have
not yet been. But instead of using the term Χριστιανόν, he now
says, *such as I am.* He holds out himself now standing before

[1] Comp. the mode of expression in Luke's narrative, Acts xiv. 9.

them as an inviting type and example of what they were to become. This holding one's self out as an example is a permissible—
nay, under certain circumstances, an enjoined pride for the Christian, if indeed it may be called *pride;* for it is a pride in God,
and for God's honour, and acts with emphatic power for the testimony. Let every witness for Christ prove himself, whether he
can publicly and privately desire for all his hearers that they
should be such as *he is.* " Behold in me what Christians are !"
is the apostle's holy and joyful appeal to all. Thus stands the
happy, joyful witness, with royal dignity even in his fetters : he
would not exchange his " bonds" for all the pomp of the king.

Vers. 30–32. Paul's words failed to touch the hearts either of
the king or the governor. When Paul had concluded these earnest
words,[1] the king immediately rose up. The prisoner's language
was too confident, and had touched him too closely ; he failed even
in retaining the laudable emotion which he had so distinctly expressed in ver. 28. It is often thus. Paul might have very justly
said, that much was still wanting in Agrippa. Agrippa had that
day heard " this man," and what he wished for the king and all
them that heard him. But if he were to follow out the unexpected
effect produced in him by Paul's language (the sudden expression
of which effect he now perhaps regretted), he would be led too far.
Paul's last words on the point, " such as I am," had completely
enlightened him. He was frightened both at himself and the ideas
which had been communicated to him, and *rose up. His* departure
is followed by that of the *governor, Bernice, and they that sat with
him. And when they were gone aside* into some other room, leaving
the prisoner—whom they might, of course, have sent away—standing
alone in the hall, and thus, as it were, flying from the victorious
orator, *they talked between themselves.* The whole of their usual
course of feeling and inconceivable indifference towards God's
truth, their air of superiority and politic way of looking at things,
appear to have returned to them as soon as they no longer had the
apostle before their eyes. *This man !*—so speak the tribunes and
chief men of the city, who now give their opinions. This man !—
so also speaks Agrippa, who now is quite in accord with Festus as
to the eloquent madness of this Christian. The whole matter ultimately turns to a discussion as to Paul's person, in order to decide

---

[1] As Da Costa remarks, " The witness, free and king-like, although in
bonds, *had the last word* almost spontaneously, as it were, in opposition to the
king, the governor, the chief men, and the accusers "

(according to the intention named in ch. xxv. 26) what account of
the prisoner could be sent to the emperor. The rest of the company courteously confirm the governor's previous (ch. xxv. 25)
opinion, and say : *This man doeth nothing worthy of death or of
bonds*—the bonds which were so touchingly mentioned by Paul as
his last though unintentional complaint. Agrippa quite agrees in
this compassionate kind of praise, but adds an ingenious reproach,
saying, " *This man might have been set at liberty, if he had not
appealed unto Cæsar.* Thou, O Festus, might have freed him !"
The unfortunate prisoner had thus prejudiced his own cause.
After Festus had accepted his appeal, Paul could not, of course,
be set free.[1] But why did not Festus immediately release the
innocent man (ch. xxv. 7, 8), instead of forcing him to resort to a
conditional appeal in order to please the Jews (ver. 9)? Why did
he accept and confirm this appeal, as if it were *unconditional?*
Agrippa's reproach, therefore, ought to have touched Festus' conscience, who perhaps in the whole affair received a fitting lesson
how a man should act, so as to be not *partly*, but *quite* just ; and
so as not only to *appear*, but *be* equitable. As far as king Agrippa
was concerned, thus much at least was attained by his hearing
the apostle's discourse, that the king did not persecute the Christians, but rather protected those whom he had *almost* joined ; for
at the outbreak of the Jewish war he gave them succour, and
received them kindly into his territory. Thus, by the operation of
a discourse delivered in the spirit of joyfulness, the captive apostle
protected many of his free brethren in that land which he was so
shortly to quit.

[1] " Nam adpellatione potestas judicis, a quo adpellatum est, cessare incipit
ad absolvendum non minus, quam ad condemnandum. Crimina enim integra
servanda sunt cognitioni superioris " (Grotius). The remark which Bengel adds
can scarcely apply : " Accedebat timor offendendi Judæos."

XXVIII.

PAUL'S ADDRESS TO HIS COMPANIONS IN HIS VOYAGE.

(CHAP. XXVII. 21-26.)

ENCOURAGEMENT GIVEN TO HIS SHIPMATES WHEN IN DANGER, BY COMMUNICATING TO THEM A REVELATION WHICH HAD BEEN AFFORDED HIM.

CH. xxvii. 1-8. Luke does not inform us how long the apostle was compelled to wait in Cæsarea before it was determined how and when he was to be sent to Rome. But by his entering so suddenly on the matter, he leads us to believe that the period was not a protracted one. With graceful modesty, Luke for a long time had omitted to make mention of himself in conjunction with Paul. Now, however, he includes in the narrative both himself and also Aristarchus of Thessalonica, who is subsequently spoken of as Paul's fellow-prisoner (Col. iv. 10), and as his fellow-labourer (with Luke, Philem. 24). Luke writes: "And when it was determined that *we* should sail into Italy"—whatever was decided on for Paul, applied also to his companions, who voluntarily accompanied him from a feeling of love—Paul and "certain other prisoners" with whom he was now associated were delivered over to Julius, a centurion of the *cohors Augusta;* and as no special ship could be found for the entire voyage, their passage was entrusted (as far as the coast of Asia) to a ship of Adramyttium, which was accustomed to frequent the Asiatic waters, or rather the seaports, harbours, and commercial towns of Asia Minor. The day following they reached Sidon, where (either for shipping or unshipping goods) a short stay was made; and Julius, actuated by kindly feelings, permitted his unknown although honourable prisoner to visit the disciples there, and with their help to furnish himself with provisions for the voyage. But the wind would not allow them to sail straight across the sea (as in ch. xxi. 2, 3): they therefore proceeded coastwise along the shores of Cyprus, and then for a short distance across the sea, so as, passing by Cilicia and Pamphylia,[1] to come to Myra (or Limyra) in Lycia. Here

---

[1] So that the apostle from his ship might perhaps have perceived and hailed the sphere of his previous ministry.

the centurion found an Alexandrine ship destined for Italy
(Rome) (laden, according to ver. 38, with wheat from Egypt),
which had probably been driven in here by the wind. Into this
ship the centurion now puts his prisoners, as the first vessel went
on further to Mysia. Even now the voyage does not go on pros-
perously; and after sailing along the coast for many days, they
ultimately reach Cnidus, the promontory of Caria, and then Sal-
mone (*Capo Salomon*), the eastern point of Crete. "And hardly
passing it," they come to a haven on the south side of the island,
close by the city of Lasea, which port, by reason of its name—
"The Fair Havens"—seemed to invite a stay.

Vers. 9–13. *Now when much time was spent,* sailing became
more and more dangerous. In November the sea was actually
closed to the ancients; and now, the fast-day or Day of Atonement
of the Jews being passed, it was well advanced in October. Now
we see that the faithful witness before princes and kings was no
novice in sailing over the seas of this world, and without either
fanaticism or unnecessary boldness, judiciously advised that which
his experience ("thrice I suffered shipwreck," etc., 2 Cor. xi.
25, 26) suggested as the best thing to be done.[1] He addresses
to the ship's company a few words of necessary warning, and says
to them decisively and emphatically, "*Sirs, I perceive that this
voyage* (under these circumstances, unless God sends some help,
which is not rashly to be looked for) *will be with hurt and much
damage, not only of the lading and ship, but also of our lives.*"
Paul says here "*our* lives," for the angel of his God had not as yet
given him any certain promise, and he felt bound to use his ordinary foresight. From the Lord's word he knew certainly and
surely that he was to testify in Rome; yet was he thus permitted to
speak to the people, and to include his own person in the common
danger. But Paul's advice fared as so often is the case with wise
counsel: the supposed practical knowledge of others, in the zeal
of their superiority, declined to listen to true knowledge and good
advice. The captain, with confidence in his skill, trusted that he
could carry the ship through; the owner, actuated by the desire of
gain, wished to hurry as much as possible; and the centurion (on
whose command the whole matter depended) believed what these

---

[1] That the writers of the Scriptures of the New Testament were men of
action more than mere learning, is exemplified by Baumgarten, when he says:
"If we consider the most learned among them all, he excels in acquaintance
with the sea, and practical knowledge of the winds."

two said, "more than the things which were spoken by Paul."
"The Fair Havens" appeared to them to be a place not sufficiently
commodious to winter in. In this doubtful position all are called
in to give their opinion; and the greater part decided upon taking
a middle course, that is, to leave the port they were in, "if by any
means they might attain to Phenice, and there to winter,"—this
harbour of Crete lying well sheltered from the south-west to the
north-west. *And when the south wind blew softly, supposing that
they had attained their purpose* (δόξαντες τῆς προθέσεως κεκρα-
τηκέναι), *loosing thence, they sailed close by Crete.*

Vers. 14–19. It soon appeared how good the advice of Paul
had been, and how unfortunately their own plans had turned out.
Not long after their confident departure, there arose, blowing
against the island (ἔβαλε κατ᾽ αὐτῆς, scil. Κρήτης), a tempestuous
east wind, called Εὐροκλύδων. Now began the terrible storm,
during which we see the apostle joyfully prevailing over all the
fears of his companions, and from which they were to be saved
for his sake. To Paul the storm was a glorification of his faith
in his God; but to the others it was a punishment for their
obstinacy, and a chastisement on account of their sins. It was,
too, a proof of the truth and power of the God whom Paul served,
—the God who thus manifested Himself to be the God of all of
them.

The wind laid hold of the ship, so that the latter could not
make head against it: they therefore abandoned the vessel to the
winds and waves, and were drifted along by them. The ship was
driven away from Phenice into the vicinity of the island of Clauda
(or Cauda, Gauda), near Crete. There they[1] had much difficulty
in getting possession of the boat (either sent to help, or just let
down from the ship). With the assistance of the boat they then
took measures for safety, binding cords round the bottom of the
ship; but fearing lest they should be driven on to one of the
African quicksands, they preferred to let down the mast,[2] and thus
surrender themselves to the waves with somewhat less danger.

---

[1] The *we* might perhaps, as in ver. 19 (reading ἐῤῥίψαμεν), be intended to
intimate the manual labour of the apostle and his companions (Baumgarten);
but it is more natural to look at it as nothing but the mode of expression
adopted in the account of the voyage: αὐτόχειρες in ver. 19 has also another
sense.

[2] Or the rigging, as Mr. Smith of Jordanhill maintains in his learned work
on this chapter (*Voyage and Shipwreck of St. Paul*).

But the tempest tossed them about more and more furiously, so that on the next day they threw overboard goods (the least necessary things first) in order to lighten the ship. On the third day, almost in despair, they also threw overboard the tackling of the ship; αὐτόχειρες, as those who would do themselves an injury.[1] Many a one, when God's storms beat upon and try our life's bark, must get rid of something more than ballast, and relinquish even the goods and implements which are seemingly most necessary for us.

Vers. 20, 21. Amid all the fury of the elements, the apostle and his brethren turned to the Lord with heart and eyes, both for themselves and their companions. Without was darkness and the deep; faith alone could overcome the timid weakness of the flesh, and could hope, and pray, and ultimately receive a revelation of comfort. For many days they saw neither the sun by day nor the (moon and) stars by night. "No small tempest lay on us, and all hope that we should be saved was then taken away." Thus writes Luke, an eye-witness of the events, who probably did not hear of Paul's revelation any sooner than all the rest, and had likewise given up all hope of life. Now was the moment arrived for the apostle to be comforted, and through him the others also; now, in the midst of the stormy waves, Paul's God majestically revealed Himself for all who would believe in Him; now God's angel is sent to His faithful servant, and promises deliverance out of the jaws of death. From the effects of toil, anxiety, and dejection (perhaps also from sea-sickness), they had fasted for a long time; but in the midst of the starving crowd Paul stood up as a comforter, and spake to them.

There is a good reason for the apostle commencing his words of consolation with a reproach: this commencement certainly did not arise from his pride, but rather from the wisdom of that love which prayed to God for the deliverance of all. God helps men out of their danger in order that they may acknowledge Him in the help, and not boast of their own cleverness; previously, therefore, in the danger they must confess their own guilt and foolishness. This is one reason why Paul in the first place directs the attention of the men to the hurt and damage which they had brought upon themselves. There is, however, another reason, which is more closely connected with the consolation itself. If

[1] Αὐτοχειρία at least occurs for self-murder, αὐτόχειρ specially for doing injury or killing with one's own hand.

these men, almost devoid as they are of hope, are to be comforted,
it is necessary that they should believe Paul's words : the sure way
to bring them to this belief was to remind them of his *previous*
words of *warning*, which had now turned out so entirely *true.*
Paul thus renders himself of more weight in the eyes of his companions, so as to be able to convey comfort to their hearts, although
previously they had despised his warning. This somewhat cutting
reproach is so well grounded by the reference to the present result
of their disobedience, that no man can say anything against it.
῞Υβρις and ζημία are the same words which Paul made use of in
his warning (ver. 10). The former points to the existing *position
of danger*, the toil and anxiety arising from the ascendancy of the
storm (*injuria tempestatis*, the harm which without distinction
affected both the ship and those in it) ; but ζημία is the resulting
and lasting *loss* and *injury* to goods, body, or life. The toil and
anxiety had now been experienced for several days, and the injury
(vers. 17–19) had not been trifling. It had indeed much the
appearance that, as Paul had said, the safety not only of the ship
and cargo, but also of their lives, would be a questionable matter.

Vers. 22, 23. *And now* I tell you something different, which
will, however, turn out just as true as my former words. I then
exhorted you with a warning remonstrance : ye would not hear
me ; and behold what danger you are in ! Now *I exhort you to be*
undismayed and *of good cheer; for there shall be no loss of any life
among you, but of the ship.* How confident and bold is this language of the man of God ! It was evident enough to them that
the ship would and must be lost ; but that not one should perish
out of the 276 souls—how could this be possible ? And by what
means was this known to and perceived by this man, who at all
events had so well foreseen the present danger ? The danger proceeded from natural causes, and his warning against it was probable
from a human point of view ; but how was the deliverance to come
to pass which appeared almost impossible ? These questions are
anticipated by the apostle, who continues with much dignity : *For
there stood by me this* (last) *night the angel of God*—the ambassador,
or messenger, of the God—*whose I am, and whom I serve.* How
beautiful is the quiet certainty of the apostle amid the dangers of
the raging sea ! *I am God's* is the loftiest and inmost confidence
of piety ; *I serve Him* is the consequent appeal to the vitality of his
worship. In referring to his " service," Paul is perhaps alluding
to his service as a witness, of which indeed this journey to Rome

formed a part; but he also directs the attention of the ship's crew
to his *outward* worship. They had perhaps noticed him fearlessly
rendering this homage to his God (ver. 35). He thus seems to say
to them, that this God whom he had reverentially worshipped in
their presence was the God who had sent to him the messenger of
promise, and would help His servant (Dan. vi. 16, 20), and not him
alone, but all the others as well. Remark how the apostle not only
acknowledges before the heathen who were present Israel's true
and only God, but also declares that His messenger, the " Jewish
angel," was *really existing.* How indeed could he avoid doing so,
as the angel *had actually appeared* to him ? But a foolish criticism
thinks it knows better, and says that Paul *dreamed!*

Ver. 24. The messenger repeated the purport of the Lord's
words recorded in ch. xxiii. 11, and confirmed the δεῖ that was
there expressed. Now he says μὴ φοβοῦ instead of merely θάρσει;
for Paul's flesh and blood trembled perhaps at the storm, although
his spirit rested calmly on his God. Paul thus kindly confesses
before his frightened companions, that even to *him* the angel had
said, " Fear not."—*Thou must be brought before Cæsar.* By these
words the angel expressly proves that the apostle's appeal was an
act of true obedience to the impulse of the Spirit, and was the way
that was right and well-pleasing to God in order to attain to the
delivery of the prescribed testimony. The angel, too, sets a mighty
and divine *" must"* against all the probabilities of opposing nature.
As regards the hearers, however, these words must have immediately
conferred some importance on the person of the apostle, and im-
parted to them a certainty of his innocence; for the angel, who
began with the words, " Fear not, Paul," cannot have intended
that the emperor would condemn him.—*And, lo, God hath given
thee all them that sail with thee.* In communicating this wondrous
gift, the angel with justice expresses a wondering " lo." In God's
sight, Paul is the master and steersman of the ship, and all the
others merely sail *with him;* and because Paul *must* be saved, but
would not willingly escape alone when all these sinners were swept
away, and in pitying love had cared for and prayed for his companions, therefore God hears the prayer of His servant, and *gives
them all to him,* all of whom would have perished if they had not
sailed with Paul. As is recorded in ch. xxv. 11, no man could or
dare give Paul to the Jews in order that he might be put to death;
but the Lord now gives Paul 275 souls in order that they may
live. In discerning in this " giving" an answer to prayer on the

part of the living God, who at the loving intercession of a faithful servant averts the calamities that were actually taking place, may we not in faith assume that many a one of those saved were not delivered merely from the dangers which awaited their *lives* and *bodies?* We may be sure that the apostle felt very specially bound to testify to and teach the hearts and consciences of them that were thus given to him.

Vers. 25, 26. After the clear and distinct reasons for the first exhortation (ver. 22) have been stated, the latter is again repeated with the addition of a *wherefore;* and a belief in the revelation they had heard is thus kindly and prudently awakened in the men. In the first place, the apostle himself says, " I believe,"—thus preceding them all in his belief, as he subsequently (vers. 35, 36) did in taking food and giving thanks. In a communication of this kind, the firm personal faith of the narrator much tends to kindle the faith of the hearers ; Paul therefore assures the men of *his own* conviction in the matter, that everything would take place just as he had been told by the angel. " I believe God," he would say, " for the angel's words are equivalent to God's own word, and that is positive and certain." At " The Fair Havens" I told you something which ye would not believe ; and lo, for His mercy's sake, God hath disproved *my* words, at which contradiction I gladly rejoice ; nay, I prayed that the things I said to you might not prove true. But now *God* hath sent a message to *me* for you all, and what He says must unfailingly take place. Paul does not look upon the nocturnal vision as merely an uncertain dream, but as the sure word of God through His angel : he knew well enough how to distinguish between an angel and a dream. The God whom he serves is not called by Paul *his* God ; he describes Him generally as the one true God—the God indeed of all them that sailed with him, although they did not serve Him, who holds in His hand both their life and death, and now desires to manifest Himself as the merciful God of every one of them. But whilst he thus summons the men to believe, like him, in this God, he also makes it clear to their understandings by an explanatory and corroborative sign, which showed the possibility of safety for the crew although the vessel might be lost, and adds a more definite prediction as a warranty of the fact that God had actually spoken to him. " We must, however," he says, " be stranded, and suffer shipwreck on a certain island—one already determined on ; but we shall be able from the shattered wreck to get safe to land." And observe ye all the more certainly, that what I say unto you is based on this special circumstance which I now announce to you. The chief design, however, of these words is to point out to a doubting mind the possibility, καθ' ὃν τρόπον the promised improbability should take place, and more forcibly to confirm the certainty of a special divine revelation in the case of one who is inclined to believe.

Vers. 27–29. As Luke, having been an eye-witness, continues to relate the further course of events down to the exact fulfilment of Paul's prediction, we notice, in the first place, that the crew paid special attention to the last words of the pious prisoner; for as soon as they found they were near the land, they began to dread the foretold shipwreck. Fourteen days and nights they had been tossed about on the Adriatic Sea (taken in its ancient and wider sense, as the sea between Crete and Sicily); then at midnight the sailors supposed they were approaching some coast. The sounding-line first showed twenty fathoms, and immediately afterwards only fifteen fathoms. Fearing, therefore, that, as foretold, they would be stranded on the rocks, they cast four anchors (small ones, such as the ancients used) out of the stern, and longingly waited for the light of day.

Vers. 30–32. Soon after, the sailors, impelled by their great fear, conceived the idea of not waiting for the daylight, and faithlessly resolved to save themselves only, and to abandon the others to their fate. Under the pretence that they wished to cast out another anchor from the bows of the ship, they let down the boat into the sea, in order to escape in the gloom of the night. The promised deliverance was not intended to be effected in this way. Paul, who was watching wakefully during the night, saw through this disgraceful plot, and called out to the centurion and his soldiers, that if the sailors who were leaving did not remain faithful to their duty in the ship as long as their services were required, none of them would be saved. We see, therefore, that God's promises are conditional: in this case, the use of ordinary means, and a faithful perseverance in duty to the very last, were both requisite. Paul, by requiring the stay of the sailors, retracts his words, and says, " Except these remain, *ye* cannot be saved." He does not say " we," for *his own* deliverance remained certain ; but God's *gift* of all the others was recalled, unless the latter would believe and obey their preserver. The sudden words, which disclosed to the soldiers both the artful plot and the peril it would involve, excited them to a rash and wrong action. The soldiers hastily cut loose the boat, which they might have used just as well as the sailors, and let it beat to pieces on the adjacent rocks.

Vers. 33–37. Although the boat was lost, the ship was now firmly anchored, and they waited for the day, to see where they were, and how matters stood. Paul, as if he were now the lord and master of the ship, exhorts the fainting men, ere it was day, to take a comforting and strengthening meal. Fourteen days had been passed in anxious waiting, and during the whole time they had eaten nothing in a regular and orderly way. Paul therefore thus addresses them : *Wherefore I pray you to take some meat,* for this will tend to your support and health, and consequent preservation.[1] These words of the apostle may teach us the same thing which he urged in ver. 21, viz. that if a man looks for God's help, he must use the ordinary means ; and as regarded Paul's shipmates, that weakness from hunger, and a hope of escape from a shipwrecked ship, were two things which could not well exist together. The real intention in this case, that the people should be strengthened by the meal for the swimming which was afterwards necessary (vers. 43, 44), was concealed by Paul, in order that they might the more joyfully eat their food. That their faith might be awakened and their appetite excited, and also that the meal might be solemnly sanctified, Paul first began to eat, after he had, in the midst of the danger, *given thanks to God in the presence of them all.* Paul stands before God as the priest for all his fellow-voyagers, and for them prays that He would bless their food. His words and his eating made them all be of good cheer ; and before daybreak, a joyful meal, which was surely well-pleasing to God, was partaken of by the 276 distressed persons. The brotherly, or rather fatherly and loving, conduct of Paul to the many and various anxious souls in this peril of the sea, is held up here as an example, in contrast to the narrow-minded or high-flown piety, which in a similar case would prefer to preach with many and vain words, and in the meantime would forget the most necessary solicitude for the sinners who need both bodily and mental sustenance. To act and encourage as Paul did on this occasion, is a testimony which will touch the heart more forcibly than any lengthy, extraneous teaching and chiding.

Vers. 38–41. The satisfied and invigorated men now began again to do all that was in their power. The ship is again light-

[1] Ὑπάρχειν πρός τινος, to belong to or be fit for anything ; τῆς ὑμετέρας σωτηρίας, the sure preservation predicted for you.

ened, by throwing overboard the whole of the cargo of wheat. Day at last arrives; but the land lying before them is unknown to all. The only thing to be noticed is, that there is a shallow creek not far off, " into which they were minded, if possible, to thrust in the ship." The anchors are now again taken up, and the ship is again committed to the mercy of the sea: the rudder-bands are loosed,[1] and the sail being set up to the wind, they endeavoured, with all the seamanship they possessed, to reach the shore. All, however, was of no avail; and the sentence that the ship must be lost (ἀποβολὴ τοῦ πλοίου), by running upon some island, had been declared to them in vers. 22 and 26. Nevertheless they only did what was right, in showing devotion to their charge up to the very last; and even if they had possessed a much firmer faith in Paul's prediction than perhaps was the case, it would notwithstanding have been their duty so to do. Although God has said to thee that thy vessel shall be wrecked, thou hast no exact knowledge of the *when*, *where*, and *how*, and must therefore do thy best to steer and sail so long as thou art permitted. Thus best will agree God's special ways and the order of things as pointed out to us. The foretold fate soon came to pass. They run upon some shallow spot (a sandbank or reef), and the ship strikes upon it; *the forepart stuck fast and remained immoveable, but the hinder part was broken with the violence of the waves.*

Vers. 42-44. The loss of the ship was soon decided; and now the matter in question was, that there should " be no loss of any man's life" (ver. 22). But now again does human wickedness endeavour to frustrate the counsel of divine love, which had decreed that *all* should be saved. On this occasion it was the soldiers' cruelty, just as before it was the sailors' selfishness; and now the prisoners were to be killed before the sea swept them away. The barbarous conclusion that the soldiers arrived at in this the extremity of their danger, is to kill the prisoners, lest any of them should escape by swimming. Should the soldiers be fortunate enough to save themselves, if they had allowed the prisoners to escape, they would have to suffer in the place of the latter (*vid.* ch. xii. 19). What a one-sided miserable officiousness, which looks to itself only, and is quite ready to sacrifice others! What cold-blooded barbarity, which, even in the immediate prospect of death, would commit murder to screen themselves from the consequences of a scarcely possible contingency! Paul, all of whose words had

---

[1] The larger ships of the ancients had rudders both before and behind.

hitherto been verified, had declared that *all* were to be saved *for his* (Paul's) *sake;* and now they desire to kill him " who *must* be brought before Cæsar," as he had before said, lest he should be saved.   Remark what kind of people these were with whom Paul sailed, whom he so lovingly prayed for—whom, too, he so kindly encouraged, after they had been given him by God.   The more humane centurion (ver. 3) (who is himself saved only for the apostle's sake) desires to save Paul, and on his account the other prisoners also.   He therefore forbids the wicked intention, and assuming a vigorous command over the final measures to be taken, orders that those who could swim should first leap overboard and make their way to land, and that the rest should endeavour to save themselves on boards or other broken pieces of the ship.   We are not told to which of these two classes Paul, Luke, and Aristarchus belonged: it is, however, very plain that no special outward help was vouchsafed to the apostle; but that, like all the rest, he had to swim for his life, or to float to shore as well as he could on some plank.   Supposing now that the words of the angel had never been recorded, how natural everything would have seemed!   How little suspicion we should have had of the wonderful connection which existed between Paul's prayers, and the fact that all his companions had been *given by God* to *one* of the swimmers struggling among all the rest!   Luke, who had previously related the revelation which predicted the events, now most emphatically and instructively closes his narrative : *And so it came to pass, that they all escaped safe to land.*

XXIX.

PAUL'S WORDS TO THE CHIEF MEN OF THE JEWS IN ROME.

(CHAP. XXVIII. 17–20.)

INVITATION TO A SPECIAL CONVERSATION AS TO THE REAL CAUSE OF HIS UNDESERVED CAPTIVITY.

CH. xxviii. 1–10. Malta, the island which in modern times is so well adapted and so often selected as a central point of missions, was the place at which Paul arrived as one among 276 shipwrecked

persons, all thoroughly wetted and chilled after their narrow escape.
The islanders (of Carthaginian origin), who (as foreigners) were
called in the Greek language *barbarians*, compassionately and
promptly did all they could for the unfortunate men.   Paul, however, being unwilling to avail himself of the services of others,
without rendering some personal assistance, brought some fuel for
the fire.   An adder (or viper) that was in the wood crept out and
fastened on his hand; then the deep *incognito* in which the apostle
was travelling was again surprisingly manifested, and subsequently
the vacillating folly of the poor islanders was also shown.   Paul is
a *prisoner*, and a venomous serpent fastens on his hand—this was
quite sufficient to give a mistaken direction to the people's dark
ideas of divine retribution, and to make them think, This hand
has certainly committed murder!   The murderer must surely die;
and although he has escaped the sea, yet *vengeance* (or the goddess
of Justice, Δίκη, the Νέμεσις of whom even these barbarians knew
something[1]) has not suffered (εἴασε) to live, as if it were already
all over with him!   But how could either adders or even lions
injure him, who was before the emperor to bear testimony of the
Lord, who shall tread the young lion and the adder under His feet?
Paul indeed had once been a murderer (according to his own confession to Agrippa, ch. xxvi. 10), but mercy had not only allowed
him to live, but had also given him a new life.   According to the
Lord's promise (Mark xvi. 18), all His faithful witnesses were to
be enabled to take up serpents without injury.   The apostle shakes
off the venomous beast into the fitting place for it: either it had
not bitten him (which, however, from the expressions used in vers.
3 and 4 is highly improbable), or the bite did not injure him.   The
islanders who were standing round, being well acquainted with the
nature of their serpents, waited some time for his becoming inflamed
by the venom, or for his sudden death; and then altering their
opinion, they thought that he was a god.[2]   The inhabitants of Lystra
had done just the reverse: first, they sacrificed to Paul as a god,
and then they stoned him (ch. xiv. 13, 18, 19).   These " barbarians " had no idea of a *man of God*—something that was inter-

---

[1] According to the ancient belief and feeling, which was indeed based on
truth, serpents were the special instruments of divine punishment.

[2] The gods were supposed to appear as strangers, perhaps also with serpents as signs.   Æsculapius, the god of physicians, who ruled over the serpent,
and Hercules, who crushed serpents in his cradle, and subsequently was a
deliverer from hydras and lions, were both specially worshipped in Melita.

mediate between God and sinners.   Soon, however, Paul showed himself to be in Malta a true Æsculapius and Hercules, ἀλεξίκακος and σωτήρ, all for the honour of his God.   The πρῶτος, or commander of the island,[1] kindly received all the shipwrecked men[2] into his country-house : his hospitality was repaid by Paul, by his laying his healing hands on the commander's sick father, and thus fulfilling the remainder of the promise in Mark xvi. 18.   This miracle brings all the sick in the island to Paul, and all are healed.[3] Now again beam forth the power and glory of the apostle : the prisoner is now a miraculous benefactor, and the supposed murderer is a dispenser of life.   Then must the ship's company indeed have wondered !   Those who were healed gave them ample fees, for at their departure they loaded them with all things necessary for them.

Vers. 11–15. After three months of the worst season of the year were past, they resumed their voyage in another Alexandrian ship, which sailed under the name, image, and protection of *Castor* and *Pollux*, the gods of navigation.   They were therefore under the best auspices, although their present fortunate voyage was vouchsafed to them only by Paul's God, who, however, did *not* command the apostle to insult or assail the image of the twin deities.   At Syracuse they tarried three days, at Rhegium only one day ; the favourable south wind (thus bringing the unfortunate voyage to a happy termination) wafted them from thence in two days to Puteoli (now Puzzuoli), the rich Campanian trading town, near Naples, and the usual landing-place for the Egyptian ships. *Where we found brethren*, writes Luke with joyful reminiscence ; for this meeting was something much better than all the friendship, honour, and sustenance which they had met with at Melita.   It

---

[1] If it may be justly supposed that the Romans were the possessors of Malta ; indeed, it has been found out that πρῶτος was the title of the chief authority there.

[2] The ἡμᾶς in ver. 7 could hardly be intended to apply only to Paul, Luke, and Aristarchus, differently from the whole of the previous narrative.   Even in ver. 10 the "*we*" does not appear to us to mean only the three Christians, but to be a kind of intermediate expression.   In vers. 11, 12, 13, the "*we*" evidently points to the whole of the company of travellers ; and not before vers. 14, 15, does it decidedly assume the narrower sense.   In ver. 16 it again applies to the whole company.   This hospitality on the part of the commander could only have been brought about through Julius the centurion ; but then it would certainly extend to him in the first place, and to many others.

[3] Luke relates this with complete repudiation of his own poor art as a physician ; in ver. 8, however, he describes the disorder accurately and technically.

must have been a complete refreshment after their protracted intercourse with the wicked ship's company ! Faith in Christ had
indeed preceded the apostle in Italy and Rome ; Aquila and Priscilla
had been labouring there, and the Epistle to the Romans had
already been written from Corinth. What a moment it must have
been for the apostle, when he first embraced his Italian brethren,
and found Christ even on his way to Cæsar ! It was natural that
the brethren should request the sojourn of such beloved guests,
and it was equally natural that the centurion should have at once
granted their request. *And so*—thus refreshed, comforted, and
honoured—*we went toward* the long-looked-for *Rome.*[1]

The brethren in Rome, who abode in the love and community
of the Spirit, although not yet united into an actual church, soon
heard of the arrival of the great apostle and epistle-writer, and
hastened to meet him. All come who can—some to the *Forum
Appii,* eight miles from Rome, and some to the *Tres Tabernas,* two
miles nearer the city. These were the brethren of whom Paul had
written : " Without ceasing I make mention of you always in my
prayers ; making request (if by any means now at length I might be
able by the will of God) to come unto you. For *I long to see you,*
that I may impart unto you some spiritual gift, to the end ye may
be established ; that is, that *I may be comforted* together with you,
by the *mutual faith both of you and me*" (Rom. i. 9-12). When
Paul saw these brethren in the faith, he *gave thanks* to his faithful
Guide, and *took courage, and was comforted* by their presence, as he
had hoped and prayed might be the case ; ἔλαβε θάρσος, obtained
a new and fuller confidence in the humble though victorious and
blessed progress of God's kingdom in the kingdom of this world.
We cannot, however, go so far as Baumgarten in the idea that,
during the whole journey from Cæsarea to the " Three Taverns,"
the apostle was under the influence of great grief and depression
about Israel and Jerusalem : his whole conduct on the way forbids
this view. There is, however, a truth which we may gather from
these words—that now, all at once, the gracious will of God to set
Rome in the place of Jerusalem was presented to his mind in a
more vivid way than at any former time ; but in this idea we must
not forget the words of the Lord, ch. xxiii. 11. This feeling of
fresh courage is, however, most justly to be referred to a slight

---

[1] Εἰς τὴν Ῥώμην. But subsequently in ver. 16, ὅτε δὲ ἤλθομεν εἰς Ῥώμην.
This was a more important and decisive moment for Rome than when it was
said, " Hannibal ante portas !"

degree of relief from the anxiety which had just now come upon
the apostle, on his close approach to the mighty metropolis of
heathendom and its emperor Nero, already considered as the type
of antichristian opinions.

Vers. 16, 17. In Rome all the rest of the prisoners were placed
in due course under the charge of the *Præfectus Prætorio;* but
Paul, about whom both Festus in writing, and Julius by word of
mouth, had given a favourable account, was permitted exceptionally
to live *by himself* (cf. ver. 30), accompanied only by a soldier who
guarded him (cf ch. xxii. 30).   Paul devoted only three days to
rest and prayer, as well as to private and refreshing intercourse with
his longed-for brethren ; then, as the witness of Christ, according
to the Scriptures, both to " the people " and the Gentiles, he forthwith takes a public step.   On this occasion, too, after all that had
occurred in Jerusalem and Cæsarea, it might be said to the Jews
in Rome, " To you first, who are the children of the prophets and
of the covenant, hath God sent His Son Jesus" (ch. iii. 25, 26).
It is probable that the apostle not only looked for the same obstinacy
as existed in the Jews of Palestine, but perhaps also suspected that
evil reports and accounts as to his character had been sent to the
Jews in Rome (ver. 21).   The circumstance that he had appealed
from the Jewish to the Roman jurisdiction would be both suspicious
and odious to them.   At all events, he at least desires to make a
public commencement of intercourse, and confidently and lovingly
to anticipate their hostility.   Either because, as a prisoner, he
thought his visiting them might be troublesome and offensive,
or—which from vers. 23 and 30 is more probable—he was not in
fact permitted to go far from his lodging, and least of all with
the soldier accompanying him could visit the synagogue, he requested the chief men among the Roman Jews to come to him at
his house.   And when they came, he introduced himself and his
matter in the following way.

Vers. 17–19. The apostle speaks kindly to them, as a brother
to brethren, and with candid confidence first assures them of his
innocence.   " I am indeed, as ye see, a captive to the Romans ;
but although I was delivered as a prisoner from Jerusalem to the
Romans, *I have committed nothing against our people*, or the *customs
of our fathers.*" [1]   This is the first general information which he
gives as to his captivity : " I," he says, " am no apostate or evil-

---

[1] From this Liebetrut correctly infers that Paul openly observed the Jewish
law, especially the Sabbath.

doer, as might well appear;" his words also tend to anticipate any
evil reports such as those recorded in ch. xxi. **21, 28.** He now
adds the second necessary information as to his *appeal* to the
emperor, and again even more forcibly asserts his innocence; but
that, nevertheless, he does not desire to complain of his nation
which persecuted him without any just cause. He only points
to his being given up into the hands of the Romans (like his
Lord) by the rather indefinite words δέσμιος παρεδόθην,[1] and says
nothing about the tumult which called forth Lysias' interference,
or of the conspiracy, to protect him from which he was sent to the
governor; for it is by no means his intention to make any complaint. He now tells somewhat more in detail how the Romans
would have let him go (both for the sake of money, ch. xxiv. 26,
and also for the sake of justice, ch. xxv. 7, 8, xxvi. 32), *because
there was* (in fact) *no cause of death in me*, and consequently none
could be legally proved. When he speaks of the *necessity* for the
appeal to the emperor being caused by an ἀντιλέγειν of the Jews,
he intends that the latter, with their repeated accusations and abuse,
would not allow the Roman judge to set him free, but that this
judge, by the question which he put to him with a view of pleasing
the Jews (ch. xxv. 9), actually *constrained him to appeal.* We
must therefore thus understand his words: " I was *not* constrained
by the opposing Jews, but by the judge, owing to or through the
continued opposition of the Jews to his letting me go." But *how*
was he constrained? This he omits in this preliminary declaration.
He does not desire to have a general discussion with the Jews as
to matters of justice and injustice, and the whole course of his
trial (which was a matter to come before Cæsar); but he longs
to talk to them about his own faith and Israel's Messiah. Against
the Jews he says nothing more than what is quite indispensable,
and this as mildly and indefinitely as possible; viz., that at their
instigation he was undeservedly placed in the hands of the Romans,
and that they had *spoken against* his being set free. Now he fully
protests that he does not desire to accuse his nation,[2] which was
nevertheless dear and precious to him. Neither did he intend his
present words as any complaint of unjust treatment, nor would he
before the emperor say anything which would injure the Jews.
Could enduring patience say anything kinder as regards either the
past or the future?

[1] Which refers back to Agabus' words (ch. xxi. 11), δήσουσι καὶ παραδώσουσι.
[2] His own nation: it is ἔθνος, and not λαός, as in ver. 17.

Ver. 20. Not only because I am guiltless, but also because I am friendly inclined towards my hostile nation (διὰ ταύτην οὖν τὴν αἰτίαν, since both my case and my disposition are what I have just declared), *have I called for you, to see you* (that is, to greet you as brethren), *and to speak with you* in friendly confidence. This is the only right interpretation of the first sentence, in which παρακαλεῖν takes the meaning (rather unusual in the New Testament) of *advocare, invitare,* and προσλαλῆσαι applies to the apostle; cf. the answer in ver. 22, "We desire to hear from thee what thou thinkest." It appears to us that the translation is very unsuitable which runs, "(Because I am innocent and well inclined towards you), I have requested you to come to me, and to speak with me." In this rendering the whole of the real aim and leading idea of the apostle's language is lost; and his aim was simply this, that he desired to speak familiarly with them. And what was it he desired to speak of? Was it of himself and his righteous conduct? This the apostle had already spoken of in ver. 19. It would have savoured of pride to summon the chief men of the Jews for this purpose. No, it was of his own *convictions of faith,* which the Jews had accused, persecuted, and spoken against in his person, which also were the real cause of the captivity he was compelled to endure: this is the subject on which Paul desired to speak *from the Scriptures* to the chief Jews in Rome, and to this all he had hitherto said was to be the necessary introduction. But did the account of Paul's faith apply to all the Jews in Rome, and their rulers? Very much, of course; for it is the *hope of Israel,* which Paul according to the Scripture (ch. xxiv. 14, 15), and in its actual and present *fulfilment* (ch. xxvi. 6-9), believingly held (ch. xxvi. 22, 23): it is the *kingdom of God,* now manifested in *Jesus,* of which he desired to speak to them out of the law of Moses and out of the prophets. He wishes, in Rome, to commence the same testimony which he had been compelled to discontinue in Jerusalem and Cæsarea.

Vers. 21, 22. Even in the first reply to the apostle's friendly greeting and invitation there seems to be something invidious: it is not altogether straightforward and true. For the moment the innocence of the prisoner is allowed in an apparently friendly way; but even in this the commencement is only partly true. "As regards the first subject of thy speech (thy innocence), we have," they say, "received no letters about thee from Judea." This might perhaps have been true, although the sending round of letters, implying suspicion and warning on the part of the Jews, began not long after. But their words, "Neither any of the brethren that have come (from Judea) have showed or (only) spoken any harm of thee, that is, have neither related anything that has happened, nor have expressed their opinions to thy detriment," contain a surprising assertion, which in their express denial must be set down as a silly falsehood, and the very reverse of the truth.[1] It can in no way be reconciled with the words that follow : " For as concerning this sect (of thine), *we know* that everywhere it is spoken against." Paul's person and name were of too important a character, and the things which during more than two years had occurred in reference to him formed too essentially the chief matter in the attacks against Christianity, for no account of these events to have reached them ; and the apostle to the Gentiles must neces-sarily have been spoken of. We see, therefore, that in an artful, although courteous way, the chief Jews make themselves out more ignorant and impartial than they really were, in order to be able subsequently to speak against "this sect" the more accurately. They do not with candid eagerness accept the further conference, but say, "We would willingly *hear from thee;* we consider it as only fair and right—ἀξιοῦμεν—that we should allow thee to tell us *what thou thinkest* "—ἃ φρονεῖς.   In the cautious and indefinite expression "what thou thinkest," instead of "the hope of Israel" (ver. 20), the second and worse half of their reply begins to betray itself,—the part, namely, which refers to the proposed conference. They somewhat sharply continue : "For as concerning *this sect,* we know that *everywhere* it is *spoken against."* Remark the well-chosen expression *sect,* with which they themselves also speak against the "hope of Israel." " Now indeed," they seem to say, " we can very well imagine that the Jews have spoken against thee ; for thy sect, as we very well know, is everywhere spoken against."[2] With this last sentence the Jews conclude their hypocritical, vacil-lating reply : for, in *their* opinion, the fact that Israel everywhere spoke against it, was not a sign of any good matter, but rather of

---

[1] Some have looked upon this assertion as true, and explain it by the de-crease or stoppage of the communication between Jerusalem and Rome after the Jews were driven out of Rome (ch. xviii. 2) by Claudius. They returned by degrees, and quietly, at the time of Nero.

[2] The chiefs of the Jews had at least some acquaintance with the small Christian community in Rome, and testify indirectly to their opposition even to them.

something evil; and after such a reply, Paul might certainly prepare himself for being similarly spoken against.   But verily in
God's sight it is plainly a sign and a seal of heavenly truth when
that truth is on earth everywhere spoken against; and it is a
characteristic of God's *right way*, that the numberless sectarians of
this world combine in calling it a "sect."   Inasmuch as this utterance of the Roman Jews is found in the last chapter of the Acts
of the Apostles, it forms a personally noteworthy conclusion for us
readers.   Christianity was then the mere opinion held by a Jewish
sect, about which the first thing said in Rome was, *It is confessedly
everywhere spoken against.*   Now it is the religion of the world, the
national and popular faith of not a few of the countries of the
earth!   It is spreading everywhere, for else why should the *speaking against it* be *everywhere* necessary?   But as soon as it is no
longer everywhere spoken against by the natural man, as soon as
the little flock of saints becomes blended with whole nations of
nominal Christians, and the vital, regenerating faith is mixed up
with mere ecclesiastical dogmas and pedantic or scientific opinions,
and thus becomes almost extinct; then must the true church again
come forth as a *sect*, and must again submit to be everywhere
spoken against.   And this is in fact the ever protesting and continually recommencing course of separation, by which alone the
true church of Jesus can maintain its position on earth, so long at
least as the present state of things endures.

XXX.

PAUL'S LAST WORDS TO THE JEWS.

(CHAP. XXVIII. 25–28.)

TESTIMONY AS TO THE CONSUMMATION OF THE PREDICTED OB-
DURACY OF THE PEOPLE, AND THE TRANSFER OF GOD'S
SALVATION TO THE GENTILES.

VERS. 23, 24. On the day which the Jews themselves had appointed, considerable numbers of them, and not merely their chief
men, came to the apostle's house.   Paul, who had already written
to the Roman Christians as to Israel's obduracy, now, as a faithful

witness even to the obdurate, like Isaiah and all the prophets, and
the Saviour Himself, felt it no hardship to speak to them during
the whole day, *from morning till evening*.   Point after point in succession, patiently and copiously, *he expounded to them* (ἐξετίθετο ;
cf. ch. xi. 4, xviii. 26), and *testified* most variously in detail and as
a whole as to the *kingdom of God*, its promise, its true signification,
and real fulfilment.   First, how the promise of God's kingdom was
to be understood in itself ; and next, how it was to be found only
in Jesus.   Thus, in all the zeal of love, and even against hope, in
all the faithfulness of his ministry, he sought *to persuade* them, in
kindly and earnest conversation, that the kingdom of God can come
and be fulfilled in Jesus only.   He spoke to them *of Jesus* out of the
law of Moses and out of the prophets, and laid before them God's
words and works, promise and fulfilment, letter and spirit, Old and
New Testament, all thoroughly agreeing one with the other, just as
the Spirit of Jesus had taught, and continued to teach, his own heart.
The immediate result was at least somewhat encouraging.   *Some*
allowed themselves to be persuaded, and assented for the moment
to the things which were spoken ; but *some* absolutely *believed not*.
But even the πείθεσθαι of the first was no real πιστεύειν, as was
evident immediately afterwards, and served only as a bitter vindication of their opposition : they were persuaded, and yet they obeyed
not ; they saw, and yet they would not perceive !

Ver. 25. *And when they agreed not among themselves*, even those
that assented to the apostle's words gave up their belief, so that
they might not become a sect, and *all were going away*.   Then
Paul, after many propositions and much talking on the part of
wranglers, waverers, and opposers, spoke to them *one word*, which
at the conclusion he was not permitted to keep back from them.
As he had already done at Antioch (ch. xiii. 40, 46), so he did
here.   He points them to Israel's predicted obduracy against God's
salvation, and to its equally predicted transfer to the Gentiles.
This was the *last word* which *must necessarily* be everywhere spoken
as a testimony to the opposing Jews, from synagogue to synagogue,
since everywhere the word of God had been first preached to them.
Thus also had the Saviour Himself closed His ministry to them
(Matt. xxi. 43).   Now the time was everywhere come for the
great transition to take place, and for Israel to be given over to
its impending judgment.   The last solemn declaration which the
apostle of the Gentiles made before all Jerusalem (ch. xxii. 21), and
at Cæsarea to the last king of the Jews, was also his *last word* to the

Jews at Rome, and generally his and the Spirit's *last words to the Jews* as a body. The Jews themselves everywhere made it the last, and after it would hear nothing further. Remark how significantly the apostolic history closes at this point, and how fully the testimony reverts to the same *Old Testament Scriptures* from which (ch. ii. 16) it proceeded.

This *one word*, which drove the Jews away, may be divided into two parts. First, Ye are obdurate and blinded; secondly, The kingdom of God passes over to the Gentiles. Both these facts were often predicted; but only as regards the *first* does the apostle quote to them the prophet Isaiah: the *second* he himself freely and briefly declares to them. In the quotation he avails himself of a confirmatory expression which the Saviour Himself used in a similar utterance (Matt. xv. 7): καλῶς—*well* is it said. Only in this καλῶς the apostle *applies* it solely to the Jews present, and says, "Well spake the Holy Ghost unto the *fathers*" (on the contrary, in Matt. xv. 7 it is, περὶ ὑμῶν). In the *first* and *last* quotation in the Acts of the Apostles[1] (ch. i. 16 and here) it is certified to us that the *Holy Ghost*—the same who, proceeding from the risen Jesus, works, lives, and testifies in His church—hath spoken *through* the prophets of Jesus, and everything which relates to Jesus (τὰ περὶ τοῦ Ἰησοῦ, ver. 23). The words "*by* Esaias the prophet *to* our fathers"[2]—although the passage quoted really contains God's word *to* Isaiah *about* the fathers—are thus shaped in order that by the διά the prophet may be subordinated to the Spirit. That which was written *of* the fathers was in fact also intended *for* them and *to* them. The children are, however, like their fathers; much indeed that was spoken to the fathers was really *prophecy*, and applied still more to the children, as particularly the passage quoted here.

Vers. 26, 27. In ch. vi. of the prophet Isaiah we read of the *sending* of the prophet to *those who will not understand him,* although his lips had been touched with the "live coal" taken from the altar. We see clearly from this (even if many other passages of the New Testament did not expressly certify to the

---

[1] Matthew also, at the end of his Gospel, reverts to the *formula citandi* of the commencement.

[2] It is not to be read ὑμῶν instead of ἡμῶν. In this we agree with Baumgarten, but not in the strange inference he draws therefrom—that by these words the apostle included *himself* in the obduracy, and that by *his* conversion the return of Israel to their God was likewise guaranteed! The expression "*our* fathers" is simply natural, as coming from a Jew speaking to Jews.

reference), that not only the first hearers and readers are intended, but also all those that follow, to whom indeed Isaiah was also sent, inasmuch as every prophet was fundamentally a type of Christ. The Jews, therefore, who misapprehended and rejected Christ both in Scripture and the words spoken to them, and absolutely would not receive God's word of salvation (יְשַׁע יְהוּ), are also meant.

The words of the passage are here accurately quoted from the Septuagint, with the exception of the transposition of the αὐτῶν from ὠσί to ὀφθαλμούς, and the more forcible emphasis given in Πορεύθητι πρὸς τὸν λαὸν τοῦτον καὶ εἰπόν instead of πορεύθητι καὶ εἰπὸν τῷ λαῷ τούτῳ (לֵךְ וְאָמַרְתָּ לָעָם הַזֶּה). This is the only one among the three quotations of this passage in the New Testament in which the *address to Isaiah* is included, for in this it is specially suitable. The expression *this people* describes the abiding validity of the word even for the then present Jews, and together with the previous words " to our fathers" forcibly denotes that this people from their fathers downwards have been refractory, and even under the influence of God's last wonders and testimonies still remain so (cf. Stephen's words, ch. vii. 51, 52). Next, the words " Go unto this people" have here their special application as regarded Paul, who had just come to Rome, and was circumstanced much as Isaiah was in respect to the Jews. The *imperative* in the Hebrew text, running, " Hear ye indeed, but understand not," and the direction to Isaiah, " Harden ye their hearts," is altered in the Greek to the *future* and the *aorist*: this is a quite correct interpretation (it is therefore also retained in Matt. xiii. 14 and John xii. 40, but somewhat altered). The forcible and certain *futurum* is an *imperative* in the prophecy, and every imperative of God is nothing but a forcibly expressed future. Isaiah could not, and God would not, harden any man's heart; but the word of the prophet, and through him of God, finds or effects this obduracy, even involuntarily, although not without prescience. Ἀκούειν and συνιέναι, βλέπειν and εἰδέναι, bear the same relation to one another (in Hebrew שָׁמַע and בִּין, רָאָה and יָדַע); but understanding is, in fact, only a true *hearing*, and perceiving a true *seeing*, and the groundwork of a right understanding lies in the *heart*: if *this* be hardened, the ears hear not, and the eyes see not. This is all intimated in the second verse, and the altered position of its words. Remark, further, how at first the external follows the internal—*heart, ears, eyes;* and then it is the reverse in the way of salvation—*eyes, ears,* and *heart.* The uncircumcised in *heart* are on this account " of uncircumcised *ears,*" and the ears are the doors that admit God's word to the heart: there finally results therefrom a closing and covering of the *eyes*— a complete blindness and κατάνυξις. Obduracy of the heart is punished with deafness of the ears, and the deafness with blindness of the eyes. This is the course of development of obduracy in all its stages. "Who hath ears to hear," but from malice in his heart will not make use of them, and does not desire to hear, "from him shall be taken even that which he hath" (Matt. xiii. 9, 12, 13). That which is said in Rom. i. 21–28 about the heathen world, applies in its fulfilment to Israel likewise. If the obdurate *heart* is to be helped by conversion, there is no other way than that the *eyes* should first again be opened (Acts xxvi. 18) ; then will the ears again be able to hear, and the heart to *understand*, and again to be *turned* to God. But the impossibility of this salvation is here very severely and mournfully derived fr__ the complete and utter blindness : μήποτε ἴδωσι . . . καὶ ἰάσωμ__ αὐτούς. This severe language, which indeed borders on irony, i_ equivalent to saying that the eyes which are sunk in sleep cannot be either soon or easily awakened, and that consequently the obduracy which has taken possession of the heart actually *renders impossible* the *help* which would come through God's salvation, preventing it, if not for ever, at least for a long period. We might then well ask, as the apostle must have asked in his spirit, and also Isaiah asked in ch. vi. 11 : Lord ! how long ? For the answer to the question, read in Isaiah the verses which follow (11–13). Compare Isa. lix. 20, and see how it is explained in Rom. xi. 26. This comforting view Paul had already written of as a mystery, when addressing the Roman Christians ; here, however, he considers the eyes of the Jews as closed, and expresses his thought in the same passage which the Saviour had already declared to be fulfilled (Matt. xiii. 14), and with which John also closes his account of Jesus' testimony to the Jews (ch. xii. 39–41).

Ver. 28. Paul now adds his *second* word, and, in full apostolic authority, he himself continues as a prophet.—*Be it known therefore unto you*, as the last thing which ye must both see and hear, *that the* (or rather, more emphatically, *this* [1]) *salvation of God is sent unto the Gentiles* in your stead, for *ye* have despised it. Besides *this* salvation there is none other. *It is already known to you* that the "hope of Israel" is spoken against by all Israel ; now, therefore, be it further known unto *you* that the *Gentiles* will believe it and

---

[1] We retain the τοῦτο here, as very emphatically placed.

receive it. Ἀπεστάλη, the transfer, has already long begun. I am especially sent to the Gentiles ; and now this transfer is to take place as regards Rome, the chief city of the Gentiles, since ye Jews even here have shown yourselves to be obdurate. Ye would not perceive and recognise "God's salvation" either in Isaiah, who so clearly and more than all the other prophets testified of it, or in the law and prophets, or even in Jesus, who was Himself *it.* Wherever and however it was sent unto you, ye *would not hear* it. Behold, the Gentiles are now God's people, for they will not treat those sent unto them as Israel treated her Isaiahs, but they will *hear* them with believing obedience. This consolatory prospect, which stands in striking contrast to the words recorded in ch. xxii. 18, is derived by Paul from Jesus' promise (ch. xxvi. 18); but the believing obedience of the Gentiles is also predicted in many places in the prophets.

Ver. 29. These were Paul's *last words* to the Jews, and the result was that they *departed.* They left God's word and testimony, and the light of His countenance ; and *among themselves*, now given up to their own folly, they *had great reasoning.* Πολλὴν συζήτησιν, or ζήτησιν—much *disputation* because they had rejected the truth, much vacillating *asking* and *seeking* because they had relinquished that which was sure and certain. The reader must not take it amiss if we give an entirely general application to this verse. Here, at the conclusion of this book, written by the Holy Ghost through the hands of Luke, every detail becomes a matter for special application. Does not Israel now stand in this συζήτησις even down to the present day? And not Israel only, but all those in Christendom who have fallen away from the faith, learned and unlearned, divines and laics? Ah! they have, like the Jews in Rome, *departed* from the Man and the Book, through whom alone, and in which alone, are the words of eternal life.

Vers. 30, 31. But Paul, and God's testimony through him, suffered no injury through Israel's departure. In order that the kingdom of God should be duly proclaimed in the capital of the world-wide empire, the imperial decision [1] was some time delayed, and for *two whole years* Paul remained in an easy captivity *in his own hired house.* Without distinction of nation or position, he received *all* who came to him, by whatever impulse their visit might be produced. Thus at Rome he *preached* the *kingdom of God,*

---

[1] If the sentence had been one of condemnation and not of acquittal, how could Luke have concluded his book in the way he has done?

teaching all those things which concerned the *Lord* of that kingdom, *Jesus* as *Christ*. The kingdom of God, which was promised in the Old Testament, is perfected in the New Testament in and through Jesus. There is no kingdom of God without Jesus; but where Jesus is, there ultimately will the kingdom of God have its full consummation. He who will proclaim the kingdom, let him teach of Jesus; and he who teaches of Jesus, let him not forget to proclaim the kingdom.[1] With all joy and confidence within, and without "no man forbidding him." With these words doth Luke joyfully conclude his Acts of the Apostles, and in the last verse reverts again to his commencement (ch. i. 3),—thus stating at the conclusion the whole theme of his book; and this theme is *the kingdom of God in Jesus*, first testified to and taught by the Risen One Himself (ch. i. 3), then at His command proclaimed by the apostles to "the uttermost parts of the earth," after the *kingdom*, through Israel's unbelief, had been taken away from the chosen people (ch. i. 6–8). The course of the gospel *from Jerusalem to Rome* embraces the whole historical scope of the book;[2] and if, with Rieger, we ask, "When will it again return to Jerusalem?" we may find our question provisionally answered in the Epistle to the Romans, the succeeding book of the New Testament in our arrangement. This reveals, both as regards Jew and Gentile, the whole of God's plan for setting up His kingdom, which is righteousness, joy, and peace in the Holy Ghost.

---

[1] "To preach the kingdom of God, and to teach about Jesus—*that* is representing the *whole* of the gospel" (Rieger). It has been elsewhere said, "It is the circumference and the centre."

[2] "In the face of the great main point of all, the person of Paul himself falls into the background." Lechler thus very appropriately vindicates this conclusion of the Acts of the Apostles, which gives us no further information as to the fate of the apostle and the result of his appeal.

www.ingramcontent.com/pod-product-compliance
Lightning Source LLC
Chambersburg PA
CBHW060447100426

42812CB00025B/2718